TO THE STUDENT

This text was created to provide you with a high-quality educational resource. As a publisher specializing in college texts for business and economics, our goal is to provide you with learning materials that will serve you well in your college studies and throughout your career.

The educational process involves learning, retention, and the application of concepts and principles. You can accelerate your learning efforts, utilizing the study guide accompanying this text.

The study guide is designed to improve your performance and the course by highlighting key points in the text and providing you with assistance in mastering basic concepts.

Check your local bookstore, or ask the manager to place an order for you today.

We at Irwin sincerely hope that this text package will assist you in reaching your goals both now and in the future.

Management
Theory and Application

The Irwin Series in
Management and The Behavioral
Sciences

L. L. Cummings and
E. Kirby Warren   Consulting Editors

Management
Theory and Application

Leslie W. Rue, Ph.D.
Professor of Management
College of Business Administration
Georgia State University

Lloyd L. Byars, Ph.D.
Professor and Chairman
Department of Management and Organizational Behavior
Graduate School of Business Administration
Atlanta University

1989 Fifth Edition

IRWIN

Homewood, Illinois 60430

Sponsoring editor: William R. Bayer
Associate editor: Sheila Smith
Project editor: Jean Roberts
Production manager: Carma W. Fazio
Designer: Diane M. Beasley
Compositor: Arcata Graphics/Kingsport
Typeface: 10/12 Bembo
Printer: R. R. Donnelley & Sons Company

LIBRARY OF CONGRESS
Library of Congress Cataloging-in-Publication Data

Rue, Leslie W.
    Management: theory and application / Leslie W. Rue, Lloyd L.
Byars.—5th ed.
        p. cm.
    Includes bibliographies and index.
    ISBN 0-256-06896-8
    1. Management.   I. Byars, Lloyd L.   II. Title.
HD31.R797 1989
658—dc19   88–13213
                                                        CIP

Printed in the United States of America

2 3 4 5 6 7 8 9 0 DO 5 4 3 2 1 0 9

To Penny and Linda

PREFACE

Since the publication of the fourth edition of this text, much has happened in the management field. Strategic management—making decisions concerning the future direction of an organization and implementing those decisions—has received increasing attention by managers in all organizations. The ethics used by the managers of many organizations have been called into question by the public at large; this has led to an increased emphasis on the ethical content of managerial decisions. Finally, business organizations continue to recognize the importance and growth of international business activities.

Because of these changes and because of the evolving nature of the study of management, we have made major revisions in this fifth edition. Relying on the suggestions of professors who have used our text, reviewers who provided valuable insights, and our own thoughts, we have retained the strongest parts of previous editions and strengthened the weaker parts. The text has been reorganized: We eliminated some material, updated and revised other material, and added new material. The major changes are summarized below.

This fifth edition focuses on the different types of skills necessary to be a successful manager. The text is organized into five major sections instead of the previous six. Section 1, "A Foundation for the Management Process," serves as an introduction to and a foundation for studying the field of management. The major change in Section 1 is that it includes chapters on international management and communication skills. The reason for moving the chapter on international management to the front is to reflect the increased emphasis being placed on this topic by both academicians and practitioners. Communication skills have been moved to Section 1 because of their importance in performing all other skills in management. Section 2, "Decision-Making and Planning Skills," begins with a totally revised chapter on decision making. This chapter has been placed at the front of Section 2 because, like communication skills, decision-making skills are required in performing all other management skills. In addition, Section 2 includes a new chapter focusing on the importance of strategic management. Section 3, "Organizing and Staffing Skills," contains two chapters on organizing skills, one on staffing skills, and one on developing people. Section 4, "Human Relations Skills," contains six chapters. It includes chapters on motivation, leadership, appraising and rewarding performance, work groups, conflict and stress, and managing change and organizational culture. The chapter on appraising and rewarding performance has been added to this section because it illustrates one of management's most effective methods of motivating and providing leadership to employees. The management of change and organizational culture has been added to this section because the application of human relations skills to these areas is essential for organizational success. Finally, Section 5, "Controlling Skills," discusses the role of managerial control in the management process. General control methods as well as operations control methods are explained. Management information systems are discussed as tools used by management to provide both control and planning information.

Several other aspects of the text should be mentioned. We have continued our practice of providing realism in the text by using numerous examples throughout. We use several real-life examples, called "Managers at Work," in each chapter. These examples are current and relate directly to the chapter material. We still provide an experiential exercise for each chapter. Several of these exercises have been updated or changed as a result of feedback from adopters and reviewers. This edition contains one in-depth incident at the end of each chapter. An additional incident is provided in the Instructor's Manual for use with most chapters. Finally, new or updated, comprehensive, real-life cases are provided at the end of each section.

As in the previous editions, we are indebted to our families, friends, colleagues, and students for the assistance we have received. Unfortunately, space limits us to mentioning only a few.

Matt Amano
Oregon State University

Gilbert Brookins
Siena College

Jeffrey Cornwall
University of Wisconsin—Oshkosh

Kathy Daruty
LA Pierce College

Gaber Abou El Enein
Mankato State University

Scott King
Sinclair Community College

Bruce Meyers
Western Illinois University

Thomas Myers
Piedmont Virginia Community College

Thomas Rakestraw
Youngstown State University

Joe Santora
Essex County College

We would also like to thank those who contributed to our marketing research:

Robert Archibald
Lakehead University

Mary Elizabeth Beres
Mercer University

John Casey
Herkimer County Community College

Ronald Clemment
Murray State University

Ed Giermack
College of DuPage

Robert D. Hay
University of Arkansas—Fayetteville

Aprile Holland
Brenau College

Henry Houser
Auburn University

Bruce Kemelgor
University of Louisville

John Kohl
San Jose State University

Rick Lester
University of North Alabama

Daniel McAllister
University of Las Vegas

Joseph Mano
Montgomery College—Rockville

Margaret Naumes
Skidmore College

Herb Oestreich
San Jose State University

Wendall Roye
Franklin Pierce College

Sterling Sessions
Weber State College

Special thanks go to Gwendolyn Donaway of Atlanta University and Loyce McCarter of Georgia State University for typing and editing this manuscript. We are excited about this edition and hope that it will be exciting to you. We are interested in any feedback that you might be inclined to send.

Leslie W. Rue
Lloyd L. Byars

Leslie W. Rue is professor of management in the College of Business Administration at Georgia State University. He received his Bachelor of Industrial Engineering (with honor) and his Master of Industrial Engineering from Georgia Institute of Technology. He received his Ph.D. in Management from Georgia State University. Dr. Rue's dissertation involved a study of the long-range planning practices of 400 U.S. and Canadian firms. Dr. Rue currently teaches in the undergraduate, the M.B.A. and the Doctoral programs at Georgia State University. He regularly teaches courses in principles of management and business policy/strategic management, and he has also taught human resource management and operations management.

Prior to joining Georgia State University, Dr. Rue was on the faculty of the School of Business, Indiana University at Bloomington, Indiana. He has worked as a data processing project officer for the U.S. Army Management Systems Support Agency, in the Pentagon, and as an industrial engineer for Delta Airlines. In addition, Dr. Rue has worked as a consultant and trainer to numerous private and public organizations in the areas of planning, organizing, and strategy.

Dr. Rue is the author of over 40 published articles, cases, and papers that have appeared in academic and practitioner journals. In addition to this book, he has coauthored seven other textbooks in the field of management. Several of these books have gone into multiple editions.

Dr. Rue has just celebrated his 20th wedding anniversary and has three teenaged children. His hobbies include the restoration of antique furniture and antique wooden speedboats.

Lloyd L. Byars received his Ph.D. from Georgia State University. He also received a Bachelor of Electrical Engineering and a Master of Science in Industrial Management from Georgia Tech. He has taught at Georgia State University and is currently professor and chairman of the Department of Management and Organizational Behavior at the Graduate School of Business Administration of Atlanta University.

Dr. Byars has published articles in leading professional journals and is also the author of four textbooks which are used in colleges and universities. He serves on the editorial review board of the *Journal of Systems Management* and the *Journal of Management Case Studies.*

Dr. Byars has worked as a trainer and consultant to many organizations, including: Duke Power Company, Georgia Kraft Company, Kraft, Inc., South Carolina Electric and Gas Company, the University of Florida—Medical School, the Department of the Army, and the U.S. Social Security Administration. Dr. Byars also serves as a labor arbitrator, certified by both the Federal Mediation and Conciliation Service and the American Arbitration Association. He has arbitrated cases in the United States, Europe, Central America, and the Caribbean.

CONTENTS

SECTION 3

Organizing and Staffing Skills   246

10   *Organizing Work*   250

Reasons for Organizing.   Division of Labor.   Authority, Power,
and Responsibility.   Sources of Authority.   Centralization versus
Decentralization.   Principles Based on Authority: *Delegation—The
Parity Principle.   Unity of Command.   Scalar Principle.   Span of
Management.   The Exception Principle.*

11   *Organization Structures*   272

Strategy and Structure.   Departmentation: *Functional.   Product.
Geographic.   Customer.   Other Types.*   Line Structure.   Line and
Staff Structure: *Line and Staff Conflict.*   Matrix Structure.   Flat
versus Tall Structures.   Committees: *Advantages.   Disadvantages.
Effectively Using Committees.   Boards of Directors.*   Simple Form,
Lean Staff.   A Contingency Approach.

12   *Staffing: Securing the Right People*   300

Human Resource Planning: *Job Analysis and Skills Inventory.
Forecasting.   Transition.   Legal Considerations.*   Integrating
Organizational Objectives, Strategy, Structure, and Human
Resource Requirements.   Recruitment: *Promotion from Within.
External Sources.   Legal Influences.*   Selection: *Who Makes the
Decision?   Legal Influences.   Selection Procedure.   Testing.
Polygraph Tests.   Drug Testing.   Reference Checking.   Employment
Interview.   Physical Examination.   Personal Judgment.*   Transfers,
Promotions, and Separations.   The Dynamics of Staffing.

Decision Support Systems (DSS).   MIS Components.   Developing an MIS: The Design Phase.   The Implementation Phase. Organization/People Strategies.   Information Centers.   Criticisms of MIS.   Computer Ethics.   Cautions Concerning MIS.

Incident   Overburdened with Paperwork, 608
Management Skill–Building Exercise   Recall, 609

SECTION 5 CASE   The Norge Division of Magic Chef, 610

Management
Theory and Application

1 A Foundation for the Management Process

1 Management, Entrepreneurship, and Small Business

2 The Management Movement

3 International Business and Management

4 Social Responsibility and Ethics

5 Communication Skills: Transmitting Understanding

SECTION 4				SECTION 5	
Human Relations Skills 14 Motivating 15 Leading 16 Appraising and Rewarding Performance 17 Work Groups 18 Conflict and Stress 19 Change and Culture	=	Management Foundation	+	Controlling Skills 20 Controlling 21 Operations Control 22 Management Information Systems	=	Improved Organizational Performance

*S*ection 1 provides both an introduction to and a foundation for studying the field of management. Management exists in all organizations—private, public, and not-for-profit—and the success of any organization is dependent on the expertise and skills of its management.

Chapter 1 defines the concepts of management and manager. Three common approaches used to analyze the management process are: (1) categorizing the functions (work) performed by management, (2) the roles that managers perform, and (3) the skills required of managers in performing the job of management. Each of these approaches is described in this chapter. The increasing role of women and minorities in management is described, and the importance of entrepreneurship and small business is discussed.

Chapter 2 presents a chronological development of the management discipline. The management pioneers are presented in perspective with the events of their day. Emphasis is placed not so much on what and when events happened as on why they happened.

Chapter 3 focuses on the increasing internationalization of business activity. Strategies used by organizations to move into international business activities and cultural differences in international management are discussed.

Chapter 4 explains the concept of social responsibility. Arguments for and against social responsibility are presented and analyzed. The important concept of ethics as related to management is discussed in detail.

Chapter 5 emphasizes the importance of effective communication in management. Both formal and informal communication systems in organizations are analyzed.

1 Management, Entrepreneurship, and Small Business

LEARNING OBJECTIVES

After studying this chapter,
you should be able to:

1 Define management.

2 Describe the levels of management.

3 List the reasons for studying management.

4 Discuss three basic approaches to studying management.

5 Explain how principles of management are developed.

6 Describe the increasing role of women and minorities in management.

7 Define entrepreneur.

8 Explain how to develop entrepreneurship in large and medium-sized organizations.

9 Discuss the significance of small business management.

The next day, Moses sat as usual to hear the people's complaints against each other, from morning to evening.

When Moses' father-in-law saw how much time this was taking, he said, "Why are you trying to do all this alone, with people standing here all day long to get your help?"

"Well, because the people come to me with their disputes, to ask for God's decisions," Moses told him. . . .

"It's not right!" his father-in-law exclaimed. "You're going to wear yourself out—and if you do, what will happen to the people? Moses, the job is too heavy a burden for you to try to handle all by yourself.

"Now listen, and let me give you a word of advice. . . .

"Find some capable, godly, honest men who hate bribes and appoint them as judges, 1 judge for each 1,000 people; he in turn will have 10 judges under him, each in charge of 100; and under each of them will be 2 judges, each responsible for the affairs of 50 people; and each of these will have 5 judges beneath him, each counseling 10 persons. Let these men be responsible to serve the people with justice at all times. Anything that is too important or complicated can be brought to you. But the smaller matters, they can take care of themselves. That way it will be easier for you because you will share the burden with them."

THE LIVING BIBLE*

*O*ver the years, some organizations have grown to be extremely large and profitable, while others have gone bankrupt. Some organizations have diversified into many new business activities, while others have not. Managers at Work 1–1 illustrates the changes that have occurred in several organizations from their initial date of incorporation.

Numerous reasons can be given for the success or failure of any particular organization. Unquestionably, an organization's management plays a critical role in its success or failure. Thus, the overriding purpose of this book is to identify, discuss, and show through examples the skills necessary to become a successful manager.

MANAGEMENT DEFINED

Management has been defined in many ways—and even today there is no universally accepted definition. One often used is "getting things done through others." Another popular definition holds that management is the efficient

MANAGERS AT WORK 1–1

ORGANIZATION	DATE OF INCORPORATION AND INITIAL PRODUCTS/ SERVICES	STATUS AS OF 1988
Coca-Cola Company	Incorporated on September 5, 1919. Primary product was soft drink concentrates and syrups.	World's largest manufacturer and distributor of soft drink concentrates and syrups. Also manufactures and distributes Minute Maid juices and Hi-C fruit drinks. Produces and distributes motion pictures through Columbia Pictures, which was acquired in 1982. Entered the production of television features by acquiring Embassy Communications and Tandem Productions in 1985.
Delta Air Lines, Inc.	Incorporated on December 31, 1930, as Delta Air Corp. Primary service was agricultural dusting operations in the South and Mexico.	Air carrier providing air transportation for passengers, freight, and mail over routes throughout the United States and abroad.
Federal Express	Incorporated on June 24, 1971. Primary service was delivery of packages and documents.	Company provides the same basic service.
IBM	Incorporated on June 15, 1911, as computing-tabulating-recording company. Primary products were time clocks and tabulating machines.	Largest manufacturer of information-handling systems in world. Some of its products include data processing machines and systems, information processors, electric and electronic typewriters, copiers, dictation equipment, and educational and testing materials.
W. T. Grant	Incorporated on November 27, 1937. Primary service was operating a chain of popular-priced department stores.	Company is bankrupt. The number of stores reached 1152. However, in 1976 the company declared bankruptcy and went out of business.

utilization of resources. In this book, we will use the following definition of management:

Management — form of work that involves guiding or directing a group of people toward organizational goals or objectives.

Management is a form of work that involves guiding or directing a group of people toward organizational goals or objectives.[1]

LEVELS OF MANAGEMENT

As can be seen from the introductory quote, the need for different levels of management dates back to biblical times. Figure 1–1 shows the three levels of management that were suggested to Moses. In today's organizations, there are still basically three levels of management.

Top management of private enterprise organizations usually includes the chairman of the board, president, and senior vice presidents. This level of management establishes the goals of the organization and the policies necessary to achieve these goals. Middle management includes all employees below the top management level who manage other managers. Middle management develops departmental goals and policies necessary to achieve the organizational goals. The final level of management is the supervisor. The supervisor manages

F I G U R E 1–1   Partial Organizational Chart from Exodus

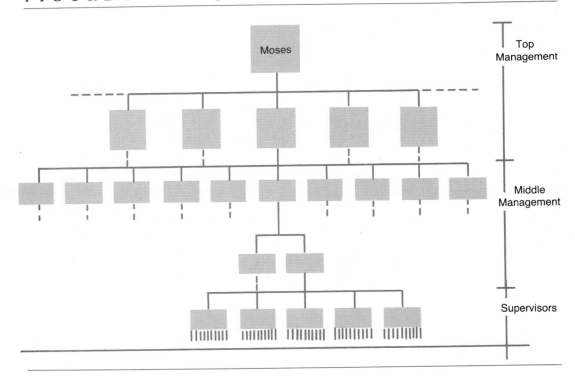

operative employees—those who physically produce an organization's goods and services.

WHY STUDY MANAGEMENT?

The most obvious reason for studying management is that many of the students reading this book will ultimately occupy positions of management in some organization. Effective management is important to all types of organizations; large and small corporations, universities, hospitals, churches, foundations, fraternities, and sororities, to identify a few. It is hoped that the study of the material in this next will prepare you for a successful career in management in a large or small organization.

Another less obvious (but equally important) reason for studying management is the profound impact that effective management can have on productivity. **Productivity,** which is defined as the output per person hour of input, affects our standard of living, rate of inflation, employment, and international competitive standing. Numerous factors influence the level of productivity. Figure 1–2 depicts some of the more important factors. None of these factors is totally separate from the others. For example, the changing resource base has certainly affected the thrust of R&D efforts toward improving the fuel efficiency of automobiles. The efficiency of management and work force are, of course, interrelated. Government regulations affect all the variables.

However, the one factor with the potential for the greatest impact on productivity is the efficiency of management. For example, a former Motorola plant in Franklin Park, Illinois, illustrates what the U.S. worker can do under effective management. Under Motorola, the plant had 140 defects for every 100 TV sets that passed down the assembly line. In 1974, Matsushita Electric Industrial Company bought the plant. The Japanese kept the same labor force;

Productivity— output per person-hour of input.

FIGURE 1–2   Factors Influencing Productivity

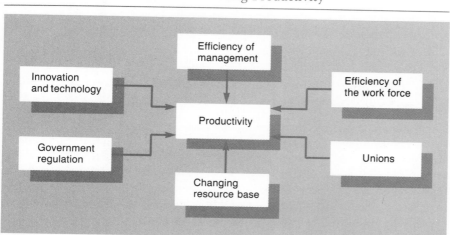

Functions of management—activities a manager performs in doing the work of management: planning, organizing, staffing, leading and controlling.

Planning—deciding what objectives to pursue during a future time period and what to do in order to achieve those objectives.

Organizing—grouping activities, assigning activities, and providing the authority necessary to carry out the activities.

Staffing—determining human resource needs and recruiting, selecting, training, and developing human resources.

Leading—directing and channeling human behavior toward the accomplishment of objectives.

Controlling—measuring performance against objectives, determining causes of deviations, and taking corrective action where necessary.

they even hired Motorola's vice president of engineering as president of the new subsidiary. In 1980, the reject rate was down to between 4 and 6 per 100 TV sets. The number of warranty claims had been reduced eightfold! What happened? A new management made drastic changes. Automation was increased; workers were asked to think about what they were doing and how it could be done better.[2]

APPROACHES TO ANALYZING MANAGEMENT

Several approaches have been used to analyze the management process. Three common approaches examine management by categorizing the *functions* (work) performed by management, the *roles* that managers perform, and the *skills* required of managers in performing the job of management. Each of these categories is discussed below.

Management Functions

Management is a form of work. The *manager* is the person who performs this work; in doing it, the manager performs certain activities. These activities are often grouped into conceptual categories called the **functions of management.** These categories are:

1. **Planning**—deciding what objectives to pursue during a future time period and what to do in order to achieve those objectives.
2. **Organizing**—grouping activities, assigning activities, and providing the authority necessary to carry out the activities.
3. **Staffing**—determining human resource needs and recruiting, selecting, training, and developing human resources.
4. **Leading**—directing and channeling human behavior toward the accomplishment of objectives.
5. **Controlling**—measuring performance against objectives, determining causes of deviations, and taking corrective action where necessary.

The functions of management are merely categories for classifying knowledge about management. Because management functions overlap, it is difficult to classify them purely as planning, organizing, staffing, leading, or controlling. In Figure 1–3, several managerial activities are classified under the different functions of management. However, this does not imply that managers perform each of these activities sequentially for each function. Figure 1–4 indicates the relative amount of emphasis placed on each function by different levels of management.

F I G U R E 1–3 Functions of Management

Planning

1. Perform self-audit—determine the present status of the organization.
2. Survey the environment.
3. Set objectives.
4. Forecast future situation.
5. State actions and resource needs.
6. Evaluate proposed actions.
7. Revise and adjust the plan in light of control results and changing conditions.
8. Communicate throughout the planning process.

Organizing

1. Identify and define work to be performed.
2. Break work down into duties.
3. Group duties into positions.
4. Define position requirements.
5. Group positions into manageable and properly related units.
6. Assign work to be performed, accountability, and extent of authority.
7. Revise and adjust the organizational structure in light of control results and changing conditions.
8. Communicate throughout the organizing process.

Staffing

1. Determine human resource needs.
2. Recruit potential employees.
3. Select from the recruits.
4. Train and develop the human resources.
5. Revise and adjust the quantity and quality of the human resources in light of control results and changing conditions.
6. Communicate throughout the staffing process.

Leading

1. Communicate and explain objectives to subordinates.
2. Assign performance standards.
3. Coach and guide subordinates to meet performance standards.
4. Reward subordinates, based on performance.
5. Praise and censure fairly.
6. Provide a motivating environment by communicating the changing situation and its requirements.
7. Revise and adjust the methods of leadership in light of control results and changing conditions.
8. Communicate throughout the leadership process.

Controlling

1. Establish standards.
2. Monitor results and compare to standards.
3. Correct deviations.
4. Revise and adjust control methods in light of control results and changing conditions.
5. Communicate throughout the control process.

Management Roles

Henry Mintzberg has proposed another method of examining what managers do by introducing the concept of managerial roles.[3] A **role** is defined as an organized set of behaviors belonging to an identifiable job.[4] But remember that the delineation of managerial working roles is essentially a categorizing process—just as it was with the managerial functions.

Mintzberg identifies 10 managerial roles, which he divides into three major groups: interpersonal roles, informational roles, and decisional roles. Figure 1–5 illustrates Mintzberg's approach to categorizing the roles of a manager. The manager's position is the starting point for defining a manager's roles.

Role – organized set of behaviors belonging to an identifiable job.

F I G U R E 1–4   Relative Amount of Emphasis Placed on Each Function
of Management

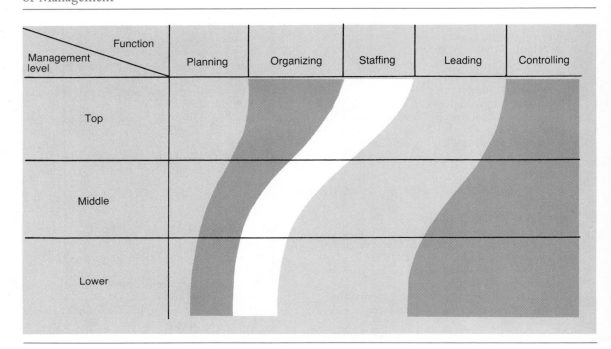

Formal authority gives the position status. Authority and status together generate certain interpersonal roles for a manager. The interpersonal roles in turn determine the informational roles of the manager. Finally, access to information, authority, and status place the manager at a central point in the organizational decision-making process. Figure 1–6 defines each of Mintzberg's 10 managerial roles.

Mintzberg further suggests that the management level and the types of work that the manager directs significantly influence the variety of roles that the manager must assume.[5] For example, managers at lower levels of the organization spend more time in the disturbance handler and negotiator roles and less time in the figurehead role. On the other hand, the chief executive of an organization concentrates more on the roles of figurehead, liaison, spokesperson, and negotiator.[6]

Management Skills

Another approach to examining the management process is in terms of the types of skills required to perform the work. Five basic skills have been identified:

Decision-making skills – involve searching the environment for conditions requiring a decision, analyzing possible courses of action, and choosing a course of action.
Administrative skills – involve understanding and performing the organizing, staffing, and controlling functions of management.

F I G U R E 1–5
Roles of a Manager

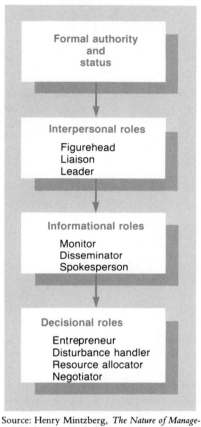

Source: Henry Mintzberg, *The Nature of Managerial Work* (New York: Harper & Row, 1973), p. 59.

1. **Decision-making skills**—involve searching the environment for conditions requiring a decision, analyzing possible courses of action, and choosing a course of action.
2. **Planning skills**—involve deciding what objectives to pursue during a future time period and how to achieve those objectives.
3. **Administrative skills**—involve understanding and performing the organizing, staffing, and controlling functions of management.
4. **Human relations skills**—involve understanding human behavior and being able to work well with people.
5. **Technical skills**—involve specialized knowledge, analytical ability within that specialty, and the ability to use tools and techniques of that specific discipline.

Human relations skills – involve understanding human behavior and being able to work well with people.

Technical skills – involve specialized knowledge, analytical ability within that specialty, and the ability to use tools and techniques of that specific discipline.

FIGURE 1–6   Definitions of Managerial Roles

Interpersonal
1. Figurehead: Manager represents the organizational unit in all matters of formality.
2. Liaison: Manager interacts with peers and other people outside the organizational unit to gain information and favors.
3. Leader: Manager provides guidance and motivation to the work group and also defines the atmosphere in which the work group will work.

Informational
1. Monitor: Manager serves as a receiver and collector of information.
2. Disseminator: Manager transmits special information within the organization.
3. Spokesperson: Manager disseminates the organization's information into its environment.

Decisional
1. Entrepreneur: Manager's role is to initiate change.
2. Disturbance handler: Role the manager must assume when the organization is threatened, such as conflicts between subordinates, the sudden departure of a subordinate, or the loss of an important customer.
3. Resource allocator: Manager decides where the organization will expend its resources.
4. Negotiator: Role the manager assumes when the organization finds itself in major, nonroutine negotiations with other organizations or individuals.

Source: Adapted from Henry Mintzberg, *The Nature of Managerial Work* (New York: Harper & Row, 1972), pp. 54–99.

In practice, management skills are so closely interrelated that it is difficult to determine where one begins and another ends. However, it is generally agreed that lower-level managers need more technical skills than managers at higher levels. Human relations skills are essential to effective management at all levels. Finally, decision-making, planning, and administrative skills become increasingly important as a person moves up the managerial ladder.

Each approach to examining the management process looks at the process from a different perspective. Each has its merits. But in the final analysis, a successful manager must: (1) understand the work that is to be performed (the management functions); (2) understand the organized set of behaviors to be performed (the managerial roles); and (3) master the skills involved in performing the job (the managerial skills). Thus, these approaches to analyzing management are not mutually exclusive—they are necessary and complementary approaches.

PRINCIPLES OF MANAGEMENT

Principle—accepted rule of action.

Since the formal study of management began, numerous concepts have been promulgated as principles of management. A **principle** is defined as "a basic truth or law."[7]

Numerous laws or principles exist in the physical sciences. Examples include the law of gravity, Ohm's law, and the law of action and reaction. These laws were developed through a careful research process involving controlled

FIGURE 1–7   Controlled Experiment Process

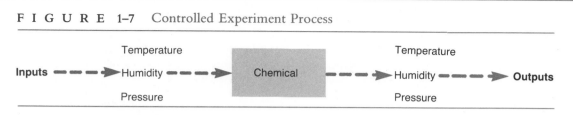

experimentation. In this process the researcher sets up an experiment in which control can be maintained on many of the input variables. For instance, in a chemical experiment the researcher may control input variables such as temperature, humidity, and pressure in order to determine the effect of change in one of these variables on a chemical. By varying one of the input factors and measuring the corresponding change in the other factors, the researcher can establish a relationship between the changes and the chemical. Figure 1–7 illustrates this process.

After the experiment has been repeated many times with identical results, the initial ideas (called hypotheses in scientific terminology) of the researchers are converted into laws or principles. Furthermore, after a hypothesis has been accepted as law, the law can be used to develop other laws.

Unfortunately, one of the major problems in developing principles of management is that it is very difficult to conduct a controlled experiment in a management environment. Cost and the inability to place absolute controls on one of the primary inputs—people—make controlled experimentation difficult. Unable to use the time-tested method of scientific experimentation to develop laws, the remaining logical alternative is to use observation and deduction. This is the method by which most principles of management have been developed. However, a word of caution is appropriate. Management principles are much more subject to change and interpretation than are the laws of the physical sciences. For instance, the management principle of "unity of command" states that an employee should have one and only one manager. However, there are examples of organizational structures that violate this principle and seem to work effectively. Thus, management principles must be viewed as guides to action and not laws that must be followed without exception. In summary, management principles should be followed, except where a deviation can be justified on the basis of sound logic.

MISCONCEPTIONS ARE COMMON

The practice of management is concerned with human behavior—and everyone seems to have their own ideas about management, especially its problems. Usually these ideas are based on personal experience and are defended with vigor.

To illustrate how each of us develops our own ideas about management

F I G U R E   1–8   True-False Test of Human Behavior

1. People probably never learn anything while they are deeply asleep.
2. Genius and insanity have little or no relationship to each other.
3. Better college students make less money after graduation than average students.
4. A person who learns rapidly remembers longer than a person who learns slowly.
5. All people in America are born equal in capacity for achievement.
6. Teaching a child to roller-skate very early in life gives the child a permanent advantage in this skill.
7. People are definitely either introverted or extroverted.
8. After you learn something, you forget more of it in the next few hours than in the next several days.
9. Famous people tend to be born of poor but hardworking parents.
10. Lessons learned just before going to sleep are remembered better than those learned early in the morning.
11. On the average, people of 45 are more intelligent than those of 20.
12. The tendency to imitate is probably learned.
13. There is a law of compensation in nature; for example, blind people are born with a highly developed sense of touch.
14. An especially favorable environment can probably raise a person's IQ a few points.
15. People born blind and having their sight restored as adults perceive the world almost immediately as we see it.

Answers: (1)T; (2)T; (3)F; (4)F; (5)F; (6)F; (7)F; (8)T; (9)F; (10)T; (11)F; (12)T; (13)F; (14)T; (15)F.

Source: Adapted from Gregory A. Kimble and Norman Garmezy, *Principles of General Psychology* (New York: Ronald Press, 1963), p. 4. Copyright © 1963 by the Ronald Press Company.

and human behavior, a true-false test of human behavior is given in Figure 1–8. The answers to the questions have been empirically verified. However, the natural tendency is to believe our intuition even at the expense of refuting scientific investigation. The same is true in management. Many ideas and fads appear which are nothing more than seat-of-the-pants propositions. These do have some value, for they lead to hypotheses that can be researched. But the student and practitioner of management must learn to separate management fact from fiction.

INCREASING ROLE OF WOMEN AND MINORITIES IN MANAGEMENT

During the 1980s, increasing emphasis has been placed on the role of women and minorities in management. Government legislation has most certainly been one of the strongest factors in this emphasis. Table 1–1 shows the growth of the civilian labor force between 1976 and 1986. As you can see, the percentage of women in the civilian labor force has grown faster than the rate of growth of the total number of people employed. During the 1982–95 period, the number of women and minorities in the labor force is projected to continue

T A B L E 1–1 Employed Civilian Labor Force (Numbers in Thousands)

	1976	1986	PERCENTAGE INCREASE
Total employed	88,752	109,597	23.48%
Men (black and white)	53,138	60,892	14.59
Women (black and white)	35,615	48,706	36.75
Minorities (male and female)	9,899	10,980	10.92

Source: Adapted from *Employment and Earnings,* U.S. Department of Labor, Bureau of Labor Statistics, January 1987; and *Handbook of Labor Statistics,* U.S. Department of Labor, Bureau of Labor Statistics, December 1983.

to grow faster than the overall labor force. And women, both black and white, will account for about two thirds of the labor force *growth* during the 1980s and 90s.[8]

Table 1–2 shows a breakdown by sex and race for people employed in executive, administrative, and managerial jobs. As can be seen, men continue to hold a larger share of these jobs. Furthermore, males continue to dominate top-level management jobs in most large organizations. However, this will not likely be the case if the trends indicated in Table 1–1 continue. And the trends are likely to continue.

T A B L E 1–2 Employment in Executive, Administrative, and Managerial Jobs, 1986 (Numbers in Thousands)

	NUMBER OF EXECUTIVE, ADMINISTRATIVE, AND MANAGERIAL JOBS	PERCENT OF TOTAL	TOTAL EMPLOYMENT	PERCENT OF TOTAL
Total	12,642		109,597	
Men	7,990	63.2	60,892	55.6
Women	4,652	36.8	48,706	44.4
Minorities (male and female)	1,137	8.9	10,814	9.8

Source: Adapted from *Employment and Earnings,* U.S. Department of Labor, Bureau of Labor Statistics, January 1987; and *Handbook of Labor Statistics,* U.S. Department of Labor, Bureau of Labor Statistics, December 1983.

ENTREPRENEURSHIP AND MANAGEMENT

A basic distinction is often made between a manager and an entrepreneur. The **entrepreneur** conceives the idea of what product or service to produce, starts the organization, and builds it to the point where additional people

Entrepreneur – conceives the idea of what product or service to produce, starts the organization, and builds it to the point where additional people are needed.

MANAGERS AT WORK 1–2

Mark Kay Ash—Founder and Chairman of the Board, Mary Kay Cosmetics, Inc.

In August 1963, Mary Kay Ash retired after a 25-year, direct-sales career. She was tired and disillusioned after years of hard work that had led only to the degree of success allowed women in the 1960s. "I thought that by starting a little business, I could give women an opportunity I had been denied." Her product was a homemade cosmetic that Mary Kay had been using since 1953. "I knew nothing about administration," Mary Kay admits. "Still don't. Luckily my husband did, and he agreed to take care of the business end of the company. I was free to handle everything else."

One month before the company was to open for business, while having breakfast and going over financial figures for the new venture, Mary Kay's husband and business partner suffered a fatal heart attack. Mary Kay was grief-stricken, confused, and scared.

However, with the help of her sons Richard and Ben, Mary Kay proceeded with her plans to open the company. It opened its doors on Friday the 13th in 500 square feet of rented space. "I never intended for the company to be more than a local business that gave women a fair chance to be successful," she says of the company that has spread to every state and several foreign countries, including Canada and Australia. In 1983, Mary Kay Cosmetics controlled about 3 percent of total cosmetics sales and 10 percent of total skin care sales nationwide. Mary Kay Cosmetics is also included in *The 100 Best Companies to Work for in America.*

How did Mary Kay do all of this? She has four guidelines: (1) good use of time (when the company was young, she started the "five o'clock club," saying it was possible to gain 10 hours each week by getting up 2 hours earlier than normal on five mornings); (2) organization (she makes a "must do" list every evening for the following day); (3) priorities ("When God is first, family is second, and job is third, everything goes right."); and (4) self-confidence ("You can do it!" is her motto.).

Source: Lynne Morgan Sullivan, "Mary Kay Ash," *Sky Magazine,* 1984, pp. 47–51.

are needed. At this point, the entrepreneur can either make the transformation to professional manager or can hire one. A *professional manager* performs the basic management functions for the ongoing organization. Entrepreneurs, then, are usually associated with relatively small business organizations; professional managers are generally associated with medium- to large-sized firms. Note, however, that an entrepreneur must perform many—if not all—of the basic management functions in starting and building an organization.

Under a broad definition—a definition that includes not only persons running a business full-time but also those doing so part-time—about 13 million Americans are engaged in some entrepreneurial activity. These 13 million entrepreneurs represent about 14 percent of all nonagricultural workers in the United States. Part-time entrepreneurs have increased fivefold in recent years.[9] Managers at Work 1–2 describes one of America's well-known entrepreneurs.

Importance of Entrepreneurship and Small Business

As was stated earlier, entrepreneurs are usually associated with small business organizations. In the mid-1980s, there were approximately 16.9 million businesses in the United States. Using the size standards set by the U.S. Small Business Administration (SBA), approximately 99 percent of these businesses are small.

The SBA size standards are established primarily to define eligibility for SBA programs and federal procurement purposes. Size standards vary by industry. Factors that are examined for the purpose of setting size standards include maximum size of firms in the industry, average firm size, the extent of industry dominance by large firms, the number of firms, and the distribution by firm size of sales and employees in the industry. The SBA sets size standards in industries by either the number of employees or sales volume in millions of dollars.

Using the SBA standards, small businesses employ 53 percent of the U.S. work force, contribute 42 percent of all sales, and are responsible for 38 percent of the gross national product. Furthermore, small businesses provide about 67 percent of initial job opportunities. Thus, it is likely that a significant percentage of the students reading this book will initially accept a job with a small business or start a small business. Figure 1–9 describes some differences between small and large businesses.

ENTREPRENEURSHIP IN LARGE AND MEDIUM-SIZED ORGANIZATIONS

An increasing emphasis is being placed on developing the entrepreneurial traits of innovation and a willingness to take risks, among managers and employees in large and medium-sized organizations. The need for innovation and risk taking in larger organizations was illustrated in a National Science Foundation study. It found that small organizations produced about 4 times as many innovations per R&D dollar as medium-sized organizations and about 24 times as many as large organizations.[10]

Yet, many large organizations like IBM, 3M, GE, and Bristol-Myers have enviable records of innovation. They have done this by encouraging an entrepreneurial spirit among their people. In a study of America's "excellent companies," Thomas Peters and Robert Waterman, Jr., identified several

F I G U R E   1–9   Roles of Small Business Managers versus Large Business Managers

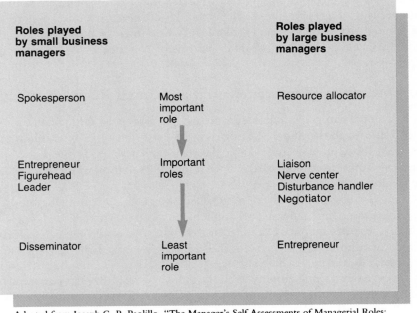

Roles played by small business managers		Roles played by large business managers
Spokesperson	Most important role	Resource allocator
Entrepreneur Figurehead Leader	Important roles	Liaison Nerve center Disturbance handler Negotiator
Disseminator	Least important role	Entrepreneur

Source: Adapted from Joseph G. P. Paolillo, "The Manager's Self Assessments of Managerial Roles: Small vs. Large Firms," *American Journal of Small Business* 8 (January–March 1984), pp. 58–64.

characteristics essential for the development of an entrepreneurial spirit within larger organizations.[11] First, organizations must develop a system that supports and encourages people to champion their new ideas or products. Three types of champions have been identified. **A product champion** is a fanatic who believes in the specific product or idea that he or she has in mind. The **executive champion** shields the new product or idea from the organization's natural tendency to reject new products or ideas. The **godfather** is typically an aging leader in the organization who provides the role model for championing.

Next, organizations that encourage entrepreneurship tolerate failures. These organizations seem to understand that some failures are to be expected when innovation is encouraged. Persistence in the face of failure and encouragement by management after a failure are key elements in developing entrepreneurship.

Finally, effective systems of communication encourage entrepreneurship. The absence of barriers to communication is essential.

ORGANIZATION OF THE BOOK

This book is divided into five basic sections:

Section 1: A Foundation for the Management Process.
Section 2: Decision-Making and Planning Skills.

Product champion – fanatic who believes in the specific product or idea that he or she has in mind.

Executive champion – shields a new product or idea from the organization's natural tendency to reject new products or ideas.

Godfather – typically an aging leader in the organization who provides the role model for championing.

Section 3: Organizing and Staffing Skills.
Section 4: Human Relations Skills.
Section 5: Controlling Skills.

Section 1 is an overview of the management process and the basic skills of management. Chapter 1 defines management and describes the functions, roles, and skills of management. The importance of entrepreneurship in organizations and small business management is also discussed. Chapter 2 presents a historical view of the management process. Chapter 3 describes the significance of the increasing internationalization of business. Chapter 4 focuses on social responsibility and ethics in management. Finally, Chapter 5 stresses the importance of communication skills in management.

Section 2 analyzes the decision-making and planning skills of management. Chapter 6 focuses on the decision-making skills of management. Chapter 7 discusses the importance of objectives to developing effective planning skills. Chapter 8 describes the strategic management process in detail. Then, Chapter 9 discusses applying planning skills to the production and operations processes that produce an organization's goods or services.

Section 3 analyzes the organizing and staffing skills of management. Organizing and the development of organizational structures are described in Chapters 10 and 11. Chapter 12 is concerned with staffing. The importance of developing employees is described in Chapter 13.

Section 4 analyzes the human relations skills that are essential for managers. Chapter 14 develops an understanding of motivation. Chapter 15 describes the importance of leadership in achieving improved organizational performance. Appraising and rewarding performance is discussed in Chapter 16. Chapter 17 explains work groups and organizations. Chapter 18 describes approaches to managing conflict and stress. Finally, managing organizational change and culture is discussed in Chapter 19.

Section 5 analyzes the importance of control systems in the management process. Chapter 20 describes the controlling function of management. The application of managerial control in the production and operations process is described in Chapter 21. Finally, the importance and role of management information systems is discussed in Chapter 22.

SUMMARY

LEARNING OBJECTIVE 1

Define Management.
Management is a form of work that involves guiding or directing a group of people toward organizational goals or objectives.

LEARNING OBJECTIVE 2

Describe the Levels of Management.
Three levels of management exist. Top management establishes the goals of the organization and the policies necessary to achieve these goals. Middle

management develops departmental goals and policies necessary to achieve the organizational goals. The supervisor manages operative employees.

LEARNING OBJECTIVE 3

List the Reasons for Studying Management.

The first reason is that many of the students reading this book will ultimately occupy a position in management. A second reason is that effective management has a profound impact of productivity which influences our standard of living, rate of inflation, employment, and international competitive standing.

LEARNING OBJECTIVE 4

Discuss Three Basic Approaches to Studying Management.

Three common approaches to studying the management process include categorizing the functions (work) performed by management, the roles that managers perform, and the skills required of managers in performing the job of management.

LEARNING OBJECTIVE 5

Explain How Principles of Management are Developed.

Normally, principles are developed through a controlled experiment process. However, management principles are developed through observation and deduction.

LEARNING OBJECTIVE 6

Describe the Increasing Role of Women and Minorities in Management.

During the 1982–95 period, the number of women and minorities in the labor force is projected to grow faster than the overall labor force. Women and minorities are also likely to increase in executive, administrative, and managerial jobs.

LEARNING OBJECTIVE 7

Define Entrepreneur.

An entrepreneur conceives the idea of what product or service to produce, starts the organization, and builds it to the point where additional people are needed.

LEARNING OBJECTIVE 8

Explain How to Develop Entrepreneurship in Large and Medium-Sized Organizations.

First, organizations must develop a system that supports and encourages people to champion their new ideas or products. They must also tolerate failures. Finally, they must have effective communication systems.

LEARNING OBJECTIVE 9

Discuss the Significance of Small Business Management.

Using SBA size standards, approximately 99 percent of all U.S. businesses are small businesses. Small businesses employ 53 percent of the U.S. work force, contribute 42 percent of all sales, and are responsible for 38 percent of the gross national product.

REVIEW QUESTIONS

1. What is management?
2. Describe the levels of management.
3. Name and describe the basic management functions.
4. Outline the roles of a manager.
5. Define the basic skills required in management.
6. How are principles of management developed?
7. Explain how the composition of the managerial work force is changing in terms of sex and race.
8. Distinguish between a professional manager and an entrepreneur.
9. What are three essential characteristics necessary for developing an entrepreneurial spirit in larger organizations?
10. What factors are examined by the SBA in setting size standards for small businesses?

DISCUSSION QUESTIONS

1. Management has often been described as a univeral process, meaning that the basics of management are transferable and applicable in almost any environment. Comment on this statement.
2. How does one decide who is and who is not a manager in a given organization? For example, is the operator of a one-person business, such as a corner grocery store, a manager?
3. Do you think that management can be learned through books and study or only through experience?
4. Discuss the following statement: "All entrepreneurs are managers, but not all managers are entrepreneurs."

REFERENCES & ADDITIONAL READINGS

[1] Throughout this book, the terms *goals* and *objectives* will be used interchangeably.

[2] Jeremy Main, "The Battle for Quality Begins," *Fortune*, December 29, 1980, p. 32.

[3] Henry Mintzberg, "The Manager's Job: Folklore and Fact," *Harvard Business Review*, July–August 1975, pp. 49–61.

[4] T. R. Sarlin and V. L. Allen, "Role Theory," in *The Handbook of Social Psychology*, 2nd ed., vol. 1, ed. G. Lindzey and E. Aronson (Reading, Mass.: Addison-Wesley Publishing, 1968), pp. 488–567.

[5] Henry Mintzberg, *The Nature of Managerial Work* (New York: Harper & Row, 1972), pp. 54–99.

[6] For more information on the roles of managers, see John P. Kotter, *The General Managers* (New York: Free Press, 1982).

[7] The American Heritage Dictionary (Boston: Houghton Mifflin Company, 1982).

[8] *Employment Projections for 1995,* U.S. Department of Labor, Bureau of Labor Statistics, March 1984, p. 4.

[9] "Facts about Small Business," Fact Sheet 40, U.S. Small Business Administration, July 1987.

[10] Lucien Rhodes and Cathryn Jakobson, "Small Companies: America's Hope for the 1980s," *Inc.,* April 1981, p. 44.

[11] Much of the following material is drawn from Thomas J. Peters and Robert H. Waterman, Jr., *In Search of Excellence* (New York: Harper & Row, 1982), pp. 202–9.

SELECTED MANAGEMENT & RELATED PERIODICALS

Selected periodicals from this list are referenced throughout the text. This list is given so the student will have a listing of the more commonly referenced management and related periodicals.

Academy of Management Journal

Academy of Management Review

Administrative Management

Administrative Science Quarterly

Business Horizons

California Management Review

Canadian Business Review

Columbia Journal of World Business

Decision Sciences

Forbes

Fortune

Journal of Small Business Management

Harvard Business Review

Human Resource Management

Industrial and Labor Relations Review

Journal of Applied Behavioral Science

Journal of Applied Psychology

Journal of Business

Journal of Human Resources

Journal of Management Studies

Journal of Systems Management

Long-Range Planning

Management Accounting

Management International Review

Management of Personnel Quarterly

Management Review

Management Science

Managerial Planning

Michigan Business Review

Monthly Labor Review

Organizational Behavior and Human Performance

Organizational Dynamics

Personnel

Personnel Administrator

Personnel Management

Personnel Psychology

Public Administration Review

S.A.M. Advanced Management Journal

Sloan Management Review

Strategic Management Journal

Supervisory Management

Training and Development Journal

The Wall Street Journal (newspaper)

INCIDENT

The Expansion of Blue Streak

A rthur Benton started the Blue Streak Delivery Company five years ago. Blue Streak initially provided commercial delivery services for all packages within the city of Unionville (population 1 million).

Art started with himself, one clerk, and one driver. Within three years, Blue Streak had grown to the point of requiring 4 clerks and 16 drivers. It was then that Art decided to expand and provide statewide service. He figured that this would initially require the addition of two new offices, one located at Logantown (population 500,000) in the southern part of the state and one at Thomas City (population 250,000) in the northern part of the state. Each office was staffed with a manager, two clerks, and four drivers. Because both Logantown and Thomas City were within 150 miles of Unionville, Art was able to visit each office at least once a week and personally coordinate the operations in addition to providing general management assistance. The statewide delivery system met with immediate success and reported a healthy profit for the first year.

The next year, Art decided to expand and include two neighboring states. Art set up two offices in each of the two neighboring states. However, operations never seemed to go smoothly in the neighboring states. Schedules were constantly being fouled up, deliveries were lost, and customer complaints multiplied. After nine months, Art changed office managers in all four out-of-state offices. Things still did not improve. Convinced that he was the only one capable of straightening out the out-of-state offices, Art began visiting them once every two weeks. This schedule required Art to spend at least half of his time on the road traveling between offices.

After four months of this activity, Art began to be very tired of the constant travel; operations in the two neighboring states still had not improved. In fact, on each trip Art found himself spending all his time putting out fires that should have been handled by the office managers.

Art decided to have a one-day meeting which all of his office managers would attend to discuss problems and come up with some answers. At the meeting, several issues were raised. First, all of the managers felt that Art's visits were too frequent. Second, most of the managers did not seem to know exactly what Art expected them to do. Finally, each of the managers felt that they should have the authority to make changes in their office procedures without checking with Art before making the change.

Questions

1. What suggestions would you offer to Art to improve his operation?

2. What management skills must Art master if he is to resolve his problems and continue to grow?

EXERCISE

Success of a Business

Have each student go to the library and bring back to class an actual example of an entrepreneurial business or a small business. Possible sources of information include *Venture, Inc.*, *Business Week,* or *The Wall Street Journal.*

Each student should then prepare a 5-minute report on the following:

a. History of the organization.
b. Main product of the organization.
c. Reasons for success.
d. Role of management.

2 The Management Movement

LEARNING OBJECTIVES

*After studying this chapter,
you should be able to:*

1 Identify why management did not emerge
as a recognized discipline until the 20th
century.

2 Describe the events that led to the U.S.
Industrial Revolution.

3 Discuss the role that the "captains of
industry" played in the development of
modern organizations.

4 Define scientific management and
outline the role that Frederick W.
Taylor and his contemporaries played
in its development.

5 Summarize Henri Fayol's
contributions to modern management.

6 Discuss the human relations thrust
in management with emphasis on the
role of the Hawthorne experiments.

7 Define the management process
period, the management theory
jungle, the systems approach, and
the contingency approach.

8 Explain why emphasis is currently
being placed on the international
aspects of management.

9 Summarize the major points made
in the book *In Search of Excellence*.

History is useful to us not because it provides us with final answers about the fate of man, but because if offers us an inexhaustible storehouse of lifestyles, civilizational modes, and ways of acting that we can draw on as we face the future. History gives us balance, patience, and a deeper understanding of what it means to live and die. History cannot save us in any ultimate sense, but it can deepen our understanding of humanity's potentialities and limitations.

ARTHUR N. GILBERT ★

An understanding of the history of any discipline is necessary to understand where the discipline currently is and where it is going. Management is no exception. Many of today's managerial problems began in the early management movement. Understanding their historical evolution helps the modern manager to cope with them. It also helps today's managers develop a feel for why the managerial approaches that worked in earlier times do not necessarily work today. The challenge to present and future managers is not to memorize historical names and dates; it is to develop a feel for why and how things happened—and to apply this knowledge to the practice of management.

Although some management was needed centuries ago, very little sophisticated management was needed prior to the 19th century. Traffic lights were not needed—and therefore not invented—before automobile travel reached a certain level of sophistication. And management, as it now exists, was not needed or even known before the maturing of the corporate form of organization. The development of management thought and concepts is an example of people responding to the needs of their environment. The environment that led up to and surrounded the emergence of management thought is the subject of this chapter.

U.S. INDUSTRIAL REVOLUTION

Daniel Wren has described the Industrial Revolution in America as having three facets: power, transportation, and communication.[1] The steam engine, developed and perfected by James Watt in England in the late 18th century, came to America shortly thereafter. The steam engine provided more efficient and cheaper power; it allowed factories to produce more goods at cheaper prices; it increased the market for goods. And the steam engine allowed factories

★ Arthur N. Gilbert, *In Search of a Meaningful Past* (Boston: Houghton Mifflin, 1972), p. 2.

to be located away from water power. This alone had a profound effect on the development of this country. Now factories could be located near their suppliers, customers, and the most desirable labor markets instead of only near rivers.

Transportation growth began with the development of canals around 1755. America's first railroad charter was obtained by John Stevens in 1815. But he lacked financial support and did not build the first railroad until 1830.[2] A railroad boom then followed in the late 1840s. The track mileage increased from just under 6,000 miles in 1848 to over 30,000 miles by 1860.[3] As the railroad network grew, so did the size of individual rail companies. By 1855, at least 13 rail companies operated and maintained more than 200 miles of track. By the mid–1850s, the railroad industry had clearly established itself as America's first big business. It was the first industry whose scope of operations extended beyond the local area.[4] Although textiles were America's first entry into the industrial age they were basically a local business with much smaller financial needs than rail companies.[5] Unlike local industries, railroad networks often spanned hundreds of miles, creating control and communication problems. Facilities could not be inspected in a matter of hours; decisions had to be made within a rapidly changing framework; scheduling became complicated. Beyond the day-to-day operating decisions, other management decisions became more complex. Long-range decisions had to be made about the expansion of facilities, new equipment purchases, and how to finance these operations.

Unlike the textile industry, which was transplanted from Europe, there were few precedents to guide the managers of the railroad companies.[6] Thus, rail company managers were the first in this country to need a sophisticated approach to management.

The railroads also made another significant contribution to the development of management: they created national and increasingly urban markets. Urban and industrial centers sprang up all along their miles of tracks. Thus, by providing rapid movement of raw materials and finished goods, railroads made a truly national market possible.

The third facet of the American Industrial Revolution—communication— was primed in 1844 by Samuel F. B. Morse's invention of the telegraph. Using the telegraph, managers could coordinate and communicate with speed and efficiency.

By 1860, the year generally thought of as the start of the Industrial Revolution in this country, power, transportation, and communication had advanced to the point that they served as an inducement to the entrepreneur.

CAPTAINS OF INDUSTRY

During the last 25 years of the 19th century, an important change took place in American industry. The economy shifted from mainly agrarian to one more involved with manufactured goods and industrial markets.[7] This was

Captains of industry –dominated and built corporate giants during the last 25 years of the 19th century; included John D. Rockefeller, James B. Duke, Andrew Carnegie, Cornelius Vanderbilt, and others.

a direct result of the urbanization brought about by a nationwide railroad system.

American business during this period was dominated and shaped by **captains of industry.** These captains of industry included men like John D. Rockefeller (oil), James B. Duke (tobacco), Andrew Carnegie (steel) and Cornelius Vanderbilt (steamships and railroads). Unlike the laissez-faire attitudes of previous generations, these men often pursued profit and self-interest above all else. While their methods have been questioned, they did obtain results. Under these men giant companies were formed through mergers in both the consumer and producer goods industries. They created new forms of organizations and introduced new methods of marketing. For the first time, nationwide distributing and marketing organizations were formed. The birth of the corporate giant also altered the business decision-making environment.

For the empire building and methods of the captains of industry, previous management methods no longer applied. Government began to regulate business. In 1890, the Sherman Antitrust Act, which sought to check corporate practices "in restraint of trade," was passed.

By 1890, previous management methods were no longer applicable to U.S. industry. No longer could managers make on-the-spot decisions and maintain records in their heads. Corporations had become large scale, with national markets. Communication and transportation had expanded and greatly helped industrial growth. Technological innovations contributed to industrial growth: The invention of the internal combustion engine and the use of electricity as a power source greatly speeded industrial development at the close of the 19th century.

However, despite what seemed an ideal climate for prosperity and productivity, wages were low.[8] Production methods were crude; worker training was almost nonexistent. There were no methods or standards for measuring work. Work had not been studied to determine the most desirable way to complete a task. The psychological and physical aspects of a job—like boredom, monotony, and fatigue—were not studied or even considered in the design of most jobs.

At this point in the development of management, the engineering profession made significant contributions. Engineers designed, built, installed, and made operative the production systems. It was only natural, then, for them to study the methods used in operating these systems.

SCIENTIFIC MANAGEMENT AND F. W. TAYLOR

The development of specialized tasks and of departments within organizations had come with the rapid industrial growth and the creation of big business. One person no longer performed every task but rather specialized in performing only a few tasks. This created a need to coordinate, integrate, and systematize

MANAGERS AT WORK 2–1

Father of Scientific Management

Frederick Winslow Taylor was born in Germantown, Pennsylvania, in 1856 of Quaker-Puritan stock. His parents wanted him to be a lawyer like his father and hence enrolled him at Phillips Exeter Academy to prepare for Harvard. Though Taylor passed the Harvard exams with honors, his poor health and eyesight forced him to take up an apprenticeship as a pattern-maker and machinist with the Enterprise Hydraulic works at Philadelphia in 1874. He was not paid at the start of his four-year apprenticeship because his father was a "man of means"; by the time he completed the apprenticeship, his pay was $3 per week. In spite of the low pay, Taylor turned out to be a diligent and sincere worker. Even as a youth he had developed a sense of self-control, character, and an ability to handle dull and tiresome tasks. At the end of his apprenticeship period, Taylor joined Midvale Steel as a common laborer and rose to machinist, to gang boss of the machinists, to foreman of the shop, to master mechanic in charge of repairs and maintenance throughout the plant, and to chief engineer in the short span of six years. This was quite an achievement for a person who had no formal training in management. Occupationally and otherwise, those 12 years which Taylor spent at Midvale were eventful. Apart from winning the U.S. Amateur doubles tennis championship in 1881, Taylor earned a mechanical engineering degree from Stevens Institute in 1883. After a three-year stint as general manager at Manufacturing Investment Company, Taylor set up practice as a consulting engineer for management. It was as a consultant to Bethlehem Steel Company that Taylor made his greatest contribution to management with his time and motion studies. Taylor published *Shop Management* in 1903 and three years later was elected president of the American Society of Mechanical Engineers. The world of management was indeed poorer when Taylor died of pneumonia a day after his 59th birthday. The epitaph at his grave in Philadelphia reads "Frederick W. Taylor, Father of Scientific Management" and rightly so.

Source: Daniel A. Wren, *The Evolution of Management Thought* (New York: Ronald Press, 1972).

the work flow. The time spent on each item could be significant if a company was producing several thousand items. Increased production plus the new need for integrating and systematizing the work flow caused engineers to begin to study work flows and job content.

The spark generally credited with igniting the interest of engineers to general business problems was a paper presented in 1886 by Henry Towne, president of the Yale and Towne Manufacturing Company, to the American Society of Mechanical Engineers. Towne stressed that engineers should be concerned with the financial and profit orientation of the business as well as their traditional technical responsibilities.[9] A young mechanical engineer named Frederick Winslow Taylor was seated in the audience. As you will see in Managers at Work, 2–1, Taylor had a profound impact on the development of management.

Taylor's first job was as an apprentice with the Enterprise Hydraulic Works of Philadelphia.[10] Here Taylor learned pattern making and machining. Upon finishing his apprenticeship in 1878, Taylor joined Midvale Steel Company as a common laborer. In six short years, he rose through eight positions to chief engineer. During his earlier years at Midvale, Taylor worked with and observed production workers at all levels. It did not take him long to figure out that many workers put forth less than 100 percent effort. Taylor referred to this behavior of restricting output as **soldiering.** Because soldiering was in conflict with Taylor's Quaker-Puritan background, it was hard for him to understand and accept. He decided to find out why workers soldiered.

Soldiering – describes the actions of employees who intentionally restrict output.

Taylor quickly saw that workers had little or no reason to produce more—most wage systems of that time were based on attendance and position. Piece-rate systems had been tried before but generally failed because of poor use and weak standards. Taylor believed a piece-rate system would work—if the workers believed that the standard had been fairly set and that management would stick to that standard. Taylor wanted to use scientific and empirical methods rather than tradition and custom for setting work standards. Taylor's efforts became the true beginning of scientific management.

Taylor first formally presented his views to the Society of Mechanical Engineers in 1895.[11] His views were expanded in book form in 1903 and in 1911.[12] **Scientific management,** as developed by Taylor, was based upon four main principles:

Scientific management – philosophy of Frederick W. Taylor that sought to increase productivity and make the work easier by scientifically studying work methods and establishing standards.

1. The development of a scientific method of designing jobs to replace the old rule-of-thumb methods. This involved gathering, classifying, and tabulating data to arrive at the "one best way" to perform a task or a series of tasks.
2. The scientific selection and progressive teaching and development of employees. Taylor saw the value of matching the job to the worker. He also emphasized the need to study worker strengths and weaknesses and to provide training to improve employee performance.
3. The bringing together of scientifically selected employees and scientifically developed methods for designing jobs. Taylor believed that new and scientific methods of job design should not merely be put before an employee; they also should be fully explained by management. He believed that employees would show little resistance to changes in methods if they understood the reasons for the change—and they saw a chance for greater earnings for themselves.
4. A division of work resulting in an interdependence between management and the workers. Taylor felt that if they were truly dependent on one another, then cooperation would naturally follow.[13]

Scientific management was a complete mental revolution for both management and employees toward their respective duties and toward each other.[14]

Frederick Winslow Taylor (1865–1915)
Scientific management is actually a philosophy about
the relationship between people and work—it is not a
technique or efficiency device. Taylor's research earned
him the title "Father of Scientific Management."

It was a new philosophy and attitude toward the use of human effort. It
emphasized maximum output with minimum effort through the elimination
of waste and inefficiency at the operative level.[15] A methodological approach
was used to study job tasks. This approach included research and experimentation methods (scientific methods). Standards were set in the areas of personnel,
working conditions, equipment, output, and procedures. The managers
planned the work; the workers performed it. The result was closer cooperation
between managers and workers.

The scientific study of work also emphasized specialization and division
of labor. Thus, the need for an organizational framework became more and
more apparent. The concepts of line and staff were developed. In an effort
to motivate workers, wage incentives were developed in most scientific management programs. Once standards were set, managers began to monitor

MANAGERS AT WORK 2–2

A Steelworker Made Management History

In 1899, a man named Henry Noll loaded 48 tons of pig iron in one day as part of a scientific management experiment conducted by Frederick W. Taylor for Bethlehem Steel. From that experiment, Taylor developed a high-incentive work program with a set sequence of work and rest motions. The program—described in Taylor's *Principles of Scientific Management*—was designed to more than triple the amount a worker could load in a day. The Taylor method was adopted by companies all over the country.

When the results of the experiment were published, Henry Noll—under the pseudonym "Schmidt"—was described only as an ambitious and healthy 27-year-old man. In a social commentary published 12 years later, Upton Sinclair described Taylor's method as inhumane and accused him of unfairly inducing "Schmidt" to perform 362 percent more work for 61 percent more pay.

In response to the criticism, Taylor and others made several unsuccessful attempts to find Henry Noll, and rumors began to surface that he had died of overexertion. In 1914, he was finally found and pronounced healthy by a physician. Henry Noll—"Schmidt"— died a natural death in 1925.

Source: Ann Kovalenko, *The Sunday Call–Chronicle,* Allentown, Pa., December 6, 1964.

actual performance and compare it with the standards. Thus began the managerial function of control.

Scientific management is a philosophy about the relationship between people and work—not a technique or an efficiency device. Taylor's ideas and scientific management were based on a concern not only for the proper design of the job but also for the worker. This has often not been understood. Taylor and scientific management were (and still are) attacked as being inhumane and interested only in increased output. The key to Taylor's thinking was that he saw scientific management as benefiting both management and the worker equally: Management could achieve more work in a given amount of time; the worker could produce more—and hence earn more—with little or no additional effort. In summary, Taylor and other scientific management pioneers believed that employees could be motivated by economic rewards, provided that those rewards were related to individual performance. Managers at Work 2–2 provides an interesting story related to Frederick Taylor.

OTHER SCIENTIFIC MANAGEMENT PIONEERS

Several disciples and colleagues of Taylor helped to promote scientific management. Carl Barth was often called the most orthodox of Taylor's followers.

He worked with Taylor at Bethlehem Steel and followed him as a consultant when Taylor left Bethelehem. Barth did not alter or add to scientific management in any great manner. Rather, he worked to popularize Taylor's ideas.

Morris Cooke worked directly with Taylor on several occasions. Cooke's major contribution was to apply scientific management to educational and municipal organizations. Cooke worked hard to bring management and labor together through scientific management. His thesis was that labor was as responsible for production as management. Cooke believed that increased production would improve the position of both.[16] Thus, Cooke broadened the scope of scientific management and helped gain the support of organized labor.

Henry Lawrence Gantt worked with Taylor at Midvale Steel and at Bethelehem Steel. Gantt is best known for his work in production control; the "Gantt chart" is still in use today. Gantt was also one of the first management pioneers to state publicly the social responsibility of management and business. He believed that the community would attempt to take over business if the business system neglected its social responsibilities.[17]

Frank and Lillian Gilbreth were important to the early management movement as a husband-and-wife team and as individuals. Frank Gilbreth's major area of interest was the study of motions and work methods. Lillian Gilbreth's primary field was psychology.

Following Frank's untimely death in 1924 (he was in his mid-50s), Lillian continued their work for almost 50 years until her death in 1972. Because of her many achievements (see Figure 2–1), Lillian Gilbreth became known as the "First Lady of Management."

By combining motion study and psychology, the Gilbreths contributed greatly to research in the areas of fatigue, monotony, micromotion study, and morale.

Harrington Emerson, who coined the term *efficiency engineer,* was one of the first to recognize the importance of good organization. Emerson felt that waste and inefficiency were eroding the American industrial system. He believed that organization and scientific management could eliminate most waste and inefficiency. Emerson also developed organized management consulting at a time when consulting engineers were still mainly concerned with technical rather than managerial problems.

FAYOL'S THEORY OF MANAGEMENT

Henri Fayol, a Frenchman, was the first to issue a complete statement on a theory of general management. Born of relatively well-to-do parents, Fayol graduated as a mining engineer. He started in 1860 as a junior executive of a coal mining and iron foundry company. In 1888, the company was near bankruptcy. Fayol took over as managing director and rapidly turned the company into a financially sound organization. After retirement in 1918, Fayol lectured and popularized his theory of administration. He became especially

F I G U R E 2–1   Achievements of Lillian M. Gilbreth—the "First Lady of Management"

Phi Beta Kappa graduate from University of California 1900 and first woman to give the university's Commencement Day Address.

Received her Ph.D. degree from Brown University becoming the first woman in the United States to receive a doctorate in psychology.

Doctoral dissertation, *The Psychology of Management,* was published as a book in 1914.

Became president of Gilbreth, Incorporated in 1924.

Became professor of management at the Purdue School of Mechanical Engineering in 1935, the first woman to hold such an appointment. Was selected American Woman's Association "Woman of the Year" in 1948.

First woman to be named an honorary member of the American Society of Mechanical Engineers.

First woman elected to the National Academy of Engineering.

Served on Committees under five U.S. Presidents.

Received over 20 honorary degrees.

Lillian M. Gilbreth (1878–1972)   **Frank B. Gilbreth** (1868–1924)

The Gilbreths, inspired by Taylor and scientific research, were among the first to use motion picture films to study hand and body movements to eliminate wasted motion. Frank is best known for his work in minimizing motion in bricklaying.

interested in applying administrative theory to government. Fayol's major work *Administration Industrielle et Generale,* was published in 1916.[18] Unfortunately, this work was not translated into English until 1930 and then in only a very limited number of copies. The book was not readily available in English until 1949.

Possibly Fayol's greatest contribution was his discussion of management principles and elements. Fayol gave the following 14 "principles of management." (He stressed flexibility in the application of these principles and that allowances should be made for different and changing circumstances.)

1. Division of work—concept of specialization of work.
2. Authority—formal (positional) authority versus personal authority.
3. Discipline—based on obedience and respect.
4. Unity of command—each employee should receive orders from only one superior.
5. Unity of direction—one boss and one plan for a group of activities having the same objective.
6. Subordination of individual interests to the general interest—plea to abolish the tendency of placing individual interest ahead of the group interest.
7. Remuneration—mode of payment of wages was dependent on many factors.
8. Centralization—degree of centralization desired depended on the situation authority and the formal communication channels.
9. Scalar chain (line of authority)—shows the routing of the line of authority and formal communication channels.
10. Order—ensured a place for everything.
11. Equity—resulted from kindness and justice.
12. Stability of tenured personnel—called for orderly personnel planning.
13. Initiative—called for individual zeal and energy in all efforts.
14. Esprit de corps—stressed the building of harmony and unity within the organization.

Fayol developed his list of principles from the practices he had used most often in his own work. He used them as broad and general guidelines for effective management. His real contribution was not the 14 principles themselves—many of these were the products of the early factory system—but rather his formal recognition and synthesis of these principles.

In presenting his "elements of management," Fayol was probably the first to outline what today are called the functions of management. Fayol listed planning, organizing, commanding, coordinating, and controlling as elements of management. He most emphasized planning and organizing because he viewed these elements as primary and essential to the other functions.

The works of Taylor and Fayol are essentially complementary. Both men believed that proper management of personnel and other resources was the key to organizational success. Both used a scientific approach to management. Their major difference was in their orientation. Taylor stressed the management of operative work, while Fayol stressed the management of organization.

PERIOD OF SOLIDIFICATION

**Period of solidi-
fication** – oc-
curred in the 1920s
and 30s; manage-
ment became rec-
ognized as a disci-
pline.

The 1920s and most of the 30s was a **period of solidification** and populariza-tion of management as a discipline. The acceptance of management as a respect-able discipline was gained through several avenues. Universities and colleges began to teach management; by 1925, most schools of engineering were offering classes in management.[19] Professional societies began to take an interest in management. Much of the management pioneers' work was presented through the American Society of Mechanical Engineers; after the turn of the century, many other professional societies began to promote management. In 1912, the Society to Promote the Science of Management was founded. The society was reorganized in 1916 as the Taylor Society. In 1936, it merged with the Society of Industrial Engineers to form the Society for the Advancement of Management, still a viable organization. The American Management Associa-tion was founded in 1923.

The first meeting of management teachers, sponsored by the Taylor Society, was held in New York in December 1924.[20] The participants agreed that the first course in management should be called Industrial Organization and Management—they could not agree on what should be required in a manage-ment curriculum. After this meeting, professors began writing textbooks in the field of management.

During the 1930s, management teachers and practitioners began to stress organization. *Onward Industry!* by J. D. Mooney and A. C. Reiley appeared in 1931 and generated interest in the historical development of organizations. Several other books in this era focused on the organizing function. By the mid-1930s, management was truly a recognized discipline. The major events leading to this are summarized in Figure 2–2.

F I G U R E 2–2 Significant Events Contributing to the Solidification of Management

- First conference on "Scientific Management," October 1911.
- First doctoral dissertation on subject of scientific management by H. R. Drury at Columbia University, 1915.
- Founding of professional management societies: Society to Promote the Science of Management, 1912; Society of Industrial Engineers, 1917; American Management Association, 1923; Society for Advancement of Management, 1936.
- First meeting of management teachers, December 1924.

THE HUMAN RELATIONS THRUST

The Great Depression saw unemployment in excess of 25 percent. Afterwards, unions sought and gained major advantages for the working class. In this period, known as the Golden Age of Unionism, legislatures and courts actively supported organized labor and the worker. Figure 2–3 contains a summary of the major pro-union laws passed during the 1920s and 30s.

F I G U R E 2–3   Significant Pro-Union Legislation during the 1920s and 1930s

Railway Labor Act of 1926	Gave railway workers the right to form unions and engage in collective bargaining; established a corresponding obligation for employers to recognize and collectively bargain with the union.
Norris–La Guardia Act of 1932	Severely restricted the use of injunctions to limit union activity.
National Labor Relations Act of 1935 (Wagner Act)	Resulted in full, enforceable rights of employees to join unions and to engage in collective bargaining with their employer, who was legally obligated to do so.
Fair Labor Standards Act of 1938	Established minimum wages and required that time-and-a-half wages be paid for hours worked over 40 in one week.

Organized labor and workers were attracting more attention. Therefore, emphasis began to be placed on understanding workers and their needs—it was the birth of the human relations movement. The earlier lack of emphasis on human relations was made prominent by the now famous Hawthorne Studies.[21]

The Hawthorne Studies

The **Hawthorne studies** began in 1924 when the National Research Council of the National Academy of Sciences began a project to define the relationship between physical working conditions and worker productivity. The Hawthorne Plant of Western Electric in Cicero, Illinois, was the study site. First, the researchers lowered the level of lighting, expecting productivity to decrease. To their astonishment, productivity increased. Over the next several months, the researchers repeated the experiment by testing many different levels of lighting. Regardless of the level of light, output was found to increase.

Baffled by the results, in early 1927 the researchers called in a team of psychologists from Harvard University led by Elton Mayo. Over the course

Hawthorne studies—series of experiments conducted in 1924 at the Hawthorne Plant of Western Electric of Cicero, Illinois: production increased in no relationship to environment but rather to psychological and social conditions.

of the next five years, hundreds of experiments were run involving thousands of employees. In these experiments the researchers altered such variables as wage payments, rest periods, and length of workday. The results were similar to those obtained in the illumination experiments—production increased in no obvious relationship to the environment. After much analysis, the psychologists concluded that other factors besides the physical environment affected worker productivity. They found that workers reacted to the psychological and social conditions at work—such as informal group pressures, individual recognition, and participation in the making of decisions. The significance of effective supervision to both productivity and employee morale was also identified and emphasized.

While the methods used and the conclusions reached by the Hawthorne researchers have been questioned, they did generate great interest in the human problems in the workplace and focused attention on the human factor.[22]

At the same time, Mary Parker Follett spurred the human relations movement. Mary Follett was not a businesswoman in the sense of managing her own business. But her writings and lectures did have great impact on many business and government leaders. While concerned with many aspects of the management process, her basic theory was that the fundamental problem of any organization was to build and maintain dynamic, yet harmonious, human relations within the organization.[23] In 1938, Chester Barnard (president

These Hawthorne studies workers didn't know it when this picture was snapped, but they were destined to become identified with one of the most famous experiments in human behavior. Begun in 1924, the Hawthorne studies continued until 1933.

of New Jersey Bell Telephone for many years) published a book which combined a thorough knowledge of organization theory and sociology.[24] Barnard viewed the organization as a social structure. He stressed the psychosocial aspects of organizations. Effectively integrating traditional management and the behavioral sciences, Barnard's work had a great impact on both managers and teachers of management.

THE PROFESSIONAL MANAGER

The career manager, or professional manager, did not exist until the 1930s. Until this time, managers could be placed into one of three categories: owner-managers, captains of industry, or financial managers. The owner-managers dominated until after the Civil War. The captains of industry controlled organizations from the 1880s through the turn of the century. The financial managers operated much the same as the captains of industry, except they often did not own the enterprises they controlled and operated. The financial managers dominated from around 1905 until the early 1930s, when public confidence in business organizations was severely weakened by the Great Depression.

During this time of weakened public confidence, people began to enter managerial jobs to perform those functions rather than because they owned the business. Thus emerged the professional manager. The **professional manager** is a career person who does not necessarily have a controlling interest in the enterprise for which he or she works. Professional managers realize their responsibility to three groups: employees, stockholders, and the public. With expanded technology and more complex organizations, the professional manager became more and more prevalent.

Professional manager – career manager who does not necessarily have a controlling interest in the organization and who realizes a responsibility to employees, stockholders, and the public.

CHANGING STYLES OF MANAGEMENT

As organizations grew in size and complexity, managers began stressing the importance of workers and their needs. As managers studied the worker and developed theories about worker behavior, new styles and methods of managing emerged.

One innovative style of managing was that of James F. Lincoln. The serious illness of his brother forced Lincoln to assume the top management position of the Lincoln Electric Company in 1913.[25] He knew little about managing a business and had no top management experience. But Lincoln remembered his former football days and the cooperation needed on the gridiron. He sought the help of his employees in managing the company.

Lincoln realized that effective cooperation required rewards. Thus he designed a plan that coupled an incentive system with a request for cooperation.

Lincoln emphasized the basic need of all individuals to express themselves. Specifically, the plan contained the following components:

1. An advisory board of employees.
2. A piece-rate method of compensation wherever possible.
3. A suggestion system.
4. Employee ownership of stock.
5. Year-end bonuses.
6. Life insurance for all employees.
7. Two weeks of paid vacation.
8. An annuity pension plan.
9. Promotion policy.

The development of the Lincoln Electric Company can be attributed to its innovative management. It certainly has been successful. For several decades, Lincoln workers have consistently been among the highest paid in their industry in the world—they have averaged almost double the total pay of employees in competing companies. Lincoln's selling price has consistently been lower than any comparable product. And the company has consistently paid a dividend since 1918. Managers at Work 2–3 provides some additional information about Lincoln Electric.

Another innovative manager, Henry Dennison (1877–1952), felt that the strengths of an organization came from its members and that the sources of power are the incentives, habits, and traditions that influence people in an organization.[26] Dennison believed that an organization has greatest strength if: all of its members are strongly motivated; their actions lose no effectiveness by frictions, conflicts, or unbalance; and their actions move in a single direction, reinforcing each other. He believed that management's primary purpose was to provide conditions under which employees work most readily and effectively. Instead of designing an organizational structure first, Dennison advocated finding "like-minded" people, grouping them, and then developing the total organizational structure. In summary, Dennison believed that management attention must focus on causes and effects in the field of human behavior. Dennison successfully practiced his management approach in the 1920s and 1930s at the Dennison Manufacturing Company, which was also one of the early companies to implement the Taylor system of scientific management.

Charles McCormick and William Given, Jr., were top managers who applied a human relations philosophy to their organizations. Both McCormick's and Given's styles of management were based on worker involvement in the decision-making process.

McCormick, the manufacturer of spices and extracts, developed and made famous the **McCormick multiple-management plan.**[27] This plan used participation as a training and motivating tool by selecting 17 promising young people from various departments within the company to form a junior board

McCormick multiple-management plan – developed by Charles McCormick; uses participation as a training and motivational tool by selecting promising young employees from various company departments to form a junior board of directors.

MANAGERS AT WORK 2–3

Productivity Policy at Lincoln Electric

John C. Lincoln founded Lincoln Electric Company in 1895 as a manufacturer of electric motors with a capital of $200. Today, after nine decades, Lincoln Electric has grown into the largest manufacturer of welding machines and electrodes. In 1914, James F. Lincoln, John's younger brother, became active head of the firm. Lincoln Electric's long-term policy on employee relations has been based on what James once said, "Labor and management are properly not warring camps; they are parts of one organization in which they must and should cooperate fully and happily." Despite the lack of latest automation, Lincoln Electric's Cleveland plant has achieved the desired goal of business with higher productivity. This has been primarily due to Lincoln's attitude toward employees which is reflected in the following statement:

If money is to be used as an incentive, the program must provide that what is paid to the worker is what he has earned. The earnings of each must be in accordance with accomplishment.

Keeping this in view, Lincoln relies on its so-called Million Dollar Men. These are skilled machine operators who supervise the work of as many as five machines at once. With higher productivity and each Million Dollar Man making $80,000 in a good year, Lincoln has been able to reduce millions of dollars on capital investment.

Source: Arthur Sharplin, *Strategic Management* (New York: McGraw-Hill, 1985), pp. 466–87; "America's Best Managed Factories," *Fortune,* May 28, 1984, pp. 16–24.

---

of directors. The junior board met with the senior board once a month and submitted its suggestions. Beside the immediate benefits of providing suggestions, the junior board provided early identification of management talent, opened communication lines, and relieved senior board members of much of the detailed planning and research. The huge success of the junior board led to the creation of sales and factory boards that operated in much the same way.

Using the term **bottom-up management,** Given, president of American Brake Shoe and Foundry Company, encouraged widespread delegation of authority to gain the involvement of "all those down from the bottom up."[28] Given's approach promoted considerable managerial freedom in decision making, the free interchange of ideas, and the recognition that managerial growth involves some failure. Given believed that the judgment, initiative, and creativeness of all employees in an organization provide a better end result than the autocratic administration of any single individual.

In 1938, Joseph Scanlon developed a productivity plan that gave employees

Bottom-up management – philosophy popularized by William B. Given, which encouraged widespread delegation of authority to solicit the participation of all employees from the bottom to the top.

Scanlon plan – incentive plan developed in 1938 by Joseph Scanlon to give workers a bonus for tangible savings in labor costs.

a bonus for tangible savings in labor costs. The **Scanlon plan** was unique in at least three respects: (1) Joint management and union committees were formed to discuss and propose labor-saving techniques. (2) Group rewards— not individual rewards—were made for suggestions. (3) Employees shared in reduced costs rather than increased profits.[29] Scanlon believed that participation was desirable not just to create a feeling of belonging but also to show clearly the role of employees and unions in suggesting improvements.

Many of the emerging styles of management of the 1930s and 40s had distinct differences. But most were based on the human relations thrust, especially on participation. The emergence of the professional manager and the rapidly rising standard of living led to a greater concern for the employee and hence to the development of participative forms of management. The professional manager realized that a greater concern for the worker would most likely result in greater productivity and therefore greater profits. The rising standard of living made workers more mobile, increased the employment options open to them, and made them less likely to settle for a strictly authoritarian environment.

MANAGEMENT PROCESS PERIOD

Process approach to management – focuses on the management functions of planning, controlling, organizing, staffing, and leading.

During the late 1940s, management thought began to move toward the idea of a **process approach to management.**[30] This was an attempt to identify and define a process for attaining desired objectives. The process approach led management to become primarily concerned with identifying and refining the functions or components of the management process. For this reason, the process approach is sometimes referred to as the "functional approach."

As we have said, Henri Fayol was the first management scholar to present explicitly a functional analysis of the management process. Fayol listed planning, organizing, commanding, coordination, and control as functions of management.

Oliver Sheldon, an Englishman, also gave an early breakdown of the management process.[31] In 1923, Sheldon saw management as the determination of business policy, the coordination of the execution of policy, the organization of the business, and the control of the executive.

Ralph C. Davis was the first American to publish a functional breakdown of the management process.[32] He subdivided it into three functions: planning, organizing, and controlling.

All of these management scholars made early reference to a functional approach to management. But the concept was not widely accepted until Constance Storrs' translation made Fayol's work readily available in 1949. Thus Fayol was truly responsible for fathering the process approach to management.

At the same time, process management was gaining acceptance as a teachable discipline. Before, while accepted as a discipline, it had been modeled after certain successful individuals. The functional approach offered a new, logical, concrete method of presenting management.

A second generation of management process thinkers evolved after the 1949 translation of Fayol's work. They taught management via the functional approach. Most management texts of the 1950s presented management as a series of functions and principles that could be learned and synthesized in a logical fashion.

The early to mid-1950s was an era of almost complete agreement about the composition and teachings of management. The management process, or functional, approach was the accepted method for the study of management.

THE MANAGEMENT THEORY JUNGLE

The late 1950s saw a new era in the study of management. Uneasy with the process approach to management, production management and industrial engineering scholars began testing mathematical and modeling approaches to quantify management. As a result, mathematical and decision theory schools of thought developed for the study of management. The decision theory school was based largely on economic theory and the theory of consumer choice. The mathematical school viewed management as a system of mathematical relationships. At the same time, behavioral scientists were studying management as small-group relations; they depended heavily on psychology and social psychology. Drawing on the work of Chester Barnard and sociological theory, another school saw management as a system of cultural interrelationships. An empirical school of thought was developed by those scholars using the case approach. Their basic premise was that effective management could be learned by studying the successes and failures of other managers.

Harold Koontz was the first management scholar to discuss clearly this fragmentation movement.[33] Koontz accurately referred to this division of thought as the **management theory jungle.** Many conferences and discussions followed Koontz's analysis in an attempt to untangle the theory jungle and to unite the various schools of thought. While some progress was made, a unified theory of management has not been realized.

THE SYSTEMS APPROACH

The fragmentation period of the late 1950s and early 60s was followed by an era of attempted integration. Many management theorists sought to use a "systems approach" in order to integrate the various management schools.

Management theory jungle – term developed by Harold Koontz; refers to the division of thought that resulted from the multiple approaches to studying the management process.

Systems approach to management – views the human, physical, and informational facets of the manager's job as linking to form an integrated whole.

The **systems approach to management** was viewed as "a way of thinking about the job of managing . . . [which] provides a framework for visualizing internal and external environmental factors as an integrated whole."[34] The manager was asked to view the human, physical, and informational facets of the manager's job as linked in an integrated whole.

One popular thrust was to use a systems approach to integrate the other schools of management into the traditional functional approach. The idea was to integrate the human relations and mathematical approaches into the appropriate functional areas. Thus while studying planning, a systems approach might include mathematical forecasting techniques.

Other systems approaches were much more grand and were based on general systems theory. These versions attempted to analyze management in terms of other disciplines and cultures. Comparative management evolved because of the multinational firms and the need for managing in diverse fields.[35]

The term *systems approach* has been overused by many. Yet, a holistic view of the management process has special merit for today's students and practitioners of management. They must learn to integrate the different management functions and topics. For example, successful managers must understand both the function of planning and how to relate planning to the other management functions.

THE CONTINGENCY APPROACH

Contingency approach to management – theorizes that different situations and conditions require different management approaches.

The 1970s were characterized by the so-called contingency approach. In the **contingency approach to management,** different situations and conditions require different management approaches. Proponents believe that there is no one best way of managing; the best way depends on the specific circumstances. Recognizing the rarity of a manager who thinks that one way of managing works best in *all* situations, one might ask, "What is new about this approach?"

What is new is that contingency theorists have often gone much farther than simply saying "it all depends." Many contingency theories outline in detail the style or approach that works best under certain conditions and circumstances. Contingency theories—many are discussed in this book—have been developed in areas such as decision making, organizational design, leadership, planning, and group behavior.

THE INTERNATIONAL AND GLOBAL MOVEMENT

In recent years, many U.S. companies have turned to the international arena for new markets and profits. For example, in 1986, the 100 largest U.S. multinationals had sales of $383 billion outside the United States.

Of this group of 100 largest multinationals, 10 companies realized more than 50 percent of their revenues from international markets and 60 companies realized between 25 and 50 percent of their revenues from international markets.[36] As U.S. companies have been expanding internationally, more foreign companies have been entering the U.S. market. Leading this group have been the Japanese, Taiwanese, and Koreans. Even companies that do not trade directly in the international and global markets are often greatly affected by foreign competition. As a result, U.S. managers have and are being forced to think in the terms of international and global rather than local or national markets.

IN SEARCH OF EXCELLENCE

In 1982 Thomas J. Peters and Robert H. Waterman, Jr., released a book, **In Search of Excellence,** that has since become the best-selling management-related book ever published.[37] Working as management consultants at a time in which Japanese management styles were receiving worldwide attention

In Search of Excellence – book by Thomas J. Peters and Robert H. Waterman, Jr., identifies 36 companies with an excellent 20-year performance record over a 20-year period. The authors formulated eight characteristics of excellence after interviewing managers in each company.

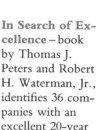

Thomas J. Peters   **Robert H. Waterman**

Reacting to the attention Japanese management style was receiving, Peters and Waterman researched six American industries: high technology, general industry, service, project management, consumer goods, and resource-based industries. Their study identified eight "attributes of excellence."

(in the late 1970s), Peters and Waterman asked the question, can't we learn something from America's most successful companies? Using a combination of subjective criteria and six measures of financial success covering a 20-year period (1961 through 1980), the authors identified a final subsample of 36 American companies. According to the authors' criteria, these companies had demonstrated excellent performance over the 20-year time frame being studied. Most of the 36 companies in the final subsample were well known companies such as IBM, McDonalds, Delta Airlines, and Eastman Kodak.

After interviewing each company in the subsample and analyzing their findings, Peters and Waterman identified the eight "attributes of excellence" (summarized in Figure 2–4).

While Peters and Waterman's work has been criticized as being overly subjective and not based on sound research methods, it has caused many managers to rethink their ways of doing things.[38] Specifically, Peters and Waterman re-emphasized the value of on-the-job experimentation and creative thinking, the need to place the customer first, and the need to treat employees

F I G U R E   2–4   Peters and Waterman's Eight Characteristics of Excellent Companies

CHARACTERISTICS OF EXCELLENCE	DESCRIPTION OF CHARACTERISTICS
1. A bias for action	A tendency to get on with things. A willingness to experiment.
2. Close to the customer	The provision of unparalleled quality/service. A willingness to listen to the customer.
3. Autonomy and entrepreneurship	Encouragement of practical risk taking and innovation. Tolerance of a reasonable number of mistakes as a part of the innovative process.
4. Productivity through people	Rank and file employees are viewed as the root source of quality and productivity gains. Employees are treated with respect and dignity. Enthusiasm and trust are encouraged.
5. Hands on; value driven	The company philosophy and values are clearly communicated. Managers take a "hands-on" approach.
6. Stick to the knitting	Companies diversify only into businesses that are closely related. Emphasis is on internal growth as opposed to mergers.
7. Simple form; lean staff	Companies have simple structure with clear lines of authority. Headquarters staff are kept small.
8. Simultaneous loose-tight properties	Autonomy is pushed down to the lowest levels but at the same time certain core values are not negotiable.

Source: Thomas J. Peters and Robert W. Waterman, *In Search of Excellence* (New York: Harper & Row, 1982), pp. 13–16.

MANAGERS AT WORK 2–4

The "Excellent Companies" Revisited

In the two years after *In Search of Excellence* was published, at least 14 of the "excellent" companies highlighted by Peters and Waterman had lost some of their luster. Of the 14 companies that stumbled, 12 were inept in adapting to fundamental changes in their markets. Some maintain that overadherence to Peters and Waterman's eight characteristics, which do not emphasize reacting to broad economic and business trends, may have contributed to their problems. Others, including Peters and Waterman, argue that these companies ran into trouble because they strayed from the principles that had been key to their earlier successes. At least two lessons can be drawn from the experiences of these companies: (1) the excellent companies of today will not necessarily be the excellent companies of tomorrow, and (2) good management requires much more than merely following any one set of rules.

Source: "Who's Excellent Now?" *Business Week,* November 5, 1984, pp. 76–78.

---

as human beings. Managers at Work 2–4 discusses what has subsequently happened to some of Peters and Waterman's "excellent companies."

This chapter summarizes the major events that impacted management discipline from the 19th century to the present. But the discipline did not develop and mature at the same rate in all parts of the country. Similarly, it did not develop from a series of discrete happenings; rather it grew from a series of major and minor events. Figure 2–5 presents a chronological summation of the major and related events in the management movement.

F I G U R E   2–5   Major Components and Related Events of the Management Movement

MANAGEMENT MOVEMENT COMPONENT	RELATIVE MAJOR EVENTS
U.S. Industrial Revolution (prior to 1875)	Steam power (1790–1810). Railroad boom (1830–50). Telegraph (1844).
Captains of industry (1875–1900)	Formation of corporate giants: John D. Rockefeller (oil). James B. Duke (tobacco). Andrew Carnegie (steel). Cornelius Vanderbilt (shipping and railroads).

F I G U R E 2–5   *(concluded)*

MANAGEMENT MOVEMENT COMPONENT	RELATIVE MAJOR EVENTS
Scientific management era (1895–1920)	Henry Towne, "The Engineer as Economist," 1886. Frederick W. Taylor's work (1895–1915): Carl Barth. Morris Cooke. Henry Lawrence Gantt. Frank and Lillian Gilbreth. Harrington Emerson. Henri Fayol, *Administration Industrielle et Generale,* 1916.
Period of solidification (1920 to early 1930s)	Founding of professional management societies (1920s). Mooney and Reiley, *Onward Industry!* 1931.
Human relations movement (1931 to late 1940s)	Hawthorne Studies, led by Elton Mayo (1924–32). Mary Parker Follett (1920–33). Chester Barnard, *Functions of the Executive,* 1938.
Management process period (early 1950s to early 1960s)	Storrs' translation of Fayol's work (1949). Ralph Davis, *Top Management Planning,* 1951. George Terry, *Principles of Management,* 1953. Koontz and O'Donnell, *Principles of Management,* 1955.
Management theory jungle (early to late 1960s)	Process approach. Quantitative approaches. Behavioral approaches.
Systems approach (late 1960s to early 1970s)	Integrating the various approaches to the study of management.
Contingency approach (1970s)	Theorizes that different situations and conditions require different management approaches.
International movement (1970s–1980s)	Increased awareness of international and global markets and managerial approaches.

SUMMARY

This chapter attempts to present the major events that contributed to what we today know as modern management. The purpose is to provide the student with an historical perspective and foundation.

LEARNING OBJECTIVE 1

Identify Why Management Did Not Emerge as a Recognized Discipline until the 20th Century.

Just as traffic lights were not needed before cars, management, as it now exists, was not needed before organizations became complex. Prior to the late 19th and early 20th centuries, most organizations were relatively simple. Industrialization and mass production brought on large and complex organizations.

LEARNING OBJECTIVE 2

Describe What Events Led Up to the U.S. Industrial Revolution.

Three major events led up to and set the stage for the U.S. Industrial Revolution: (1) the invention of the steam engine by James Watt in the late 18th century; (2) the development and expansion of the railroads in the early to mid-1800s; and (3) the invention of the telegraph by Samuel F. B. Morse in 1844.

LEARNING OBJECTIVE 3

Discuss the Role That the Captains of Industry Played in the Development of Modern Organizations.

The captains of industry, including such men as John D. Rockefeller, James B. Duke, Andrew Carnegie, and Cornelius Vanderbilt, built great companies. They introduced nationwide distributing and marketing methods. Because of the size and dominance of these companies, the relationship between business and government was altered forever. Government passed legislation which sought to check corporate practices in restraint of trade.

LEARNING OBJECTIVE 4

Define Scientific Management and Outline the Role That Frederick W. Taylor and His Contemporaries Played in Its Development.

Scientific management is a philosophy and attitude toward the use of human effort; it seeks to maximize output with minimum effort through the elimination of waste and inefficiency at the operative level. Frederick W. Taylor was the major figure responsible for popularizing scientific management through his writings and consulting. Several contemporaries of Taylor helped spread Taylor's philosophy through their own efforts. The most prominent of these included Carl Barth, Morris Cooke, Henry Gantt, Frank and Lillian Gilbreth, and Harrington Emerson.

LEARNING OBJECTIVE 5

Summarize Henri Fayol's Contributions to Modern Management.

While Henri Fayol's contributions were many, the most significant was his development of management principles and elements. The 14 principles developed by Fayol are still applicable today, and his five management elements are very similar to today's functions of management.

LEARNING OBJECTIVE 6

Discuss the Human Relations Thrust in Management with Emphasis on the Role of the Hawthorne Experiments.

Following the Great Depression, more emphasis began to be placed on understanding workers and their needs. The Hawthorne studies, which began in 1924 and lasted until 1932, focused attention on human relations and specifically the psychological and sociological aspects of work. Mary Parker Follett also helped to popularize the human relations movement.

LEARNING OBJECTIVE 7

Define the Management Process Period, the Management Theory Jungle, the Systems Approach, and the Contingency Approach.

The management process period took place between the late 1940s into the late 1950s. During this period, management thought was primarily concerned with identifying and refining the functions or components of the management process. The management theory jungle was first clearly identified by Harold Koontz. The management theory jungle referred to the fact that many different approaches were being taken in the late 1950s and early 60s to the study of management. The systems approach was an attempt to integrate the various approaches to management. The systems approach views the human, physical, and informational facets of the manager's job as linking together to form an integrated whole. The contingency approach to management theorized that different situations and conditions require different management approaches and that no one approach works best in all situations.

LEARNING OBJECTIVE 8

Explain Why Emphasis Is Currently Being Placed on the International Aspects of Management.

In today's world many U.S. companies have turned to the international arena for new markets and profits. Even those companies that do not trade internationally are often greatly impacted by imports or exports from other countries. Thus, almost all companies are affected today to some degree by the international aspects of management.

LEARNING OBJECTIVE 9

Summarize the Major Points Made in the Book In Search of Excellence.

The authors of *In Search of Excellence* identified eight characteristics of excellent companies (see Figure 2–4). In general, these eight characteristics emphasize the value of on-the-job experimentation and creative thinking, the need to place the customer first, and the need to treat employees as human beings.

REVIEW QUESTIONS

1. What were the three facets of the Industrial Revolution in America? Discuss the impact of each of these facets on the development of industry as it is today.
2. What effect did the captains of industry have on the relationships between government and industry?
3. What is scientific management? Discuss the four main principles of scientific management.
4. Discuss the major contribution to scientific management of Morris Cooke, Henry Lawrence Gantt, Frank and Lillian Gilbreth, and Harrington Emerson.
5. What was Henri Fayol's major contribution to the management movement?
6. Discuss the impact of the Hawthorne Studies on management thought.

7. Describe in detail the following approaches to the management process: Lincoln Electric Company, McCormick multiple-management plan, bottom-up management, and the Scanlon plan.
8. What is the process approach to management? Discuss some of the major contributors to this approach.
9. Discuss the factors which led to the management theory jungle.
10 What is the systems approach to the management process?
11. Describe the contingency approach to managing.
12. Name the eight characteristics of successful companies as reported by the authors of *In Search of Excellence*.

DISCUSSION QUESTIONS

1. Why did the professional manager not emerge until the 20th century?
2. How were Taylor and Fayol's approaches to the management process different, and how were they similar?
3. Why do you think Taylor and scientific management have been misunderstood by many people as being inhumane?

4. "Successful managers adapt their style to the situation." Discuss your views on this statement.
5. Discuss your views on the following statement: The eight characteristics identified by the authors of *In Search of Excellence* are nothing more than good common sense.

REFERENCES & ADDITIONAL READINGS

[1] Daniel Wren, *The Evolution of Management Thought,* 2nd ed. (New York: Ronald Press, 1979), p. 90.

[2] Dorothy Gregg, "John Stevens: General Entrepreneur," in *Men in Business,* ed. William Miller (New York: Harper & Row, 1957), pp. 120–52.

[3] Alfred D. Chandler, Jr., "The Railroads: Pioneers in Modern Corporate Management," *Business History Review,* Spring 1965, p. 17.

[4] Wren, *The Evolution of Management Thought,* pp. 93–94.

[5] Chandler, "The Railroads," pp. 17–19.

[6] Ibid., p. 21.

[7] Alfred D. Chandler, Jr., "The Beginnings of 'Big Business' in American Industry," *Business History Review,* Spring 1959, p. 3.

[8] Harry Kelsey and David Wilderson, "The Evolution of Management Thought" (unpublished paper, Indiana University, Bloomington, 1974), p. 7.

[9] Henry R. Towne, "The Engineer as Economist," *Transactions,* ASME 7 (1886), pp. 428–32.

[10] Frank Barkley Copley, *Frederick W. Taylor: Father of Scientific Management,* vol. 1 (New York: Harper & Row, 1923), pp. 77–79.

[11] Frederick W. Taylor, "A Piece-Rate System," *Transactions,* ASME 16 (1895), pp. 856–83.

[12] Frederick W. Taylor, *Shop Management* (New York: Harper & Row, 1903); Frederick W. Taylor, *The Principles of Scientific Management* (New York: Harper & Row, 1911).

[13] *Scientific Management: Address and Discussions at the Conference on Scientific Management at the Amos Truck School of Administration and Finance* (Norwood, Mass.: Plimpton Press, 1912), pp. 32–35.

[14] John F. Mee, *Management Thought in a Dynamic Economy* (New York: New York University Press, 1963), p. 411.

[15] John F. Mee, "Seminar in Business Organization and Operation" (unpublished paper, Indiana University, Bloomington), p. 5.

[16] Wren, *The Evolution of Management Thought,* p. 188.

[17] Henry L. Gantt, *Organizing for Work* (New York: Harcourt Brace Jovanovich, 1919), p. 15.

[18] Henri Fayol, *Administration Industrielle et Generale* (Paris: The Societe de l'Industrie Minerale, 1916). First translated into English by J. A. Coubrough, *Industrial and General Administration* (Geneva: International Management Institute, 1930). Later translated by Constance Storrs, *General and Industrial Management* (London: Sir Isaac Pitman & Sons, 1940).

[19] John F. Mee, "Management Teaching in Historical Perspective," *Southern Journal of Business,* May 1972, p. 21.

[20] Ibid., p. 22.

[21] For a detailed description of the Hawthorne Studies, see Fritz G. Roethlisberger and William J. Dickson, *Management and the Worker* (Cambridge, Mass.: Harvard University Press, 1939).

[22] For example, see Alex Carey, "The Hawthorne Studies: A Radical Criticism," *American Sociological Review,* June 1967, pp. 403–16.

[23] Henry C. Metcalf and L. Urwick, eds., *Dynamic Administration: The Collected Papers of Mary Parker Follett* (New York: Harper & Row, 1940), p. 21.

[24] Chester I. Barnard, *The Functions of the Executive* (Cambridge, Mass.: Harvard University Press, 1938).

[25] Charles W. Brennan, *Wage Administration,* rev. ed. (Homewood, Ill.: Richard D. Irwin, 1963), p. 289.

[26] Henry S. Dennison, *Organization Engineering* (New York: McGraw-Hill, 1931).

[27] Charles P. McCormick, *Multiple Management* (New York: Harper & Row, 1949).

[28] William B. Given, Jr., *Bottom Up Management* (New York: Harper & Row, 1949).

[29] Joseph Scanlon, "Enterprise for Everyone,"

Fortune, January 1950, pp. 41, 55–59; Wren, *The Evolution of Management Thought,* p. 330.

[30] Mee, *Management Thought,* p. 53.

[31] Oliver Sheldon, *The Philosophy of Management* (London: Sir Isaac Pitman & Sons, 1923).

[32] Ralph C. Davis, *The Principles of Business Organizations and Operations* (Columbus, Ohio: H. L. Hedrick, 1935), pp. 12–13.

[33] Harold Koontz, "The Management Theory Jungle," *Academy of Management Journal,* December 1961, pp. 174–88.

[34] Richard A. Johnson, Fremont E. Kast, and James E. Rosenzweig, *The Theory and Management of Systems* (New York: McGraw-Hill, 1963), p. 3.

[35] Wren, *The Evolution of Management Thought,* pp. 463–64.

[36] "The 100 Largest U.S. Multinationals," *Forbes,* July 27, 1987, pp. 152–56.

[37] Thomas J. Peters and Robert H. Waterman, Jr., *In Search of Excellence* (New York: Harper & Row, 1982).

[38] For a criticism of *In Search of Excellence,* see Daniel T. Carroll, "A Disappointing Search for Excellence," *Harvard Business Review,* November–December 1983, pp. 78–88.

INCIDENT

Granddad's Company

The J.R.V. Company, which manufactures industrial tools, was founded in 1905 by James R. Vail, Sr. Currently, James R. Vail, Jr., is the president of the company; his son Richard is executive vice president. James Jr. has run the company for the past 30 years in a fashion very similar to that of his father.

When the company was founded, James Sr. had been a big supporter of scientific management. He had organized the work very scientifically with the use of time and motion studies to determine the most efficient method of performing each job. As a result, most jobs at J.R.V. were highly specialized and utilized a high degree of division of labor. In addition, there was always a great emphasis on putting people in jobs that were best suited for them and then providing adequate training. Most employees are paid on a piece-rate incentive system, with the standards set by time and motion studies. James Jr. has largely continued to emphasize scientific management since he took over. All employees now receive two weeks paid vacation and company insurance. Also, J.R.V. employees are generally paid an average wage for their industry. The present J.R.V. building was constructed in 1920. But it has had several minor improvements, such as the addition of fluorescent lighting and an employees' lunchroom.

James Jr. is planning to retire in a few years. Recently, he and Richard, his planned successor, have disagreed over the management of the company. Richard's main argument is that times have changed and that time and motion studies, specialization, high division of labor, and other company practices are obsolete. On the other hand, James Jr. argues that J.R.V. has been successful under its present management philosophy for many years. Change would be "foolish."

Questions

1. Do you agree with Richard?

2. Are the principles of scientific management applicable in today's organizations?

EXERCISE

What Have We Learned?

The following are excerpts from a speech made by Frederick W. Taylor in 1911:*

> If any of you will get close to the average workman in this country—close enough to him so that he will talk to you as an intimate friend—he will tell you that in his particular trade if, we will say, each man were to turn out twice as much work as he is now doing, there could be but one result to follow: namely, that one half the men in his trade would be thrown out of work.
>
> This doctrine is preached by almost every labor leader in the country and is taught by every workman to his children as they are growing up; and I repeat, as I said in the beginning, that it is our fault more than theirs that this fallacy prevails.
>
> While the labor leaders and the workmen themselves in season and out of season are pointing out the necessity of restriction of output, not one step are we taking to counteract that fallacy; therefore, I say, the fault is ours and not theirs.

A. Do you think that Taylor's position is equally applicable today? Be prepared to justify your answer.

C. Jackson Grayson, chairman of the American Productivity Center in Houston, has warned that if management and labor cannot make their relationship less adversarial, "then we won't get the full, long-term kick in productivity that we desperately need."†

B. Looking at Taylor's and Grayson's remarks, which were made approximately 63 years apart, one has to wonder what we have learned. Many other similar comparisons could be made. Why do you think that managers don't seem to learn as much as they could from the past?

---

* *Scientific Management: Address and Discussions* (Norwood, Mass., Plimpton Press, 1912), pp. 23–24.
† "The Revival of Productivity," *Business Week*, February 13, 1984, p. 100.

3 International Business and Management

LEARNING OBJECTIVES

*After studying this chapter,
you should be able to:*

1 Describe the basic strategies used by organizations to move into international business.

2 Define exporting and importing.

3 Define a parent organization and a host country.

4 Discuss the importance of cultural differences in international management.

5 Explain the problem of foreign exchange rates.

6 Define a tariff and a quota.

7 Describe a multinational corporation (MNC).

8 List the factors that have been credited for the success of Japanese management.

9 Explain the principles of Theory Z management.

*Of the 500 largest industrial corporations in the United States, at least 25
earn more than half of their profits overseas. Today, 68 of the 156 largest
multinational organizations are U.S. firms.*

DAVID RICKS AND VIJAY MAHAJAN*

**Comparative
advantage** –
country produces
those goods and
services it can pro-
duce more effi-
ciently or cheaply
than other
countries.

An important factor in the management of any organization is the increasing internationalization of business activity. International business activities range from exporting goods to other nations to establishing manufacturing
operations in other nations. These activities present new challenges to managers.

While not all organizations are directly involved in international business
activities, events that impact on American organizations occur almost daily
in other nations. Thus, it is increasingly important that all managers understand
the nature of international business activity.

The trading of goods and services across national boundaries results from
the principle of comparative advantage. A country has a **comparative advantage** when it can produce goods and services more efficiently or cheaply
than other countries. Factors determining a country's comparative advantage
include the presence of natural resources, adequate quality and quantity of
labor and capital, available technology, and the costs of these resources.

INTERNATIONAL BUSINESS INVOLVEMENT

Generally, the decision to extend an organization's operations to other countries
has two objectives: profit and stability. In terms of profit, international operations give organizations the chance to meet the increasing demand for goods
and services in foreign countries. In addition, new sources of demand (in
other countries) for an organization's output may have a stabilizing effect on
the organization's production process.

Organizations deciding to move into international operations can usually
be classified as following one of four basic strategies:

1. Exploit a Technological Lead. When an organization creates a new
product, it at first enjoys a distinct competitive advantage. As the product
becomes less unique and this advantage erodes, the organization often attempts

*David A. Ricks and Vijay Mahajan, "Blunders in International Marketing: Fact or Fiction,"
Long-Range Planning, February 1984, p. 78.

to build new markets elsewhere. In addition, as costs begin to play a more critical part in the production of the product, the organization often sets up production and/or marketing facilities nearer to the markets it is serving.

2. Exploit a Strong Trade Name. A successful product often induces organizations to set up operations on an international basis. Foreign brands often are considered better—as a result of snob appeal or on the basis of superior quality. This is especially evident in the foreign car market.

3. Exploit Advantages of Scale. Larger organizations can more easily assemble the funds, physical assets, and human resources needed to produce and distribute goods on a larger scale than can smaller organizations.

4. Exploit a Low-Cost Resource. When costs of production are a critical concern, an organization may set up international operations in areas where the resource and/or labor costs are relatively lower than they are domestically.

EXPORTING AND IMPORTING

An organization may become involved in international business activities by exporting, importing, or manufacturing in a foreign country.

Exporting refers to the selling of an organization's goods in another country; **importing** is the purchasing of goods or services from a foreign company. Some of the more common reasons for exporting and importing are listed in Figure 3–1.

Organizations that make a commitment to selling their products overseas must decide how to organize their exporting/importing activities. The organizational structure that is used depends on how critical these activities are to the overall organization. The organization may establish its own internal structure. This requires special expertise in international accounting, finance, marketing, and law. As a result, many organizations either cannot or do not desire to establish such divisions. Some contract with an outside person who is sometimes called a combination export-import manager. An **export-import manager** serves a group of exporting/importing organizations and handles all activities involved in the exporting/importing of the organization's goods or services.

Over time, many organizations find that it is economically better to expand their production operations overseas than to continue exporting goods to their markets abroad. Furthermore, in recent years, less-developed countries have sought local production of goods. As a result, American organizations are finding that they must produce in these countries in order to maintain their overseas markets.

The ways in which international organizations expand their production

Exporting – selling an organization's goods or services to another country.

Importing – purchasing goods or services from foreign companies.

Export-import manager – serves a group of exporting/importing organizations and handles all activities involved in the exporting/importing of their goods or services.

F I G U R E 3–1   Reasons for Exporting and Importing Goods

WHY EXPORT?

1. If the production process requires high volume to reduce cost per unit, the home market may be too small to absorb the output. Thus, the output may be sold overseas. Stoves, for example, are purchased by households only when needed to replace an old one or when a new home is built. To restrict selling stoves only to the U.S. market could limit the number of stoves demanded below that amount which is cost efficient to produce.
2. The demand for the firm's product may be seasonal and irregular. By expanding the firm's market to other countries, production costs may be lowered by more effective production scheduling.
3. All products undergo what is called the product life cycle: When the product is first introduced, there is usually a big demand and the introducing firm is the only supplier. As the product reaches maturity, this competitive edge is reduced and can be maintained only by creating new markets, where it reenters the growth stage.
4. In selling goods overseas, the organization may not face competition as stiff as it does in the United States; thus, its marketing costs may be reduced. By selling its established goods in new overseas markets, the organization is also able to increase its profits without risking new-product development.

WHY IMPORT?

1. The goods may be needed but not available in the importing country (e.g., crude oil).
2. Many foreign-made products have prestige value and are demanded by the home market (e.g., French perfumes, sports cars from Germany).
3. Some foreign goods are less expensive due to lower production costs.

Parent organiza-tion – organization that extends its operations beyond its nation's boundaries.

Host country – country in which a foreign organiza-tion does business.

activities differ in the degree of control retained by the **parent organization** (the organization extending its operations beyond its nation's boundaries). The country which it is entering is referred to as the **host country.** The parent company may set up assembly operations in a foreign country: Parts are exported overseas, and the finished product is assembled there. Also, the parent organization may contract with a foreign organization to produce its product, but retain control over the marketing of the product in that country. Licensing arrangements are an extension of this latter type of expan-sion. The parent organization enters into an agreement with a foreign organiza-tion, licensing it to produce and market the parent organization's product in return for a set percentage of sales revenues. Often, the parent organization provides technical and/or managerial support to the foreign organization. Managers at Work 3–1 describes a licensing agreement between Bethlehem Steel and two European steelmakers.

PROBLEMS IN INTERNATIONAL BUSINESS ACTIVITIES

When an organization decides to extend its operations abroad, some new problems must be dealt with if the activities are to be managed effectively.

MANAGERS AT WORK 3-1

Bethlehem Steel Corporation

Agreements have been signed between Bethlehem Steel Corporation of the United States and two European steelmakers for licenses to manufacture Bethlehem's aluminum-zinc alloy coated sheet. Ensidesa (Empress Siderargica Nacional SA) of Madrid, Spain, and La Magona D'Italia of Florence, Italy, announced the agreement in April 1984. The coated sheet is used in the building and roofing industry, automotive and appliance markets, and for solar heating panels.

Both European companies are major producers of sheet steel, Ensidesa being the largest integrated steel company in Spain and La Magona being Italy's main precoated sheet steel producer. This agreement brings to 13 the number of licenses granted for this technology by Bethlehem Steel. Many of the world's largest steelmakers have signed agreements, including those in Japan, Australia, and Canada.

Source: Adapted from *Iron and Steel International,* June 1984, p. 74.

Cultural Differences

In order to understand the differences between U.S. and international management, it is necessary to understand differences in culture. Obviously, U.S. managers and French managers do not see the world in the same way because they come from different cultures. **Culture** can be defined as "something that is shared by all or almost all members of some social group, something that the older members of the group try to pass on to the younger members, and something (as in the case of morals, laws, and customs) that shapes behavior or structures one's perception of the world."[1] In other words, people living in different countries develop different values and different ways of relating to each other. For example, North Americans tend to stand far apart while talking; Middle Easterners stand close. In some cultures bribery is condoned in certain business situations; North Americans consider bribery to be a crime. Scheduled meeting times and punctuality is expected by North Americans; but in the Middle East and China the people have more relaxed views of time.[2]

Sexual bias also can pose problems in the international management environment. Many times, a woman who appears to be the appropriate choice for an overseas managerial position will not be acceptable in terms of that country's biases. She might have difficulty maintaining the respect of her fellow employees as well as subordinates, and the result might be failure of the operation. Women are now slowly beginning to attain high management positions in

Culture – beliefs, key values, understandings, and norms that members of a group share.

MANAGERS AT WORK 3–2

Japanese Women: A Push for Job Equality

Japan frequently is considered among the most modern industrial nations of the world. Still, it has lagged behind many countries in its attitude toward women employees, especially as managers. Many companies will not hire women for any office position other than clerical or as a receptionist. They earn less than men in comparable positions, and they seldom are promoted. In addition, they many times are expected to report early for work to prepare the morning tea. Through the years, however, a slow progression of women into some managerial ranks has occurred.

In April 1986, an equal employment law took effect. The bill was controversial, with opponents claiming it would legislate away ingrained culture and mores. Designed to ban discrimination against women in hiring and promotion, the legislation also was intended to remove restrictions on overtime and late-night work for managerial women.

In keeping with Japan's cultural traditions, though, married working women still have to assume responsibility for housework, cooking, and child care. The result can be an emotional and physical burden, and many women consider marriage to be incompatible with a professional career.

Source: Adapted from Janice James Miller and John A. Kilpatrick, *Issues for Managers: An International Perspective* (Homewood, Ill.: Richard D. Irwin, 1987), p. 116.

some countries, but only after years of inferior job status. Japanese women exemplify this, as shown in Managers at Work 3–2.

Numerous cultural differences influence the social, economic, technical, and political environment of a country. Success in the international business environment requires that these differences be recognized in managing international business activities.

Payment for International Transactions

Foreign exchange rate – the rate of exchange for one currency to another currency, e.g., French francs to American dollars.

International trade requires exchanging currency from one country into that of another. **Foreign exchange rates** (the rate of exchange for one currency to another currency, e.g., French francs to American dollars) present certain problems as the rates fluctuate in value. In fact, a change in foreign exchange rates can wipe out profits earned on an international transaction.

The problem of foreign exchange rates arises because of the time lag between the time of a sale and the delivery of and payment for the product or service. Because two different countries are involved and the changes in supply and demand for the two currencies vary, the importer can pay a different amount

FIGURE 3–2   Effects of Exchange Rates Changes on Importers and Exporters

	EFFECT WHEN CONTRACT STATED IN IMPORTER'S CURRENCY		EFFECT WHEN CONTRACT STATED IN EXPORTER'S CURRENCY	
RATE CHANGE	IMPORTER	EXPORTER	IMPORTER	EXPORTER
1. Importer currency strengthens.	No effect.	Receives more units of domestic currency after conversion.	Must pay fewer units of domestic currency.	No effect.
2. Exporter currency strengthens.	No effect.	Receives fewer units of domestic currency after conversion.	Must pay more units of domestic currency to purchase foreign currency.	No effect.

Source: Janice James Miller and John A. Kilpatrick, *Issues for Managers: An International Perspective* (Homewood, Ill.: Richard D. Irwin, 1987), p. 65.

than originally expected. Figure 3–2 shows the effects of exchange rates changes on importers and exporters.

Tariffs

Tariffs are government-imposed taxes charged on goods imported into, or exported from, a country. They serve (1) to raise revenues for the country or (2) to protect the country's producers from the competition of imported goods. The tariffs charged on parts are often less than those charged on finished goods. Therefore, foreign assembly operations (discussed earlier) have become quite popular.

Tariffs – government-imposed taxes charged on goods imported into, or exported from, a country.

Quotas

A **quota** establishes the maximum quantity of a product that can be imported (or exported) during a given time period. A quota can be set in physical or in value terms. Quotas can be imposed unilaterally, or they can be negotiated on a voluntary basis. Voluntary negotiation generally means that the quotas have been negotiated with threats of even worse restrictions if voluntary cooperation is not forthcoming.

Quotas – the maximum quantity of a product that might be imported (or exported) during a given time period.

Government Control over Profits

A firm owning facilities in another country naturally expects to receive profits from its operations. The amount of profits the parent company receives is often controlled by the host country's government, which regulates the access foreigners have to its currency.

Taxation

Firms operating in another country are subject to that country's laws and regulations. As taxes are a primary source of government revenue, many countries tax foreign investments located within their boundaries. These taxes may be quite high, since some of these foreign countries have few other businesses to tax.

MULTINATIONAL CORPORATIONS (MNCs)

Multinational corporation (MNC) – any business organization that maintains a production, assembly, sales, or service presence in two or more countries.

The multinational corporation (MNC) has become a well-known entity in international business. Yet a common definition of that entity does not seem to exist. Measures used to determine if a business is multinational include percentage of total sales accounted for by majority-owned foreign affiliates, percentage of earnings due to foreign operations, and percentage of new capital investment destined for overseas facilities.[3] However, for the purposes of this book, an **MNC** is defined as any business that maintains a production, assembly, sales, or service presence in two or more countries.[4]

The internationalization of American companies has been dramatic, with companies such as IBM, Eastman Kodak, Exxon, Bank America, and American Express having large and growing international activities. The same kind of experience can be observed among non-American multinationals such as Volkswagen, Nestlé, British Petroleum, Phillips, Toyota, Olivetta, and numerous others. Managers at Work 3–3 describes one of the largest U.S. MNCs.

Problems Facing MNCs

As would be expected, MNCs must deal with the normal problems in international business activities, such as tariffs, quotas, cultural differences, taxation, payment for international transactions, and government control over profits. Each of these problems was discussed earlier in this chapter. However, MNCs also face other difficult and challenging problems. Managers at Work 3–4 shows how Walt Disney solved a problem unique to MNCs.

MANAGERS AT WORK 3–3

Exxon: An International Giant

Virtually every American has heard the name Exxon. The huge oil company is an international manufacturer and marketer of energy and industrial products. Exxon explores for and produces crude oil and natural gas, mines for coal and other minerals, and manufactures petroleum-based chemical and other industrial products. Exxon is such a mammoth presence in the American economy that it is frequently viewed as an all-American institution.

To the surprise of many, Exxon is more international than American. Exxon has operations in 80 countries other than the United States. In 1986, a full 72 percent of Exxon's approximate 70 billion in sales and almost three quarters of all its profits were made outside the United States.

Source: "The 100 Largest U.S. Multinationals," *Forbes*, July 27, 1987, pp. 152–56.

Human Rights. Should Ford Motor Co. and General Electric close their South African plants as long as apartheid exists in that country? Should Coca-Cola establish minimum labor standards for all of its bottlers around the world to prevent abuses of workers in certain countries? Such questions present dilemmas for managers of MNCs which are accompanied by ethical predicaments and hard choices. Most MNCs have yet to develop a coherent, effective response to the challenge of human rights.[5] In each specific situation, management of an MNC must strike a balance between the interests and ideals of all of its various publics. There are no clear and easy choices.

Terrorism. Over the past decade, MNCs have become a favorite target of numerous forms of terrorism. The U.S. Central Intelligence Agency (CIA) has concluded that "because of the tighter security measures that have been introduced at U.S. military and diplomatic installations, the continuing lure of lucrative ransom and extortion payments, and the symbolic value of U.S. firms (e.g., as 'capitalistic foreign exploiters' of the local working class), there is a real danger that terrorist attacks on the U.S. business community abroad will become even more frequent in the future."[6] Forms of terrorism include but are not limited to kidnapping of executives of MNCs, bombings, assassinations, and hijackings.

One way MNCs defend against terrorism is to increase security. It is now fairly standard practice for executives of MNCs in such high-risk cities as Paris, Rome, New York, and Mexico City to be accompanied by at least one bodyguard. Measures have also been taken to ensure a high level of security for

MANAGERS AT WORK 3–4

Walt Disney's Solution to Blocked Funds

One of the problems that MNCs face is the problem of blocked funds. This happens when a government puts a ban on sending local currency out of the country. A government may do this to protect (hold down) the supply of its currency on foreign exchange markets; holding the supply *down* is equivalent to trying to hold the price *up*.

Suppose a country has trouble meeting interest payments on foreign debt. Local subsidiaries may wish to change local currency for scarce foreign currencies, as when a firm in Mexico wishes to exchange pesos for dollars in order to send profits to a parent firm elsewhere. The government may then "block" the exchange of pesos for dollars and use the dollars (earned through the export of petroleum to the United States, for example) to pay the interest.

Airlines are examples of firms that are hurt by this because they are required by law to accept local currency in payment for air transportation. The company may be forced to sell the currency at a big discount, hold the currency even though it is falling in value, quit operations altogether, or find some productive way to trade or invest the currency. For the firm, the question may then become what to do with the funds that it has earned but can't send out of the country.

One solution is illustrated by Walt Disney, Inc., the American film company. Shortly after World War II, Disney earned large amounts of yen in Japan by showing cartoons. Since they could not at that time convert yen to dollars, they solved the problem by selling the yen to American firms wanting to invest in Japanese markets. Disney got dollars, and the American firms were able to make their investments in yen.

Source: Adapted from Janice James Miller and John A. Kilpatrick, *Issues for Managers: An International Perspective* (Homewood, Ill.: Richard D. Irwin, 1987), p. 68.

the MNCs plants and other productive assets. Finally, most MNCs now have substantial insurance coverage to protect themselves against financial losses as a result of terrorism.

Marketing Practices. The approach used by many MNCs has been to simply take products designed to meet consumer needs and desires at home and market them in foreign markets. The tendency has been to treat foreign countries as an extension of the U.S. marketplace, which creates very significant potential for conflict. For example, should a drug banned in the United States be sold by an MNC in an underdeveloped country? Should infant formula— safe to use in developed countries—be advertised, promoted, and sold in underdeveloped countries, where poverty and illiteracy may make the product unsafe? Pricing, distribution, advertising and promotion, and product quality and safety often pose unique problems for managers in the international environment.

Some MNCs have attempted to better understand the unique nature of a country's market by extending the concept of consumer affairs departments to foreign markets. For example, Coca-Cola has expanded its consumer affairs departments to its foreign subsidiaries. In order to consider the worldwide nature of its market, Gillette has a vice president of product integrity who can veto product introductions, order packaging changes, and stop advertising claims for any Gillette division anywhere in the world.

Managers in MNCs

Using local nationals in management positions in foreign operations seems preferable to using only nonlocal managers. Two reasons given for this are lower costs and more thorough knowledge of the culture and market. In some countries, the development of local management is legally required by the host government as a condition of entry.

LEARNING FROM FOREIGN MANAGEMENT

As U.S. companies have expanded internationally, many foreign companies have entered the U.S. market. Leading this group are the Japanese. Because of Japan's phenomenal economic success since World War II, managers began to study the Japanese management style.

Japanese Management

At least five factors have been credited for the success of the Japanese management style:

1. Emphasizing the flow of information and initiative from the bottom up.
2. Making top management the facilitator of decision making rather than the issuer of edicts.
3. Using middle management as the impetus for, and shaper of, solutions to problems.
4. Stressing consensus as the way of making decisions.
5. Paying close attention to the personal well-being of employees.[7]

Many American, Canadian, and European companies have adopted these principles of Japanese management. William Ouchi has named this style of

Theory Z – Japanese management style which features lifetime employment, limited promotions, nonspecialized careers, and collective decision making.

management Theory Z. **Theory Z** organizations generally use the following principles:

1. Lifetime employment: Employees are not laid off during recessions. Rather, paychecks are pared down for all employees, including management.
2. Evaluation and promotion: Promotions often only come every 10 years in Japanese companies. But no one seems to resent this, since everyone is treated the same way.
3. Nonspecialized careers: Japanese managers do not specialize, and they regularly move from one department to another.
4. Collective decision making: Japanese managers make decisions through a tedious process of collective decision making.[8]

Lessons to Be Learned

Peter Drucker has outlined six lessons which he feels can be learned from foreign management, especially Western European and Japanese. These lessons are:[9]

1. Foreign managements increasingly demand responsibility from their employees.
2. Foreign managements have thought through their benefits policies more carefully and, especially in Japan and Germany, structure benefits according to the needs of recipients.
3. Foreign managements take marketing more seriously in that they attempt to know what is value for the customer.
4. Foreign managements base their marketing and innovation strategies on the systematic and purposeful abandonment of the old, the outworn, and the obsolete.
5. Foreign managements keep separate and discrete those areas where short-term results are the proper measurement and those where results should be measured over longer time spans—innovation, product development, product introduction, manager development, etc.
6. Managers in large Japanese, German, and French companies see themselves as national assets and leaders responsible for the development of proper policies in the national interest.

Drucker readily admits that each of those lessons is American in origin. However, reexamining and possibly reinstituting practices developed earlier is never bad, especially when they have been emulated so successfully by foreign managements.

SUMMARY

LEARNING OBJECTIVE 1

Describe the Basic Strategies Used by Organizations to Move into International Business.

Four basic strategies are employed. These are: exploit a technological lead; exploit a strong trade name; exploit advantages of scale; and exploit a low-cost resource.

LEARNING OBJECTIVE 2

Define Exporting and Importing.

Exporting refers to the selling of an organization's goods in another country. Importing is the purchasing of goods or services from a foreign company.

LEARNING OBJECTIVE 3

Define a Parent Organization and a Host Country.

A parent organization refers to the organization that is extending its operations beyond its nation's boundaries. The country which a parent organization is entering is referred to as the host country.

LEARNING OBJECTIVE 4

Discuss the Importance of Cultural Differences in International Management.

Culture is something that is shared by all or almost all members of some social group, something that the older members of the group try to pass on to the younger members, and something that shapes behavior or structures one's perception of the world. Cultural differences must be recognized and considered in managing international business activities.

LEARNING OBJECTIVE 5

Explain the Problem of Foreign Exchange Rates.

The problem of foreign exchange rates arises because of the time lag between the time of a sale and the delivery of and payment for the good or service. Because two different countries are involved and the changes in supply and demand for the two countries vary, the importer can pay a different amount than originally expected.

LEARNING OBJECTIVE 6

Define a Tariff and a Quota.

Tariffs are government-imposed taxes charged on goods imported into, or exported from, a country. A quota establishes the maximum quantity of a product that can be imported (or exported) during a given time period.

LEARNING OBJECTIVE 7

Describe a Multinational Corporation (MNC).

An MNC is any business that maintains a production, assembly, sales, or service presence in two or more countries.

LEARNING OBJECTIVE 8

List the Factors That Have Been Credited for the Success of Japanese Management.

The five factors are: emphasizing the flow of information and initiative from the bottom up; making top management the facilitator of decision making rather than the issuer of edicts; using middle management as the impetus for, and sharer of, solutions to problems; stressing consensus as the way of making decisions; and paying close attention to the personal well-being of employees.

LEARNING OBJECTIVE 9

Explain the Principles of Theory Z Management.

The following principles are generally followed by Theory Z organizations: lifetime employment; promotions often come only every 10 years; nonspecialized careers; and collective decision making.

REVIEW QUESTIONS

1. In what ways may an organization enter into international business activities?
2. What are four basic strategies used by organization that decide to move into international operations?
3. What is exporting? Importing?
4. What are tariffs? Quotas?
5. Describe some problems faced by organizations in international business activities.
6. What is a multinational corporation (MNC)?
7. Describe some unique problems faced by MNCs.
8. What factors have been credited for the success of the Japanese management style?
9. Outline six lessons that can be learned from foreign management.

DISCUSSION QUESTIONS

1. Do you think that the old saying "When in Rome, do as the Romans do" applies to international business activities?

2. What problems would you face if you were asked to serve as manager in a foreign country?

3. What are some management practices that are typical in the U.S. that would be difficult to apply in foreign countries?

REFERENCES & ADDITIONAL READINGS

[1] Nancy J. Adler, *International Dimensions of Organizational Behavior* (Boston, Mass.: Kent Publishing Company, 1986), pp. 8–9.

[2] Examples are drawn from Raymond V. Lesikar, *Basic Business Communication* 4th ed. (Homewood, Ill.: Richard D. Irwin, 1988), p. 103.

[3] Thomas N. Gladwin and Ingo Walter, *Multinationals under Fire* (New York: John Wiley & Sons, 1980), p. 2.

[4] Ibid., p. 2.

[5] Ibid., p. 131.

[6] Directorate of Intelligence, U.S. Central Intelligence Agency, "International Terrorism in 1976," RP77–10034U (Washington, D.C.: July 1977), p. 4.

[7] Richard Tanner Johnson and William Ouchi, "Made in America Under Japanese Management," *Harvard Business Review,* September–October 1974, p. 62.

[8] For example, see William Ouchi, *Theory Z: How American Business Can Meet the Japanese Challenge* (Reading, Mass.: Addison-Wesley Publishing, 1981).

[9] Peter F. Drucker, "Learning from Foreign Management," *The Wall Street Journal,* June 4, 1980, p. 1.

INCIDENT

Staying at Home

With the increased interest in doing business overseas, many large organizations have found it necessary to assign Americans to managerial positions in other countries. The prospect of seeing the world at the company's expense has enticed many Americans to seek overseas assignments in the past. Furthermore, overseas assignment has been used by organizations as a mechanism by which managers are groomed for higher-level positions when they are returned to America. Equally appealing has been the "hardship pay" awarded to those relocated managers to help ease the transition into another society for them and their families. In the past, these managers and their families generally have been relocated in European countries such as England, France, and Belgium.

However, many organizations have found recently that they are having trouble recruiting managers for overseas assignments. The opportunities, while plentiful, are increasingly being turned down. While some organizations have attempted to solve this problem by filling managerial positions from within the country in which they are operating, many others are reluctant to do so. These organizations feel that it is necessary to have managers who understand the workings of the American parent company as well as the complexities of international business. While local people may serve well in lower-level managerial positions, organizations are hesitant to place them in higher positions of authority.

The problem for these organizations is a perplexing one. It is especially critical since most new foreign opportunities are in the middle East and the underdeveloped countries, where capable local human talent does not exist in great quantities. Even if organizations wanted to use local people in these managerial positions, it is unlikely that they would possess the abilities and experience to perform successfully in these positions.

Questions

1. Why are firms facing this problem? Why would individuals today be less likely to accept overseas assignments?

2. What would an individual consider in deciding whether or not to accept an overseas assignment?

3. Can organizations do anything about this problem? Can they make the opportunity of an overseas assignment any more attractive for American managers?

EXERCISE

Blunders

Multinational corporations have on occasion experienced unexpected troubles due to culture, language, and custom differences. The following examples demonstrate problems encountered by some companies with regard to product and company names:*

A. When Chevrolet introduced its Nova in Puerto Rico, sales were less than brisk. When spoken, the word *Nova* sounded like *"no va,"* which in Spanish means "it doesn't go."

B. Ford introduced a low-cost truck, the Fiera, into some less developed countries and also experienced slow sales. Unfortunately, *Fiera* meant "ugly old woman" in Spanish.

C. A private Egyptian airline, Misair, proved to be rather unpopular with Frenchmen. When pronounced in French, the name means "misery."

D. The phonetic pronunciation of Esso in Japanese means "stalled car." Obviously this name did not go over well in Japan.

Questions

1. Assume that you have been considering opening a McDonald's franchise in either Central America or Spain. Develop a list of internationally related factors that you would need to investigate in evaluating the feasibility of this idea.

2. Prioritize the list you developed in question 1.

---

* These examples are taken from David A. Ricks, *Big Business Blunders: Mistakes in Multinational Marketing* (Homewood, Ill.: Richard D. Irwin, 1983), pp. 37–47.

4 Social Responsibility and Ethics

LEARNING OBJECTIVES

After studying this chapter, you should be able to:

1 Define social responsibility.

2 List the arguments for social responsibility.

3 List the arguments against social responsibility.

4 Define a social audit.

5 Define consumerism.

6 Define corporate philanthropy.

7 Explain the concept of business ethics.

*Then the Lord said to Cain, "Where is Abel your brother?" And he said,
"I do not know. Am I my brother's keeper?"*

G E N E S I S   4 : 9 ★

*A*re business organizations expected to concern themselves with social
issues that are broader than producing and selling goods and services?
If they are, what specific issues should be addressed?

Should managers be expected to apply ethical standards in their day-to-
day business decisions? If they are, what ethical standards should be applied?
The purpose of this chapter is to examine the social responsibility of organizations and the importance of ethics in management.

DEFINING SOCIAL RESPONSIBILITY

**Social responsi-
bility** – moral and
ethical content of
managerial and
corporate deci-
sions over and
above the prag-
matic require-
ments imposed by
legal principle and
the market econ-
omy.

Social responsibility is concerned with how individuals and organizations
deal with current social issues. The general public has a rather broad and
all-inclusive definition of the social responsibility of business organizations.
The public seems to feel that managers and business organizations should
provide leadership in rebuilding cities, wiping out poverty, controlling crime,
and cutting government red tape. In short, social responsibility has come to
mean participation in a multitude of issues and problems. Presently, no universally accepted definition exists for the term. In this book, social responsibility
is defined as "the moral and ethical content of managerial and corporate
decisions over and above the pragmatic requirements imposed by legal principle
and the market economy."[1] Managers at Work 4–1 shows what some organizations are and are not doing in social responsibility decisions.

SOCIAL RESPONSIBILITY— A HISTORICAL PERSPECTIVE

The idea that business has a responsibility other than producing goods and
services is not new. In 1919, Henry L. Gantt stated his belief that the community
would attempt to take over business if the business system neglected its social
responsibilities.[2] Another early management writer who discussed social re-

★ *New American Stand Bible* (Nashville, Tenn.: Thomas Nelson Publishers, 1977).

MANAGERS AT WORK 4–1

Awards and Razzes

The Council on Economic Priorities, which monitors the social actions of corporations, presented awards to eight companies for their good conscience and also gave dishonorable mention to four companies. Those receiving awards were:

- Sara Lee, Polaroid, and General Mills for their charitable contributions.
- IBM and Amoco for their community action programs.
- Avon Products for promoting women and minorities into management.
- Johnson & Johnson and Ford Motor Company for disclosure of information.
- Polaroid also received an award for pulling out of South Africa before it was fashionable.

Those given dishonorable mention were:

- A. H. Robins for its handling of the Dalkon Shield disputes.
- American Cyanamid for having no women or minority directors.
- Litton Industries for its puny charitable contributors.
- Mobil for its lack of disclosure.

Source: Adapted from: "CEP Salutes Nine, Razzes Four," *Business and Society Review,* Spring 1987, p. 64.

sponsibility was Oliver Sheldon. Writing in 1923, Sheldon stressed that management has a social responsibility:

> It is important, therefore, early in our consideration of management in industry, to insist that however scientific management may become, and however much the full development of its powers may depend upon the use of the scientific method; its primary responsibility is social and communal.[3]

However, concern for social responsibility was rare during this early period.

Changes began to occur in the late 1930s and early 40s. Shorter workweeks and safer working conditions were some of the first changes. Many of these early social responsibility changes were precipitated by labor unions. In effect, labor unions pressured organizations to consider factors other than just profitability.

In 1948, the theme of the annual Harvard Business School Alumni Association meeting was "business responsibility." In 1958, the American Management Association surveyed 700 companies concerning their "managerial creed or statement of basic objectives."[4] Nearly every company expressed the belief that they had a responsibility to society. In the 1950s and 60s, more and more organizations and managers expressed concern about the social responsibilities of organizations. However, few socially responsible programs were actually implemented until the late 1960s.

Looking back, the attitudes of managers toward social responsibility seem to have gone through three historical phases.[5] Phase 1, which dominated until the 1930s, emphasized the belief that a business manager had but one objective—to maximize profits. Phase 2, from the 1930s to the early 60s, stressed that managers were responsible not only for maximizing profits but also for maintaining an equitable balance among the competing claims of customers, employees, suppliers, creditors, and the community. Phase 3, still dominant today, contends that managers and organizations should involve themselves in the solutions of society's major problems. Figure 4–1 describes these three phases in more depth.

SOCIAL RESPONSIBILITY TODAY

Today's organizations and managers still question the exact nature of their social responsibility. Major arguments for and against the social responsibility of business organizations are presented in Figure 4–2. The following sections of this chapter discuss in detail some of the more important arguments.[6]

Arguments for Social Responsibility

1. It is in the best interest of the business. The future of business organizations depends on good relationships with the society in which they operate. If organizations fail to act in the area of social responsibility, then society will act against business organizations. Boycotting products and picketing the organization—even violence against the organization—are examples of actions that can be taken. By extension, if public pressure becomes too strong, then government will force the organization to take responsibility.

2. Social actions can be profitable. No clear evidence now seems to support a cause-and-effect relationship between social responsibility and profits.[7] Indirectly, though, it seems logical that donations to higher education, hiring disadvantaged persons, taking part in urban renewal projects, and aiding conservation programs should help the long-term profitability of all organizations.

3. Being socially responsible is the ethical thing to do. Business is an integral part of society; so, many people argue that being socially responsible is a moral obligation of organizations. Proponents feel organizations are morally responsible to provide safe products, clean up streams, and conserve natural resources. Thus, if the public-at-large feels that being socially responsible is the ethical thing to do, it can be expected that managers and organizations will feel the same way.

Arguments against Social Responsibility

1. It might be illegal. Milton Friedman has argued that the only responsibility of business is to maximize profits for shareholders.[8] This assumes that managers are agents of the stockholders and that the diversion of funds to

FIGURE 4–1   Historical Phases of Attitudes of Managers toward Social Responsibility

ATTITUDES	PHASE 1 PROFIT-MAXIMIZING MANAGEMENT (1800 TO 1920s)	PHASE 2 TRUSTEESHIP MANAGEMENT (LATE 1920s TO EARLY 1960s)	PHASE 3 QUALITY-OF-LIFE MANAGEMENT (LATE 1960s TO PRESENT)
Orientation:	1. Raw self-interest.	1. Self-interest. 2. Contributors' interest.	1. Enlightened self-interest. 2. Contributors' interests. 3. Society's interests.
Economic values:	What's good for me is good for my country. Profit maximizer. Money and wealth are most important. Let the buyer beware *(caveat emptor)*. Labor is a commodity to be bought and sold. Accountability of management is to the owners.	What's good for organizations and management is good for our country. Profit satisficer. Money is important, but so are people. Let us not cheat the customer. Labor has certain rights which must be recognized. Accountability of management is to the owners, customers, employees, suppliers, and other contributors.	What is good for society is good for our company. Profit is necessary, but. . . . People are more important than money. Let the seller beware *(caveat venditor)*. Employee dignity has to be satisfied. Accountability of management is to the owners, contributors, and society.
Technological values:	Technology is very important.	Technology is important, but so are people.	People are more important than technology.
Social values:	Employee personal problems must be left at home. I am a rugged individualist, and I will manage my business as I please. Minority groups are inferior to whites. They must be treated accordingly.	We recognize that employees have needs beyond their economic needs. I am an individualist, but I recognize the value of group participation. Minority groups have their place in society, and their place is inferior to mine.	We hire the whole person. Group participation is fundamental to our success. Minority group members are people, as you and I are.
Political values:	That government is best which governs least.	Government is a necessary evil.	Business and government must cooperate to solve society's problems.
Environmental values:	The natural environment controls the destiny of people.	People can control and manipulate the environment.	We must preserve the environment in order to lead a quality life.
Aesthetic values:	Aesthetic values? What are they?	Aesthetic values are OK, but not for us.	We must preserve our aesthetic values, and we will do our part.

Source: Adapted from Robert D. Hay, Edmund R. Gray, and James E. Gates, *Business and Society: Cases and Text* (Cincinnati: South-Western Publishing, 1976), pp. 10–11.

activities that do not contribute to profits may be illegal. This viewpoint was held by most managers and was supported by the courts for a long time. For instance, in 1919, a Michigan court declared that business was to be operated primarily for the profit of stockholders. The court forced the company to declare a dividend, which it had not done for many years.

F I G U R E 4–2   Arguments for and against Social Responsibility

MAJOR ARGUMENTS FOR SOCIAL RESPONSIBILITY

1. It is in the best interest of the business to promote and improve the communities where it does business.
2. Social actions can be profitable.
3. It is the ethical thing to do.
4. It improves the public image of the firm.
5. It increases the viability of the business system. Business exists because it gives society benefits. Society can amend or take away its charter. This is the "iron law of responsibility."
6. It is necessary to avoid government regulation.
7. Sociocultural norms require it.
8. Laws cannot be passed for all circumstances. Thus, business must assume responsibility to maintain an orderly legal society.
9. It is in the stockholder's best interest. It will improve the price of stock in the long run, because the stock market will view the company as less risky and open to public attack and therefore award it a higher price-earnings ratio.
10. Society should give business a chance to solve social problems that government has failed to solve.
11. Business is considered, by some groups, to be the institution with the financial and human resources to solve social problems.
12. Prevention of problems is better than cures—so let business solve problems before they become too great.

MAJOR ARGUMENTS AGAINST SOCIAL RESPONSIBILITY

1. It might be illegal.
2. Business plus government equals monolith.
3. Social actions cannot be measured.
4. It violates profit maximization.
5. Cost of social responsibility is too great and would increase prices too much.
6. Business lacks social skills to solve societal problems.
7. It would dilute business's primary purposes.
8. It would weaken U.S. balance of payments, because price of goods will have to go up to pay for social programs.
9. Business already has too much power. Such involvement would make business too powerful.
10. Business lacks accountability to the public. Thus, the public would have no control over its social involvement.
11. Such business involvement lacks broad public support.

Source: R. Joseph Monsen, Jr., "The Social Attitudes of Management," in *Contemporary Management: Issues and Viewpoints,* ed. Joseph W. McGuire (Englewood Cliffs, N.J.: Prentice-Hall, 1974 © 1974), p. 616. Adapted by permission of Prentice-Hall, Inc.

This argument has been considerably weakened over the years. A 1935 amendment to the Internal Revenue Code allowed corporations to deduct up to 5 percent of net profits for social purposes. And in 1953, the New Jersey Supreme Court upheld the right of the A. P. Smith Company to give funds to Princeton University against the desires of some stockholders. The court stated, "It is not just a right but a duty of corporations to support higher education in the interest of the long-range well-being of their stockholders because the company could not hope to operate effectively in a society which is not functioning well."

2. Business plus government equals monolith. Proponents of this argument feel that business should make profits and government should spend tax money to attack social problems. They argue that socially motivated business activities s..limate and compromise the profit motive. Proponents of this argument feel that if business assumes more and more social responsibility, then there could ultimately be very little functional difference between business and government. Without this functional difference, society would be dominated by one unopposed and unstoppable monolith.

3. Social actions cannot be measured. If managers do have a social responsibility other than to maximize profits for stockholders, how do they know what it is? Can they decide how great a burden they are justified in placing on themselves or their stockholders to serve that social interest? Also, who should decide what is good for society? Proponents of this argument feel that management cannot accurately measure the benefits of social action; also, it is fruitless to continue spending money without measuring the return on the investment.

The financial audit has been used traditionally to measure the profit performance of organizations. The need for measuring an organization's social responsibility has led to the idea of a social audit. A **social audit** attempts to report, in financial terms, an organization's expenditures and investments for social purposes. This is done by categorizing the socially related expenses and investments in terms of income, expenses, assets, and liabilities.[9] However, the problems of placing a dollar value on social investments are complex and subject to individual interpretation. Some business organizations have used the following methods to show socially responsible activities:

1. Narrative disclosure of social responsibility efforts in footnotes of financial statements.
2. Adding to traditional financial statements to include the costs of specific social responsibility efforts.
3. Special reports covering pollution, occupational health, equal employment, and other areas of activity.

Social audit – attempt to report in financial terms the expenditures and investments made by an organization for social purposes.

ACTIONS NECESSARY TO IMPLEMENT SOCIAL RESPONSIBILITY

The biggest obstacle to organizations assuming more social responsibility is pressure by financial analysts and stockholders. They push for steady increases in earnings per share on a quarterly basis. Concern about immediate profits makes it difficult to invest in areas that cannot be accurately measured and still have returns which are long run in nature. Furthermore, pressure for short-term earnings impacts on corporate social behavior; most companies

MANAGERS AT WORK 4-2

Cure for River Blindness

River blindness is a disease that afflicts 18 million people in developing countries and permanently blinds 500,000 people each year. The disease is spread by black flies which breed near fast-flowing tropical streams—hence the name river blindness. In 1987 Merck & Co. announced that it will begin distributing ivermectin, a drug that halts river blindness. Moreover, Merck declared that it would donate enough of the new drug through the World Health Organization (WHO) to wipe out river blindness by the year 2000. WHO has for decades mounted spraying campaigns to kill the black flies. However, the campaigns were never totally effective. Ivermectin does a much better job because it kills the parasites carried by the flies.

Source: Adapted from "Miracle Worker," *Time,* November 2, 1987, p. 78.

are geared to short-term profit goals. Budgets, objectives, and performance evaluations are often based on short-run considerations. Management may state a willingness to lose some short-term profit to achieve social objectives. However, managers who sacrifice profit and seek to justify these actions on the basis of corporate social goals may find stockholders unsympathetic.

Organizations should also carefully examine their cherished values—short-run profits and others—to ensure that these concepts are in tune with the values held by society. This should be a constant process, because the values held by society are ever changing.

Organizations should reevaluate their long-range planning and decision-making processes to ensure that they fully understand the potential social consequences. Plant location decisions are no longer merely economic matters. Environmental impact and job opportunities for the disadvantaged are examples of other factors that may be considered.

Organizations should seek to aid both governmental agencies and voluntary agencies in their social efforts. This should include technical and managerial help as well as monetary support. Technological knowledge, organizational skills, and managerial competence can all be applied to solving social problems.

Organizations should look at ways to help solve social problems through their own business. Many social problems stem from the economic deprivation of a fairly large segment of our society. Attacking this could be the greatest social effort of organizations. Managers at Work 4–2 describes the actions of Merck & Co. in solving a major health problem.

In order for business organizations to implement social responsibility programs successfully, society must also meet certain basic responsibilities. These are summarized in Figure 4–3.

F I G U R E 4–3 Responsibility of Society to Business in Implementing Social Responsibility Programs

1. *Set rules that are clear and consistent.* Society must define organizations' boundaries; minimum standards expected to be met or exceeded; and performance criteria. Society must be consistent in its expectations for corporate social responsibility through the various governmental regulations affecting this area.
2. *Keep the rules within the bounds of technical feasibility.* Business cannot do the impossible. However, many of today's regulations are unworkable in practice. Extreme environmental restrictions have, on occasion, set standards surpassing those of Mother Nature.
3. *Make sure rules are economically feasible; recognize that society itself must be prepared to pay the cost—not only of their implementation by business but also their administration by government.* Ultimately, it is the people who must pay, either through higher prices or taxes.
4. *Make rules prescriptive, not retroactive.* There is a present trend toward retroactivity in an attempt to force retribution for the past—to make today's rules apply to yesterday's ball game.
5. *Make rules goal seeking, not procedure prescribing.* Tell organizations to devise the best, most economical, and most efficient way to get there.

Source: Adapted from Jerry McAfee, "Responsibilities Shared by Corporations and Society," *Credit and Financial Management*, May 1978, p. 31.

HOW SOCIALLY RESPONSIBLE ARE TODAY'S ORGANIZATIONS?

Regardless of the arguments against social responsibility, organizations—either on their own or through pressures from the government or consumers—are becoming more aware of their social responsibilities. Figure 4–4 summarizes many issues now seen as legitimate social concerns of organizations. The commitments of organizations in three of these areas are discussed next.

Consumerism

Consumerism is a social movement that seeks to redress the perceived imbalance in the marketplace between the buyer and the seller. Initially, the consumer movement sought to correct this through legislation; it was very successful in getting laws passed relating to product safety and consumer information. The **Federal Fair Packaging and Labeling Act of 1966** regulates labeling procedures for businesses. The **Truth in Lending Act of 1967** regulates the extension of credit to individuals. The **Consumer Product Safety Act of 1972** protects consumers against unreasonable risks of injury associated with consumer products. In fact, more consumer legislation was enacted from 1965 to 1980 than during the previous 189 years.[10]

Consumerism – social movement that seeks to redress the perceived imbalance in the marketplace between buyers and sellers.

Fair Packaging and Labeling Act of 1967 – regulates labeling procedures for businesses.

Truth in Lending Act of 1967 – regulates the extension of credit to individuals.

Consumer Product Safety Act of 1972 – protects consumers against unreasonable risks of injury associated with consumer products.

F I G U R E 4–4   Issues That Are Social Concerns
of Organizations

External issues—may or may not have been directly caused by business:
1. Poverty.
2. Drug abuse.
3. Decay of cities.
4. Community relations.
5. Philanthropy.

External issues—caused by economic activity of business.
1. Environmental pollution.
2. Safety and quality of goods and services (consumerism movement).
3. Social impact of facilities closings.
4. Site locations of new facilities.

Internal issues—directly related to economic activity.
1. Equal employment opportunity.
2. Occupational safety and health.
3. Quality of work life.

Society of Consumer Affairs Professionals in Business (SOCAP) – promotes professionalism among consumer affairs managers.

National Environment Policy Act of 1969 – committed the federal government to preserving the country's ecology, established a White House Council on Environmental Quality, and required filings of environmental impact statements.

Council on Environmental Quality – assists and advises the president on environmental issues.

Spurred by the consumer movement and legislation, more and more companies are taking action on consumer affairs. One action establishes consumer affairs departments to handle consumer complaints and concerns. Well over 600 corporations and trade associations have formed consumer affairs departments. Firms such as Whirlpool, General Motors, Ford, American Motors, Zenith, Eastman Kodak, J. C. Penney, Sears, General Foods, and Giant Foods are generally thought to be effectively responding to consumers. Furthermore, the **Society of Consumer Affairs Professionals in Business (SOCAP)** has been organized to promote professionalism among consumer affairs managers.

Environmentalism

During the 1960s and 70s, protection of the environment became an important political issue. It resulted not only in stricter application of earlier laws but also in several new laws designed to improve the environment. Figure 4–5 outlines several key laws that influence business activities in relation to the environment.

The key legislation in environmental protection was the **National Environmental Policy Act of 1969.** The law went into effect on January 1, 1970; it committed the government to preserving the country's ecology, established a White House **Council on Environmental Quality,** and required filings of environmental impact statements (EIS) for any major federal action that could greatly affect the quality of the human environment. This law requires the president to submit an annual report to Congress on environmental quality. The Council on Environmental Quality assists in the preparation of the environmental quality report and advises the president on environmental issues.

F I G U R E   4–5   Laws Relating to Environmental Protection

DATE	NAME	PURPOSE
December 17, 1963	Clean Air Act	To improve, strengthen, and accelerate programs for the prevention and abatement of air pollution.
November 3, 1966	Clean Water Restoration Act of 1966	To provide technical and financial assistance in the development of waste treatment, water purification, and water quality control programs.
January 1, 1970	National Environmental Policy Act of 1969	To establish a national policy on the environment and to establish a Council on Environmental Quality.
October 27, 1972	Noise Control Act of 1972	To control the emission of noise harmful to the human environment.
December 16, 1974	Safe Drinking Water Act	To assure that the public is provided with safe drinking water.
October 11, 1976	Toxic Substances Control Act	To regulate business and protect human health and the environment by requiring testing and necessary use restrictions on certain chemical substances.
October 21, 1976	Resource Conservation and Recovery Act	To provide technical and financial assistance to develop management plans and facilities for the recovery of energy and other resources from discarded materials and to regulate the management of hazardous waste.

Environmental Impact Statements (EIS) require agencies of the federal government to submit a written report of proposed actions that affect the human environment. They must give an environmental analysis of the proposal, outline alternative methods of meeting the agency's goals, describe the existing environment, and analyze the environmental impact anticipated from the alternative proposals.

Environmental impact statements (EIS) – written report required of federal government agencies on proposed actions that affect the human environment.

Environmental Protection Agency (EPA) – interprets and administers the environmental protection policies of the federal government.

As a result of this legislation, the **Environmental Protection Agency (EPA)** was created in July 1970 by the order of the president. The EPA combines the environmental protection functions of the federal government which had been scattered among the Interior, Agriculture, and Health, Education and Welfare departments and the Atomic Energy Commission. Today, the EPA interprets and adminsters the environmental protection policies of the federal government; it also has authority to approve or disapprove all environmental impact statements.

Changing interpretations of the law by the EPA and complaints that the laws are too strict and costly have made environmental protection controversial. For example, the Council on Environmental Quality estimates the cumulative costs of environmental protection legislation to be $735 billion between 1979 and 1988.[11] As a result, a growing number of people feel the need for reform of regulatory rules and procedures. However, reform will not mean that environmental concerns will disappear. Environmental protection will continue to be a major social concern of business organizations.

Philanthropy

Corporate Philanthropy – donations of money, property, or work by organizations to needy persons or for socially useful purposes.

Corporate philanthropy involves donations of money, property, or work by organizations to needy persons or to socially useful purposes. Companies can use one or more of three methods to make their donations. First, contributions can be made directly by the company. Second, a company foundation can be created to handle the philanthropic program. Numerous organizations use this approach. For example, Apple Computer Company has the Apple Education Foundation; General Electric has the General Electric Foundation. A final method for making contributions is for a company to establish a Clifford trust. Under a **Clifford Trust,** the company turns over some of its assets for a set period—usually it is a little more than 10 years—during which all of the income earned by the assets goes to charity. At the end of the set period, the assets revert to the company.

Clifford Trust – company turns over some of its assets for a set time period during which all of the income earned on the assets goes to charity.

In the past, companies have directed their philanthrophic efforts toward education, the arts, and the United Way. However, in the 1980s, the federal government has repeatedly exhorted private enterprise organizations to play a greater role in the support of nonprofit organizations and altruistic causes.

How has business responded? Some say organizations have made significant contributions. Others argue that they have not done enough. Exact figures on total corporate giving are hard to determine. However, it was estimated that corporate charitable giving was over $3 billion annually in the early 1980s.[12] It is expected that corporate philanthropic efforts will continue to increase well into the 1990s.

BUSINESS ETHICS

Social responsibility deals with how individuals and organizations handle current social issues. Business ethics are concerned with the day-to-day behavior standards of individuals and organizations. **Ethics** are standards or principles of conduct used to govern the behavior of an individual or group of individuals. Ethics are generally concerned with questions of right and wrong or with moral duties. Ethical standards can be developed by an individual, a group of individuals, or society. Laws are ethics formalized by a society; they are usually concerned with principles of conduct. Organizational ethics, however, generally deal more with the behavior of individuals or groups of individuals not covered by the law.

Ethics – standards or principles of conduct that govern the behavior of an individual or a group of individuals.

Why Is a Code of Ethics Needed?

Due to the adverse publicity that many organizations have received, society is demanding a code of ethics for organizations. Many people believe that if organizations do not develop their own code, the issue will be forced by public opinion or even government regulation. In fact, the **Foreign Corrupt Practices Act** was passed in 1977. This law makes it illegal to obtain or retain business through payments to influence foreign officials and governments improperly. It is not, however, limited to businesses operating abroad nor to illegal foreign payments. It has significant internal accounting control and recordkeeping requirements that apply to the domestic operations of businesses. The act requires that a company's books and records accurately and fairly reflect transactions in reasonable detail. The company's internal accounting controls must provide reasonable assurances that:

Foreign Corrupt Practices Act of 1977 – prohibits American companies operating abroad from bribing foreign officials, political candidates, and party leaders; requires company books and records to accurately and fairly reflect transactions.

- Transactions are carried out in an authorized manner.
- Transactions have been reported and recorded to permit correct preparation of financial statements and to maintain accurate records of assets.
- Access to assets is in accordance with management's authorization.
- Inventories of assets occur periodically and appropriate action is taken to correct discrepancies.

A code of ethics also reduces the organizational pressures to compromise personal ethics for the sake of organizational goals. One study indicated that managers do feel pressured to compromise personal standards to achieve company goals. In this study, Archie B. Carroll found that 50 percent of top-level managers, 65 percent of middle-level managers, and 84 percent of lower-level managers feel this pressure.[13]

Lastly, a code of ethics in organizations appeals to the ethical needs of people within organizations. Research shows that people generally want and need to be ethical in their business lives as well as their private lives.[14] Furthermore, most want to be part of an organization whose purpose and activity are beneficial to society.

Corporate Codes of Ethics

The **Judeo–Christian ethic** is generally considered to be the basis of Western ethical standards. Its primary goal is love—including love of God and neighbor.

Judeo–Christian ethic – generally the basis of Western ethical codes; primary goal is love—including love of God and neighbor.

MANAGERS AT WORK 4–3

Cummins Practice on Ethical Standards

For Cummins, ethics rests on a fundamental belief in people's dignity and decency. Our most basic ethical standard is to show respect for those whose lives we affect and to treat them as we would expect them to treat us if our positions were reversed. This kind of respect implies that we must:

1. Obey the law.
2. Be honest—present the facts fairly and accurately.
3. Be fair—give everyone appropriate consideration.
4. Be concerned—care about how Cummins' actions affect others, and try to make those effects as beneficial as possible.
5. Be courageous—treat others with respect even when it means losing business. (It seldom does. Over the long haul, people trust and respect this kind of behavior and wish more of our institutions embodied it.)

Source: This material is drawn from Oliver F. Williams, "Business Ethics: A Trojan Horse?" *California Management Review*, Summer 1982, p. 20.

James F. Lincoln, founder of the highly successful Lincoln Electric Company, commented on the ethics of organizations: "Do unto others as you would have them do unto you. This is not just a Sunday school idea, but a proper labor-management policy."[15] His statement is a logical starting point for developing a corporate code of ethics.

Codes of ethics should be formal, written, and communicated to all employees. The Cummins Engine Company, for example, has given considerable time, thought, money, and energy to develop its corporate ethical codes. Their formal, written set of policies is called *Cummins Practices*.[16] *Cummins Practices* deal with ethical standards, questionable payments, meals, gifts and discounts, financial representations, customs declarations, supplies selection, and employee involvement in political campaigns and noncorporate political activities. Each section discusses a practice, details responsibility for the practice, and lists persons to consult for more information and advice. The *Cummins Practice on Ethical Standards* is summarized in Managers at Work 4–3.

A wide range of issues can be covered under a code of ethics; but rules in themselves are not always enough to handle all problems. For example, in the Gospel of Mark, Chapter 2, verses 23–28, and Chapter 3, verses 1–6, Jesus faced conflicting obligations. On the one hand, there was the obligation to follow the rules of the Sabbath observance, which forbade a wide range of activities. On the other hand, there were disciples who were hungry and followers to be healed. Jesus did not deny the validity of the rules of the

MANAGERS AT WORK 4–4

Code of Ethics South Central Bell and Southern Bell*

South Central Bell and Southern Bell's code of ethics outlines specific actions required of employees in the areas of privacy of communications, fair competition, conflict of interest, internal company accounting procedures, proprietary information, company funds, political contributions, company property, company records, computer systems, espionage, sabotage, and drugs.

The document also states:

Each employee, alone, is responsible for his or her actions. For each, integrity is a personal liability. No one will be permitted to justify an illegal act by claiming it was ordered by someone in higher management. No one, regardless of level, is ever authorized to direct an employee to commit an illegal or unethical act.

* Southern Bell and South Central Bell were reorganized in 1984 and are now Bell South.

Source: Public company documents.

Sabbath. He decided that, in that case, the needs of life took priority over worship obligations and rest requirements.[17]

Codes of conduct do not end value conflicts. Organizations still need to have a formal mechanism to assist managers in resolving value conflicts in light of the corporate code. For example, Cummins Engine has a department of corporate responsibility to assist its managers. Managers may also need more education in business ethics. One way of institutionalizing a corporate code of ethics is through an ethics training program within the management development program.

Finally, the corporate code of ethics must be followed by all levels of management. Having a written code does more harm than good if management does not put into practice what is written. "Actions speak louder than words" is an old statement that is especially true in codes of conduct. Managers at Work 4–4 summarizes the code of ethics of South Central Bell and Southern Bell. It also specifically states that each person is responsible for his own behavior.

SUMMARY

LEARNING OBJECTIVE 1

Define Social Responsibility.

Social responsibility is the moral and ethical content of managerial and corporate decisions over and above the pragmatic requirements imposed by legal principle and the market economy.

LEARNING OBJECTIVE 2

List the Arguments for Social Responsibility.

The arguments for social responsibility are: It is in the best interest of the business; social actions can be profitable; being socially responsible is the ethical thing to do.

LEARNING OBJECTIVE 3

List the Arguments against Social Responsibility.

The arguments against social responsibility are: It might be illegal; business plus government equals monolith; and social actions cannot be measured.

LEARNING OBJECTIVE 4

Define a Social Audit.

A social audit attempts to report, in financial terms, an organization's expenditures and investments for social purposes.

LEARNING OBJECTIVE 5

Define Consumerism.

Consumerism is a social movement that seeks to redress the perceived imbalance in the marketplace between the buyer and the seller.

LEARNING OBJECTIVE 6

Define Corporate Philanthropy.

Corporate philanthropy involves donations of money, property, or work by organizations to needy persons or to socially useful purposes.

LEARNING OBJECTIVE 7

Explain the Concept of Business Ethics.

Business ethics are concerned with the day-to-day behavior standards of individuals and organizations. Ethics are standards or principles of conduct used to govern the behavior of an individual or group of individuals.

REVIEW QUESTIONS

1. What is social responsibility?
2. Outline three major arguments for social responsibility.
3. Outline three major arguments against social responsibility.
4. What are some obstacles to organizations becoming more socially responsible?
5. Categorize the issues that are now considered to be legitimate social concerns of organizations.
6. What is consumerism?
7. What actions have organizations taken in environmental protection?
8. What methods can companies use to make charitable contributions?
9. What are ethics?
10. Give some reasons why a code of ethics is needed in organizations.

DISCUSSION QUESTIONS

1. Do you feel that organizations and managers should be evaluated with regard to social responsibility?
2. "Profits, not social responsibility, must be the primary concern of managers." Discuss.
3. What are some ethical questions that you

have faced in college? What basis did you use to resolve them?

4. Do you agree with the statement of James F. Lincoln: "Do unto others as you would have them do unto you. This is not just a Sunday School ideal, but a proper labor-management policy"? Why or why not?

REFERENCES & ADDITIONAL READINGS

[1] Robert H. Bork, "Modern Values and Social Responsibility," *MSU Business Topics,* Spring 1980, p. 7.

[2] Henry L. Gantt, *Organization for Work* (New York: Harcourt Brace Jovanovich, 1919), p. 15.

[3] Oliver Sheldon, *The Philosophy of Management* (Marshfield, Mass.: Pitman Publishing, 1966), p. xv (originally published in London in 1923 by Sir Isaac Pitman and Sons).

[4] Stewart Thompson, *Management Creeds and Philosophy: Top Management Guides in Our Changing Economy,* Research Study No. 32 (New York: American Management Association, 1958).

[5] For a different perspective, see Steven L. Wartick and Philip L. Cochran, "The Evolution of the Corporate Social Performance Model," *Academy of Management Review,* October 1985, pp. 758–69.

[6] For more discussion on the arguments for and against social responsibility, see Clarence C. Walton, "Corporate Social Responsibilities: The Debate Revisited," *Journal of Economics and Business* 34 (1982), pp. 173–87.

[7] See, for instance, Kenneth E. Aupperle, Archie B. Carroll, and John D. Hatfield, "An Empirical Examination of the Relationship between Corporate Social Responsibility and Profitability," *Academy of Management Journal,* June 1985, pp. 446–63.

[8] Milton Friedman, "Does Business Have a Social Responsibility?" *Magazine of Bank Administration,* April 1971, p. 14.

[9] See, for instance, Meinolf Dierkes and Ariane Berthoin Antal, "Whither Corporate Social Reporting: Is It Time to Legislate?" *California Management Review,* Spring 1986, pp. 106–21.

[10] Hiram C. Barksdale and William D. Perreault, Jr., "Can Consumers Be Satisfied?" *MSU Business Topics,* Spring 1980, p. 19.

[11] Tom Alexander, "A Simpler Path to a Cleaner Environment," *Fortune,* May 4, 1981, p. 239.

[12] James A. Joseph, "Directing the Flow of Corporate Largesse," *Business and Society Review,* Summer 1982, p. 42.

[13] Archie B. Carroll, "Managerial Ethics: A Post-Watergate View," *Business Horizons,* April 1975, p. 77.

[14] James Weber, "Institutionalizing Ethics into the Corporation," *MSU Business Topics,* Spring 1981, p. 48.

[15] C. Roland Christensen, Norman A. Berg, and Malcolm S. Salter, *Policy Formulation and Administration,* 8th ed. (Homewood, Ill.: Richard D. Irwin, 1980), p. 591.

[16] This material is drawn from Oliver F. Williams, "Business Ethics: A Trojan Horse?" *California Management Review,* Summer 1982, p. 19.

[17] Ibid., p. 16.

INCIDENT

Poletown, USA*

In 1981, General Motors decided to invest $500 million for a new facility to boost its production of Cadillacs and Fisher body frames. The plant was to take 500 acres of land located in an old and historic area of Detroit called Poletown, as well as part of an adjacent area and a portion of the site occupied by one of Chrysler's defunct Dodge plants.

Since 6,000 new jobs and the potential for better dividends and better products were attractive prospects, Detroit's leaders worked hard to move the project forward; Michigan desperately needed jobs and Detroit needed tax income in the face of an impoverished state budget. But the people of Poletown, mostly elderly, protested. They wanted to keep their houses and their old church.

Since the early days of its formation, the United Automobile Workers (UAW) has had a reputation as being a socially responsible union. From 1979 to 1981, union membership had dropped from 1.5 million to 1.25 million. Its income had fallen by nearly a million per month. It had just sacrificed over $1 million in negotiated wages and benefits in a last-ditch effort to save jobs at Chrysler. Should the union support General Motors by favoring construction of the new plant? Or should it back the citizens of Poletown? The union wrestled with these questions. M. L. Douglas, vice president of Local 22, finally responded. "We have feelings about uprooting a lot of older people, but with the way things are going now, we cannot afford to lose those jobs."

The church faced another problem. John Cardinal Dearden, leader of the archdiocese, was known for his liberal views. By virtue of his own personality and priestly commitment, it could be reasonably inferred that because of the perceived needs of the poor and elderly, the Cardinal's response would be in their favor. Through a church bulletin, the parishioners learned that an agreement had been signed on February 16, 1981, with the city of Detroit. The diocese would sell the two churches of Poletown. Reactions were initially stunned surprise—and then anger. One parishioner expressed the common revulsion when he said, "They have sold us out to the city and to General Motors for 30 pieces of silver."

Questions

1. Were General Motors, the city of Detroit, the UAW, and John Dearden acting socially responsible?

2. Should the good of the larger number be used as rationale for social responsibility?

* Source: Adapted from Clarence C. Walton, "Corporate Social Responsibility: The Debate Revisited," *Journal of Economics and Business* 34 (1982), pp. 184–85.

EXERCISE

*Truthfulness in Advertising**

*A*dvertising claims may be totally inaccurate ("sticker price is a low $5,998" may omit all transportation costs, state taxes, dealer charges, and factory options, which together add 25 percent to 30 percent to the price of a car). Other claims are greatly exaggerated ("12-hour relief from sore throat pain"), verbally misleading ("you'll have to eat 12 bowls of Shredded Wheat to get the vitamins and nutrition in 1 bowl of Total"), or visually misleading (healthy, active people shown in pleasant social situations to advertise liquor, beer, or cigarettes).

Question

From magazines, newspapers, or television, select an advertisement you believe to be untruthful. Be prepared to describe why you feel the claims are untruthful and into what group (inaccurate, exaggerated, or misleading) you think they fall.

---

* Source: La Rue Tone Hosmer, *The Ethics of Management* (Homewood, Ill.: Richard D. Irwin, 1987), p. 86.

5 Communication Skills: Transmitting Understanding

LEARNING OBJECTIVES

After studying this chapter,
you should be able to:

1 Define communication.

2 Describe the interpersonal communication process.

3 Define semantics and explain its role in the interpersonal communication process.

4 Define perception.

5 Explain the concept of feedback in communication.

6 Describe organizational communication systems.

7 Define downward communication systems.

8 Define upward communication systems.

9 Explain the importance of the grapevine.

10 Discuss the communication process in an international management setting.

A naturalist discovered that baboons have a language consisting of shrill alarm cries, contented chucklings and grunts, dissatisfied barks, silly happy chatterings, mourning wails for their dead, cries denoting pain, groans of dread, and calls for assembly and for action. He observed that at night there was a continuous soft mumbling among them which sounded so much like human talk that he was almost convinced that they were capable of articulated speech. A native confirmed this for him: "Baboons can talk," he said. "But they won't do it in front of men for fear they will put them to work."

JOHN DENTON SCOTT*

Breakdowns in the communication process are said to cause divorces, wars, racial problems, business failures, and other problems too numerous to mention. Within organizations, there are endless places where poor communication can be costly if not disastrous. Therefore, poor communication is often named the culprit when any organizational problem arises. It may very well be the cause of the problem; but it is sometimes only a symptom of a more complex problem. Poor communication can be used as a scapegoat for other problems.

Good communication is not a cure-all for all organizational problems. It will not, for instance, make up for poor planning. However, even good plans must be communicated. Thus good communication is an essential element in achieving excellent performance.

Communication has been estimated to occupy between 50 and 90 percent of the manager's time.[1] Unfortunately, however, research has revealed that as much as 70 percent of all business communications fail to achieve their intended purpose.[2]

WHAT IS COMMUNICATION?

Communication—transfer of information that is meaningful to those involved; the transmittal of understanding.

The problem in defining communication is best shown by the fact that one study found over 95 definitions of the term.[3] Many were supposed to be "the one true" definition. In this book, **communication** is defined as the transfer of information that is meaningful to those involved—in general, the transmittal of understanding. Communication can occur in many forms ranging from face-to-face contact involving facial expressions and body movements

* Adapted from John Denton Scott, "Speaking Wildly," *Reader's Digest*, May 1977, p. 144.

to written messages. One author states that communication occurs when a person takes something into account, whether it was something someone did or said or did not do or say, whether it was some observable event, some internal condition, the meaning of something being read or looked at, some feeling mixed with some past memory—literally anything that can be taken into account by human beings in general and that person in particular.

Communication in organizations can be viewed in one of two perspectives: between individuals (interpersonal communication) and within the formal organization structure (organizational communication). These two basic forms are interdependent: interpersonal communication is almost always a part of organizational communication.

INTERPERSONAL COMMUNICATION

Effective communication between individuals, especially between a manager and subordinates, is critical to achieving organizational goals and, as a result, to effectively managing people. **Interpersonal communication** occurs between individuals. It is an interactive process that involves a person's effort to attain meaning and to respond to it. It involves sending and receiving verbal and nonverbal messages. These come not only from other people but also from the physical and cultural settings of both the sender and the receiver.

Interpersonal communication—communication between individuals.

The basic purpose of interpersonal communication is to transmit ideas, thoughts, or information so that the sender of the message both is understood and understands the receiver. Figure 5–1 diagrams this dynamic and interactive

F I G U R E 5–1 Interpersonal Communication Process

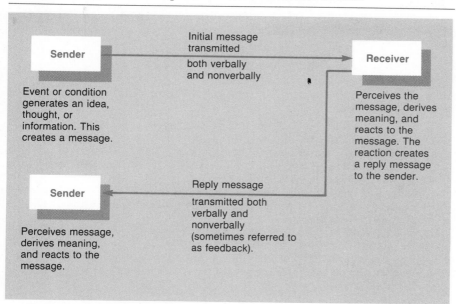

process. An event or condition generates an idea, thought, or information. The desire to share the information or to inform another person about it provides the need to communicate. The sender then creates a message and transmits it both verbally and nonverbally. It is perceived and interpreted by the receiver. Hopefully, the receiver creates a reply message with a response or reaction to the initial message. This reply message may cause the sender to have responses which lead to a repeat of the process.

Often, many factors interfere and cause this process to fail. Some of the causes of communication failure are: different interpretations of the meaning of words (semantics), differences in perception, poor listening habits, inadequate feedback, and differences in the interpretation of nonverbal communications.

Semantics

Semantics – science or study of the meaning of words and symbols.

Semantics is the science or study of the meaning of words and symbols. Words themselves have no real meaning. They have meaning only in terms of peoples' reactions to them. A word may mean very different things to different people, depending on how it is used. In addition, a word may be interpreted differently, depending on the facial expressions, hand gestures, and voice inflection used.

The problems involved in semantics are of two general types. Some words and phrases invite multiple interpretations. For example, Figure 5–2 shows different interpretations of the word *fix*. Another problem is that groups of people in specific situations often develop their own technical language, which may or may not be understood by outsiders. For example, physicians, government, and military employees are often guilty of using acronyms and abbreviations that only they understand.

F I G U R E 5–2   Interpretations of the Word *Fix*

An Englishman visits America and is completely awed by the many ways we use the word *fix*. For example:

1. His host asks him how he'd like his drink fixed. He meant *mixed*.
2. As he prepares to leave, he discovers that he has a flat tire and calls a repairman who says he'll fix it immediately. He means *repair*.
3. On the way home, he is given a ticket for speeding. He calls his host, who says, "Don't worry, I'll fix it." He means *nullify*.
4. At the office the next day, he comments on the cost of living in America, and one of his cohorts says, "It's hard to make ends meet on a fixed income." He means *steady* or *unchanging*.
5. He has an argument with a co-worker. The latter says, "I'll fix you." He means *seek revenge*.
6. A cohort remarks that he is in a fix. He means *condition* or *situation*.
7. He meets a friend at his apartment who offers to "fix him up" with a girl. You know what that means.

Words are the most common form of interpersonal communication. Because of the real possibility of misinterpretation, words must be carefully chosen and clearly defined for effective communication.

Perception

Perception also plays an important role in interpersonal communication. **Perception** basically refers to how a message is processed by a person. Each individual's perception is unique; so people often perceive the same situation in entirely different ways.

Perception in communication depends primarily on three factors: personality, previous experience, and a stimulus (see Figure 5–3). The mix of these factors creates a unique perception for each person. The stimulus is the information received, whether it is conveyed in writing, verbally, or another way. Perception of the received information is modified by the individual's personality, previous experience, and other factors. Therefore, different people react differently to the same message, because no two have the same personal experiences, memories, likes, and dislikes. In addition, the phenomenon of selective perception often distorts the intended message: People tend to listen to only part of the message, blocking out the rest for a number of reasons.

Two illustrations found in many introductory psychology texts show the influence of perception. Please answer the following questions before proceeding.

1. What characteristics do you perceive of the woman in Figure 5–4?
2. In Figure 5–5(A), what shape is the largest?
3. In Figure 5–5(B), which line—*AX, CX, CB,* or *XD*—is the longest?

About 60 percent of the people who see Figure 5–4 for the first time see an attractive, apparently wealthy young woman. About 40 percent see an ugly, poor old woman. (Figure 5–6 shows both figures clearly.) In Figure

Perception— how a person processes a message; influenced by the person's personality and previous experience and unique for each individual.

F I G U R E 5–3   Perception Development in Communication

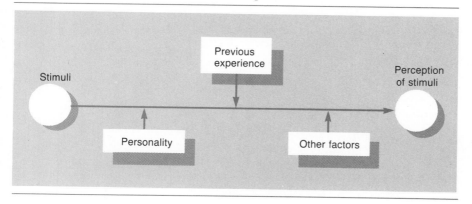

F I G U R E 5–4   Picture of a Woman

Source: Edwin G. Boring, "A New Ambiguous Figure," *American Journal of Psychology,* July 1930, p. 444. Also see Robert Leeper, "A Study of a Neglected Portion of the Field of Learning—The Development of Sensory Organization," *Journal of Genetic Psychology,* March 1935, p. 62. Originally drawn by cartoonist W. E. Hill and published in *Puck,* November 8, 1915.

F I G U R E 5–5   Shapes for Perception

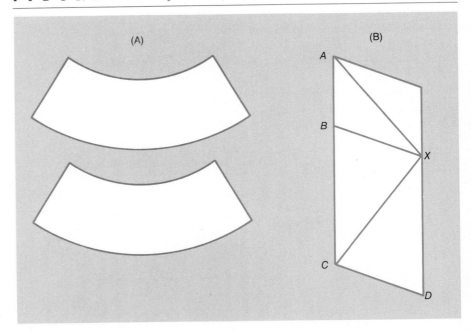

Source: Gregory A. Kimble and Normal Garmezy, *General Psychology* (New York: Ronald Press, 1963), pp. 324–25.

F I G U R E 5–6   Clear Picture of the Young and the Old Woman

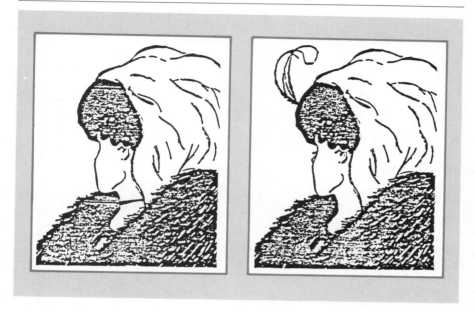

Source: Robert Leeper, "A Study of a Neglected Portion of the Field of Learning—The Development of Sensory Organization," *Journal of Genetic Psychology.* March 1935, p. 62.

5–5, both shapes in A are the same size; in B, the lines *AX, CX, CB,* and *XD* are of equal length. Obviously, if differences in perception exist in viewing physical objects, more subtle forms of communication such as facial expressions and hand gestures leave much room for differences in perception. Managers at Work 5–1 gives a humorous example of differences in perception.

Listening—An Important Factor

Communication depends on the ability not only to send but also to receive messages. So the ability to listen effectively greatly enhances the communication process. Tests indicate that immediately after listening to a 10-minute oral presentation, the average listener has heard, comprehended, accurately evaluated, and retained about half of what was said. Within 48 hours, that drops another 50 percent to a 25 percent effectiveness level. By the end of a week, that level goes down to about 10 percent or less.[4]

Effective listening is not natural to most people. How well a person listens very much depends on the listener's attitude toward the speaker. The listener who respects the intelligence of the speaker and expects to profit from the communication will be more likely to listen effectively.

Daydreaming and concern with other matters also often keep individuals from listening to what a speaker is saying. It has been suggested that at any

MANAGERS AT WORK 5–1

Perception in the Examination Room

A woman of 35 came in one day to tell me that she wanted a baby but that she had been told that she had a certain type of heart disease which might not interfere with a normal life but would be dangerous if she ever had a baby. From her description, I thought at once of mitral stenosis. This condition is characterized by a rather distinctive rumbling murmur near the apex of the heart and especially by a peculiar vibration felt by the examining finger on the patient's chest. The vibration is known as the "thrill" of mitral stenosis.

When this woman had been undressed and was lying on my table in her white kimono, my stethoscope quickly found the heart sounds I had expected. Dictating to my nurse, I described them carefully. I put my stethoscope aside and felt intently for the typical vibration which may be found in a small but variable area of the left chest.

I closed my eyes for better concentration and felt long and carefully for the tremor. I did not find it, and with my hand still on the woman's bare breast, lifting it upward and out of the way, I finally turned to the nurse and said: "No thrill."

The patient's eyes snapped open, and with venom in her voice she said: "Well, isn't that just too bad? Perhaps it's just as well you don't get one. That isn't what I came for."

My nurse almost choked, and my explanation still seems a nightmare of futile words.

Source: Frederic Loomis, *Consultation Room* (New York: Alfred A. Knopf, 1939), p. 47.

given point in a college lecture, 20 percent of both men and women are thinking about sex, 60 percent are off on some mental trip of their own, and only the remaining 20 percent are concentrating on the professor.[5]

Other barriers to effective listening include: mentally arguing with points being made by the speaker before the talk is finished; getting impatient with listening, and preferring active involvement by talking; lack of interest in the message; and other negative reactions toward the speaker.

Effective listening habits can be developed. Summarized below are some tips to improve listening skills:

1. Relax and clear your mind if someone is speaking, so that you're receptive to what they're saying.

2. Never assume that you've heard correctly, because the first few words have taken you in a certain direction. Most listening mistakes are made by people who only hear the first few words of a sentence, finish the sentence in their own minds, and miss the second half.

3. Learn to speed up your point of contact as a listener. The second you

hear a sound coming from another person, concentrate quickly on the first few words. That will get you started correctly.

4. Don't tune out a speaker just because you don't like his or her looks, voice, or general demeanor. Stay open to new information.

5. Don't overreact emotionally to the speaker's words or ideas—especially those that may run contrary to your usual thinking. Hear the other person out.

6. Before forming a conclusion, let the speaker complete his or her thought. Then, evaluate by distinguishing in your mind specific evidence presented (good) versus generalities (bad).

7. Part of listening is writing things down that are important. You should always have a piece of paper, a pencil, a notebook, or a card in your pocket. Throughout the day, many important things are discussed. But by the close of business, you don't remember the details. How many of you have found a phone number on a scrap of paper in your handwriting with no name attached? So, take notes to listen, to remember later, and to document, if necessary.

8. People will often say one thing and mean something else. As you grow in your listening sophistication it is important to listen for *intent* as well as *content*. This gets back to the absorption process we talked about before. Watch as you listen. Be sure that the speaker's eyes, body, and face are sending signals that are consistent with the speaker's voice and words. If something sounds out of sync, get it cleared up. Many people are afraid of looking foolish if they ask for clarification because it will seem as if they weren't paying attention. Better to have the speaker repeat a message on the spot than to set off a chain reaction of misunderstanding.

9. Human communication goes through three phases: reception (listening), information processing (analyzing), and transmission (speaking). When you overlap any of those, you may short-circuit the reception (listening) process. Try to listen without *over*analyzing. Try to listen without interrupting the speaker.

10. The other major failing of people in listening is simple distraction. To listen correctly you must be able to reprioritize immediately. The second you hear sound coming towards you, focus and say to yourself: "This is important." Keep your eye on the speaker. Don't fiddle with pens, pencils, papers, or other distractions.[6]

Managers at Work 5–2 tells how Sperry Univac sponsored seminars in good listening habits.

Feedback

Effective communication is a two-way process. Information must flow back and forth between sender and receiver. The flow from the receiver to the

MANAGERS AT WORK 5–2

Sperry Univac: "The Computer People Who Listen"

It all started as an advertising slogan, "We understand how important it is to listen." Before undertaking the advertising campaign, however, Sperry management decided that the campaign should not be hollow. Management decided that efforts had to be made to ensure that people in the company really did listen to customers. Senior managers throughout Sperry were given seminars in good listening habits. Once the advertisements stressing Sperry's commitment to good listening and to training good listeners appeared on television, employees from throughout the company requested the training. Since then, over 10,000 employees have taken the training.

The 10 bad listening habits that the Sperry training program attempts to eliminate are:

1. Calling the subject uninteresting.
2. Criticizing the speaker's delivery or mannerisms.
3. Getting stimulated by something the speaker says.
4. Listening primarily for facts.
5. Trying to outline everything.
6. Faking attention.
7. Allowing interfering reactions.
8. Avoiding difficult material.
9. Letting emotion-laden words arouse personal antagonism.
10. Daydreaming.

One of the clear lessons learned from Sperry's experience is that people are much less efficient listeners than they imagine.

Source: Adapted from *International Management,* February 1981, pp. 201–21. Permission of McGraw-Hill International Publications Company Limited. All rights reserved.

Feedback – flow of information from receiver to sender that indicates if the message was received as intended by sender.

sender is called **feedback.** It allows the sender to know if the receiver has received the correct message; it also lets the receiver know if he or she has the correct message. For example, asking a person if he or she understands a message often puts that person on the defensive and can result in little feedback. Instead of asking if a person understands a message, it is much better to request that the receiver explain what he or she has heard.

In an experiment designed to show the importance of feedback, a person was asked to describe a series of rectangles (see Figure 5–7) to a group of people.[7] The experiment was conducted two different ways. First, the sender described the rectangles. The listeners could not ask questions or see the sender; thus, there was no feedback. In the second trial, the sender could see the listeners, and the listeners could ask questions. Thus, feedback was present.

The results showed that lack of feedback increased the speed of transmission.

F I G U R E 5–7   Rectangles in Communication Experiment

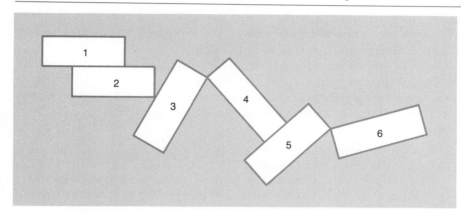

Source: Reprinted from *Managerial Psychology* by Harold J. Leavitt by permission of The University of Chicago Press © 1972 by *(copyright holder)*.

However, feedback caused the accuracy and the listeners' degree of confidence in the accuracy to improve greatly. In summary, feedback in the communication process takes more time but improves the quality of the communication.

Nonverbal Communication

Humans have a unique capacity for conveying meaning through silence and other nonverbal means of expression as well as through speech. Gestures, vocal intonations, facial expressions, and body posture are all used to communicate at the **nonverbal** level.

Some studies have indicated that from 60 to 93 percent of a message's overall effect comes from nonverbal communication.[8] This suggests that people are not good "nonverbal liars." In other words, people communicate nonverbally that part of the message which they wish least to communicate. Further, visual clues often lead to more accurate judgments about the meaning of a message than do vocal cues.

Nonverbal communication – conscious or unconscious behavior of the individual sending a message that is perceived consciously or subconsciously by the receiver.

ORGANIZATIONAL COMMUNICATION SYSTEMS

Organizational communication occurs within the formal organizational structure. In general, organizational communication systems are downward, upward, and lateral (horizontal). Overlapping these three formal systems is the informal communication system called the *grapevine*.

Organizational communication – communication occurring within the formal organizational structure.

Two Early Approaches

Management pioneer Henry Fayol (see Chapter 2) was one of the first writers to analyze the communication process. He recognized that communication via the formal chain of command could produce unnecessary distortion. In Figure 5–8, suppose that F would like to transmit a message to G. Following the formal chain of command, the message would go from F to B to C to G. It is easy to see the potential for distortion. Fayol proposed a shortcut between F and G. He stated the need for the shortcut (called Fayol's gangplank, or bridge) as follows:

> Allow the two employees . . . to deal, at one sitting and in a few hours, with some question or other which via the scalar chain would . . . inconvenience many people, involve masses of paper, lose weeks or months to get to a conclusion less satisfactory generally than the one which could have been obtained via direct contact.[9]

Chester Barnard also stressed the importance of communication in organizations.[10] In fact, he felt that it was basic to the existence of an organization—essential for establishing its authority structure. He contended that an employee can and will accept a communication as authoritative only if four conditions are met: the employee (1) understands the communication, (2) believes it to be consistent with the purpose of the organization, (3) believes it to be compatible with his or her personal interest as a whole, and (4) is physically and mentally able to comply with the communication. Barnard's coupling of authority with the communication process led to his development of the acceptance theory of authority, discussed in Chapter 10.[11]

Communication Patterns

Figure 5–9 shows six communication patterns which can exist in an organization. Each falls into one of two classes, depending on the presence or lack

F I G U R E 5–8   Fayol's Gangplank Concept

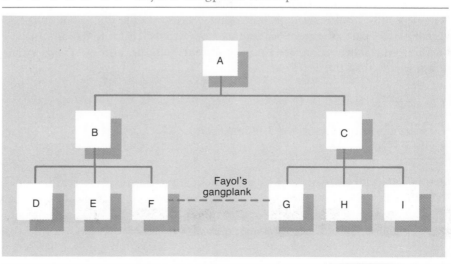

F I G U R E 5–9   Communication Patterns

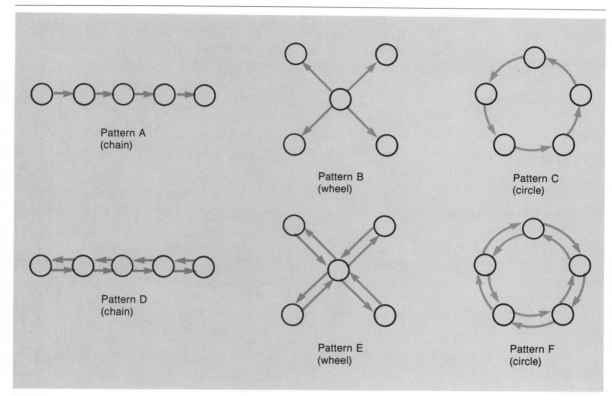

of feedback. No pair of individuals can exchange messages in patterns A, B, and C; in other words, no feedback can occur. They do not encourage good coordination or the exchange of ideas.

Any pair of individuals in patterns D, E, and F can exchange messages either directly or indirectly. Thus, feedback can occur. Such patterns have advantages and disadvantages as outlined in Figure 5–10. The following conclusions about patterns of communication networks can be drawn from the figure.

1. They affect the accuracy and speed of messages.
2. They affect the task performance of the group.
3. They affect the satisfaction of group members.

Thus, no one communication pattern is best for all situations. The most effective one for a given situation depends on the required speed, accuracy, morale, and organization structure. For instance, the wheel pattern is most desirable in situations requiring a clear-cut leader and rapid decisions.

Numerous studies have researched the relationships between the pattern of the network and the communication process. Primarily, these studies have indicated that the network pattern is important in determining the effectiveness of the communication process.

F I G U R E 5–10 Advantages and Disadvantages of
Communication Patterns

Characteristics	Chain	Wheel	Circle
Speed	Fast	Fast	Slow
Accuracy	Good	Good	Poor
Organization	Slowly emerging but stable organization	Almost immediate and stable organization	No stable form of organization
Emergency of leader	Marked	Very pronounced	None
Morale	Poor	Very poor	Very good

Downward Communication Systems

Downward communication — transmitting information from higher to lower levels of the organization through the chain of command.

Traditional views of the communication processes in organizations have been dominated by **downward communication** systems. Such systems transmit information from higher to lower levels of the organization. The chain of command determines the flow of downward information. Policy manuals, bulletins, organizational magazines, job descriptions, and directives are all examples of downward communication.

Often, downward communication systems are assumed to be better than studies indicate that they actually are. For example, it has been reported that much of the material in employee handbooks and manuals is not understandable to the average employee.[12]

One important choice that must be made in such systems is the medium to use. Written communication is less likely to be filtered and provides an official record; but it does not enable immediate feedback. Oral communication provides no record and is subject to filtering; but it does facilitate immediate feedback. Figure 5–11 offers some guidelines for when to use oral and written communications.

F I G U R E 5–11   Effective Communication Methods

METHOD OF COMMUNICATION	SITUATIONS	
	MOST EFFECTIVE	LEAST EFFECTIVE
Oral communication by itself.	Reprimanding employees. Resolving work-centered disputes.	Communicating information requiring future action. Communicating information of a general nature. Communicating directives or orders. Communicating information about an important policy change. Communicating with your immediate superior about work problems. Promoting a safety campaign.
Written communication by itself.	Communicating information requiring future action. Communicating information of a general nature.	Communicating information requiring immediate action. Commending an employee for noteworthy work performance. Reprimanding an employee for poor performance. Resolving work-related disputes.
Oral, then written communication.	Communicating information requiring immediate action. Communicating directives or orders. Communicating information about an important policy change. Communicating with your immediate superior about work-related problems. Promoting a safety campaign. Commending an employee for noteworthy work performance.	

Source: Dale Level, Jr., "Communication Effectiveness: Method and Situation," *Journal of Business Communication*, Fall 1972, pp. 19–25.

Upward Communication Systems

Upward communication systems transmit information from the lower levels of the organization to the top. An upward communication system should help management judge the effectiveness of their downward communications and enable them to learn about organizational problems. Four major areas of information should be communicated from below: (1) the activities of subordinates in terms of their achievements, progress, and future plans; (2) unresolved work problems in which subordinates may need help currently or in the future; (3) suggestions or ideas for improvements within work groups or the organization as a whole; and (4) the feelings of subordinates

Upward communication – originates at the lower levels of the organization and flows toward the top.

FIGURE 5–12   Techniques Used in Upward Communication

Informal inquiries or discussion with employees.
Exit interviews.
Discussion with first-line supervisors.
Grievance or complaint procedures.
Grapevine.
Union representatives.
Counseling.
Formal meeting with employees.
Suggestion system.
Formal attitude surveys.
Question-and-answer column in employee publication.
Gripe boxes.
Hot-line system

about their jobs, associates, and the organization. Figure 5–12 lists several forms of upward communication.

The key to effective upward communication systems appears to be a superior-subordinate relationship in which subordinates do not feel that they will be penalized for candor. Subordinates often conceal and distort their real feelings, problems, opinions, and beliefs because they fear disclosure may cause the superior to punish them in some way. In fact, trust in one's superior appears to be a key variable in effective upward communication systems. Managers at Work 5–3 describes suggestion systems at Pitney Bowes.

Ideally, the organizational structure should provide for both upward and downward communication systems. Communication should flow in both directions through the formal organizational structure. Unfortunately, communication from the bottom does not flow as freely as communication from the top. Some deterrents to effective upward communication are:

1. Management fails to respond when subordinates bring up information or problems. Failure to respond will ultimately result in no communication.

2. Managers tend to be defensive about less-than-perfect actions. When subordinates see this defensiveness, information will be withheld.

3. The manager's attitude plays a critical role in the upward communication process. If the manager is really concerned and really listens, then upward communication improves.

4. Physical barriers can also inhibit the upward communication process. Separating a manager from his or her subordinates creates communication problems.

5. Time lags between the communication and the action can inhibit upward communication. If it takes months for the various levels of management to approve an employee's suggestion, upward communication is hindered.

MANAGERS AT WORK 5-3

Suggestion Boxes at Pitney Bowes

Pitney Bowes has two separate programs that reward employees for offering ideas: a suggestion system in which the company splits realized savings with the employee who had the idea, and the Job Opportunities Employee Referred Program, which uses cash and travel bonuses as incentives for employees to nominate specific individuals from outside the company to fill vacant positions.

The suggestion system is simple. Employees who have ideas to improve efficiency or reduce costs submit them to management. If the idea is implemented and saves money, the employee is rewarded with half the savings (up to a maximum of $50,000 paid over a two-year period).

The employee referral program pays the employee $1,000 for each referred candidate hired. All the $1,000 recipients are then put into a pool, and an employee selected by random drawing earns a vacation for two.

Source: Adapted from "Suggestion Boxes with a Difference," *Personnel Journal*, January 1986, p. 11.

Horizontal, or Lateral, Communication

The upward and downward communication systems generally follow the formal chain of command within the organization. However, greater size and complexity increase the need for communication across the lines of the formal chain of command. This is referred to as **horizontal** or **lateral communication.** Horizontal communication is essential to coordination among departments and to the proper functioning of the upward and downward communication systems.

Specialized departments (such as engineering, marketing research, and quality control) perform functions such as gathering data, issuing reports, preparing directives, coordinating activities, and advising higher levels of management. Such specialized departments are generally quite active in horizontal communication because their activities influence several chains of command rather than one. Departments that depend on one another for achieving their respective goals also need horizontal communication. Finally, matrix structures require much horizontal communication.

Interdepartmental committee meetings and distribution of written reports are two of the more commonly used methods of horizontal communication. A word of caution about memoranda that cross departmental lines: Too many memos and reports—an excess of paperwork—lead to new communication problems. The recipient of too many memoranda may end up not reading even the important ones.

Horizontal (lateral) communication – transmitting information across the lines of the formal organization's chain of command.

Grapevines

Many informal paths of communication also exist in organizations. These informal channels are generally referred to as **grapevines.** During the Civil War, intelligence telegraph lines hung loosely from tree to tree looked similar to a grapevine. Messages sent over these lines were often garbled; thus, any rumor was said to be "from the grapevine."[13] The organization grapevine often results from the organization's informal work groups.

Although generally not sanctioned formally, the grapevine always exists. As the name suggests, it does not follow the organizational hierarchy. It may go from secretary to vice president or from engineer to clerk. Not limited to nonmanagement personnel, the grapevine also operates among managers and professional personnel.

The grapevine generally has a poor reputation because it is regarded as a rumor factory. However, rumors and the grapevine are not identical. Rumors are only part of the grapevine—the part not based on fact or authority. Managers should correct all rumors as quickly as possible.

In normal work situations, over three-fourths of grapevine information is accurate.[14] The errors can, of course, completely change the information; so the grapevine probably produces more misunderstanding than its small percentage of wrong information indicates.

Some suggestions to aid management in effectively using the grapevine follow.

1. The grapevine is a permanent part of the formal organizational structure. It should be used to facilitate effective communication.
2. Managers should have a knowledge of what the grapevine is communicating and why.
3. Managers' inputs into the grapevine are spread to a greater number of employees—most employees hear grapevine information for the first time from management. Therefore, all levels of management should be provided with total and accurate information so that the messages they communicate through the grapevine are accurate.[15]

Communication in International Management

In addition to the cultural differences that exist in the international management environment there exists the obvious problems of dealing with different languages. There are over 3,000 languages spoken on earth, and about 100 of these are official languages of nations.

Fortunately for us, English is the primary language used in international business. This is not to say that other languages are not used, however. When business executives have a common language, whatever it may be, they are likely to use it. For example, a business executive from Iraq dealing with an executive from Saudi Arabia would communicate in Arabic, for

Arabic is their common language. For the same reason, an executive from Venezuela would use Spanish in dealing with an executive from Mexico. The point is that when executives have no common language, they are likely to use English. Clearly, English is the leading international language, and its leadership continues to grow.

Even though we can take comfort in knowing that ours is the most commonly used language in international business, we must keep in mind that it is not the primary language of many of those using it. Many of these users have had to learn English as a second language and are not likely to be as fluent as we are. In addition, they are probably going to have problems in understanding us.

There are no simple answers to communicating in international management, although there are two things you should keep in mind. One, learn the culture of the people with whom you communicate. Two, write and speak clearly and simply. Most people you will deal with have learned English in school and will not understand jargon or slang. Remembering these simple rules is important since the trend for expansion into international markets continues to strengthen.[16]

S U M M A R Y

LEARNING OBJECTIVE 1

Define Communication.
Communication is the transfer of understanding.

LEARNING OBJECTIVE 2

Describe the Interpersonal Communication Process.
Interpersonal communication occurs between individuals. It is an interactive process that involves a person's effort to attain meaning and to respond to it. It involves sending and receiving verbal and nonverbal messages.

LEARNING OBJECTIVE 3

Define Semantics and Explain Its Role in the Interpersonal Communication Process.
Semantics is the science or study of the meaning of words and symbols. Because of the real possibility of misinterpretation, words must be carefully chosen and clearly defined for effective communication.

LEARNING OBJECTIVE 4

Define Perception.
Perception basically refers to how a message is processed by an individual. Perception of the received information is modified by the individual's personality, previous experience, and other factors.

LEARNING OBJECTIVE 5

Explain the Concept of Feedback in Communication.

Feedback is the flow of information from the receiver to the sender. In order for communication to be effective, information must flow back and forth between sender and receiver.

LEARNING OBJECTIVE 6

Describe Organizational Communication Systems.

Organizational communication occurs within the formal organizational structure. In general, organizational communication systems are downward, upward, and horizontal.

LEARNING OBJECTIVE 7

Define Downward Communication Systems.

Downward communication systems transmit information from higher to lower levels of the organization. The chain of command determines the flow of downward information. Policy manuals, bulletins, organizational magazines, job descriptions, and directives are all examples of downward communication.

LEARNING OBJECTIVE 8

Define Upward Communication Systems.

Upward communication systems transmit information from the lower levels of the organization to the top. Four major areas of information should be communicated from below: the activities of subordinates in terms of their achievements, progress, and future plans; unresolved work problems in which subordinates may need help currently or in the future; suggestions or ideas for improvements within work groups or the organization as a whole; and the feelings of subordinates about their jobs, associates, and the organization.

LEARNING OBJECTIVE 9

Explain the Importance of the Grapevine.

The grapevine is the informal paths of communication that overlap the formal organizational structure. Although generally not sanctioned formally, the grapevine always exists.

LEARNING OBJECTIVE 10

Discuss the Communication Process in an International Management Setting.

Even though English is the most commonly used language in business, it is important to realize that it is not the primary language of all who use it. When communicating in an international setting it is important to know the culture of the people and to write and speak clearly and simply, avoiding the use of jargon and slang.

REVIEW QUESTIONS

1. What is communication?
2. Define interpersonal communication.
3. What is semantics?
4. What is perception, and what role does it play in communication?
5. What is feedback, and how does it affect the communication process?
6. Give some suggestions for improving listening habits.
7. What is the importance of nonverbal communication in interpersonal communication?
8. Identify the contributions of Henri Fayol and Chester Barnard to the understanding of the communication process.
9. Describe three conclusions which can be drawn concerning communication patterns in organizations.
10. Describe the following organizational communication systems:
    a. Downward communication systems.
    b. Upward communication systems.
    c. Horizontal, or lateral, communication systems.
    d. Grapevines.

DISCUSSION QUESTIONS

1. Describe some ways in which the grapevine can be used effectively in organizations.
2. Explain why the following question is raised frequently by many managers: "Why didn't you do what I told you to do?"
3. Discuss the following statement: "Meanings are in people, not words."
4. "Watch what we do, not what we say." Is this a good practice in organizations? Explain.
5. Poor communication of the organization's goals is often given as the reason for low performance of the organization. Do you think that this is usually a valid explanation?

REFERENCES & ADDITIONAL READINGS

[1] Henry Mintzberg, *The Nature of Managerial Work* (New York: Harper & Row, 1973), p. 38.

[2] Ralph W. Weber and Gloria E. Terry, *Behavioral Insights for Supervisors* (Englewood Cliffs, N.J.: Prentice-Hall, 1975), p. 138.

[3] F. E. X. Dance, "The Concept of Communication," *Journal of Communication* 20 (1970), pp. 201–10.

[4] Roger Ailes, *You Are the Message* (Homewood, Ill.: Dow Jones-Irwin, 1988), p. 47.

[5] David R. Hampton, Charles E. Sumner, and Ross A. Webber, *Organizational Behavior and the Practice of Management,* 4th ed. (Glenview, Ill.: Scott, Foresman, 1978), p. 117.

[6] Ailes, *You Are the Message,* pp. 50–51.

[7] Harold J. Leavitt, *Managerial Psychology,* 4th ed. (Chicago: University of Chicago Press, 1978), p. 116.

[8] Herta A. Murphy and Herbert W. Hildebrandt, *Effective Business Communications,* 4th ed. (New York: McGraw Hill, 1984), pp. 29–30.

[9] Henri Fayol, *General and Industrial Management,* trans. Constance Storrs (London: Sir Isaac Pitman & Sons, 1949), p. 35.

[10] Chester I. Barnard, *The Functions of the Executive* (Cambridge, Mass.: Harvard University Press, 1938).

[11] For additional discussion on organizational communication, see J. S. Leipzig and E. More, "Organizational Communication: A Review and Analysis of Three Current Approaches to Field," *Journal of Business Communication,* Fall 1982, pp. 77–92.

[12] See L. McCallister, "Predicted Employee Compliance to Downward Communication," *Journal of Business Communication,* Winter 1983, pp. 67–79.

[13] Keith Davis and John W. Newstrom, *Human Behavior at Work: Organizational Behavior* (New York: McGraw-Hill, 1985), p. 315.

[14] Ibid., p. 315.

[15] For additional information on the grapevine, see J. L. Esposito and R. L. Rosnow, "Corporate Rumors: How They Start and How to Stop Them," *Management Review,* April 1983, pp. 44–49.

[16] For additional information, see Raymond V. Lesikar, *Basic Business Communication,* 4th ed. (Homewood, Ill.: Richard D. Irwin, 1988).

INCIDENT

Unions—Why?

George Abbott, 53 years old, sat back in his chair, totally bewildered. He had just been told by his first-shift supervisor Alice Moore that the paperworkers union was rapidly gaining support in the mill that he had managed for over 20 years. The way things were going, it looked like they would have enough supporters to demand an election within the next week. He couldn't believe it. The Marlan Textile Mill was a small mill, employing about 50 relatively unskilled employees. The work force was predominantly comprised of middle-aged females living in the small, rural, southern town of Tyson, where the mill was located.

Abbott could not understand why they would do this to him. He had always thought his employees were happy with the conditions at the mill. It was a small operation and was more like a large family than a place of employment. Surely, if there was something causing them to be so dissatisfied that they felt they had to turn to a union, he would have been aware of it. It made no sense whatsoever to him.

George: Alice, I just can't understand it. I can't help but take it personally. Why, I've done everything I could to see that they would get a fair deal. What could it be?

Alice: Well, George, I don't really know for sure, but rumor has it that it's not more money that they're after. Half of them couldn't earn near what you pay them anywhere else, and they know it. And I can tell you, they do appreciate it. I can't figure it out either. Everyone that's talked to me about the whole situation has agreed that you've been real fair with them.

George: Then why the union? I mean, they just didn't wake up one morning and say "Hey, let's unionize!" Something must be wrong—it just doesn't make sense.

Alice: You know, George, I've only been at the mill two months now. But I've heard that they've been asking for years for more washroom facilities. This may sound crazy, but I wonder what that might have had to do with it. I've heard a lot of talk about that lately.

George: No, we're in compliance with OSHA standards. Sure, at least once a month, someone suggests that additional washroom facilities be made available and the existing ones be made "prettier." But I don't take those suggestions seriously. You know, when I implemented the suggestion box, I knew people would feel like they had to participate. Asking for more washrooms is just one of the first things that would come into a woman's mind. You know how those ladies are. They want to be sure that I know they're interested in the company; so they feel like they have to make their share of suggestions. They don't really need another washroom.

Questions

1. What communication system has failed?

2. What do you think of George's perception of the situation? Is his perception typical of some managers?

EXERCISE

Your Listening Ratio

Do you talk more than you listen? Rate yourself on the talk/listen ratio chart. Then ask two family members or two friends to score you. Also, have your boss or two co-workers score you.

Check the line of the ratio best representing the percent of the time you generally:

TALK	LISTEN	
10	90	_____
20	80	_____
30	70	_____
40	60	_____
50	50	_____
60	40	_____
70	30	_____
80	20	_____
90	10	_____

Compare your self-assessment with the way others rated you. If there are major discrepancies in the scores, the more accurate numbers are the ones reflecting how others view you. Their perception is what's real.

In general, though, you should strive to listen 60 to 70 percent of the time and talk 30 to 40 percent. The reason for this bias toward listening is that most people listen but don't really *hear*. We therefore need to overcompensate—and listen more—to improve our comprehension.

Source: Rober Ailes, *You Are the Message* (Homewood, Ill.: Richard D. Irwin, 1988), pp. 45–46.

C A S E

*Mary Kay Cosmetics, Inc.**

Mary Kay Cosmetics, Inc. (MKY) is a manufacturer and distributor of cosmetics and skin care products. The story of MKY is, to a large extent, the story of Mary Kay Ash's life.

Mary Kay was born Mary Kathlyn Wagner in Hot Wells, a small town in south Texas. At age seven she was helping to support her family and her invalid father, while her mother ran the family restaurant in a Houston suburb.

Graduation from high school meant the end of formal education, even though Mary Kay had graduated from Reagan High School in Houston with honors and hoped to attend college. She was soon married to Ben Rogers. The marriage lasted 11 years and resulted in the birth of three children: Marilyn in 1935; Ben, Jr., in 1936; and Richard in 1943. World War II meant months of separation from her husband, who had been drafted and was unable to send home more than a few dollars each month. For a while during the time Ben was in the service, Mary Kay attended classes at the University of Houston, but her college career was cut short due to the responsibility of caring for the small children.

To make ends meet, Mary Kay went to work part-time for Stanley Home Products in Houston selling household specialties at parties in homes. She had a natural aptitude for selling and quickly became one of her company's leading sales representatives. Mary Kay learned that people liked to talk to her and that her positive attitude enabled her to overcome most of the obstacles she encountered in sales.

In 1953, after 13 years, Mary Kay left Stanley and went to work for World Gifts Company in Dallas selling decorative accessories. She moved up in this organization to the position of national training director. After 10 years with World Gifts, Mary Kay was working 60-hour weeks and making $25,000 a year. A disagreement over proposed policy changes at World Gifts prompted Mary Kay to retire in 1963. She had spent almost 25 years in direct selling.

Retirement was very unpleasant for Mary Kay. She was unhappy with nothing to do, and within a few days after leaving World Gifts, she began writing down all the direct-selling techniques she had learned in her 25 years in sales. After spending two weeks on this task, she spent another two weeks compiling a list of problems she had encountered in selling, ways of solving these problems, and how she would do things differently in the future if she

---

* Written by Sexton Adams, North Texas State University, and Lloyd L. Byars, Atlanta University.

had the opportunity. Her initial intent was to put this material in a book that would help women sell.

In reviewing and editing the notes she had written, Mary Kay realized that she had prepared everything needed to operate a sales organization. The only thing missing was a product.

Several years earlier, while working for Stanley Home Products, Mary Kay had conducted a demonstration of her company's products one evening to a group of approximately 20 women in a home in one of the suburbs of Dallas. The hostess for the party kept the guests after Mary Kay's demonstration to present them with gifts of little jars of skin treatment—several creams she had prepared using formulas she had been given by her grandfather, who had at one time operated a local tannery. Mary Kay was anxious to try the skin treatment herself. She took several of the jars, which were of various sizes and shapes. The creams smelled terrible, but they worked. These creams were eventually to become the first of the Mary Kay product line.

THE BEGINNING OF THE COMPANY

Shortly after the completion of her writing, Mary Kay and her second husband, George Hallenbeck, whom she had married in 1963, decided to use Mary Kay's sales and problem-solving techniques and to go into business. George's background included sales and administration. The idea of starting a new business appealed to both of them. The formulas for the skin creams Mary Kay had been given several years earlier were purchased for $500. The woman who owned the formulas had been attempting to market them by herself but had not been successful.

The process of organizing the new company was under way. Mary Kay's husband was to be the administrator. He was in the process of planning the physical facilities and caring for other matters regarding the operation of the business, while Mary Kay was preparing the final draft of the sales manual, designing and ordering containers, and recruiting salespeople. One month before the business was to open, George died of a heart attack.

Mary Kay discussed her situation with her children; Richard, who was then a 20-year-old insurance salesman in Houston, moved to Dallas and helped his mother start the company in September 1963, with $500 capitalization. Richard, who had attended North Texas State University for a year and a half as a marketing major, was in charge of administration and finance. Mary Kay's duties included training, merchandising, and selling. Six months later, Ben, Mary Kay's older son, joined the business to take care of warehousing and shipping. Ben later became the vice president for merchandising but left the company in 1978.

The new company, Beauty by Mary Kay, opened with two full-time employees—Mary Kay and Richard, who drew a salary of $250 a month to start—and nine women who sold the initial skin care products being made with the purchased formulas. One of MKY's strategies from the beginning was that each sales representative (who was called a beauty consultant) would buy her own products at approximately 50 percent of retail, pay for all products in advance, and carry a sufficient amount of products with her to fill all orders on the spot. Thus, the company had no accounts payable and no accounts receivable.

The small staff of beauty consultants was successful, both in selling and in recruiting new beauty consultants. The number of people added became so large that a system was established to advance some of the beauty consultants to the position of training director. An incentive compensation plan was devised which enabled beauty consultants who became sales managers to draw an override on the commissions earned by the beauty consultants they recruited and trained. The number of beauty consultants grew from the original 9 to 318 in 1964, just one year after the company began operation. Sales for the first year amounted to $198,514. The second year, sales exceeded $800,000. The growth continued at an astonishingly rapid pace both in the number of consultants and sales. MKY went public in 1967.

In 1969, it was necessary to add 102,000 square feet to the manufacturing facility in Dallas. Additional space has been added several times. A new distribution center was added in Dallas, and in the late 1960s, plans for expansion of sales and distribution centers outside the southwest were begun. In the 1970s, expansion was first made into the California market with the opening of a branch in Los Angeles designed to serve the western states. The move westward was tremendously successful, and MKY soon had more beauty consultants in California than in Texas. An Atlanta branch was opened in 1972, and a third branch was opened in Chicago in 1975. In 1978 the first office outside the United States was opened in Toronto.

Attempts to broaden international operations beyond Canada led to the opening of a subsidiary in Australia, and in 1980, a wholly owned subsidiary in Argentina. During September, 1984, the company began operations in the United Kingdom.

PRODUCT LINE

The initial product line at MKY consisted of skin care products for women. Since 1976, there has been a gradual move toward diversification of products and additions to the Mary Kay line. In 1980, the Skin Care Line was diversified to meet the needs of the different consumers whose skin types were not alike. Colors were updated to reflect the colors in fashion. The sunscreen was reformulated, and in 1981, MKY introduced the Body Care System. This line has also been expanded to include toiletry items, accessories, and hair care products. The skin care products for women still account for 50 percent of the sales revenue and probably will remain the major income producers. Today the products at MKY are still primarily oriented toward skin care rather than the high-fashion market. During the past several years, MKY has experimented in the market of skin care products and toiletry items for men. These are marketed under the product name Mr. K.

MANAGEMENT AND PHILOSOPHY

The primary reason for the success of MKY was the motivating reason for starting the company. "This company was really begun to give women an opportunity to advance, which I was denied, when I worked for others." This opportunity to become successful and the rewards provided for hard work are evident in the slogan, "I can, I will, I must," which Mary Kay instills in all her employees, particularly during the training seminars. "I train the sales force by example and by relationship."

Although the sales force is independent, it maintains a strong and intimate relationship with the company. The organization of the sales force is the brainchild of Mary Kay herself. One of the more subtle activities which takes place at an annual seminar conducted by MKY is the recruitment of new beauty consultants. A portion of each seminar is reserved for explaining the MKY sales organization, compensation, and incentive plan.

Recognizing a lag in the sales force and a loss of competitive edge in 1978, MKY changed its compensation program. In addition to the markup they receive on the products they sell, sales managers are also eligible for a series of commissions based on their monthly unit sales. To become a sales manager, the beauty consultant must recruit 24 women into the organization to become consultants. The sales manager is then eligible to participate in a training program and later become a sales director. Sales directors spend time on independent sales, but they also manage, train, and recruit other sales consultants. "We expect sales directors to sell a minimum level of $3,000 wholesale products per month, which is $6,000 retail." Mary Kay says that if a sales director falls short of that goal for two consecutive months, then the company contacts that woman to see how it can help. New sales managers come to Dallas for one week of training and return from time to time during the year for special training programs, the highlight of the year being the annual seminar. It consists of workshops conducted by outstanding beauty consultants and directors. Used not only during the seminar, but also at other times during the year are training materials such as guides, manuals, tape cassettes, flip charts, films, and other materials developed by the MKY staff.

The annual seminar is a major attraction for MKY employees. It is held in Dallas for three days each August. This spectacle is a combination consisting of beauty pageant, awards night, party, the sharing of ideas, classes, goal-setting, leadership training, and even bookkeeping. Each person attends the meeting at her own expense, and they come from all states, Puerto Rico, Canada, Australia, and Argentina. The awards include mink coats, diamond rings, diamond bumblebee pins, watches, luggage, typewriters, pocket calculators, exotic vacations, and the yearlong use of pink Cadillacs and Buick Regals.

FUTURE OF MKY

MKY has a somewhat uncertain future. Exhibit 1 shows a disturbing trend.

E X H I B I T   1

	AVERAGE NUMBER OF BEAUTY CONSULTANTS	NET SALES ($000)	NET INCOME ($000)
1982	173,137	$304,275	$35,372
1983	195,671	323,758	36,654
1984	173,101	277,500	33,781
1985	145,493	248,970	21,286
1986	141,113	255,016	(46,206)

In December 1985, MKY stockholders approved a management buyout, led by Mary Kay Ash, of the outstanding stock of the company. The buyout was valued at between $304 million and $315 million. The announcement also attributed MKY's declining sales and profits in part to a scarcity of women eager to sell beauty products door-to-door.

Also, during 1986, MKY liquidated its United Kingdom subsidiary due to its continued failure to meet performance expectations.

2 Decision-Making and Planning Skills

=

Management Foundation

+

=

Improved Organizational Performance

*S*ection 2 deals specifically with decision-making and planning skills.

Chapter 6 is developed on the premise that all managers, regardless of their level in an organization, must make decisions. Conditions for making decisions, as well as intuitive and rational approaches to making decisions, are discussed. Major emphasis is placed on how to make creative decisions. The chapter closes with a discussion of participation in decision making.

Chapter 7 introduces and discusses the concepts of objectives, strategies, and plans. A major portion of this chapter is devoted to defining these concepts and clarifying the relationships among them. Several different types of plans are discussed.

Chapter 8 focuses on the strategic management process and how it relates to today's managers. A strategic management model is presented and used to familiarize the reader with this process. Special attention is devoted to the forecasting of environmental factors.

Chapter 9 applies planning concepts to the operations function. The operations function includes the design, operation, and control of facilities and resources directly involved in the production of the organization's goods or services. Chapter 9 concentrates on the design and operation of operating systems. Product/service design, process selection, site location, physical layout, and job design are all discussed, along with several methods and techniques for handling these tasks.

6 The Manager as Decision Maker

LEARNING OBJECTIVES

*After studying this chapter,
you should be able to:*

1 Explain the difference between decision making and problem solving.

2 List the different conditions under which managers make decisions.

3 Explain the intuitive approach to decision making.

4 Discuss the rational approach to decision making with particular emphasis on its limitations.

5 Define creativity and innovation; outline the basic stages in the creative process.

6 Describe several specific tools and techniques that can be used to foster creative decisions.

7 List the six steps in creative decision making.

8 Explain the role that values play in making decisions.

9 Summarize the positive and negative aspects of group decision making.

"Executive" derives from a Latin word meaning to do *and the Oxford dictionary defines it in terms of "the action of carrying out or carrying into effect." Neither of these approaches would suggest that the main responsibility and function of the executive is to make decisions. Yet in modern business and industry, this is precisely what is expected. Executives are rewarded and evaluated in terms of their success in making decisions.*

D A V I D W . M I L L E R A N D M A R T I N K . S T A R R*

S ome authors use the term *decision maker* to mean manager. Although managers are decision makers, the converse is not necessarily true. Not all decision makers are managers. For example, a person sorting fruit or vegetables is required to make decisions, but not as a manager. However, all managers, regardless of their positions in the organization, must make decisions in the pursuit of organizational goals. In fact, decision making pervades all of the basic management functions: planning, organizing, staffing, leading, and controlling. Although different types of decisions are required for these functions, they all require decisions. Thus, to be a good planner, organizer, staffer, leader, and controller, a manager must first be a good decision maker.

Herbert Simon, a Nobel prize winner, has described the manager's **decision process** in three stages: (1) intelligence, (2) design, and (3) choice.[1] The intelligence stage involves searching the environment for conditions requiring a decision. The design stage entails inventing, developing, and analyzing possible courses of action. Choice, the final stage, refers to the actual selection of a course of action.

The decision process stages show the difference between management and nonmanagement decisions. Nonmanagement decisions are concentrated in the last (choice) stage. The fruit or vegetable sorter has only to make a choice as to the size or quality of the goods. Management decisions place greater emphasis on the intelligence and design stages. If the decision-making process is viewed as only the choice stage, then managers spend very little time making decisions. If, however, the decision-making process is viewed as not only the actual choice but also the intelligence and design work needed to make the choice, then managers spend most of their time making decisions.

Decision process—process that involves three stages: intelligence, design, and choice. Intelligence is searching the environment for conditions requiring a decision. Design is inventing, developing, analyzing possible courses of action. Choice is the actual selection of a course of action.

*Adapted from David W. Miller and Martin K. Starr, *Executive Decisions and Operations Research* (New York: Harper & Row, 1960), p. 10.

DECISION MAKING VERSUS PROBLEM SOLVING

The terms *decision making* and *problem solving* are often confused, and therefore, need to be clarified. As indicated in the introductory paragraph, **decision making,** in its narrowest sense, is the process of choosing from among various alternatives. A *problem* is any deviation from some standard or desired level of performance. **Problem solving** is, then, the process of determining the appropriate responses or actions necessary to alleviate a problem. Problem solving necessarily involves decision making since all problems can be attacked in numerous ways and the problem solver must decide which is best. On the other hand, all decisions do not involve problems (such as the person sorting fruit or vegetables). However, from a practical perspective, almost all managerial decisions do involve solving or at least avoiding problems. Because of this, it is usually not necessary to distinguish between managerial decision making and managerial problem solving.

Decision making – in its narrowest sense, is the process of choosing from among various alternatives.

Problem solving – the process of determining the appropriate responses or actions necessary to alleviate a problem.

The Decision Maker's Environment

A manager's freedom to make decisions depends largely on the manager's position within the organization and on its structure. In general, higher-level managers have more flexibility and discretion. The patterns of authority outlined by the formal organization structure also influence the flexibility of the decision maker.

Another important factor of decision-making style is the purpose and tradition of the organization. For example, a military organization requires a different style of decision making than a volunteer organization.

The organization's formal and informal group structures affect decision-making styles. These groups may range from labor unions to advisory councils.

A final subset of the environment includes all the decision maker's superiors and subordinates. The personalities, backgrounds, and expectations of these people influence the decision maker.

Figure 6–1 shows the major environmental factors that affect decision makers in an organization.

Successful managers must develop an appreciation for the different environmental forces that both influence them and are influenced by their decisions. They must develop a multilevel view (organization, group, and individual) of decision making. To always have a single-level view—whether it be the organization's, a group's, or the individual's—will not result in optimal decisions. Managers who view decisions only from the organizational perspective— who have no appreciation for the groups and individuals making up the organization—will eventually experience problems with their employees.

"Country Club" managers, who are concerned only about their employees and neglect the organization's objectives in their decisions, will probably not keep their jobs. The same is true of managers who become overly concerned

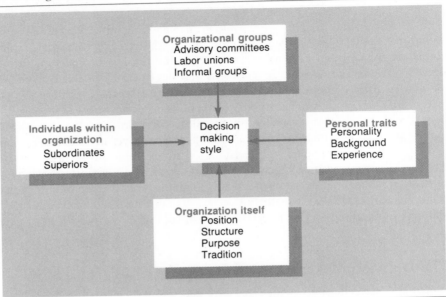

with organizational groups and neglect either the individual's or the organization's objectives.

CONDITIONS FOR MAKING DECISIONS

Decisions are not always made with the same amount of available information. The best decision often depends on what happens at a later time. Take the simple decision of whether or not to take an umbrella when going outside. The more desirable alternative is determined by whether or not it rains; but this is not under the control of the decision maker.

Table 6–1 gives combinations of alternatives and states of nature with their respective outcomes for the individual trying to decide whether or not to take an umbrella outside.

Situation of certainty –
situation that occurs when a decision maker knows exactly what will happen and can often calculate the precise outcome for each alternative.

Certainty

Knowing exactly what will happen places the decision maker in a **situation of certainty.** In such a situation, the decision maker can often calculate the precise outcome for each alternative. If it is raining, the person knows the state of nature—and therefore knows the best alternative (take an umbrella).

T A B L E 6–1   Umbrella Decision: Alternatives and States of Nature

	STATE OF NATURE	
ALTERNATIVE	**NO RAIN**	**RAIN**
Take umbrella	Dry, but inconvenient	Dry
Do not take umbrella	Dry	Wet

Risk

Unfortunately, the state of nature is not always known in advance. The decision maker can often obtain—at some cost—information on the state of nature. The desirability of getting the information is figured by weighting the costs of obtaining the information against its value. A decision maker is in a **situation of risk** if the relative probabilities associated with each state of nature are known. If the weather forecaster has said there is a 40 percent chance of rain, the decision maker is operating in a situation of risk.

The precise probabilities of the various states of nature usually are not known. However, reasonably accurate ones based on historical data and past experiences can often be calculated. When no such data exists, it is difficult to estimate probabilities. In such cases, one approach is to survey individual opinions.

Under conditions of risk, expected value analysis can be used by the decision maker. With this technique the expected payoff of an act can be mathematically calculated. One shortcoming of expected value analysis is that it represents the average outcome if the event is repeated a large number of times. That is of little help if the act only takes place once. For example, airplane passengers are not interested in the average fatality rates. Rather they are interested in what happens on their particular flight.

Uncertainty

With no knowledge of the relative probabilities of the respective states of nature, decision makers operate in a **situation of uncertainty.** For example, a person going to New York who had not heard a weather forecast for New York would have no knowledge of the likelihood of rain and, hence, would not know whether or not to carry an umbrella.

If the decision maker has little or no knowledge about which state of nature will occur, one of three basic approaches may be taken. The first is to choose the alternative whose best possible outcome is the best of all possible outcomes for all alternatives. This is an optimistic, or gambling approach—it is sometimes called the **maximax** approach. A decision maker using this approach would not take the umbrella, since the best possible outcome is no rain and no umbrella.

A second approach for dealing with uncertainty is to compare the worst possible outcomes for each of the alternatives and select the one which is

Situation of risk – situation that occurs when the decision maker is aware of the relative probabilities of occurrence associated with each alternative.

Situation of uncertainty – situation that occurs when a decision maker operates without knowing the relative probabilities of occurrence of the respective alternatives.

Maximax approach – sometimes called optimistic or gambling approach to decision making, to select the alternative whose best possible outcome is the best of all possible outcomes for all alternatives.

T A B L E 6–2   Possible Approaches to Making Decisions under Uncertainty

APPROACH	HOW IT WORKS	RELATED TO THE UMBRELLA EXAMPLE
Optimistic or gambling approach (Maximax)	Choose the alternative whose best possible outcome is the best of all possible outcomes for all alternatives.	Do not take umbrella.
Pessimistic approach (Maximin)	Compare the worst possible outcomes of each of the alternatives and select the alternative whose worst possible outcome is least bad.	Take umbrella.
Risk-averting approach	Choose the alternative which has the least variation among its possible alternatives.	Take umbrella.

Maximin approach – to compare the worst possible outcomes for each of the alternatives and select the one which is least bad. This is a pessimistic approach to decision making.

Risk-averting approach – to choose the alternative with the least variation among its possible outcomes.

least bad. This is a pessimistic approach—sometimes called the **maximin** approach. In the umbrella example, the decision maker would compare the worst possible outcome of taking an umbrella to that of not taking an umbrella. The decision maker would then decide to take an umbrella, since it is better to carry an unneeded umbrella than to get wet.

The final approach is to choose the alternative with the least variation among its possible outcomes. This is a **risk-averting approach** and makes for more effective planning. If the decision maker chooses not to take an umbrella, the outcomes can vary from being dry but inconvenienced to being dry. Thus, the risk-averting decision maker would take an umbrella to be sure of staying dry. Table 6–2 gives the different approaches to making a decision under conditions of uncertainty.

The specific approach used by the decision maker under conditions of uncertainty depends on the individual's aversion to risk and the consequences of a bad decision.

TIMING THE DECISION

To properly time a decision, the need for a decision must be recognized. That is not always easy. The manager may simply not be aware of what is

MANAGERS AT WORK 6-1

There Is No Other Way

Back in 1978, Chairman Orin E. Atkins of Ashland Oil sold most of the company's crude oil–producing reserves and some chemical businesses for $1.2 billion. Immediately following the sale, crude oil prices continued to rise, and many people questioned whether Atkins made the right decision.

According to Atkins, he had to do it. Ashland did not have enough crude oil or cash to become a major force in the industry. In 1978, Ashland had to buy 94 percent of its oil on the open market, and its sales and assets were only a fraction of those of the industry leaders—Texaco and Exxon.

With the proceeds of the sale, Atkins paid off some debts and purchased a pollution control equipment business and an insurance business—all part of a plan to improve the company's financial condition and reduce the influence of the remaining petroleum business. Says Atkins, "There is no question that if we had held those assets, we could have got more for them. We simply had no choice."

Source: Maurice Barnfather, *Forbes,* March 30, 1981, p. 41.

going on, or the problem requiring a decision may be camouflaged. Once the need is realized, the decision must be properly timed. Some managers always seem to make decisions on the spot; others tend to take forever in deciding even a simple matter. The manager who makes quick decisions runs the risk of making bad decisions. Failure to gather and evaluate available data, to consider people's feelings, and to anticipate the impact of the decision can result in a very quick but poor decision. Just as risky is the other extreme; the manager who listens to problems, promises to act, but never does. Nearly as bad is the manager who responds only after an inordinate delay. Other familiar types are: the manager who never seems to have enough information for a decision; the manager who frets and worries over even the simplest decisions; and the manager who refers everything to superiors.

Knowing when to make a decision is complicated because different decisions have different time frames. For instance, a manager generally has more time to decide committee appointments than he has to decide what to do when three employees call in sick. No magic formula exists to tell managers when a decision should be made or how long it should take. The important thing is to see the importance of properly timing decisions. Managers at Work 6–1 shows that managers sometimes must make decisions even when they know the timing is poor. Managers at Work 6–2 shows how the ability to make rapid decisions benefited Johnson & Johnson in 1982.

MANAGERS AT WORK 6–2

Crisis Decision Making at Johnson & Johnson

In September 1982, a psychopathic killer laced 44 capsules of Extra-Strength Tylenol with fatal amounts of cyanide and randomly inserted the packages on store shelves in the Chicago area. Within a three-day period, seven people died.

Although the manufacturer, Johnson & Johnson, was completely blameless in the tragedy, corporate management was faced with a crisis of gigantic proportion. The Tylenol product had accounted for $450 million in sales the year before and contributed over 15 percent to company profits. How top management handled the crisis would impact the reputation of the company and, ultimately, the survival of the Tylenol brand.

Chairman Burke quickly formed a seven-member strategy team that met twice daily during the first six weeks of the crisis. A few of the many decisions the team made during the crisis were:

- To conduct an extensive product recall at a cost of $100 million.
- To stop all Tylenol advertising.

- To promote the trustworthiness of the organization through the use of the media. Burke appeared on the "Phil Donahue Show," and "60 Minutes" filmed a strategy session.
- To modify product packaging to make it tamperproof.
- To begin the product comeback (several weeks later) with a 30-city video press conference via satellite.

In the weeks immediately following the tragedy, Tylenol's share of the over-the-counter analgesic market fell from 35 percent to 4.5 percent. By June 1983, Tylenol had recovered 27 percent of the market. As of January 1984, Tylenol had captured 32 percent of the market.

Sources: Mitchell Leon, "Tylenol Fights Back," *Public Relations Journal,* March 1983, pp. 10–14; "Speedy Recovery for Tylenol," *Marketing and Media Decisions,* June 1983, p. 36; Leonard Snyder, "An Anniversary Review and Critique: The Tylenol Crisis," *Public Relations Review,* Fall 1983, pp. 24–34; Johnson & Johnson, Annual Report, 1983.

THE INTUITIVE APPROACH TO DECISION MAKING

Intuitive approach–when managers make decisions largely based on hunches and intuition.

When managers make decisions solely on hunches and intuition (the **intuitive approach**), they are practicing management as if it were wholly an art based on feelings. Sadly, this happens in many situations. Managers sometimes become so emotionally attached to certain positions that almost nothing will change their minds. They develop the "don't bother me with the facts—my mind is made up" attitude. George Odiorne has isolated the following emotional attachments which can adversely affect decision makers:

1. They fasten on the big lie and stick with it.
2. They are attracted to scandalous issues and heighten their significance.
3. They press every fact into a moral pattern.
4. They overlook everything except the immediately useful.
5. They have an affinity for romantic stories and find such information more significant than any other kind, including hard evidence.[2]

Such emotional attachments can be very real and can lead to poor decisions. They most often affect managers or decision makers living in the past, who either will not or cannot modernize. An example is the manager who insists on making decisions just as the founder of the company did 50 years ago.

Odiorne offers two suggestions for managers and decision makers engulfed by emotional attachments.[3] First, become aware of biases and allow for them. Undiscovered biases do the most damage. Second, seek out independent opinions. It is always good to ask the opinion of some person who has no vested interest in the decision.

THE RATIONAL APPROACH TO DECISION MAKING

The physical sciences have provided an alternative approach to decision making which can be adapted to management problems. The **rational approach** (sometimes called the scientific approach) to decision making includes the following steps:

1. Recognize the need for a decision.
2. Establish, rank, and weigh criteria.
3. Gather available information and data.
4. Identify possible alternatives.
5. Evaluate each alternative with respect to all criteria.
6. Select the best alternative.

Once the need for making the decision is known, criteria must be set for expected results of the decision. These criteria should then be ranked and weighed according to their relative importance.

Next, factual data relating to the decision should be collected. After that, all alternatives that meet the criteria are identified. Each is then evaluated with respect to all criteria. The final decision is based on the alternative which best meets the criteria.

Rational approach – includes the following steps: recognize the need for a decision; establish, rank, and weigh criteria; gather available information and data; identify possible alternatives; evaluate each alternative with respect to all criteria; and select the best alternative.

Limitations of the Rational Approach

The rational approach to decision making is certainly an improvement over the intuitive approach; but it is not without its problems and limitations.

The rational approach is based on the concept of *economic man*. This concept postulates that people behave rationally and that their behavior is based on the following assumptions:

1. People have clearly defined criteria, and the relative weights which they assign to these criteria are stable.
2. People have knowledge of all relevant alternatives.
3. People have the ability to evaluate each alternative with respect to all the criteria and arrive at an overall rating for each alternative.
4. People have the self-discipline to choose the alternative which rates the highest (they will not manipulate the system).

Often these assumptions are not very realistic. Decision makers do not always have clearly defined criteria for making the decision. Even when criteria are clearly defined, people often cannot agree on the importance of the different criteria. For example, factors important to the person making the decision may not be equally important to other affected parties.

Another problem is that many decisions are based on limited knowledge of the possible alternatives. For example, everyone has agonized over a particular decision only to later discover that he or she never even considered one or more of the best possibilities. Even when information is available, it is usually less than perfect. Because the quality and quantity of available information is often less than desired, evaluating or predicting the outcomes for various alternatives can be extremely difficult. When information is extremely limited, predicting outcomes may be only slightly better than guessing.

A final problem is the temptation to manipulate or ignore the gathered information and choose a favored—but not necessarily the best—alternative. This occurs when the decision maker chooses a particular alternative "because I like it."

Due to the limitations of the rational approach, most decisions—even when the rational approach is followed—still involve some judgment. Thus in making decisions, the manager generally uses a combination of science and art.

A SATISFICING APPROACH

Principle of bounded rationality – assumes that people have the time and cognitive ability to process only a limited amount of information upon which to base decisions.

Believing the assumptions of the rational approach to be generally unrealistic, Herbert Simon, in attempting to understand how managerial decisions are actually made, formulated his **principle of bounded rationality.** Simon's principle of bounded rationality states that "the capacity of the human mind for formulating and solving complex problems is very small compared with the size of the problems whose solution is required for objectively rational behavior—or even for a reasonable approximation to such objective rationality."[4] Basically, the principle of bounded rationality states that there are definite limits to human rationality. Based on the principle of bounded rationality, Simon proposed a decision model of the "administrative man," with the following assumptions:

1. A person's knowledge of alternatives and criteria are limited.
2. People act on the basis of a simplified, ill-structured, mental abstraction of the real world; this abstraction is influenced by personal perceptions, biases, and so forth.
3. People do not attempt to optimize but will take the first alternative which satisfies their current level of aspiration. This is called *satisficing*.
4. An individual's level of aspiration concerning a decision fluctuates upward and downward, depending on the values of the most recently found alternatives.

The first assumption is a synopsis of the principle of bounded rationality. The second assumption follows naturally from the first. If limits do exist to human rationality, then an individual must make decisions based on limited and incomplete knowledge. The third assumption also naturally follows from the first assumption. If the decision maker's knowledge of alternatives is incomplete, then the individual cannot optimize but only satisfice. **Optimizing** means selecting the best possible alternative; **satisficing** means selecting the first alternative that meets the decision maker's minimum standard of satisfaction. Assumption four is based on the belief that the criteria for a satisfactory alternative is determined by the current level of aspiration. **Level of aspiration** refers to the level of performance that a person expects to attain and it is determined by the person's prior successes and failures.

Figure 6–2 represents the satisficing approach to decision making. If the decision maker is satisfied that an acceptable alternative has been found, that alternative is selected. Otherwise the decision maker searches for an additional alternative. In Figure 6–2, the double arrows indicate a two-way relationship: The value of the new alternative is influenced by the value of the best previous alternative; the value of the best previous alternative is, in turn, influenced by the value of the new alternative. As indicated by the arrows, a similar two-way relationship exists between the value of the new alternative and the current level of aspiration. The net result of this evaluation determines whether or not the decision maker is satisfied with the alternative. Thus, the "administrative man" selects the first alternative that meets the minimum satisfaction criteria and makes no real attempt to optimize.

Optimizing – selecting the best possible alternative.

Satisficing – selecting the first alternative that meets the decision maker's minimum standard of satisfaction.

Level of aspiration – level of performance that a person expects to attain. It is determined by the person's prior successes and failures.

MAKING CREATIVE DECISIONS

If the rational approach to decision making is based on unrealistic assumptions and the intuitive and satisficing approaches often result in less than optimal decisions, what can managers do to improve their decision-making process? The authors of *In Search of Excellence* and others strongly suggest that successful

F I G U R E 6–2   Model of the Satisficing Approach

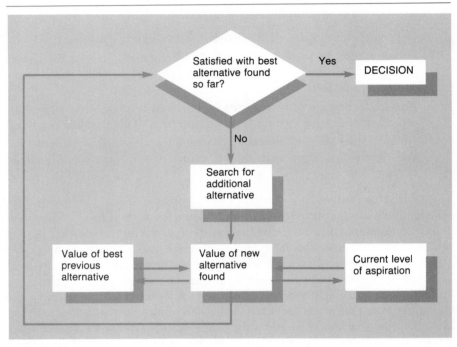

Source: Adapted from James G. March and Herbert A. Simon, *Organizations* (New York: John Wiley & Sons, 1958), p. 49.

companies encourage creative decisions and innovation on the part of their managers.[5] The purpose of this section is to discuss some techniques and methods for fostering creative decisions within an organization.

The Creative Process

Creativity – coming up with an idea that is new, original, useful or satisfactory to its creator or to someone else.

Innovation – process of applying a new and creative idea to a product, service, or method of operation.

Creativity and innovation, while similar, are not exactly the same. **Creativity** is the thinking process involved in producing an idea or concept that is new, original, useful, or satisfying to its creator or to someone else. Innovation is doing new things. Creativity involves coming up with a new idea, while **innovation** involves implementing the new idea.

The creative process generally has four basic stages: (1) preparation, (2) incubation, (3) illumination, and (4) verification.[6] Preparation involves the hard, conscious, systematic, and often fruitless examination of a problem or area of study. The preparation stage involves getting ready to solve a particular problem. Preparation not only requires being aware of a problem area but also requires study of the problem area. The stage during which the individual or group is not consciously thinking about the problem forms the incubation stage. Unconscious mental exploration of the problem occurs during incubation. The illumination stage occurs with the appearance of the solution and is generally a very sudden occurrence. Finally, the verification stage of creativity involves testing and refining the solution.

For most people, the above four stages overlap each other as different problems are explored. A manager reading the morning mail may be accumulating knowledge in preparation for solving one problem, may be at the incubation stage on another problem, and also may be verifying another problem.

Establishing a Creative Environment

Probably the single most important factor that influences creativity and innovation by organizational members is the climate or environment in which they work. It is the manager who sets the tone of the environment. If a manager is genuinely interested in creative ideas, most employees are aware of it. The opposite is also true; most employees realize when a manager is not interested in creativity.

One factor that often inhibits creativity is fear of the consequences of failure. Failures are to be expected. If someone is fired every time an innovative effort fails, word quickly gets around and innovation is discouraged. Thus, it has been suggested that in areas of a business where risk is a factor in growth, special ground rules be established that permit innovative managers and employees to function without fear of being fired if they fail. Managers at Work 6–3 describes how the 3M Company has attempted to do this.

Another factor that fosters creativity and innovation is the development of effective communication systems throughout the organization.[7] Rigid adherence to the formal channels of communication jeopardizes innovation. Upward and lateral communication must be fostered and encouraged.

Finally, the management of an organization must realize that highly creative and innovative people often do not fit the typical organization mold. They generally shun highly regulated situations. They are often egoistic and can frequently be obnoxious. Thomas J. Watson, founder of IBM, stated his opinion on this issue: "We are convinced that any business needs its wild ducks. And in IBM, we try not to tame them."[8]

Tools to Foster Creativity

In addition to establishing the proper environment, there are several available techniques that can assist managers in encouraging creativity. The following sections describe some of these techniques.

Brainstorming. Alex F. Osborn developed brainstorming as an aid to producing creative ideas for an advertising agency. Basically, **brainstorming** involves presenting a problem to a group of people and allowing them to present ideas for solution to the problem. Brainstorming is intended to produce a large quantity of ideas or alternatives and generally follows a definite procedure.

In the first phase, members of the group are asked to present ideas off the top of their heads. The group is told that quantity is desired and that

Brainstorming – involves presenting a problem to a group and allowing them to produce a large quantity of ideas for its solution; no criticisms are allowed initially.

MANAGERS AT WORK 6–3

3M Company

3M is 39th on the Fortune 500 list with sales of $8.6 billion in 1986. Its businesses include graphic systems, abrasives, adhesives, building materials, chemicals, protective products, printing products, static control, recording materials, electrical products, and health care products. The largest segment of its business is tape and allied products, amounting to about 17 percent of sales. The following story describes how the tape business started.

The salesmen who visited the auto plants noticed that workers painting new two-toned cars were having trouble keeping the colors from running together. Richard G. Drew, a young 3M lab technician, came up with the answer: masking tape, the company's first tape. In 1930, six years after Du Pont introduced cellophane, Drew figured out how to put adhesive on it, and Scotch tape was born, used initially for industrial packaging. It didn't really begin to roll until another imaginative 3M hero, John Borden, a sales manager, created a dispenser with a built-in blade.

Source: Adapted from Thomas J. Peters and Robert H. Waterman, Jr., *In Search of Excellence* (New York: Harper & Row, 1982), p. 228; and "The Fortune 500 Largest U.S. Industrial Corporations," *Fortune*, April 27, 1987, p. 364.

they should not be concerned about the quality of their ideas. Four basic rules for the first phase are:

1. No criticism of ideas is allowed.
2. No praise of ideas is allowed.
3. No questions or discussion of ideas is allowed.
4. Combinations and improvements on ideas that have been previously presented are encouraged.

Gordon technique – differs from brainstorming in that no one but the group leader knows the exact nature of the real problem under consideration. A key word is used to describe a problem area.

During the second phase, the merits of each idea are reviewed. This review often leads to additional alternatives. Furthermore, alternatives with little merit are eliminated in this phase. In the third phase, one of the alternatives is selected. Frequently, the alternative is selected through group consensus.

Gordon Technique. William J. J. Gordon developed a technique for the consulting firm of Arthur D. Little, Inc. to spur creative problem solving. The technique was initially devised to get creative ideas on technical problems. The **Gordon technique** differs from brainstorming in that no one but the group leader knows the exact nature of the real problem under consideration. A key word is used to describe a problem area; the group then explores that area, using the key word as a starting point. For instance, the word *conservation* may be used to start a discussion on energy conservation. The key word would direct discussion and suggestions on conservation to other areas in addition to the one under question. Proponents of the Gordon technique argue that it gives better quality ideas because the discussion is not limited to one particular area as with the brainstorming technique.

Nominal Grouping Technique (NGT). The **nominal grouping technique** is a highly structured technique designed to keep personal interactions at a minimum. It involves the following steps:

1. *Listing:* Each group member, working alone, develops a list of probable solutions to a group task.
2. *Recording:* Each member offers an item from his or her listing in a round-robin manner to the group leader who records the ideas on a master list in full view of the group. The round-robin process continues until all items on each person's list have been recorded by the leader.
3. *Voting:* Each member records on an individual ballot his or her preference with respect to the priority or importance of the times appearing on the master list.

No verbal interaction is allowed during the first three steps. The results of the voting are tabulated, and scores are posted on the master list.

4. *Discussion:* Each item is then discussed for clarification and evaluation.
5. *Final voting:* Each member votes a second time with respect to the priority of the ideas generated.[9]

The NGT has been found to generate more unique ideas than brainstorming. However, both the NGT and brainstorming suffer from the problem that occurs when the participants are so close to the problem that they are blind to what appear to be obvious solutions.[10]

Brainwriting. Under the **brainwriting** approach, group members are presented with a problem situation and then asked to jot their ideas down on paper without any discussion. The papers are not signed. The papers are then exchanged with others, who build upon the ideas and pass the papers on again until all have had an opportunity to participate.

Input-Output Scheme. This technique was developed by General Electric for use in solving energy-related problems. The first step under the **the input-output scheme** is to list the desired output. Once the desired output has been agreed upon, the next step is to list all possible combinations of inputs which could lead to the desired output. After the list of possible inputs has been exhausted, the group then discusses and ranks the desirability of the different possibilities. This process continues until one input eventually emerges as the preferred approach.

Nominal grouping technique (NGT) – highly structured technique for solving group tasks; minimizes personal interactions to encourage activity and reduce pressures toward conformity.

Brainwriting – group is presented with a problem situation and members anonymously write down ideas, then exchange papers with others who build upon ideas and pass them on until all have participated.

Input-output scheme – list desired output, then list all steps required to attain this. These steps are then discussed and their desirability prioritized until one output emerges.

Synectics –
requires the partic-
ipants to fantasize
about how a par-
ticular problem
could be solved if
there weren't any
fiscal or technical
constraints. Of-
ten, at least one or
two of these solu-
tions can be re-
fined into quite
practical solutions.

Synectics. **Synectics** is a relatively new technique used in creative problem solving. One method used in synectics is called "goal wishing" and requires the participants to fantasize about how a particular problem could be solved if there weren't any fiscal or technical constraints. After developing a list of wishful solutions, the participants are encouraged to come up with the most absurd solutions they can imagine. Often, at least one or two of these solutions can be refined into quite practical solutions.

A word of caution must be offered in the use of any of these techniques: Much controversy exists regarding their effectiveness as aids to creativity. Two researchers addressed this issue: "The evidence on balance does not seem encouraging enough to propose that managers who are seeking an extremely creative idea to help them on a problem situation should resort to a brainstorming session."[11] On the other hand, these same researchers concluded that brainstorming may be effective at generating a wider variety of solutions to a problem.

In conclusion, none of the previously described techniques is a complete answer for improving creativity within organizations. Each should be viewed as a tool that can help in some situations when the proper environment has been established.

A Model for Creative Decision Making

The purpose of this section is to present a practical model that can lead to better and more creative decisions.[12] While this model incorporates parts of the rational approach, its emphasis is on encouraging the generation of new ideas. Figure 6–3 outlines the different stages of this model.

F I G U R E 6–3   Model for Creative Decision Making

STAGE		
1	Recognition	To investigate and
2	Fact finding	eventually define a
3	Problem finding	problem or decision situation.
4	Idea finding	To generate possible alternatives or solutions (ideas).
5	Solution finding	To identify criteria and evaluate ideas generated in stage 4.
6	Acceptance finding	Work out a plan for implementing a chosen idea.

Source: Bruce Meyers (unpublished paper, Western Illinois University, 1987).

Stage 1: Recognition. When a problem or a decision situation exists, it is useful first to describe the circumstances in writing. A good approach is to simply write out the facts in narrative form. This stage should include a description of the present situation, as well as when and where pertinent events occurred or will occur.

Stage 2: Fact Finding. After the decision situation has been described in written form, the next step is to systematically gather additional information concerning the current state of affairs. Questions asked in this stage usually begin with *who, what, where, when, how many, how much,* or similar words. The intent of the fact-finding stage is to organize available information about the decision situation.

Stage 3: Problem Finding. The fact-finding stage is primarily concerned with the present and past; the problem-finding stage is oriented toward the future. In a sense this stage might be viewed as problem redefining or problem analysis. The overriding purpose of this stage is to rewrite or restate the problem in a manner that will encourage more creative solutions. In light of stages 1 and 2 above, the decision maker should attempt to restate the problem in several different ways, with the ultimate goal of encouraging a broader range of solutions. For example, the decision situation, Shall I use my savings to start a new business? could be restated as, In what ways might I finance my new business? The first statement elicits a much more narrow range of possible solutions than does the second. Shall I fire this employee? could be changed to, Should I transfer, punish, retrain, or fire this employee, or should I give him/her another chance?

After listing several restatements of the problem, the decision maker should select the one that most closely represents the real problem and has the greatest number of potential solutions. At this point, the decision situation should be defined in such a manner as to suggest multiple solutions.

Stage 4: Idea Finding. The purpose of this stage is to generate a number of different alternatives for the decision situation. In this stage a form of brainstorming is used, following two simple rules: (1) no judgment or evaluation is allowed, and (2) all ideas presented must be given consideration. The purpose of these rules is to encourage the generation of alternatives, regardless of how impractical they may seem at first. A good approach is for the decision maker to list as many ideas as possible that relate to the problem.

The decision maker should then go back and consider what might be substituted, combined, adopted, modified, eliminated, or rearranged to transform any of the previously generated ideas into additional ideas.

Stage 5: Solution Finding. The purpose of this stage is to identify the decision criteria and to evaluate the potential ideas generated in stage 4. The first step in this stage is for the decision maker to develop a list of potential decision criteria by listing all possibilities. Once a list of potential criteria has been developed, the decision maker should pare down the list by selecting the most appropriate criteria. Naturally the decision maker should aim for a manageable number of criteria (normally fewer than seven). The next step is to evaluate each idea generated in stage 4 against the selected criteria. Many ideas from stage 4 can usually be eliminated by simple inspection. The remaining ideas should then be evaluated against each criterion using some type of rating scale. After each idea has been evaluated against all criteria, the best solution is usually obvious.

Stage 6: Acceptance Finding. The purpose of this last stage is to identify what needs to be done in order to successfully implement the chosen idea or solution. Not only does this stage address the *who, when, where,* and *how* questions but it should also attempt to anticipate potential objections to the decision.

While the above model is certainly not perfect, it does encourage managers to go beyond bounded rationality and to make better decisions than by following the satisficing approach.

THE ROLE OF VALUES IN DECISION MAKING

Value – a conception, explicit or implicit, defining what an individual or group regards as desirable. People are not born with values but rather they acquire and develop them early in life.

A **value** is a conception, explicit or implicit, defining what an individual or group regards as desirable.[13] Values play an important role in the decision-making process. People are not born with values but rather they acquire and develop them early in life. Parents, teachers, relatives, and others influence an individual's values. As a result, every manager and employee brings a certain set of values to the workplace.

A person's values have an impact on the selection of performance measures, alternatives, and choice criteria in the decision process. Differences in values often account for the use of different performance measures. For example, a manager primarily concerned with economic values would probably measure performance differently than a manager primarily concerned with social values. The former might look only at profit, the latter might think only of customer complaints. Differences in values might also generate different alternatives. A viable alternative to one person might be unacceptable to another because of differences in values. Because the final choice criteria depend on the performance measures used, they are also affected by values. For example, consider the question of laying off excess employees. Managers with dominant economic values would probably lay them off much quicker than would managers with high social values.

George England, who has conducted very extensive research on the role of values in the decision-making process, has identified three major categories of values (see Figure 6–4).[14]

F I G U R E   6–4   England's Major Categories of Values

The pragmatic mode:	Suggests that an individual has an evaluative framework that is primarily guided by success-failure considerations.
The ethical-moral mode:	Implies an evaluative framework consisting of ethical considerations influencing behavior toward actions and decisions which are judged to be right, and away from those judged to be wrong.
The affect, or feeling, mode:	Suggests an evaluative framework which is guided by hedonism. One behaves in ways that increase pleasure and decrease pain.

Source: George England, "Personal Value Systems of Managers and Administrators," *Academy of Management Proceedings*, August 1973, pp. 81–94.

He reported the following:

1. There are large individual differences in personal values within every group studied. In the different countries studied, some managers have a pragmatic orientation, some have an ethical-moral orientation, and some have an affect, or feeling, orientation. Some managers have a very small set of values; others have a large set and seem to be influenced by many strongly held values.

2. Personal value systems of managers are relatively stable and do not change rapidly. Edward Lusk and Bruce Oliver repeated one of England's earlier studies and reported that values of managers had changed very little during the six years covered by their study.[15]

3. Personal value systems of managers are related to and/or influence the way managers make decisions. For example, those who have profit maximization as an important goal are less willing to spend money on cafeteria and rest room improvements than those who do not have profit maximization as an important value.

4. Personal value systems of managers are related to their career success as managers. Successful American managers favor pragmatic, dynamic achievement-oriented values; less successful managers prefer more static and passive values.

5. There are differences in the personal values of managers working in different organizational contexts. For example, the personal values of U.S. managers were found to be different from those of labor leaders.

6. Overall, the value systems of managers in the different countries studied were similar; yet, there were some distinct differences. The data suggest that cultural and social factors—as opposed to level of technological and industrial

development—are more important in explaining value differences and similarities.[16]

The work of England and others clearly establishes the importance that values play in the decision-making process of managers. His and other more recent studies show that values may differ from culture to culture and that these differences may have a profound effect on resulting decisions.[17] To make sound decisions, today's managers must not only be aware of their own values; they also must know those of others inside and outside the organization.

PARTICIPATION IN DECISION MAKING

Most managers have opportunities to involve their subordinates and others in the decision-making process. One pertinent question is, Do groups make better decisions than individuals? Another is, When should subordinates be involved in making managerial decisions?

Group Decision Making

Everyone knows the old axiom that two heads are better than one. Empirical evidence generally supports this view—with a few minor qualifications. Group performance is frequently better than that of the average group member.[18] Similarly, groups can often be successfully used to develop innovative and creative solutions to problems. Groups also take longer to solve problems than does the average person.[19] Thus, group decisions are generally better when avoiding mistakes is more important than speed.

Group performance is generally superior to that of the average group member for two basic reasons. First, the sum total of the group's knowledge is greater; second, the group has a much wider range of alternatives in the decision process.

Group decision making also has other benefits. It facilitates and increases acceptance of the decision by group members, especially when a change is being implemented. A more complete understanding of both the decision and alternative solutions results from group decision making. This is especially helpful when those who must implement the decision participate in the process. Managers at Work 6–4 presents an example of such a situation.

However, some potential drawbacks can greatly limit the effectiveness of group decision making. One person may dominate or control the group. This occurs frequently when the president or other higher-ups in the organization take part in the decision process. Because of their presence many other members become inhibited. The social pressures of conformity can also inhibit group members.

Competition can develop within the group to such an extent that winning an issue becomes more important than the issue itself. A final hazard results

MANAGERS AT WORK 6–4

Workers Participation in Decision Making at AT&T

AT&T ranks as one of the 10 largest U.S. Industrial Corporations, and its plant in Richmond, Virginia is recognized as one of the best-run plants. A high degree of automation at this plant has not eliminated the need for initiative or imagination on the workers' part. Employees at every level in the plant make suggestions (and are encouraged to do so) on the methods to be adopted for improvement in operations. At one time, workers in one particular department found that the machines were being underutilized because of longer waiting times for replacement of worn-out parts by the maintenance staff. The workers arrived at a solution by deciding to handle the replacement job themselves, much to the delight of the maintenance staff for whom this was a mundane, low-priority task.

Source: "America's Best-Managed Factories," *Fortune*, May 28, 1984, pp. 16–24.

from the dynamics of group decision making. Groups tend to accept the first potentially positive solution and give little attention to others.

One other trait of group decision making compares the risk that people will take alone and in a group. Laboratory experiments have shown that unanimous group decisions are consistently more risky than the average of the individual decisions.[20] This is somewhat surprising since group pressures often inhibit the members. Possibly people feel less responsible for the outcome of a group decision than when they act alone.

Figure 6–5 summarizes the positive and negative aspects of group decision making.

F I G U R E 6–5   Positive and Negative Aspects of Group Decision Making

POSITIVE ASPECTS

1. The sum total of the group's knowledge is greater.
2. The group possesses a much wider range of alternatives in the decision process.
3. Participation in the decision-making process increases the acceptance of the decision by group members.
4. Group members better understand the decision and the alternatives considered.

NEGATIVE ASPECTS

1. One individual may dominate and/or control the group.
2. Social pressures to conform can inhibit group members.
3. Competition can develop to such an extent that winning becomes more important than the issue itself.
4. Groups have a tendency to accept the first potentially positive solution, while giving little attention to other possible solutions.

▟ S U M M A R Y

This chapter discusses three different approaches to decision making: the rational approach, the satisficing approach, and the creative approach. Several specific tools and techniques that can aid in the decision–making process was also presented.

L E A R N I N G   O B J E C T I V E   1

Explain the Difference between Decision Making and Problem Solving.

In its narrowest sense, decision making is the process of choosing from various alternatives. Problem solving is the process of determining the appropriate responses or actions necessary to alleviate a deviation from some standard or desired level of performance. From a practical perspective almost all managerial decisions involve solving or avoiding problems, and therefore, it is not necessary to distinguish between managerial decision making and managerial problem solving.

L E A R N I N G   O B J E C T I V E   2

List the Different Conditions under Which Managers Make Decisions.

Managers normally make decisions under conditions of certainty, risk, or uncertainty.

L E A R N I N G   O B J E C T I V E   3

Explain the Intuitive Approach to Decision Making.

The intuitive approach is followed when managers make decisions based on hunches and intuition. Emotion and feeling play a major role when following this approach.

L E A R N I N G   O B J E C T I V E   4

Discuss the Rational Approach to Decision Making with Particular Emphasis on Its Limitations.

The rational approach involves the following six steps: (1) recognize the need for a decision; (2) establish, rank, and weigh the criteria; (3) gather available information and data; (4) identify possible alternatives; (5) evaluate each alternative with resepct to all criteria; and (6) select the best alternative. Often the assumptions on which the rational approach is based are not very realistic. For example, the criteria are not always clearly defined; all possible alternatives are not always known; the different alternatives are often difficult to evaluate; and people do not always have the discipline to choose the best alternative even when it has been identified.

L E A R N I N G   O B J E C T I V E   5

Define Creativity and Innovation; Outline the Basic Stages in the Creative Process.

Creativity is the thinking process involved in producing an idea or concept that is new, original, useful, or satisfying to its creator or someone else.

Innovation is doing new things. The creative process generally has four stages: (1) preparation, (2) incubation, (3) illumination, and (4) verification.

LEARNING OBJECTIVE 6

Describe Several Specific Tools and Techniques That Can Be Used to Foster Creative Decisions.

Tools that can be used to foster creative decisions include: brainstorming, the Gordon technique, the nominal grouping technique, brainwriting, the input-output scheme, and synectics.

LEARNING OBJECTIVE 7

List the Six Steps in Creative Decision Making.

The model for creative decision making encompasses the following six steps: (1) recognition, (2) fact finding, (3) problem finding, (4) idea finding, (5) solution finding, and (6) acceptance finding.

LEARNING OBJECTIVE 8

Explain the Role That Values Play in Making Decisions.

A manager's values have an impact on the selection of performance measures, alternatives, and choice criteria in the decision process.

LEARNING OBJECTIVE 9

Summarize the Positive and Negative Aspects of Group Decision Making.

Positive aspects include: (1) The sum total of the group's knowledge is greater; (2) the group possesses a much wider range of alternatives in the decision process; (3) participation in the decision-making process increases the acceptance of the decision by group members; and (4) group members better understand the decision and the alternatives considered. Negative aspects include: (1) One individual may dominate and/or control the group; (2) social pressures to conform can inhibit group members; (3) competition can develop to such an extent that winning becomes more important than the issue itself; (4) groups have a tendency to accept the first potentially positive solution, while giving little attention to other possible solutions.

REVIEW QUESTIONS

1. What are the three stages in the decision-making process?
2. What is the difference between decision making and problem solving?
3. Distinguish between the decision situations of certainty, risk, and uncertainty.
4. Discuss the intuitive approach to decision making.
5. Discuss the rational approach to decision making.
6. What criticisms can be made concerning the rational approach to decision making?
7. Discuss the satisficing approach to decision making. What is the difference between satisficing and optimizing?
8. Describe the following aids to creativity:

  a. Brainstorming
  b. Gordon technique
  c. Nominal grouping technique
  d. Brainwriting
  e. Input-output scheme
  f. Synectics

9. Describe a model for creative decision making.
10. What are values? Is there any relationship between values and managerial success?
11. Outline some positive and negative aspects of group decision making.

DISCUSSION QUESTIONS

1. Do you agree that many managers only attempt to satisfice rather than optimize in making decisions? Support your answers with examples.
2. How can managers' values affect their decisions? Be specific.
3. What factors do you think affect the amount of risk that a manager is willing to take when making a decision?
4. Comment on the following statement: Groups always make better decisions than individuals acting alone.
5. Suppose you are the head of a committee charged with choosing where to locate a new "teen center" in your community. Your task force is made up of eight adults. Describe how you might go about your task.

REFERENCES & ADDITIONAL READINGS

[1] Herbert A. Simon, *The New Science of Management Decision* (New York: Harper & Row, 1960), p. 2.

[2] George S. Odiorne, *Management and the Activity Trap* (New York: Harper & Row, 1974), pp. 128–29; George S. Odiorne, *The Change Resisters* (Englewood Cliffs, N.J.: Prentice-Hall, 1981), pp. 15–25.

[3] Odiorne, *Management and the Activity Trap,* pp. 142–44.

[4] Herbert A. Simon, *Model of Man* (New York: John Wiley & Sons, 1957), p. 198.

[5] Thomas J. Peters and Robert H. Waterman, Jr., *In Search of Excellence* (New York: Harper & Row, 1982), pp. 12–13; also see Harold J. Leavitt, *Corporate Pathfinders* (Homewood, Ill.: Dow Jones-Irwin, 1986).

[6] Graham Walles, *The Art of Thought* (New York: Harcourt Brace Jovanovich, 1976), p. 80.

[7] Peters and Waterman, *In Search of Excellence,* p. 223.

[8] Thomas J. Watson, *A Business and Its Beliefs* (New York: McGraw-Hill, 1963), p. 28.

[9] Gene E. Burton, Dev S. Pathok, and David B. Burton, "The Gordon Effect in Nominal Grouping," *University of Michigan Business Review,* July 1978, p. 8.

[10] Ibid., p. 7.

[11] T. Richards and B. L. Freedom, "Procedures for Managers in Idea-Deficient Situations: An Examination of Brainstorming Approaches," *Journal of Management Studies,* February 1978, pp. 43–55.

[12] The basis for this model and much of the discussion was contributed by Bruce Meyers, associate professor of management at Western Illinois University.

[13] William D. Guth and Renato Tagiuri, "Personal Values and Corporate Strategy," *Harvard Business Review,* September–October 1965, pp. 124–25.

[14] George England, "Personal Value Systems of Managers and Administrators," *Academy of Management Proceedings,* August 1973, pp. 81–94.

[15] Edward J. Lusk and Bruce L. Oliver, "American Managers' Personal Value Systems Revisited," *Academy of Management Journal,* September 1974, pp. 549–54.

[16] England, "Personal Value Systems," pp. 82–87.

[17] For example, see H. S. Badr, E. R. Gray, and B. L. Kedia, "Personal Values and Managerial Decision Making: Evidence from Two Cultures," *Management International Review,* Fall 1982, pp. 65–73.

[18] Irving Lorge, David Fox, Joel Davitz, and Marlin Brenner, "A Survey of Studies Contrasting the Quality of Group Performance and Individual Performance, 1930–1957," *Psychological Bulletin,* November 1958, pp. 337–72; Frederick C. Miner, Jr., "Group versus Individual Decision Making: An Investigation of Performance Measures, Decision Strategies, and Process Losses/Gains," *Organizational Behavior and Human Performance,* February 1984, pp. 112–24.

[19] M. E. Shaw, "A Comparison of Individuals and Small Groups in the National Solution of Complex Problems," *American Journal of Psychology,* July 1932, pp. 491–504; Lorge et al., "A Survey of Studies."

[20] M. Wallach, N. Kogan, and D. J. Bem, "Group Influence on Individual Risk Taking," *Journal of Abnormal and Social Psychology,* August 1962, pp. 75–86; N. Kogan and M. Wallach, "Risk Taking as a Function of the Situation, the Person, and the Group," in *New Directions of Psychology,* vol. 3, ed. G. Mardler (New York: Holt, Rinehart & Winston, 1967).

INCIDENT

Getting Out of the Army

Jay Abbott is confident that his future will be secure and financially rewarding should he decide to remain in the army. He entered more than 10 years ago as a commissioned officer after completing his college education on an ROTC scholarship. Jay, 31 years old, has progressed to the rank of captain and is currently being considered for promotion to major. He has no reason to believe he will not be promoted. He has been successful in all of his appointments, is well liked by everyone—his peers, superiors, and subordinates—and has an unblemished record.

However, at the 10-year mark, Jay had second thoughts about staying in the army and has been thinking about leaving ever since. He has felt more and more resentful that the army has affected a large part of his personal life. Although he had always preferred to wear his hair shorter than that of most young men, he resented the fact that even if he wanted to let it grow out or have sideburns, he couldn't do it. It was the principle of the whole idea—the intrusion of the army into this personal life. The fact that this intrusion extended to the behavior of his wife and children bothered him even more.

Jay's wife Ellen was finishing her master's thesis. This took up a large portion of her free time; yet her lack of involvement in the officers' clubs was frowned upon. There was just no such thing as a private family life in his position. He didn't even have much time to spend with the family. His job required long hours of work, including weekend duty—which left little time for his wife and two daughters, aged seven and nine. Another problem was that Ellen, holding a degree in design engineering, was unable to pursue any kind of real career—something that was important to both of them.

These thoughts raced through Jay's mind over and over again as he tried to decide what would be best for him and his family. There were a lot of positive factors about the army, he kept reminding himself: he was already earning $31,000 a year; with his near-certain promotion, this would be raised to $35,000. Also he was being recommended for the Army's Command and General Staff College. There was little chance he would not be approved; completing the program would make his future even brighter. If he stayed, he'd be able to retire in just 10 more years (at age 41) with a permanent retirement income of half his final salary plus free medical and dental coverage. By then, he figured, he would probably be a lieutenant colonel with a base pay of around $48,000; at worst, he would retire a major. At 41, there would be plenty of time to devote to a second career should he so desire.

But, Jay could argue, regardless of how attractive the benefits seemed, salaries in the armed services had not kept pace with the rising rate of inflation: Congress had held the lid on raises at 5 percent. Furthermore, he did not look for any change in their posture in the next few years. In fact, Jay had read several newspaper articles indicating that Congress was considering reducing benefits for the armed services—the 20-year retirement specifically.

Jay had done some checking around. He learned that the training and experience received in the army was valuable to civilian employers. Commissioned in the signal corps, he had vast experience in the area of telecommunications. He had recently completed a tour as an instructor in a service school. He had also been in many positions of leadership during his term in the army. At 31, he probably had more firsthand managerial experience than most civilian managers. He knew that large organizations were currently hiring young ex-military officers at salaries of $5,000 to $10,000 higher than recent college graduates.

Questions

1. What should Jay do?
2. What factors should be considered in Jay's decision?
3. What role would values play in Jay's decision?

EXERCISE

Risk Aversion

This exercise illustrates how different decision makers react differently to similar risks. Draw the following set of axes on a piece of paper:

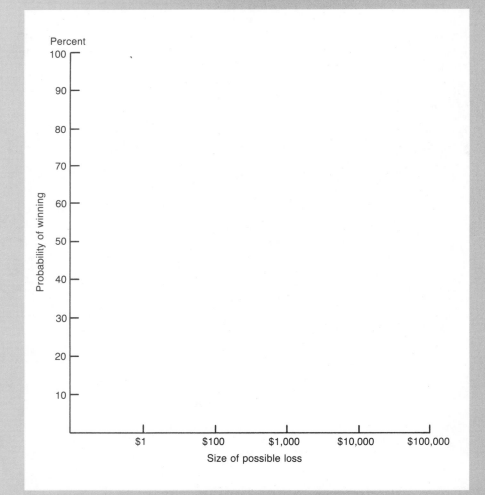

Assume you are faced with a decision on whether to play or not to play a game of chance. You will play the game once and only once. If you win, you will get $2. If you lose, you will have to pay $1. Would you be willing to play if the probability of winning the game is 80 percent? How about 50

percent? 40 percent? 30 percent? Find the lowest probability of winning for which you would be willing to play the game for one time only. Put a dot above the $1 on the graph at the probability that you select. Repeat the process for each of the following games:

REWARD FOR WINNING	PENALTY FOR LOSING
$ 20	$ 10
200	100
2,000	1,000
20,000	10,000
200,000	100,000

Note: Players cannot declare bankruptcy if they lose. They must give up one third of their earnings until the debt is fully paid.

A. Connect the dots on your graph and compare the curves drawn by various individuals in the class.
B. Do you consider yourself to be a risk taker or a risk averter?
C. How do you think that your affinity for risk might affect your ability to be a good manager?

7 Objectives, Strategy, and Plans

Of course, objectives are not a railroad timetable. They can be compared to the compass bearing by which a ship navigates. The compass bearing itself is firm, pointing in a straight line toward the desired port. But in actual navigation, the ship will veer off its course for many miles to avoid a storm. She will slow down to a walk in a fog and heave to altogether in a hurricane. She may even change destination in midocean and set a new compass bearing toward a new port—perhaps because war has broken out, perhaps only because her cargo has been sold in midpassage. Still, four-fifths of all voyages end in the intended port at the originally scheduled time. And without a compass bearing, the ship would neither be able to find the port nor be able to estimate the time it will take to get there.

P E T E R F . D R U C K E R *

Planning – the process of deciding what objectives to pursue during a future time period and what to do to achieve those objectives. Planning has two major segments: setting objectives, and formulating a strategy for reaching those objectives.

Planning is the process of deciding what objectives to pursue during a future time period and what to do to achieve those objectives. Before studying the planning process in depth, it is necessary to clearly understand the terms *objective, strategy,* and *policy.* All are a part of, or relate directly to, the planning process.

Many differences exist about the meanings of these terms. Not only do their definitions and meanings vary widely, but there is also much confusion over how the terms relate to each other. This chapter will clear up some of this confusion.

OBJECTIVES

Objectives (goals) – statements outlining what you are trying to achieve; they give an organization and its members direction.

If you don't know where you're going, how will you know when you get there? Objectives and goals, as stated in Chapter 1, are used interchangeably in this book. (Some authors describe objectives as being somewhat more specific and short range than are goals.) **Objectives** are statements outlining what you are trying to achieve; they give an organization and its members direction and purpose. Few managers question the importance of objectives, only what the objectives should be.

Management is a form of work that involves guiding or directing a group of people toward organizational goals or objectives—the process centers around organizational objectives. Management cannot be properly practiced without

* Peter F. Drucker, *The Practice of Management* (New York: Harper & Row, 1954), pp. 60–61.

pursuing specific objectives. Managers today and in the future must concentrate on where they and their organizations are headed.

It is also important to realize that managers and employees at all levels in an organization should have objectives; everyone should know what he or she is trying to achieve. One key for organizational success is for the objectives at all different levels to mesh together. The next section presents a method for accomplishing this.

A Cascade Approach

The key to ensuring that objectives properly relate to one another is the manner in which they are set. One desirable approach to setting objectives is to have the objectives "cascade" down through the organization.

1. The objective-setting process begins at the top with a clear, concise statement of the central purpose or mission of the organization.
2. Long-range organizational goals are formulated from this statement.
3. The long-range goals lead to the establishment of more, short-range performance objectives for the organization. When tied to a specific time period, such as a year, these performance objectives become the basis for, and an integral part of, the objectives of the chief executive and the top management team.
4. Derivative objectives are then developed for each major division or department.
5. Objectives are then established for the various subunits in each major division or department.
6. The process continues on down through the organizational hierarchy.[1]

This **cascade approach** to goal setting, depicted in Figure 7–1, does not imply autocratic or "top down" management. It merely ensures that the objectives of individual units within the organization are in phase with the major objectives of the organization. It coordinates the entire objective-setting process.

Cascade approach – ensures that the objectives of individual units within the organization are in phase with the major objectives of the organization.

Organizational Mission

An organization's mission is actually the broadest and highest level of objectives. **Mission** defines the basic **purpose** or purposes of the organization (for this reason, the terms *mission* and *purpose* are often used interchangeably). Basically, an organization's mission outlines why the organization exists. A mission statement usually includes a description of the organization's basic products and/or services and a definition of its markets and/or sources of revenue.

Mission (purpose) – defines the basic purpose(s) of an organization— why the organization exists.

F I G U R E 7–1   Cascade Approach to Objective Setting

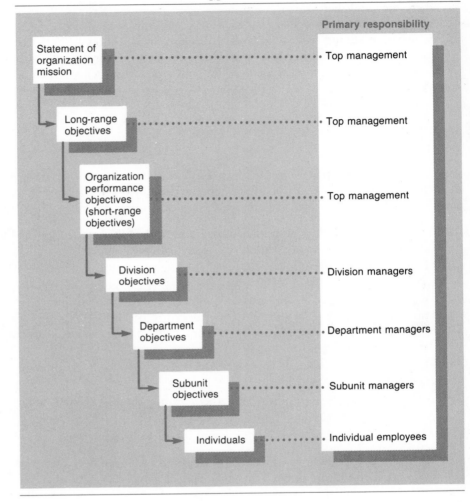

Defining *mission* is crucial. It is also more difficult than one might imagine. Peter Drucker emphasizes that an organization's purpose should be examined and defined not only at its inception or during difficult times but also during successful periods.[2] If the railroad companies of the early 1900s or the wagon makers of the 1800s had made developing a firm position in the transportation business their organizational purpose rather than sticking strictly to the rail or wagon business, they might today hold the same economic positions that they enjoyed in earlier times.

Drucker argues that an organization's purpose is not determined by the organization itself but by its customers.[3] Customer satisfaction with an organization's product or service defines the purpose more than does the organization name, statutes, or articles or incorporation. Drucker outlines three questions that need to be answered to define an organization's present business. First, management must identify the customers—where they are, how they buy, and how they can be reached. (Is the customer retail or wholesale?) Second, management must know what the customer buys: Does the Rolls-Royce owner buy transportation or prestige? Finally, what is the customer looking for in the product? For example, does the homeowner buy an appliance from Sears, Roebuck & Co. because of price, quality, or service?

Management must also identify what the future business will be and what it should be. Drucker presents four areas to investigate. The first is market potential: What does the long-term trend look like? Second, what changes in market structure might occur because of economic developments, changes in styles or fashions, or competition? For example, how have oil prices affected the automobile market structure? Third, what possible changes will alter the customers' buying habits? What new ideas or products might create new customer demands or change old demands? Consider, for example, the impact of the minicalculator on the sale of slide rules and hand-cranked adding machines. Finally, what customer needs are not being adequately served by available products and services? The success of the Xerox Corporation is a well-known example of identifying and filling a current customer need. As indicated in the cascade approach, all objectives are derived from the organization's mission.

Long-Range and Short-Range Objectives

Long-range objectives generally go beyond the current fiscal year of the organization. Long-range objectives must support and not conflict with the organizational mission. But they may be quite different from the organizational mission and still support it. For instance, the organizational mission of a fast-food restaurant might be to provide rapid hot food service to a certain area of the city. One long-range objective might be to increase sales to a specific level within the next four years. Obviously, this objective is quite different from the organizational mission; but it still supports the mission.

Short-range objectives should be derived from an in-depth evaluation of long-range objectives. Such an evaluation should result in a listing of priorities of the long-range objectives. Then short-range objectives can be set to help achieve the long-range objectives.

All levels within the organization should set objectives based on the long-range and short-range objectives of the organization. Objectives at any level must be coordinated with, and subordinated to, the objectives of the next higher level. All objectives are then synchronized and not working against each other.

Objectives should be clear, concise, and quantified when possible. Affected

Long-range objectives – go beyond the current fiscal year— must support and not conflict with the organizational mission.

Short-range objectives – generally tied to a specific time period of a year or less and are derived from an in-depth evaluation of long-range objectives.

personnel should clearly understand what is expected. Objectives should span all major areas of the organization, not just a single area. The problem with one overriding objective is that it is often achieved at the expense of other desirable objectives. While objectives in different areas may serve as checks on each other, they should be reasonably consistent with each other. Objectives should be dynamic; they should be reevaluated as the environment and opportunities change. Objectives for organizations normally fall into one of four general categories: (1) profit oriented, (2) service to customers, (3) employee needs and well-being, and (4) social responsibility. Even nonprofit organizations must be concerned with profit in the sense that they generally must operate within a budget. The following areas represent potential areas for establishing objectives in most organizations:[4]

1. *Profitability.* Measures the degree to which the firm is attaining an acceptable level of profits; expressed in terms of profits before or after taxes, return on investment, earnings per share, or profit-to-sales ratios, among others.

2. *Markets.* Reflects the firm's position in its marketplace, expressed in terms of share of the market, dollar or unit volume in sales, or niche in the industry.

3. *Productivity.* Measures the efficiency of internal operations expressed as a ratio of inputs to outputs, such as number of items or services produced per unit of time.

4. *Product.* Describes the introduction or elimination of products or services; expressed in terms of when a product or service will be introduced or dropped.

5. *Financial resources.* Reflects goals relating to the funding needs of the firm; expressed in terms of capital structure, new issues of common stock, cash flow, working capital, dividend payment, and collection periods.

6. *Physical facilities.* Concerned with the physical facilities of the firm; expressed in terms of square feet of office or plant space, fixed costs, units of production, or other similar measurements.

7. *Research and innovation.* Reflects the research, development, and/or innovation aspirations of the firm; usually expressed in terms of dollars to be expended.

8. *Organization structure.* Describes objectives relating to changes in the organizational structure and related activities; expressed in terms of a desired future structure or network of relationships.

9. *Human resources.* Concerned with the human resource assets of the organization; expressed in terms of absenteeism, tardiness, number of grievances, and training.

10. *Social responsibility.* Refers to the commitments of the firm regarding society and the environment; expressed in terms of types of activities, number of days of service, or financial contributions.

Managers at Work 7–1 discusses some objectives of the Goodyear Tire & Rubber Company.

MANAGERS AT WORK 7–1

Goodyear's Objectives

Goodyear, the Akron-based tire manufacturing giant, earned a profit of $305.5 million on $9.7 billion sales in 1983. However, the company's stock fell from $36.875 in December 1982 to $26.75 by the end of the following year. To stabilize Goodyear's position and increase its profitability, Chairman Robert E. Mercer, at the beginning of 1984, set the following objectives:

1. Achieve a $15 billion sales within the next five years.
2. Boost return on sales to 5 percent.
3. Increase shareholders' equity to 15 percent (it stood at 10.1 percent in 1983).

While he believed that the first objective would not be difficult to achieve (keeping in view the increase in car sales all around), Mercer felt that the latter two goals might be beyond reach as long as the company's main business was geared to the cyclical tire industry. In order to attain the objectives, Mercer decided to diversify into aerospace, oil, and gas, which should provide faster growth and higher profit margins.

Source: "The King of Tires Is Discontented," *Fortune*, May 28, 1984, pp. 64–70.

Management by Objectives (MBO)

One approach to setting objectives that has enjoyed considerable popularity is the concept of **management by objectives.** MBO is a philosophy based on converting organizational objectives into personal objectives. It assumes that establishing personal objectives elicits employee commitment, which leads to improved performance. The MBO process is summarized in Figure 7–2. MBO has also been called management by results, goals and control, work planning and review, and goals management. All these programs are similar and follow the same basic process.

The objective-setting process in MBO is best accomplished by using the cascade approach to objective setting that was outlined in Figure 7–1. Setting objectives from top to bottom creates an integrated hierarchy of objectives throughout the entire organization. It ensures that the various levels within the organization have a common direction.

In MBO, the objective-setting process requires involvement and collaboration among the various levels of the organization; this joint effort has beneficial results. First, people at each level become more aware of organizational objectives. The better they understand the organization's objectives, the better they see their roles in the total organization. Second, the objectives for an

Management by objectives (MBO) – superior and subordinate jointly define the objectives and responsibilities of the subordinate's job; superior uses them to evaluate subordinate's performance; subordinate's rewards are directly related to performance.

F I G U R E 7–2   The MBO Process

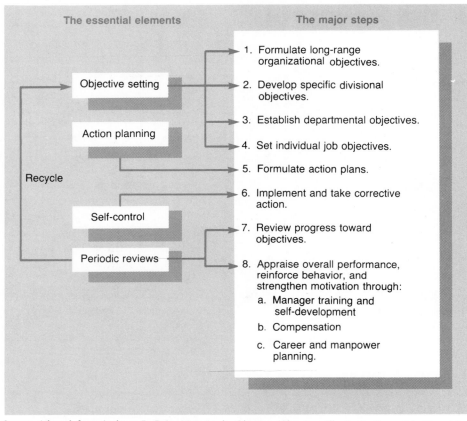

Source: Adapted from Anthony P. Raia, *Managing by Objectives* (Glenview, Ill.: Scott, Foresman). Copyright 1974 by Scott, Foresman & Co. Reprinted by permission of the publisher.

individual are jointly set by the person and the superior; there are give-and-take negotiating sessions between them. Achieving self-formulated objectives can improve motivation and, thus, job performance.

Setting objectives in MBO is not always easy, and problems occur frequently. Often the most difficult problem is deciding the specific areas in which to set objectives. The guidelines offered in Figure 7–3 should help in this process.

After the objectives have been jointly established, a plan of action for achieving them should be developed. This involves the following:

1. Determine the major activities necessary to accomplish the objectives.
2. Establish subactivities necessary for accomplishing the major activities.

F I G U R E 7–3 Guidelines for Establishing Individual Objectives

1. Adapt your objectives directly to organizational goals and strategic plans. Do not assume that they support higher-level management objectives.
2. Quantify and target the results whenever possible. Do not formulate objectives whose attainment cannot be measured or at least verified.
3. Test your objectives for challenge and achievability. Do not build in cushions to hedge against accountability for results.
4. Adjust the objectives to the availability of resources and the realities of organizational life. Do not keep your head either in the clouds or in the sand.
5. Establish performance reports and milestones that measure progress toward the objective. Do not rely on instinct or crude benchmarks to appraise performance.
6. Put your objectives in writing and express them in clear, concise, and unambiguous statements. Do not allow them to remain in loose or vague terms.
7. Limit the number of statements of objectives to the most relevant key result areas of your job. Do not obscure priorities by stating too many objectives.
8. Communicate your objectives to your subordinates so that they can formulate their own job objectives. Do not demand that they do your goal setting for you.
9. Review your statements with others to assure consistency and mutual support. Do not fall into the trap of setting your objectives in a vacuum.
10. Modify your statements to meet changing conditions and priorities.
11. Do not continue to pursue objectives which have become obsolete.

Source: Adapted from Anthony P. Raia, *Managing by Objectives* (Glenview, Ill.: Scott, Foresman). Copyright 1974 by Scott, Foresman & Co. Reprinted by permission of the publisher.

3. Assign primary responsibility for each activity and subactivity.
4. Estimate time requirements necessary to complete each activity and subactivity.
5. Identify additional resources required for each activity and subactivity.

After establishing objectives and outlining the actions necessary to accomplish them, individuals are allowed to pursue their objectives essentially in their own manner. Therefore, MBO is largely a system of self-control. Of course, there are policy constraints on individuals; but basically, people achieve goals through their own abilities and effort.

Periodic progress reviews are an essental ingredient of MBO. This includes giving each employee feedback on actual performance as compared to planned performance (objectives). The importance of this personal feedback cannot be overestimated.

The manner in which the feedback is given is important. If it is hostile, performance may be reduced. Reviews should not be used to degrade the individual. Performance appraisal under MBO is discussed further in Chapter 16, "Appraising and Rewarding Performance."

Many organizations proudly proclaim that they have successfully implemented MBO when, in fact, they have met very few of the actual requirements.

MANAGERS AT WORK 7–2

Management by Objectives at Alcan

Roy Gentles, president and chief executive officer of Alcan Aluminum Corporation, is proud of Alcan's MBO process. The steps they follow are:

1. Each divisional and functional head performs a needs analysis in his or her area and generates a list of about 10 potential objectives.
2. The divisional and functional heads then whittle the lists down to the two or three objectives that are the most important to the total corporation and send that list to Gentles.
3. In a management meeting, Gentles and

his staff reduce the list of 30–35 objectives to 8–10 most important corporate objectives.
4. The new corporate objectives then *cascade* back down through the organization. At this point, the divisional and functional areas are responsible for defining and coordinating any activities necessary to accomplish the objectives.

Source: Roy A. Gentles, "Alcan's Integration of Management Techniques Raises Their Effectiveness," *Management Review,* April 1984, pp. 31–33.

To summarize, an MBO system in its simplest form must meet the following three minimum requirements:

1. Individual objectives are jointly set by the subordinate and the superior.
2. Individuals are periodically evaluated and receive feedback concerning their performance.
3. Individuals are evaluated and rewarded on the basis of objective attainment.

Managers at Work 7–2 describes how Alcan Aluminum Corporation implemented MBO.

Strategy – outlines the basic steps that management plans to take in order to reach an objective or set of objectives. Outlines how management intends to achieve its objectives.

STRATEGY

The word **strategy** originated with the Greeks around 400 B.C.; it pertained to the art and science of directing military forces.[5] A strategy outlines the basic steps that management plans to take in order to reach an objective or set of objectives. In other words, strategy outlines how management intends to achieve its objectives.

Types of Strategies

Strategies exist at different levels in an organization; they are classified according to the scope of what they are intended to accomplish. Strategies that address what businesses a multibusiness organization will be in and how resources will be allocated among those businesses are referred to as **corporate strategies.** They are established at the highest levels in the organization, and they involve a long-range time horizon. **Business strategies** focus on how to compete in a given business. Narrower in scope than a corporate strategy, business strategy generally applies to a single business unit. A third level of strategy is the functional strategy. Functional strategies are narrower in scope than business strategies. **Functional strategies** deal with the activities of the different functional areas of a business—production, finance, marketing, personnel, and the like. Usually, functional strategies are in effect for a relatively short period of time—often one year or less. They must support business-level strategies; but they are mainly concerned with "how to" issues. Managers at Work 7–3 discusses how an unwise functional strategy has crippled an entire company.

Sometimes, the term strategy is used for the entire organization. Such overall strategy is also called its grand strategy. A **grand strategy** describes the way that the organization will puruse its objectives, given the threats and opportunities in the environment and the resources and capabilities of the organization. A grand strategy outlines how the organization as a whole intends to compete. Three factors have a major impact on an organization's grand strategy: (1) the external environment; (2) the internal situation; and (3) the objectives being pursued. A grand strategy attempts to bring these elements together to provide direction for the organization in the face of changing conditions. Figure 7–4 summarizes the different types of strategies and illustrates the hierarchial relationships.

POLICIES

Policies are broad, general guides to action which constrain or direct objective attainment. In this light, policies channel how management should order its affairs and its attitude toward major issues: they dictate the intent of those who guide the organization. In other words, policies define the universe from which future strategies and plans are derived. "It is the policy of the public relations department to answer in writing all written customer complaints" is an example of such a policy.

Policies are generally less action oriented than strategies and usually have a longer life. They do not indicate exactly how to attain objectives; rather they outline the framework within which the objectives must be pursued.

Policy statements often contain the words *to ensure, to follow, to maintain, to promote, to be, to accept,* and similar verbs. For example, the ABC Company

---

Corporate strategies – address what businesses an organization will be in and how resources will be allocated among those businesses.

Business strategies – focus on how to compete in a given business.

Functional strategies – concerned with the activities of the different functional areas of a business.

Grand strategy – describes the way the organization will pursue its objectives, given the threats and opportunities in the environment and its own resources and capabilities.

Policies – broad, general guides to action which constrain or direct objective attainment.

MANAGERS AT WORK 7–3

Strategic Muddle at Transco

Strategies make or mar an organization. A company often sinks or swims depending on the strategies and policies it adopts.

In the late 1970s the natural gas market experienced severe shortages and skyrocketing prices, primarily due to government controls. Angry consumers, who couldn't get enough gas to heat their homes, picketed Transco Energy Company's headquarters in Houston. Panic stricken, Transco, like many other pipeline companies, subsequently entered into costly, long-term purchase contracts with producers. This functional strategy resulted in agreements that called for payments of $10 for every 1,000 cubic feet of gas, and included take–or–pay clauses which obligated the company to pay for the gas even if it didn't need it. This strategy has since backfired. As of September 1987, natural gas was plentiful, demand was weak, and the going price was only $1.40 per thousand cubic feet. Because of its contracts, Transco is stuck with a huge liability to producers for high-priced gas it refuses to take. The company's earnings have plummeted from a high of $140 million in 1981 to a $4.3 million loss in 1986. To quote George S. Slocum, the new chief executive of Transco Energy Company, "Transco just can't win." The big question is whether Transco can ride out this crisis. Whatever happens, Slocum can be sure that his first year as CEO won't be his easiest.

Source: "Can Transco Wriggle Out of the 'Take-or-Pay' Mess?" *Business Week*, September 28, 1987, pp. 66–67.

---

may have a policy "to accept all returns that are accompanied by a sales slip." Such a policy is a general guideline for pursuing company objectives related to profit and sales.

Policies exist at all levels of an organization. A typical organization has some policies that relate to everybody in the organization and some that relate only to certain parts of the organization. A policy such as "this company will always try to fill vacancies at all levels by promoting from within" would relate to everyone in the organization. On the other hand, the previously described policy requiring that all customer complaints be answered in writing relates only to departmental personnel.

Procedure – series of related steps or tasks expressed in chronological order for a specific purpose.

Procedures and Rules

Procedures and rules differ from policies only in degree. In fact, they may be thought of as low-level policies. A **procedure** is a series of related steps

F I G U R E 7–4   Pyramid of Strategies

Corporate Strategy

Addresses what businesses an organization will be in and how resources will be allocated among those businesses.

Business Strategy

Focuses on how to compete in a given business.

Functional Strategy

Concerned with the activities of the different functional areas of the organization; short-range, step-by-step methods to be used (tactics).

or tasks expressed in chronological order for a specific purpose. Procedures define in step-by-step fashion the methods by and through which policies are achieved. They outline precisely how a recurring activity must be accomplished. Procedures allow for little flexibility and deviation. A company's policy may be to accept all customer returns submitted within one month of purchase; company procedures would outline exactly how a return should be processed. Well-established, formal procedures are often known as *standard operating procedures* (SOPs).

Rules require specific and definite actions for a given situation. Rules leave little doubt about what is to be done. They permit *no* flexibility and deviation. Unlike procedures, rules do not have to specify sequence. For example, "No smoking in the conference room" is a rule.

Procedures and rules, then, are actually subsets of policies. All provide some kind of guidance. The differences lie in the ranges of applicability and the degree of flexibility. A no-smoking rule is much less flexible than a procedure for handling customer complaints; the latter is likewise less flexible than a hiring policy.

> **Rules** – require specific and definite actions for a given situation. They permit no flexibility or deviation.

PLANNING

Planning, as discussed earlier, is the process of deciding what objectives to pursue during a future time period and what to do to achieve those objectives. Thus, the process has two major segments: (1) setting objectives; and (2) formulating a strategy for reaching those objectives. Planning is the management function that produces and integrates objectives, strategies, and policies. Planning answers three basic questions:

1. Where are we now?
2. Where do we want to be?
3. How can we get there from here?

The first question calls for an assessment of the present situation. The second question involves determining the desired objectives. The final question requires an outline of actions and an analysis of the financial impact on those actions. It should be stressed that planning is concerned with future implications of current decisions and not with decisions to be made in the future.[6] The planner should examine how current decisions will limit the scope of future actions.

Some authors separate the objective-setting process from the planning process. In such cases, planning is viewed in the more narrow sense of determining a course of action toward some predetermined goal or objective. For example, it is not uncommon for top management to dictate the objectives for a division or department and then ask the respective manager to develop a plan for attaining the objectives. In this light, planning compares to the formulation of business and functional strategies as defined in the previous chapter. At the upper levels of management, the planning process usually does involve the setting of objectives. At the very top levels of management, planning compares to the formulation of a grand strategy. Whether or not the objective-setting process is viewed as an integral part of the planning process or as a precedent of it, objectives must be set before the planning process can be completed. It is not possible to outline a course of action for reaching some objective if one does not know what the objective is.

Why Plan?

Planning is the primary management function; it is inherent in everything a manager does. It is futile for a manager to attempt to perform the other management functions without having a plan. Managers who attempt to organize without a plan will find themselves reorganizing on a regular basis. The manager who attempts to staff without a plan will be constantly hiring and firing employees. Motivation is almost impossible in an organization with continuous reorganization and high employee turnover.

Planning enables a manager or organization to affect rather than accept the future. By setting objectives and charting a course of action, the organization commits itself to "making it happen." This allows the organization to affect the future. Without a planned course of action, the organization is much more likely to sit back, let things happen, and then react to these happenings in a crisis mode. Managers at Work 7–4 demonstrates how Procter & Gamble is trying to positively affect its future through planning.

MANAGERS AT WORK 7–4

Planning for the Future at Procter & Gamble

Procter & Gamble, the colossus of Cincinnati (1986 sales: $15.4 billion), suffered a reduction in profits for fiscal year 1985 ending in June as compared to the previous year. While sales increased from $12.9 billion in 1984 to $13.6 billion in 1985, net earnings declined from $890 million to $635 million during the same period. This reduction in profits was the first in 33 years. The reason for reduced profits was increased spending to launch four big products and to step up research and development. Procter & Gamble's plan to achieve higher growth was based on research to market superior products. Another aspect of Procter & Gamble's master plan was to spend about 30 percent of the $1 billion capital budget on cost-saving projects and to expand production capacity ahead of time. Both of these actions had a negative effect on short-term profit, but Procter & Gamble is betting that they will have a positive long-range effect on profits.

Source: "Procter & Gamble's Comeback Plan," *Fortune*, February 4, 1985, pp. 30–37; Annual Reports of the Procter & Gamble Company for 1984, 1985, 1986.

Planning provides a means for actively involving personnel from all areas of the organization in the management of the organization. Involvement produces a multitude of benefits. First, input from throughout the organization improves the quality of the plans—good suggestions can come from any level in the organization. Involvement in the planning process also enhances the overall understanding of the organization's direction. Knowing the big picture can minimize friction between departments, sections, and individuals. For example, through planning, the sales department can understand and appreciate the objectives of the production department and their relationship to organizational objectives. Involvement in the planning process fosters a greater personal commitment to the plan; the plan becomes "our" plan rather than "their" plan. Positive attitudes created by involvement also improve overall organizational morale and loyalty.

Planning can also have positive effects on managerial performance. Studies have demonstrated that employees who stress planning earn very high performance ratings from supervisors.[7] They have also shown that planning has a positive impact on the quality of work produced.[8] While some have proved inconclusive, several studies have reported a positive relationship between planning and certain measures of organizational success such as profits and goals.[9] One explanation that would fit all the findings to date is that good planning—as opposed to the mere presence or absence of a plan—is related to organizational success.

A final reason for planning is the mental exercise required to develop a plan. Many people believe that the experience and knowledge gained throughout the development of a plan are more important than the plan itself. Preparing and developing a plan requires managers to think in a future- and contingency-oriented manner; this can result in great advantages over managers who are static in their thinking.

Formal Planning

All managers plan. The difference lies in the methods they employ and the extent to which they plan. Most planning is carried out on an informal or casual basis. This occurs when planners do not record their thoughts but rather carry them around in their heads. A **formal plan** is a written, documented plan developed through an identifiable process.

Formal plan – a written, documented plan developed through an identifiable process.

The need for formal planning is not limited to large organizations; small ones can realize the same benefits. Of course, formal planning processes can vary greatly from large to small organizations and even among similar-sized organizations. One might have a 2-page formal plan; another a 100-page document. The appropriate degree of sophistication depends on the needs of the individual managers and the organization itself. The environment, size, and type of business are factors which typically affect the planning needs of an organization.

Who Should Plan?

Formal planning is not reserved strictly for top-level managers. Formal planning should be practiced by all levels of management—from first-line supervisors right up to the chairman of the board. Of course, the detail and type of plan varies greatly with the level and responsibility of the manager. For example, first-line supervisors normally prepare plans to aid in meeting the objectives of their departments. Such plans might include a day-by-day breakdown of what needs to be done. Middle-level managers also prepare plans to aid in the accomplishment of their objectives. Normally, the plans of middle management are for a longer duration and are more comprehensive than those of managers working beneath them. Top-level managers develop plans that guide the entire organization.

Short-range plans – generally cover up to one year.

Long-range plans – start at the end of the current year and extend into the future. In practice, most long-range plans span at least three to five years into the future.

Planning Horizon: Short Range versus Long Range

Short-range plans generally cover up to one year. **Long-range plans** start at the end of the current year and extend into the future. How long should a long-range plan be? The question cannot be answered specifically. The right time frame varies with the organization and the nature of the specific environment and activity. What may be long range when operating in a rapidly changing environment may be short range when operating in a relatively static environment. In practice, most long-range plans span at least three to five years, with some extending as far as 20 years into the future. While long-range planning is possible at any level in the organization, it is primarily carried out at the top levels of the organization.

Functional Plans

In addition to being long range or short range, plans are often classified by function or use. The most frequently encountered types of **functional plan** are sales and marketing plans, production plans, financial plans, and personnel plans. Sales and marketing plans are for developing new products/services and selling both present and future products/services. Production plans deal with producing the desired products/services on a timely schedule. Production/operations planning is discussed in depth in Chapter 9. Financial plans primarily deal with meeting the financial commitments and capital expenditures of the organization. Personnel plans, discussed in Chapter 12, relate to the human resource needs of the organization. Many functional plans are interrelated and interdependent. For example, a financial plan would obviously be dependent on production, sales, and personnel plans.

Functional plans – originate from the functional areas of an organization like production, marketing, finance, and personnel.

Operational versus Strategic Plans

Strategic planning is the process which sets forth organizational objectives to be achieved, strategies and policies needed to reach those objectives, and short-range plans to make sure that the strategies are successfully implemented. For all practical purposes, then, strategic planning is analogous to top-level long-range planning. The terms *strategic planning, (top-level) long-range planning,* and *corporate planning* basically mean the same thing and are interchangeable.

Strategic planning covers a relatively long period of time and affects many parts of the organization. It includes the formulation of mission and objectives, and the selection of the means by which the objectives are to be attained.

Operational or **tactical planning** is short-range planning and concentrates on the formulation of functional plans. Production schedules and day-to-day plans are examples of operational plans. However, the distinctions between strategic and operational planning are relative, not absolute. The major difference is the level at which the planning is done. Strategic planning is primarily done by top-level managers; operational planning is done by managers at all levels in the organization and especially by middle- and lower-level managers. Strategic planning is covered in much greater depth in the next chapter.

Strategic planning – analogous to top-level long-range planning; covers a relatively long period of time; affects many parts of the organization; includes the formulation of objectives and the selection of the means by which they are to be attained.

Operational or tactical planning – short-range planning; done primarily by middle- to lower-level managers, it concentrates on the formulation of functional plans.

SUMMARY

This chapter defines and discusses the importance of organizational objectives, defines and illustrates the concept of strategy, and explains the reasons for and types of organizational planning. The relationship among organizational objectives, strategies, and plans is also discussed.

LEARNING OBJECTIVE 1

Explain What an Objective Is and Describe the Cascade Approach for Setting Objectives.

An objective is a statement outlining what you are trying to achieve. Under the cascade approach for setting objectives, the objective-setting process begins at the top with a clear statement of mission. Long-range goals are then formulated from this statement. Derivative objectives are then developed for each major division or department and then for the various subunits. This process continues down throughout the organizational hierarchy.

LEARNING OBJECTIVE 2

Define Organizational Mission and Explain How Mission Relates to Long- and Short-Range Objectives.

Mission defines the basic purpose or purposes of the organization and usually includes a description of the organization's basic products and/or services and a definition of its markets and/or sources of revenue. An organization's mission is actually the broadest and highest level of objectives. It is from the mission that all long-range and short-range objectives are derived.

LEARNING OBJECTIVE 3

Describe Management by Objectives and Identify Its Basic Requirements.

MBO is a philosophy based on converting organizational objectives into personal objectives. The basic requirements of an MBO system are: (1) that individual objectives are jointly set by the subordinate and the superior; (2) individuals are periodically evaluated and receive feedback concerning their performance; and (3) individuals are evaluated and rewarded on the basis of objective attainment.

LEARNING OBJECTIVE 4

Define Strategy and Distinguish between Corporate, Business, and Functional Level Strategies.

A strategy outlines the basic steps that management plans to take in order to reach an objective or set of objectives. Corporate strategies address what businesses a multibusiness organization will be in and how resources will be allocated among those businesses. Business strategies focus on how to compete in a given business. Functional strategies deal with the activities of the different functional areas of a business.

LEARNING OBJECTIVE 5

Differentiate between Policies, Procedures, and Rules.

Policies are broad, general guides to action which constrain or direct objective attainment. A procedure is a series of related steps or tasks expressed in chronological order for a specific purpose. A rule is a type of policy that requires specific and definite actions to be taken or not taken in a given situation. Procedures and rules are actually subsets of policies.

LEARNING OBJECTIVE 6

Define Managerial Planning and Distinguish between Formal and Informal Planning.

Managerial planning is the process of deciding what objectives to pursue during a future time period and what to do to achieve those objectives. Formal planning occurs when a written, documented plan is developed through an identifiable process. Informal planning does not produce a written document.

LEARNING OBJECTIVE 7

Differentiate between Long-Range and Short-Range Plans.

What is considered long range in one environment may be short range in another environment; the time frame varies with the organization and the nature of its specific environment. However, short-range plans generally cover up to one year and long-range plans start at the end of the current year and extend into the future.

LEARNING OBJECTIVE 8

Contrast Strategic Planning with Operational Planning.

Strategic planning covers a relatively long period of time; affects many parts of the organization; includes the formulation of objectives and the selection of the means by which the objectives are to be obtained. Operational or tactical planning is short range and concentrates on the formulation of functional strategies.

REVIEW QUESTIONS

1. What is the purpose of organizational objectives?
2. Describe the cascade approach to setting objectives.
3. What questions must be answered in identifying an organization's present business? What area must be investigated in identifying an organization's future business?
4. List several areas in which objectives might be set by an organization.
5. What is management by objectives? What are the three minimum requirements of an MBO system?
6. What is a corporate strategy? A business strategy? A functional strategy?
7. What is the purpose of a grand strategy?

8. What are policies?
9. What is planning? What questions does planning answer?
10. Discuss the relationship between objectives and planning. Give an example of this relationship.
11. Why is it necessary to plan? Distinguish between formal and informal planning. How is most planning conducted?

DISCUSSION QUESTIONS

1. What percentage of managers do you think have a clear understanding of what they are supposed to do? How might this percentage be improved?
2. Many managers believe: Policy should always be made at the top. What do you think?
3. "How can we develop long-range objectives and strategies when we do not know where we are going tomorrow?" is a question often posed by managers. How would you answer this question?
4. Discuss the following statement: Planning is something managers should do when they have nothing else to do.

REFERENCES & ADDITIONAL READINGS

[1] Anthony Raia, *Managing by Objectives* (Glenview, Ill: Scott, Foresman, 1974), p. 30.

[2] Peter F. Drucker, *The Practice of Management* (New York: Harper & Row, 1954), p. 51.

[3] Ibid., pp. 50–57.

[4] Raia, *Managing by Objectives,* p. 38.

[5] George A. Steiner, *Top Management Planning* (New York: Macmillan, 1969), p. 237.

[6] David C. D. Rogers, *Corporate Strategy and Long-Range Planning* (Ann Arbor, Mich: Landis Press, 1973), p. 12.

[7] J. J. Hemphill, "Personal Variables and Administrative Styles," *Behavioral Science and Educational Administration* (Chicago: National Society for the Study of Education, 1964), chap. 8.

[8] A. L. Comrey, W. High, and R. C. Wilson, "Factors Influencing Organization Effectiveness: A Survey of Aircraft Workers," *Personnel Psychology* 8 (1955), pp. 79–99.

[9] For a discussion of these studies, see John A. Pearce II, Elizabeth B. Freeman, and Richard D. Robinson, Jr., "The Tenuous Link between Formal Strategic Planning and Financial Performance," *Academy of Management Review,* October 1987, pp. 658–73.

INCIDENT

Hudson Shoe Company

Mr. John Hudson, president of Hudson Shoe Company, and his wife spent the month of February on a long vacation in Santo Oro in Central America. After two weeks, Mr. Hudson became restless and started thinking about an idea he had considered for several years but had been too busy to pursue—entering the foreign market.

Mr. Hudson's company, located in a midwestern city, was started some 50 years earlier by his father, now deceased. It has remained a family enterprise, with his brother David in charge of production, his brother Sam the comptroller, and his brother-in-law Bill Owens taking care of product development. Bill and David share responsibility for quality control; Bill often works with Sam on administrative matters and advertising campaigns. Many competent subordinates are also employed. The company has one of the finest reputations in the shoe industry. Their integrity of product is to be envied and is a source of great pride to the company.

During John's stay in Santo Oro, he decided to visit some importers of shoes. He spoke to several and was most impressed with Señor Lopez of Bueno Compania. After checking Señor Lopez's bank and personal references, his impression was confirmed. Señor Lopez said he would place a small initial order if the samples proved satisfactory. John immediately phoned his office and requested that they rush samples of their best numbers to Señor Lopez. These arrived a few days before John left for home. Shortly after arriving home, John was pleased to receive an order for 1,000 pairs of shoes from Señor Lopez.

John stayed in touch with Lopez by telephone; within two months after the initial order, Hudson Shoe received an order for 5,000 additional pairs of shoes per month. Business continued at this level for about two years until Señor Lopez visited the plant. He was impressed and increased his monthly order from 5,000 to 10,000 pairs of shoes.

This precipitated a crisis at Hudson Shoe Company, and the family held a meeting. They had to decide whether to increase their capacity with a sizable capital investment or drop some of their customers. They did not like the idea of eliminating loyal customers but did not want to make a major investment. David suggested that they run a second shift, which solved the problem nicely.

A year later, Lopez again visited and left orders for 15,000 pairs per month. He also informed them that more effort and expense was now required on his part for a wide distribution of the shoes. In addition to his regular 5 percent commission, he asked John for an additional commission of $1 per pair of shoes. When John hesitated, Lopez assured him that Hudson could raise their selling price by $1 and nothing would be lost. John felt uneasy but went along because the business was easy, steady, and most profitable. A few of Hudson's smaller customers had to be dropped.

By the end of the next year, Lopez was placing orders for 20,000 pairs per month. He asked that Hudson bid on supplying boots for the entire police force of the capital city of Santo Oro. Hudson received the contract and within a year, was supplying the army and navy of Santo Oro and three other Central American countries with their needs.

Again, several old Hudson customers could not get their orders filled. Other Hudson customers were starting to complain of late deliveries. Also, Hudson seemed to be less willing to accept returns at the end of the season or to offer markdown allowances or advertising money. None of this was necessary with their export business. However, Hudson Shoe did decide to cling to their largest domestic customer—the largest mail order chain in the United States.

In June of the following year, Lopez made a trip to Hudson Shoe. He informed John that in addition to his $1 per pair, it would be necessary to give the Minister of Revenue $1 per pair if he was to continue granting import licenses. Moreover, the defense ministers, who approved the army and navy orders in each country where they did business, also wanted $1 per pair. Again, selling prices could be increased accordingly. Lopez informed John that shoe manufacturers in the United States and two other countries were most anxious to have this business at any terms. John asked for 10 days to discuss this with his partners. Lopez agreed and returned home to await their decision. The morning of the meeting of the board of directors of the Hudson Shoe Company, a wire was received from the domestic chain stating that they would not be buying from Hudson next season. John Hudson called the meeting to order.

Questions

1. What were the objectives of Hudson Shoe?

2. What policies existed?

3. Do you agree with Hudson's strategy?

4. What would you do if you were John Hudson?

EXERCISE

Baker's Business

Y ou are the manager of the Baker Company, a small national company engaged in the manufacture and distribution of household gadgets such as bottle openers and ice crackers. The company is 60 years old and was founded by your spouse's grandfather. Baker became unionized six years ago and is still located in its original building (which has been slightly modernized and added on to). The company's income statement for last year and some additional information are given in Exhibits 1 and 2.

A. With regard to the Baker Company, rank the following general objectives in the relative order of importance that you think the company should follow (1 = Most important; 6 = Least important).

      1. To continue to grow.

      2. To provide for employee welfare (pay good wages, provide attractive fringe benefits, maintain present work forces, safety, etc.).

      3. To increase profits by increasing sales and/or reducing costs.

      4. To stay ahead of the competition.

      5. To maintain satisfactory operations: smooth production, schedules, deliveries, etc.

      6. To produce quality products and thus promote the reputation of the company.

B. Write a specific objective statement for each of the general areas listed in A. Make any assumptions necessary for realistic objectives.

E X H I B I T   1

BAKER COMPANY
1988 Income Statement

Total sales of 826,000 units at $5.60 . . . . $4,626,000

Cost of goods sold

	UNITS		RATE		
Raw materials					
Opening inventory	349,000	@	$2.308	$ 805,000	
Purchases	825,000	@	2.280	1,881,000	
Total available	1,174,000	@	2.288	2,686,000	
Less closing inventory	349,000	@	2.288	799,000	
Work in progress					
Material	825,000	@	2.288	1,888,000	
Labor (.382 hours per unit)	825,000	@	4.800	1,512,000	
Fixed costs	825,000	@	0.655	540,000	
Total	825,000	@	4.776	3,940,000	
Opening inventory	140,000	@	3.500	490,000	
Total in process	965,000				
Less closing inventory	132,000	@	3.500	462,000	
Finished goods					
Manufactured	833,000	@	4.764	3,968,000	
Opening inventory	441,000	@	4.768	2,103,000	
Total available	1,274,000	@	4.765	6,071,000	
Less closing inventory	448,000	@	4.765	2,135,000	
Cost of goods sold	826,000	@	4.765		3,936,000
Gross margin					690,000
Other expenditures					
Marketing				210,000	
Research and development				125,000	
Market research information				5,000	
Total other expenditures					340,000
Taxable income					350,000
Income taxes					182,000
Net profit after taxes					$ 168,000

E X H I B I T 2 Baker Company Statistics

Sales and net profits (for previous five years):

YEAR	SALES	NET PROFIT
1987	$4,649,000	$181,000
1986	4,760,000	188,000
1985	5,040,000	218,000
1984	4,561,000	119,000
1983	4,328,000	(48,000)

Miscellaneous data (1988):

Salaried workers	21
Wage-earning employees	180
Avoidable resignations	
Salaried	7
Wage earners	38
Worker-days lost	
Voluntary work stoppages	980
Accidents	12
Absences	620
Grievances filed[*]	19
New products introduced[†]	7
Increase in new customers	12%
Increase in customer complaints	19%
Market share	25%

[*] Eleven were settled at the local level. Of the eight grievances settled by arbitration, seven were in favor of the company.

[†] Average over the past five years has been four new products.

8 Strategic Management

LEARNING OBJECTIVES

After studying this chapter,
you should be able to:

1 Define strategic management and explain its relationship to strategic planning.

2 Discuss the roles of different levels of management in the strategic management process.

3 Name the three phases of the strategic management process.

4 Outline the five major chronological stages of the strategic management process.

5 Summarize the importance of assessing the external environment.

6 Name the three basic types of forecasts.

Once upon a time there were two pigs (a third one had gone to market and disappeared) who were faced with the problem of protecting themselves from a wolf.

One pig was an old-timer in this wolf-fending business, and he saw the problem right away—just build a house strong enough to resist the huffing and puffing he had experienced before. So, the first pig built his wolf-resistant house right away out of genuine, reliable lath and plaster.

The second pig was green at this wolf business, but he was thoughtful. He decided he would analyze the wolf problem a bit. He sat down and drew up a matrix (which, of course, is pig latin for a blank sheet of paper) and listed the problem, analyzed the problem into components and possibilities of wolf strategy, listed the design objectives of his wolf-proof house, determined the functions that his fortress should perform, designed and built his house, and waited to see how well it worked.

All this time, the old-timer pig was laughing at the planner pig and vehemently declined to enter into this kind of folly. He had built wolf-proof houses before, and he had lived and prospered, hadn't he? He said to the planner pig, "If you know what you are doing, you don't have to go through all that jazz." And with this, he went fishing or rooting or whatever it is that pigs do in their idle hours.

The second pig worked on his system anyway and designed for predicted contingencies.

One day the mean old wolf passed by the two houses (they both looked the same—after all, a house is just a house). He thought that a pig dinner was just what he wanted. He walked up to the first pig's house and uttered a warning to the old-timer, which was roundly rejected, as usual. With this, the wolf, instead of huffing and puffing, pulled out a sledge hammer, knocked the door down, and ate the old-timer for dinner.

Still not satisfied, the wolf walked to the house of the pig who had developed a strategy and repeated his act. Suddenly, a trap door in front of the house opened, and the wolf dropped into a deep, dark pit, never to be heard from again.

Morals: 1.   *They are not making wolves like they used to.*
          2.   *It's hard to teach old pigs new tricks.*
          3.   *If you want to keep the wolf away from your door, you'd better develop a strategic plan.*

ROGER A. KAUFMAN*

---

* Adapted from Roger A. Kaufman, "Why System Engineering? A Fable" (original source unknown).

*T*he rate of change in the environment has increased in modern times. Therefore, it is more and more important for managers to keep their plans and strategies current. The process used to do this for the overall organization is referred to as strategic management. In essence, **strategic management** is the application of the basic planning process at the highest levels of the organization. Through the strategic management process, top management determines the long-run direction and performance of an organization by ensuring careful formulation, proper implementation, and continuous evaluation of plans and strategies. In essence, strategic management is the process that encompasses the development, implementation, and continuous evaluation of strategic plans.

It is entirely possible to prepare a formal plan with a well-defined strategy and not practice strategic management. With such a situation, the plan could become outmoded as changes occur in the environment. Avon (see Managers at Work 8–1) is an example of how one company's plan became obsolete. Practicing strategic management does not ensure that an organization will meet all changes successfully—but it does increase the odds.

Although guided by top management, successful strategic management involves many different levels in the organization. For example, top management may ask middle- and lower-level managers for input when formulating top-level plans. Once top-level plans have been finalized, different organizational units may be asked to formulate plans for their respective areas. A proper strategic management process helps ensure that plans throughout the different levels of the organization are coordinated and mutually supportive.

Setting the organization's mission; defining what business or businesses the organization will be in; setting objectives; developing, implementing, and evaluating strategies; and adjusting these components as necessary are all involved in the strategic management process. While the basic process is similar in most organizations, differences exist in the formality of the process, levels of managerial involvement, and degree of institutionalization of the process.

All organizations engage in the strategic management process either formally or informally. Organizations that consciously engage in strategic management generally follow some type of formalized process for making decisions and taking actions that affect their future direction. In the absence of a formal process, strategic decisions are made in a piecemeal fashion. An informal approach to strategy, however, does not necessarily mean that the organization doesn't know what it is doing. It simply means the organization does not engage in any type of formalized process for initiating and managing strategy.

Strategic management – formulation, proper implementation, and continuous evaluation of strategic plans—these determine the long-run direction and performance of an organization.

MANAGERS AT WORK 8–1

Changing Environment for Avon

The typical Avon sales representative has always been a housewife who wants to earn pocket money on a flexible schedule. Her customers are other women in her community who more often than not, are home during the day. The success of Avon's door-to-door sales business has been largely dependent on recruiting good sales representatives—and a lot of them.

In the 1970s, economic conditions dictated two paychecks for many families, and social changes brought about a greater variety of job opportunities for women. The result was record numbers of women entering the full-time job market. For Avon, the changes dealt a double blow—its customer base and potential sales force began to disappear. After suffering a sharp decline in sales and earnings, Avon is now beginning to rethink its sales approach.

Source: "For Avon, Everything Depends on Recruiting," *Financial World*, December 31, 1983, pp. 28–29.

RESPONSIBILITY FOR STRATEGIC MANAGEMENT

Successful strategic management involves the cooperation of several levels in the organization. While the earlier discussed definition of strategic management emphasizes the role of top managers, any successful strategic management effort requires the active involvement of *all* levels of management. The roles of the different levels of management in the strategic management process are discussed below.

The Role of Top Management

Top management, and particularly the chief executive officer (CEO), must take the lead in establishing the strategic management process. George Steiner, a nationally recognized expert on strategic management, has stated, "There can and will be no effective formal strategic planning in an organization in which the chief executive does not give it firm support and make sure that others in the organization understand his depth of commitment."[1] This statement leaves little room for doubt concerning the importance of the CEO's involvement. In addition to being personally committed to the process, the CEO must make sure that others in the organization are aware of this commitment. This emphasizes the fact that a CEO's commitment must include hands-on involvement. A good example is J. C. Penney, Inc., which is known for the excellence of its planning process. Donald V. Siebert, Penney's former

MANAGERS AT WORK 8–2

Strategic Management at Ford: Centers of Excellence

"To look beyond one's nose" is an old adage. Every organization has to look ahead for growth, stability, and prosperity. Recently Ford Motor Company has been one of the most profitable car companies in the world. From a profitability standpoint, Ford sped past its bigger rival, General Motors Corporation, in 1986, earning $3.3 billion on $62.7 billion in sales versus GM's $2.9 billion on $102.8 billion in sales. For the first half of 1987, Ford's $2.9 billion in profits topped the combined earnings of both GM and Chrysler Corporation.

In an effort to keep such momentum going into the 1990s and beyond, Ford has committed itself to strategic management. Chief Executive Donald Peterson, the mild-mannered engineer who turned Ford Motor Company around, is reorganizing his design and engineering teams into what he calls "Centers of Excellence." Located in different countries, the centers will work on key components for cars. Designers in each market will then style exteriors and passenger compartments to appeal to local tastes. Each car usually will be built on the continent where it is to be sold. Through strategic management, Peterson hopes to avoid duplicating efforts and to capitalize on the expertise of Ford's specialists.

Source: "Can Ford Stay on Top?" *Business Week,* September 20, 1987, pp. 78–86.

chairman and CEO, described the system and his commitment to it in these words: "We did our first formal five-year planning around 1963, and since then, our projections have been updated annually. . . . Our goal is to set guidelines for delegated decision making to give our operating managers an idea of what (top) management expects."[2] Many attempts at strategic management have failed because a CEO professed commitment but never became personally involved in the process.

Other members of the organization take their cues from the CEO. If he or she demonstrates involvement, others are likely to follow. Unfortunately, the reverse is also true: if the CEO exhibits a lack of involvement, others will interpret this as a sign of disinterest. The importance of the CEO and the top management's active involvement cannot be overstated. Managers at Work 8–2 describes how the CEO of Ford Motor Company is using strategic management to guide Ford into the future.

The Role of Middle- and Lower-Level Managers

In many cases middle- and lower-level managers do not have to be concerned about how to design and manage the planning systems, as this is done at top levels in the organization. However, any successful strategic management effort is dependent on inputs and cooperation from middle- and lower-level managers.[3] There is also evidence that middle- and lower-level managers are being asked to assume a more active role in the strategic management process.[4]

At the very least, middle- and lower-level managers must understand the strategic management process and system well enough to be able to provide the inputs required of them. The inputs naturally vary from situation to situation, but they often relate to operating capabilities. For example, are there enough machines to supply the demand for the product? Will we have enough personnel to service a 10 percent increase in customers? Middle- and lower-level managers typically provide information to top management relating to the internal and external analyses and to the selection of long-range and intermediate-range objectives. The most visible involvement of middle- and lower-level managers is in implementing the chosen corporate and business strategies by formulating and carrying out the necessary functional strategies.

Middle- and lower-level managers should know what role they are expected to play in the strategic management process. They should also be aware of corporate level plans so that their operating plans can be properly formulated. Involving these managers in the strategic management process not only provides needed information but also greatly reduces resistance to any changes that may result from the process.

Strategic planning – covers a relatively long period of time; affects many parts of the organization; includes the formulation of objectives and the selection of the means by which they are to be attained.

Formulation phase – first phase in strategic management, where the initial strategic plan is developed.

Implementation phase – second phase in strategic management, where the strategic plan is put into effect.

Evaluation phase – third phase in strategic management, where the implemented strategic plan is monitored, evaluated, and updated.

PHASES OF STRATEGIC MANAGEMENT

The strategic management process is composed of three major phases: (1) formulating the **strategic plan,** (2) implementing the strategic plan, and (3) evaluating the strategic plan. The **formulation phase** is concerned with developing the initial strategic plan. The **implementation phase** involves implementing the strategic plan that has been formulated. The **evaluation phase** stresses the importance of continuously evaluating and updating the strategic plan after it has been implemented. Each of the three phases of the strategic management process is critical to its success. A breakdown in any one area can easily cause the entire process to fail.

A STRATEGIC MANAGEMENT MODEL

Although different organizations may use somewhat different approaches to the strategic management process, most successful approaches share several common components and a common sequence. The components and sequences represented in Figure 8–1 can be used to describe the strategic management process.[5] As indicated by the categories listed in bold print in the center of Figure 8–1, the strategic management process includes five chronologial stages:

F I G U R E 8–1   The Strategic Management Process

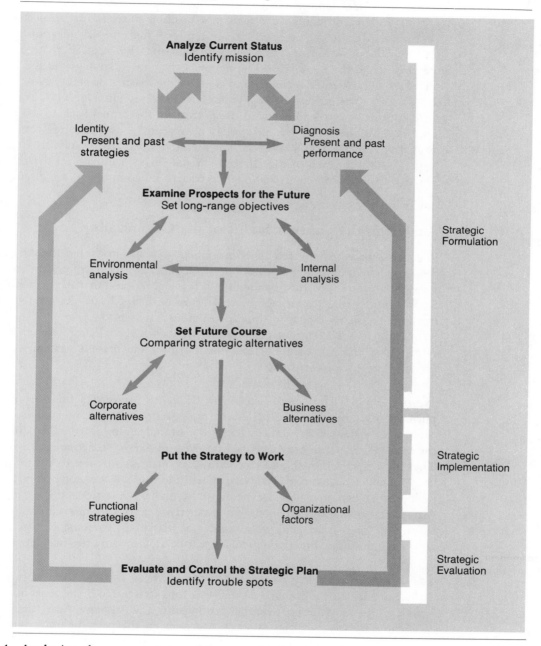

1. Analyzing the current status of the organization.
2. Examining the prospects for the future.
3. Setting the future course.
4. Putting the strategy to work.
5. Evaluating and controlling the strategic plan.

The logic behind this breakdown is that any organization must first analyze and clearly understand its current situation. Once an organization has a firm grip on its present status, it is then in a position to examine prospects for the future. After future prospects have been identified, the organization must set a future course through careful evaluation and choice of alternatives. In the next stage, the organization implements the chosen strategy. In the final stage, the organization evaluates and controls the selected strategy. Note that the strategic management process is presented as an iterative process, as indicated by the arrows leading from the bottom of the model back to the top. The implication is that the process is never-ending and requires constant evaluation, updating, and revising. The double-headed arrows indicate a two-way relationship: each of the affected variables has an impact on the other. The five major components and their respective subcomponents are discussed in greater depth in the following sections.

Analyzing the Current Status of the Organization

Regardless of whether strategic management is being instituted for the first time in a new or existing organization, the organization's current performance, mission, and strategy must be identified. It is only logical that these variables be analyzed before the organization's future is mapped out. As obvious as this may be, many managers appear to ignore this step.

In Figure 8–1, three groups of variables are shown as the major determinants of an organization's current status: mission, past and present strategies, and past and present performance.

Identifying Mission. As discussed in Chapter 7, *mission* defines the basic purposes of the organization. Ideally, an organization's mission is clearly recognized and widely known throughout the organization. Even when this is the case, however, an organization may wish to alter or redefine its mission. Thus, an organization should periodically evaluate its mission to ensure that the mission is current. In situations where the mission has not been clearly defined, it is absolutely necessary to do so. In small organizations, this normally requires the owner or owners to define exactly what the organization is trying to produce and/or sell and what market or markets it is trying to serve. In large organizations, these same issues must be identified by top management.

Identifying Past and Present Strategies. It is a well-known fact that Sears Roebuck & Co. embarked on a conscious strategy to upgrade its quality image in the 1960s. Prior to implementing this new strategy, Sears first had to identify clearly what its strategy had been in the past. In other words, before a strategic change can be developed and implemented, the past and present strategies must be clarified.

General questions to be addressed include the following: Has past strategy been consciously developed? If not, can past history be analyzed to identify what implicit strategy has evolved? If so, has the strategy been recorded in written form? In either case, a strategy or series of strategies, as reflected by the organization's past actions and intentions, should be identified.

Diagnosing Past and Present Performance. In order to evaluate how past strategies have worked and to determine whether strategic changes are needed, the organization's performance record must be examined. How is the organization currently performing? How has the organization performed over the last several years? Is the performance trend moving up or down? These are all questions that management must address before attempting to formulate any type of future strategy. Evaluating an organization's performance usually involves some type of in-depth financial analysis and diagnosis.

Examining the Prospects for the Future

The first step in looking toward the future is to decide what the long- and intermediate-range objectives should be in light of the current mission. However, these objectives cannot be accurately established without examining the internal and external environments. Thus, establishing the long- and intermediate-range objectives and analyzing the internal and external environments are concurrent processes that influence each other. These circular relationships are shown by the two-way arrows in Figure 8–1.

Setting Long-Range Objectives. Given the mission, what does the organization hope to achieve and accomplish over the long term? In establishing long-range objectives, the emphasis is on corporate- and divisional-level objectives, as opposed to departmental objectives.

The first step is to decide which areas of the organization's business should be covered by objectives. As discussed in Chapter 7, common choices include sales, market share, costs, product introductions, return on investment, and societal goals. Once the areas for objectives have been decided on, the next step is to determine the desired magnitudes and associated time frames for accomplishment.

Conducting an Internal Analysis. The basic idea in conducting an internal analysis is to perform an objective assessment of the organization's current strengths and weaknesses. What things does the organization do well? What things does the organization do poorly? From a resource perspective, what are the organization's strengths and weaknesses?

As emphasized earlier, the process of setting long-range objectives is influenced by the results of the internal analysis. Similarly, the internal analysis should focus on factors affected by the long-range objectives. Thus, there is a circular relationship between these variables.

Assessing the External Environment. An organization's **external environment** consists of everything outside the organization, but the focus of this assessment is on the external factors that have an impact on its business.

External environment – all of those factors that exist outside of the organization that have an impact or effect on the organization.

Such factors are classified by their proximity to the organization: they are either in its broad environment or in its competitive environment. Broad environmental factors are somewhat removed from the organization but can still influence it. General economic conditions, social, political, and technological trends represent common factors in the broad environment. Factors in the competitive environment are close to and come in regular contact with the organization. Stockholders, suppliers, competitors, labor unions, and customers represent members of the competitive environment.

Assessing the external environment emphasizes the fact that organizations do not operate in a vacuum and are very much affected by their surroundings. Because of the uncertainties involved in forecasting the future impact of environmental factors, this is one of the most difficult and yet more critical parts of the strategic management process. The section at the end of this chapter discusses some of the forecasting methods used by organizations to predict the impact of external factors. This portion of the model concludes the reflective part of the strategic management process. Having analyzed its current status and examined its prospects for the future, the organization is then in a position to consider its future course.

Setting the Future Course

Setting the future course involves generating possible strategic alternatives, based on the mission and long-range objectives, and then selecting the most promising alternative.

Comparing Strategic Alternatives. The goal in this phase of the process is to identify the feasible strategic alternatives (in light of everything that has been done up to this point) and then to select the best alternative. Given the mission and long-range objectives, what are the feasible strategic alternatives? The internal and external environmental analyses also place limitations on the feasible strategic alternatives. For example, the results of an internal financial analysis could severely limit an organization's options for expansion. Similarly, the results of an external analysis of population trends might also limit an organization's expansion plans. Once a set of feasible alternatives has been defined, the final strategic choice must then be made.

The evaluation and final choice of an appropriate strategic alternative involves the integration of the mission, objectives, internal analysis, and external analysis. In this phase an attempt is made to select the overall, or grand, strategy that offers the organization its best chance to achieve its mission and objectives through actions that are compatible with its capacity for risk and its value structure. Once the grand strategy has been identified, additional substrategies must then be selected to support it.

In the case of diversified, multibusiness organizations, comparing strategic alternatives involves assessing the attractiveness of each of the different businesses as well as the overall business mix. The next step is to evaluate specific alternative strategies for each business unit. Thus, the emphasis in this phase of the model is on the need for generating strategic alternatives at both the corporate level and the business level.

Putting the Strategy to Work

The fourth section of the model emphasizes the importance of translating planned strategy into organizational actions. Given that the grand strategy and supporting substrategies have been clearly identified, what actions must be taken to implement these strategies? Strategy implementation involves everything that must be done to put the strategy in motion successfully. Necessary actions include determining and implementing the most appropriate organizational structure, developing short-range objectives, and establishing functional strategies.

Implementing Strategy: Organizational Factors. Not only does an organization have a strategic history, but it also has existing structures, policies, and systems. Although each of these factors can change as a result of a new strategy, each must be assessed and dealt with as part of the implementation process.

Even though an organization's structure can always be altered, the associated costs may be very high. For example, a reorganization might result in substantial hiring and training costs for newly structured jobs. Thus, from a very practical standpoint, an organization's current structure places certain restrictions on how a strategy should be implemented.

The strategy must fit with current organizational policies, or the conflicting policies must be modified. Often, past policies heavily influence the extent to which future policies can be altered. For example, it has been the policy of the A. T. Cross Company (manufacturers of the world-renowned writing instruments) to unconditionally guarantee its products for life. This policy is well known and is now expected by many of the company's customers. Because of these expectations, it would now be very difficult for Cross to discontinue its guarantee policy.

Similarly, organizational systems that are currently in place can affect how the strategy might best be implemented. These systems can be either formal or informal. Examples include information systems, compensation systems, communication systems, and control systems. These systems are discussed at length in later chapters of this book.

Implementing Strategy: Functional Strategies. As defined in Chapter 7, functional strategies are the means by which the business strategy is operationalized. Functional strategies outline the specific short-range actions to be taken by the different functional units of the organization (production, marketing, finance, personnel, etc.) in order to implement the business strategy.

The purpose of functional strategies is to make the corporate- and business-level strategies a reality.

The formulation of functional strategies plays a major role in determining the feasibility of the corporate- and business-level strategies. If sound functional strategies cannot be formulated and implemented, it may be that the corporate- and/or business-level strategies need to be reworked. As the old saying goes, the functional strategies are the point where "the rubber meets the road."

Evaluating and Controlling the Strategic Plan

After things have been put into motion, the next challenge is to monitor continuously the organization's progress toward its long-range objectives and mission. Is the grand strategy working, or should revisions be made? Where are problems likely to occur? The emphasis here is on making the organization's managers aware of the problems that are likely to occur and of the actions that should be taken if these problems do occur. A recent survey found that a significant number of firms that do engage in strategic planning do not provide for a system to track the plan.[6] This indicates that strategic control and evaluation are areas on which many organizations need to work.

FORECASTING ENVIRONMENTAL FACTORS

Almost all managers have some way of forecasting or anticipating the future—especially as it relates to their jobs and areas of responsibility. For example, a top-level manager may want to forecast the future demand for a certain product. A first-line supervisor may need to forecast next week's production. Generally, a forecast tells a manager what to expect in view of the current and predicted situation.

Event outcome forecasts – try to predict the outcome or result of a highly probable future event.

Event timing forecasts – try to predict when a known event will occur.

Time series forecasts – basing a prediction or trend on historical data.

Types of Forecasts

Almost all forecasts can be placed in one of three classes: (1) **event outcome forecasts,** (2) **event timing forecasts,** and (3) **time series forecasts.**[7] Event outcome forecasts are concerned with predicting the outcome of a highly probable future event. Some examples of event outcome forecasts are: What will be the total cost for building our new plant? How much will it cost to market the new product being developed? or Who will take over as department manager when Mr. Jones retires next year?

Event timing forecasts are concerned with predicting when a given event will occur. Examples of event timing forecasts include the following: When will we have a new model of product X? When will we be able to get the property rezoned? or When will the new equipment arrive?

Frontlines

Laura Henderson, founder and president of Prospect Associates.

I ntrapreneurship occurs when employees are given free rein to develop their own products and the financial support to bring them to market. This concept was first refined, and the term coined, by enterpreneur Gifford Pinchot III and has been informally adopted by Laura Henderson, founder and president of Prospect Associates, Rockville, Maryland.

Henderson's company provides professional and technical services to the biomedical community, including communications, library searches, database services, and data analysis to the National Institutes of Health. Henderson adopted intrapreneurship when she realized she lacked the range of technical skills and knowledge needed for Prospect to grow. She hired a staff of experts who were willing to take responsibility for their own area of the company.

The implementation of intrapreneurship, coupled with an American society that has become more health conscious, has enabled Prospect Associates to grow from 15 to 150 employees in nine years and to realize 1988 fiscal year sales of $7.8 million. (Chapter 1)

Students believe the young and the educated are today's entrepreneurs.

THE ENTREPRENEUR'S CHANGING IMAGE

R ags To Riches—Good-Bye Horatio Alger. Hello Donald Trump. Unlike past generations, today's youth no longer perceives entrepreneurs as "rags to riches" success stories. Like such silver-spoon successes as Trump, "riches to riches" may be more on target. According to a recent survey by Research & Forecasts Inc. in New York, 89 percent of college students believe entrepreneurs come from middle-income or well-to-do backgrounds. A majority of the 502 students polled (53 percent) also believe that entrepreneurs are college graduates, and 8 percent think they have postgraduate degrees. Almost half (42 percent) think that today's typical entrepreneurs are under 30 years old. (Chapter 1)

HOW STUDENTS PERCEIVE ENTREPRENEURS

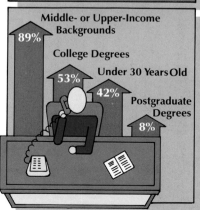

89% Middle- or Upper-Income Backgrounds

53% College Degrees

42% Under 30 Years Old

8% Postgraduate Degrees

A QUESTION OF TURF

As entrepreneurs we are always negotiating for something. Negotiating on your own turf means you control the environment, which can be a crucial advantage. I learned the hazards of the other fellow's turf in my ealier position as president of Benrus Corp. Kuwait's national soccer team had won the Pan-Arabic championships, and a rich men's sporting club wanted 6,000 digital watches, which it was going to give to the national players and the club's members. I decided to ask for 30 dinar ($22) per watch; I would let them get me down to 20 dinar. The president and I had barely said hello when he announced that his best offer was $8 a watch. After some unproductive talk he insisted we watch the soccer game. The only time he spoke was during the infrequent time-outs. The president was using the soccer game to control the ebb and flow of our own match. In the end, I persuaded the president to raise his offer by all of 25 cents per watch. The Kuwaitis had done their homework and found out from industry sources that we were discontinuing that line of watches and would be happy to unload them at any reasonable price. Combining that knowledge with their ability to keep me off balance throughout the negotiations had made them invincible. (Chapter 3)

Courtesy of Remington.

Victor Kiam

"Negotiation means using the facts, the ground and human nature."

Innovative people often display a "greed for new things" writes management expert Peter Drucker. Drucker feels that creativity can become systematic in an organization, making a company breakthrough-prone. It is important to "focus managerial vision on opportunity. If problems are the only thing being discussed, opportunity will die of neglect." The development of breakthrough ideas is closely tied to positive attitude. Managers must set the right mood to get creative results. (Chapters 5 and 6)

Courtesy of Jerry Bauer

Courtesy of UPI/Bettman Newsphotos.

It's risky to deviate from the standards that made you successful, as Chrysler Corp. recently discovered. A federal grand jury found that Chrysler executives had been driving cars with the odometers disconnected. These cars, some with thousands of miles on them, others in accidents and repaired, were being sold as new. What happened to the good corporate practice of having executives test drive cars off the assembly lines? The executives lost sight of the company standards of honesty and integrity that had made Chrysler successful, exploiting this practice and using the cars for personal purposes. Once ethical standards have been set, it is critical that they be reflected in the routine activities of an organization. They serve as important guideposts by which a company reaches its goals. (Chapter 4)

PUTTING AN END TO MEMO MADNESS

One company has abolished memos and created a new form of communication that forces people to talk, not type.

If you're an employee at ATI Medical Inc., and you're caught writing a memo, you may find yourself out of a job. "Memos don't serve any purpose," says Paul Stevenson, president of the Glendale, California–based company that rents medical equipment to hospitals. "They waste valuable time and file space, and hinder communication between employees." The no-memo policy instigated by Stevenson when he founded the company five years ago, doesn't mince words—it states that violators will be fired.

Instead of memos, Stevenson uses "PAPCOEs"—a reverse acronym that stands for "enunciations of corporate policies and procedures." While memos are churned out at a moment's notice, PAPCOEs are an event—only 12 have been written in the company's history. "The sole purpose of PAPCOEs is to state a policy change," says Stevenson. "Policies are the only things that need to be written down and kept on record." Unlike memos, PAPCOEs can't be sent to just a few people. "That's what we have talking for," says Stevenson. "You can't get feedback from a slip of paper."

"So far the no-memo policy has worked beautifully," says

Stevenson, whose company now has 150 employees, 30 offices, and sales of $14 million. "It saves hours of time each week and, most important, everyone at ATI has learned to talk to each other. And that means more ideas are generated and then put into action." (Chapter 5)

Courtesy of ATI Medical.

THE TRUTH ABOUT COMMUNICATING

Spreading the Word. How well a company performs may depend on how good its internal lines of communication are, according to a study conducted by Hay Research for Management in Philadelphia. The study found that 79 percent of middle-management employees in high-performing companies were satisfied with the amount of internal information they got, compared with 69 percent at low-performing companies. Among professional employees (computer programmers, data processors, and accountants) at these high-performing

SKILLS VALUED BY M.B.A.s

COMMUNICATION 89% SKILLS

INITIATIVE 86%

INTUITION 50%

CUNNING 4%

M.B.A. students feel that communication is more important than cunning.

organizations, 64 percent were satisfied, compared with only 34 percent at less successful firms. Because of this growing awareness of internal

communication needs, managers can use employee feedback to make improvements in this area.

Speak for Yourself. Even those about to enter the work force are placing a greater emphasis on communication. According to a survey conducted by the Los Angeles–based Graduate Management Admission Council, 89 percent of the 2,000 first-year M.B.A. students polled felt that good communication skills were "very important" to their future success as managers; initiative was a close second with 86 percent. Good intuition was rated "very important" by 50 percent. At the low end of the survey were traits such as cunning (4 percent). (Chapter 5)

Frontlines

Courtesy of The Clorox Company.

TRUST YOUR INSTINCTS

Developing intuitive decision-making skills in managers can lead to increased corporate productivity, according to *Small Business Report*. Because today's business environment is characterized by rapid change, decisions based solely on factual reports might soon become obsolete. Increasingly, managers often must act quickly to respond to emerging trends. Companies that encourage managers to use their intuitive skills in problem-solving meetings will gain an edge over the competition. Managers who display the strongest intuitive capabilities should also be given projects that make the most of their ability. (Chapter 6)

In 1957 Hewlett-Packard established the following policy statements:

1 Have objectives.
2 Explain and teach them.
3 Gain agreement, with modification if necessary.
4 Have everyone share in the success of achievement.
5 Be egalitarian to assure that communications are open.

They serve to reinforce the principles of cooperative management—the concept of leading, not directing. They stress a management style that is informal, with give and take discussion, lack of private offices, casual dress, and the universal use of first names. (Chapter 7)

Courtesy of Hewlett-Packard Company.

STRATEGIC BOUNDARIES

Managers don't have to feel trapped by well-thought-out strategic plans. Although few managers would deny the need for a long-term plan, many fear it will become a straitjacket if followed too rigidly. The *Harvard Business Review* suggests looking at your strategic course not as a constraint but as a general

Courtesy of Anheuser-Busch Companies, In

framework within which you can take advantage of the unexpected. The *Review* recommends stepping back every few days and writing down a summary of what your department has been doing. How do the daily dilemmas fit into the broader picture? This will allow you to revise your goals in light of new information or changing circumstances. (Chapters 7 and 8)

MANAGERS AT WORK 8–3

Atari's Failure to Predict Market Downturn

Atari has the dubious distinction of being the video game industry's biggest loser. In 1982, the industrywide sales of video games were a strong 7 million units. At that time, Atari was the number-one video game producer, owning approximately 43 percent of the market. In 1983, customer interest in video games waned considerably, and sales plummeted to 3 million units. Although industrywide losses from the decline in demand and price markdowns totaled $1.5 billion, Atari lost $539 million—roughly one third of the total industry loss. In order to survive, Atari was forced to cut back on virtually all long-term R&D projects and reduce personnel from 7,000 to 2,500 in less than one year.

Source: "A Game Plan for Survival at Atari," *Business Week,* April 9, 1984, p. 32; *The Wall Street Journal,* June 10, 1982, p. 33; *Advertising Age,* February 7, 1983, p. 3.

Time series forecasts attempt to project future trends or values based on historical data. An example of time series forecasts is: Based on past growth patterns, what do we predict the population in a certain area will be in 1995?

Forecasting Methods

Forecasting methods and levels of sophistication vary greatly. The methods employed may vary from educated guesses to computer projections using sophisticated statistical analyses. Several factors determine the most appropriate methods of forecasting. These factors include the nature of the desired forecast, the available expertise, and the available financial resources.

Many managers forecast the future based on experience and past events. Typically, a manager might examine what happened during the last few years and then project this into the future. This method has one obvious drawback: the past may not be representative of the future.

Another popular method of forecasting is to use a **jury of executive opinion.** With this method, several managers get together and devise a forecast based on their pooled opinions. The advantage is simplicity; the disadvantage is that it is not necessarily based on facts.

Statistics and mathematical methods represent the most advanced and reliable approach to forecasting. The advent and recent adaptiveness of electronic computers have made statistical and mathematical forecasting not only possible but accessible. A major drawback is the cost of gathering and analyzing data. Another drawback is that many such analyses require expertise in the field of mathematics, statistics, and computers.

Jury of executive opinion–managers get together and share opinions—from these a forecast is devised.

Statistics and mathematical forecasting methods–data is gathered and interpreted. Requires expertise in math, statistics, and the computer, and can be expensive.

MANAGERS AT WORK 8–4

Computerized Forecasting at Mrs. Fields Cookies

Mrs. Fields, Inc., the cookie company, achieved a profit of 18.5 percent on $87 million sales in 1986, up from $72.6 million a year earlier. The recipe for the success lies in the fact that the 500 company-owned stores in 37 states are controlled by computerized operations linked to the company headquarters. Each of the stores' performance is monitored by its computerized Day Planner Program. This program makes hourly product sales projections based on the previous year's performance and other influencing factors. Influencing factors include such things as holidays, sale days, school days, etc. The computer also aids the store managers with crew scheduling, equipment maintenance, crew applicant interviews, and personnel administration.

Source: "Mrs. Fields Secret Ingredient," *Inc.,* October 1987, pp. 65–70.

The Appendix at the end of this chapter discusses, in greater detail, several of the most frequently used forecasting techniques. Managers at Work 8–3 tells how inaccurate forecasts led to major problems for Atari.

Managers at Work 8–4 describes how one company uses computers to forecast sales.

SUMMARY

This chapter introduces and describes the concept of strategic management. The roles of top, middle, and lower levels of managers in the strategic management process are discussed. Particular emphasis is given to forecasting pertinent variables in the organization's environment.

LEARNING OBJECTIVE 1

Define Strategic Management and Explain Its Relationship to Strategic Planning.
Strategic management is the process of determining the long-run direction and performance of an organization by ensuring careful formulation, proper implementation, and continuous evaluation of plans and strategies. In essence, strategic management is the process that encompasses the development, implementation, and continuous evaluation of strategic plans.

LEARNING OBJECTIVE 2

Discuss the Roles of Different Levels of Management in the Strategic Management Process.
The CEO and top levels of management must give the strategic management process their firm support, and they must communicate this support to

all levels of management. The CEO is the person charged with making strategic management happen. Middle and lower levels of managers must understand the strategic management process and system so that they can provide the input required of them and carry out the necessary implementation strategies. There is evidence that middle- and lower-level managers are becoming increasingly involved in the strategic management process.

LEARNING OBJECTIVE 3

Name the Three Phases of the Strategic Management Process.

The three major phases of the strategic management process are: (1) formulating the strategic plan, (2) implementing the strategic plan, and (3) continuously evaluating and updating the strategic plan.

LEARNING OBJECTIVE 4

Outline the Five Major Chronological Stages of the Strategic Management Process.

The five chronological stages of the strategic management process are: (1) analyzing the current situation, (2) examining the prospects for the future, (3) setting the future course, (4) putting the strategic plan to work, and (5) evaluating and controlling the strategic plan.

LEARNING OBJECTIVE 5

Summarize the Importance of Assessing the External Environment.

Organizations do not operate in a vacuum and are very much affected by changes in their environment. Because of the uncertainties involved in forecasting the future input of environmental factors, this is one of the most difficult, and yet more critical, parts of the strategic management process.

LEARNING OBJECTIVE 6

Name the Three Basic Types of Forecasts.

Almost all forecasts can be classified as one of three types: (1) event outcome forecasts, (2) event timing forecasts, and (3) time series forecasts.

REVIEW QUESTIONS

1. What is strategic management?
2. Who is the one person in an organization most responsible for successfully implementing strategic management?
3. What is required of middle- and lower-level managers in the strategic management process?
4. Name the three major phases of the strategic management process.
5. Recount the five chronological stages of the strategic management process.
6. What are the three classes of forecasts?
7. How does a jury of executive opinion work?

DISCUSSION QUESTIONS

1. Can you resolve the dilemma that strategic planning is easiest where environmental change is least but more useful where environmental change is greatest? How?

2. If you were serving as a strategic management consultant, how might you answer this question: How can I plan for next year when I don't even know what I'm going to do tomorrow?

3. With the rapid pace of change in today's world, why should management even try to forecast the future?

4. What are some of the problems that a top-level manager might experience in attempting to coordinate the plans of various subunits?

REFERENCES & ADDITIONAL READINGS

[1] George B. Steiner, *Strategic Planning: What Every Manager Must Know* (New York: Free Press, 1979), p. 80.

[2] Chester Burger, *The Chief Executive: Realities of Corporate Leadership* (Boston: CBI, 1978), p. 110.

[3] Daniel H. Gray, "Uses and Misuses of Strategic Planning," *Harvard Business Review,* January–February 1986, p. 91.

[4] "The New Breed of Strategic Planner," *Business Week,* September 17, 1984, pp. 62–68.

[5] The model used in this section is from Leslie W. Rue and Phyllis G. Holland, *Strategic Management: Concepts and Experiences* (New York: McGraw-Hill, 1986), pp. 57–62.

[6] Joel E. Ross and Ronnie Silverblatt, "Developing the Strategic Plan," *Industrial Marketing Management,* May 1987, p. 108.

[7] C. W. J. Granger, *Forecasting in Business and Economics* (New York: Academic Press, 1980), pp. 6–10.

INCIDENT

Strategic Planning by a Student

Susan Good is a senior majoring in management at the local university. She is an excellent student with a 3.4 out of a 4.0 grade point average. However, she really hasn't decided on what she wants to do. Her interviews for jobs through the university placement office have confused her even more. Each interviewer has asked her what she wants to do, and she really has had no adequate answer. Because of her dilemma, Susan went to see Professor Chapman, one of her management professors, and discussed the problem with him. His reply was, "Your problem is not all that unusual. Many students feel the same way. Why don't you use some of the strategic planning concepts you have learned in management and develop a personal career plan?"

Questions

1. Can strategic planning concepts be used for personal career planning?
2. Develop a five-year career plan for your own career.

EXERCISE

Developing a Strategic Plan

*A*ssume you have just purchased the Baker Company, discussed in the exercise at the end of Chapter 7.

1. Based on the information available in the exercise, current economic conditions, and local environmental conditions, outline a one-year strategic plan for the Baker Company. Be sure to follow the strategic management model.
2. What additional information would you like to have, if it were available?
3. What do you think are the weakest parts of your plan? How would you strengthen these parts?
4. Be prepared to present your plan to the class.

   List the types of information and analysis that you would do if you were preparing a full-blown strategic plan. A detailed plan is not required.

APPENDIX

Forecasting Techniques

All forecasting techniques can be classified as either qualitative or quantitative. **Qualitative techniques** are based primarily on opinions and judgments. **Quantitative techniques** are based primarily on the analysis of data and the use of statistical techniques. The following sections discuss several different qualitative and quantitative techniques.

Qualitative Techniques

Jury of Executive Opinion. With this method, several managers get together and devise a forecast based on their pooled opinions. Advantages of this method are simplicity and low cost. The major disadvantage is that the forecast is not necessarily based on facts.

Sales Force Composite. Under the sales force composite method, a forecast of sales is determined by combining the sales predictions of experienced salespeople. Because salespeople are in constant contact with customers, they are often in a position to accurately forecast sales. Advantages of this method are the relatively low cost and simplicity. The major disadvantage is that sales personnel are not always unbiased, especially if their sales quotas are based on sales forecasts.

Customer Evaluation. This method is similar to the sales force composite except that it goes to customers for estimates of what the customers expect to buy. Individual customer estimates are then pooled to obtain a total forecast. This method works best when a small number of customers make up a large percentage of total sales. Drawbacks are that the customer may not be interested enough to do a good job and that the method has no provisions for including new customers.

Delphi Technique. The Delphi technique is a method for developing a consensus of expert opinion. Under this method, a panel of experts is chosen to study a particular question. The panel members do not meet as a group and may not even know the identity of other panel members. Panel members are then asked (usually by mailed questionnaire) to give their opinions concerning certain future events or forecasts. After the first round of opinions has

Qualitative techniques – type of forecasting technique based primarily on opinions and judgments.

Quantitative techniques – type of forecasting technique based primarily on the analysis of data and the use of statistical technique.

been collected, the coordinating person summarizes the different opinions and sends this information to the different panel members. Based on this information, panel members are asked to rethink their earlier responses and make a second forecast. This same procedure then continues until a consensus is reached or until the responses do not change appreciatively. The Delphi technique is relatively inexpensive and moderately complex.

Anticipatory Surveys. This method is used when mailed questionnaires, telephone interviews, or personnel interviews are used to forecast future buyer intentions. In reality, this is a form of sampling, in that those surveyed are intended to represent some larger population. Potential drawbacks of this method are that stated intentions are not necessarily carried out and that the sample surveyed does not represent the population. This method is usually accompanied by medium costs and medium complexity.

Quantitative Techniques

Time Series Analysis. This technique forecasts future demand based on what has happened in the past. The basic idea of time series analysis is to fit a trend line to past data and then to extrapolate this trend line into the future. Sophisticated mathematical procedures are used to derive this trend line and to identify any seasonal or cyclical fluctuations. Usually a computer program is used to do the calculations required by a time series analysis. One advantage of time series analysis is that it is based on something other than opinion. This method works best when a significant amount of historical data is available and when the environmental forces are relatively stable. The disadvantage is that the future may not be like the past.

Regression Modeling. Regression modeling is a mathematical forecasting technique in which an equation with one or more input variables is derived to predict another variable. The variable being predicted is called the *dependent variable*. The input variables used to predict the dependent variable are called *independent variables*. The general idea of regression modeling is to determine how changes in the independent variables affect the dependent variable. Once the mathematical relationship between the independent variables and the dependent variable has been determined (in the form of an equation), future values for the dependent variable can be forecast based on known or predicted values of the independent variables. The mathematical calculations required to derive the equation are extremely complex and almost always require the use of a computer. Regression modeling is relatively complex and expensive.

Econometric Modeling. Econometric modeling is one of the most sophisticated methods of forecasting. In general, econometric models attempt to mathematically model an entire economy. Most econometric models are based on numerous regression equations which attempt to describe the relationships between the different sectors of the economy. Very few organizations are capable of developing their own econometric models. Those organizations that do use econometric models usually hire the services of consulting groups or companies that specialize in econometric modeling. Econometric modeling is very expensive and complex and is, therefore, primarily used only by very large organizations.

9 Operations Planning

LEARNING OBJECTIVES

*After studying this chapter,
you should be able to:*

1 Define operations management.

2 Describe an operating system and identify the two basic types of operating systems.

3 Differentiate between product/service design, process selection, and site-selection decisions.

4 Describe and give an example of the two basic classifications of physical layouts.

5 Explain the sociotechnical approach to job design.

6 Outline the three major steps for developing an aggregate production plan.

7 Summarize the differences between resource allocation and activity scheduling.

An initial step in the planning process is to determine the character of the output of the enterprise. Once this decision is made, the way the output is created must be set. To complete the planning of the system, techniques for acquiring and using the necessary resources have to be chosen. The resources considered in making the planning decisions may be financial, may be physical (machinery or equipment), or may be human. The role of the human element is considered from a motivational standpoint and in regard to its importance in job design and job performance.

ARTHUR C. LAUFER*

Operations management – application of the basic concepts and principles of management to those segments of the organization that produce the goods and/or services.

Operations planning – designing the systems of the organization that produce goods or services; planning the day-to-day operations within these systems.

Operations management, which evolved from the field of production or manufacturing management, deals with the application of the basic concepts and principles of management to those segments of the organization that produce the goods and/or services of the organization. Traditionally, the term *production* brings to mind such things as smokestacks, machine shops, and the manufacture of real goods. Operations management is the management of the producing function in any organization—private or public, profit or nonprofit, manufacturing or service. **Operations planning** is concerned with designing the systems of the organization that produce the goods or services and with the planning of the day-to-day operations that take place within these systems. This chapter first discusses the basic design-related aspects of operations and then discusses the planning of the day-to-day operations.

THE IMPORTANCE OF OPERATIONS MANAGEMENT

The operations function is only one part of the total organization; however, it is a very important part. The production of goods and/or services often involves the largest part of an organization's financial assets, personnel, and expenses. The operations process also usually takes up an appreciable amount of time. Thus, because of the resources and time consumed by operations, the management of this function plays a critical role in achieving the organization's goals.

Effective operations managers directly influence worker output by (1) building group cohesiveness and individual commitment and (2) making sound

---

* From Arthur C. Laufer, *Operations Management* (Cincinnati: South-Western Publishing, 1975), p. 172.

MANAGERS AT WORK 9–1

Facilities Planning at McDonald's

The main function of each McDonald's hamburger outlet is the fast delivery of a consistently high-quality product in a clean facility. One of the keys to McDonald's phenomenal success is the detailed facility layout and planned used of materials. Storage and preparation space are designed specifically for the existing mix of products, which discourages the owner from supplementing the menu. All products are prepackaged and premeasured to ensure uniformity. Food is cooked on equipment designed to make an optimum amount without waste. McDonald's even uses a special wide-mouthed scoop to fill a bag with exactly the right amount of french fries. The scoop prevents costly overfilling but creates an impression of abundance. The facilities are planned in such detail that employee discretion is virtually eliminated.

Source: Theodore Levitt, "Production-Line Approach to Service," *Harvard Business Review*, September–October 1972, p. 41.

---

technical and administrative decisions. Both have become more complex and important in recent years. Society wants not only improved productivity but also an enriched work environment. At the same time, social changes have increased the cultural gap between younger workers and established managers. The human problems confronting operations management have therefore become more important and more difficult.

Most operations managers no longer manage in a stable environment with standard products. Changing technology and a strong emphasis on low costs have altered the technical and administrative problems they confront. The modern operations manager must deal not only with low costs but also product diversity, high quality, short lead times, and a rapidly changing technology. As a result, their problems are now greater and require much more managerial talent than ever before. Managers at Work 9–1 describes the role of operations planning in the success of McDonald's.

OPERATING SYSTEMS AND ACTIVITIES

Operating systems consist of the processes and activities necessary to turn inputs into goods and/or services. Operating systems exist in all organizations; they are made up of people, materials, facilities, and information. The end result of an operating system is to add value by improving, enhancing, or rearranging the inputs. Many operating systems take a collection of parts and form them into a more valuable whole. For example, an automobile is a group of separate parts formed into a more valuable whole.

Operating system – consists of the processes and activities necessary to transform various inputs into goods and/or services.

In some situations, the operating system breaks something down from a larger quantity to smaller quantities with more value. A metal shop cuts smaller parts from larger sheets of metal; a butcher produces steaks, hamburger, and other cuts from a side of beef. Both break down a larger quantity into smaller quantities with more value.

A third type of operating system produces services by turning inputs into more useful outputs. Here, emphasis is usually placed more on labor and less on materials. For example, a television repair shop uses some materials but the primary value results from the repairer's labor.

Figure 9–1 presents a simplified model of an operating system. The operating system is broader and more inclusive than just the conversion or transformation process. It includes not only the design and operation of the process but also many of the activities needed to get the various inputs (such as product design and scheduling) into the transformation process. Many of the activities necessary to get the outputs out of the transformation process (such as inventory control and materials distribution) are also included.

F I G U R E   9–1   Simplified Model of an Operating System

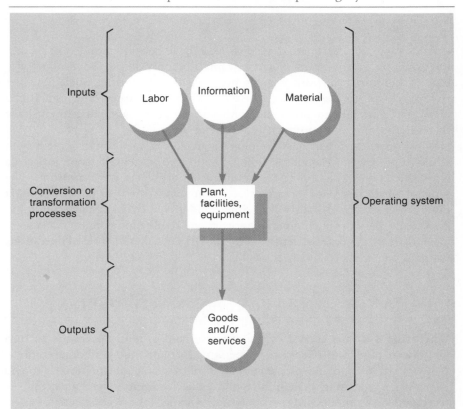

Basic Types of Operating Systems

There are two basic types of operating systems. One is based on continuous flows, the other on intermittent flows. Organizations with **continuous flows** generally have a standardized product or service. This product or service is often advertised and is immediately available to the customer. The post office, paper mills, petroleum refineries, assembly plants, and fast-food outlets with standardized products (such as McDonald's) are examples. The continuous type of operation has relatively large volumes of identical or similar products/services flowing through similar stages of the operating system.

The second type of operating system, the **intermittent flow** (or job shop) type, produces customized products and services. Because of its customized nature, organizations using an intermittent operating system usually do not keep an inventory of finished products or offer standardized services. Intermittent flow systems include special-order fabrication shops, hospitals, advertising agencies, and dental offices.

With economies of scale, specialized labor, and high equipment use, the continuous flow system usually results in lower unit costs than the intermittent flow system. However, continuous flow systems usually require special-purpose equipment which is less flexible and usually more expensive than general-purpose equipment. An example is the customized equipment and machinery used in an automobile assembly plant.

Continuous flow – operating system used by companies that produce large amounts of similar products/services flowing through similar stages of the operating system.

Intermittent flow – operating system used when customized products and services are produced.

PRODUCT/SERVICE DESIGN

An organization's product or service determines the design of its operating systems. The design of new product/service or the redesign of an existing product/service may cause extensive systems redesign, equipment change, new personnel, and so on. Again, referring to the automobile industry, consider the redesign necessary just to change from one year's models to the next year's models. The design can be functionally sound, yet not economical to produce. Of course, specific functional design objectives must be achieved; however, several alternative designs are often available. When such choices exist, production costs should certainly be one criterion used in the decision.

Historically, design engineers have encountered conflict with operations managers. Design engineers are technically oriented and sometimes may lack concern for production methods and costs. On the other hand, operations managers may care more about production costs and requirements than about the functional requirements of the product. Such conflict can be minimized through good communication which fosters an appreciation by both the engineer and the manager of the common objective of producing a functional product or service at the minimum cost.

Managers at Work 9–2 describes how Pitney Bowes integrated engineering design with purchasing and manufacturing to help avoid designs that look good on paper but can't be produced.

MANAGERS AT WORK 9–2

Avoiding Undeliverable Designs at Pitney Bowes

"A design is effective only if it's effective in the manufacturing community. Purchasing and quality are where you plant the seeds of an effective design." These are the words of Frank E. Seestrom, who is director of engineering for electronic meters at Pitney Bowes' advanced development center in Norwalk, Connecticut. Sal Cargino is a resident purchasing manager who, with a full staff, supports Seestrom and about 400 other engineers.

Carbino regularly meets with engineers and also takes plenty of road trips. The purpose of Carbino's advanced purchasing group is to handle new product buying, from breadboards to prototypes to pilot runs through the first production run. At that point the responsibility shifts to the appropriate production buying group. Having Carbino and his group work directly with the engineers helps avoid designs that no one can produce. In addition to working with the design engineers, Carbino and his staff are also constantly interacting with manufacturing and quality engineers.

Source: Adapted from "How Pitney Bowes Avoids Undeliverable Designs," *Purchasing,* March 27, 1986, pp. 87–90.

PROCESS SELECTION

Process selection – specifies in detail the processes and sequences required to transform inputs into products or services.

Process selection includes a wide range of decisions about the specific process to be used, the basic sequences of the process, and the equipment to be used. As suggested earlier, the product/service design decisions and the process selection decisions should be closely coordinated.

The processes and equipment used can play a large role in whether the product or service is competitive. The importance of the process selection decision has become magnified in some industries with the advent of robotics. This has clearly been shown in the steel and automotive industries: the Japanese steel and automotive industries have much more modern production processes than their American counterparts. Managers at Work 9–3 describes a fully automated production facility at IBM.

Once the overall type of operations process has been selected, specific decisions are needed regarding such factors as whether to use general or special-purpose equipment, to make or to buy the components, and how much to automate. In equipment decisions, several factors beyond normal cost should be considered:

1. Availability of operators.
2. Training required for operators.

MANAGERS AT WORK 9–3

Fully Automated Computer Plant at IBM

IBM has many firsts to its credit. One of the more recent pioneering activities undertaken by IBM is the development of a fully automated computer plant. The production of the IBM PC convertible is a milestone in the computer industry. It is the first computer to be built entirely by robots. Technically, the process is known as flexible automation, which makes use of modular workstations that can be programmed to perform a variety of tasks. From receiving dock to shipping dock, the machine is assembled, tested, packed, and shipped without any manual interference. The production line is designed to make not only the PC convertible but any electronic product that is no bigger than 2 feet by 2 feet by 14 inches. By using such high-tech equipment, IBM has been able to cut costs and remain competitive. An equally important contribution of this facility is the plant's ability to respond with unprecedented swiftness to the almost monthly shifts in the computer market.

Source: "IBM's No-Hands Assembly Line," *Fortune,* September 15, 1986, 105–9.

3. Maintenance record and potential.
4. Availability of parts and services.
5. Supplier assistance in installation and debugging.
6. Compatibility with existing equipment.
7. Flexibility of equipment in handling product variation.
8. Safety of equipment.
9. Expected delivery date.
10. Warranty coverage.

In process selection, the overriding objective is to specify in detail the most economical processes and sequences required to transform the inputs into the desired product or service. Managers at Work 9–4 describes how Digital Equipment Corporation uses expert systems to assist in several decisions related to process selection.

SITE SELECTION

Management should carefully consider site location. It is easy to become overly engrossed in the operating details and techniques and ignore the importance of site location. Location is an ongoing question; it does not occur

MANAGERS AT WORK 9–4

Expert Systems at Digital

Expert systems enable less experienced employees to arrive at judgments that are as sound as an expert's. These systems make use of artificial intelligence—the technology that tries to get computers to think the way people do. At the heart of these systems there is an innovative software program that embodies the rules specialists use to make decisions. Digital Equipmant Corporation (DEC) was one of the earliest companies to introduce expert systems to run its operations. Developed over a decade, DEC has utilized 40 big expert systems in its operations. The earliest system developed by DEC was XCON, which helps engineers in selecting the right mix of cables, disk drives, power packs, and cabinets to use on certain computers to meet its customers' requirements. Other expert systems have been developed by DEC. While XSEL helps computer salesmen to order the right combination of components, XFL aids in laying out the site for a computer installation, CDX gives expert advice on reviving a crashed computer system, AI Spear is a warning system for maladies in tape drives, and Dispatches plots the shortest path through several destinations. It is believed that DEC saves more than $25 million a year through the help of expert systems.

Source: "Now, Live Experts on a Floppy Disk," *Fortune*, October 12, 1987, pp. 69–82.

only when a facility is outgrown or obsolete. Location decisions relate to offices, warehouses, service centers, and branches, as well as the parent facility. Each site-selection decision involves the total production-distribution system of the organization. Therefore, not only the location of new facilities should be examined; the location of present facilities should also be regularly reviewed for the most effective production-distribution system.

Several options exist for expanding capacity when the present facility is overcrowded:

1. Subcontract work.
2. Add another shift.
3. Work overtime.
4. Move operation to a larger facility.
5. Expand present facility.
6. Keep current facility and add another facility elsewhere.

A decision to move the entire operation to a larger facility or to add another facility elsewhere means management is faced with a location decision. Figure 9–2 lists several factors to consider when locating a new facility. The final

FIGURE 9–2   Factors to Be Considered in Site Location

1. Revenue.
   a. Location of customers and accessibility.
   b. Location of competitors.
2. Operating costs.
   a. Price of materials.
   b. Transportation costs: materials, products, people.
   c. Wage rates.
   d. Taxes: income, property, sales.
   e. Utility rates.
   f. Rental rates.
   g. Communication costs.
3. Investment.
   a. Cost of land.
   b. Cost of construction.
4. Other limiting factors.
   a. Availability of labor with appropriate skills.
   b. Availability of materials, utilities, supplies.
   c. Union activity.
   d. Community attitudes and culture.
   e. Political situation.
   f. Pollution restrictions.
   g. Climate.
   h. General living conditions.

site choice will have to be a compromise among these factors. For example, the decision in 1987 by RJR Nabisco to move its headquarters from Winston-Salem, North Carolina, to Atlanta, Georgia, was partially based on the fact that Atlanta is much more accessible from a transportation standpoint.

PHYSICAL LAYOUT

Physical layout is essentially the process of planning the optimum physical arrangement of facilities, which includes personnel, operating equipment, storage space, office space, materials-handling equipment, and room for customer service and movement. Physical layout integrates all of the previous planning of the design process into one physical system. Physical layout decisions are needed for a number of different reasons:

1. Construction of a new or additional facility.
2. Obsolescence of current facilities.
3. Changes in demand.
4. Development of a new or redesigned product or process.
5. Personnel considerations: frequent accidents, poor working environment, or prohibitive supervisory costs.

Physical layout – process of planning the optimum physical arrangement of facilities—including personnel, operating equipment, storage space, office space, materials-handling equipment, and room for customer or product movement.

Demand forecasts for the product or service must be considered in establishing the productive capacity of the organization. The costs of running short on space and equipment must be balanced with the costs of having idle space and equipment. A good approach is to match space needs with estimates of future demand but purchase equipment only as it is needed. This allows quick capacity expansion and avoids the costs of idle equipment.

Basic Layout Classifications

Process physical layout – equipment or services of a similar functional type are arranged or grouped together.

Most layouts are either process oriented or product oriented. Process layouts are generally used in intermittent flow operating systems. In a **process layout,** equipment or services of a similar functional type are arranged or grouped together: All X-ray machines are grouped together; all reproduction equipment is grouped together; all drilling machines are grouped together; and so forth. Custom fabrication shops, hospitals, and restaurants are usually arranged in this fashion. With a process layout, a product/customer moves from area to area for the desired sequence of functional operations. When the product or service is not standardized or when the volume of similar products or customers in service at any one time is low, a process layout is preferred because of its flexibility.

Product physical layout – equipment or services are arranged according to the progressive steps by which the product is made or the customer is served.

Product layouts usually occur in continuous flow operating systems. In a **product layout,** equipment or services are arranged according to the progressive steps by which the product is made or the customer is serviced. A product layout is generally used when a standardized product is made in large quantities. The assembly line is the ultimate product layout. Automobile assembly plants, cafeterias, and standardized testing centers are normally product layout oriented. In a product layout, all the equipment or services necessary to produce a product or completely serve a customer are located in one area. Figure 9–3 lists the major advantages of both process and product layouts.

F I G U R E 9–3   Advantages of Process and Product Layout

ADVANTAGES OF PROCESS LAYOUT:

1. Lower investment in equipment and personnel because of less duplication (do not need the same machine or person doing the same thing in two different areas).
2. Adaptable to demand fluctuations.
3. Worker jobs are not as repetitive or routine.
4. Layout is conducive to incentive pay systems.
5. Allows for the production of a greater variety of products with a smaller capital base.
6. Failures of equipment or people do not hold up successive operations.

ADVANTAGES OF PRODUCT LAYOUT:

1. Relatively unskilled labor may be utilized.
2. Training costs are low.
3. Materials-handling costs are usually low.
4. Smaller quantities of work in process.
5. Operations control and scheduling are simplified.

Computer-Assisted Physical Layout

Various computer programs have been developed to aid in designing physical layouts. Most computer approaches to the process-oriented layout stress the relative placement of like components subject to certain criteria; materials-handling cost is the most frequently used criterion. Computer programs for product-oriented layouts attempt to assign tasks to workstations so that the work load is balanced among the different stations along the line.

JOB DESIGN

Job design specifies the work activities of an individual or group of individuals. Job design answers the question of how the job is to be performed, who is to perform it, and where it is to be performed.

The job design process can generally be divided into three phases:

1. The specification of individual tasks.
2. The specification of the method of performing each task.
3. The combination of individual tasks into specific jobs to be assigned to individuals.[1]

Phases 1 and 3 determine the content of the job, while phase 2 indicates how the job is to be performed.

Job design – designates the specific work activities of an individual or group of individuals.

Job Content

Job content is the sum of all the work tasks the jobholder may be asked to perform. Starting with the scientific management movement, job content focused almost totally on the process by which the job was done. This usually meant minimizing short-run costs by minimizing the unit operation time. The obvious problem with this approach is that the job can become overly routine and repetitive, which leads to motivational problems in the form of boredom, absenteeism, turnover, and perhaps low performance. (These problems and some potential solutions are discussed in Chapters 14 and 16.) One fact greatly complicates the job design process: different people react differently to similar jobs. In other words, what is boring and routine to one person is not necessarily boring and routine to another.

Job content – aggregate of all the work tasks the job holder may be asked to perform.

Job Methods

The next step is to determine the precise methods to be used to perform the job. The optimum **job method** is a function of the manner in which the human body is used, the arrangement of the workplace, and the design of

Job method – manner in which the human body is used, the arrangement of the workplace, and the design of the tools and equipment used.

the tools and equipment used.[2] The main purpose of job method design is to find the one best way to do a job. Normally, job methods are determined after the basic process and physical layout have been determined.

Motion study is used in designing jobs. It involves determining the necessary motions and movements for performing a job or task and then designing the most efficient method for putting these motions and movements together.

Job methods designers have traditionally concentrated on manual tasks. However, the basic concept of finding the one best way applies to all types of jobs.

The Physical Work Environment

The physical work environment—temperature, humidity, ventilation, noise, light, color, etc.—can have an impact on employee performance and safety. Studies clearly show that adverse physical conditions do have a negative effect on performance; but the degree of influence varies from person to person.

The importance of safety in the design process was reinforced by the **Occupational Safety and Health Act (OSHA)** of 1970. Designed to reduce job injuries, the act gives very specific federal safety guidelines for almost all U.S. organizations.

Occupational Safety and Health Act (OSHA) of 1970 – designed to reduce job injuries; established specific federal safety guidelines for almost all U.S. organizations.

In general, the work area should allow for normal lighting, temperature, ventilation, and humidity. Baffles, acoustical wall materials, and sound absorbers should be used to reduce unpleasant noises. Exposure to less than ideal conditions should be limited to short periods of time. This will minimize possible physical or psychological damage to the workers.[3]

Sociotechnical Approach

The sociotechnical concept was first introduced in the 1950s by Eric Trist and his colleagues at the Tavistock Institute of Human Relations in London, England.[4] The **sociotechnical approach** rests on two premises:[5] (1) In any organization that requires people to perform certain tasks, there is a joint system operating—this joint system combines the social and technological systems; and (2) the environment of every sociotechnical system is influenced by a culture, its values, and a set of generally accepted practices. The concept stresses that the technical system, the related social system, and the general environment should all be considered when designing jobs.

Sociotechnical approach – approach to job design that considers both the technical system and the accompanying social system.

The sociotechnical approach is very situational; few jobs have identical technical requirements, social surroundings, and environments. This approach requires that the job designer carefully consider the role of the worker within the system, the task boundaries, and the autonomy of the work group. Using the sociotechnical approach, Louis Davis has developed the following guidelines for job design:

1. The need for the content of a job to be reasonably demanding for the worker in terms other than sheer endurance and yet provide some variety (not necessarily novelty).
2. The need for being able to learn on the job and to go on learning.
3. The need for some minimum area of decision making that the individual can call his own.
4. The need for some minimal degree of social support and recognition at the workplace.
5. The need to be able to relate what the individual does and what he produces to his social life.
6. The need to feel that the job leads to some sort of desirable future.[6]

DAY-TO-DAY OPERATIONS PLANNING

Designing an effective operating system does not ensure that it will operate efficiently. The day-to-day operations must also be planned and then carried out. This is called production planning. **Production planning** includes aggregate production planning, resource allocation, and scheduling. Its overriding purpose is to maintain a smooth, constant flow of work from start to finish—so that the product or service will be completed in the desired time at the lowest possible cost.

> Production planning – concerned primarily with aggregate production planning, resource allocation, and activity scheduling.

Aggregate Production Planning

Aggregate production planning deals with overall operations and with balancing the major parts of the operating system. Its primary purpose is to match the organization's resources with the demands for its goods or services. Specifically, the plan should find the production rates which satisfy demand requirements while minimizing the costs of work force and inventory fluctuations. Aggregate production plans generally look 6 to 18 months into the future.

> Aggregate production planning – concerned with overall operations and balancing major sections of the operating system; matches organization's resources with demands for its goods and services.

The first step to take in developing an aggregate production plan is to obtain a demand forecast for the organization's goods or services. The second step involves evaluating the impact of the demand forecasts on the organization's resources—plant capacity, work force, raw materials, and the like. The final step is to develop the best plan for using the organization's current and expected resources for meeting the forecast demand. The aggregate production plan determines production rates, work force needs, and inventory levels for the entire operating system over a specified time period. Management at Work 9–5 describes how Honeywell has used computers in its aggregate planning process.

MANAGERS AT WORK 9–5

Aggregate Production Planning with Computers at Honeywell

Honeywell's Small System and Peripherals Division manufactures circuit boards, subassemblies, cables and assembles terminals and minicomputers. In such a highly competitive market characterized by short product life cycles and complex manufacturing processes, planning is an essential but difficult task.

Honeywell has developed a comprehensive, computerized, medium- to long-range planning system to help estimate future manpower and equipment requirements. When market forecasts are entered as the independent variable, the system can be used to generate labor and equipment projections. The projected requirements are used to justify expenditures on new equipment and facilities and to plan manpower adjustments. The benefits of such a system are that manpower and equipment are added only when needed and that management has a realistic basis for making planning decisions.

Source: Kelvin Cross, "Manufacturing Planning with Computers at Honeywell, *"Long-Range Planning,* December 1984, pp. 66–75.

Resource Allocation

Resource allocation – efficient allocation of people, materials, and equipment in order to meet the demand requirements of the operating system.

Resource allocation is the efficient allocation of people, materials, and equipment in order to meet the demand requirements of the operating system. It is the natural outgrowth of the aggregate production plan. The materials needed must be determined and ordered; the work must to distributed to the different departments and workstations; personnel must be allocated; and time allotments must be set for each stage of the process.

Due to resource scarcities, resource allocation has become critical in recent times. Increased competition, both domestic and foreign, has also increased its importance. Proper resource allocation can mean great cost savings, which can give the needed competitive edge.

Numerous mathematical and computer-assisted tools and techniques can assist in resource allocation. Linear programming, critical path method (CPM), and program evaluation and review technique (PERT) are some of the most often used. (CPM and PERT are discussed in the Appendix to this chapter.)

Routing – finds the best path and sequence of operations for attaining a desired level of output with a given mix of equipment and personnel.

Routing. **Routing** finds the best path and sequence of operations for attaining a desired level of output with a given mix of equipment and personnel. Routing looks for the best use of existing equipment and personnel through careful assignment of these resources. An organization may or may not have to analyze its routing system frequently; it depends on the variety of products or services being offered.

Flowcharts and diagrams are used to locate and end inefficiencies in a process by analyzing the process in a step-by-step fashion. Most charting procedures divide the actions in a given process into five types: operations, transportations, inspections, delays, and storages. Figure 9–4 defines each of these types of actions. Two types of charts frequently used are the assembly chart and the flow process chart.

Assembly charts depict the sequence and manner in which the various parts of a product or service are assembled. A **flow process chart** outlines what happens to the product as it moves through the operating facility. Flow process charts can also map the flow of customers through a service facility. Figure 9–5 shows a flow process chart for the processing of a form for an insurance company.

Assembly chart – depicts the sequence and manner in which the various components of a product or service are assembled.

Flow process chart – outlines what happens to a product or service as it progresses through the facility.

F I G U R E 9–4   Flowcharting Activities

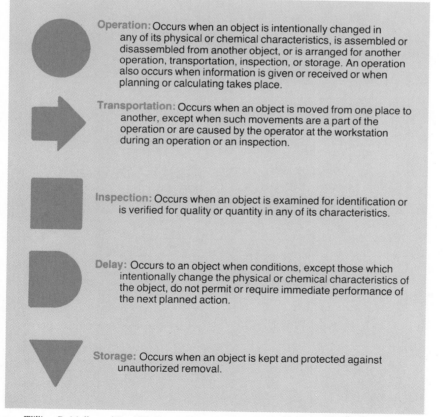

Operation: Occurs when an object is intentionally changed in any of its physical or chemical characteristics, is assembled or disassembled from another object, or is arranged for another operation, transportation, inspection, or storage. An operation also occurs when information is given or received or when planning or calculating takes place.

Transportation: Occurs when an object is moved from one place to another, except when such movements are a part of the operation or are caused by the operator at the workstation during an operation or an inspection.

Inspection: Occurs when an object is examined for identification or is verified for quality or quantity in any of its characteristics.

Delay: Occurs to an object when conditions, except those which intentionally change the physical or chemical characteristics of the object, do not permit or require immediate performance of the next planned action.

Storage: Occurs when an object is kept and protected against unauthorized removal.

Source: William R. Mullee and David B. Porter, "Process-Chart Procedures," in *Industrial Engineering Handbook*, 2nd ed., ed. H. B. Maynard (New York: McGraw-Hill, 1963), pp. 2–21.

FIGURE 9–5 Flow Process Chart: Present Method for Completing Authorization-to-Investigate Form

		Summary	
Operation	Complete authorization to	Sheet __1__ of __1__ Sheets	● Operation	7
Product	investigate form		▶ Transport	4
Depts.	Property Loss	Charted By ___Joe Millard___	■ Inspect	1
Drawing No. ___N.A.___ Part No. ___N.A.___		Date ___9/14___	◗ Delay	1
Quantity	One form in triplicate		▽ Store	—
		Approved By ___Jim Street___	Vertical distance	—
			Horizontal distance	180 ft.
Present ___✓___ Proposed _____		Date ___9/15___	Time (hours)	16.000

No.	Dist. Moved (Feet)	Worker Time (Hours)	Symbols	Description
1		.200	●▶■◗▽	Remove Claim Dept's. request from in-basket and identify client.
2	55	3.250	●▶■◗▽	Walk to filing area, locate file, and return to desk. Locate pertinent information in client file.
3		.500	●▶■◗▽	Type information on authorization to investigate form (form no. 3355).
4		.500	●▶■◗▽	Walk to section leader's desk.
5	35	.200	●▶■◗▽	Wait for signature.
6		.500	●▶■◗▽	Walk back to desk.
7	35	.200	●▶■◗▽	Tear form apart into separate sheets.
8		.200	●▶■◗▽	Prepare regional investigator's copy for mailing; place in mail basket on desk.
9		1.750	●▶■◗▽	Prepare Claims Dept's. copy for routing; place in mail basket on desk.
10		1.500	●▶■◗▽	Place one copy in client's file.
11		.200	●▶■◗▽	Walk to filing area, refile, and return to desk.
12	55	2.250	●▶■◗▽	
13			●▶■◗▽	
14			●▶■◗▽	

Source: From *Production and Operations Management* by Norman Gaither. Copyright © 1980 by The Dryden Press. Reprinted by permission of CBS College Publishing.

Activity Scheduling

Activity scheduling develops the precise timetable to be followed in producing the product or service. It also includes dispatching work orders and expediting critical and late orders. Scheduling does not involve deciding how long a job will take (part of job design); rather it determines when the work is to be done. Scheduling is the link between system design and operations planning and control. Once the initial schedule has been set, the system is ready for operation. Of course, scheduling is an ongoing activity in an operating system.

A scheduling system design must be based on knowledge of the operating system for which it is being designed. Scheduling for intermittent systems is very complex because of the larger number of individual orders or customers that must flow through the system. Many types of scheduling tools—such as the Gantt chart, the critical path method, and the program evaluation and review technique—have been developed to help overcome scheduling problems (each of these is discussed in the Appendix to this chapter).

Scheduling for high-volume continuous flow systems is often a process of matching the available resources to the production needs as outlined by the aggregate plan. Computer simulation is used to assist in the scheduling of continuous flow systems by estimating the impact of different scheduling decisions on the system.

> **Activity scheduling** – develops the precise timetable to be followed in producing a product or service.

SUMMARY

This chapter introduces the major concepts relating to operations management. Operations planning and its importance to the overall success of the organization are discussed. The major activities involved in designing and then implementing an operating system are presented.

LEARNING OBJECTIVE 1

Define Operations Management.

Operations management is the application of the basic concepts and principles of management to those segments of the organization that produce the goods and/or services of the organization.

LEARNING OBJECTIVE 2

Describe an Operating System and Identify the Two Basic Types of Operating Systems.

An operating system consists of the processes and activities necessary to transform various inputs into goods and/or services. The two basic types of operating systems are those based on continuous flows and those based on intermittent flows. Continuous flow systems generally have a standardized product or service. Intermittent flow systems usually produce customized products and services.

LEARNING OBJECTIVE 3

Differentiate between Product/Service Design, Process Selection, and Site Selection Decisions.

Product/service design decisions are those decisions that deal with how the product or service will be designed. The design must be such that it can be economically produced. Process selection includes a wide range of decisions concerning the specific process to be used, the basic sequences of the process, and the equipment to be used. Site-selection decisions are concerned with where to locate a new or additional facility.

LEARNING OBJECTIVE 4

Describe and Give an Example of the Two Basic Classifications of Physical Layouts.

The two basic types of layouts are process layouts and product layouts. With a process layout, the equipment or services of a similar functional type are arranged or grouped together. Custom fabrication shops and hospitals are examples of organizations that use process layouts. With a product layout, the equipment or services are arranged according to the progressive steps by which the product is made or the customer is serviced. Automobile assembly plants and cafeterias are examples of organizations that use product layouts.

LEARNING OBJECTIVE 5

Explain the Sociotechnical Approach to Job Design.

The sociotechnical approach to job design considers not only the technical system and the task to be done but also the accompanying social system.

LEARNING OBJECTIVE 6

Outline the Three Major Steps for Developing an Aggregate Production Plan.

The first step in developing an aggregate production plan is to obtain a demand forecast for the organization's goods or services. The second step involves evaluating the impact of the demand forecasts on the organization's resources. The third step is to develop the best plan for using the organization's current and expected resources for meeting the forecasted demand.

LEARNING OBJECTIVE 7

Summarize the Differences between Resource Allocation and Activity Scheduling.

Resource allocation is concerned with the efficient allocation of people, materials, and equipment in order to meet the demand requirements of the operating system. This includes distributing the work load and determining how much time should be allotted for each stage in the production process. Activity scheduling develops the precise timetable to be followed when producing the product or service. Activity scheduling does not involve determining how long a job will take but rather it determines when the work is to be done.

REVIEW QUESTIONS

1. What is operations management?
2. Describe an operating system.
3. Describe the two basic types of operating systems.
4. What is the overriding objective of the process selection decision?
5. Discuss several factors that should be considered in site location.
6. What is a process-oriented layout? A product-oriented layout?
7. The job design process can generally be divided into what three phases?
8. What is the sociotechnical approach to job design? Give some guidelines for job design, using the sociotechnical approach.
9. What is production planning?
10. Define aggregate production planning.
11. What is the difference between resource allocation and activity scheduling?

DISCUSSION QUESTIONS

1. Explain how you might take a production line approach (transferring the concepts and methodologies of operations management) to a service organization such as a fast-food restaurant.
2. Does process selection in service industries such as restaurants and hotels differ from process selection in manufacturing? If so, how?
3. Why should all of the phases involved in designing an operating system be integrated?
4. Discuss the following statement: Most production planning is a waste of time because it all depends on demand forecasts, which are usually inaccurate.

REFERENCES & ADDITIONAL READINGS

[1] Louis E. Davis, "Job Design and Productivity: A New Approach," *Personnel,* March 1957, p. 420.

[2] Richard A. Johnson, William T. Newell, and Roger C. Vergin, *Production and Operations Management: A Systems Concept* (Boston: Houghton Mifflin, 1974), p. 204.

[3] Ibid., p. 206.

[4] Peter B. Vaill, "Industrial Engineering and Socio-Technical Systems," *Journal of Industrial Engineering,* September 1967, p. 535.

[5] Louis E. Davis and James C. Taylor, *Design of Jobs,* 2nd ed. (Santa Monica, Calif.: Goodyear Publishing, 1979), pp. 98–99.

[6] Louis E. Davis, *Job Satisfaction—A Socio-Technical View,* Report 515-1-69 (Los Angeles: University of California, 1969), p. 14.

INCIDENT

The Lines at Sam's

Sam Baker owns and manages a cafeteria on Main Street in Dawsonville. He has been in business for almost two years. During his two years of operation, Sam has identified several problems that he has not been able to solve. One is the line that always seems to develop at the checkout register during the rush hour. Another problem is that customers are constantly complaining that the size of the helpings and the size of the pie slices vary tremendously from customer to customer. A third problem that has been disturbing Sam is the frequency with which the cafeteria runs out of "choice dishes." The final problem perplexing Sam is the fact that every Sunday at noon, when a large crowd arrives after church, Sam invariably runs short of seating space.

Sam has worked at other food establishments for the past 15 years; most of them have experienced similar problems. In fact, these and other related problems have come to be expected and are therefore accepted practice for the industry. After all, Sam's former boss used to say, "You can't please everybody all the time." Sam is wondering if he should take the industry's position and just accept these problems as an inherent part of the business.

Questions

1. Do you have any suggestions for Sam? If so, what are they?

2. Can you think of other service-oriented industries that seem to take the same view toward their problems as Sam's industry?

EXERCISE

Disseminating Confidential Information

*E*very month, you are responsible for collating and stapling 500 copies of a four-page document. The documents must then be placed in manila envelopes which are sealed and have the word *CONFIDENTIAL* written on each. The four pages are printed on one side only and are numbered sequentially.

A. Assume you have a manual stapler and a felt marker at your disposal. Draw a sketch of how you would arrange your workplace for doing this task and describe the procedure you would use.

B. Assume you have the authority (within reason) to make changes in the equipment, materials, and processes used, as long as the basic task of organizing the information and labeling it as confidential is accomplished. What suggestions would you make?

APPENDIX

Gantt Chart

Gantt chart – control device that graphically depicts work planned and work accomplished in their relation to each other and to time.

Critical path method (CPM) – planning and control technique that graphically depicts the relationship between the various activities of a project; used when time durations of project activities are accurately known and have little variance.

Performance evaluation and review technique (PERT) – planning and control technique that graphically depicts the relationships between the various activities of a project; used when the durations of the project activities are not accurately known.

The **Gantt chart** is the oldest and simplest method of graphically showing both expected and completed production. Developed by Henry L. Gantt in the early 1900s, the main feature of the Gantt chart is that work planned and work accomplished are shown in their relation to each other and in relation to time. Figure 9A–1 presents a typical Gantt chart.

Gantt charts emphasize the element of time by readily pointing out any actual or potential slippages. One criticism of the Gantt chart is that it can require considerable time to incorporate scheduling changes such as rush orders. To accommodate such scheduling changes rapidly, mechanical boards using movable pegs or cards have been developed.

Critical Path Method (CPM) and Program Evaluation and Review Technique (PERT)

The Gantt chart concept formed the foundation for network analysis.[1] The most popular network analysis approaches are the **critical path method (CPM)** and **program evaluation and review technique (PERT).** These two techniques were developed almost simultaneously in the late 1950s. CPM grew out of a joint study by Du Pont and Remington Rand Univac to determine how to best reduce the time required to perform routine plant overhaul, maintenance, and construction work.[2] PERT was developed by the Navy in conjunction with representatives of Lockheed Aircraft Corporation and the consulting firm of Booz Allen & Hamilton to coordinate the development and production of the Polaris weapons system.

CPM and PERT are both techniques which result in a graphical network representation of a project. The graphical network is composed of activities and events. An activity is the work necessary to complete a particular event, and it usually consumes time. Events denote a point in time, and their occurrence signifies the completion of all activities leading into the event. All activities originate and terminate at events. Activities are normally represented by arrows in a network, while events are represented by a circle. The dashed

---

[1] There is evidence that there were other forerunners to CPM and PERT. See Edward R. Marsh, "The Harmonogram of Karol Adamiecki," *Academy of Management Journal,* June 1975, pp. 358–64.

[2] Joseph J. Moder and Cecil R. Phillips, *Project Management with CPM and PERT* (New York: Van Nostrand Reinhold, 1970), p. 6.

FIGURE 9A–1 Gantt Chart with Heavy Lines Indicating Work Completed

Activity Description	Dec. 1972				Jan. 1973					Feb. 1973				Mar. 1973				Apr. 1973				May
	4	11	18	25	2	8	15	22	29	5	12	19	26	5	12	19	26	2	9	16	23	7 1

Source: Adapted from Elwood S. Buffa, *Modern Production Management*, 4th ed. (New York: John Wiley & Sons, 1973), p. 576.

F I G U R E   9A–2   Project Represented by Gantt Chart and a Project Network

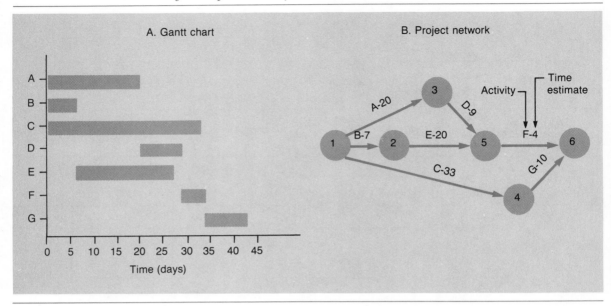

arrows in a project network, called dummies, show dependencies or precedence relationships. They simply denote that the starting of an activity or set of activities depends on the completion of another activity or set of activities.

Figure 9A–2 shows a simple project represented by both a Gantt chart and a project network. The *project network* has two distinct advantages over the Gantt chart: (1) The dependencies of the activities on each other are noted explicitly, and (2) the activities are shown in greater detail.

The path through the network that has the longest duration (based on a summation of estimated individual activity times) is referred to as the critical path. If any activity on the critical path lengthens, then the entire project duration lengthens.

The major difference between CPM and PERT centers around the activity time estimates. CPM is used for projects whose activity durations are accurately known and whose variance in performance time is negligible. On the other hand, PERT is used when the activity durations are more uncertain and variable. CPM is based on a single estimate for an activity duration, where PERT is based on three time estimates for each activity: an optimistic (minimum) time, a most likely (modal) time, and a pessimistic (maximum) time.

Project network analysis can provide information beyond simple project planning and control. By knowing the critical activities, the project manager can best allocate limited resources and can make more accurate time-cost trade-offs.

CASE

*Harley-Davidson**

The unique form of transportation known as the motorcycle has been an integral part of American life now for nearly a century. Sadly, only one American motorcycle manufacturing concern, Harley-Davidson, whose corporate logo reflects the American ideals of strength, freedom, and patriotism in a majestic bald eagle poised for flight, continues to produce American-made motorcycles. Harley-Davidson competes alone against a vast array of Japanese- and European-built motorcycles which have captured a large share of Harley-Davidson's domain: large, powerful, sport and cruising motorcycles. Undaunted and refusing to relinquish its hold on its proud heritage, the company that began at the turn of the century with its namesakes William A. Davidson, Walter C. Davidson, Arthur Davidson, and William S. Harley, carries on today as the producer of what many people consider the finest motorcycles ever made.

BEGINNINGS

The bicycle was the immediate predecessor of the motorcycle. By the close of the 19th century, bicycle racing had become quite a celebrated sport, and the first experimental "motor bicycles" had appeared in Europe. The first commercially produced motorcycle in the United States did not appear until 1901.

It was not long after this that two young childhood friends from Milwaukee, Wisconsin—William Harley and Arthur Davidson—turned their inquisitive minds to the development of a motor-powered bicycle of their own. By the spring of 1903 the first prototype model was completed. It was capable of speeds of almost 25 miles per hour.

Realizing the limits of simply attaching a small motor to a bicycle frame, the two original entrepreneurs designed a whole new bicycle from the ground up with a frame made of heavy-gauge tubing, a lengthened wheelbase, and the now-standard two-stroke DeDion gasoline engine. This became the first commercial Harley-Davidson motorcycle.

William and Arthur were now joined by the remaining Davidson brothers, William and Walter. Erecting a 10 by 15 foot wooden shed in the backyard of the family home and painting "Harley-Davidson Motor Co." on the door,

---

* This case was prepared by Nabil A. Ibrahim, Ph.D., Augusta College.

these four young men quietly heralded a new chapter in American transportation history.

Enlisting the aid of an uncle, James McLay, who possessed the necessary capital, the four young visionaries built the first major production facility at the corner of 27th and Chestnut streets in the industrial sector of Milwaukee. By 1906, production was approaching 50 machines a year, all of which were quickly snapped up by Milwaukee residents. As the first mass-produced inexpensive automobile was not yet available, motorcycles were an attractive substitute. On September 22, 1907, the Harley-Davidson Motor Company of Milwaukee was legally incorporated and entered the growing field of American motorcycle producers.

By spring 1908, factory floor space had increased to 5,000 square feet and production had reached 456 machines a year, produced by some 36 employees. The industry was somewhat crowded, with about 33 different manufacturers. Only several were considered at high enough quality to really compete with Harley-Davidson. A major marketing achievement occurred in 1909 when Arthur Davidson demonstrated his machine to a convention of rural free delivery mail carriers, who promptly switched in large numbers from their Wagners to Harley-Davidsons. By the mid-teens there were many American companies manufacturing motorcycles, but the "Big Three" were Indian, Excelsior, and, in third place, Harley-Davidson.

Motorcycle racing had become a serious sport before the end of the first decade of the 20th century, and Walter Davidson immediately recognized the advertising potential. Entering himself in the 1908 endurance run against 84 other riders, sponsored by the infant Federation of American Motorcyclists, he finished the grueling 24-hour course with a perfect score of 1,000.

Europe was already in the throes of World War I, and almost all motorcycle production there had been diverted to military use. While it was not immediately apparent, a subtle difference in motorcycle design had been taking place between the European and American machines. The American-made motorcycle required greater durability and more power than was necessary for European machines. American roads—where they existed—were mostly unpaved; and distances between cities were greater. As a result, the American-designed motorcycle that evolved was better suited to wartime duties than the usually smaller, lighter, and more fragile European machine.

America entered World War I in April 1917, and the motorcycle industry switched immediately to military production. The war provided a huge market for motorcycles equipped with sidecars for use by the allied forces, and the government placed large orders with the Milwaukee-based Harley-Davidson.

The 1920s brought a decline in popularity of the motorcycle, as affordable automobiles had at last become a reality. While domestic demand declined, overseas interest picked up, and by 1927, 50 percent of all American-made motorcycles made their way to Europe. By this time, Harley-Davidson's top-of-the-line model was the 74 "Cruising J," constituting the backbone of Harley-Davidson as the industry leader.

The close of the Great Depression was marked by two bitter events: unionization of Harley-Davidson's workers, and the death of William Davidson. Nevertheless, year-end production for 1937 reached 11,674 units, an increase over 1936 of nearly 3,000 machines. Over 50 percent of this output was sold overseas.

During the 1930s, Harley-Davidson concentrated production into two main motorcycle types which formed the mainstay of the line for the next three decades. The 61E "Big Twin" was perfected despite initial faults, and the 45 model, although less in demand than the "Big Twin," still saw much service as a utility vehicle fitted with a sidecar.

By 1940, because of wartime production for the government, the main Juneau Avenue production facility was expanded and put into round-the-clock production. Shortly afterwards, the company lost another original founder, President Walter Davidson. He was succeeded in the leadership of Harley-Davidson by his son William Davidson. A third founder, William Harley, died in 1943.

Harley-Davidson's cumulative war production was stupendous, rolling out 88,000 machines before the cancellation of the government contracts. A side effect of the war effort was increased awareness of the Harley-Davidson motorcycle by thousands of GIs who learned to ride on Army motorcycles. This eventually translated into more sales in the domestic market after the war.

THE POSTWAR ERA

The early postwar period saw the beginning of serious inroads by imported motorcycles into the American market. Although an import tariff of 8 percent was levied in the United States, exported Harley-Davidsons felt the weight of a 33 percent to 50 percent tariff.

Arthur Davidson, the last of the original founders, died in the early 1950s. The decade also ushered in the first significant threat to the company from imports.

But despite the imports, Harley-Davidson managed to continue to sell all it produced. A new introduction, the Harley-Davidson 125, a smaller machine designed to compete against the imports, sold 10,000 in its first year of production. However, as an ominous note of things to come, a November 1959 issue of *Cycle Magazine* featured an advertisement introducing the Honda; a small machine, 50 cc, it featured electric starting. The first advertising line read, "You meet the nicest people on a Honda."

The mid-1960s brought Harley-Davidson to a precarious position—it claimed only 6 percent of the market, although sales were a record high amount of $31 million. At this time it was decided to offer stock to the public. Control of the corporation remained in the hands of the surviving members of the Harley and Davidson families, who held a majority of the tendered stock.

Despite the injection of capital, Harley-Davidson continued on shaky financial ground through the mid-1960s, and in 1967 it was decided to put the company up for sale to a conglomerate. American Machine and Foundry (AMF) acquired Harley-Davidson, but Harley-Davidson management and most of its staff were retained.

The acquisition of Harley-Davidson by AMF brought about a harsh reappraisal of Harley Davidson's problems. While the four original founders had run the company well in the early years and managed to survive the Great Depression, their deaths and replacement by their descendants was not the best thing for the company. Control was spread out among too many Harleys and Davidsons, some of whom lacked the ability to function in upper-level management. Harley-Davidson's production facilities were outdated and badly in need of modernization and retooling. The problem of Harley-Davidson's management was not addressed during this period, but critical renovation and retooling of the production facilities was accomplished. The product line was also expanded somewhat with the introduction in 1970 of the "Superglide." At this time a new logo was also introduced: a broad ribboned number 1, carrying a symbol of the American flag together with the slogan, "The All-American Freedom Machine."

In addition to the retooling of the Milwaukee facilities, AMF opened another production outlet in York, Pennsylvania. With an expanded product line and new facilities, 1973 was a record year for the industry and for Harley-Davidson. It was generally believed that the greatly increased demand was primarily due to the baby-boomers who were maturing into driving and motorcycling age.

The increased output and transition from more traditional, craftsmanlike production to modern assembly line techniques brought on a sharp rise in quality control problems. Riders began to discern a distinct difference between Milwaukee and York machines, mainly because about half of the York-made machines were defective in some respect. These various problems, coupled with AMF's huge capital infusion into Harley-Davidson that had yet to show a substantial return, caused AMF's management to begin considering getting rid of Harley-Davidson.

THE EARLY 1980s

Signaling the end of an era, Harley-Davidson's top management, led by Vaughn Beals, made the company private again in 1981 by separating it from the AMF conglomerate in exchange for $80 million. The company immediately began an aggressive advertising campaign which included such slogans as "Motorcycles by the people, for the people," and stressed an almost patriotic theme to encourage the public to support this veteran American industry. They instantly turned the reorganized company in a new direction through marketing and more dealer cooperation in updating present products and developing additional models.

During this period the country was experiencing an economic recession, and motorcycles were among the first products to be affected. In Japan, however, production increased at a very rapid pace. American buyers purchased approximately 800,000 units during 1981. The effect was drastic for the sales of domestic motorcycles. Harley-Davidson, having never been very competitively priced, was hurt.

With a month-long plant shutdown in 1982 to reduce inventories, and with falling sales throughout the country, Harley-Davidson faced a severe cash-flow problem. Many dealers, whose inventories were taking up floor space and were eating up interest, were now offering models at prices near their own factory cost.

At this time Vaughn Beals, president of Harley-Davidson, announced that the country's oldest motorcycle manufacturer faced bankruptcy; he began to cut company operations. Meanwhile, many dealers were complaining of quality control problems and were deluging the factory with warranty demands.

THE 1982 TARIFF

Despite several drastic cost-saving efforts, the company was still teetering on the edge of disaster. In September 1982, Harley-Davidson took its complaints before the Federal Trade Commission (FTC), claiming the Japanese were dumping large motorcycles in the United States at very cheap prices and were threatening Harley-Davidson with bankruptcy.

In April 1983, President Ronald Reagan took the advice of the FTC and raised the tariffs and imposed quotas for five years on motorcycles over 700 cc in displacement. This was said to be the most aggressive trade restraint ever taken by the United States.

Harley-Davidson took two bold steps in 1986 by changing from a private to a public company, and by acquiring the Holiday Rambler Corporation. As part of a new diversification strategy, Holiday Rambler was seen as an excellent opportunity, because both companies are manufacturing intensive and both produce leading recreational vehicles. They both sell products to very committed groups of people whose lifestyles are heavily influenced by their recreational activities. One final reason for this acquisition was to diversify into an industry that is without Japanese competition.

ASSUMING A COMPETITIVE POSTURE

In order to successfully compete with imported motorcycles, the company undertook significant engineering programs that made dramatic improvements in its V-twin engine designs and, at the same time, resulted in markedly lowered production costs. In addition, the company substantially broadened its product line, offering 16 heavyweight models as compared with only 3 models in 1976. Also, Harley-Davidson reorganized its plant under a system that borrowed heavily from the Japanese style of management. The system, which stressed worker involvement in the manufacturing process, just-in-time manufacturing, and statistical control of operations, became a model for many other companies. An extensive quality control campaign was also introduced.

As a result, the company raised the percentage of motorcycles leaving its production lines without defects from about 50 percent to more than 98 percent, and there was a sharp drop in the number of warranty claims and consumer complaints. In one year, the company was able to lower its break-even point by one third, from 53,000 to 35,000 units annually.

By 1986, Harley-Davidson's share of the U.S. market for heavyweight motorcycles moved up to 33 percent—it had dipped from 42 percent in 1976 to 23 percent in 1983. For all types of motorcycles, the company's share increased from 12.5 percent in 1983 to 19.4 percent in 1986.

The company also began a program to assist dealers in remodeling their dealerships. Each new store was designed for improved traffic flow as well as for increased appeal to a much larger number of people.

In March 1987, the company concluded that its competitive position had improved so much that it asked President Reagan to end its tariff and quota protection a year early. Indeed, Harley-Davidson's motorcycle business was profitable in 1986 for the first time since the company's managers bought it from AMF in 1981. Vaughn Beals was quoted saying: "We're profitable again. We're capitalized. We're diversified. We don't need any more help." A few weeks later, the company announced that, for the first quarter in 1987, it had sales of $162 million and a net income of $5.2 million. These compared with $70 million in sales for the first quarter in 1986 and a net loss of $0.16 million.

3 Organizing and Staffing Skills

10 Organizing Work

11 Organization Structures

12 Staffing

13 Developing People within Organizations

=

Management Foundation

+

=

Improved Organizational Performance

S ection 3 analyzes the organizing and staffing skills of management. These are the skills involved in defining and structuring the work to be done and then employing the appropriate people to fill the established jobs.

Chapter 10 is the first of two chapters related to the organizing function. It introduces that function through a discussion of division of labor. Authority is presented as the concept most central to the organizing function. The delegation process and its importance in the management process are discussed.

Chapter 11 builds on the basic concepts of Chapter 10 and presents several types of organization structures. This chapter also develops the idea that the most appropriate organization structure depends on the organization's strategy, the particular technology employed, the rate of change in the environment, and other dynamic factors.

Chapter 12 deals with the staffing function of management. Human resource planning, recruitment, selection, and other personnel-related activities are discussed.

Chapter 13 emphasizes the importance of developing people. The role of the manager in orienting new employees is described. In addition, the role of the manager in training new and longer-term employees is discussed. Finally, methods used by organizations to develop the skills of managers are presented.

10 Organizing Work

LEARNING OBJECTIVES

*After completing this chapter,
you should be able to:*

1 Define organization and differentiate between a formal and informal organization.

2 Explain the importance of the organizing function.

3 List the advantages and the major disadvantage of horizontal division of labor.

4 Distinguish between authority, power, and responsibility.

5 Explain the concept of centralization versus decentralization.

6 List five principles of organization that are related to authority.

7 Identify several reasons why managers are reluctant to delegate.

If the employer fails to apportion the work among his assistants, it is likely that they will duplicate one another's work. If he neglects to distinguish between the kinds of work as promptly as the amount of endeavor permits, he will lose the advantages of specialization. If he delays too long in appointing supervisors, with the result that the task of oversight exceeds his capacity, the work will not be as well done as it might. Any of these errors reduces, if it does not prevent, the success of the enterprise. In each case, organization has been neglected; it has not performed its mission as a means to a more effective concerted endeavor.

ALVIN BROWN*

Organization – group of people working together in some concerted or coordinated effort to attain objectives.

Organizing – the grouping of activities necessary to attain common objectives and the assignment of each grouping to a manager who has the authority necessary to supervise the people performing the activities.

Informal organization – aggregate of the personal contacts and interactions and the associated groupings of people working within the formal organization.

*M*ost work today is accomplished through organizations. An **organization** is a group of people working together in some type of concerted or coordinated effort to attain objectives. As such, an organization provides a vehicle for implementing strategy and accomplishing objectives that could not be achieved by individuals working separately. The process of **organizing** is the grouping of activities necessary to attain common objectives and the assignment of each grouping to a manager who has the authority necessary to supervise the people performing the activities.[1] Thus, organizing is basically a process of division of labor accompanied by appropriate delegation of authority. As illustrated in the above introductory quote, proper organizing results in the better use of resources.

The framework which defines the boundaries of the formal organization and within which the organization operates is the organization structure. A second and equally important element of an organization is the informal organization. The **informal organization** refers to the aggregate of the personal contacts and interactions and the associated groupings of people working within the formal organization.[2] The informal organization has a structure, but it is not formally and consciously designed. The informal organization is discussed in greater depth in chapter 17.

REASONS FOR ORGANIZING

One of the primary reasons for organizing is to establish lines of authority. This creates order within the group. Absence of authority almost always leads to chaotic situations where everyone is telling everyone else what to do.

* Alvin Brown, *Organization of Industry* (Englewood Cliffs, N.J.: Prentice-Hall, 1947), p. 15.

Second, organizing improves the efficiency and quality of work through synergism. *Synergism* occurs when individual or separate units work together to produce a whole greater than the sum of the parts. Synergism results when three people working together produce more than four people working separately. Synergism can result from division of labor or from increased coordination, both of which are products of good organization.

A final reason for organizing is to improve communication. A good organization structure clearly defines channels of communication among the members of the organization. Such a system also ensures more efficient communications.

DIVISION OF LABOR

Organizing is basically a process of division of labor. The merits of dividing labor have been known for centuries. Taking the very simple task of manufacturing a pin, Adam Smith in 1776 demonstrated how much more efficiently the task could be performed through division of labor.[3]

Labor can be divided either vertically or horizontally. Vertical division of labor is based on the establishment of lines of authority and defines the levels that make up the vertical organizational structure. In addition to establishing authority, vertical division of labor facilitates the flow of communication within the organization.

Horizontal division of labor is based on specialization of work. The basic assumption underlying horizontal division of labor is that by making each worker's task specialized, more work can be produced with the same effort through increased efficiency and quality. Specifically, horizontal division of labor can result in the following advantages:

1. Fewer skills required per person.
2. Easier to supply the skills required for selection or training purposes.
3. Repetition or practice of the same job develops proficiency.
4. Efficient use of skills by primarily utilizing each worker's best skills.
5. The ability to have concurrent operations.
6. More conformity in the final product if each piece is always produced by the same person.

The major problem with horizontal division of labor is that it can result in job boredom and even degradation of the worker. An extreme example of horizontal division of labor is the automobile assembly line. It is not hard to imagine the behavioral problems associated with such an assembly line. When examining horizontal division of labor, it is necessary to identify two dimensions of the job: scope and depth.

Job scope refers to the number of different types of operations performed. In performing a job with narrow scope the worker would perform few operations and repeat the cycle frequently. The negative effects of jobs lacking in

Job scope – number of different types of operations performed on the job.

scope vary with the person performing the job but can result in more errors and lower quality.

Job depth refers to the freedom of employees to plan and organize their own work, to work at their own pace, and to move around and communicate as desired. A lack of job depth can result in job dissatisfaction and work avoidance which can in turn lead to absenteeism, tardiness, and even sabotage.

Job depth – freedom of employees to plan and organize their own work, to work at their own pace, and to move around and communicate as desired.

A job can be high in job scope and low in job depth or vice versa. For example, newspaper delivery involves the same few operations each time, but there is considerable freedom in organizing and pacing the work. Thus, the job is low in scope but high in depth. Of course, many jobs are low (or high) in both job scope and job depth.

Division of labor is not more efficient or even desirable in all situations. At least two basic requirements must exist for the successful use of division of labor. The first requirement is a relatively large volume of work. Enough volume must be produced to allow for specialization and also to keep each employee busy. A second basic requirement is stability in the volume of work, employee attendance, quality of raw materials, product design, and production technology.

AUTHORITY, POWER, AND RESPONSIBILITY

Authority – right to command and expend resources.

Power – ability to command or apply force; not necessarily accompanied by authority.

Responsibility – accountability for the attainment of objectives, the use of resources, and the adherence to organizational policy.

Authority is the right to command and expand resources. Lines of authority serve to link the various organizational components. Unclear delegation of authority is a major source of confusion and conflict within an organization.

Many people confuse power with authority. **Power** is the ability to command or apply force and is not necessarily accompanied by authority. Power is derived from the control of resources. A man with a pistol may have the power to shoot another, but he does not have the right to do so. Similarly, managers may have the power to make frivolous expenditures, but they do not have the right to do so. However, it is true that authority and power often accompany each other.

Responsibility is accountability for the attainment of objectives, the use of resources, and the adherence to organizational policy. Once responsibility is accepted, it becomes an obligation to perform assigned work. The term *responsibility* as used here should not be confused with the term *responsibilities* as in the context of defining job duties.

SOURCES OF AUTHORITY

Authority has traditionally been viewed as a function of position, flowing from top to bottom through the formal organization. According to this view, people hold authority because they occupy a certain position; once removed from the position, they lose their authority. Taking this theory one step further, one can say that the American people, through the Constitution and laws, represent the ultimate source of authority in this country. The Constitution and laws guarantee the right of free enterprise. The owners of a free enterprise organization have the right to elect a board of directors and top management. Top management selects middle-level managers. This process continues down to the lowest person in the organization. This traditional view of authority is also called the formal theory of authority.

A second theory of authority was first outlined in 1926 by Mary Parker Follett and popularized in 1938 by Chester Barnard.[4] Called the acceptance theory of authority, this theory maintains that a manager's source of authority lies with his or her subordinates, because they have the power to either accept or reject the manager's command. Presumably, if the subordinate does not accept the authority of the manager, it does not exist. Both Follett and Barnard viewed disobeying a communication from a manager as a denial of authority by the subordinate.

CENTRALIZATION VERSUS DECENTRALIZATION

There are limitations to the authority of any position. These limitations may be external, in the form of laws, politics, or social attitudes, or they may be internal, as delineated by the organization's objectives or by the job description. The tapered concept of authority states that the breadth and scope of authority become more limited as one descends the scalar chain (see Figure 10–1).

The top levels of management establish the shape of the funnels in Figures 10–1 and 10–2. The more authority that top management chooses to delegate, the less conical the funnel becomes. The less conical the funnel, the more decentralized is the organization. **Centralization** and **decentralization** refer to the degree of authority delegated by upper management. This is usually reflected by the numbers and kinds of decisions made by the lower levels of management. As they increase, the degree of decentralization also increases. Thus, an organization is never totally centralized or totally decentralized: it falls along a continuum ranging from highly centralized to highly decentralized. Looking at Figure 10–2, the organization represented by the diagram on the left is much more centralized than that represented by the right-hand diagram.

The answer to the question of how much an organization should decentralize depends on the specific situation and organization. Decentralization allows for more flexibility and quicker action. It also relieves executives from time-consuming detail work. It often results in higher morale by allowing lower levels of management to be actively involved in the decision-making process. The major disadvantage of decentralization is the potential loss of control. Duplication of effort can also accompany decentralization.

Because no magic formula exists for determining the appropriate degree

Centralization – little authority is delegated to lower levels of management.

Decentralization – a great deal of authority is delegated to lower levels of management.

F I G U R E 10–1   Tapered Concept of Authority

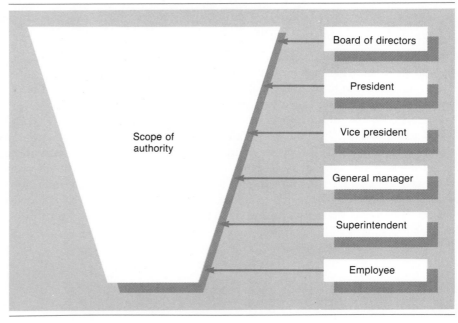

F I G U R E 10–2   Centralized versus Decentralized Authority

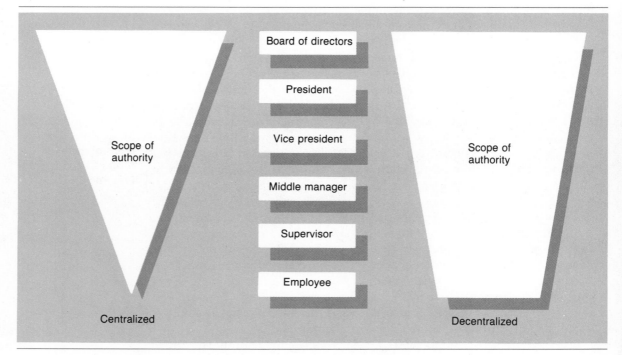

MANAGERS AT WORK 10–1

Regionalization of Campbell Soup

The Campbell Soup can is probably the most durable symbol of American mass marketing. For more than half a century, Campbell has used standardization, volume production, and national brand identity to produce and sell a line of products across the United States. For better marketability, Campbell has cooked up a new approach. Instead of developing a single set of products and marketing programs to use throughout the United States, Campbell is tailoring its products to fit different regions of the country—and even individual neighborhoods within a city. This is being done despite of the fact that this approach, called regionalization, can drive up both

manufacturing and marketing costs by reducing economies of scale. In pursuing regionalization, Campbell has carved the country into 22 regions. In each of these regions there is a combined sales and marketing force which no longer operates merely as an extension of the corporate office. Every regional office is managed as an autonomous profit center with its own mix of advertising and promotion. One major result of regionalization has been to decentralize by pushing decision making down to levels closer to the consumer.

Source: "Marketing's New Look," *Business Week,* January 26, 1987, pp. 64–69.

of decentralization, top management must periodically evaluate its particular situation in light of the advantages and disadvantages of greater decentralization. Managers at Work 10–1 describes how Campbell Soup has decentralized through regionalization.

PRINCIPLES BASED ON AUTHORITY

Because authority is a key element in management and organizations, numerous related principles have been developed. Before proceeding, recall from Chapter 1 that management principles are suggested guides rather than ironclad laws.

Delegation—The Parity Principle

Can authority be delegated? Can responsibility be delegated? There is little debate concerning the delegation of authority—it can and should be delegated. For example, a manager might very well choose to delegate the authority to subordinates to make expenditures, without approval, up to a stipulated amount. But, considerable debate often arises with regard to the delegation of responsibility. A close analysis of this debate generally reveals that it is more the result of semantics than of a misunderstanding of the concepts involved. Those contending that responsibility cannot be delegated support their answer by stating that managers can never shed the responsibilities of their jobs by passing them on to subordinates. Those contending that responsibility can be delegated justify their position by pointing out that managers can certainly make subordinates responsible to them for certain actions.

Both parties are correct. Managers can delegate responsibilities to subordinates in the sense of making subordinates responsible to them. However, this delegation to subordinates does not make managers any less responsible to their superiors. Delegation of responsibility does not mean abdication of responsibility by the delegating manager. Responsibility is not like an object which can be passed from individual to individual. Suppose a loan manager for a bank decided to delegate to the loan officers the responsibility for ensuring that all loans are processed within a 10-day limit as stated by bank policy. Loan managers can certainly make loan officers accountable (responsible) to them in this matter. At the same time, loan managers are no less accountable to their bosses.

Parity principle – states that authority and responsibility coincide.

The **parity principle** states that authority and responsibility must coincide. Management must delegate sufficient authority so subordinates can do their jobs. At the same time, subordinates can be expected to accept responsibility only for those areas within their authority.

Both authority and responsibility must be accepted by subordinates before the delegation process has been completed. Management sometimes expects employees to seek and assume responsibility that they have not been asked to assume and then to bid for the necessary authority. Such a system leads to guessing games which do nothing but create frustration and waste energy.

A manager's resistance to delegating authority is natural. There are several reasons why they are reluctant. Unfortunately, many managers subscribe to the old saying, "If you want something done right, do it yourself!" Such an attitude reveals that the manager does not have a grasp of the management process and has done a poor job of selecting and developing subordinates. Managers who attempt to do everything themselves find that their time is continually consumed by rather unimportant tasks and that they do not have time to do important tasks. Newly appointed managers tend to adopt this attitude. They fear failure unless they do each task personally.

A second reason often given for not delegating is that it is easier for a manager to do a task than to teach a subordinate how to do it. This might be true the 1st time a particular task has to be done, but what about the 10th or 20th time? Delegating often does involve some initial investment of time; however, this investment is usually recouped quickly through subsequently saved time.

A third reason why managers are reluctant to delegate is the fear that a subordinate will look so good that he or she might replace the manager. To good managers, such fears are totally unfounded. A manager's performance is, for the most part, a reflection of the performance of subordinates. If a manager's subordinates look good, the manager looks good; if the subordinates look bad, the manager looks bad.

A fourth reason that causes managers to shy away from delegating is the human attraction for power. Most people like the feel of power which often accompanies authority. To many managers, there is a certain degree of satisfaction in having the power and authority to grant or not grant certain requests.

Yet another reason that managers are reluctant to delegate is that they often feel comfortable doing those things that should be delegated. This is especially a problem with people recently promoted into management. It is only natural that many new managers feel more comfortable doing the same tasks that they did before they became managers.

In spite of all the reasons for not delegating, there are some very strong reasons why a manager should delegate. Several phenomena occur when a manager successfully delegates. The manager's time is freed to pursue other tasks, and the subordinates gain feelings of belonging and being needed. These feelings often lead to a genuine commitment on the part of the subordinates. Another reason to delegate is that it is one of the best methods for developing subordinates and satisfying customers. Pushing authority down the organization also allows employees to deal more effectively with customers. For example, some department stores give their salespeople the authority to make exchanges and refunds right on the floor, while others force customers to go to the credit department. Most customers much prefer the first situation. The importance of satisfying the customer should not be minimized. Thomas Peters and Robert Waterman, Jr., in their study of America's excellent companies, identified "close to the customer" as one of the eight identifiable attributes of excellent companies.[5]

Unfortunately, the tendency of many delegating managers is to delegate only simple, unimportant tasks. The following quote from Robert Townsend illustrates this point:

> Many give lip service, but few delegate authority in important matters. And that means all they delegate is dog-work. A real leader does as much dog-work for his people as he can: He can do it, or see a way to do without it, 10 times as fast. And he delegates as many important matters as he can because that creates a climate in which people grow.[6]

Successful delegation involves delegating matters which stimulate the subordinates.

How to Delegate. In order to successfully delegate, a manager must decide which tasks can be delegated. A good way for a manager to identify which tasks might be delegated is to first analyze how he or she spends his or her time. This can usually be done by keeping a daily time log indicating how time is actually spent. By carefully studying a time log, a manager can often identify the functions and duties that can be delegated and those that cannot. Once a manager has determined which tasks can be delegated, he or she should decide which subordinates can handle each task. In order to best assign tasks to subordinates, managers must be well acquainted with the skills of their immediate subordinates. When a manager has decided what tasks can be delegated to which subordinates, the next step is to grant authority to make commitments, use resources, and take the actions necessary to perform the tasks. This is often the most difficult step in the delegation process for all of the reasons mentioned in the previous section. The final steps in the delegation process are to make the subordinates responsible and to control the delegation. Subordinates can be made responsible by clearly creating an obligation on their part. The delegation can be controlled by monitoring it regularly and ensuring that it does not revert to the delegating manager. Figure 10–3 summarizes the steps in the delegation process.

F I G U R E   10–3   Steps in the
Delegation Process

---

1. Analyze how you spend your time.
2. Decide which tasks can be assigned.
3. Decide who can handle each task.
4. Delegate the authority.
5. Create an obligation (responsibility).
6. Control the delegation.

Probably the most nebulous part of the delegation process centers around the question, How much authority should be delegated? As mentioned previously, management must delegate sufficient authority to allow the subordinate to perform the job. Precisely what can and cannot be delegated depends on the commitments of the manager and the number and quality of subordinates. A general rule of thumb is to delegate authority and responsibility to the lowest organization level that has the competence to accept them. Managers at Work 10–2 describes how good delegation habits have contributed to the success of Applied Energy Services, Inc.

Unity of Command

Unity-of-Command principle – states that an employee should have one and only one immediate manager.

The **principle of unity of command** states that an employee should have one and only one immediate manager. The difficulty of serving more than one superior has been recognized for thousands of years. Recall the Sermon on the Mount, when Jesus said, "No man can serve two masters."[7]

In its simplest form, this problem arises when two managers tell the same subordinate to do different jobs at the same time. The subordinate is thus placed in a no-win situation. Regardless of which manager the employee obeys, the other will be dissatisfied. The key to avoiding problems with unity of command is make sure that employees clearly understand the lines of authority that directly affect them. All too often, managers assume that

MANAGERS AT WORK 10–2

Profile: Roger Sant, Applied Energy Services, Inc.

Our management style is unique compared to others in "heavy industry." Each of our plants is divided into five or seven autonomous work groups, called *families* by the workers. Each family organizes itself, operates itself, makes improvements, and is ultimately responsible to a plant manager. The workers regularly take the initiative in thinking of ways to improve company operations. Instead of only telling workers what to do, this environment allows them to think and act on their own. We utilize lean management and employee innovation to make it cheaper for the utilities to buy from us than to produce kilowatts themselves. It seems to work. Sales for 1987: $38 million; contracted for 1988: $80 million.

Source: Adapted from "Success," May 1988, p. 10.

employees understand the lines of authority when in fact they do not. For example, does the industrial relations manager in plant A report directly to the general manager of plant A or to the corporate vice president of industrial relations? In this type of situation, which is not unusual, the industrial relations manager in plant A normally will report directly to the plant A general manager and have a consultative type of relationship with the corporate vice president of industrial relations.

Scalar Principle

The **scalar principle** states that authority in the organization flows one link at a time, through the chain of managers ranging from the highest to lowest ranks. Commonly referred to as the chain of command, the scalar principle is based on the need for communication and the principle of unity of command.

The problem with circumventing the scalar process is that the link bypassed in the process may have very pertinent information. For example, suppose that Jerry goes directly above his immediate boss Ellen to Charlie for permission to take his lunch break 30 minutes earlier. Charlie, believing it to be reasonable, approves Jerry's request—only to later find out that the other two people in Jerry's department had also rescheduled their lunch breaks. Thus, the department would be totally vacant from 12:30 to 1 o'clock. Ellen, the bypassed manager, would have known about the other rescheduled lunch breaks.

A common misconception is that every action must painfully progress through every link in the chain, whether its course is upward or downward.

Scalar principle—states that authority in the organization flows, one link at a time, through the chain of managers ranging from the highest to lowest ranks; also called chain of command.

This point was refuted many years ago by Lyndell Urwick, an internationally known management consultant:

> Provided there is proper confidence and loyalty between superiors and subordinates, and both parties take the trouble to keep the other informed in matters in which they should have a concern, the "scalar process" does not imply that there should be no shortcuts. It is concerned with authority, and provided the authority is recognized and no attempt is made to evade or to supersede it, there is ample room for avoiding in matters of action the childish practices of going upstairs one step at a time or running up one ladder and down another when there is nothing to prevent a direct approach on level ground.[8]

As Fayol stated, years before Urwick, "It is an error to depart needlessly from authority, but it is an even greater one to keep to it when detriment to the business ensues."[9] Both men are simply saying that in certain instances, one can and should shortcut the scalar chain if it is not done in a secretive or deceitful manner.

Span of Management

Span of management – number of subordinates a manager can effectively manage; also called span of control.

The **span of management** (also called the span of control) refers to the number of subordinates a manager can effectively manage. Although the British World War I general, Sir Ian Hamilton, is usually given credit for developing the concept of a limited span of control, there are numerous related examples throughout history (see Managers at Work 10–3). Sir Ian argued that a narrow span of management (with no more than six subordinates reporting to a manager) would enable the manager to get the job accomplished in the course of a normal working day.[10]

In 1933, V. A. Graicunas published a classic paper that analyzed subordinate-superior relationships in terms of a mathematical formula.[11] This formula was based on the theory that the complexities of managing increase geometrically as the number of subordinates increases arithmetically. Graicunas's reasoning was that not only did the number of single relationships increase but so did the number of direct group relationships and cross relationships. Table 10–1 shows the total number of potential relationships envisioned by Graicunas. (Managers at Work 10–4 provides some interesting personal information about Graicunas.)

Based on his personal experience and the works of Sir Ian and Graicunas, Urwick first stated the concept of span of management as a management principle in 1938: "No superior can supervise directly the work of more than five, or at the most, six subordinates whose work interlocks."[12] As will be seen, Urwick's concept is not exactly applicable in all situations.

Since the publication of Graicunas's and Urwick's works, the upper limit of five or six subordinates has been continuously criticized as being too restrictive. Many practitioners and scholars contend that there are situations in which more than five or six subordinates can be effectively supervised. Their beliefs

MANAGERS AT WORK 10–3

Historical Development of Span of Management

There is some evidence that the Egyptians practiced a form of "span of management." In the earliest Egyptian dynasties, a pharaoh's death meant that his workers and servants were killed and buried with him. As the civilization evolved, that unusual custom was replaced with the idea of burying carvings that symbolized the servants. Interestingly, excavated carvings of servants have indicated that there was a ratio of about 10 servants to each supervisor.

Source: Daniel A. Wren, *The Evolution of Management Thought,* 2nd ed. (New York: John Wiley & Sons, 1979.)

have been substantiated by considerable empirical evidence showing that the limit of five or six subordinates has been successfully exceeded in many situations.[13] Urwick has suggested that these exceptions can be explained by the fact that senior workers often function as unofficial managers or leaders.[14]

In view of recent evidence, the span-of-management concept has been revised to state that the number of people who should report directly to any one person should be based upon the complexity, variety, and proximity of the jobs, the quality of the people filling the jobs, and the ability of the manager. Complexity basically refers to the job scope and job depth of the jobs being managed. Naturally, the more complex the jobs being managed, the lower the appropriate span of management. Variety relates to the number of different types of jobs being managed. For example, are all the subordinates doing the same or similar jobs, or are they doing very different jobs? The more variety that is present, the lower the appropriate span of management.

T A B L E 10–1   Graicunas's Direct, Cross, and Group Relationships

NUMBER OF SUBORDINATES	NUMBER OF DIRECT SINGLE RELATIONSHIPS	NUMBER OF CROSS RELATIONSHIPS	NUMBER OF DIRECT RELATIONSHIPS BETWEEN GROUPS	NUMBER OF TOTAL RELATIONSHIPS
1	1	0	0	1
2	2	2	2	6
3	3	6	9	18
4	4	12	28	44
5	5	20	75	100
6	6	30	186	222
7	7	42	441	490
8	8	56	1,016	1,080

MANAGERS AT WORK 10-4

The Life of Vytautas Andrius Graicunas

Information about the life of Vytautas Graicunas, the developer of the span of control, is sketchy and often ambiguous. Although Graicunas is frequently described as a Lithuanian or French mathematician, he was actually born, raised, and educated in Chicago. After completing degrees in accounting and mechanical engineering, he helped start several factories in the United States and Europe. While attending a meeting of the International Committee for Scientific Management in Paris in 1929, Graicunas met Lyndall F. Urwick, and they collaborated on the classic essay about the span of control—"Relationship in Organization."

During the Second World War, Graicunas was a major in the U.S. Air Corps and adviser to the Lithuanian Air Force. Although little information is available about his activities between 1940 and 1947, it is suspected that he served with the U.S. Office of Strategic Services. While on a business trip to Moscow in 1947, Graicunas was arrested by the Soviet Secret Police. After interrogation and torture, Graicunas went on a starvation strike and died.

Source: Arthur G. Bedeian, "Vytautas Andrius Graicunas—a Biographical Note," *Academy of Management Journal,* June 1974, p. 347.

The physical dispersion or the proximity of the jobs being managed also influences the span of management. If the subordinates are all working in rather close proximity, such as in one room, the span of management would be greater than if they are spread over the city or state. Quality of the people refers to the fact that some people need and require closer supervision than do others. The final contingent factor, the ability of the manager, refers to the skill of the manager in performing managerial duties.

Thus, in situations where workers are engaged in simple, repetitive operations in close proximity, the span of management could be very large. In situations involving highly diversified and technical work, the span of management might be as low as three or four.

While much thought is given to ensuring that a manager's span of management is not too great, the opposite situation is often overlooked. All too frequently in organizations, situations develop in which only one subordinate is reporting to a particular manager. While this situation might very well be justified under certain circumstances, it often results in an inefficient and "top-heavy" organization. The pros and cons of flat organizations (wide spans of management, few levels) versus tall organizations (narrow spans of management, many levels) are discussed at length in the next chapter. Figure 10-4 summarizes the factors affecting the manager's span of management.

F I G U R E 10–4 Factors Affecting the Span of Management

FACTOR	DESCRIPTION	RELATIONSHIP TO SPAN OF CONTROL
Complexity	Job scope Job depth	Inverse*
Variety	Number of different types of jobs being managed	Inverse*
Proximity	Physical dispersion of jobs being managed	Direct†
Quality of subordinates	General quality of the subordinates being managed	Direct†
Quality of manager	Ability to perform managerial duties	Direct†

* As the factor of complexity (or variety) increases, the span of management decreases.

† As the factor of proximity (or quality) increases, the span of management increases.

The Exception Principle

The exception principle (also known as management by exception) is closely related to the parity principle. The **exception principle** states that managers should concentrate their efforts on matters that deviate significantly from normal and let subordinates handle routine matters. The idea here is that managers should concentrate on those matters that require their abilities and not become bogged down with duties that their subordinates should be doing. The exception principle can be hard to comply with when incompetent or insecure subordinates refer everything to their superiors because they are afraid to make a decision. On the other hand, the superior should refrain from making everyday decisions which have been delegated to a subordinate.

> **Exception principle** — states that managers should concentrate on matters that deviate significantly from normal and let subordinates handle routine matters; also called management by exception.

/S U M M A R Y

This chapter introduces the organizing function and illustrates how organization is achieved through division of labor. The delegation process, principles of authority, and the advantages and disadvantages of centralization versus decentralization are also presented.

L E A R N I N G O B J E C T I V E 1

Define Organization and Differentiate between a Formal and Informal Organization.

An organization is a group of people working together in some type of concerted or coordinated effort to attain objectives. As such, an organization provides a vehicle for accomplishing objectives that could not be achieved by individuals working separately. The framework that defines the boundaries of the formal organization and within which the organization operates is the organization structure. The informal organization refers to the aggregate of the personal contacts and interactions and the associated groupings of people working within the formal organization. The informal organization has a structure, but it is not formally and consciously designed.

LEARNING OBJECTIVE 2

Explain the Importance of the Organizing Function.
The organizing function determines how organizational resources will be employed to achieve goals. It also establishes lines of authority, improves the efficiency and quality of work through synergism, and improves communication by defining channels of communication in the organization.

LEARNING OBJECTIVE 3

List the Advantages and the Major Disadvantage of Horizontal Division of Labor.
Horizontal division of labor can result in the following advantages: (1) fewer skills are required per person; (2) it is easier to supply the skills required for selection or training purposes; (3) repetition or practice of the same job develops proficiency; (4) there is efficient use of skills by primarily utilizing each worker's best skills; (5) it allows concurrent operations; and (6) there is more conformity in the final product if each piece is always produced by the same person. The major disadvantage of horizontal division of labor is that it can result in job boredom and even degradation of the worker.

LEARNING OBJECTIVE 4

Distinguish between Authority, Power, and Responsibility.
Authority is the right to command and expend resources. Lines of authority serve to link the various organizational components together. Power is the ability to command or apply force and is not necessarily accompanied by authority. Power is derived from the control of resources. Responsibility is accountability for the attainment of objectives, the use of resources, and the adherence to organizational policy. Once responsibility is accepted, it becomes an obligation to perform assigned work.

LEARNING OBJECTIVE 5

Explain the Concept of Centralization versus Decentralization.
Centralization and decentralization refer to the degree of authority delegated by upper management. This is usually reflected by the numbers and kinds of decisions made by the lower levels of management. As they increase, the degree of decentralization also increases. Thus, an organization is never totally centralized or totally decentralized: it falls along a continuum ranging from highly centralized to highly decentralized.

LEARNING OBJECTIVE 6

List Five Principles of Organization That Are Related to Authority.

Five principles of organization related to authority are: (1) the parity principle, (2) principle of unity of command, (3) the scalar principle, (4) span of management, and (5) the exception principle.

LEARNING OBJECTIVE 7

Identify Several Reasons Why Managers Are Reluctant to Delegate.

A manager's resistance to delegating authority is natural. Several of the reasons why managers are reluctant to delegate include the following: (1) fear of subordinates failing (if you want anything done right around here, do it yourself); (2) it is easier for a manager to do the task than to teach a subordinate how to do it; (3) fear of the subordinate looking too good; (4) the human attraction for power; and (5) the manager often feels comfortable doing those things that should be delegated.

REVIEW QUESTIONS

1. What is an organization? Define the management function of organizing. Define organizational structure. What is an informal organization?
2. Discuss the reasons for organizing.
3. What is the difference between horizontal and vertical division of labor? What is the difference between job scope and job depth?
4. Define authority, power, and responsibility.
5. Discuss two approaches to viewing the sources of authority.
6. What is the difference between a highly centralized and a highly decentralized organization?
7. What is the parity principle?
8. Describe three components of the delegation process.
9. Why are many managers reluctant to delegate authority?
10. What is the unity-of-command principle?
11. What is the scalar principle?
12. What is the span of management?
13. What is the exception principle?

DISCUSSION QUESTIONS

1. Do you think that division of labor has been emphasized too much in today's highly mechanized and efficient society?
2. Comment on the following statement which is attributed to Robert Heinlein:

   A human being should be able to change a diaper, plan an invasion, butcher a hog, conn a ship, design a building, write a sonnet, balance accounts, build a wall, set a bone, comfort the dying, take orders, give orders, cooperate, act alone, solve equations, analyze new problems, pitch manure, program a computer, cook a tasty meal, fight efficiently, die gallantly. Specialization is for insects.

3. The Que Company has 712 employees and annual sales of $11.2 million. The entire company is located in one office building

on Main Street. Based on this information, what can you say about the degree of centralization of authority in this organization?

4. As a manager, do you think you would prefer a relatively large (more than seven) or small (seven or less) span of management? Why, and what are the implications of your choice?

REFERENCES & ADDITIONAL READINGS

[1] Harold Koontz and Cyril O'Donnell, *Management: A Systems and Contingency Analysis of Managerial Functions,* 6th ed. (New York: McGraw-Hill, 1976), p. 274.

[2] Chester L. Barnard, *Functions of the Executive* (Cambridge, Mass.: Harvard University Press, 1938), pp. 114–15.

[3] Adam Smith, *The Wealth of Nations* (New York: Modern Library, 1917), (originally published in 1776).

[4] Mary Parker Follett, *Freedom and Co-Ordination* (London: Management Publication Trust, 1949), pp. 1–15 (the lecture reproduced in *Freedom and Co-Ordination* was first delivered in 1926); Barnard, *Functions,* p. 163.

[5] Thomas J. Peters and Robert H. Waterman, Jr., *In Search of Excellence* (New York: Harper & Row, 1982), pp. 14, 156–99.

[6] Robert Townsend, *Further up the Organization* (New York: Alfred A. Knopf, 1984), p. 50.

[7] *The Holy Bible,* Revised Standard Version, Matthew 6:24.

[8] L. F. Urwick, *The Elements of Administration* (New York: Harper & Row, 1943), p. 46.

[9] Henri Fayol, *General and Industrial Management* (London: Sir Isaac Pitman & Sons, 1949), p. 36 (first published in 1916).

[10] Sir Ian Hamilton, *The Soul and Body of an Army* (London: Edward Arnold, 1921), p. 229.

[11] V. A. Graicunas, "Relationship in Organization," *Bulletin of the International Management Institute* (Geneva: International Labour Office, 1933), reprinted in *Papers on the Science of Administration,* ed. L. Gulick and F. L. Urwick (New York: Institute of Public Administration, 1937), pp. 181–87.

[12] L. F. Urwick, "Scientific Principles and Organizations," *Institute of Management Series No. 19* (New York: American Management Association, 1938), p. 8.

[13] For a brief discussion of such situations, see Leslie W. Rue, "Supervisory Control in Modern Management," *Atlanta Economic Review,* January–February 1975, pp. 43–44.

[14] L. F. Urwick, "V. A. Graicunas and the Span of Control," *Academy of Management Journal,* June 1974, p. 352.

INCIDENT

Taking Over Dad's Business

Casey Ice Company had been in operation for over 50 years manufacturing ice for all purposes, ranging from crushed ice for sale in convenience stores to 300-pound block ice for industrial use. As with all seasonal industries, the company's daily operations were in a state of flux, with long hours of work required during the busy season. The company employed anywhere from 75 to 125 people ranging from unskilled labor to sales and supervisory personnel.

Mr. Albert had managed the plant for the past 30 years, ever since he had purchased it from an old friend. He performed all of the jobs in the plant, working right along with the workers and spending very little time in the office looking at "those figures and crazy ideas that have no business in an ice plant." Mr. Albert's philosophy was aptly described by his frequently made observation that "this is an old-fashioned business, and we're going to run it in an old-fashioned way." Mr. Albert's words were law. That he knew everything there was to know about making ice could not be disputed. He used his expertise and position to run all aspects of the operation, trusting few if any of the other employees. Recently he had fired Ben Porter on the spot for "laying out" on Labor Day. Ben tried to explain that he had worked 33 days straight with no time off and, further, that his supervisor had given him permission to take the day off. But his explanation was to no avail. Mr. Albert simply stated that no supervisor had the authority to give him the day off.

Two months ago, Mr. Albert suffered a heart attack and died while loading a truck with ice. His daughter, Christie, who had been living on the West Coast, had been considering going into business for herself for some time and was now considering the possibility of replacing her father. She hadn't been home much during the past few years, as she had been busy pursuing her own career in advertising. But she remembered how much the company had meant to her father and felt somewhat obligated to carry on and expand his organization.

In October, Christie arrived at the Casey Ice Company, walked in the door, and saw a sign posted on the wall directly in front of her: "We got one rule—do what you're told." It had been a long time since she'd walked through that door, but she knew she'd never seen the sign before. Tearing it down, she proceeded to walk through the plant talking to the employees and supervisors.

The situation was bordering on chaos; nobody seemed to be working. As the day progressed, she learned that nobody really knew what they were supposed to do. "Mr. Albert had always assigned the jobs first thing each morning" was the most common answer she received when asking what was going on. Absenteeism and tardiness were major problems; there were no policies, procedures, or rules for her to refer to. When she tried to get information from the supervisors, she learned that her father hadn't really used supervisors as subordinates who directed the work force.

Christie retreated to the office for the rest of the day to study the records regarding company operations. The investigation proved even more alarming than her conversation with the employees. Her father had kept all the books with the help of an old friend who was a CPA. It took some time to decipher the meaning behind the figures she found.

The annual turnover rate averaged about 75 percent over the past five years, which explained why the daily work log revealed that many employees spent a substantial part of their time training new employees. The financial statements revealed that the company had lost a considerable amount of money due to decreasing sales over the past two years. In fact, sales for last year were down $327,000 from the previous year. On the other hand, Christie knew that the Casey Ice Company was the only large ice company in the major metropolitan area (550,000 population). She later learned that many vendors, dissatisfied with late deliveries and even forgotten deliveries, discontinued buying ice from Casey and purchased ice machines. Further, one employee of Casey revealed to Christie that during the ice shortage on July 4 last year, Casey Ice Company's prices rose 100 percent for a two-week period because Mr. Albert believed "if they want it bad enough, they'll pay for it." This, the employee suggested, resulted in even more vendors discontinuing use of the company's services.

The records also revealed a significant problem existed in the industrial market for ice. Casey Ice Company once served a large number of industrial users; in fact, over half of Casey's customers used to be industrial users. However, the number of industrial users had gradually dwindled over the years. Today, industrial ice services comprised a little under 12 percent of the total business.

Christie sat back in the leather chair, resting her feet on the desk. Her father had been so proud of Casey Ice Company. None of this made any sense—how could he have let things get into such a state? But more importantly, what could she do to get things moving again?

Questions

1. What can Christie do to straighten things out?

2. What principles of organization have been violated?

EXERCISE

Minor Errors

R ecently you have noticed that one of the staff members on the same level as your boss has been giving you a hard time concerning reports that you submit to her. Having reviewed recent reports, you have discovered a few minor errors that you should have caught; but in your opinion, they are not significant enough to warrant the kind of criticism you've been receiving. Your boss and this particular manager have a history of bad relations, which may be one reason for her attitude and actions.

As you think about how to best handle the situation, you consider these alternatives:

1. Talk to the manager in private and ask her why she is being so critical.
2. Do nothing. It is probably a temporary situation; to bring undue attention to it will only make matters worse.
3. Since your boss may get involved, discuss it with her and ask advice on what to do.
4. Work harder to upgrade the reports; make sure there will be nothing to criticize in the future.
5. Discuss it with your boss, but minimize or down play the situation by letting her know that you feel that constructive criticism of this type is usually healthy.

Other alternatives may be open to you, but assume that these are the only ones you have considered.

A. *Without discussion* with anyone, decide which of these approaches you would take now. Be prepared to defend your choice.
B. What principle of organization most closely relates to this situation?
C. To what extent do you think this is an organization problem as opposed to a personality problem?

11 Organization Structures

LEARNING OBJECTIVES

*After completing this chapter,
you should be able to:*

1 Describe the general relationship between an organization's strategy and its structure.

2 Identify the different types of departmentation.

3 Distinguish between a line structure, a line and staff structure, and a matrix structure.

4 Explain what is meant by a flat structure versus a tall structure.

5 List several advantages and disadvantages of committees.

6 Discuss the following phrase: simple form, lean staff.

7 Describe a contingency approach to organizing.

One man draws out the wire, another straightens it, and a third cuts it, a fourth points it, a fifth grinds it at the top for receiving the head; to make the head requires two or three distinct operations; to put it on is a peculiar business, to whiten the pins is another; it is even a trade by itself to put them into the paper, and the important business of making a pin is, in this manner, divided into 18 distinct operations, which, in some manufactory, are all performed by distinct hands; though in others the same man will sometimes perform two or three of them. I have seen a small manufactory of this kind where 10 men only were employed and where some of them consequently performed two or three distinct operations. But though they were very poor and therefore but indifferently accommodated with the necessary machinery, they could, when they exerted themselves, make among them about 12 pounds of pins a day.

ADAM SMITH[*]

Many people believe that a good manager or a good employee should be able to perform well regardless of the organization structure and environment. The belief is that if managers or employees are good enough, then they can overcome any obstacles the organization structure might present. Others believe that given the right organization structure, anyone should be able to perform in an acceptable fashion. The truth lies somewhere in between. An appropriate **organization structure** certainly helps to achieve good performance.

Organization structure – framework that defines the boundaries of the formal organization and within which the organization operates.

STRATEGY AND STRUCTURE

A major part of an organization's strategy for attaining its objectives deals with how the organization is structured. Chapter 10 discussed the basic organizational concepts of division of labor and the establishment of appropriate authority relationships. The structure of an organization is reflected in how groups compete for resources, where responsibilities for profits and other performance measures lie, how information is transmitted, and how decisions are made. In addition to clarifying and defining strategy through the delegation of authority and responsibility, the structure of the organization can either facilitate or inhibit strategy implementation.

[*] Adam Smith, *An Inquiry into the Nature and Causes of the Wealth of Nations,* vol. 1 (London: A. Strahan and T. Cadell, 1776), pp. 7–8.

In a ground-breaking study of organizational strategy, Alfred D. Chandler described a pattern in the evolution of organizational structures.[1] The pattern was based on studies of Du Pont, General Motors, Sears Roebuck & Co., and Standard Oil Company, with corroborating evidence from many other firms. The pattern Chandler described was that of changing strategy, followed by administrative problems, leading to decline in performance, revised structure, and a subsequent return to economic health. In summary, Chandler concluded that structure follows strategy. In other words, Chandler found that changes in strategy ultimately led to or resulted in changes in the organization's structure. Chandler's work related particularly to growth and to the structural adjustments that were made to maintain efficient performance during market expansion, product-line diversification, and vertical integration.

Although subsequent research has supported the existence of a relationship between strategy and structure, it is clear that strategy is not the only variable that has a bearing on structure.[2] It can safely be concluded that the process of matching structure to strategy is complex and should be undertaken with a thorough understanding of the historical development of the current structure, the requirements of the organization's environment and technology, and the political relationships that might be affected.[3] The process of departmentation, which is the primary means used to structure an organization, is discussed in the next section.

DEPARTMENTATION

While thousands of different organization structures exist, almost all are built on the concept of departmentation. **Departmentation** involves grouping activities into related work units. The work units may be related on the basis of work functions, product, customer, geography, technique, or time.

Departmentation – grouping activities into related work units.

Functional

Functional departmentation occurs when organization units are defined by the nature of the work. Although different terms may be used, most organizations have three basic functions—production, sales, and finance. Production refers to the actual creation of something of value, either goods or services or both. The distribution of goods or services created is usually referred to as sales or marketing. Finally, any organization, manufacturing or service, must provide the financial structure necessary for carrying out its activities.

Functional departmentation – organizational units are defined by the nature of the work.

Each of these basic functions may be broken down as necessary. For instance, the production department may be split into maintenance, quality control, engineering, manufacturing, and so on. The marketing department may be grouped into advertising, sales, and market research. (Figure 11–1 charts a typical functional departmentation.)

F I G U R E   11–1   Functional Departmentation

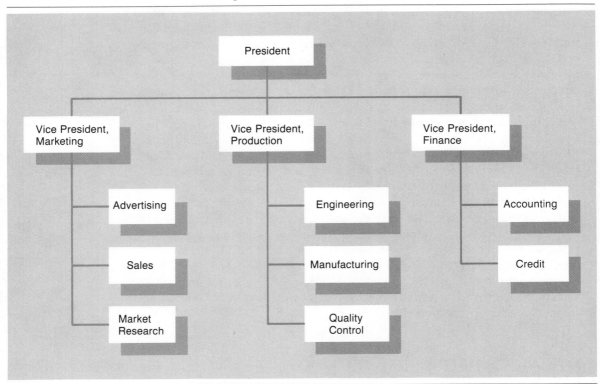

The primary advantage of functional departmentation is that it allows for specialization within functions. It also provides for efficient use of equipment and resources. Functional departmentation, however, can be accompanied by some negative effects. Members of a functional group may develop more loyalty to the functional group's goals than to the organization's goals. If the group's goals and the organization's goals are not mutually supportive, such activity can lead to problems. Conflict may also develop between different departments striving for different goals. This type of conflict is discussed in greater depth in Chapter 18.

Product

Product departmentation—all activities necessary to produce and market a product or service are under one manager.

Under **departmentation by product** or service, all the activities needed to produce and market a product or service are usually under a single manager. This system allows workers to identify with a particular product and thus develop esprit de corps. It also facilitates managing each product as a distinct profit center. Product departmentation provides opportunities for training for executive personnel by letting them experience a broad range of functional activities. Problems can arise if departments become overly competitive to

F I G U R E 11–2 Product Departmentation

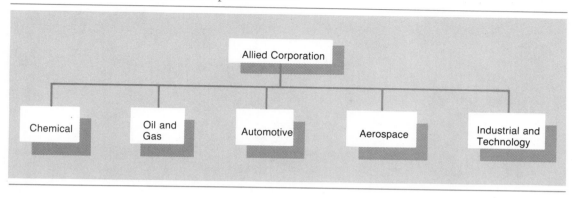

the detriment of the overall organization. A second potential problem is that facilities and equipment may have to be duplicated. Product departmentation adapts best to large, multiproduct organizations. Figure 11–2 illustrates product departmentation at the Allied Corporation.

Geographic

Geographic departmentation is most likely to occur in organizations that maintain physically dispersed and autonomous operations or offices. Departmentation by territories permits the use of local workers and/or salespeople. This can create customer goodwill and an awareness of local feelings and desires. It can also provide a high level of service. Of course, having too many geographic locations can be very costly.

Geographic departmentation – organizational units are defined by territories.

Customer

Another type, **customer departmentation,** is based on division by customers served. A common example is an organization which has one department to handle retail customers and one department to handle wholesale or industrial customers. (Figure 11–3 shows departmentation by customer for Johnson & Johnson.) This type of departmentation has the same advantages and disadvantages as product departmentation. For example, if the Professional Group and the Pharmaceutical Group in Figure 11–3 became too competitive with each other for corporate resources, the organization's overall performance could be damaged.

Customer departmentation – organizational units are based on division by customers served.

Other Types

Several other types of departmentation are possible. Departmentation by simple numbers is practiced when the most important ingredient to success is the number of workers. Organizing for a local United Way drive might be an

F I G U R E 11–3   Customer Departmentation

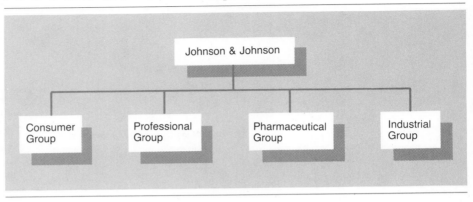

example. Departmentation by process or equipment is another possibility. A final type of departmentation is by time or shift. Organizations that work around the clock may use this type of departmentation.

Departmentation is practiced not only for division of labor but also to improve control and communications. Typically, as an organization grows in size, it adds levels of departmentation. A small organization may have no departmentation at first. As it grows, it may departmentalize first by function, then by product, then by geography. As illustrated in Figure 11–4, many different department mixes are possible for a given organization. Which one is best depends on the specific situation.

Another factor that affects an organization's structure is conducting business in the international arena. Managers at Work 11–1 describes how Ampex, Citicorp, Dow, and Honda differ in their organization's foreign market operations.

LINE STRUCTURE

Line structure—organization structure with direct vertical lines between the different levels of the organization.

The most important aspect of the **line structure** is that the work of all organizational units is directly involved in producing and marketing the organization's goods or services. The simplest organization structure, it has vertical links between the different levels of the organization. All members of the organization receive instructions through the scalar chain. One advantage is a clear authority structure which promotes rapid decision making and prevents passing the buck or blaming someone else. A disadvantage is that it may force managers to perform too broad a range of duties. It may also cause the organization to become too dependent on one or two key persons who are capable of performing many duties. Because of its simplicity, line structure exists most frequently in small organizations. Figure 11–5 represents a simplified line structure.

F I G U R E 11–4 Possible Departmentation Mixes for a Sales Organization

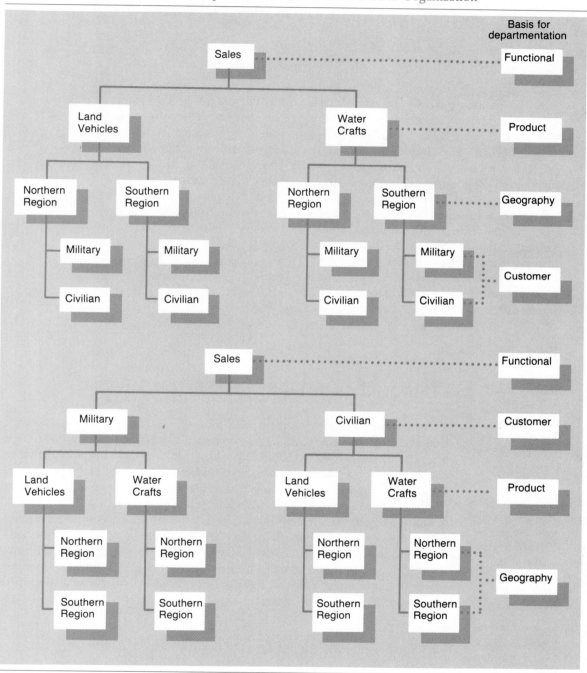

MANAGERS AT WORK 11-1

The Conduct of International Business

Ampex, Citicorp, Dow, and Honda have a lot in common. They export something of value from their home countries and also produce abroad. They implement overseas activities via wholly owned foreign subsidiaries, joint ventures, and licensing arrangements that display obvious dependence on the parent company. They generally center their R&D at home. But Ampex, Citicorp, Dow, and Honda differ in important ways, too. Ampex produces abroad to export back to the U.S. market in some cases. Its R&D is centered in the home market, while Dow, Citicorp, and

Honda conduct product application and consumer research in foreign markets. The four companies exhibit very different organization structures at the top: the divisionalizing of Ampex is on a product basis; that of Citicorp and Dow, on a hybrid product, customer, and/or geographic basis; and that of Honda, on a functional basis.

Source: Robert Grosse and Duane Kujawa, *International Business: Theory and Managerial Applications* (Homewood, Ill.: Richard D. Irwin, 1987), p. 9.

LINE AND STAFF STRUCTURE

Line and staff structure – organization structure that results when staff specialists are added to a line organization.

Staff functions – advisory and supportive in nature; designed to contribute to the efficiency and maintenance of the organization.

Line functions – functions and activities directly involved in producing and marketing the organization's goods or services.

The addition of staff specialists to a line-structured organization creates a **line and staff structure.** As a line organization grows in size, staff assistance often becomes necessary. **Staff functions** are advisory and supportive in nature; they contribute to the efficiency and maintenance of the organization. **Line functions** are directly involved in producing and marketing the organization's goods or services. They generally relate directly to the attainment of major organizational objectives, while staff functions contribute indirectly. Staff people are generally specialists in one field, and their authority is normally limited to that of making recommendations to line people. Typical staff functions include research and development, personnel management, employee training, and various "assistant to" positions. Figure 11–6 shows a simplified line and staff organization structure.

Line and Staff Conflict

The line and staff organization allows much more specialization and flexibility than the line organization; however it sometimes creates conflict. The potential problem of a line-staff conflict should not be taken lightly. A 1960s study

F I G U R E 11–5 A Simplified Structure

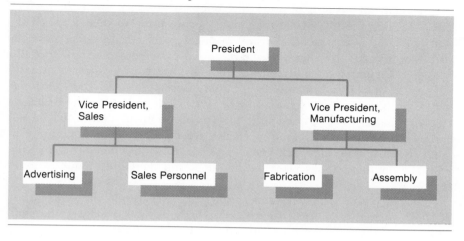

by the American Management Association found that 41 out of 100 companies reported some form of line–staff conflict.[4] There is no reason to believe that this is a lesser problem today.

Some staff specialists resent the fact that they may be only advisers to line personnel and have no real authority over the line. At the same time, line managers, knowing that they have final responsibility for the product,

F I G U R E 11–6 A Simplified Line and Staff Structure

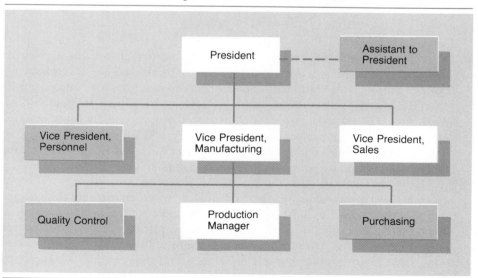

are often reluctant to listen to staff advice. Many staff specialists feel that they should not be in a position of having to sell their ideas to the line. They feel that the line managers should openly listen to their ideas. If the staff specialist is persistent, the line manager often resents even more the staff's "always trying to interfere and run my department." The staff specialist who does not persist often becomes discouraged because "no one ever listens."

Another factor in line and staff conflict is that line and staff personnel may be different in orientation and behavior. For example, line managers are often older, have worked their way up through the ranks, and do not have a college education.[5] Staff specialists usually are young and highly educated. Because they may lack line experience, they are often accused of not knowing anything about what the line does and therefore "living in ivory towers."

Reducing and ending line-staff conflict that is harming the organization depends on the building of mutual trust between line managers and staff. The first step in building this relationship is to develop a clear understanding of the lines of authority and the responsibilities of each group. If this is successful, each group should appreciate the fact that they can both maximize their performance only through cooperation.

In some organizations, staff specialists are encouraged to obtain some line experience by working on projects or committee assignments with line departments. With some experience in line management, staff specialists can better understand the problems facing the line managers that they work with and support. In other companies, corporate staff positions are occupied by line managers for a limited time period. For example, IBM fills most of its corporate staff positions with line managers who are rotated back to line jobs after a maximum of three years.[6]

MATRIX STRUCTURE

The matrix (also called project) form of organization has recently evolved; it is a way of forming project teams within the traditional line-staff organization. A project is "a combination of human and nonhuman resources pulled together in a temporary organization to achieve a specified purpose."[7] The marketing of a new product and the construction of a new building are examples of projects. Because projects have a temporary life, a method of managing and organizing them was sought so that the existing organization structure would not be totally disrupted and would maintain some efficiency.

Matrix structure – hybrid organization structure in which individuals from different functional areas are assigned to work on a specific project or task. Also called project form of organization.

Under the **matrix structure,** those working on a project are officially assigned to the project *and* to their original or base department. A manager is given the authority and responsibility for meeting the project objectives in terms of cost, quality, quantity, and time of completion. The project manager is then assigned the necessary personnel from the functional departments of the parent organization. Thus, a horizontal-line organization develops for the project within the parent vertical-line structure. Under such a system, the functional personnel are assigned to and evaluated by the project manager while they work on the project. When the project or their work is done, the functional personnel return to their departments. Figure 11–7 shows a matrix structure.

F I G U R E 11–7　Illustrative Matrix Structure

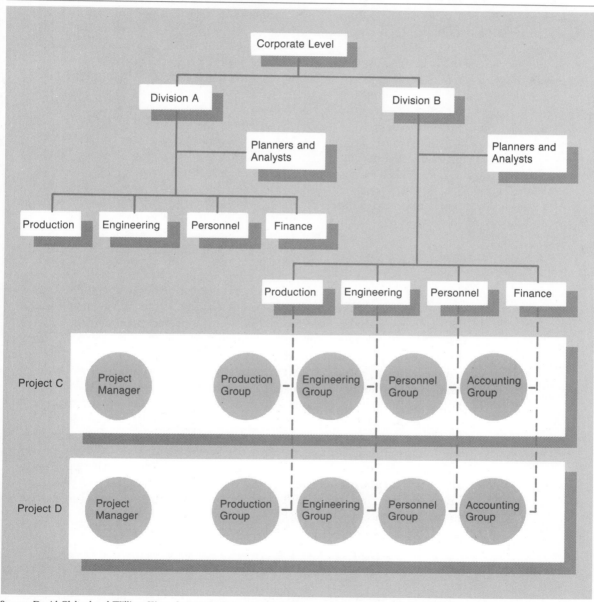

Source: David Cleland and William King, *Systems Analysis and Project Management,* 3rd ed. (New York: McGraw-Hill, 1983), p. 279.

MANAGERS AT WORK 11-2

Matrix Management at Crane Plastics

In the late 1970s, Crane Plastics, Inc. was struggling through a difficult transition in its manufacturing operations. Crane was beginning to make its own plastic compound for its diverse line of vinyl siding and custom extrusion products, and the changeover required intense collaboration among departments. Gary Fulmer, executive vice president of Crane, introduced matrix management at this stage. Far from expecting a total turnaround with a huge profit, Fulmer was simply hoping to quell the chaos that had erupted.

A prime weakness of a matrix structure is the feeling among team members that they are being forced to work for two bosses at the same time: their normal supervisors and the project team leader. The project at Crane is headed by Howard Bennett, whose rank is on par with vice presidents of other departments in the company. Bennett's status as vice president underscores Crane's commitment to the matrix approach, and it gives Bennett the clout to fend off the department-versus-department power plays that have plagued other companies' attempts to implement a matrix structure.

Source: "Team Players," *Inc.,* September 1984, pp. 140–44.

A major advantage of matrix structure is that the mix of people and resources can readily be changed as project needs change. Other advantages include the emphasis placed on the project by use of a project team and the relative ease with which project members can move back into the functional organization once the project has ended.

One serious problem is that matrix structure can result in a violation of the principle of unity of command. A role conflict can develop if the authority of the project manager is not clearly delineated from that of the functional managers. In such a case, the people assigned to the project might receive conflicting assignments from their project manager and their functional managers. A second problem occurs when the personnel assigned to a project are still evaluated by their functional manager, who usually has little opportunity to observe their work on the project. Managers at Work 11–2 describes how Crane Plastics, Inc. successfully implemented a matrix structure in part of its organization.

FLAT VERSUS TALL STRUCTURES

The previous chapter discussed the different factors that influence a manager's span of control (span of management). A closely related concept is the idea of a flat versus a tall organization structure. Many studies have compared the desirability of flat structures versus tall structures. A **flat structure** has relatively few levels and relatively large spans of management at each level; a **tall structure** has many levels and relatively small spans of management (see Figure 11–8). A classic study in this area was conducted by James Worthy.[8] Worthy studied the morale of over 100,000 employees at Sears Roebuck & Co. during a 12-year period. His study noted that organizations with fewer levels and wider spans of management offer the potential for greater job satisfaction. A wide span of management also forces the manager to delegate authority and to develop more direct links of communication—another plus. Peters and Waterman emphasize that the number of middle-management levels is one of the biggest contrasts between Japanese and American companies.[9] In general, the Japanese have far fewer middle managers and much flatter structures. For example, there are only 5 levels between the chairman and the first-line supervisor at Toyota; there are 15 at Ford.

On the other hand, Carzo and Yanouzas found that groups operating in a tall structure had significantly better performance than those operating in a flat structure.[10] Other studies have also shown conflicting results. Therefore, one cannot conclude that all flat structures are better than all tall structures (or vice versa).[11] Recalling from Chapter 10 that the most appropriate span of management is dependent on several situational variables, this is exactly what one would expect to find. There are advantages and disadvantages associated with both flat and tall structures. Which is most appropriate depends on the specific situational variables. Managers at Work 11–3 describes how Apple Computer reduced the number of levels in its organization structure.

Flat structure – organization with few levels and relatively large spans of management at each level.

Tall structure – organization with many levels and relatively small spans of management.

F I G U R E 11–8 Flat versus Tall Structures

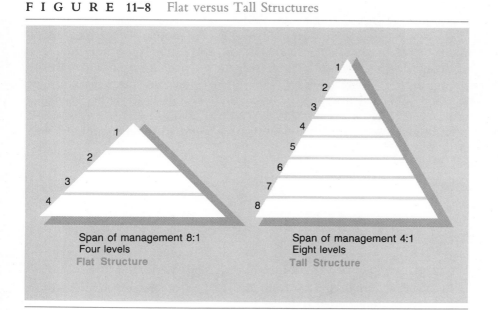

Span of management 8:1
Four levels
Flat Structure

Span of management 4:1
Eight levels
Tall Structure

MANAGERS AT WORK 11–3

Flat and Decentralized Apple Computer

Before 1984, Apple was organized into five divisions with centralized manufacturing and marketing for all products. In 1984, Chief Executive Officer John Scully created two decentralized divisions organized around the company's two major products.

Another very important element of Apple's organization structure is the minimum number of management layers. Apple's sales per employee ratio is an amazing $300,000 per employee. A computer company of comparable size, Intel Corporation, has a sales-to-employee ratio of $100,000 per employee.

Source: "Apple's New Crusade," *Business Week,* November 26, 1984, pp. 146–56.

COMMITTEES

Committee – organization structure in which a group of people are formally appointed, organized, and superimposed on the line or line and staff structure to consider or decide certain matters.

A **committee** is a group of people formally appointed and organized to consider or decide certain matters. A form of matrix structure, they are superimposed on the existing line or line and staff structure. Committees can be permanent (standing) or temporary and are usually in charge of, or supplementary to, the line and staff functions.

A temporary, or ad hoc, committee is generally appointed to deal with a specific problem or problems; it studies the problem, makes its recommendations, and then is dissolved. The permanent, or standing, committee usually acts more in a purely advisory capacity to certain organizational units or managers. When committees have the authority to order rather than just recommend, they are called plural executive committees. Plural executive committee privileges are usually reserved for very high-level committees such as the board of directors.

Advantages

Committees have many of the same advantages as matrix structures. Primary advantages are:

1. The formation of a committee places emphasis on the problem.
2. Expertise can be drawn from many areas of the organization; thus, better solutions often result.

3. Group decisions are often better than individual decisions.
4. Committee members are often motivated by being involved.
5. Better coordination and communication often result because all affected parties can be represented.
6. Consolidation of authority from several areas of the organization exists to make decisions.

Disadvantages

Everyone has heard the following old sayings: A committee is a collection of the unfit appointed by the unwilling to do the unnecessary, and A camel is a horse invented by a committee. Committees can have many positive features; they can also have many drawbacks if not properly managed. Some potential drawbacks are:

1. They can be excessively time-consuming and costly.
2. They tend to compromise when agreement is not easily reached. Such compromise decisions are often mediocre in quality.
3. They can result in divided responsibility with no one feeling personally responsible.
4. They can result in a tyranny of the minority. For example, one very strong-minded and vocal member can often control the entire committee.

Effectively Using Committees

Managers can do many things to avoid the pitfalls and increase the efficiency of a committee. The first step is to define clearly its functions, scope, and authority. Obviously, the members must know the purpose of the committee if it is to function effectively. If it is a temporary committee, the members should be informed of its expected duration. This will help avoid prolonging the life of the committee unnecessarily.

In addition, careful thought should go into the selection of the committee members and chairperson. Size is always an important variable; generally, committees become more inefficient as they grow in size. A good rule of thumb is to use the smallest group necessary to get the job done. It is more important to select capable members than representative members. It is also important to pick members from the same approximate organizational level. Members from higher levels may inhibit the actions and participation of the other members. Figure 11–9 lists several methods for selecting committee members and chairpeople and outlines good and bad points for each method.

Once a committee has been properly set up, there are other things a manager can do to ensure that it functions effectively. The manager should encourage participation from all members. All too often, one or two members do 90

F I G U R E   11-9   Methods of Selecting Committees

METHOD	ADVANTAGES/DISADVANTAGES
Appointment of chairperson and members.	Promotes sense of responsibility for all. May result in most capable members. Members may not work well together.
Appointment of chairperson who chooses members.	Will probably get along well. Lack of sense of responsibility by members. May not be most capable or representative.
Appointment of members who elect chairperson.	Lack of sense of responsibility by chairperson. May not choose best chairperson for the job. Election of chairperson may lead to split in the committee.
Volunteers.	Will get those who have greatest interest in the outcome (or those who are the least busy). Lack of responsibility. Potential is great for splits among members of the committee.

percent of the work. Because much committee work involves meetings, emphasis should be placed by the chairperson on the conduct of all committee meetings. Each meeting should be carefully planned, with an agenda sent out in advance. This helps the members prepare for the meeting; they can also see that the meeting is not going to be a waste of time. It is equally important to stick to the agenda and not run the meeting past the allotted time. Once the meeting is in progress, careful minutes should cover the major points and recommendations. These minutes should be given to all committee members at a later date. The committee chairperson should design a reporting system to ensure that all follow-up actions are taken. Finally, the committee should periodically reevaluate the need for the committee.

Boards of Directors

Board of directors – carefully selected committee that reviews major policy and strategy decisions proposed by top management.

A **board of directors** is, in reality, a type of committee that is responsible for reviewing the major policy and strategy decisions proposed by top management. Although most boards restrict their inputs to the policy and strategy level and do not participate in the day-to-day operation of the organization, their degree of involvement varies widely from board to board. Boards are used strictly as figureheads in some organizations, contributing little to the organization. However, because of the potential contribution that the board can make, its members should be carefully chosen. Directors do not necessarily need to own stock; they should be chosen primarily for what they can and will contribute to the organization. Usually boards of directors are paid a nominal fee for their services. Recent lawsuits against boards of directors concerning their liabilities regarding the day-to-day operation of the organization have increased the risks of serving on boards. (See Managers at Work 11–4.) Thus, boards are becoming more active than they have been in the

MANAGERS AT WORK 11–4

Stockholder Sues Board of Directors

A Martin Marietta Corp. shareholder sued the company's directors, charging they breached their fiduciary duties to the company and its stockholders in their fight against Bendix Corporation's tender offer. The shareholder charged the defensive tender offer by Marietta directors was made to perpetuate themselves in office—it denied holders the right to sell their stock at advantageous prices.

Source: "Marietta Holder Sues Board over Its Defense against Bendix Offer," *The Wall Street Journal,* January 11, 1983, p. 12.

past. Moreover, some people now require liability insurance coverage before they will serve on a board of directors. Managers at Work 11–5 shows that boards of directors do not always agree with top management.

SIMPLE FORM, LEAN STAFF

As an organization grows and has success, it tends to evolve into a more and more complex structure. Just how this takes place varies; frequently, a major cause is an increase in staff positions, especially at high levels. Many managers seem to feel a need for more staff and a more complex structure as the organization grows. They seem inclined to equate staff size with success.

In their observations, Peters and Waterman found that many of the best-performing companies had managed to maintain a simple structure with a small staff (see Figure 11–10).[12] One reason for this is that a simple form with a lean staff better allows an organization to adjust to a fast-changing environment. A simple form with a lean staff is also conducive to innovation. A simple form and a lean staff are naturally intertwined, in that one breeds the other: A simple form requires fewer staff, and a lean staff results in a simple form.

Peters and Waterman outline four characteristics or practices that enable organizations to maintain a simple form and a lean staff:[13]

1. Extraordinary divisional integrity. Each division has its own functional areas, including product development, finance, and personnel.
2. Continual formation of new divisions and rewards for this practice.
3. A set of guidelines which determine when a new product or product line will become an independent division.

MANAGERS AT WORK 11-5

Board and CEOs Disagree on Merger Plans

In January 1985, Occidental Petroleum Corporation and Diamond Shamrock Corporation announced plans to merge. The merger was to involve a one-for-one stock exchange and the creation of a new holding company with Occidental's chairman Armand Hammer as the new chairman and chief executive officer. Diamond Shamrock's chairman and chief executive officer William Bricker and Armand Hammer had agreed to the merger and thought both boards would support it. However, when each board met to vote on the merger, there was very little support. Occidental's board reluctantly accepted the proposal over the adamant objections of two directors. Diamond Shamrock directors rejected the proposal unanimously. Within a few days of the initial announcement, all merger plans were canceled.

Source: "Occidental, Diamond Shamrock Cancel Merger Plan Hours after Announcing It," *The Wall Street Journal,* January 8, 1985; "Diamond Shamrock Chief Says Concern Isn't for Sale but Notes Vulnerability," *The Wall Street Journal,* January 9, 1985.

4. Moving people and even products among divisions on a regular basis without causing disruption.

Peters and Waterman postulate that the successful organizations of the future will be variations of the simple, divisionalized line and staff structure and that they will have the above characteristics.

F I G U R E   11-10   Example of Companies with Lean Staffs

Emerson Electric has 54,000 employees and fewer than 100 in its corporate headquarters.
Dana employs 35,000 and reduced its corporate staff from about 500 in 1970 to around 100 in 1982.
Schlumberger, the $6 billion diversified oil service company, has a corporate staff of 90.
Intel, which enjoys $1 billion in sales, has virtually no staff; temporary staff assignments are given to line officers.
ROLM manages a $200 million business with about 15 people in the corporate headquarters.

Source: Thomas J. Peters and Robert H. Waterman, Jr., *In Search of Excellence* (New York: Harper & Row, 1982), pp. 311–12.

A CONTINGENCY APPROACH

Even if one accepts the merits of a simple form with a lean staff (as discussed in the last section), research has clearly shown that there is no one structure suitable for all situations. An earlier section in this chapter indicated that there is a relationship between strategy and structure but that there are also several other factors that can influence this relationship.

The knowledge that there is no one best way to organize—the design is conditional—has led to a **contingency (situational) approach** to organizing. In a study dealing with organization structure and environment, Lawrence and Lorsch concluded that different organizations in different environments require different kinds of organization structures at various stages in their growth.[14] As we discussed earlier in this chapter, strategy is one factor that has a major influence on the most appropriate structure for an organization. Figure 11–11 shows many of the other variables that can have an impact on what is the most appropriate organization structure. While studies have investigated most of these variables, the results have often been inconclusive.[15] The important thing is to realize that each situation must be evaluated in light of these variables and then structured accordingly.

Contingency approach to organization structure—states that the most appropriate structure depends on the technology used, the rate of environmental change and other dynamic forces.

F I G U R E 11–11 Variables Affecting Appropriate Organization Structure

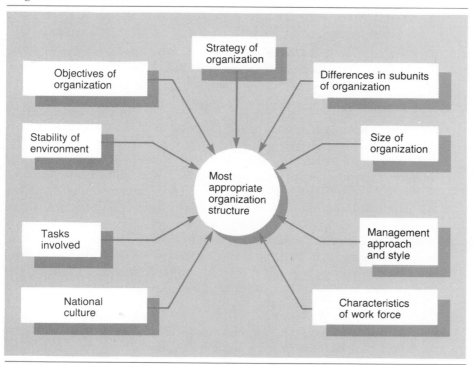

Once management adopts a contingency view, it will begin to thoroughly analyze the relevant variables and then choose the appropriate structure; it is essentially a matching process. Because each of the interacting forces is dynamic, top management should periodically analyze and appraise their structure in light of any relevant changes.

SUMMARY

This chapter describes several types of organization structures and introduces several variables that affect structure. The effective use of committees and boards of directors is discussed. The relationship between strategy and structure is explored and a contingency model for designing organization structures is presented.

LEARNING OBJECTIVE 1

Describe the General Relationship between an Organization's Strategy and Its Structure.

Early research by Chandler reported that changes in strategy ultimately lead to changes in an organization's structure. Although subsequent research has supported an existence of some relationship between strategy and structure, it is clear that strategy is not the only variable—but has a bearing on structure.

LEARNING OBJECTIVE 2

Identify the Different Types of Departmentation.

Departmentation refers to the grouping of activities into related work units. Departmentation may be undertaken on the basis of work function, product, customer, geography, or time worked (shift).

LEARNING OBJECTIVE 3

Distinguish between a Line Structure, a Line and Staff Structure, and a Matrix Structure.

A line structure is the simplest organization structure; it has direct vertical links between the different organizational levels. The addition of staff specialists to a line organization creates a line and staff structure. Staff functions are advisory and supportive in nature; line functions are directly involved in producing and marketing the organization's goods or services. A matrix structure is a hybrid structure in which individuals from different functional areas are assigned to work on a specific project or task. Under a matrix structure, those working on a project are officially assigned to the project and to their original or base department.

LEARNING OBJECTIVE 4

Explain What Is Meant by a Flat Structure versus a Tall Structure.

A flat structure has relatively few levels and relatively large spans of management at each level; a tall structure has many levels and relatively small spans of management.

LEARNING OBJECTIVE 5

List Several Advantages and Disadvantages of Committees.

The primary advantages of committees are: (1) the formation of a committee places emphasis on the problem; (2) expertise can be drawn from many areas of the organization; thus, better solutions often result; (3) group decisions are often better than individual decisions; (4) committee members are often motivated by being involved; (5) better coordination and communication often result because all affected parties can be represented; and (6) consolidation of authority from several areas of the organization exists to make decisions.

The primary disadvantages of committees are: (1) they can be excessively time-consuming and costly; (2) they tend to compromise when agreement is not easily reached (such compromise decisions are often mediocre in quality); (3) they can result in divided responsibility with no one feeling personally responsible; (4) they can result in a tyranny of the minority. For example, one very strong-minded and vocal member can often control the entire committee.

LEARNING OBJECTIVE 6

Discuss the Following Phrase: Simple Form, Lean Staff.

An organization with a simple form and lean staff better allows the organization to adjust to a fast-changing environment. Because of the absence of bureaucracy, this type of structure is also conducive to innovation and new ideas.

LEARNING OBJECTIVE 7

Describe a Contingency Approach to Organizing.

The contingency approach to organization states that the most appropriate structure depends on many situational variables, including strategy, objectives, environment, size, technology, and employee characteristics. When taking a contingency approach, a manager should first analyze these variables and design a structure to fit the situation.

REVIEW QUESTIONS

1. Discuss the relationship between an organization's strategy and its structure.
2. Describe:
   a. Functional departmentation.
   b. Product departmentation.
   c. Geographic departmentation.
   d. Customer departmentation.
3. What are line functions? What are staff functions?

4. Explain:
   a. Line structure.
   b. Line and staff structure.
   c. Matrix structure.
5. What factors contribute to the potential conflict between line and staff personnel in a line and staff organization? How can the potential for destructive conflict be reduced?

6. What are the advantages of a flat structure? What are the advantages of a tall structure?

7. What are the advantages associated with committees? What are the disadvantages? How can committees be made more effective?

8. Describe four characteristics or practices that enable organizations to maintain a simple form and a lean staff.

9. What is the contingency approach to organizing?

DISCUSSION QUESTIONS

1. How can you justify the use of a matrix structure since it clearly violates the unity-of-command principle?

2. Do you think that the contingency approach to organizing is a useful concept that can be implemented, or is it really a cop-out?

3. Discuss this statement: When the appropriate organization structure is determined, the firm no longer has to worry about structure.

4. How would you respond to the following statement: There is no way to grow and keep the corporate staff small.

REFERENCES & ADDITIONAL READINGS

[1] A. D. Chandler, *Strategy and Structure* (Cambridge, Mass.: MIT Press, 1962).

[2] Some relevant research includes J. Child, "Organization Structure, Environment, and Performance: The Role of Strategic Choice," *Sociology* 6 (1972), pp. 1–22; and R. Rumelt, *Strategy, Structure, and Economic Performance* (Boston: Harvard Business School, Division of Research, 1974).

[3] Leslie W. Rue and Phyllis G. Holland, *Strategic Management: Concepts and Experiences* (New York: McGraw-Hill, 1986), p. 631.

[4] Ernest Dale, *Organization* (New York: American Management Association, 1962), p. 67.

[5] M. Dalton, "Conflict between Staff and Line Managerial Officers," *American Sociological Review*, June 1950, pp. 342–51; James A. Belasco and Joseph A. Alutto, "Line-Staff Conflicts: Some Empirical Insights," *Academy of Management Journal*, December 1969, p. 477.

[6] Thomas J. Peters and Robert W. Waterman, Jr., *In Search of Excellence* (New York: Harper & Row, 1982), p. 312.

[7] David Cleland and William King, *Systems Analysis and Project Management,* 3rd ed. (New York: McGraw-Hill, 1983), p. 187.

[8] James Worthy, "Organization Structure and Employee Morale," *American Sociological Review* 15 (1956), pp. 169–79.

[9] Peters and Waterman, *In Search of Excellence,* p. 313.

[10] Carzo Rocco, Jr., and John Yanouzas, "Effects of Flat and Tall Organization Structure," *Administrative Science Quarterly* 14 (1969), pp. 178–91.

[11] Dan R. Dalton, William D. Todor, Michael J. Spendolini, Gordon J. Fielding, and Lyman W. Porter, "Organization Structure and Performance: A Critical Review," *Academy of Management Review*, January 1980, pp. 49–54.

[12] Peters and Waterman, *In Search of Excellence,* pp. 306–17.

[13] Ibid. p. 310.

[14] Paul Lawrence and Jay Lorsch, "Differentiation and Integration," *Administrative Science Quarterly*, June 1967, pp. 1–47.

[15] For a review of some of these, see Mariann Jelinek, "Technology, Organizations, and Contingency," *Academy of Management Review,* January 1977, pp. 17–26; Peter H. Grinyer and Masoval Yasai-Ardekani, "Strategy, Structure, Size, and Bureaucracy," *Academy of Management Journal,* September 1981, pp. 471–86; David F. Gillespie and Dennis S. Mileti, "Technology and the Study of Organizations: An Overview and Appraisal," *Academy of Management Review,* January 1977, pp. 7–16; Louis Fry, "Technology-Structure Research: Three Critical Issues," *Academy of Management Journal,* September 1982, pp. 532–53.

INCIDENT

Who Dropped the Ball?

In October 1975, the Industrial Water Treatment Company (IWT) introduced KELATE, a new product that was 10 times more effective than other treatments in controlling scale buildup in boilers. The instantaneous demand for the new water treatment KELATE required that IWT double its number of service engineers within the following year.

The sudden expansion caused IWT to reorganize their operations. Previously, each district office had been headed by a district manager who was assisted by a chief engineer and two engineering supervisors. In 1976, this structure was changed. The district manager now had a chief engineer and a manager of operations. Four engineering supervisors (now designated as group leaders) were established. They were to channel all work assignments through the manager of operations, while all engineering-related problems were to be handled by the chief engineer. Each group leader supervised 8 to 10 field service engineers (see Exhibit 1).

Bill Marlowe, district manager for the Southeast District, has just received a letter from an old and very large customer, Sel Tex, Inc. The letter revealed that when Sel Tex inspected one of their boilers last week, they found that the water treatment was not working properly. When they contacted IWT's service engineer for their area, Wes Smith, they were told that he was scheduled to be working in the Jacksonville area the rest of the week but would get someone else down there the next day. When no one showed up, Sel Tex was naturally upset—after all, they were only requesting the engineering service they had been promised.

Bill Marlowe, upset over the growing number of customer complaints that seemed to be crossing his desk in recent months, called Ed Jones, chief engineer, into his office and showed him the letter he had received from Sel Tex.

Ed: Why are you showing me this? This is a work assignment foul-up.

Bill: Do you know anything about this unsatisfactory condition?

Ed: Sure, Wes called me immediately after he found out. Their concentration of KELATE must have gone up, since they're getting corrosion and oxygen on their tubes. I told Peter Adinaro, Wes's group leader, about it, and I suggested he schedule someone to visit Sel Tex.

Bill: OK, Ed, thanks for your help. [*Bill then calls Peter Adinaro into his office.*]

E X H I B I T   1   Partial Organizational Chart for IWT

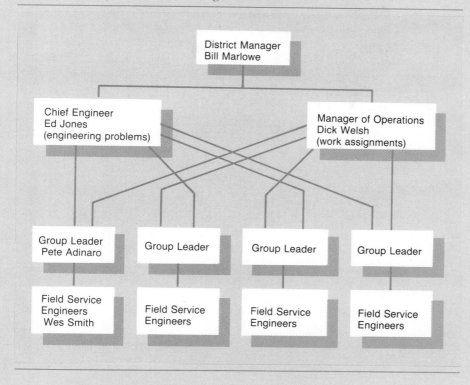

Bill: Peter, two weeks ago Ed asked you to assign someone to visit Sel Tex because of a tube corrosion problem they are having. Do you remember?

Peter: Oh sure! As usual, Wes Smith called Ed instead of me. I left a message for Dick to assign someone there because my whole group was tied up and I couldn't spare anyone. I thought Dick would ask another group leader to assign someone to check it out.

Bill: Well, thanks for your help. Tell Dick to come on in here for a second.

Dick Welsh, manager of operations, came into Bill's office about 20 minutes later.

Bill: Dick, here's a letter from Sel Tex. Please read it and tell me what you know about the situation.

Dick: [*After reading the letter.*] Bill, I didn't know anything about this.

Bill: I checked with Pete, Wes's group leader, and he tells me he left a message for you to assign someone since his group was all tied up. Didn't you get the message?

Dick: Have you taken a look at my desk lately? I'm flooded with messages. Heck, I'm the greatest message handler of all times. If I could schedule my people without having all the engineering headaches unloaded on me, I wouldn't have all these messages. Sure, it's possible that he left a message but I haven't seen it. I will look for it though. Anyway, that letter sounds to me like they've got an engineering problem, and Ed should contact them to solve it.

Bill: I'll write Sel Tex myself and try to explain the situation to them. You and I will have to get together this afternoon and talk over some of these difficulties. See you later, Dick.

Questions

1. What are the problems that Bill Marlowe faces?

2. Are the problems related to the way IWT is organized or are they related to the employees?

3. How could these problems be resolved?

EXERCISE

Organize

Suppose you have just been hired as the vice president in charge of sales for COMBO Enterprise, Inc. COMBO manufactures, sells, and distributes both land and water vehicles. The land vehicles are bicycles powered by a two-horsepower, two-cycle engine. Basically, you have developed a method to adapt an off-the-shelf chain saw motor to a popular French-produced bicycle. The water vehicles use the same chain saw motor adapted to a standard canoe which is fitted with a special propeller and rudder.

The advantage over the available competition is that, due to the light weight of the motor being used, the bicycles and canoes can also be used manually with very little loss of efficiency as compared to nonmotorized bicycles and canoes. Your market surveys have shown that there is a large market for such a product.

COMBO serves both civilian and military markets for both the land and water vehicles.

Presently, COMBO has a plant in a medium-sized eastern city and one in a medium-sized western city. The eastern plant handles all business east of the Mississippi River, while the western plant handles business west of the Mississippi.

A. Design what you think would be the best way to organize the sales (marketing) division of the company.
B. Design an alternate structure for your division.
C. Why did you prefer one structure over the other?
D. Design a matrix structure (if you did not use one in A or B) for this situation. What would be the pros and cons of such a structure in this situation?

12 Staffing: Securing the Right People

LEARNING OBJECTIVES

After studying this chapter,
you should be able to:

1 Outline the human resource planning process.

2 Define job analysis, job description, job specification, and skills inventory.

3 Define equal employment opportunity.

4 Describe the recruitment process.

5 Define affirmative action plan.

6 Discuss reverse discrimination.

7 Define tests, test validity, and test reliability.

8 Explain polygraph and drug testing.

9 Discuss the types of employment interviews.

Every aspect of a firm's activities is determined by the competence, motivation, and general effectiveness of its human organization

RENSIS LIKERT*

Staffing – securing and developing human resources for the jobs created by the organizing function.

Staffing involves securing and developing people to perform the jobs which have been created by the organizing function. The goal of **staffing** is to obtain the best available people for the organization and to develop the skills and abilities of those people. Obtaining the best available people generally involves forecasting personnel requirements and recruiting and selecting new employees. Developing the skills and abilities of an organization's employees involves employee development as well as the proper use of promotions, transfers, and separations. The staffing function is complicated by numerous government regulations. Furthermore, many of these regulations are subject to frequent change.

Unfortunately, many of the staffing activities have traditionally been conducted by human resource/personnel departments and have been considered relatively unimportant by line managers. However, securing and developing qualified personnel should be a major concern of all managers, as it involves the most valuable asset of an organization—human resources.

HUMAN RESOURCE PLANNING

Human resource (personnel) planning (HRP) – process of getting the right number of qualified people into the right job at the right time.

Human resource planning (HRP), also referred to as personnel planning, has been defined as the process of "getting the right number of qualified people into the right job at the right time."[1] Put another way, HRP is "the system of matching the supply of people—internally (existing employees) and externally (those to be hired or searched for)—with the openings the organization expects to have for a given time frame."[2]

HRP involves applying the basic planning process to the human resource needs of an organization. Once organizational plans are made and specific objectives set, the HRP process attempts to define the human resource needs to meet the organization's objectives.[3]

The first basic question addressed by the planning process—Where are we now?—is frequently answered in human resource planning by using job analyses and skills inventories.

*Rensis Likert, *The Human Organization* (New York: McGraw-Hill, 1967), p. 1.

Job Analysis and Skills Inventory

Job analysis is the process of determining, through observation and study, the pertinent information relating to the nature of a specific job. The end products of a job analysis are a job description and a job specification. A **job description** is a written statement that identifies the tasks, duties, activities, and performance results required in a particular job. A **job specification** is a written statement that identifies the abilities, skills, traits, or attributes necessary for successful performance in a particular job. In general, it can be said that a job specification identifies the qualifications of an individual who could perform the job. Job analyses are frequently conducted by specialists from the human resource department. However, managers should have input into the final job descriptions for the jobs they are managing.

Through conducting job analyses, an organization defines its current human resource needs on the basis of current and/or newly created jobs. The purpose served by a **skills inventory** is to consolidate information about the organization's current human resources. The skills inventory contains basic information on all the employees of an organization, giving a comprehensive picture of the individual. Through analyzing the skills inventory, the organization can assess the current quantity and quality of its human resources.

Thomas Patten has outlined seven broad categories of information that may be included in a skills inventory:[4]

1. Personal data history: age, sex, marital status, etc.
2. Skills: education, job experience, training, etc.
3. Special qualifications: memberships in professional groups, special achievements, etc.
4. Salary and job history: present salary, past salary, dates of raises, various jobs held, etc.
5. Company data: benefit plan data, retirement information, seniority, etc.
6. Capacity of individual: scores on tests, health information, etc.
7. Special preferences of individual: location or job preferences, etc.

The popularity of computerized skills inventories has risen in recent years. Today, many large organizations such as IBM, RCA, and the U.S. Civil Service Commission have computerized skills inventory systems.[5] The primary advantage of a computerized skills inventory is that it offers a quick and accurate evaluation of the skills that are available within the organization. Combining the information provided by job analysis and the skills inventory enables the organization to evaluate the present status of its human resources.

Because the type of information required about management personnel sometimes differs from that required about nonmanagerial employees, some organizations maintain a separate management inventory. In addition to biographical data, a management inventory often contains the following information: work experience, product knowledge, industrial experience, formal

Job analysis – process of determining, through observation and study, information relating to the nature of a specific job.

Job description – written statement that identifies the tasks, duties, activities, and performance results required in a particular job.

Job specification – written statement that identifies the abilities, skills, traits, or attributes necessary for a particular job.

Skills inventory – contains basic information on all employees of an organization.

education, training courses, foreign language skills, relocation limitations, career interests, and performance appraisals.

In addition to appraising the current status of its human resources, anticipated changes in the current work force due to retirements, deaths, discharges, promotions, transfers, and resignations must be considered. Certain changes in personnel can be estimated accurately and easily, while other changes are not so easily forecast. Changes such as retirements can be forecast reasonably accurately from information in a skills inventory. Others, such as transfers and promotions, can be estimated by taking into account such factors as the ages of individuals in specific jobs and the requirements of the organization. Individuals with potential for promotion can and should be identified. Factors such as deaths, resignations, and discharges are much more difficult to predict. However, past experience and historical records can often provide helpful information in these areas. Planned training and development experiences should also be considered when evaluating anticipated changes.

Forecasting

Human resource forecasting – process that determines future human resource needs.

The second basic question addressed in the planning process is: Where does the organization want to go? **Human resource forecasting** attempts to answer this question with regard to the organization's human resource needs. It is a process that attempts to determine the future human resource needs of the organization in light of the organization's objectives. Some of the many variables that are considered in forecasting human resource needs include sales projections, skills required in potential business ventures, composition of the present work force, technological changes, and general economic conditions. Due to the critical role human resources play in attaining organizational objectives, all levels of management should be involved in the forecasting process.

Human resource forecasting is presently conducted largely on the basis of intuition; the experience and judgment of the manager is used to determine future human resource needs. This assumes that all managers in the organization are aware of the future plans of the total organization. Unfortunately, this is not true in many cases. For instance, a decision to increase the number of sales representatives in an organization could very likely have human resource implications for all units of the organization. Ideally, an increase in the number of sales representatives would generate more sales, which would then require increased production and increased invoicing to customers. Then, the production and accounting departments would need to increase their human resources.

Various mathematical and statistical techniques are also used to project future personnel needs. A simple example of such a method is the use of sales forecasts to determine human resource needs.

Transition

The human resource forecast results in a statement of what the organization's human resource needs are in light of its plans and objectives. These human resource needs are referred to as aggregate human resource requirements. The skills inventory, management inventory, and job descriptions derived from job analyses define the current quantity and quality of the organization's human resources.

The final phase of human resource planning—the transition—is to determine how the organization can obtain the quantity and quality of human resources required to meet its objectives as reflected by the human resource forecast. The difference between the aggregate human resource requirements and the current level of human resources available to the organization is referred to as the net human resource requirements. The net human resource requirements may be either positive or negative.

The organization engages in several transitional activities in order to bring its current level of human resources in line with forecast requirements. These activities include recruiting and selecting new employees, developing current and/or new employees, promoting or transferring employees, laying off employees, and discharging employees. Other factors that must be considered when determining how forecast human resources will be attained include organizational policies on promotions, transfers, layoffs, and discharges. Generally, the coordination of these activities is delegated to a human resource or personnel department within the organization.

Legal Considerations

Government regulation now plays a vital role in human resource planning. Discriminatory personnel practices by many organizations led to this. Four significant government bills in this area are the Equal Pay Act of 1963; the Civil Rights Act of 1964; the Age Discrimination in Employment Act of 1968, as amended in 1978; and the Rehabilitation Act of 1973.

The **Equal Pay Act of 1963,** which became effective in June 1964, prohibits wage discrimination on the basis of sex. The law states: "No employer . . . shall . . . discriminate . . . between employees on the basis of sex by paying wages . . . at a rate less than the rate at which he pays wages to employees of the opposite sex . . . for equal work on jobs the performance of which requires equal skill, effort, and responsibility and which are performed under similar working conditions."[6]

Title VII of the Civil Rights Act of 1964 is designed to eliminate employment discrimination related to race, color, religion, sex, or national origin in organizations that conduct interstate commerce. The 1978 Civil Rights Act Amendment to Title VII prohibits discrimination in employment because of pregnancy, childbirth, or related medical conditions. The act as amended covers the following types of organizations:

1. All private employers of 15 or more people.
2. All educational institutions, public and private.
3. State and local governments.
4. Public and private employment agencies.

Equal Pay Act of 1963 – effective in June 1964; prohibits wage discrimination on the basis of sex.

Civil Rights Act of 1964 – Title VII of this act was designed to eliminate employment discrimination based on race, color, religion, sex, or national origin in organizations that conduct interstate commerce.

MANAGERS AT WORK 12–1

Sears' Costly Win in a Hiring Suit

When Sears Roebuck & Co. was charged with discrimination in 1973, its officers felt that the matter would be quickly resolved considering its affirmative action program. However, Sears was wrong. At one point, the EEOC demanded as much as $600 million in settlement money to rid Sears of the charges. Sears decided to fight.

After more than 12 years and $20 million, Sears is nearing the end of its struggle. In February 1986, U.S. District Court Judge

John A. Norbberg ruled that Sears had proved that its affirmative action program far exceeded the requirements of federal law. Shortly after the judge's decision, Sears asked the judge for attorney's fees and other expenses as compensation from the EEOC.

Source: Adapted from Steve Weiner, "Sears' Costly Win in a Hiring Suit," *The Wall Street Journal,* March 18, 1986, p. 28.

---

5. Labor unions with 15 or more members.

6. Joint labor-management committees for apprenticeship and training.

Equal employment opportunity – right of all people to work and advance on the basis of merit, ability, and potential.

The Civil Rights Act was passed by Congress to establish guidelines for ensuring equal employment opportunities for all people. **Equal employment opportunity** refers to the right of all people to work and to advance on the basis of merit, ability, and potential. One of the major focuses of equal employment opportunity efforts has been to identify and eliminate discriminatory employment practices. Such practices are any artificial, arbitrary, and unnecessary barriers to employment when the barriers operate to discriminate on the basis of sex, race, or other impermissible classification.

Two federal agencies—the Equal Employment Opportunity Commission (EEOC) and the Office of Federal Contract Compliance Programs (OFCCP)—have major responsibility for enforcing equal opportunity legislation. The EEOC was created by the Civil Rights Act. It investigates complaints of discrimination, develops guidelines to enforce the act, and takes legal action against organizations using discriminatory employment practices.

Managers at Work 12–1 describes how Sears Roebuck & Co. resisted legal action taken against the company by the EEOC.

The OFCCP within the U.S. Department of Labor is responsible for ensuring equal employment opportunity among federal contractors and subcontractors, which includes most major businesses in the United States. A special clause in their contracts makes equal employment opportunity an integral part of their agreements. Women, minorities, members of religious and ethnic groups, handicapped persons, Vietnam veterans, and disabled veterans of all wars are protected by the equal opportunity requirements in federal government contracts.

The **Age Discrimination in Employment Act** went into effect on June 12, 1968. Initially, it was designed to protect individuals 40–65 years of age from discrimination in hiring, retention, compensation, and other conditions of employment. In 1978, the act was amended and coverage was extended to individuals up to age 70. Specifically, the act now forbids mandatory retirement at age 65 except in certain circumstances. The **Rehabilitation Act of 1973** prohibits discrimination in hiring of the handicapped by federal agencies and federal contractors.

Union contracts also influence human resource planning when they contain clauses regulating transfers, promotions, discharges, and so on.

Age Discrimination in Employment Act of 1968 – amended in 1978; protects individuals from 40 to 70 years of age from discrimination in hiring, retention, compensation, and other conditions of employment.

Rehabilitation Act of 1973 – prohibits discrimination in the hiring of the handicapped by federal agencies and federal contractors.

INTEGRATING ORGANIZATIONAL OBJECTIVES, STRATEGY, STRUCTURE, AND HUMAN RESOURCE REQUIREMENTS

Figure 12–1 graphically illustrates the basic relationships among organizational objectives, strategy, structure, and human resource requirements. As this figure shows, establishing organizational objectives, formulating a strategy

F I G U R E 12–1 Organizational Objectives, Strategy, Structure, and Human Resource Requirements

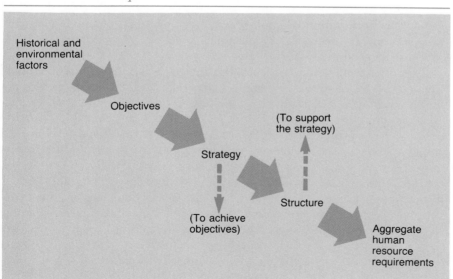

Source: The authors are indebted to Professor Bruce Meyers of Western Illinois University for the development of this diagram.

to achieve those objectives, and developing an organizational structure to support the strategy are necessary prerequisites to determining an organization's aggregate human resource requirements.

Net human resource requirements are determined by comparing the aggregate human resource forecasts to the present human resources in light of anticipated changes. If the net requirements are positive, the organization implements the processes of recruitment, selection, and training and development. If the requirements are negative, proper adjustments must be made through attrition, layoffs, or discharges. As these changes take place, they should be recorded in the skills inventory.

RECRUITMENT

Recruitment —
process of seeking and attracting a supply of people from which qualified candidates for job vacancies can be selected.

Recruitment involves the activities of seeking and attracting a supply of people from which qualified candidates for job vacancies can be selected. The amount of recruitment that must be done by an organization is determined by the difference between the forecast human resource needs and the talent available within the organization. After the decision to recruit has been made, the sources of supply must be explored.

Promotion from Within

If an organization has been doing an effective job of selecting employees, one of the best sources of supply for job openings is its own employees. Promotion from within is a policy that many organizations follow. In fact, some of the best managed organizations, such as Delta Airlines and IBM, have a strict promotion-from-within policy.

Promotion from within has several advantages. First, an organization should have a good idea about the strengths and weaknesses of its own employees. Employee morale and motivation are positively affected by internal promotions, assuming such promotions are perceived as being equitably related to performance. Finally, most organizations have a sizable investment in their employees; using the abilities of present employees to their fullest extent improves the organization's return on its investment.

Peter Principle —
idea popularized by Lawrence Peter, that managers tend to be promoted to their level of incompetence.

Certain potential dangers must be acknowledged before adopting a policy of promotion from within. One danger has been popularized by Lawrence Peter: Managers tend to be promoted to their level of incompetence.[7] According to the **Peter Principle,** successful managers are continually promoted until they finally reach a level at which they are unable to perform. The Peter Principle can and does occur in organizations. However, knowing the present skills of employees (skills inventory) and knowing the skills required by a new job (job analysis) minimizes the occurrence of the Peter Principle.

MANAGERS AT WORK 12–2

Employee Referrals at Lanier Business Products

Lanier Business products netted 150 new people for field sales and service jobs through an employee referral program. The eight-month effort awarded a special coffee mug to each referring employee and a camera if the referred candidate was hired. Employees also received the usual referral cash award, which varies according to the position.

In addition, Lanier districts across the country were broken into competing leagues. The top winner in a league received a 3-day, expense-paid vacation at a resort, and the grand prize winner won 10 days in Monte Carlo with such extras as a flight on the Concorde and a trip on France's new high-speed train.

This employee search campaign effort reportedly yielded people at half the usual cost per hire. The usual 12-interviews-to-1-hire ratio dropped a little over 5-to-1.

Source: Adapted from "HRM Update," *Personnel Administrator,* August 1985, p. 20.

A second danger involves the inbreeding of ideas. When all vacancies are filled from within, caution must be taken to ensure that new ideas and innovations are not stifled by attitudes such as "we've never done it before" or "we did all right without it."

External Sources

Organizations have a wide range of external sources available for obtaining personnel. Probably the most widely used method for obtaining external personnel is the "Help Wanted" advertisement. Recruitment on college and university campuses is also used by many organizations. Other sources for obtaining personnel include employment agencies (public and private), management consulting firms, employee referrals, and labor unions. Managers at Work 12–2 illustrates an employee referral program at Lanier Business Products.

Legal Influences

The previously discussed legislation has also had a profound impact on the recruitment activities of organizations. For example, reliance on "word of mouth" or "walk in" methods of recruitment has been ruled by the courts to be a discriminatory practice where females and minorities are not well represented at all levels within the organization.[8]

The EEOC offers the following suggestions to help eliminate discrimination in recruitment practices:[9]

- Maintain a file of unhired female and minority applicants who are potential candidates for future openings. Contact these candidates first when an opening occurs.
- Utilize females and minorities in recruitment and the entire human resource process.
- Place classified ads under "Help Wanted" or "Help Wanted, Male-Female" listings. Be sure that the content of ads does not indicate any sex, race, or age preference or qualification for the job.
- Advertise in media directed toward women and minorities.
- All advertising should include the phrase "equal opportunity employer."

SELECTION

The purpose of selection is to choose from those who are available the individuals most likely to succeed on the job. The process is entirely dependent on proper human resource planning and recruitment. Only when an adequate pool of qualified candidates is available can the selection process function effectively. The ultimate objective of the selection process is to match the requirements of the job with the qualifications of the individual.

Who Makes the Decision?

The responsibility for hiring is assigned to different levels of management in different organizations. Often, the human resource/personnel department does the initial screening of recruits, but the final selection decision is left to the manager of the department with the job opening. Such a system relieves the manager of the time-consuming responsibility of screening out unqualified and uninterested applicants. Less frequently, the human resource/personnel department is responsible for both the initial screening and the final decision. Many organizations leave the final choice to the immediate manager, subject to the approval of higher levels of management. In small organizations, the owner or the top manager often makes the choice.

An alternate approach is to involve peers in the selection decision. Traditionally, peer involvement has been used primarily with professionals and those in upper levels of management, but it is becoming more popular at all levels of the organization. Under this approach, co-workers have an input into the final selection decision.

Peer and managerial involvement normally is desirable not only for identifying talent but also for facilitating the acceptance of the new employee by the work group. Experience has shown that co-workers may have negative reactions toward the new employee if the selection is made solely by the human resource department. On the other hand, supervisors and peer groups are often more committed to helping new workers succeed if they have some input into their selection.

The selection process has been of primary interest to the government, as evidenced by the number of laws and regulations in effect that prohibit discrimination in the selection of employees. One action that is frequently required of organizations is the development of an affirmative action plan.

An **affirmative action plan** is a written document outlining specific goals and timetables for remedying past discriminatory actions. All federal contractors and subcontractors with contracts over $50,000 and 50 or more employees are required to develop and implement written affirmative action plans which are monitored by OFCCP. While Title VII and EEOC do not require any specific type of affirmative action plan, court rulings have often required affirmative action when discrimination has been found.

> **Affirmative action plan** – written document outlining specific goals and timetables for remedying past discriminatory actions.

A number of basic steps are involved in the development of an effective affirmative action plan. Figure 12–2 presents the EEOC's suggestions for developing an affirmative action plan.

Organizations without affirmative action plans will find that it makes good business sense to identify and revise employment practices that have discriminatory effects, before the federal government requires such action. Increased legal action and the record of court-required affirmative action emphasize the advantage of writing and instituting an affirmative action plan.

However, the growing number of **reverse discrimination** suits may have a significant impact on affirmative action programs. Reverse discrimination is the alleged preferential treatment for one group (minority or female) over another group (white male) rather than merely providing equal opportunity. The first real test case in this area was the Bakke case of 1978.[10] Allen Bakke, a white male, brought suit against the medical school of the University of California at Davis. He charged that he was unconstitutionally discriminated against when he was denied admission to the medical school while some minority applicants with lower qualifications were accepted. The Supreme Court ruled in Bakke's favor, but at the same time upheld the constitutionality of affirmative action programs.

> **Reverse discrimination** – alleged preferential treatment for one group (minority or female) over another group (white male) rather than merely providing equal opportunity.

In another case in 1979, the Supreme Court heard a challenge—brought by a white worker, Brian F. Weber—to an affirmative action plan collectively bargained by a union and an employer.[11] This case questioned whether Title VII of the Civil Rights Act of 1964 as amended prohibited private employers from granting racial preference in employment practices. The Court, in a 5-

F I G U R E   12–2   EEOC's Suggestions for Developing an Affirmative Action Plan

1. The chief executive officer of an organization should issue a written statement describing his or her personal commitment to the plan, legal obligations, and the importance of equal employment opportunity as an organizational goal.
2. A top official of the organization should be given the authority and responsibility for directing and implementing the program. In addition, all managers and supervisors within the organization should clearly understand their own responsibilities for carrying out equal employment opportunity.
3. The organization's policy and commitment to the policy should be publicized both internally and externally.
4. Present employment should be surveyed to identify areas of concentration and underutilization and to determine the extent of underutilization.
5. Goals and timetables for achieving the goals should be developed to improve utilization of minorities, males, and females in each area where underutilization has been identified.
6. The entire employment system should be reviewed to identify and eliminate barriers to equal employment. Areas for review include: recruitment, selection, promotion systems, training programs, wage and salary structure, benefits and conditions of employment, layoffs, discharges, disciplinary action, and union contract provisions affecting these areas.
7. An internal audit and reporting system should be established to monitor and evaluate progress in all aspects of the program.
8. Company and community programs that are supportive of equal opportunity should be developed. Programs might include training of supervisors on their legal responsibilities and the organization's commitment to equal employment and job and career counseling programs.

Source: *Affirmative Action and Equal Employment*, vol. 1 (Washington, D.C.: U.S. Equal Employment Opportunity Commission, 1974), pp. 16–64.

to-2 opinion, held that it did not and that the voluntary quota was permissible. The Weber decision also hinted at the Court's criteria for a permissible affirmative action plan: (1) the plan must be designed to break down old patterns of segregation; (2) it must not involve the discharge of innocent third parties; (3) it must not have any bars to the advancement of white employees; and (4) it must be a temporary measure to eliminate discrimination.

Another Supreme Court decision in 1984 was concerned with a conflict between a seniority system and certain affirmative action measures taken by the City of Memphis, Tennessee.[12] In 1981, budget deficits caused layoffs of personnel in the city's fire department. The layoffs were to be based on seniority. The district court issued an injunction ordering the city to refrain from applying the seniority system because it would decrease the percentage of black employees in certain jobs. However, the Supreme Court ruled that the Memphis Fire Department could not insulate blacks from layoffs and demotions. This decision did not ban the use of affirmative action programs, but did indicate that a seniority system may limit the use of certain affirmative action measures.[13]

F I G U R E   12–3   Steps in the Selection Process

STEPS IN SELECTION PROCESS	POSSIBLE CRITERIA FOR ELIMINATING POTENTIAL EMPLOYEE
Preliminary screening from application blank, résumé, employer records, etc.	Inadequate educational level or performance/experience record for the job and its requirements.
Preliminary interview	Obvious disinterest and unsuitability for job and its requirements.
Testing	Failure to meet minimum standards on job-related measures of intelligence, aptitude, personality, etc.
Reference checks	Unfavorable reports from references regarding past performance.
Employment interview	Inadequate demonstration of ability or other job-related characteristics.
Physical examination	Lack of physical fitness required for job.
Personal judgment	Intuition and judgment resulting in the selection of a new employee.

Some guidance on the issue of reverse discrimination and affirmative action has been given in the *Bakke, Weber,* and *Memphis* cases. However, the issue is far from settled, and more court cases are likely in the future.

Selection Procedure

Figure 12–3 is a suggested procedure for selecting employees. The preliminary screening and preliminary interview eliminate candidates who are obviously not qualified for the job. In the preliminary screening of applications, personnel data sheets, school records, work records, and similar sources are reviewed to determine characteristics, abilities, and the past performance of the individual. The preliminary interview is then used to screen out unsuitable or uninterested applicants who passed the preliminary screening phase.

Testing

One of the most controversial areas of staffing is employment testing. **Tests** provide a sample of behavior that is used to draw inferences about the future behavior or performance of an individual. Many tests are available to organizations for use in the selection process.[14] Tests used by organizations can be grouped into the following general categories: aptitude, psychomotor, job knowledge and proficiency, interests, psychological, and polygraphs.

Aptitude tests measure a person's capacity or potential ability to learn. *Psychomotor tests* are used to measure a person's strength, dexterity, and coordination.

Test – sample of behavior used to draw inferences about the future behavior or performance of an individual.

Job knowledge tests measure the job-related knowledge possessed by the applicant. *Proficiency tests* measure how well the applicant can do a sample of the work that is to be performed. *Interest tests* are designed to determine how a person's interests compare with the interests of successful people in a specific job. *Psychological tests* attempt to measure personality characteristics. *Polygraph tests,* popularly known as "lie detector tests," record physical changes in the body as the test subject answers a series of questions. By studying recorded physiological measurements, the polygraph examiner then makes a judgment as to whether the subject's response was truthful or deceptive.

Employment testing is legally subject to the requirements of validity and reliability. **Test validity** refers to the extent to which a test predicts a specific criterion. For organizations, the criterion usually used is performance on the job. Thus, test validity generally refers to the extent to which a test predicts future job success or performance. The selection of criteria to define job success or performance is a most difficult problem, and its importance cannot be overstated. Obviously, test validity cannot be measured unless satisfactory criteria exist.

Test reliability refers to the consistency or reproducibility of the results of a test. Three methods are commonly used to determine the reliability of a test. The first method, called test-retest, involves testing a group of people and then retesting them at a later date. The degree of similarity between the sets of scores determines the reliability of the test. The second method, called parallel forms, entails giving two separate but similar forms of the test. The degree to which the sets of scores coincide determines the reliability of the test. The third method, called split halves, divides the test into two halves to determine if performance is similar on both halves. Again, the degree of similarity determines the reliability. All of these methods require statistical calculations for determining the degree of reliability of the test.

In the past, organizations have frequently used tests without establishing their validity or reliability. As a result of such practices, testing came under a great deal of attack. The previously discussed Civil Rights Act of 1964 includes a section specifically related to the use of tests:

> nor shall it be an unlawful employment practice for an employer to give and to act upon the results of any professionally developed ability test provided that such a test, its administration, or action upon the results is not designed, intended, or used to discriminate because of race, color, religion, sex, or national origin.[15]

Two Supreme Court decisions have had a profound impact on the use of testing by organizations. First, in the case of *Griggs* v. *Duke Power Company,* the Court ruled that any test which has an adverse impact on women or minority group applicants must be validated as job related, regardless of whether an employer intended to discriminate.[16] In *Albermarle Paper Company* v. *Moody,* the Supreme Court placed the burden on the employer to show that its tests are in compliance with EEOC guidelines for testing.[17]

Finally, in 1978, the EEOC, the Civil Service Commission, the Department of Justice, and the Department of Labor adopted a document titled "Uniform

Test validity – extent to which a test measures what it purports to measure (generally, how well it predicts future job success or performance).

Test reliability – consistency or reproducibility of the results of a test.

Guidelines on Employee Selection Procedures."[18] These guidelines established the federal government's position concerning discrimination in employment practices. The guidelines explain what private and public employers must do to prove that their selection procedures, including testing, are nondiscriminatory.[19]

Polygraph Tests

The **polygraph,** popularly known as the lie detector, is a device that records physical changes in the body as the test subject answers a series of questions. The polygraph records fluctuations in blood pressure, respiration, and perspiration on a moving roll of graph paper. The polygraph operator makes a judgment as to whether the subject's response was truthful or deceptive by studying the physiological measurements recorded on the paper.

Polygraph – device that records physical changes in the body as test subject answers questions; also known as lie detector.

The use of a polygraph rests on a series of cause-and-effect assumptions: stress causes certain physiological changes in the body; fear and guilt cause stress; lying causes fear and guilt. The theory behind the use of a polygraph test assumes a direct relationship between the subject's responses to the questions and the physiological responses recorded on the polygraph. However, the polygraph machine itself does not detect lies; it only detects physiological changes. The operator must interpret the data recorded by the machine. Thus, it is the operator, not the machine, that is the real lie detector.

Over the last several years serious questions have been raised about the validity of polygraph tests. Difficulties involve situations in which a person lies without guilt (a pathological liar) or lies believing the response to be true. Furthermore, it is difficult to prove that the physiological responses recorded by the polygraph occur only because a lie has been told. In addition, some critics argue that the use of the polygraph violates fundamental principles of the Constitution: the right of privacy, the privilege against self-incrimination, and the presumption of innocence. As a result of these questions and criticisms, Congress has recently passed legislation that severely restricts the use of commercial polygraph (effective December 27, 1988). Managers at Work 12–3 describes a substitute approach to polygraph being used by many companies.

Drug Testing

The past few years have seen a proliferation of drug-testing programs. Programs have been instituted not only to screen job applicants, but also to test current employees for drug use. It has been estimated that about 20 percent of the Fortune 500 companies have either instituted drug-testing programs or are contemplating instituting them.[20]

As a result of these programs, numerous lawsuits have been filed on the legality of drug testing. Generally, it can be concluded that a drug-testing program is on stronger legal ground if it is limited to job applicants. Further-

MANAGERS AT WORK 12–3

A Substitute for Polygraph

One offshoot of the concern (and recent legislation) about using polygraph for personnel selection purposes has been the development of a number of psychological tests designed to measure honesty. Most of these psychological tests are written tests, known as paper-and-pencil honesty or integrity tests. These tests require the participant to answer a number of questions in writing. It has been estimated that, in 1987, approximately 2.5 million pre-employment honesty tests were administered by over 6,000 employers.

TrueTest is a test recently developed by InterGram, Inc., with the assistance of Dr. John B. Miner. The initial development and validation of the test utilized some 1,700 people. TrueTest, composed of 82 items, was specifically designed to avoid discrimination against any group on the basis of sex or minority status. InterGram reports extensive studies have shown that TrueTest can discern the dishonest job applicant with 84 percent effectiveness.

Source: Company Documents from InterGram, Inc.

more, testing of current employees should not be on a random basis. Probable cause such as a dramatic change in behavior or a sudden increase in accident rates should be established before testing. In addition, test results should be protected to ensure confidentiality.[21] Managers at Work 12–4 summarizes the drug-testing program of the National Basketball Association. (NBA).

Reference Checking

Reference checking can take place either before or after the diagnostic interview. Many organizations realize the importance of reference checking and provide space on the application form for listing references. Most prospective employers contact individuals from one or more of the three following categories: personal, school, or past employment references. For the most part, contacting individuals who are personal references has limited value because generally no applicant is going to list someone who will not give a positive recommendation. Contacting individuals who have taught the applicant in a school, college, or university is also of limited value for similar reasons. Previous employers are clearly the most used source and are in a position to supply the most objective information.

Reference checking is most frequently conducted by telephone. However,

MANAGERS AT WORK 12-4

Drug-Testing Program in the National Basketball Association (NBA)

In 1983, the NBA and the National Basketball Players Association (NBPA) adopted a simple but tough drug-testing program. A player who comes forth voluntarily with a drug (cocaine or heroin) problem is given treatment with no penalty. If a player comes forth a second time, he receives treatment, but his pay is suspended. If he comes forth a third time, he is banned from the game. A player who fails to come forth voluntarily, and is caught using drugs, is immediately banned from further play. Players who refuse to take a drug test are also banned, as are players involved in distributing drugs. Players who are banned can apply for reinstatement after two years; if they are drug free at that time, they will probably be reinstated.

Source: Adapted from Paul D. Staudoher, "Drug Abuse Program in Professional Sports: Lessons for Industry," *Personnel*, October 1987, p. 48.

many organizations will not answer questions about a previous employee unless the questions are put in writing. The amount and type of information that a previous employer is willing to divulge vary from organization to organization. The least that can be accomplished is to verify the previous employment. Other information that might be obtained includes reasons for leaving and whether or not the organization would be willing to rehire the person and why.

Government legislation has significantly influenced the process of reference checking. The Privacy Act of 1974 prevents government agencies from making their employment records available to other organizations without the consent of the individual involved. The Fair Credit and Reporting Act (FCRA) of 1971 requires private organizations to give job applicants access to information obtained from a reporting service. It is also mandatory that an applicant know that a check is being made. Because of these laws, most employment application forms now contain statements which must be signed by the applicant to authorize the employer to check references and conduct investigations.

Employment Interview

The employment interview is used by virtually all organizations as an important step in the selection process. Its purpose is to supplement information gained in other steps in the selection process to determine the suitability of an applicant for a specific opening in the organization. It is important to remember that all questions asked during an interview must be job related. Equal employment opportunity legislation has placed limitations on the types of questions that can be asked during an interview.

Types of Interviews. Several different types of interviews are used by organizations. The structured interview is conducted using a predetermined outline. Through the use of this outline, the interviewer maintains control of the interview so that all pertinent information on the applicant is covered systematically. Advantages to the use of structured interviews are that it provides the same type of information on all interviewees and allows systematic coverage of all questions deemed necessary by the organization. Furthermore, research studies have recommended the use of a structured interview to increase reliability and accuracy.[22]

Unstructured interviews are conducted using no predetermined checklist of questions. This type of interview uses open-ended questions such as: Tell me about your previous job. Interviews of this type pose numerous problems, such as a lack of systematic coverage of information, and are very susceptible to the personal biases of the interviewer. This type of interview, however, does provide a more relaxed atmosphere.

Three other types of interviewing techniques have been used to a limited extent by organizations. The stress interview is designed to place the interviewee under pressure. In the stress interview, the interviewer assumes a hostile and antagonistic attitude toward the interviewee. The purpose of this type of interview is to detect the highly emotional person. In board (or panel) interviews, two or more interviewers conduct the interview. Group interviews, in which several interviewees are questioned together in a group discussion, are also sometimes used. Board interviews and group interviews can involve either a structured or unstructured format.

Problems in Conducting Interviews. Although interviews have widespread use in selection procedures, a host of problems exist. The first, and certainly one of the most significant, problems is that interviews are subject to the same legal requirements of validity and reliability as other steps in the selection process.

Furthermore, the validity and reliability of most interviews is questionable. One of the primary reasons for this seems to be that it is easy for the interviewer to become either favorably or unfavorably impressed with the job applicant for the wrong reasons. Several common pitfalls may be encountered in interviewing a job applicant. Interviewers, like all people, have personal biases. These biases play a role in the interviewing process. For example, a qualified male applicant should not be rejected merely because the interviewer dislikes long hair on males.

Closely related is the problem of the **halo effect,** which occurs when the interviewer allows a single prominent characteristic to dominate judgment

Halo effect – occurs when interviewers allow a single prominent characteristic to dominate their judgment of all traits.

of all other traits. For instance, it is often easy to overlook other characteristics when a person has a pleasant personality. However, merely having a pleasant personality does not necessarily ensure that the person will be a good employee.

Overgeneralizing is another common problem. An interviewee may not behave exactly the same way on the job as during the interview. The interviewer must remember that the interviewee is under pressure during the interview and that some people just naturally become nervous during an interview.

Conducting Effective Interviews. Problems associated with interviews can be partially overcome through careful planning. The following suggestions are offered to increase the effectiveness of the interviewing process.

Careful attention must be given to the selection and training of interviewers. They should be outgoing and emotionally well-adjusted persons. Interviewing skills can be learned, and the persons responsible for conducting interviews should be thoroughly trained in these skills.

The plan for the interview should include an outline specifying the information to be obtained and the questions to be asked. The plan should also include room arrangements. Privacy and some degree of comfort are important. If a private room is not available, the interview should be conducted in a place where other applicants are not within hearing distance.

The interviewer should also attempt to put the applicant at ease. The interviewer should not argue with the applicant or put the applicant on the spot. A brief conversation about a general topic of interest or offering the applicant a cup of coffee can help ease the tension. The applicant should be encouraged to talk. However, the interviewer must maintain control and remember that the primary goal of the interview is to gain information that will aid in the selection decision.

The facts obtained in the interview should be recorded immediately. Generally, notes can and should be taken during the interview.

Finally, the effectiveness of the interviewing process should be evaluated. One way to evaluate effectiveness is to compare the performance ratings of individuals who are hired against assessments made during the interview. This cross-check can serve to evaluate the effectiveness of individual interviewers as well as the total interviewing program.

Physical Examination

Many organizations require a physical examination before an employee is hired. Its purpose is not only to determine whether the applicant is physically capable of performing the job but also to determine the applicant's eligibility for group life, health, and disability insurance. Because of the expense, physical examinations are normally given as one of the last steps in the selection process. Their expense has also caused many organizations to have applicants complete a health questionnaire when they fill out their application form. If no serious medical problems are indicated on the medical questionnaire, the applicant is not normally required to have a physical examination.

The Rehabilitation Act of 1973 has caused many employers to reexamine the physical requirements for many jobs. The act prohibits discrimination against handicapped persons; it requires government contractors to take affirmative action to employ qualified handicapped persons—persons who, with reasonable accommodations, can perform the essential functions of a job. This act does not prohibit employers from giving medical exams. However, it does encourage employers to make medical inquiries which are directly related to the applicant's ability to perform job-related functions and encourages employers to make reasonable accommodations in helping handicapped people to perform the job.

Personal Judgment

The final step in the selection process is the personal judgment required to select one individual for the job. (Of course, the assumption is that at this point there will be more than one individual qualified for the job.) A value judgment, using all of the data obtained in the previous steps of the selection process, must be made in selecting the best individual for the job. If previous steps have been performed correctly, the chances of success in this personal judgment are dramatically improved.

The individual making the personal judgment should also recognize that in some cases, none of the applicants are satisfactory. If this occurs, the job should be redesigned, more money should be offered to attract more qualified candidates, or other actions should be taken. Caution should be taken against accepting the best individual who has been seen, if the individual is not what is needed to do the job.

TRANSFERS, PROMOTIONS, AND SEPARATIONS

The final step in the human resource planning process involves transfers, promotions, and separations. **Transfers** involve moving an employee to another job at approximately the same level in the organization, with basically the same pay, performance requirements, and status. Planned transfers can serve as an excellent development technique. Transfers can also be helpful in balancing varying departmental work load requirements. The most common problem relating to transfers occurs when a "problem" employee is unloaded on an unsuspecting manager. Training, counseling, or corrective discipline of the employee may eliminate the need for such transfers. If the employee cannot be rehabilitated, discharge is usually preferable to transfer.

Transfer – moving an employee to another job at about the same level, with about the same pay, performance requirements, and status.

A **promotion** moves an employee to a job involving higher pay, status, and thus higher performance requirements. The two basic criteria used by most organizations in promotions are merit and seniority. Union contracts often require that seniority be considered in promotions. Many organizations prefer to base promotions on merit as a way of rewarding and encouraging performance. Obviously, this assumes that the organization has a method for evaluating performance and determining merit. An organization must also consider the requirements of the job under consideration, not just the employee's performance in previous jobs. Success in one job does not automatically ensure success in another job. Both past performance and potential must be considered. This also lessens the probability of the occurrence of the Peter Principle.

A **separation** involves either voluntary or involuntary termination of an employee. In voluntary terminations, many organizations attempt to determine why the employee is leaving, by using exit interviews. This type of interview provides insights into problem areas that need to be corrected in the organization. Involuntary separations should be made only as a last resort. When a company has hired an employee and invested resources in the employee, termination results in a low return on the organization's investment. Training and counseling often are tried before firing an individual. However, when rehabilitation fails, the best course of action is usually termination, because of the negative impact a disgruntled or misfit employee can have on others in the organization.

Promotion – moving an employee to a job with higher pay, status, and thus higher performance requirements.

Separation – voluntary or involuntary termination of an employee.

THE DYNAMICS OF STAFFING

Because organizations are dynamic, the staffing process is subject to continual changes. The activities involved in the staffing function must continuously be reevaluated in light of changing conditions, both internal and external. Internal conditions include changing job requirements, changing technology, retirements, deaths, resignations, terminations, and promotions. External conditions include government regulations, general economic conditions, industry competition, and resource availability. These conditions and the changes they cause must be adequately considered so that the level of human resources can be maintained in order to achieve organizational objectives. The critical link between an organization's human resources and the achievement of organizational goals is reflected in the general consensus that even if the physical assets of an organization were suddenly destroyed, the human organization, if properly staffed, could rebuild and maintain an ongoing and viable organization.

This chapter has presented what could be considered an ideal staffing model. It should not be concluded, however, that most organizations follow this model: Many do not.

▟ SUMMARY

LEARNING OBJECTIVE 1

Outline the Human Resource Planning Process.
Human resource planning is a process of getting the right number of qualified people into the right job at the right time. Once organizational plans are made and specific objectives are set, human resource planning attempts to define the human resource needs to meet the organization's objectives.

LEARNING OBJECTIVE 2

Define Job Analysis, Job Description, Job Specification, and Skills Inventory.
Job analysis is the process of determining, through observation and study, the pertinent information relating to the nature of a specific job. A job description is a written statement that identifies the tasks, duties, activities, and performance results required in a particular job. A job specification is a written statement that identifies the abilities, skills, traits, or attributes necessary for successful performance in a particular job. A skills inventory contains basic information on all employees of an organization.

LEARNING OBJECTIVE 3

Define Equal Employment Opportunity.
Equal employment opportunity refers to the right of all people to work and to advance on the basis of merit, ability, and potential.

LEARNING OBJECTIVE 4

Describe the Recruitment Process.
Recruitment involves the activities of seeking and attracting a supply of people from which qualified candidates for job vacancies can be selected.

LEARNING OBJECTIVE 5

Define an Affirmative Action Plan.
An affirmative action plan is a written document outlining specific goals and timetables for remedying past discriminatory actions.

LEARNING OBJECTIVE 6

Discuss Reverse Discrimination.
Reverse discrimination is the alleged preferential treatment for one group (minority or female) over another group (white male) rather than merely providing equal opportunity.

LEARNING OBJECTIVE 7

Define Tests, Test Validity, and Test Reliability.
Tests provide a sample of behavior that is used to draw inferences about the future behavior or performance of an individual. Test validity refers to the extent to which a test predicts a specific criterion. Test reliability refers to the consistency or reproducibility of the results of a test.

LEARNING OBJECTIVE 8

Explain Polygraph and Drug Testing.

The polygraph is a device that records physical changes in the body as the test subject answers a series of questions. Drug-testing programs are generally on stronger legal grounds if they are limited to job applicants. Testing of current employees should not be done on a random basis. Test results should be confidential.

LEARNING OBJECTIVE 9

Discuss the Types of Employment Interviews.

A structured interview is conducted using a predetermined outline. Unstructured interviews are conducted using no predetermined checklist of questions. In the stress interview, the interviewer assumes a hostile and antagonistic attitude in order to place the interviewee under stress. In board (or panel) interviews, two or more interviewers conduct the interview. Group interviews involve having several interviewees questioned together in a group discussion.

REVIEW QUESTIONS

1. How does staffing relate to the organizing function?
2. What is human resource planning?
3. What is a job analysis? A job description? A job specification? A skills inventory?
4. What is human resource forecasting?
5. Describe a model of the human resource planning process.
6. Describe the purpose of the following government legislation:
   a. Equal Pay Act of 1963.
   b. Civil Rights Act of 1964.
   c. Age Discrimination in Employment Act of 1968, as amended in 1978.
7. What is equal employment opportunity?
8. Define affirmative action plan.
9. What is recruitment? Describe some sources of recruitment.
10. What is selection? Describe the steps in the selection process.
11. What is test validity?
12. What is test reliability? What methods are commonly used to determine test reliability?
13. What is a polygraph test?
14. What are the general requirements for a legal drug test?
15. What is reference checking?
16. Describe two basic types of interviews.
17. Discuss some common pitfalls in interviewing.
18. What is a transfer? A promotion? A separation?

DISCUSSION QUESTIONS

1. Discuss the following statement: An individual who owns a business should be able to hire anyone and shouldn't have to worry about government interference.
2. Discuss your feelings on reverse discrimination.
3. Many managers believe that line managers should not have to worry about human

resource needs and that this should be handled by the human resource department. What do you think?

4. One common method of handling problem employees is to transfer them to another department of the organization. Discuss your feelings on this practice.

REFERENCES & ADDITIONAL READINGS

[1] C. F. Russ, Jr., "Manpower Planning Systems: Part I," *Personnel Journal,* January 1982, p. 41.

[2] Ibid.

[3] For a description on how Robbins & Meyers, Inc. does human resource planning, see David R. Leigh, "Business Planning Is People Planning," *Personnel Journal,* May 1984, pp. 44–45.

[4] Thomas H. Patten, *Manpower Planning and the Development of Human Resources* (New York: John Wiley & Sons, 1971), p. 243.

[5] For a detailed discussion on skills inventories, see Donald C. Doele and Carlton W. Dukes, "Skills Inventories and Promotion Systems," *Handbook of Human Resources Administration,* 2nd ed., ed. Joseph J. Famularo (New York: McGraw-Hill, 1986), pp. 18-1–18-21.

[6] "Equal Pay for Equal Work under the Fair Labor Standards Act," *Interpractices Bulletin* (Washington, D.C.: U.S. Department of Labor, 1967), Title 29, pt. 800.

[7] Lawrence J. Peter and R. Hall, *The Peter Principle* (New York: Bantam Books, 1969).

[8] *Parham* v. *Southwestern Bell Telephone Company,* 433 F2d 421 (8th Cir. 1970).

[9] *Affirmative Action and Equal Employment,* Vol. 1 (Washington, D.C.: U.S. Equal Opportunity Employment Commission, 1974), pp. 30–31.

[10] *University of California Regents* v. *Bakke,* 483 U.S. 265 (1978).

[11] *United Steelworkers* v. *Weber,* 99 S. Ct. 2721 (1979).

[12] *Memphis Firefighters, Local 1974* v. *Stotts,* 104 S. Ct. 2576 (1984).

[13] Theresa Johnson, "The Future of Affirmative Action: An Analysis of the Stotts Case," *Labor Law Journal,* October 1985, p. 788.

[14] For a detailed description of a large number of tests, see *Tests and Reviews* (Highland Park, N.J.: Gryphon Press, 1974).

[15] Title VII, Section 703(h), Civil Rights Acts of 1964.

[16] *Griggs* v. *Duke Power Company,* U.S. Supreme Court (1971).

[17] Thaddeus Holt, "A View from Albermarle," *Personnel Psychology,* Spring 1977, p. 71. Also see "EEOC Guidelines on Employment Testing," *Federal Register,* August 1, 1970, p. 12333.

[18] "Uniform Guidelines on Employee Selection Procedures," *Federal Register,* August 25, 1978, pp. 38290–315.

[19] For a more in-depth discussion on the current state of testing, see Dale Yoder and Paul D. Staudohar, "Testing and EEO: Getting Down to Cases," *Personnel Administrator,* February 1984, pp. 67–74.

[20] Donald J. Petersen, "The Ins and Outs of Implementing a Successful Drug-Testing Program," *Personnel,* October 1987, pp. 52–53.

[21] Ibid., p. 53.

[22] E. D. Pursell, M. A. Champion, and S. R. Gaylord, "Structured Interviewing: Avoiding Selection Problems," *Personnel Journal,* November 1980, p. 908.

INCIDENT

The Employment Interview

Jerry Sullivan is the underwriting manager for a large insurance company located in the Southwest. Recently, one of his best employees had given him two weeks' notice of her intention to leave. She was expecting a baby within a very short time period, and she and her husband had decided that she was going to quit work and stay home with her new baby and her other two young children.

Today Jerry was scheduled to start interviewing applicants for this job. The first applicant was Barbara Riley. She arrived at the company's office promptly at 9 A.M., the time scheduled for her interview. Unfortunately, just before she arrived, Jerry received a phone call from his boss, who had just returned from a three weeks' vacation. He wanted Jerry to bring him up to date on what had been going on. The telephone conversation lasted 30 minutes. During this time, Barbara Riley was seated in the company's reception room.

At 9:30, Jerry went to the reception room and invited her into his office. The following conversation occurred:

Jerry: Would you like a cup of coffee?

Barbara: No, I've already had one.

Jerry: You don't mind if I have a cup, do you?

Barbara: No, go right ahead. [*Jerry pauses, and rings his secretary Dorothy Cannon.*]

Jerry: Dorothy, would you fix me a cup of coffee?

Dorothy: I'll bring it in shortly. You have a call on Line 1.

Jerry: Who is it?

Dorothy: It's Tom Powell, our IBM representative. He wants to talk to you about the delivery date on our new word processor.

Jerry: I'd better talk to him. [*Turning to Barbara.*] I'd better take this call. I'll only be a minute. [*He picks up his phone.*] Well, Tom, when are we going to get our machines?

This phone conversation goes on for almost 10 minutes. After hanging up, Jerry turns again to Barbara to resume the interview.

Jerry: I'm sorry, but I needed to know about those machines. We really do need them. We only have a short time, so why don't you just tell me about yourself.

At that point, Barbara tells Jerry about her education, which includes an undergraduate degree in psychology and an M.B.A. which she will be receiving shortly. She explains to Jerry that this will be her first full-time job. Just then the phone rings, and Jerry's secretary tells him that his next interviewee is waiting.

Jerry: [*Turns to Barbara.*] Thank you for coming in. I'll be in touch with you as soon as I interview two more applicants for this job. However, I need to ask you a couple of quick questions.

Barbara: OK.

Jerry: Are you married?

Barbara: I am divorced.

Jerry: Do you have children?

Barbara: Yes, two boys.

Jerry: Do they live with you?

Barbara: Yes.

Jerry: The reason I am asking is that this job requires some travel. Will this pose a problem?

Barbara: No.

Jerry: Thanks, and I'll be in touch with you.

Questions

1. Outline the inadequacies of this interview.
2. What information did Jerry learn?
3. How do you feel about Jerry's last questions?

EXERCISE

The T-Test

Y ou will be given one minute to copy the letter T on a blank sheet of paper as many times as possible. The exercise is timed, and exactly one minute is permitted.

A frequency distribution will then be developed by your instructor (or the class) to show how well the class performed.

A. What is the shape of the distribution?
B. Why is the distribution shaped in this manner?
C. Why would some students have performed better and some worse?
D. How would you feel about using this test as a selection device? What problems can you see with using it?

13 Developing People within Organizations

LEARNING OBJECTIVES

*After studying this chapter,
you should be able to:*

1 Define human asset accounting.

2 Describe orientation.

3 Define training.

4 Explain the steps necessary to ensure that job training is effective.

5 Discuss vestibule training, apprenticeship training, and programmed instruction.

6 List and define the most popular methods of management development.

7 Describe an assessment center.

8 List the steps involved in the evaluation of training and management development.

Few organizations would admit that they can survive without it—yet some act as though they could.

Everyone knows what it is—yet management, unions, and workers often interpret it in light of their own job conditions.

It is going on all the time—yet much of it is done haphazardly.

It is futile to attempt it without the needed time and facilities—yet often those responsible for it lack either or both.

It costs money—yet at times there is not adequate budgetary appropriation for it.

It should take place at all levels—yet sometimes it is limited to the lowest operating levels.

It can help everyone do a better job—yet those selected for it often fear it.

It is foolish to start it without clearly defined objectives—yet this is occasionally done.

It cannot be ignored without costing the company money—yet some managers seem blind to this reality.

It should permeate the entire organization and be derived from the firm's theory and practice of management—yet sometimes it is shunted off to one department that operates more or less in isolation from the rest of the business.

F. A. PHILLIPS, W. M. BERLINER, AND J. J. CRIBBIN[*]

Newly hired employees must be introduced to the organization and to their jobs. They must be trained to perform their jobs. Furthermore, current employees must regularly have their skills updated and must learn new skills. An organization should also be very concerned about developing the skills of its management team. The introductory quote to this chapter rather humorously describes the incongruencies that can exist between what managers say or feel about employee development and what they actually do. Regardless of what many organizations do, however, the development of human resources is a key managerial responsibility.

Human asset accounting – attempt to place a value on an organization's human assets by measuring the costs incurred by organizations in recruiting, hiring, training, and developing their human assets.

HUMAN ASSET ACCOUNTING

Human asset (or human resource) accounting attempts to place a value on an organization's human assets. It measures the costs incurred by organiza-

[*] F. A. Phillips, W. M. Berliner, and J. J. Cribbin, *Management of Training Programs* (Homewood, Ill.: Richard D. Irwin, 1960), pp. 5–6.

tions in recruiting, hiring, training, and developing their human assets.[1] Basically, the proponents of human asset accounting feel that the quality of the human resources in an organization should be reflected on its balance sheet.

Several methods have been suggested for finding the financial value of an organization's human resources:

1. *Start-up costs:* Derive the original costs of hiring and training personnel as well as the costs of developing working relationships.
2. *Replacement costs:* Estimate the cost of replacing current employees with others of equivalent talents and experience.
3. *Present-value method:* Multiply the present value of wage payments for the future five years times the firm's efficiency ratio (which is a measure of the firm's rate of return in relation to the average rate of return for the industry).
4. *Goodwill method:* Allocate a portion of the company's earnings in excess of the industry average (goodwill) to human resources.

Human asset accounting is not presently an acceptable accounting practice for financial reporting purposes. However, direct costing, introduced as a management technique in 1939, has become accepted managerial accounting for internal purposes, although it has never been an accepted practice for either tax or financial reporting. Thus, in order for the use of human asset accounting to become widespread, it must first be proved to be useful in practice.

ORIENTATION

Orientation is the introduction of new employees to the organization, their work unit, and their job. It comes from co-workers and the organization. The orientation from co-workers is usually unplanned and unofficial, and it can provide the new employee with misleading and inaccurate information.[2] This is one of the reasons that it is important to have an orientation provided by the organization. An effective orientation program has an immediate and lasting impact on the new employee and can make the difference between a new employee's success or failure.

Job applicants get some orientation to the organization even before they are hired, sometimes through the organization's reputation—how it treats employees and the types of products or services it provides. Also, during the selection process, applicants often see other general aspects of an organization and what their duties, working conditions, and pay will be.

After the employee is hired, the organization's formal orientation program begins. For all types of organizations, orientation should usually be conducted at two distinct levels:

Orientation—introduction of new employees to the organization, their work unit, and their job.

1. General organizational orientation—presents topics of relevance and interest to all employees.
2. Departmental and job orientation—covers topics unique to the new employee's specific department and job.

Normally, the general orientation is given by the human resource/personnel department. Departmental and job orientation is generally handled by the new employee's manager.

Organizational Orientation

Organizational orientation should cover the needs of both the organization and the employee. A good balance is essential if the orientation program is to have positive results. The organization is interested in making a profit, providing good service to customers and clients, satisfying employee needs and well-being, and being socially responsible. New employees, on the other hand, generally are more interested in pay, benefits, and specific terms and conditions of employment.

Figure 13–1 provides a listing of suggested topics for an organization's orientation program.

Departmental and Job Orientation

The content of departmental and job orientation depends on the needs of the department and the skills and past experience of the new employee. Figure 13–2 provides a checklist for departmental and job orientation programs.

Orientation Kit

Orientation kit—packet of written information given to a new employee to supplement the verbal orientation program.

Each new employee should receive a kit or packet of information to supplement the verbal orientation program. This **orientation kit** is normally prepared by the human resource department and can provide a wide variety of materials. Care should be taken in its design. Essential information should be provided, but not too much information given. Materials that might be included in an orientation kit include:[3]

Organizational chart.
Map of the organization's facilities.
Copy of policy and procedures handbook.
List of holidays and fringe benefits.
Copies of performance appraisal forms and procedures.
Copies of other required forms (e.g., expense reimbursement form).

FIGURE 13–1 Possible Topics for an Organizational Orientation Program

1. Overview of the company:
   Welcoming speech.
   Founding, growth, trends, goals, priorities, and problems.
   Traditions, customs, norms, and standards.
   Current specific functions of the organization.
   Products/services and customers served.
   Steps in getting product/service to customers.
   Scope of activities.
   Organization, structure, and relationship of company and its branches.
   Facts on key managerial staff.
   Community relations, expectations, and activities.

2. Key policies and procedures review.

3. Compensation:
   Pay rates and ranges.
   Overtime.
   Holiday pay.
   Shift differential.
   How pay is received.
   Deductions: required and optional, with specific amounts.
   Option to buy damaged products, and costs thereof.
   Discounts.
   Advances on pay.
   Loans from credit union.
   Reimbursement for job expenses.
   Tax shelter options.

4. Fringe benefits:
   Insurance:
       Medical–dental.
       Life.
       Disability.
       Workers' compensation.
   Holidays and vacations (e.g., patriotic, religious, birthday).
   Leave: personal illness, family illness, bereavement, maternity, military, jury duty, emergency, extended absence.
   Retirement plans and options.
   On-the-job training opportunities.
   Counseling services.
   Cafeteria.
   Recreation and social activities.
   Other company services to employees.

5. Safety and accident prevention:
   Completion of emergency data card (if not done as part of employment process).
   Health and first-aid clinics.
   Exercise and recreation centers.
   Safety precautions.
   Reporting of hazards.
   Fire prevention and control.
   Accident procedures and reporting.
   OSHA requirements (review of key sections).
   Physical exam requirements.
   Use of alcohol and drugs on the job.

6. Employee and union relations:
   Terms and conditions of employment review.
   Assignment, reassignment, and promotion.
   Probationary period and expected on-the-job conduct.
   Reporting of sickness and lateness to work.
   Employee rights and responsibilities.
   Manager and supervisor rights.
   Relations with supervisors and shop stewards.
   Employee organizations and options.
   Union contract provisions and/or company policy.
   Supervision and evaluation of performance.
   Discipline and reprimands.
   Grievance procedures.
   Termination of employment (resignation, layoff, discharge, retirement).
   Content and examination of personnel record.
   Communications: channels of communication—upward and downward—suggestion system, posting materials on bulletin board, sharing new ideas.
   Sanitation and cleanliness.
   Wearing of safety equipment, badges, and uniforms.
   Bringing things on to, and removing things from, company grounds.
   On-site political activity.
   Gambling.
   Handling of rumors.

7. Physical facilities:
   Tour of facilities
   Food services and cafeteria.
   Restricted areas for eating.
   Employee entrances.
   Restricted areas (e.g., from cars).
   Parking.
   First aid.
   Rest rooms.
   Supplies and equipment.

8. Economic factors:
   Costs of damage, by select items, with required sales to balance.
   Costs of theft with required sales to compensate.
   Profit margins.
   Labor costs.
   Cost of equipment.
   Costs of absenteeism, lateness, and accidents.

F I G U R E 13–2   Possible Topics for Departmental and Job Orientation Programs

1. Department functions:
   Goals and current priorities.
   Organization and structure.
   Operational activities.
   Relationship of functions to other departments.
   Relationships of jobs within the department.

2. Job duties and responsibilities:
   Detailed explanation of job, based on current job description and expected results.
   Explanation of why the job is important, how the specific job relates to others in the department and company.
   Discussion of common problems and how to avoid and overcome them.
   Performance standards and basis of performance evaluation.
   Number of daily work hours and times.
   Overtime needs and requirements.
   Extra-duty assignments (e.g., changing duties to cover for an absent worker).
   Required records and reports.
   Checkout on equipment to be used.
   Explanation of where and how to get tools, have equipment maintained and repaired.
   Types of assistance available; when and how to ask for help.
   Relations with state and federal inspectors.

3. Policies, procedures, rules, and regulations:
   Rules unique to the job and/or department.
   Handling emergencies.
   Safety precautions and accident prevention.
   Reporting of hazards and accidents.

Cleanliness standards and sanitation (e.g., cleanup).
Security, theft problems and costs.
Relations with outside people (e.g., drivers).
Eating, smoking, chewing gum, etc., in department area.
Removal of things from department.
Damage control (e.g., smoking restrictions).
Time clock and time sheets.
Breaks/rest periods.
Lunch duration and time.
Making and receiving personal telephone calls.
Requisitioning supplies and equipment.
Monitoring and evaluating employee performance.
Job bidding and requesting reassignment.
Going to cars during work hours.

4. Tour of department:
   Rest rooms and showers.
   Fire-alarm box and fire extinguisher stations.
   Time clocks.
   Lockers.
   Approved entrances and exists.
   Water fountains and eye-wash systems.
   Supervisors' quarters.
   Supply room and maintenance department.
   Sanitation and security offices.
   Smoking areas.
   Locations of services to employees related to department.
   First-aid kit.

5. Introduction to department employees

Source: Walter D. St. John, "The Complete Employee Orientation Program," Copyright May 1980, p. 377. Reprinted with permission of *Personnel Journal*, Costa Mesa, California; all rights reserved.

Emergency and accident prevention procedures.

Sample copy of company newsletter or magazine.

Telephone numbers and locations of key company personnel (e.g., security).

Copies of insurance plans.

Many organizations require employees to sign a form stating they have received and read the orientation kit. In unionized organizations, this protects the company if a grievance arises and the employee claims not to be aware of certain company policies and procedures. However, whether signing a document really encourages new employees to read the kit is questionable.

TRAINING EMPLOYEES

Training is a process that involves acquiring skills or learning concepts to increase the performance of employees. Generally, the new employee's manager has primary responsibility for training in how to perform the job. Sometimes this is delegated to a senior employee in the department. Regardless, the quality of this initial training can greatly influence the employee's job attitude and productivity.

Economic, social, technological, and governmental changes also influence the skills needed in an organization. Changes in these areas can make current skills obsolete in a short time. Also, planned organizational changes and expansions can make it necessary for employees to update their skills or acquire new ones. Managers at Work 13–1 shows the importance that McDonald's has placed on employee training.

Training – process that involves acquiring skills or learning concepts to increase employee performance.

Determining Training Needs

Training must be aimed at the achievement of some organizational objective, such as more efficient production methods, improved quality of products/services, or reduced operating costs. An organization should only commit its resources to training that can help in achieving its objectives. Deciding on specific training activities in an organization requires a systematic and accurate analysis of training needs.

A variety of methods can be used to determine an organization's training needs.[4] Company reports and records provide clues to internal trouble spots. Records on absenteeism, turnover, tardiness, and accident rates provide objective evidence of problems. Because this type of information already exists, it can be collected and examined with minimal effort and interruption of the work flow. Interviews with employees, questionnaires, and group discussions can also be used to locate training needs. Personal observations of work being performed can also give insight into performance problems that may be corrected through training.

Establishing Training Objectives

After training needs have been determined, objectives must be set for meeting these needs. Unfortunately, many training programs have no goals. "Training for training's sake" appears to be the maxim. With this philosophy, it is almost impossible to evelute the strengths and weaknesses of a training program.

In general, objectives should define the skills to be acquired or concepts to be learned from the training. They should be in writing and be measurable. Until an organization decides what results it expects from training, it cannot determine the content or method of instruction.

MANAGERS AT WORK 13–1

Hamburger University

Hamburger University is McDonald's worldwide training center located in Oak Brook, Illinois. At Hamburger University, there are seven major classrooms, eight seminar rooms, a library, and four fully functioning equipment laboratories. All of this is located on an 80-acre site with two large man-made lakes.

Hamburger University utilizes several types of audio-visual equipment, including both live and remote television, as well as all necessary restaurant equipment to enable the student to make the transition from classroom to the restaurant. Nearly 2,500 students attend Hamburger University each year.

The purpose of Hamburger University is to conduct the Advanced Operations Course (AOC) which is required for all owners/managers of McDonald's Corporation. The university is staffed by 28 professors and is taught to participants from 41 countries and territories in 7 languages. The curricular areas are Operations and Management, Equipment, and Personnel/Human Resources Skills.

Source: Public company documents, McDonald's Corporation. Conversation with the Dean at Hamburger University.

METHODS OF TRAINING

Several methods can be used to satisfy an organization's training needs and accomplish its objectives. Some of the more commonly used methods include on-the-job training, job rotation, vestibule training, apprenticeship training, classroom training, and programmed instruction.

On-the-Job Training and Job Rotation

On-the-job training (OJT) – normally given by a senior employee or supervisor; trainee is shown how to perform the job and allowed to do it under the trainer's supervision.

On-the-job training (OJT) is normally given by a senior employee or supervisor. The trainee is shown how to perform the job and allowed to do it under the trainer's supervision.

One form of on-the-job training is job rotation, sometimes called cross-training. Under OJT, an employee learns several different jobs within a work unit or department and performs each for a specified time period. One main advantage of job rotation is that it allows flexibility in the department. For example, when one member of a work unit is absent, another can perform that job.

One advantage of OJT is that no special facilities are required; also, the new employee does productive work during the learning process. Its major disadvantage is that the pressures of the workplace can cause training to be haphazard or neglected.

Several steps can be taken to ensure that job training is effective. The following five steps should be followed in any type of on-the-job training:

1. Prepare the employee for learning the job. The desire to learn a new job is almost always present in an employee. Showing an interest in the person, explaining the job's importance, and explaining why it must be done right enhance the employee's desire to learn. Knowing the employee's previous work experience in similar jobs enables the trainer to use that experience in explaining the present job or to eliminate explanations that are unnecessary.

2. Break down the work into components and identify the key points. This breakdown consists of defining the segments which make up the total job. In each segment, something is done to advance the work toward completion. The breakdown can be seen as a detailed road map which helps guide the employee through the entire work cycle in a rational, easy-to-understand manner, without injury to the person or damage to the equipment.

Any directive or information that helps the employee perform a work component correctly, easily, and safely is a key point. Key points are the "tricks of the trade" and are given to the employee to help reduce learning time. Observing and mastering the key points help the employee to acquire needed skills and perform the work more effectively.

3. Demonstrate the proper way to perform the job. Simply telling an employee how to perform a job is usually not enough. An employee must not only be told but also must be shown how to do the job. Each component of the job must be demonstrated. While each is being shown, the key points for that component should be explained. Employees should be encouraged to ask questions about each component.

4. Allow the employee to perform the job. An employee should perform the job under the guidance of the trainer. Generally, an employee should be required to explain what to do at each phase of the job. If the explanation is correct, the employee is then allowed to perform the phase. If it is incorrect, the mistake should be corrected before the employee is allowed to actually perform the phase. Praise and encouragement are essential.

5. Gradually put the employee on his or her own. When the trainer is reasonably sure that an employee can do the job alone, the employee should be allowed to work at his or her own pace and should be left alone while developing skills in performing the job. An employee should not be turned loose and forgotten. The trainer should return periodically to answer any questions and see that all is going well. An employee will have questions and will make better progress if the trainer is available to answer them and help with problems.

Figure 13–3 outlines the basic steps that should be followed in providing on-the-job training.

F I G U R E   13–3   Steps Leading to Effective On-the-Job Training

A. Determining the training objectives and preparing the training area.
   1. Decide what the trainee must be taught in order to do the job efficiently, safely, economically, and intelligently.
   2. Provide the right tools, equipment, supplies, and material.
   3. Have the workplace properly arranged, just as the employee will be expected to keep it.
B. Presenting the instruction.
   Step 1. Preparation of the trainee for learning the job:
      a. Put the trainee at ease.
      b. Find out what the trainee already knows about the job.
      c. Get the trainee interested in and desirous of learning the job.
   Step 2. Breakdown of work into components and identification of key points:
      a. Determine the segments that make up the total job.
      b. Determine the key points or tricks of the trade.
   Step 3. Presentation of the operations and knowledge:
      a. Tell, show, illustrate, and question to put over the new knowledge and operations.
      b. Instruct slowly, clearly, completely, and patiently, one point at a time.
      c. Check, question, and repeat.
      d. Make sure the trainee understands.
   Step 4. Performance tryout:
      a. Test the trainee by having him or her perform the job.
      b. Ask questions beginning with why, how, when, or where.
      c. Observe performance, correct errors, and repeat instructions, if necessary.
      d. Continue until the trainee is competent in the job.
   Step 5. Follow-up
      a. Put the trainee on his or her own.
      b. Check frequently to be sure the trainee follows instructions.
      c. Taper off extra supervision and close follow-up until the trainee is qualified to work with normal supervision.

Vestibule Training

Vestibule training – procedures and equipment similar to those used in the actual job are set up in a special working area called a vestibule.

In **vestibule training,** procedures and equipment similar to those used in the actual job are set up in a special working area called a vestibule. The trainee is then taught how to perform the job by a skilled person and is able to learn the job at a comfortable pace without the pressures of production schedules.

The primary advantage of this method is that the trainer can stress theory and use of proper techniques rather than output, and the student can learn by actually doing the job. However, this method is expensive, and the employee still must adjust to the actual production environment. Vestibule training has been used for training typists, word processor operators, bank tellers, clerks, and others in similar jobs.

Apprenticeship Training

Apprenticeship training dates back to biblical times. It is frequently used to train personnel in skilled trades, such as carpenters, bricklayers, electricians, mechanics, and tailors. The apprenticeship period generally lasts from two to five years. During this time, the trainee works under the guidance of a skilled worker but receives lower wages than the skilled worker.

Apprenticeship training – used in skilled trades; trainee works under the guidance of a skilled and licensed worker.

Classroom Training

Classroom training is conducted off the job and is probably the most familiar method of training. Classroom training is an effective means of quickly getting information to large groups with limited or no knowledge of the subject being presented. It is useful for teaching actual material, concepts, principles, and theories. Portions of orientation programs, some aspects of apprenticeship training, and safety programs are usually presented with some form of classroom instruction. However, classroom training is used more frequently for technical, professional, and managerial employees.

Programmed Instruction

The increased availability and lower cost of computers have made the use of programmed instruction more attractive. **Programmed instruction** requires the trainee to read material on a particular subject and then to answer questions about the subject. If the answers are correct, the trainee moves on to more advanced or new material. If the answers are incorrect, the trainee is required to reread the material and answer additional questions. The material in programmed instruction is presented either in text form or on computer video displays. Regardless of the type of presentation, programmed instruction provides active practice, a gradual increase in difficulty over a series of steps, immediate feedback, and an individualized rate of learning. It normally is used to teach factual information. Managers at Work 13–2 illustrates one form of computerized programmed instruction.

Programmed instruction – classroom training in which material is presented in text form or on computers; students must answer questions correctly before advancing.

MAKING TRAINING MEANINGFUL

To make all types of training more meaningful, there are several common pitfalls that a manager should avoid. Lack of reinforcement is one. An employee who is praised for doing a job well is likely to be motivated to do it well again. Praise and recognition can very effectively reinforce an employee's learning. Too many managers only point out mistakes. And they often tell

MANAGERS AT WORK 13–2

SAFECO Offers Training by Computer

SAFECO, which operates computers in various aspects of the insurance business, is offering its 6,500 insurance agents the opportunity to take training courses in the comfort of their own offices. The courses are designed so agents can take them at their convenience and work at their own speed. The most important benefit is that agents can learn in their offices while still being able to service their clients.

The first course, which teaches the use of computer terminals, was introduced in 1980. A course on private passenger auto rating has also been added since then. It can be completed in four to six hours.

Two agents who recently discovered the convenience of the computer-taught courses are Cynthia Caldwell of the Frank B. Hall Agency in Seattle and Ruth McCoy of the Torrence Insurance Agency in Longview, Washington.

Caldwell was the first agent to complete the new auto rating course; McCoy was the first to complete the course for continuing-education credits. They not only received the training in their offices; they were able to take the examinations at their terminals. When they finished, the scores flashed on the screens immediately so they didn't have to wait to find out if they had passed.

Source: Adapted from Alfred G. Haggerty, "SAFECO Offers Training by Computer," *National Underwriter* (*Property and Casualty Insurance Edition*), July 1, 1983, pp. 2, 14.

people: I'll let you know if you do the job wrong. However, people also want to know when they do the job right. Feedback regarding progress is critical to effective learning. Setting standards for trainees and measuring performance against them encourage learning.

"Practice makes perfect" definitely applies to the learning process. Too many managers try to explain the job quickly—then they expect the person to do it perfectly the first time. Having trainees perform a job or explain how to perform it focuses their concentration and helps learning. Repeating a job or task several times also helps. Learning is always aided by practice and repetition.

Managers sometimes also have preconceived and inaccurate ideas about what certain people or groups of people can or can't do (the Pygmalion effect). A manager should realize that different people learn at different rates. Some learn rapidly; some learn more slowly. A manager shouldn't expect everyone to pick the job up right away. The pace of the training should be adjusted to the trainee. Also, if a person is not a fast learner, this does not mean that the person will always be a poor performer. The manager should take the attitude that all people can learn and want to learn.

MANAGEMENT DEVELOPMENT

Management development is concerned with developing the attitudes and skills necessary to become or remain an effective manager. To be successful, it must have the full support of the organization's top executives. Management development should be designed, conducted, and evaluated on the basis of the goals of the organization, the needs of the managers involved, and probable changes in the organization's management team.

Management development – developing the attitudes and skills necessary to become or remain an effective manager.

Needs Assessment

Numerous methods have been proposed for use in assessing management development needs. The management development needs of any organization are composed of the aggregate, or overall, needs of the organization and the development needs of each manager within the organization.

Organizational needs. The most common method for determining organizational management development needs is an analysis of problem areas within the organization.[5] For example, increases in the number of grievances or accidents within an area of the organization often signal the need for management development. High turnover rates, absenteeism, or tardiness might also indicate management development needs. Projections based on the organization's objectives and on changes in its management team are also used to determine overall management development needs.

Needs of individual managers. The performance of the person is the primary indicator of individual development needs. Performance evaluations of each manager can be examined to determine areas that need strengthening. The existence of problem situations within a manager's work unit can also signal needs. Planned promotions or reassignments also often indicate the need for development.

Establishing Management Development Objectives

After the management development needs of an organization have been determined, objectives for the overall management development program and for individual programs must be established to meet these needs. Both types of objectives should be written and measurable.

One classification system for overall management development objectives involves routine, problem-solving, and innovative objectives. Routine, or regularly occurring, objectives might include supervisory training for new managers. Specifically, these might include targets for the number of trainees, hours of training, cost per trainee, and time required for trainees to reach a standard level of knowledge.

The second category of objectives is concerned with problem areas within the organization that are to be addressed through management development.

They would result from a needs assessment of management reports on such factors as absenteeism, turnover, safety, and number of grievances. Also, managers could be interviewed or polled through questionnaires.

Innovative objectives are aimed at achieving higher levels of performance with new techniques to improve the quality of management, reduce the cost of management development, or ensure more effective development activities.

The difference between problem-solving and innovative objectives is shown by the following example:

> An organization notices a sudden increase in employee grievances. To correct this, a new development program is designed to improve the human relations skills of supervisors. If the number of grievances then returns to normal or is reduced even further, the situation has been remedied. The problem-solving objective has been met. In another company, new supervisors have received most of their training in the form of classroom lectures; this method appears to be meeting the organization's needs. However, the human resource department, seeing room for improvement, starts a program of combined home study and programmed learning. If the new supervisors can now build their skills faster or at a lower cost, an innovative objective has been achieved.

After these overall management development objectives have been set, individual program goals must be identified. They should specify the skills or attitudes expected from the program. After these objectives have been established, course content and method of instruction can be specified.

Methods Used in Management Development

Understudy assignments – OJT where an individual, designated as heir to a job, learns the job from the present jobholder.

Some of the most popular methods of management development, listed in Figure 13–4, are discussed below.

Understudy Assignments. **Understudy assignments** generally are used to develop an employee to fill a specific job. The person who will someday have a specific job works for the incumbent to learn the job. The title of

F I G U R E   13–4   Selected Methods Used in Management Development

ON THE JOB	OFF THE JOB
Understudy assignments	Classroom training
Coaching	Lectures
Experience	Case studies
Job rotation	Role playing
Special projects and committee	In-basket techniques
assignments	Business games
	University and professional association
	seminars

the heir apparent is usually assistant manager, administrative assistant, or assistant to a particular manager.

There is one main advantage to understudy assignments. The heir realizes the purpose of the training and can learn in a practical and realistic situation without being directly responsible for operating results. On the negative side, however, the understudy learns the bad as well as the good practices of the incumbent. In addition, understudy assignments that last a long time can become expensive. If an understudy assignment system is used, one or more of the other management development methods should also be used.

Coaching. **Coaching** by experienced managers stresses the responsibility of all managers for developing subordinates. Experienced managers advise and guide trainees in solving management problems. Coaching should allow the trainee to develop individual approaches to management with the counsel of a more experienced person.

One advantage to coaching is that the trainee gets practical experience and sees the results of decisions. The danger is that the coach may neglect the training or pass on incorrect management practices. The coach's expertise and experience are critical to this method.

Coaching – management development conducted on the job, where experienced managers (mentors) advise and guide trainees in solving managerial problems.

Experience. Development through experience is used in many organizations. Employees are promoted into management jobs and allowed to learn on their own, from their daily experiences. The primary advantage is that the manager, trying to perform a certain job, may see the need for development and look for a way to get it. However, employees who have to learn on their own can create serious problems by making mistakes. Also, it is frustrating to try to manage without the needed background and knowledge. Serious problems can be avoided if experience is combined with other management development methods.

Job Rotation. **Job rotation** is designed to give an employee broad experience in many different areas of the organization. In understudy assignments, coaching, and experience, the trainee generally receives training and development for one particular job. In job rotation, the trainee goes from job to job within the organization, generally remaining in each from six months to a year. This technique is often used by large organizations for training recent college graduates.

Job rotation shows trainees how management principles can be applied in a cross section of environments. The training is practical; it also allows the trainee to become familiar with the company's entire operations. One disadvantage is that the trainee is often given menial work in each job. There is also a tendency to leave the trainee in each job too long.

Job rotation – employee learns several different jobs in a work unit or department and performs each for a specified time period.

Special Projects and Committee Assignments. Special projects require the employee to learn about a specific subject. For example, a trainee may be told to develop a training program on safety. This would require learning

about the present internal safety policies and problems and about the safety training done by other companies. The person must also learn to work and relate to other employees. However—and this is critical—the special assignment must provide a developing and learning experience for the trainee and not just busywork.

Committee assignments, similar to special projects, can be used if the organization has standing or ad hoc committees. An employee works with the committee on its regular duties; thus, the person develops skills in working with others and learns through the activities of the committee.

Classroom Training. Classroom training is not only used in management development programs; it is also widely used in the orientation and training activities discussed earlier in this chapter. Therefore, some of the material in this section also applies to those activities. In addition, several of the approaches used in organization development (discussed later in this chapter) involve classroom training.

Lectures. With lecturing, the trainer has control and can present the material just as desired. The lecture is useful for presenting facts; however, its value in changing attitudes and in teaching skills is somewhat limited.

Case studies. This technique was popularized by the Harvard Business School. With this method, sample situations are presented for the trainee to analyze. Ideally, the **case study** should force the trainee to think through problems, propose solutions, choose among them, and analyze the consequences of the decision. One primary advantage of the case study method is that it brings a note of realism to the instruction. However, case studies often are simpler than the real situations faced by managers. Also, when cases are discussed, there is often a lack of emotional involvement on the part of the participants; thus, attitude and behavioral changes are less likely to occur. Finally, the success of the case study method depends greatly on the skills of the instructor.[6]

One type of case study is the **incident method.** The trainee receives only the general outline of a situation. The trainer then provides more information as the trainee requests it. In theory, this method makes the trainee probe the situation and seek information, much as would be required in real life.

Role playing. In the **role-playing** method, trainees are required to act out assigned roles in a realistic situation. They learn from playing the roles. The success of this method depends on the ability of trainees to act realistically. Videotaping allows for review and evaluation of the exercise to improve its effectiveness.

In-basket techniques. This technique simulates a realistic situation. It requires the trainee to answer one manager's mail and telephone calls. Important duties are interspersed with routine matters. One call may come from an important customer who is angry; another from a local civic club requesting a donation. The trainee analyzes the situation and suggests possible actions. Evaluation is based on the number and quality of decisions and on the priorities assigned to each situation. The **in-basket technique** has been used not only

Case study – classroom training where students analyze real or hypothetical situations and suggest what to do and how to do it.

Incident method – form of case study; students are given the general outline of a situation and are given additional information only as they request it.

Role playing – trainees learn by acting out assigned roles in a realistic situation.

In-basket technique – classroom training where trainee is required to handle a manager's mail and phone calls and react accordingly.

MANAGERS AT WORK 13–3

The Looking Glass Game

"Looking Glass" is one of the oldest and most widely used business games. It was developed in a three-year, $300,000 project by social scientists at the Center for Creative Leadership, a nonprofit think tank in Greensboro, North Carolina.

Participants in the game get a chance to show their managerial skills by running for one day a make-believe glass manufacturing company with 4,000 employees and $200 million in annual sales. The Looking Glass company has three divisions. Participants make decisions on matters ranging from the important to the inconsequential: Looking Glass has a chance to make a big acquisition; the Advanced Products Division is attempting to decide where to locate a new plant; the division that makes windshields can't keep up with demand.

In recent years, more than 4,000 managers of major companies including IBM, AT&T, Union Carbide, and Monsanto have participated in the Looking Glass game.

Source: Adapted from Peter Petre, "Games that Teach You to Manage," *Fortune*, October 29, 1984, pp. 65–72.

for management development but also in assessment centers. (They are discussed later in this chapter.)

Business games. **Business games** generally provide a setting of a company and its environment and require a team of players to make operating decisions. Business games also normally require the use of computer facilities. Often, several different teams in a business game act as companies within an industry. This method forces trainees to work not only with other group members; they also must deal with competition within the industry. Advantages of business games are: they simulate reality; decisions are made in a competitive environment; feedback is provided about decisions; and decisions are made with less-than-complete data. The main problem is that many trainees simply attempt to determine the key to winning. When this occurs, the game is not used to its fullest potential as a learning device.[7] Managers at Work 13–3 describes one business game.

Business game – classroom training that provides the setting of a company and its environment and requires team players to make operating decisions.

University and Professional Association Seminars. Many colleges and universities offer both credit and noncredit courses to help meet the management development needs of various organizations. These courses range from principles of supervision to advanced executive management programs. Professional associations—such as the American Management Association—also offer a wide variety of management development programs. Many of the classroom techniques discussed in this chapter are used in these programs.

MANAGERS AT WORK 13–4

Management Development at Young & Rubicam (Y&R) Advertising Agency

To keep on top of its growth, continue to turn out its own management talent pool, and ensure that all employees at Y&R's various new and old offices remain faithful to the Y&R modus operandi, this advertising agency has found it necessary to create what would be called its own in-house college.

There are 18 separate management development programs at Y&R, covering strategy, creative print, broadcast, direct marketing, selling, lawful interviewing, performance appraisal, time management, writing, and presentation skills. One of the most grueling of the 18 courses is the Advertising Skills Workshop. Held twice a year, this course requires the Y&R managers to spend five and one-half weeks in a classroom, from 8:30 A.M. to 5:30 P.M. daily. Participants are taught the Y&R way of doing things, as well as key points in handling clients.

Throughout the course, the participants apply what they have learned to a case study which is either real or is based on a real-life situation. In a recent course, the test case was a hypothetical Better for You food line from General Foods. Ultimately, students make presentations based on what they've learned.

Source: Adapted from Christy Marshall, "Y&R a Heavy Investor in Executive Training," *Advertising Age,* March 14, 1983, p. 72.

Managers at Work 13–4 demonstrates an advertising agency's approach to employee development.

ASSESSMENT CENTERS

Assessment center —evaluates an individual's potential as a manager and determines the person's development needs based on his or her reactions in a simulated, "real world" environment.

An **assessment center** utilizes a formal procedure to evaluate a person's potential as a manager and determine that person's developmental needs. Assessment centers are used in both the selection and development of managers. Basically, these centers simulate the problems that a person might face in a real managerial situation. Presently, more than 2,000 companies use assessment centers. Because of its validity, assessment center use has continued to grow.[8] AT&T was one of the earliest and best-known users of assessment centers.

In the typical center, 10 to 15 employees of about equal rank are brought together for three to five days to work on individual and group exercises typical of a managerial job. Business games, situational problems, interviews, and cases are normally used. These exercises involve the employees in decision making, leadership, written and oral communication, planning, organizing, and motivation. Assessors observe the participants, rate their performance, and provide feedback to them about their performance and developmental needs.

Assessors are often selected from management ranks several levels above those of the participants. Also, psychologists from outside the organization often serve as assessors. For a program to be successful, the assessors must be thoroughly trained in the assessment process, the mechanics of the exercises to be observed, and the techniques of observing and providing feedback.

One attractive feature of assessment centers is extensive research showing the technique is valid in predicting managerial success.[9] Furthermore, participants learn from the feedback what their strong and weak points are, and they are often advised how to improve their skills in a particular area.

However, some operational problems can arise in using assessment centers. First, the organization must recognize that they are often more costly than other methods of management assessment and the development.[10] Problems can occur when employees come from different levels in the organization. When their differences become apparent, lower-level participants often defer in the group exercises to those at higher levels; thus, the assessment results are biased. Finally, certain "canned" exercises may only be remotely related to the on-the-job activity at the organization in question. Care must be taken to ensure that exercises used in the assessment center bring out the specific skills and aptitudes needed in the position for which participants are being assessed. Managers at Work 13–5 describes an assessment center at Burlington Northern Railway.

EVALUATING EMPLOYEE TRAINING AND MANAGEMENT DEVELOPMENT ACTIVITIES

When the results of employee training and management development are evaluated, certain benefits accrue. Less effective programs can be withdrawn to save time and effort. Weaknesses within programs can be identified and remedied.[11]

Evaluation of training and management development can be broken down into four logical steps:

1. *Reaction.* How well did the trainees like the program?
2. *Learning.* What principles, facts, and concepts were learned in the program?
3. *Behavior.* Did the job behavior of the trainees change because of the program?
4. *Results.* What were the results of the program in terms of factors such as reduced costs or reduction in turnover?

MANAGERS AT WORK 13–5

Assessment Centers at Burlington Northern Railroad (BN)

BN wanted to create a reservoir of people to compete for higher-level jobs, make sure its managers had the skills that would make them promotable, and make sure its sales representatives could gain some experience in what the management environment is all about so that they could decide whether they're cut out to compete for managerial-level positions.

The company used assessment centers to meet its needs. In 1982, BN conducted 10 assessment centers of 10 persons each. It ensured that assessments would be fair by qualifying 30 people as assessors and by having each participant assessed by four assessors.

Two weeks after each session, results were sent to the participants, showing what their pattern of performance had been, where they were strong and where they were weak, and indicating their needs for skill development.

Source: Adapted from "Sharpening Sales Skills," *Railway Age,* August 1983, pp. 56–57.

Reaction evaluation generally uses questionnaires administered at the end of the training program. Trainee reactions can be checked just after the training and again several weeks later. The major flaw in using only reaction evaluation is that the enthusiasm of trainees is not necessarily evidence of improved ability and future performance.

Learning evaluation measures how well the trainee has learned the principles, facts, and concepts presented in the program. Behavior evaluation measures how the training has influenced the employees' behavior on the job. Each requires testing of the trainee's knowledge and behavior both before and after training. Also, control groups—which do not receive the training but match the training group as closely as possible in all other respects—are required for learning and behavior evaluations. Comparison of pretest and posttest data on trainees identifies the changes in knowledge and behavior. Comparison of data from the control group and the trainee group helps to identify factors other than training that may have produced the change.

Results evaluation attempts to measure changes in variables such as turnover, absenteeism, accident rates, tardiness, and productivity. As with learning and behavior evaluation, pretests, posttests, and control groups are required in performing an accurate results evaluation.

Even when great care is taken in designing evaluation procedures, it is hard to determine the exact effect of training and management development activities on learning, behavior, and results. Because of this, the evaluation of training and management development is still limited and often superficial.

SUMMARY

LEARNING OBJECTIVE 1

Define Human Asset Accounting.

Human asset accounting attempts to place a value on an organization's human assets.

LEARNING OBJECTIVE 2

Describe Orientation.

Orientation is the introduction of new employees to the organization, their work unit, and their job.

LEARNING OBJECTIVE 3

Define Training.

Training is a process that involves acquiring skills or learning concepts to increase the performance of employees.

LEARNING OBJECTIVE 4

Explain the Steps Necessary to Ensure That Job Training Is Effective.

Five steps to be followed in any type of on-the-job training are: (1) prepare the employee for learning the job; (2) break down the work into components and identify the key points; (3) demonstrate the proper way to perform the job; (4) allow the employee to perform the job; and (5) gradually put the employee on his or her own.

LEARNING OBJECTIVE 5

Discuss Vestibule Training, Apprenticeship Training, and Programmed Instruction.

In vestibule training, procedures and equipment similar to those used in the actual job are set up in a special working area called a vestibule, where the trainee learns the job at a comfortable pace without the pressures of production schedules. Apprenticeship training generally lasts from two to five years and requires the trainee to work under the guidance of a skilled worker over this time period. Programmed instruction requires the trainee to read material on a subject and then to answer questions about the subject.

LEARNING OBJECTIVE 6

List and Define the Most Popular Methods of Management Development.

Understudy assignments require the person who will someday have a specific job to work for the incumbent to learn the job. Coaching has experienced managers advise and guide trainees in solving management problems. Job rotation gives a manager broad experience in many different areas of the organization. Role-playing requires trainees to act out assigned roles in a realistic situation. In-basket techniques require the trainee to answer one manager's mail and telephone calls. Business games generally provide a setting of a company and its environment and require a team of players to make operating decisions.

LEARNING OBJECTIVE 7

Describe an Assessment Center.

An assessment center utilizes a formal procedure to evaluate a person's potential as a manager and determine that person's development needs.

LEARNING OBJECTIVE 8

List the Steps Involved in the Evaluation of Training and Management Development.

The four steps in the evaluation of training and management development are: (1) Reaction. How well did the trainees like the program? (2) Learning. What principles, facts, and concepts were learned in the program? (3) Behavior. Did the job behavior of the trainees change because of the program? (4) Results. What were the results of the program in terms of factors such as reduced costs or reduction in turnover?

REVIEW QUESTIONS

1. What is human asset accounting?
2. What is orientation?
3. Describe the two distinct levels at which orientation is normally conducted within organizations.
4. What is training?
5. Describe the following methods of training.
   a. On-the-job.
   b. Job rotation.
   c. Vestibule.
   d. Apprenticeship.
   e. Programmed instruction.
6. What is management development?

7. Describe the following methods used in management development:
   a. Understudy assignments.
   b. Coaching.
   c. Experience.
   d. Job rotation.
   e. Special projects and committee assignments.
   f. Classroom training.
8. What is an assessment center?
9. Describe four logical steps in the evaluation of training and management development.

DISCUSSION QUESTIONS

1. Discuss the following statement: Why should we train our employees? It is a waste of money because they soon leave and another organization gets the benefits.
2. Outline a system for evaluating a development program for supervisors.

3. Discuss the following statement: Management games are fun, but you don't really learn anything from them.
4. Why are training programs generally one of the first areas to be eliminated when an organization must cut its budget?

REFERENCES & ADDITIONAL READINGS

[1] Bruce E. Meyers and Hugh H. Shane, "Human Resource Accounting for Managerial Decisions; Capital Budgeting Approach," *Personnel Administrator,* January 1984, p. 29.

[2] See, for instance, M. R. Louis, "Surprise and Sense Making: What Newcomers Experience in Entering Unfamiliar Organizational Settings," *Administrative Science Quarterly,* June 1980, pp. 226–51.

[3] Walter D. St. John, "The Complete Employee Orientation Program," *Personnel Journal,* May 1980, p. 375.

[4] S. V. Steadman, "Learning to Select a Needs Assessment Strategy," *Training and Development Journal,* January 1980, pp. 56–61.

[5] L. A. Digman, "Determining Management Development Needs," *Human Resource Management,* Winter 1980, p. 13.

[6] For an in-depth discussion on the case method, see C. Argyris, "Some Limitations of the Case Method: Experiences in a Management Development Program," *Academy of Management Review,* April 1980, pp. 291–98.

[7] For a further discussion of business games, see B. Hunter and M. Price, "Business Games: Underused Learning Tools?" *Industry Week,* August 18, 1980, pp. 52–56.

[8] L. A. Digman, "How Well-Managed Organizations Develop Their Executives," *Organizational Dynamics,* Autumn 1978, pp. 65–66. See also the entire February 1980 issue of *Personnel Administrator,* which is devoted to an analysis of assessment centers.

[9] Louis Olivas, "Using Assessment Centers for Individual and Organizational Development," *Personnel,* May–June 1980, p. 63.

[10] Donald H. Brush and Lyle F. Schoenfeldt, "Identifying Managerial Potential: An Alternative to Assessment Centers," *Personnel,* May–June 1980, p. 71.

[11] For a discussion of evaluation procedures for management development activities, see L. A. Digman, "How Companies Evaluate Management Development Programs," *Human Resource Management,* Summer 1980, pp. 9–13.

INCIDENT

Starting a New Job

Jack Smythe, branch manager for a large computer manufacturer, has just been told by his marketing manager, Bob Sprague, that Otis Brown has given two weeks' notice. When Jack had interviewed Otis, he had been convinced of the applicant's tremendous potential in sales. Otis was bright and personable, an honor graduate in electrical engineering from Massachusetts Institute of Technology who had the qualifications that the company looked for in computer sales. Now he was leaving after only two months with the company. Jack called Otis into his office for an exit interview.

Jack: Come in, Otis, I really want to talk to you. I hope I can change your mind about leaving.

Otis: I don't think so.

Jack: Well, tell me why you want to go. Has some other company offered you more money?

Otis: No. In fact, I don't have another job. I'm just starting to look.

Jack: You've given us notice without having another job?

Otis: Well, I just don't think this is the place for me!

Jack: What do you mean?

Otis: Let me see if I can explain. On my first day at work, I was told that my formal classroom training in computers would not begin for a month. I was given a sales manual and told to read and study it for the rest of the day.

The next day I was told that the technical library, where all the manuals on computers are kept, was in a mess and needed to be organized. That was to be my responsibility for the next three weeks.

The day before I was to begin computer school, my boss told me that the course had been delayed for another month. He said not to worry, however, because he was going to have James Chess, the branch's leading salesperson, give me some on-the-job training. I was told to accompany James on his calls. I'm supposed to start the computer school in two weeks, but I've just made up my mind that this place is not for me.

Jack: Hold on a minute, Otis. That's the way it is for everyone in the first couple months of employment in our industry. Any place you go will be the same. In fact, you had it better than I did. You should have seen what I did in my first couple of months.

Questions

1. What do you think about the philosophy of this company pertaining to a new employee's first few months on the job?

2. What suggestions do you have for Jack to help his company avoid similar problems of employee turnover in the future?

EXERCISE

OJT

*A*ssume you are training director for a large, local retail company. The company has seven department stores in your city. One of your biggest problems is adequately training new salesclerks. Because salesclerks represent your company to the public, the manner in which they conduct themselves is highly important. Especially critical aspects of their job include knowledge of the computerized cash register system, interaction with the customers, and knowledge of the particular products being sold.

A. Design a three-day orientation/training program for these salesclerks. Be sure to outline the specific topics (subjects) to be covered and the techniques to be used.

B. Specify what methods could be used to evaluate the success of the program.

C A S E

*The Coca-Cola Company**

A three-legged brass pot stands in the middle of one of U.S. industry's most colorful corporate legends. From this pot, Dr. John Smyth Pemberton is said to have poured a syrup which he carried to Jacobs' Pharmacy in Atlanta, Georgia, on May 8, 1886. The product was mixed with soda water and served as a fountain beverage. Sold for 5 cents a glass, Coke sales averaged 65 cents a day (13 drinks) for the remainder of 1886. Since that time, Coca-Cola has become one of the world's most common trademarks; the brass pot has been replaced by an organization selling soft drink, food, and entertainment products to people in more than 135 countries.

With 1986 revenues in excess of $8.6 billion, the company is easily the world's largest producer of soft drink beverages, producing more than 35 percent of the soft drinks consumed worldwide. In addition to sheer size, several developments during the last decade have pointed to the increasing demands on personnel and the importance of human resource development.

With the beginning of Roberto C. Giozueta's chairmanship in 1981, Coca-Cola shed its conservative image in favor of an aggressive new strategy with growth in earnings as a primary objective. With 1982 earnings of $512 million, the management team set a goal for annual earnings of $1 billion by 1990. In developing a strategy for attaining this goal, the planning process identified seven areas of particular concern—finance, competition, bottling, consumer, energy, technical, and human. To acknowledge the importance of the human factor, Chairman Goizueta made the following statement in his "Strategy for the 1980s" statement published in the company's 1982 Annual Report:

Finally, let me comment on this vision as it affects our "lifestyle"—or business behavior—as a viable international business entity. I have previously referred to the *courage* and *commitment* that will be indispensable as we move through the 1980s. To this I wish to add *integrity* and *fairness* and insist that the combination of these four ethics be permeated from top to bottom throughout our organization so that our behavior will produce leaders, good managers, and—most importantly— entrepreneurs. It is my desire that we take initiatives as opposed to being only reactive and that we *encourage intelligent individual risk taking*.

As a true international company with a multicultural and multinational employee complement, we must foster the "international family" concept which has been a part of our tradition. All employees will have equal opportunities to grow, develop, and advance within the company. Their progress will depend only on their abilities, ambition, and achievements.

* This case was prepared by Thomas K. Glenn II, Emory University. Used by permission.

To foster the growth and development of Coca-Cola personnel, the Human Resources Development (HRD) area has the objectives of "attracting, evaluating, developing, and retaining outstanding employees." Comprised of approximately 40 individuals, the HRD area is organized into four groups—Employment, Employee Training, Bottler Training, and Employee Development. In addition to full-time HRD personnel, the company retains a "faculty" made up of professors and experts in various areas who teach courses and provide specialized consultation.

Though the company is obviously dedicated to enhancing the quality of existing personnel, considerable effort is focused on the screening process prior to hiring. The employment group administers a one-and-a-half-day assessment process in evaluating an applicant's potential. Usually perceived as a positive experience, the procedure is frequently praised by applicants—some of whom do not eventually become Coke employees—for its thoroughness and effectiveness in pointing to logical career directions. Having hired individuals who meet established criteria, the company looks to the other three HRD groups—employee development, employee training, and bottler training—to provide counseling and educational assistance as necessary.

EMPLOYEE DEVELOPMENT

The Employee Development Group addresses three primary objectives: staffing, evaluation, and development. The group's role in accomplishing these objectives is viewed as an iterative process, as shown in Exhibit 1.

As suggested by Exhibit 1, the Employee Development Group develops procedures for evaluating individuals and matching them with appropriate jobs. Additionally, the group develops and conducts evaluations to assist in training, guidance, and promotions. Programs produced by Employee Development are used by the Employee and Bottler Training groups, as well as by the Employment Group in its initial screening process.

More specific objectives are itemized as follows:

1. To develop talent in depth and in advance of anticipated staffing needs, enabling the company to promote from within wherever possible.
2. To attract and retain the most qualified employees available.
3. To identify employees with demonstrated potential and see that they have the opportunity to test themselves in positions with expanded responsibilities.
4. To match job abilities to job requirements effectively.
5. To maintain integrity in the selection and promotion process.
6. To improve employee and department performance levels.

Several important principles undergird the employee development process, two of which are employee participation and employee initiative. Written policy emphasizes the necessity of employee participation at every stage of

E X H I B I T 1   Career Development System

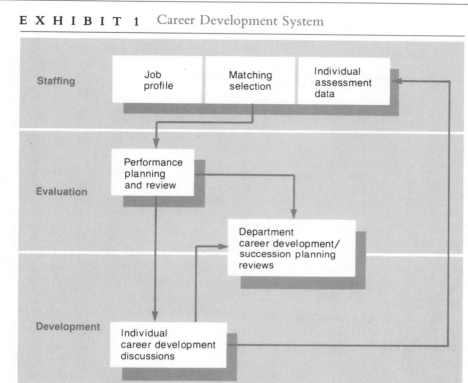

the career development process—from establishing objectives to discussing career interests and plans. Where employee initiative is concerned, it is felt that both the manager and the employee share responsibility for the employee's career. Despite the manager's role in this process, the employee must take the initiative in deciding personal goals and then making commitments to reach them.

EMPLOYEE TRAINING

Results from evaluation procedures developed by the Employee Development Group may lead a manager to conclude that certain employees need training to improve performance in their present jobs. Conversely, high-level achievers may show potential for assuming greater levels of responsibility or performing more demanding tasks. In either case, the Employee Training Group provides a wide "curriculum" of in-house training and educational programs.

To communicate the group's activities to employees throughout the organization, a course catalog (similar in format to that used by many colleges) is made available to all employees and updated periodically through the *Employee Training Update*. The catalog groups skills into various areas, such as effective

E X H I B I T 2 Partial List of
Course Offerings

Assertive Skills for On-the-Job Effectiveness
Leadership Workshop
The Changing Office Environment
Speed and Accuracy in Handling Numbers
Managing Programs and Projects
Basic Finance
Career Strategies for Managers and Professionals
The Computer: A Management Resource
The Personal Computer
Introduction to 1–2–3® from LOTUS®

business writing or project management, and lists courses which correspond to these areas. Exhibit 2 provides a partial list of courses administered by the Employee Training Group. As suggested by the course titles, programs are available for virtually all levels of employment.

In addition to performing a function that is purely educational in nature, the Employee Training Group plays a vital role in the area of communication. Three courses entitled "Orientation: The Coca-Cola Company," "Coca-Cola USA: In-Depth Orientation for Managers and Professionals," and "Employee Update" provide systematic briefings which address company history, values, policies, and recent changes.

If employees have educational needs that cannot be met by in-house programs, the Training Information Procedure (TIP) can help to find courses and seminars offered by outside sources. Such assistance ranges from providing recommendations of programs to handling registration procedures for individuals enrolling in educational institutions.

BOTTLER TRAINING

Though the Employee Training Group develops programs that are used in almost all areas of the company, a separate group within the HRD area is responsible for disseminating these and many other programs throughout the vast bottler network.

The Bottler Training Group provides an important service that is unique when compared to training facilities in many other large organizations. To better appreciate this, one must first understand some of the basic differences among types of franchise agreements.

A basic dimension of franchise agreements is their comprehensiveness. At one extreme lies the *product distribution* franchise in which franchisors provide the franchisees with goods in salable form. The franchisees operate under their own names, usually pay no franchise fee, and are frequently licensed to sell additional products offered by other franchisors. Compared with other types of franchises, product distribution agreements are not comprehensive. They seldom impose requirements on the franchisee's marketing or management activities. Such agreements simply provide a license to sell certain goods or services and are common in the marketing of furniture and home appliances.

At the other extreme lies the *pure,* or *comprehensive,* franchise. This type of arrangement provides the franchisee with a license to use a trade name, products or services to be sold, and a complete operating format. Procedures for production and quality control are usually specified, as well as design and appearance of the physical plant. Training of supervisors and employees is a frequent requirement. This type of agreement is common among fast-food franchises, of which McDonald's is a notable example.

Coca-Cola markets soft drink products through more than 1,500 bottlers worldwide. Though some of these operations are company owned, the vast majority operate under franchise agreements. The comprehensiveness of these agreements falls somewhere between the two extremes described above. The franchised bottlers purchase Coca-Cola product ingredients, pay for the privilege of using the company trademark, and agree to adhere to various production and quality control standards. Beyond these requirements, bottlers operate in a decentralized structure that allows them considerable freedom in marketing, management, and personnel decisions. In stark contrast to the McDonald's franchisee, who must attend Hamburger University, or the Burger King operator, who must enroll in Whopper College, owners of Coca-Cola bottling franchises may obtain training for themselves and/or their employees from the Bottler Training Group, from some other sources, or may simply prefer to use their own approaches to train bottling plant employees internally.

A significant implication of this arrangement is that the Bottler Training Group does not have a "captive market" for its services. As a result, the group must "sell" its programs—a situation creating incentive to develop meaningful and productive training packages. Though evaluation techniques developed by the employee Development Group and educational programs provided by the Employee Training Group are available to bottlers, Bottler Training offers additional training packages that are custom designed for bottling plant applications. Training systems are designed for seminar and in-plant video formats. Exhibit 3 provides a list of courses suggesting the industry-specific nature of the curriculum.

BASIC PHILOSOPHIES

Several characteristics appear as basic philosophies throughout the HRD area. First, there is a strong strategic planning orientation: Objectives and means of accomplishing them are carefully articulated and put in writing. Next, all HRD personnel are aware that they are performing roles which go beyond the functions of education and training. Communication and public/employee relations are of equal importance. "Selling the company" is a constant objective.

Reflecting Chairman Goizueta's statements about the importance of personal

E X H I B I T 3 Examples of
Bottler Training Courses

Line Supervisor's Training Seminar
Empty Bottle Inspection
Microbiological Testing
Distribution Management Workshop
In-Plant Safety
Forklift and Materials Handling
Product Handling on the Route
Successful Selling in a Changing Market
Managing Today's Fleet
Train-the-Trainer Workshops

initiative, HRD's operating philosophy rests on the assumption that employees will take the initiative to utilize development and training opportunities. For the most part, access to programs is limited only by the employee's desire to participate. Programs are developed for capitalizing on initiative (as opposed to developing it). As a result, entry-level screening procedures attempt to identify individuals who possess initiative from the outset.

Finally, and in keeping with the strategic planning orientation, program implementation holds a level of importance equal to that of formulation. Once a training or evaluation technique is developed and validated, procedures for administration are systematized to assure proper usage.

4 Human Relations Skills

SECTION 4

Human Relations Skills
14 Motivating
15 Leading
16 Appraising and Rewarding Performance
17 Work Groups
18 Conflict and Stress
19 Change and Culture

=

Management Foundation

+

SECTION 5

Controlling Skills
20 Controlling
21 Operations Control
22 Management Information Systems

=

Improved Organizational Performance

*A*ll decision-making, planning, organizing, and staffing skills are carried out through and depend on people for their success. Thus, the effective use of human relations skills is essential for achieving organizational objectives.

It is difficult to isolate human relations skills from other management skills. Effective plans cannot be developed without considering the people who will carry them out. Therefore, various human relations concepts are interspersed throughout this text. Section 4 emphasizes and discusses those aspects of human relations skills which are essential for managerial success.

Chapter 14 discusses current concepts and approaches to motivating people. The relationship between motivation and satisfaction is also analyzed.

Chapter 15 focuses on the human relations skills of leading or influencing human behavior. Different styles of leadership are discussed and evaluated. Several contemporary leadership theories are also presented. A strong argument is made for a situational approach to leadership.

Chapter 16 is concerned with appraising and rewarding performance—one of management's most powerful tools in encouraging employees to work hard. This chapter describes methods of appraising employee performance and systems used by organizations to reward employees.

Chapter 17 discusses both informal and formal work groups. Informal work groups are shown to be assets of the organization if properly managed. Team building and the development of quality circles are also described.

Chapter 18 focuses on conflict and stress in organizations. Conflict is presented as a normal and natural organizational activity which can produce positive results if properly managed. Stress is an inevitable occurrence in organizations. Suggestions are offered for managing stress.

Chapter 19 is designed to develop an understanding of how today's rapid pace of change affects organizations. It identifies and analyzes the role of organizational culture and its influence on organizational performance.

14 Motivating: Activating and Sustaining Human Behavior

LEARNING OBJECTIVES

After studying this chapter,
you should be able to:

1 Define motivation.

2 Define the traditional theory of motivation.

3 Explain the hierarchy of needs.

4 Discuss the achievement-power-affiliation theory of motivation.

5 Discuss the motivation-maintenance theory of motivation.

6 Discuss the preference-expectancy theory of motivation.

7 Explain reinforcement theory.

8 Define job satisfaction and organizational morale.

The early bird catches the worm. That fact
Has been into every young cranium packed
It's really absurd the talk that is heard
Of the wonderful thrift of that wonderful bird
And not the least mention is made of the worm
That equally early set out on a squirm
Except that within that most provident bird
The poor little fellow was thus early interred
Now it seems there's a word on both sides to be said
For had he but snugly remained in his bed
Or curled up for a nap
In mother earth's lap
The poor little chap
Would doubtless have lived to Methuselah's age
And another tale figured in history's page.

Moral: Maxims and rules
That are taught in the schools
Are excellent truly for governing fools
but you of your actions get up early of course
But if you're a worm don't be so absurd
*As to get up at dawn to be caught by a bird.**

S tatements and questions such as these are often expressed by managers at all levels in organizations: Our employees are just not motivated. Half the problems we have are due to a lack of personal motivation. How do I motivate my employees?

The problem of motivation is not a recent development. Research conducted by William James in the late 1800s indicated the importance of motivation.[1] James found that hourly employees could keep their jobs by using approximately 20 to 30 percent of their ability. He also found that highly motivated employees will work at approximately 80 to 90 percent of their ability. Figure 14–1 illustrates the potential influence of motivation on performance. Highly motivated employees can bring about substantial increases in performance and substantial decreases in problems such as absenteeism, turnover, tardiness, strikes, and grievances. Managers at Work 14–1 describes Deere & Co.'s approach to and benefits from motivating employees.

* "The Early Bird" (source unknown).

MANAGERS AT WORK 14-1

A Day on the Farm (Deere & Co.)

Many years ago, most of the employees who built the plows, combines, tillage equipment, and planters for Deere & Co. came from farms. Thus, they knew the ins and outs of farm equipment and how essential each piece of machinery was in determining a farmer's profitability. But now, most of the people who produce the equipment are city people; and since the equipment isn't assembled until it reaches the dealer, many workers have never even seen the assembled product.

So how can the importance of the machinery to the farmer be impressed upon these workers? Deere's answer: field trips, where employees get to meet a dealer and a farmer. They watch, and sometimes operate, the equipment on a farm. The trips have triggered improved employee suggestions, a greater attention to quality, and a better relationship between management and employees.

Source: Adopted from "A Day on the Farm," *Industry Week*, August 20, 1984, p. 25.

THE MEANING OF MOTIVATION

Motivation – causative sequence concerned with what activates human behavior, what directs this behavior, and how it is sustained.

The word **motivation** comes from the Latin word *movere*, which means to move. Numerous definiton s are given for the term. Usually included are such words as *aim, desire, end, impulse, intention, objective,* and *purpose.* These

F I G U R E 14–1 Potential Influence of Motivation on Performance

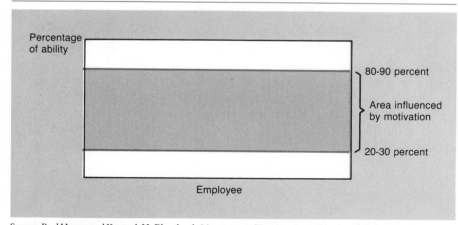

Source: Paul Hersey and Kenneth H. Blanchard, *Management of Organizational Behavior: Utilizing Human Resources,* 4th ed. (Englewood Cliffs, N.J.: Prentice-Hall, 1982), p. 4. Copyright © 1982 by Prentice-Hall, Inc. Adapted by permission.

definitions normally include three common characteristics of motivation. First, motivation is concerned with what activates human behavior. Second, motivation is concerned with what directs this behavior toward a particular goal. Third, motivation is concerned with how this behavior is sustained.[2]

Motivation can be analyzed using the following causative sequence:

$$\text{Needs} \rightarrow \text{Drives or motives} \rightarrow \text{Achievement of goals}$$

In motivation, needs produce motives which lead to the accomplishment of goals. Needs are caused by deficiencies, which can be either physical or psychological. For instance, a physical need exists when an individual goes without sleep for 48 hours. A psychological need exists when an individual has no friends or companions. Individual needs will be explored in much greater depth later in this chapter.

A motive is a stimulus which leads to an action that satisfies the need. In other words, motives produce actions. Lack of sleep (the need) activates the physical changes of fatigue (the motive) which produces sleep (the action, or in this example, inaction).

Achievement of the goal satisfies the need and reduces the motive. When the goal is reached, balance is restored. However, other needs arise which are then satisfied by the same sequence of events. Understanding the motivation sequence in itself offers a manager little help in determining what motivates people. The theories of motivation described in this chapter help to provide a broader understanding of what motivates people. They include: traditional theory; need hierarchy theory; achievement-power-affiliation theory; motivation-maintenance theory; preference-expectancy theory; and reinforcement theory.

TRADITIONAL THEORY

Traditional theory of motivation—based on the assumption that money is the primary motivator: if the reward is great enough, employees will produce more.

The **traditional theory of motivation** evolved from the work of Frederick W. Taylor and the scientific management movement that took place at the turn of this century. Taylor's ideas were based on his belief that existing reward systems were not designed to reward individuals for high production. He felt that when highly productive people discover that they are being compensated basically the same as less productive people, then the output of highly productive people will decrease. Taylor's solution was quite simple. He designed a system whereby an employee was compensated according to individual production.

One of Taylor's problems was determining a reasonable standard of performance. Taylor solved the problem by breaking jobs down into components and measuring the time necessary to accomplish each component. In this way, Taylor was able to establish standards of performance "scientifically."

Taylor's plan was unique in that he had one rate of pay for units produced up to the standard. Once the standard was reached, a significantly higher rate was paid, not only for the units above the standard but for all units produced during the day. Thus, under Taylor's system, employees could in many cases significantly increase their pay for production above the standard.

The traditional theory of motivation is based on the assumption that money is the primary motivator. Financial rewards are directly related to performance in the belief that if the reward is great enough, employees will produce more.

NEED HIERARCHY THEORY

The **need hierarchy theory** is based on the assumption that individuals are motivated to satisfy a number of needs and that money can directly or indirectly satisfy only some of these needs. The need hierarchy theory is based largely on the work of Abraham Maslow.[3]

Maslow's Need Hierarchy

Maslow felt that several different levels of needs exist within individuals and that these needs relate to each other in the form of hierarchy. Maslow's **hierarchy of needs** consists of the five levels shown in Figure 14–2.

Need hierarchy theory – based on the assumption that individuals are motivated to satisfy a number of needs and that money can satisfy only some of these needs.

Hierarchy of needs – Maslow's five levels of individual needs: physiological, safety, social, esteem (or ego), and self-actualization.

F I G U R E 14–2 Maslow's Need Hierarchy

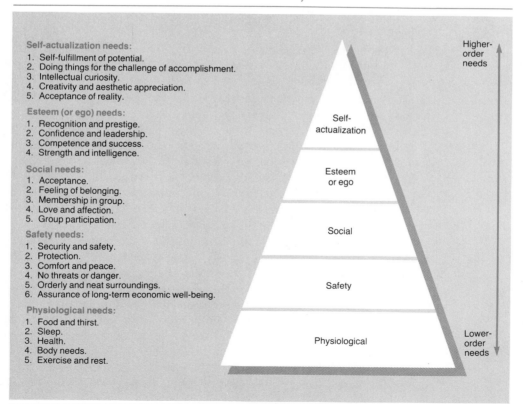

Self-actualization needs:
1. Self-fulfillment of potential.
2. Doing things for the challenge of accomplishment.
3. Intellectual curiosity.
4. Creativity and aesthetic appreciation.
5. Acceptance of reality.

Esteem (or ego) needs:
1. Recognition and prestige.
2. Confidence and leadership.
3. Competence and success.
4. Strength and intelligence.

Social needs:
1. Acceptance.
2. Feeling of belonging.
3. Membership in group.
4. Love and affection.
5. Group participation.

Safety needs:
1. Security and safety.
2. Protection.
3. Comfort and peace.
4. No threats or danger.
5. Orderly and neat surroundings.
6. Assurance of long-term economic well-being.

Physiological needs:
1. Food and thirst.
2. Sleep.
3. Health.
4. Body needs.
5. Exercise and rest.

Self-actualization

Esteem or ego

Social

Safety

Physiological

Higher-order needs

Lower-order needs

MANAGERS AT WORK 14–2

Incentive Programs at Burroughs

Burroughs Corp. is a Detroit-based computer systems/services manufacturer and marketer. Sales incentive programs at Burroughs focus mainly on rewarding members of the sales force with corporate trips to warm locations or to major sports events. Gifts, plaques, and recognition by top management are also integral parts of the program.

Two of the companywide incentive programs at Burroughs are its Worldwide Legion of Honor and the U.S. Tennis Open. The Worldwide Legion of Honor recognizes sales/marketing personnel who have achieved a minimum quota for orders and revenue and who rank as the company's top sales/marketing achievers. Each winner is allowed to bring an adult guest along on a corporate trip. Locations of the trips have included: Maui, Hawaii; Bermuda; and Palm Springs, California. The U.S. Tennis Open includes more than just marketing and salespeople. Corporate operations personnel and other staff can win the tickets and trip to the U.S. Open.

Source: Adapted from Cynthia R. Milsap, "How Burroughs Gains an Edge in Sales Force Motivation," *Business Marketing,* April 1985, pp. 50–52.

The physiological needs are basically the needs of the human body that must be satisfied in order to sustain life. These needs include food, sleep, water, exercise, clothing, shelter, and so forth.

Safety needs are concerned with protection against danger, threat, or deprivation. Since all employees have (to some degree) a dependent relationship with the organization, safety needs can be critically important. Favoritism, discrimination, and arbitrary administration of organizational policies are all actions which arouse uncertainty and therefore affect the safety needs.

The third level of needs is composed of the social needs. Generally categorized at this level are the needs for love, affection, belonging—all are concerned with establishing one's position relative to others. This need is satisfied by the development of meaningful personal relations and by acceptance into meaningful groups of individuals. Belonging to organizations and identifying with work groups are means of satisfying these needs in organizations.

The fourth level of needs is composed of the esteem needs. The esteem needs include both self-esteem and the esteem of others. These needs influence the development of various kinds of relationships based on adequacy, independence, and the giving and receiving of indications of self-esteem and acceptance. Managers at Work 14–2 illustrates Burrough's approach to motivating employees through recognition.

The highest-order need is concerned with the need for self-actualization or self-fulfillment—that is, the need of people to reach their full potential in applying their abilities and interests to functioning in their environment. This need is concerned with the will to operate at the optimum and thus receive the rewards that are the result of that attainment. The rewards may not only be in terms of economic and social remuneration, but also in terms of psychological remuneration. The need for self-actualization of self-fulfillment is never completely satisfied; one can always reach one step higher.

The Need Hierarchy Theory: Other Considerations

The need hierarchy shown in Figure 14–2 adequately describes the general order or ranking of most people's needs. However, there are several other possibilities to be considered. First, although the needs of most people are arranged in the sequence shown in Figure 14–2, differences in the sequence can occur, depending on an individual's learning experience, culture, social upbringing, and numerous other aspects of personality. Second, the strength or potency of a person's needs may shift back and forth under different situations. For instance, during bad economic times, physiological and safety needs might tend to dominate an individual's behavior; in good economic times, higher-order needs might dominate an individual's behavior.

The unconscious character of the various needs should be recognized. In addition, there is a certain degree of cultural specificity of needs. In other words, the ways by which the various needs can be met tend to be controlled by cultural and societal factors. For example, the particular culture may dictate one's eating habits, social life, and numerous other facets of life.

Finally, different methods can be used by different individuals to satisfy a particular need. Two individuals may be deficient in relation to the same physiological need; however, the way in which each chooses to satisfy that need may vary considerably.

As far as motivation is concerned, the thrust of the need hierarchy theory is that a satisfied need is not a motivator. Consider the basic physiological need for oxygen. Only when an individual is deprived of oxygen can it have a motivating effect on that person's behavior.

Many of today's organizations are applying the logic of the need hierarchy. For instance, compensation systems are generally designed to satisfy the lower-order needs—physiological and safety. On the other hand, interesting work and opportunities for advancement are designed to appeal to higher-order needs. So the job of a manager is to determine the need level that an individual employee is attempting to attain and then provide the means by which the employee can satisfy that need. Obviously, determining the need level of a particular person can be a difficult process. All people do not operate at the same level on the need hierarchy. All people do not react similarly to the same situation.

It must be pointed out that little research has been conducted to test the validity of the need hierarchy theory.[4] Its primary value is that it provides a structure for analyzing needs and, as will be seen later in this chapter, is used as a basis for other theories of motivation.

ACHIEVEMENT-POWER-AFFILIATION THEORY

Achievement-power-affilia-tion theory – holds that people have three needs: achievement, power, and affilia-tion; the level of intensity varies among individu-als; and people are motivated in situa-tions that allow them to satisfy their most intense need(s).

Closely related to the need hierarchy theory is the **achievement-power-affiliation theory,** primarily developed by David McClelland.[5] This theory holds that all people have three needs: (1) a need to achieve, (2) a need for power, and (3) a need for affiliation. The need for achievement is a desire to do something better or more efficiently than it has been done before—to achieve. The need for power is basically a concern for influencing people— to be strong and influential. The need for affiliation is a need to be liked—to establish or maintain friendly relations with others. McClelland maintains that most people have a degree of each of these needs but that the level of intensity varies. For example, an individual may be high in the need for achievement, moderate in the need for power, and low in the need for affiliation. This individual's motivation to work will vary greatly from that of another person who has a high need for power and low needs for achievement and affiliation. According to this theory, it is the responsibility of managers to recognize the dominating needs in both themselves and their employees and to integrate these differences effectively. An employee with a high need for affiliation would probably respond positively to demonstrations of warmth and support by the manager; an employee with a high need for achievement would likely respond positively to increased responsibility. Through self-analysis, managers can gain insight as to how they tend to respond to employees. They may then want to alter their response to employees to best fit the employees' needs.

MOTIVATION-MAINTENANCE THEORY

Motivation-maintenance theory – states that all work-related factors can be grouped into one or two catego-ries: *maintenance factors,* which will not produce moti-vation but can pre-vent it; and *motiva-tors,* which can encourage moti-vation.

Frederick Herzberg, Bernard Mausner, and Barbara Snyderman developed a theory of work motivation which has had wide acceptance in management circles. The theory is referred to by several names: **motivation-maintenance theory,** dual-factor theory, or motivation-hygiene theory.

Initially, the development of the theory involved extensive interviews with approximately 200 engineers and accountants from 11 industries in the Pitts-burgh area. The purpose of this work was summarized as follows:

> To industry, the payoff for a study of job attitudes would be increased productivity, decreased absenteeism, and smoother working relations. To the individual, an under-standing of the forces that lead to improved morale would bring greater happiness and greater self-realization.[6]

In the interviews, researchers used what is called the critical incident method. This involved asking subjects to recall work situations in which they had experienced periods of high and low motivation. They were asked to recount specific details about the situation and the effect of the experience over time.

It was found through analysis of the interviewees' statements that different factors were associated with good and bad feelings. The findings fell into two major categories. Those factors that were most frequently mentioned in association with a favorably viewed incident concerned the work itself. These factors were achievement, recognition, responsibility, advancement, and the characteristics of the job. But when subjects felt negatively oriented toward a work incident, they were more likely to mention factors associated with the work environment. These included status; interpersonal relations with supervisors, peers, and subordinates; technical aspects of supervision; company policy and administration; job security; working conditions; salary; and aspects of their personal life that were affected by the work situation.

The latter set of factors was called "hygiene" or "maintenance" factors because the researchers felt that they are preventive in nature. In other words, they do not produce motivation but can prevent motivation from occurring. Thus, proper attention to hygiene factors is a necessary but not sufficient condition for motivation. The first set of factors were called "motivators." The researchers contended that these factors, when present in addition to the hygiene factors, provide true motivation.

Job enlargement – involves making a job structurally larger by giving an employee more similar operations or tasks to perform.

Job rotation – practice of periodically rotating job assignments.

Job enrichment – upgrading a job with factors like more meaningful work, recognition, responsibility, and opportunities for advancement.

In summary, the motivation-maintenance theory contends that motivation comes from the individual, not from the manager. At best, proper attention to the hygiene factors keeps an individual from being highly dissatisfied but does not make that individual motivated. Both hygiene and motivator factors must be present in order for true motivation to occur. Figure 14–3 lists some examples of hygiene and motivator factors.

Job enrichment programs have been developed in an attempt to solve motivational problems by using the motivation-maintenance theory. Unlike **job enlargement,** which merely involves giving an employee more of a similar type of operation to perform, or **job rotation,** which is the practice of periodically rotating job assignments, **job enrichment** involves an upgrading of the job by adding motivator factors. Designing jobs that provide for meaningful work, achievement, recognition, responsibility, advancement, and growth is the key to job enrichment.

As can be seen from Figure 14–4, the motivation-maintenance theory is

F I G U R E 14–3 Hygiene-Motivator Factors

HYGIENE FACTORS (ENVIRONMENTAL)	MOTIVATOR FACTORS (JOB ITSELF)
Policies and administration	Achievement
Supervision	Recognition
Working conditions	Challenging work
Interpersonal relations	Increased responsibility
Personal life	Advancement
Money, status, security	Personal growth

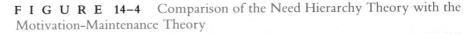

F I G U R E 14–4   Comparison of the Need Hierarchy Theory with the Motivation-Maintenance Theory

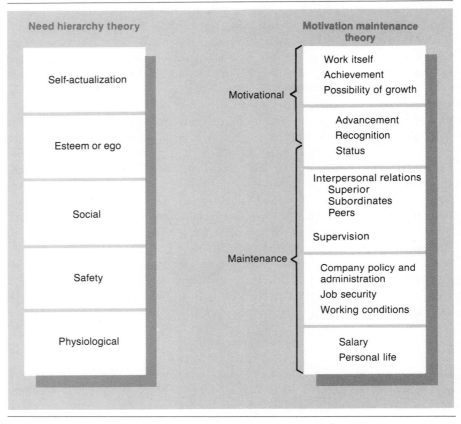

very closely related to the need hierarchy theory of motivation and so is subject to many of the same criticisms.

Preference ex-
pectancy the-
ory –holds that
motivation is
based on a combi-
nation of the indi-
vidual's *expectancy*
that increased ef-
fort will lead to in-
creased perfor-
mance which will
lead to rewards,
and the individu-
al's *preference* for
those rewards.

PREFERENCE-EXPECTANCY THEORY

An additional theory of motivation was developed by Victor H. Vroom.[7] Called the **preference-expectancy (or expectancy) theory,** Vroom's theory is based on the belief that people act in such a manner as to increase pleasure and decrease displeasure. People are motivated to work if: (1) they believe their efforts will be rewarded, and (2) they value the rewards that are being offered. The first requirement—persons need to believe that their efforts will be rewarded—can be further broken down into two separate components: (1) the expectancy that increased effort will lead to increased performance, and (2) the expectancy that increased performance will lead to increased rewards. These expectancies are developed largely from an individual's past experiences. For example, based on incidents that happened in the past, a person may feel that working harder does not produce any better results. On the other hand, even if employees believe that working harder does result in higher performance, they may not believe that higher performance is directly related to rewards.

The second part of the preference–expectancy theory is concerned with the value that the employee places on the rewards that are offered by the organization. Historically, organizations have assumed that whatever rewards are provided will be valued by employees. Even if this were true, some rewards are certainly more valued than others. In fact, certain rewards, such as a promotion which involves a transfer to another city, may be viewed negatively.

Expectancy theorists believe that individual expectancies and preferences are formed either consciously or unconsciously, but that they definitely exist in most people. The preference–expectancy theory is shown in model form in Figure 14–5.

F I G U R E 14–5   Model of Preference-Expectancy Theory

$$
\begin{aligned}
\text{Motivation} &= \begin{pmatrix} \text{Expectancy that increased} \\ \text{effort will lead to rewards} \end{pmatrix} \times \begin{pmatrix} \text{Preference of the} \\ \text{individual for the rewards} \end{pmatrix} \\[2mm]
&= \left[\begin{pmatrix} \text{Expectancy that} \\ \text{increased effort} \\ \text{will lead to increased} \\ \text{performance} \end{pmatrix} \begin{pmatrix} \text{Expectancy that} \\ \text{increased performance} \\ \text{will lead to rewards} \end{pmatrix} \right] \begin{bmatrix} \text{Preference of} \\ \text{the individual} \\ \text{for the rewards} \end{bmatrix}
\end{aligned}
$$

The following example is intended to illustrate the preference–expectancy theory. Assume that John Stone is an insurance salesman for the ABC Life Insurance Company. John has learned over the years that he completes one sale for approximately every six calls he makes. John definitely perceives a direct relationship between his effort and performance. Since John is on a straight commission, he also perceives a direct relationship between performance and rewards. Thus, his expectation that increased effort will lead to increased rewards is relatively high. Further, suppose that John's income is currently in a high tax bracket such that he gets to keep, after taxes, only 50 percent of his commissions. This being the case, he may not look upon the additional money that he gets to keep (the reward) as being very attractive. The end result is that John's preference for the additional money may be relatively low. Even when this is multiplied by his relatively high expectation of receiving the additional money, his motivation to do additional work may be relatively low.

Each of the separate components of the preference–expectancy model can be affected by the organization's practices and management. The expectancy that increased effort will lead to increased performance can be positively influenced by providing proper selection, training, and clear direction to the work force. The expectancy that increased performance will lead to rewards is almost totally under the control of the organization. Does the organization really attempt to link rewards to performance? Or are rewards based on some other variable, such as seniority? The final component—the preference for the rewards being offered—is usually taken for granted by the organization. Organizations should solicit feedback from their employees concerning the types of rewards that are valued. Since an organization is going to spend a certain amount of money on rewards (salary, fringe benefits, and so on), it should ensure the maximum return from its investment.

The development of the preference-expectancy theory is still in its infancy; many questions remain that must be answered. For example, critics attack the theory as being overly rational—humans often don't act rationally. Others say the theory ignores impulsive and expressive behavior. In spite of these criticisms, the preference-expectancy theory is currently one of the most subscribed-to theories of motivation.

REINFORCEMENT THEORY

Reinforcement theory – motivation approach based on the idea that behavior that appears to lead to a positive consequence tends to be repeated, while behavior that appears to lead to a negative consequence tends not to be repeated.

The final theory of motivation to be explored is reinforcement theory, which is closely related to preference-expectancy theory.[8] The general idea behind **reinforcement theory** is that behavior that appears to lead to a positive consequence tends to be repeated, while behavior that appears to lead to a negative consequence tends not to be repeated. A positive consequence is a reward.[9]

The current emphasis on the use of reinforcement theory in management practices is concerned with positive reinforcement. Examples include increased pay for increased performance, and praise and recognition when an employee does a good job. Generally, several steps are to be followed in the use of positive reinforcement. These steps include:

1. Selecting reinforcers that are strong and durable enough to establish and strengthen the desired behavior.
2. Designing the work environment in such a way that the reinforcing events are contingent on the desired behavior.
3. Designing the work environment so that the employee has the opportunity to demonstrate the desired behavior.[10]

The key to successful positive reinforcement is that rewards must result from performance. Several suggestions for the effective use of reinforcement have been proposed. These include the following:

MANAGER AT WORK 14–3

The "Golden Banana" Award

The Foxboro Company is a leading multinational manufacturer and distributor of instrumentation and control systems. In its early days, a technical advance was desperately needed for the survival of the company. Late one evening, a scientist rushed into the president's office with a working prototype. Dumbfounded at the elegance of the solution and bemused at how to reward it, the president bent forward in his chair, found something, leaned over the desk to the scientist, and said, "Here!" In his hand was a banana, the only reward he could immediately put his hands on. From that point on, the small "gold banana" pin has been the highest accolade for scientific achievement at Foxboro.

Source: Adapted from Thomas J. Peters and Robert H. Waterman, Jr., "How the Best-Run Companies Turn So-So Performers into Big Winners," *Management Review*, November–December 1982, p. 11.

1. All people should not be rewarded the same. In other words, the greater the level of performance by an employee, the greater should be the rewards.
2. Failure to respond to an employee's behavior has reinforcing consequences.
3. A person must be told what can be done to be reinforced.
4. A person must be told what he or she is doing wrong.
5. Reprimands should not be issued in front of others.
6. The consequences of a person's behavior should be equal to the behavior.[11]

While positive reinforcement can be used by managers to elicit and strengthen desired behavior by employees, negative reinforcement and punishment are used to reduce the frequency of undesired behavior. **Negative reinforcement** removes a negative stimulus from the environment as a consequence of behavior. **Punishment** is either the application of a negative stimulus or the removal of a pleasant factor from the environment as a consequence of behavior. Disciplinary systems within organizations are examples of systems designed to reduce undesired behavior. Generally, it has been found that positive reinforcement is more effective than negative reinforcement and punishment in producing and maintaining a desired behavior.[12] Managers at Work 14–3 gives an example of positive reinforcement.

Negative reinforcement – removes a negative stimulus from the environment as a consequence of behavior.

Punishment – either the application of a negative stimulus or the removal of a pleasant factor from the environment as a consequence of behavior.

INTEGRATING THE THEORIES
OF MOTIVATION

All of the motivation theories previously presented contain the common thread that motivation is goal-directed behavior. Although the theories may appear to be quite different, most of them are not in conflict with one another. Rather, each looks at a different segment of the overall motivational process or at the same segment from a different perspective. Figure 14–6 presents a model which reflects the overall motivational process and indicates relationships among major motivational theories.

Vroom's preference-expectancy theory is shown at the heart of the model by the three factors that are shown to influence effort; note the arrows leading to the effort box. Maslow's need hierarchy theory and the achievement-power-affiliation theory are represented in the upper left-hand corner of the model by the variable labeled "Nature and strength of current needs." The nature

F I G U R E 14–6   The Overall Motivational Process

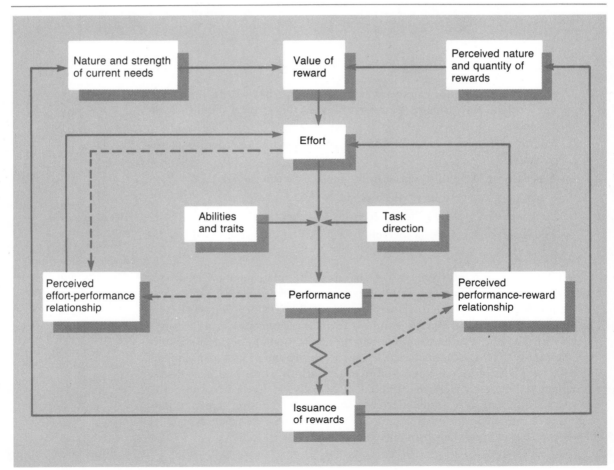

and strength of current needs reflect the individual's needs, which in turn affect the value that the person places on the reward being offered. If the reward matches the individual's needs, that person will place more value on the reward than if it does not match the need level. The motivation-maintenance theory is represented by the variable "perceived nature and quantity of rewards," which is found in the upper right-hand corner of the model. Both of these variables reflect the need for rewards to consist of both hygiene and motivator factors. For example, if only hygiene factors are provided, then the perceived nature and quantity of the rewards would only be marginal, which in turn would result in a marginal or low value placed on the reward by the individual. Issuance of rewards based on performance reinforces the person's behavior. As suggested by Figure 14–6 no single motivation theory provides all the answers.

JOB SATISFACTION

Closely related to motivation is the concept of job satisfaction. In fact, managers often view motivated employees as being synonymous with satisfied employees. There are, however, important differences between motivated employees and satisfied employees.

Job satisfaction is an individual's general attitude about his or her job. The five major components of job satisfaction are: (1) attitude toward work group, (2) general working conditions, (3) attitude toward company, (4) monetary benefits, and (5) attitude toward supervision. Other major components that should be added to these five are the individual's attitudes toward the work itself and toward life in general. The individual's health, age, level of aspiration, social status, and political and social activities can all contribute to job satisfaction. Therefore, job satisfaction is an attitude that results from other specific attitudes and factors.

Job satisfaction refers to the individual's mental set about the job. This mental set may be positive or negative, depending on the individual's mental set concerning the major components of job satisfaction. Job satisfaction is not synonymous with organizational morale. **Organizational morale** refers to an individual's feeling of being accepted by, and belonging to, a group of employees through common goals, confidence in the desirability of these goals, and progress toward these goals. Morale is related to group attitudes, while job satisfaction is more of an individual attitude. However, the two concepts are interrelated in that job satisfaction can contribute to morale and morale can contribute to job satisfaction.

The Satisfaction-Performance Controversy

For many years, managers have believed for the most part that a satisfied worker will automatically be a good worker. In other words, if management could keep all the workers "happy," good performance would automatically

Job satisfaction – individual's general attitude about his or her job.

Organizational morale – individual's feelings of being accepted by, and belonging to, a group of employees through common goals, confidence in the desirability of these goals, and progress toward them.

follow. Charles Greene has suggested that many managers subscribe to this belief because it represents "the path of least resistance."[13] Greene's thesis is that increasing employees' happiness is far more pleasant for the manager than confronting employees with their performance if a performance problem exists.

Research evidence generally rejects the more popular view that employee satisfaction leads to improved performance. The evidence does, however, provide moderate support for the view that performance causes satisfaction. The evidence also provides strong indications that: (1) rewards constitute a more direct cause of satisfaction than does performance; and (2) rewards based on current performance cause subsequent performance.[14]

Research has also investigated the relationship between intrinsic and extrinsic satisfaction and performance for jobs categorized as being either stimulating or nonstimulating.[15] The studies found that the relationship did vary, depend-

F I G U R E   14–7   Determinants of Satisfaction and Dissatisfaction

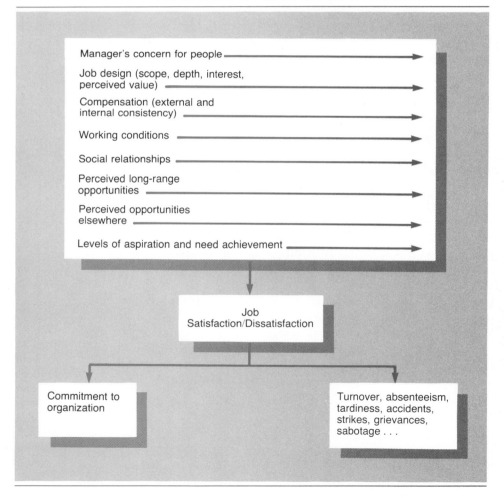

MANAGERS AT WORK 14-4

How Excellent Companies Stay That Way

At Dreyers Grand Ice Cream, every Wednesday is "ice cream day," and all employees go to the factory store and create their own ice cream treat—on the company. In addition to this, several times throughout the year a "fun day" is declared. One fun day the executives served up a barbecue to the employees. An employee singled out as working particularly hard is rewarded with a "Dreyer's Weekend," a three-day all-expense-paid weekend anywhere in or around California. Chairman and CEO T. Gary Rogers had reaped some nice benefits from this institutionalized fun. Sales have gone from $6 million to $134 million since he bought the company in 1977.

Source: Adapted from *Success*, September 1987, p. 30.

ing on whether the job was stimulating or nonstimulating. These and other studies further emphasize the complexity of the satisfaction-performance relationship. One relationship that has been clearly established is that job satisfaction does have a positive impact on turnover, absenteeism, tardiness, accidents, grievances, and strikes.[16]

In addition, recruitment efforts by employees are generally more successful if the employees are satisfied. Satisfied employees are preferred simply because they make the work situation a more pleasant environment. So, even though a satisfied employee is not necessarily a high performer, there are numerous reasons for cultivating satisfied employees.

As mentioned earlier, a wide range of both internal and external factors affect an individual's level of satisfaction. The top portion of Figure 14–7 summarizes the major factors which determine an individual's level of satisfaction (or dissatisfaction). The lower portion of the figure shows the organizational behaviors generally associated with satisfaction and dissatisfaction. Individual satisfaction leads to organizational commitment, while dissatisfaction results in behaviors detrimental to the organization (turnover, absenteeism, tardiness, accidents, etc.). For example, employees who like their jobs, supervisors, and other job-related factors will probably be very loyal and devoted employees. However, employees who strongly dislike their jobs or any of the job-related factors will probably be disgruntled and will often exhibit these feelings by being late, absent, or by taking more covert actions to disrupt the organization.

Satisfaction and motivation are not synonymous. Motivation is a drive to perform, while satisfaction reflects the individual's attitude or happiness with the situation. The factors that determine whether an individual is satisfied with the job differ from those that determine whether the individual is motivated. Satisfaction is largely determined by the comfort offered by the environment and the situation. Motivation, on the other hand, is largely determined by the value of rewards and their contingency on performance. The result of motivation is increased effort, which in turn increases performance if the individual has the ability and if the effort is properly directed. The result of satisfaction is increased commitment to the organization, which may or may not result in increased performance. This increased commitment will normally result in a decrease in problems such as absenteeism, tardiness, turnover, and strikes. Managers at Work 14–4 tells how T. Gary Rogers of Dreyers Grand Ice Cream has incorporated a motivational reward system into its corporate culture.

S U M M A R Y

L E A R N I N G   O B J E C T I V E   1

Define Motivation.

Motivation is concerned with what activates human behavior, what directs this behavior toward a particular goal, and how this behavior is sustained.

L E A R N I N G   O B J E C T I V E   2

Define the Traditional Theory of Motivation.

The traditional theory of motivation is based on the assumption that money is the primary motivation of people: if the monetary reward is great enough, employees will work harder and produce more.

L E A R N I N G   O B J E C T I V E   3

Explain the Hierarchy of Needs.

The five levels of needs are physiological, safety, social, ego, and self-actualization. The physiological needs include food, sleep, water, exercise, clothing, and shelter. Safety needs are concerned with protection against danger, threat, or deprivation. Social needs are the needs for love, affection, and belonging. Ego needs include both self-esteem and the esteem of others. Self-actualization is the need of people to reach their full potential in applying their abilities and interests to functioning in their environment.

L E A R N I N G   O B J E C T I V E   4

Discuss the Achievement-Power-Affiliation Theory of Motivation.

This theory holds that people have three needs: achievement, power, and affiliation. The level of intensity of these needs varies among individuals, and people are motivated in situations that allow them to satisfy their most intense needs.

L E A R N I N G   O B J E C T I V E   5

Discuss the Motivation-Maintenance Theory of Motivation.

This theory postulates that all work-related factors can be grouped into two categories. The first category, maintenance factors, will not produce motivation but can prevent it. The second category, motivators, encourages motivation.

LEARNING OBJECTIVE 6

Discuss the Preference-Expectancy Theory of Motivation.

This theory holds that motivation is based on a combination of the individual's expectancy that increased effort will lead to increased performance (which will lead to rewards), and the individual's preference for those rewards.

LEARNING OBJECTIVE 7

Explain Reinforcement Theory.

This theory is an approach to motivation based on the idea that behavior that appears to lead to a positive consequence tends to be repeated, while behavior that appears to lead to a negative consequence tends not to be repeated.

LEARNING OBJECTIVE 8

Define Job Satisfaction and Organizational Morale.

Job satisfaction is an individual's general attitude about his or her job. Organizational morale refers to an individual's feeling of being accepted by, and belonging to, a group of employees through common goals, confidence in the desirability of these goals, and progress toward these goals.

REVIEW QUESTIONS

1. Explain the motivation sequence.
2. Describe the following theories of motivation:
   a. Traditional theory.
   b. Need hierarchy theory.
   c. Achievement-power-affiliation theory.
   d. Motivation-maintenance theory.
   e. Preference-expectancy theory.
   f. Reinforcement theory.
3. What is job satisfaction? What are the major components of job satisfaction?
4. What is organizational morale?
5. Discuss the satisfaction-performance controversy.
6. From a managerial standpoint, what are the real benefits of having satisfied employees?

DISCUSSION QUESTIONS

1. Discuss your views on this statement: Most people can be motivated with money.
2. Do you think that a very loyal employee is necessarily a good employee?
3. As a manager, would you prefer a motivated or a satisfied group of employees? Why?
4. The XYZ Company has just decided to take all of its employees (200 in number) to Las Vegas for a three-day expense-paid weekend to show its appreciation for their high level of performance this past year. What is your reaction to this idea?
5. Discuss the following statement: A satisfied employee is one that is not being pushed hard enough.

REFERENCES & ADDITIONAL READINGS

[1] Cited in Paul Hersey and Kenneth H. Blanchard, *Management of Organizational Behavior: Utilizing Human Resources,* 4th ed. (Englewood Cliffs, N.J.: Prentice-Hall, 1982), p. 4.

[2] Richard M. Steers and Lyman W. Porter, *Motivation and Human Behavior* (New York: McGraw-Hill, 1983), pp. 3–4.

[3] Abraham H. Maslow, *Motivation and Personality,* 2nd ed. (New York: Harper & Row, 1970).

[4] Edwin A. Locke, "The Nature and Causes of Job Satisfaction," in *Handbook of Industrial and Organizational Psychology,* ed. Marvin D. Dunnette (New York: John Wiley & Sons, 1983).

[5] David C. McClelland, *The Achievement Motive* (New York: Halsted Press, 1976).

[6] Frederick Herzberg, Bernard Mausner, and Barbara Synderman, *The Motivation to Work* (New York: John Wiley & Sons, 1959), p. ix.

[7] Victor H. Vroom, *Work and Motivation* (New York: John Wiley & Sons, 1967).

[8] McGregor's Theory X and Theory Y, which some authors consider to be basic theories of motivation, are discussed in Chapter 15, "Leading: Influencing Human Behavior." The authors of this text feel that the theories more logically fit into a discussion of leadership than of basic motivation theories.

[9] Steers and Porter, *Motivation,* chap. 4.

[10] Ibid., pp. 123–24.

[11] Ibid., pp. 162–63.

[12] P. M. Podsakoff, William D. Tudor, and Richard Skov, "Effects of Leader Contingent and Noncontingent Reward and Punishment Behaviors on Subordinate Performance and Satisfaction," *Academy of Management Journal,* December 1982, pp. 810–21.

[13] Charles N. Greene, "The Satisfaction-Performance Controversy," *Business Horizons,* October 1972, p. 31. Also see D. R. Norris and R. E. Niebuhr, "Attributional Influences on the Job Performance–Job Satisfaction Relationship," *Academy of Management Journal,* June 1984, pp. 424–31.

[14] Greene, "The Satisfaction-Performance Controversy," p. 40.

[15] John M. Ivancevich, "The Performance to Satisfaction Relationship: A Causal Analysis of Stimulating and Nonstimulating Jobs," *Organizational Behavior and Human Performance* 22 (1978), pp. 350–64.

[16] Donald P. Schwab and Larry L. Cummings, "Theories of Performance and Satisfactions: A Review," *Industrial Relations,* October 1970, pp. 408–29. Also see Locke, "Job Satisfaction," p. 1343, for a complete summary of the related research.

INCIDENT

Our Engineers Are Just Not Motivated

*S*ituation: You are a consultant to the manager of mechanical engineering for a large company (8,000 employees, $200 million annual sales) that manufactures industrial equipment. The manager has been in this position for six months, having moved from a similar position in a much smaller company.

Manager: I just can't seem to get these people to perform. They are all extremely competent, but they just don't seem to be willing to put forth the kind of effort that we expect and need if this company is going to remain successful.

Consultant: What type of work do they do?

Manager: Primarily designing minor modifications to existing equipment lines to keep up with our competition and to satisfy special customer requirements.

Consultant: How do you evelute their performance?

Manager: Mainly on whether they meet project deadlines. Its's hard to evaluate the quality of their work, since most of it is fairly routine and the designs are frequently altered later by the production engineers to facilitate production processes.

Consultant: Are they meeting their deadlines reasonably well?

Manager: No, that's the problem. What's worse is that they don't really seem too concerned about it.

Consultant: What financial rewards do you offer them?

Manager: They are all well-paid—some of the best salaries for mechanical engineers that I know of anywhere. Base pay is determined mainly on the basis of seniority, but there is also a companywide profit-sharing plan. At the end of each year, the company distributes 10 percent of its profits after taxes to the employees. The piece of the pie that you get is in proportion to your basic salary. This kind of plan was used in the company I used to work for, and it seemed to have a highly motivating effect for them. They also get good vacations, insurance plans, and all the other usual goodies. I know of no complaints about compensation.

Consultant: How about promotion possibilities?

Manager: Well, all I know is that I was brought in from the outside.

Consultant: If they are so lackadaisical, have you considered firing any of them?

Manager: Are you kidding? We need them too much, and it would be difficult and expensive to replace them. If I even threatened to fire any of them for anything short of blowing up the building, my boss would come down on me like a ton of bricks. We are so far behind on our work as it is. Besides, I'm not sure that it's really their fault entirely.

Questions

1. Why are the engineers not motivated?
2. What should management do to correct the situation?

EXERCISE

Motivation-Maintenance

This exercise is designed to illustrate Herzberg's motivation-maintenance theory in terms of your personal experiences.

A. Think of a time when your were extremely motivated or "turned on" by a job (the instance could have taken place yesterday or several years ago and it could have been on a full or part-time job) and write a brief two- or three-sentence description of the situation. After you have completed the description, list the reasons that this situation had a motivational effect on you. Don't sign your name, but do pass your paper forward.

B. After completing the above, repeat the same procedure, for a situation which was highly demotivating. After all the papers have been passed forward your instructor will help you analyze them.

15 Leading: Influencing Human Behavior

LEARNING OBJECTIVES

*After studying this chapter,
you should be able to:*

1 Define leadership.

2 Discuss the relationship between power
and authority.

3 Describe the self-fulfilling prophecy in
management.

4 Define the trait theory of leadership.

5 List and define the basic leadership styles.

6 Understand the Managerial Grid.

7 Define the contingency approach to
leadership.

8 Explain the path-goal theory of leadership.

9 Define the life-cycle theory of leadership.

10 List some of the lessons that can be
learned from leadership research.

Leadership is many things. It is being patient. It is altering agendas so that new priorities get enough attention. It is being visible when things are going awry, and invisible when things are going well. It's listening carefully much of the time, frequently speaking with encouragement, and reinforcing words with believable action. It's being tough when necessary, and it's the occasional naked use of power. *

A s we saw in Chapter 14, motivation comes from inside a person. Leadership—what one person can do to influence the behavior of others—and motivation are closely related. The leadership abilities of one person can certainly affect the motivation of other people.

Each year, new information is published about leadership. Checklists have been devised to find what style of leadership is used by people. Questionnaires try to determine the style of leadership used within an organization. New teaching aids and devices are designed to improve one's leadership abilities.

All of this activity would seem to show that managers today know a great deal about the leadership process. But this is not true. Many of them appear to have a hard time performing well in leadership roles. This chapter reviews and offers a perspective on leadership styles and processes.

LEADERSHIP: WHAT IS IT?

Leadership – process of influencing the behavior of members of a group.

Leader – occupies the central role in a leadership situation; has the ability to influence the behavior of others in a given situation.

Leadership is a process of influencing the activities of members of a group in performing their tasks of goal setting and goal achievement. The ability to obtain followers and influence them makes a leader. Generally, influence is the result when one person presents information in such a way as to convince the other members of the group that their situation will be improved if they behave in a certain way. A **leader** is the person who takes the central role in this interaction by influencing the behavior of other members of the group.

Managers are in a leadership role because they can influence the behavior of members of the formal work group. However, that does not mean the manager is effective in the role. A manager's leadership can be measured by the contribution of the group toward the organization's objectives (such as increased profit or service to customers).

* Adapted from Thomas J. Peters and Robert H. Waterman, Jr., "How the Best-Run Companies Turn So-So Performers into Big Winners," *Management Review*, November–December 1982, p. 15.

Generally, there are two types of leaders in organizations: One is the formal or appointed leader (manager) who is assigned to the position by the organization; the other, the informal leader, is chosen by the group itself. Each type of leader relies on different sources of authority in performing the role. Note, however, that appointed leaders (managers) may or may not be informal leaders.

SOURCES OF AUTHORITY

The informal leader of a group is the one seen by the group as most capable of satisfying its needs. The authority of the leader can be removed, reduced, or increased, depending on the group's perceived progress toward its goals. The leader's authority may also be threatened by the emergence of different or additional goals.

A simple example of this point follows. Suppose a group of people were shipwrecked on a desolate island. The group's first goal would probably be to ensure their survival by finding food, water, and shelter. The person selected by the group as the leader would be the person seen by the group as the one who could best help the group survive. However, after this need is met, other needs will emerge. The need to escape from the island would probably emerge rather quickly. The person first selected as leader may not be perceived as the most capable to direct attainment of these new needs. In this case, the group might select a new leader. This process of changing leaders might continue, depending on the group's view of its needs.

The role of manager and the role of the previous example's leader are different. The example shows an elective, or emergent, style of leadership. Under this system, the leader must know the needs of the group and must be seen by the group as being most capable in meeting those needs. In other words, the source of authority for the leader is the group being led. In most organizations, however, a manager's source of authority does not come from the group being managed but rather from higher management. Thus, the source of authority for a manager comes from above rather than below. Managers at Work 15–1 describes a leader who emerged at a critical time in the Civil Rights movement.

POWER, AUTHORITY, AND LEADERSHIP

Power – ability or capacity to influence others to do something that they would not otherwise do.

Power is the ability to command or apply force. It is not necessarily accompanied by authority. Through **power,** people can be influenced by someone to do something that they would not otherwise do. The use of or desire for power is often viewed negatively in our society because power is often linked

MANAGERS AT WORK 15–1

Martin Luther King, Jr., and the Southern Christian Leadership Conference

Martin Luther King, Jr., came to national attention in 1955 when the 26-year-old clergyman emerged as leader of the Montgomery bus boycott, the first massive and sustained black protest in the South following the Supreme Court's decision of May 1954. King and his associates went on to form the Southern Christian Leadership Conference in 1957 and lead the Birmingham protests of 1963, which contributed to the passage of the major civil rights legislation of 1964 and 1965. King's nonviolent philosophy won him the Nobel Peace Prize in 1965. He was recognized as one of the most important leaders of the civil rights movement.

Martin Luther King's leadership skills seemed to center around his faith in God, his vision of the future of the civil rights movement, and his ability to communicate. His "I Have a Dream" speech is well remembered for its eloquence in stating a vision for the future. On April 3, 1968, King stated:

> We've got some difficult days ahead. But, it really doesn't matter with me now. Because I've been to the mountain top. I won't mind. Like anybody, I would like to live a long life. Longevity has its place. But I'm not concerned about that now. I just want to do God's will.
>
> And he's allowed me to go up to the mountain. And I've looked over, and I've seen the Promised Land. I may not get there with you, but I want you to know tonight that we as a people will get to the Promised Land.

On April 4, 1968, Martin Luther King, Jr., was assassinated.

Adapted from Martin Luther King, Jr., *The Measure of a Man* (Philadelphia: Pilgrim Press, 1968), p. 63; Melvin Drimmer, *Black History: A Reappraisal* (Garden City, N.Y.: Doubleday Publishing, 1968), pp. 440–54.

Authority – right to issue directives and expend resources.
Coercive power – based on fear.
Reward power – based on one's ability to provide rewards for compliance with one's wishes.

with the capacity to punish. There are, however, other forms of power, as shown in Figure 15–1.

Authority which exists in the formal organization, is the right to issue directives and expend resources. Authority has been viewed in the past as a function of position in the organizational hierarchy, flowing from the top to the bottom of the organization. Basically, the amount of authority that a manager has depends on the amount of **coercive, reward,** and **legitimate power** that the manager can exert in a certain position. Chester Bernard's acceptance theory of authority, discussed in Chapter 10, suggests that the source of a manager's authority lies with the subordinate: The subordinate has the power either to accept or to reject a superior's command; if the subordinate rejects the authority of a superior, it does not exist. Barnard viewed disobeying or ignoring a superior as a denial of the latter's authority. Basically,

F I G U R E 15–1 Types of Power

Coercive power	Based on fear, the subordinate does what is required to avoid punishment or some other negative outcome. The disciplinary policies of organizations generally are based on this type of power.
Reward power	Based on the ability of one individual to provide rewards, either intrinsic or extrinsic, for compliance with this individual's wishes.
Legitimate power	Based on an individual's position in the organization; thus, when joining an organization, a person accepts the fact that the boss's orders are to be carried out.
Expert power	Based on the special skill, expertise, or knowledge that a particular individual possesses.
Referent power	Exemplified by the charismatic individual who has unusual traits that allow that person to control situations.

he was referring to the degree of legitimate power that a manager commands. The coercive and reward power a manager can exert affect how much legitimate power the manager holds. Power can also be exerted up from the bottom of an organization as well as from the top down. Employees can have some power over management. For instance, they can strike or threaten a strike.

Leadership has been described in this chapter as a process of influencing the behavior of other members of the group. Leaders may use one or several types of power to influence group behavior. For instance, some political leaders use **referent power;** others use a combination of coercive, reward, and referent power—Adolph Hitler is an example. Informal leaders generally combine referent power and **expert power.** Some managers rely only on their authority—which is the combination of coercive, reward, and referent power—while others use different combinations.

Legitimate power – based on one's position in an organization.

Referent power – based on the charismatic traits or characteristics of an individual.

Expert power – based on the special skill, expertise, or knowledge of an individual.

LEADER ATTITUDES

Douglas McGregor developed two attitude profiles, or assumptions, about the basic nature of people. These attitudes were termed **Theory X** and **Theory Y;** they are summarized in Figure 15–2. McGregor maintained that many leaders in essence subscribe to either Theory X or Theory Y and behave accordingly. A Theory X leader would likely use a much more authoritarian style of leadership than a leader who believes in Theory Y assumptions. The real value of McGregor's work was the idea that a leader's attitude toward human nature has a large influence on how that person behaves as a leader.[1]

The relationship between a leader's expectations and the resulting performance of subordinates has received much attention. Generally, it has been found that if the manager's expectations are high, productivity is likely to

Theory X and Theory Y – terms coined by Douglas McGregor to describe assumptions made by managers about basic human nature.

FIGURE 15–2   Assumptions about People

THEORY X

1. The average human being has an inherent dislike of work and will avoid it if possible.
2. Because of their dislike of work, most people must be coerced, controlled, directed, or threatened with punishment to get them to put forth adequate effort toward the achievement of organizational objectives.
3. The average human being prefers to be directed, wishes to avoid responsibility, has relatively little ambition, and wants security above all.

THEORY Y

1. The expenditure of physical and mental effort in work is as natural as play or rest.
2. External control and the threat of punishment are not the only means for bringing about effort toward organizational objectives. Workers will exercise self-direction and self-control in the service of objectives to which they are committed.
3. Commitment to objectives is a function of the rewards associated with their achievement.
4. The average human being learns, under proper conditions, not only to accept but to seek responsibility.
5. The capacity to exercise a relatively high degree of imagination, ingenuity, and creativity in the solution of organizational problems is widely, not narrowly, distributed in the population.
6. Under the conditions of modern industrial life, the intellectual potentialities of the average human being are only partially utilized.

Source: Douglas McGregor, *The Human Side of Enterprise* (New York: McGraw-Hill, 1960), pp. 33–34 and 47–48. Copyright © 1960 by McGraw-Hill, Inc. Used with permission of McGraw-Hill Book Company.

Self-fulfilling prophecy (Pygmalion in management) – describes the influence of one person's expectations on another's behavior.

be high. On the other hand, if the manager's expectations are low, productivity is likely to be poor. McGregor called this phenomenon the **self-fulfilling prophecy.** It has also been called **Pygmalion in management.**

GENERAL APPROACHES TO LEADERSHIP

Many studies have been done on leadership. Some of the more important ones are discussed here.

Trait Theory

Trait theory – holds that certain physical and psychological characteristics, or traits, differentiate leaders from their groups.

Early research efforts devoted to leadership stressed what the leader was *like* rather than what the leader *did*—a **trait theory** of leadership. Many personality traits (such as originality, initiative, persistence, knowledge, enthusiasm), social traits (tact, patience, sympathy, etc.), and physical characteristics (e.g., height, weight, attractiveness) have been examined to differentiate leaders.[2]

At first glance, a few traits do seem to distinguish leaders from followers. These include being slightly superior in such physical traits as weight and height and in a tendency to score higher on tests of dominance, intelligence, extroversion, and adjustment. But the differences seem to be small, with much overlap.

Thus, the research in this area has generally been fruitless—largely because the traits related to leadership in one case usually did not prove to be predictive in other cases. In general, it can be said that traits may to some extent influence the capacity to lead. But these traits must be analyzed in terms of the leadership situation (described in detail later in this chapter).

Basic Leadership Styles

Other studies dealt with the style of the leader. They found three basic leadership styles: autocratic, laissez-faire, and democratic. The main difference among these styles is where the decision-making function rests. Generally, the **autocratic leader** makes most decisions for the group; the **laissez-faire leader** allows people within the group to make all decisions; and the **democratic leader** guides and encourages the group to make decisions. More detail about each of the leadership styles is given in Figure 15–3. (Figure 15–3 implies that the democratic style is the most desirable and productive. However, current research on leadership, discussed later in this chapter, does not necessarily support this conclusion.) The primary contribution of this research was identifying the three basic styles of leadership. Managers at Work 15–2 describes the leadership style of Lucille Ball.

Autocratic leader – makes most decisions for the group.

Laissez-faire leader – allows individuals in the group to make the decisions.

Democratic leader – guides and encourages the group to make decisions.

Dimensions of the Leadership Process

A series of studies on leadership was conducted at Ohio State University to find out the most important activities of successful leaders. The researchers wanted to find out what a successful leader does, regardless of the type of group being led: a mob, a religious group, a university, or a business organization. To do this, they developed a questionnaire called the **Leader Behavior Description Questionnaire (LBDQ).** Both the original form and variations of it are still used today.

In using the questionnaire, two leader activities emerged consistently as being the most important: consideration and initiating structure. The term *consideration* refers to the leader activity of showing concern for individual group members and satisfying their needs. The term *initiating structure* refers to the leader activity of structuring the work of group members and directing the group toward the attainment of the group's goals.

Since the Ohio State research, many other studies have been done on the relationship between the leader activities of consideration and initiating structure and their resulting effect on leader effectiveness. The major conclusions that can be drawn from these studies are:[3]

Leader Behavior Description Questionnaire (LBDQ) – developed at Ohio State University and designed to determine how successful leaders carry out their activities.

1. Leaders scoring high on consideration tend to have more satisfied subordinates than do leaders scoring low on consideration.
2. The relationship between the score on consideration and leader effectiveness depends on the group that is being led. In other words, a high

F I G U R E   15–3   Relationship between Styles of Leadership and Group Members

---

AUTOCRATIC STYLE

Leader
1. The individual is very conscious of his or her position.
2. He or she has little trust and faith in members of the group.
3. This leader believes that pay is a just reward for working and the only reward that will motivate employees.
4. Orders are issued to be carried out, with no questions allowed and no explanations given.

Group members
1. No responsibility is assumed for performance, with people merely doing what they are told.
2. Production is good when the leader is present, but poor in the leader's absence.

LAISSEZ-FAIRE STYLE

Leader
1. He or she has no confidence in his or her leadership ability.
2. This leader does not set goals for the group.

Group members
1. Decisions are made by whomever in the group is willing to do it.
2. Productivity generally is low, and work is sloppy.
3. Individuals have little interest in their work.
4. Morale and teamwork generally are low.

DEMOCRATIC STYLE

Leader
1. Decision making is shared between the leader and the group.
2. When the leader is required or forced to make a decision, his or her reasoning is explained to the group.
3. Criticism and praise are given objectively.

Group members
1. New ideas and change are welcomed.
2. A feeing of responsibility is developed within the group.
3. Quality of work and productivity generally are high.
4. The group generally feels successful.

Source: Adapted from Leland B. Bradford and Ronald Lippitt, "Building a Democratic Work Group," *Personnel* 22, no. 3 (November 1945). Copyright © 1945 by American Management Association, Inc. Reprinted by permission of the publisher.

---

score on consideration was positively correlated with leader effectiveness for managers and office staff in a large industrial firm, whereas a high score on consideration was negatively correlated with leader effectiveness for production foremen.

3. There is also no consistent relationship between initiating structure and leader effectiveness; rather, the relationship varies depending on the group that is being lead.

MANAGERS AT WORK 15–2

Lucille Ball and Desilu Productions

The television program "I Love Lucy" was the forerunner of modern-day situation comedies and was one of the most successful series ever produced for television. It gave its leading woman Lucille Ball her introduction to the business side of television and motion pictures. Lucy—no one calls her Ms. Ball—went on to become the first woman to head a major Hollywood film company, Desilu Productions, Inc.

During her early years as an actress, she studied how directors worked with cast and crew, how they motivated people, why some succeeded and others failed. "I never regretted all the B films because I was getting paid for learning. What more can one want?" Lucy's philosophy about employees is: "Anytime one of my people is unhappy, he or she is free to go; if that person is unhappy, you have nothing." Her philosophy of work is: "Set high standards for yourself, be true to them, and give it your best shot, because you'll never be able to please everybody."

Source: Adapted from Tony Velvui, "The Real Lucille Ball," *Nation's Business,* October 1981, pp. 75–78.

Likert's Work

The Institute for Social Research of the University of Michigan conducted studies to discover principles contributing both to the productivity of a group and to the satisfaction derived by group members. The initial study was conducted at the home office of the Prudential Insurance Company in Newark, New Jersey.

Interviews were conducted with 24 section heads or supervisors and 419 nonsupervisory personnel. Results of the interviews showed that supervisors of high-producing work groups were more likely:

1. To receive general rather than close supervision from their superiors.
2. To like the amount of authority and responsibility they have in their job.
3. To spend more time in supervision.
4. To give general rather than close supervision to their employees.
5. To be employee oriented rather than production oriented.

Supervisors of low-producing work groups had basically opposite characteristics and techniques. They were production oriented and gave close supervision.

Rensis Likert, then director of the institute, published the results of his years of research in the book *New Patterns of Management,* which is a classic in its field. Likert feels that there are four patterns or styles of leadership or management employed by organizations. He has identified and labeled these styles as follows:

System 1: Exploitative authoritative. Authoritarian form of management that attempts to exploit subordinates.

System 2: Benevolent authoritative. Authoritarian form of management, but paternalistic in nature.

System 3: Consultative. Manager requests and receives inputs from subordinates but maintains the right to make the final decision.

System 4: Participative. Manager gives some direction, but decisions are made by consensus and majority, based on total participation.

Likert used a questionnaire to determine the style of leadership and the management pattern employed in the organization as a whole. The results of his studies indicated that System 4 was the most effective style of management and that organizations should strive to develop a management pattern analogous to this system.

The Managerial Grid

Managerial Grid® – two-dimensional framework characterizing a leader according to concern for people and concern for production.

Robert Blake and Jane Mouton have also developed a method of classifying the leadership style of an individual.[5] The **Managerial Grid®,** depicted in Figure 15–4, is a two-dimensional framework rating a leader on the basis of concern for people and concern for production. (Notice that these activities closely relate to the leader activities from the Ohio State studies—consideration and initiating structure.) A questionnaire is used to locate a particular style of leadership or management on the grid.

Blake and Mouton identified five basic styles of management, using the Managerial Grid. *Authority-obedience*—located in the lower right-hand corner (9,1 position)—assumes that efficiency in operations results from properly arranging the conditions at work with minimum interference from other people. The opposite view; *country club management*—located in the upper left-hand corner (1,9 position)—assumes that proper attention to human needs leads to a comfortable organizational atmosphere and workplace. *Team management*—in the upper right-hand corner (9,9)—combines a high degree of concern for people with a high degree of concern for production. The other two styles on the grid are *impoverished management* (1,1) and *organization man management* (5,5). The Managerial Grid is intended to serve as a framework for managers to learn what their leadership style is and to develop a plan to move toward a 9,9 team management style of leadership.

FIGURE 15–4   The Managerial Grid®

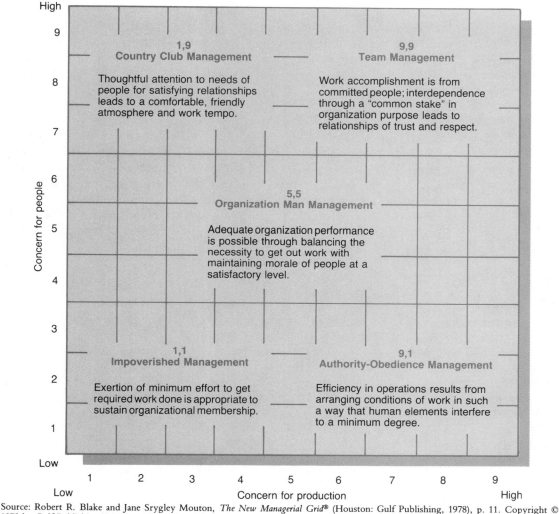

Source: Robert R. Blake and Jane Srygley Mouton, *The New Managerial Grid®* (Houston: Gulf Publishing, 1978), p. 11. Copyright © 1978 by Gulf Publishing Company. Reproduced by permission.

SITUATIONAL (CONTINGENCY) APPROACHES TO LEADERSHIP

The leadership studies discussed so far are similar in that they do not specifically address the complex differences between groups (such as production workers versus accountants) and their influences on leader behavior. To imply that a manager should be employee oriented rather than production oriented (Michigan studies) or that the leader should exhibit concern for both production and people (Blake and Mouton) does not say much about what the leader should do in particular situations. Nor does it offer much guidance for daily leadership situations. Current research is largely concerned with the style of leadership that is most effective in a particular situation.[6] This is called the **contingency approach to leadership.**

Contingency approach to leadership – holds that the most effective style of leadership depends on the particular situation.

Continuum of Leadership Behaviors

Robert Tannenbaum and Warren Schmidt contend that different combinations of situational elements require different styles of leadership. They suggest that there are three important factors, or forces, involved in finding the most effective leadership style: forces involving the manager, the subordinate, and the situation.[7] Furthermore, all of these forces are interdependent.

Figure 15–5 describes in detail the forces that affect leadership situations. Since these forces differ in strength and interaction in differing situations, one style of leadership is not effective in all situations.

FIGURE 15–5   Forces in the Leadership Situation

FORCES IN THE MANAGER	FORCES IN THE SUBORDINATES	FORCES IN THE SITUATION
Value system: How the manager personally feels about delegating, degree of confidence in subordinates.	Need for independence: Some people need and want direction, while others do not.	Type of organization: Centralized versus decentralized.
Personal leadership inclinations: Authoritarian versus participative.	Readiness to assume responsibility: Different people need different degrees of responsibility.	Work group effectiveness: How effectively the group works together.
Feelings of security in uncertain situations.	Tolerance for ambiguity: Specific versus general directions.	The problem itself: The work group's knowledge and experience relevant to the problem.
	Interest and perceived importance of the problem: People generally have more interest in, and work harder on, important problems.	Time pressure: It is difficult to delegate to subordinates in crisis situations.
	Degree of understanding and identification with organizational goals: A manager is more likely to delegate authority to an individual who seems to have a positive attitude about the organization.	Demands from upper levels of management.
	Degree of expectation in sharing in decision making: People who have worked under subordinate-centered leadership tend to resent boss-centered leadership.	Demands from government, unions, and society in general.

In fact, Tannenbaum and Schmidt argue that there is a continuum of behaviors that the manager may employ, depending on the particular situation (see Figure 15–6). Those authors further conclude that successful leaders are keenly aware of the forces that are most relevant to their behavior at a given time. Successful leaders accurately understand not only themselves but also the other persons in the organizational and social environment, and they are able to behave correctly in light of these insights.

Fiedler's Contingency Approach to Leadership

Fred Fiedler further refined the idea of a situational approach to leadership. He tried to define the particular style of leadership needed for a given situation.[8] Fiedler defined two basic styles of leadership—task motivated and relationship motivated. The task-motivated style (similar to earlier discussed ideas of concern for production and initiating structure) fulfills the leader's need for satisfaction from the performance of a task. The relationship-motivated style of leadership (similar to concern for people and consideration) fulfills the leader's need to gain satisfaction from interpersonal relationships.

F I G U R E 15–6 Continuum of Leadership Behavior

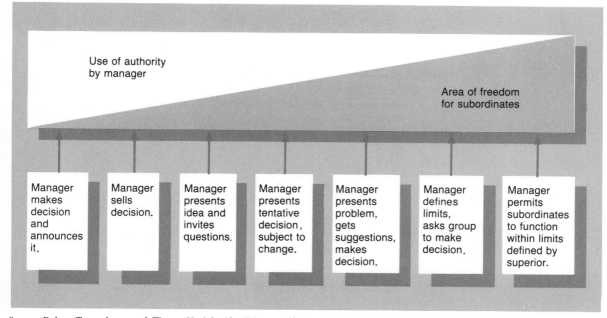

F I G U R E 15–7   Fiedler's Classification of Situations

SITUATION	1	2	3	4	5	6	7	8
Leader-member relations	Good	Good	Good	Good	Poor	Poor	Poor	Poor
Task structure	Structured	Structured	Unstructured	Unstructured	Structured	Structured	Unstructured	Unstructured
Position power	Strong	Weak	Strong	Weak	Strong	Weak	Strong	Weak

Favorable for leader   Unfavorable for leader

Fiedler used a questionnaire to find the leadership style of an individual. Respondents were asked to describe the person with whom they could work least effectively and the person with whom they could work most effectively. A person who described a least preferred co-worker in fairly favorable terms was presumed to be motivated to have close interpersonal relations with others; Fiedler classified these people as relationship-motivated leaders. On the other hand, people who rejected co-workers with whom they had difficulties were presumed to be motivated to accomplish or achieve the task: they were classified as task-oriented leaders.[9]

Fiedler next turned to the situation in which the leader was operating. He placed leadership situations along a favorable-unfavorable continuum based on three major dimensions: leader-member relations, task structure, and position power. *Leader-member relations* refer to the degree that others trust and respect the leader, and to the leader's friendliness. This compares somewhat to referent power. *Task structure* is the degree to which job tasks are structured. For example, assembly-line jobs are more structured than managerial jobs. *Position power* refers to the power and influence that go with a job. A manager has more position power who is able to hire, fire, and discipline. Position power compares to coercive, reward, and legitimate power. Using these three dimensions, an eight-celled classification scheme was developed. Figure 15–7 shows this scheme along the continuum.

Figure 15–8 shows the most productive style of leadership for each situation. In both highly favorable and highly unfavorable situations, a task-motivated

F I G U R E 15–8   Relationship of Leadership Style to Situation

SITUATION	1	2	3	4	5	6	7	8
Leader-member relations	Good	Good	Good	Good	Poor	Poor	Poor	Poor
Task structure	Structured	Structured	Unstructured	Unstructured	Structured	Structured	Unstructured	Unstructured
Leader position power	Strong	Weak	Strong	Weak	Strong	Weak	Strong	Weak
	Favorable for leader						Unfavorable for leader	
Most productive leadership style	Task	Task	Task	Relation	Relation	No data	Task or relation	Task

MANAGERS AT WORK 15–3

Lido "Lee" Anthony Iacocca and The Chrysler Corporation

Lee Iacocca joined Ford Motor Co. right out of school in 1946. After a series of marketing jobs, he was appointed as vice president and general manager of the Ford Division in 1960. By 1967, he was running all of Ford's North American car and truck operations as executive vice president and general manager. In December 1970, he was named company president and second in command to Henry Ford II. However, in 1978, he was fired by Henry Ford, after years of disputes over who should be on the management team and what the future direction of Ford's product line should be.

Later in 1978, Iacocca accepted the job as CEO of Chrysler Corporation, which was on its way to reporting a loss of $205 million on $13.6 billion in sales. Iacocca's description of what he found was as follows: "I found a mess. It was an absolute mess . . . At that point, you don't have time for strategies or philosophies. We had time to make a payroll every Friday."

Iacocca's charismatic leadership style was described as follows: "There were lots of times he had to rally the marketing troops. His speciality was speaking at company rallies. His own strength of character would mesmerize them. He's the only guy I know who can talk about the same thing four times in the same presentation and still not lose the audience's interest. People were fascinated by him."

In telling the management of Chrysler what it had to do, Iacocca says it was simple. "Our whole team had to learn one thing quickly—you're playing with live ammunition. If we have one failure, we're done. We're bankrupt."

Source: Adapted from Larry Marion, "CEO of the Year: Lee Iacocca of Chrysler," *Financial World,* March 31, 1983, pp. 22–26.

leader was found to be more effective. In highly favorable situations, the group is ready to be directed and is willing to be told what to do. In highly favorable situations, the group welcomes having the leader make decisions and direct the group. In moderately favorable situations, a relationship-motivated leader was found to be more effective. In Situation 7 (moderately poor leader-member relations, unstructured task, and strong position power), the task and relationship styles of leadership were equally productive. Thus, Fiedler has gone one step beyond Tannenbaum and Schmidt. He is shown which style of leadership is most effective in a given situation. Managers at Work 15–3 describes Lee Iacocca's style of leadership during difficult times at Chrysler Corporation.

Path-Goal Theory of Leadership

Path-goal theory of leadership – holds that the leader's role is to increase personal payoffs to subordinates for work-goal attainment, make the path to payoffs easier, increase the opportunities for satisfaction enroute, and that the effectiveness of such efforts depends on the situation.

The **path-goal theory of leadership** attempts to define the relationships between a leader's behavior and the subordinates' performance and work activities.[10] Leader behavior is acceptable to subordinates to the degree that they see it as a source of satisfaction now or as a step toward future satisfaction. Leader behavior influences the motivation of subordinates when it makes the satisfaction of their needs contingent on successful performance; and it provides the guidance, support, and rewards needed for effective performance (but which are not already present in the environment). The path-goal theory of leadership and the expectancy theory of motivation, which was described in the previous Chapter, are closely related in that leader behaviors can either increase or decrease employee expectancies.

In path-goal theory, leader behavior falls into one of the four basic types—role classification, supportive, participative, and autocratic. *Role classification leadership* lets subordinates know what is expected of them, gives guidance as to what should be done and how, schedules and coordinates work among the subordinates, and maintains definite standards of performance. *Supportive leadership* has a friendly, approachable leader who attempts to make the work environment more pleasant for subordinates. *Participative leadership* involves consulting with subordinates and asking for their suggestions in the decision-making process. *Autocratic leadership* comes from a leader who gives orders which are not to be questioned by subordinates.

Under this theory, each of these leadership behaviors results in different levels of performance and subordinate satisfaction, depending on the structure of the work tasks. Role clarification leads to high satisfaction and performance for subordinates engaged in unstructured tasks. Supportive leadership brings the most satisfaction to those who work on highly structured tasks. Participative leader behavior enhances performance and satisfaction for subordinates engaged in ambiguous tasks. Autocratic leadership behavior has a negative effect on both satisfaction and performance in both structured and unstructured task situations.

Life-Cycle Theory of Leadership

Life-cycle theory of leadership – holds that the maturity level of the followers determines the most appropriate leadership style for a situation.

Paul Hersey and Kenneth Blanchard include maturity of the followers as an important factor in style of leadership.[11] According to the **life-cycle theory of leadership,** as the level of maturity of followers increases, not only less and less structure (task) but also less and less socioemotional support (relationship) is needed in leader behavior. The maturity level of the followers is determined by their relative independence, their ability to take responsibility, and their achievement-motivation level.

Figure 15–9 shows the cycle of the basic leadership styles that should be used by the leader, depending on the maturity of the followers. The life-cycle theory proposes that as the followers progress from immaturity to matu-

F I G U R E 15–9   Life-Cycle Theory of Leadership

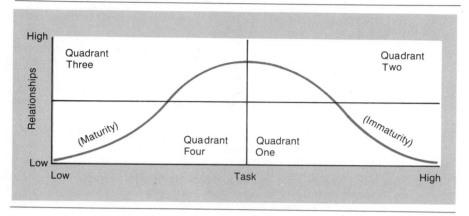

rity, the leader's behavior should move from: (1) high task–low relationships to (2) high task–high relationships to (3) low task–high relationships to (4) low task–low relationships.

LEADERSHIP AND DECISION MAKING

One key to effective decision making is the ability of the leader to select the appropriate decision-making style for each decision faced. Research and practice show that no single style of decision making works best in all situations. Successful leaders learn to match the appropriate decision-making style with the situation.

Victor Vroom and Philip Yetton addressed the problem with a very practical and useful model.[12] They developed the set of alternative decision styles shown in Figure 15–10. Each style has a code and is increasingly more participative: Style A–I has no subordinate participation, while Style G–II is almost totally participative.

Vroom and Yetton selected three variables bearing on the appropriateness of a given decision-making style: (1) the quality or rationality of the decision; (2) the acceptance or commitment by subordinates to execute the decision effectively; and (3) the amount of time required to make the decision.

Figure 15–11 shows Vroom and Yetton's model as a decision tree. The problem attributes are shown across the top of the figure. For any decision situation, start at the left-hand side and work toward the right until a terminal node is reached. When more than one decision-making style is feasible, this model chooses the style requiring the least amount of time.

Vroom and Yetton found that most leaders actually do use different decision-making styles in different situations. They also found that leaders are much more likely to break decision rules about acceptance or commitment of the

F I G U R E 15–10   Types of Management Decision Styles

A–I: You solve the problem or make the decision yourself, using information available to you at that time.

A–II: You obtain the necessary information from your subordinate(s), then decide on the solution to the problem yourself. You may or may not tell your subordinates what the problem is, while getting the information from them. The role played by your subordinates in making the decision is clearly one of providing the necessary information to you rather than generating or evaluating alternative solutions.

C–I: You share the problem with your subordinates as a group, collectively obtaining their ideas and suggestions. Then you make a decision that may or may not reflect your subordinates' influence.

G–II: You share a problem with your subordinates as a group. Together you generate and evaluate alternatives and attempt to reach agreement (consensus) on a solution. Your role is much like that of chairperson. You do not try to influence the group to adopt your solution, and you are willing to accept and implement any solution that has the support of the entire group.

Source: Victor H. Vroom, "A New Look at Managerial Decision Making," *Organizational Dynamics*, Spring 1973. © 1973 by AMACOM, a division of American Management Associations, New York, p. 67. Reprinted by permission of the publisher. All rights reserved.

decision than those designed to protect the quality of rationality of the decision. One might then conclude that typical leaders' decisions are more likely to suffer from a lack of acceptance by followers than from the quality of the decision. Similarly, leaders who learn what decision styles work best in what situations are usually going to make better decisions than those who don't.

IMPLICATIONS OF LEADERSHIP THEORIES FOR ORGANIZATIONS AND MANAGERS

How can all of these leadership theories be made relevant to the organization's need for effective managers? First, given the situational factors discussed in this chapter, it appears unlikely that a selection process will be developed to accurately predict successful leaders. The dynamic, changing nature of managerial roles further complicates the situation. Even if the initial process could select effective leaders, the dynamics of the managerial situation might make the selection invalid. Further, contrary to the conclusions of many studies, most leadership training today seems to assume that there is one best way to lead.

However, leadership training designed to help leaders or potential leaders identify the nature of the leadership situation appears to have potential in developing more effective leaders. Such training is not so much a process of changing individual traits as it is one of ensuring that the person is operating

FIGURE 15-11 Vroom and Yetton's Decision Model

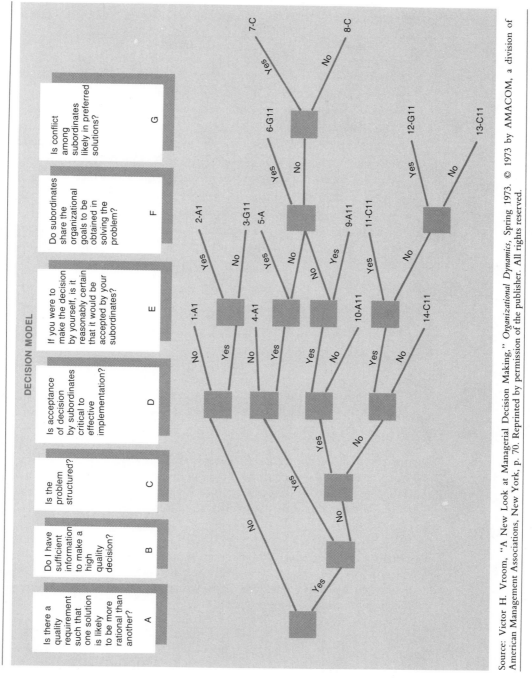

DECISION MODEL

A — Is there a quality requirement such that one solution is likely to be more rational than another?

B — Do I have sufficient information to make a high quality decision?

C — Is the problem structured?

D — Is acceptance of decision by subordinates critical to effective implementation?

E — If you were to make the decision by yourself, is it reasonably certain that it would be accepted by your subordinates?

F — Do subordinates share the organizational goals to be obtained in solving the problem?

G — Is conflict among subordinates likely in preferred solutions?

1-A1
2-A1
3-G11
4-A1
5-A
6-G11
7-C
8-C
9-A11
10-A11
11-C11
12-G11
13-C11
14-C11

Source: Victor H. Vroom, "A New Look at Managerial Decision Making," *Organizational Dynamics*, Spring 1973. © 1973 by AMACOM, a division of American Management Associations, New York, p. 70. Reprinted by permission of the publisher. All rights reserved.

in an appropriate situation or of teaching the individual how to act in a given situation. The following points on effective leadership can tentatively be made:

1. High consideration and initiating structure often provide a successful leadership style.
2. Under emergency or high-pressure situations, emphasis on initiating structure is desirable and often preferred by subordinates.
3. When the manager is the only information source for subordinates regarding their tasks, they often expect the manager to structure their behavior.
4. Subordinates have differing preferences regarding the degree of consideration and initiating structure exhibited by their managers.
5. Higher management often has set preferences regarding the leadership styles employed by lower-level managers.
6. Some managers can adjust their behavior to fit the situation; while others, in attempting to make this adjustment, appear to be fake and manipulative.

SUMMARY

LEARNING OBJECTIVE 1

Define Leadership.
Leadership is a process of influencing the activities of members of a group in performing their tasks of goal setting and goal achievement.

LEARNING OBJECTIVE 2

Discuss the Relationship between Power and Authority.
Power is the ability to command or apply force. It is not necessarily accomplished by authority. Authority, which exists in the formal organization, is the right to issue directives and expend resources.

LEARNING OBJECTIVE 3

Describe the Self-Fulfilling Prophecy in Management.
The self-fulfilling prophecy basically postulates that what a manager expects of subordinates and the way he or she treats subordinates largely determines their performance and career progress.

LEARNING OBJECTIVE 4

Define the Trait Theory of Leadership.
The trait theory of leadership emphasizes what the leader is like rather than what the leader does. Personality traits and physical characteristics are examined to differentiate leaders. Few studies have been able to support this theory.

LEARNING OBJECTIVE 5

List and Define the Basic Leadership Styles.

The autocratic leader makes most decisions for the group. The laissez-faire leader allows people within the group to make all decisions. The democratic leader guides and encourages the group to make decisions.

LEARNING OBJECTIVE 6

Understand the Managerial Grid.

The Managerial Grid is a two-dimensional framework rating a leader on the basis of concern for people and concern for production.

LEARNING OBJECTIVE 7

Define the Contingency Approach to Leadership.

The contingency approach to leadership defines two basic styles of leadership—task motivated and relationship motivated. In both highly favorable and highly unfavorable situations, a task-motivated leader was found to be more effective. In moderately favorable situations, a relationship-motivated leader was found to be more effective.

LEARNING OBJECTIVE 8

Explain the Path-Goal Theory of Leadership.

The path-goal theory of leadership attempts to define the relationships between a leader's behavior and the subordinates' performance and work activities. Leader behavior influences the motivation of subordinates when it makes the satisfaction of their needs contingent on successful performance; and it provides the guidance, support, and rewards needed for effective performance.

LEARNING OBJECTIVE 9

Define the Life-Cycle Theory of Leadership.

According to the life-cycle theory of leadership, as the maturity of followers increases, not only less and less structure but also less and less socioemotional support is needed in leader behavior.

LEARNING OBJECTIVE 10

List Some of the Lessons That Can Be Learned from Leadership Research.

The following lessons can be learned from leadership research:

High consideration and initiating structure often provide a successful leadership style.

Under emergency or high-pressure situations, emphasis on initiating structure is desirable and often preferred by subordinates.

When the manager is the only information source for subordinates regarding their tasks, they often expect the manager to structure their behavior.

Subordinates have differing preferences regarding the degree of consideration and initiating structure exhibited by their managers.

Higher management often has set preferences regarding the leadership styles employed by lower-level managers.

Some managers can adjust their behavior to fit the situation; while others, in attempting to make this adjustment, appear to be fake and manipulative.

REVIEW QUESTIONS

1. Define leadership. What is the source of a leader's authority?
2. Describe in detail the following three leadership styles:
    a. Autocratic.
    b. Laissez-faire.
    c. Democratic.
3. What was the purpose of the Ohio State leadership studies? What were the results of the Ohio State studies?
4. What was the purpose of the University of Michigan leadership studies? Explain the results of the Michigan studies.
5. Describe the Managerial Grid.
6. Describe three important forces, or factors, that Tannenbaum and Schmidt think should be considered in determining what leadership style is most effective.
7. What is Fiedler's contingency approach to leadership?
8. What is the path-goal theory of leader effectiveness?
9. What is the life-cycle theory of leadership?
10. What three variables determine the appropriateness of a given decision-making style in the Vroom and Yetton model?
11. Describe some of the implications of the studies on leadership for organizations and managers.

DISCUSSION QUESTIONS

1. Discuss the following statement: Leaders are born and cannot be developed.
2. Do you agree or disagree with this statement: Leaders must have courage. Why?
3. Do you think the variance in leadership styles of such people as Adolph Hitler, Franklin D. Roosevelt, and Martin Luther King, Jr., can be explained by any of the theories discussed in this chapter? Elaborate on your answer.
4. Explain what people mean when they use this statement: Leaders lead by example. Do you believe it? Explain your answer.

REFERENCES & ADDITIONAL READINGS

[1] For another view on Theory X and Theory Y, see T. C. Carbone, "Theory X and Theory Y Revisited," *Managerial Planning*, May–June 1981, pp. 24–27.

[2] J. D. Barrow, "The Variables of Leadership: A Review and Conceptual Framework," *Academy of Management Review*, April 1977, p. 232.

[3] Victor H. Vroom, "Leadership," in *Handbook of Industrial & Organizational Psychology,* ed. Marvin D. Dunnette (Skokie, Ill.: Rand McNally, 1976), p. 1531.

[4] Rensis Likert, *New Patterns of Management* (New York: McGraw-Hill, 1961).

[5] Robert R. Blake and Jane Srygley Mouton, *The New Managerial Grid* (Houston: Gulf Publishing, 1978); Robert R. Blake and Jane S. Mouton, "How to Choose a Leadership Style," *Training and Development Journal,* February 1982, pp. 38–45.

[6] C. L. Graeff, "The Situational Leadership Theory: A Critical Review," *Academy of Management Review,* April 1983, pp. 285–91.

[7] Robert Tannenbaum and Warren Schmidt, "How to Choose a Leadership Pattern," *Harvard Business Review,* July–August 1986, p. 129.

[8] Fred E. Fiedler, *A Theory of Leadership Effectiveness* (New York: McGraw-Hill, 1967).

[9] For more analysis on this subject, see Ramadhar Singh, "Leadership Style and Reward Allocation: Does Least Preferred Co-Worker Scale Measure Task and Relation Orientation?" *Organizational Behavior and Human Performance,* October 1983, pp. 178–97.

[10] For an in-depth analysis of the path-goal theory, see J. F. Schriesheim and C. A. Schriesheim, "Test of the Path-Goal Theory of Leadership and Some Suggested Directions for Future Research," *Personnel Psychology,* Summer 1980, pp. 349–71; and Janet Falk and Eric R. Wendler, "Dimensionality of Leader-Subordinate Interactions: A Path-Goal Investigation," *Organizational Behavior and Human Performance,* October 1982, pp. 241–64.

[11] Paul Hersey and Kenneth Blanchard, "Life-Cycle Theory of Leadership," *Training and Development Journal,* June 1979, pp. 94–100.

[12] Victor H. Vroom, "A New Look at Managerial Decision Making," *Organizational Dynamics,* Spring 1973, pp. 66–80; and Victor H. Vroom and Philip W. Yetton, *Leadership and Decision Making* (Pittsburgh: University of Pittsburg Press, 1973).

INCIDENT

Changes in the Plastics Division

Ed Sullivan was general manager of the Plastics Division of Warner Manufacturing Company. Eleven years ago, Ed hired Russell (Rusty) Means as general manager of the Plastics Division's two factories. Ed trained Rusty as a manager and feels that Rusty is a good manager, an opinion based largely on the fact that products are produced on schedule and are of such quality that few customers complain. In fact, for the past eight years, Ed has pretty much let Rusty run the factories independently.

Rusty believes strongly that his job is to see that production runs smoothly. He feels that work is work. Sometimes it is agreeable, sometimes disagreeable. If an employee doesn't like the work, he or she can either adjust or quit. Rusty, say the factory personnel, "runs things. He's firm and doesn't stand for any nonsense. Things are done by the book, or they are not done at all." The turnover in the factories is low; nearly every employee likes Rusty and feels that he knows his trade and that he stands up for them.

Two months ago, Ed Sullivan retired and his replacement Wallace Thomas took over as general manager of the Plastics Division. One of the first things Thomas did was call his key management people together and announce some major changes that he wanted to implement. These included: (1) bring the operative employees into the decision-making process; (2) establish a planning committee made up of three management members and three operative employees; (3) start a suggestion system; and (4) as quickly as possible, install a performance appraisal program agreeable to both management and the operative employees. Wallace also stated that he would be active in seeing that these projects would be implemented without delay.

After the meeting, Rusty was upset and decided to talk to Robert Mitchell, general manager of sales for the Plastics Division.

Rusty: Wallace is really going to change things, isn't he?

Robert: Yeah, maybe it's for the best. Things were a little lax under Ed.

Rusty: I liked them that way. Ed let you run your own shop. I'm afraid Wallace is going to be looking over my shoulder every minute.

Robert: Well, let's give him a chance. After all, some of the charges he's proposing sound good.

Rusty: Well, I can tell you our employees won't like them. Having them participate in making decisions and those other things are just fancy management stuff that won't work with our employees.

Questions

1. What different styles of leadership are shown in this case?

2. What style of leadership do you feel that Wallace will have to use with Rusty?

3. Do you agree with Rusty? Discuss.

EXERCISE

Insubordination?

T he company installed a new performance management system this year. You distributed the information and forms several weeks ago, and they were due to be completed two weeks ago. One manager reporting to you has not yet returned his. This morning, you ran into him in the parking lot and asked him about it. He reacted angrily with: "I haven't had time to do it—I don't have enough time to get my job done as it is, much less to take the time necessary to have my people write a bunch of meaningless information."

You asked him to stop by your office later to discuss it. As you think about how to handle this situation in the meeting, you consider several alternatives.

1. In view of his attitude and behavior, it clearly is appropriate to exercise your authority. Tell him, in no uncertain terms, that this must be done if he expects to continue as a supervisor.
2. Tell him why this program is important and use your best persuasion technique to sell him on doing it willingly.
3. Remind him that no salary increases, including his own, will be processed until the forms are completed. Establish another deadline and let him know you expect it to be done then.
4. Explain to him that appraising employee performance is a part of every supervisor's job and that he himself is being evaluated on his performance in implementing this program.
5. Tell him you understand the difficulties of his job and the shortage of time available to do it, but remind him that this is a mandatory program that has top management's backing.

Other alternatives may be open to you, but assume that these are the only ones you have considered. WITHOUT DISCUSSION with anyone, choose one of them and be prepared to defend your choice.

16 Appraising and Rewarding Performance

LEARNING OBJECTIVES

After studying this chapter, you should be able to:

1 Define performance appraisal.

2 Define performance.

3 Explain the determinants of performance.

4 List and define the nine major performance appraisal methods.

5 Discuss the common errors in making performance appraisals.

6 List some suggestions for making performance appraisal systems more acceptable legally.

7 Define compensation.

8 Explain pay equity.

9 Define job evaluation.

10 Describe wage surveys.

On the morning following each day's work, each workman was given a slip of paper informing him in detail just how much work he had done the day before, and the amount he had earned. This enabled him to measure his performance against his earnings while the details were fresh in his mind. Without this there would have been great dissatisfaction among those who failed to climb up to the task asked of them, and many would have gradually fallen off in their performance.

F R E D E R I C K   W .   T A Y L O R *

A ppraising and rewarding performance is one of management's most powerful tools for encouraging employees to work hard. As you will recall from Chapter 14, the relationship between performance and rewards is a critical component in the level of motivation of any employee.

In today's organizations, performance appraisal systems have undergone substantial changes from the method described above. The purpose of the first part of this chapter is to describe the methods used by organizations in appraising employee performance.

PERFORMANCE APPRAISAL: DEFINITION AND USES

Performance appraisal – communicating to employees how they are doing on the job and guiding their future level of effort and task direction.

Performance appraisal is a process that involves determining and communicating to an employee how he or she is performing the job and, ideally, establishing a plan of improvement. When properly conducted, performance appraisals not only let employees know how well they are performing, but should also influence their future level of effort and task direction. Effort should be enhanced if the employee is properly reinforced. The task perception of the employee should be clarified through the establishment of a plan for improvement.

One of the most common uses of performance appraisals is for making administrative decisions relating to salary increases, promotions, transfers, and sometimes demotions or terminations. For example, the present job performance of an employee is often the most significant consideration for determining whether to promote the person. While successful performance in the present job does not necessarily mean that an employee will be an effective

* F. W. Taylor, *Scientific Management* (New York: Harper & Row, 1911), p. 52.

performer in a higher-level job, performance appraisals do provide some predictive information.

Performance appraisal information can also provide needed input for determining both individual and organizational training and development needs. For example, it can be used to identify individual strengths and weaknesses. These data can then be used to help determine the organization's overall training and development needs. For an individual employee, a completed performance appraisal should include a plan outlining specific training and development needs.

Another important use of performance appraisals is to encourage performance improvement. In this regard, performance appraisals are used as a means of communicating to employees how they are doing and suggesting needed changes in behavior, attitude, skill, or knowledge. This type of feedback clarifies for employees the job expectations held by the manager. Often this feedback must be followed by coaching and training by the manager to guide an employee's work efforts.

A concern in organizations is how often performance appraisals should be conducted. One study indicated that annual performance appraisals are the most common.[1] However, there seems to be no real consensus on the question of how frequently performance appraisals should be done. The answer seems to be as often as necessary to let the employees know what kind of job they are doing and, if performance is not satisfactory, the measures that must be taken for improvement. For many employees, this cannot be accomplished through one annual performance appraisal. Therefore, it is recommended that informal performance appraisals be conducted two or three times a year in addition to the annual performance appraisal for most employees.

UNDERSTANDING PERFORMANCE

Performance refers to the degree of accomplishment of the tasks that make up an individual's job. It reflects how well an individual is fulfilling the requirements of a job. Often confused with effort, which refers to energy expended, performance is measured in terms of results. For example, a student may exert a great deal of effort in preparing for an examination and still make a poor grade. In such a case, the effort expended is high, yet the performance is low.

> **Performance –** degree of accomplishment of the tasks that make up an individual's job.

Determinants of Performance

Job performance is the net effect of an employee's effort as modified by abilities and role (or task) perceptions. This implies that performance in a given situation can be viewed as resulting from the interrelationships between effort, abilities, and role perceptions.

Effort – the energy (physical and/or mental) used by an individual in performing a task.

Abilities – stable personal characteristics used in performing job tasks.

Role (task) perceptions – the activities and behavior that people believe are necessary to perform job tasks.

Effort, which results from being motivated, refers to the amount of energy (physical and/or mental) used by an individual in performing a task. **Abilities** are personal characteristics used in performing a job. Abilities usually do not fluctuate widely over short periods of time. **Role (task) perceptions** refer to the direction(s) in which individuals believe they should channel their efforts on their jobs. The activities and behavior that people believe are necessary in the performance of their jobs define their role perceptions.

To attain an acceptable level of performance, a minimum level of proficiency must exist in each of the performance components. Similarly, the level of proficiency in any one of the performance components can place an upper boundary on performance. If employees put forth tremendous effort and have excellent abilities but lack a good understanding of their roles, performance will probably not be high in the eyes of their managers. Much work will be produced, but it will be misdirected. Likewise, an employee who puts forth a high degree of effort and understands the job but lacks ability probably will rate low on performance. A final possibility is the employee who has good ability and understanding of the role but is lazy and expends little effort. This employee's performance will also probably be low. Of course, an employee can compensate up to a point for a weakness in one area by being above average in one or both of the other areas. Managers at Work 16–1 defines performance standards for federal government employees.

Environmental Factors as Performance Obstacles

Other factors beyond the control of the employee can also stifle performance. Although such obstacles are sometimes used merely as excuses, they are often very real and should be recognized.

Some common potential performance obstacles include a lack of or conflicting demands on the subordinate's time, inadequate work facilities and equipment, restrictive policies that affect the job, lack of cooperation from others, type of supervision, temperature, lighting, noise, machine pacing, shifts, and luck.

Environmental factors should be viewed not as direct determinants of individual performance, but as modifying the effects of effort, ability, and direction (see Figure 16–1). For example, poor ventilation or worn-out equipment might very easily affect the effort exerted by an individual. Unclear policies or poor supervision can also produce misdirected effort. Similarly, a lack of training could result in underutilized abilities. One of management's greatest responsibilities is to provide employees with adequate working conditions and a supportive environment to eliminate or minimize performance obstacles.

PERFORMANCE APPRAISAL METHODS

This section will discuss each of the following performance appraisal methods:

1. Goal setting, or management by objectives.
2. Work standards approach.

MANAGERS AT WORK 16–1

U.S. Office of Personnel Management Defines Performance Standards

The U.S. Office of Personnel Management defines performance standards for federal agencies as "the expressed measures of the level of achievement established by management for the duties and responsibilities of a portion or group of positions. . . . (They) may include, but are not limited to elements (measurement factors) such as quantity, quality, and timeliness."

Several key words or phrases in this definition are further described as follows:

Expressed means that the standards must be explicit and written.

Measures of level of achievement means that standards should result in defining that performance at some rating level.

By management means that management is responsible for setting the standards.

for the duties and responsibilities of a position or group of positions, means that the standards can be tailored to individual job duties to allow for job differences.

Source: Adapted from Robert G. Pajer, "Performance Appraisal: A New Era for Federal Government Managers," *Personnel Administrator,* March 1984, p. 82.

3. Essay appraisal.
4. Critical-incident appraisal.
5. Graphic rating scale.
6. Checklist.
7. Behaviorally anchored rating scale (BARS).
8. Forced-choice rating.
9. Ranking methods.

One study, conducted for the American Management Association (AMA), of 588 organizations belonging to AMA's human resources, finance, marketing, and information systems divisions explored the frequency of use of the various appraisal methods. The method most frequently mentioned was goal setting (used by 85.9 percent). This was followed by written essay statements (81.5 percent), description of critical incidents (79.4 percent), graphic rating scales (64.8 percent), weighted checklists (56.4 percent), and behaviorally anchored rating scales (35 percent). The least used were paired comparisons (16.3 percent), forced choices (22.8 percent), and forced distribution (26.4 percent).[2]

F I G U R E 16–1   Environmental Factors That Modify Performance

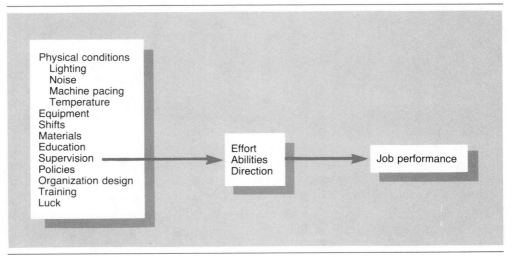

Goal Setting, or Management by Objectives (MBO)

Management by objectives (MBO) –system whereby the superior and subordinate jointly define the objectives and responsibilities of the subordinate's job; the superior uses them to evaluate the subordinates performance; and the subordinate's rewards are directly related to performance.

Management by objectives (MBO), which was introduced in Chapter 7, is an approach to performance appraisal based on setting goals. MBO is more commonly used for performance appraisal with professional and managerial employees. The following paragraphs reinforce and elaborate on the major points of MBO as related to performance appraisal.

The MBO process typically consists of:

1. Establishing clear and precisely defined statements of objectives for the work that is to be done by an employee.
2. Developing an action plan indicating how these objectives are to be achieved.
3. Allowing the employee to implement this action plan.
4. Measuring objective achievement.
5. Taking corrective action, when necessary.
6. Establishing new objectives for the future.

If an MBO system is to be successful, several requirements must be met. First, objectives should be quantifiable and measurable; objectives whose attainment cannot be measured or at least verified should be avoided where possible. Objectives should also be challenging and yet achievable, and they should be expressed in writing and in clear, concise, unambiguous language. Figure 16–2 lists some sample objectives that meet these requirements.

MBO also requires that employees have considerable input into the objective-setting process. Active participation by the employee is also essential in developing the action plan. Managers who set an employee's objectives without

F I G U R E 16–2   Sample Objectives for MBO

To answer all customer complaints in writing within three days of receipt of complaint.

To reduce order-processing time by two days within the next six months.

To implement the new computerized accounts receivable system by August 1.

input and then ask the employee, "You agree to these, don't you?" are unlikely to get high levels of employee commitment.

A final requirement for the successful use of MBO is that the objectives and action plan must serve as a basis for regular discussions between the manager and the employee concerning the employee's performance. These regular discussions provide an opportunity for the manager and employee to discuss the progress and to modify objectives when necessary.

Work Standards

The **work standards approach** to performance appraisal is most frequently used for production employees and is basically a form of goal setting for these employees. It involves setting a standard or expected level of output and then comparing each employee's performance to the standard. Generally speaking, work standards should reflect the normal output of a normal person. Work standards attempt to answer the question of what is a fair day's output? Several methods can be used for setting work standards. Some of the more common are summarized in Figure 16–3.

An advantage of the work standards approach is that the performance review is based on highly objective factors. Of course, to be effective, the

Work standards approach–a form of goal setting that involves setting a standard and then comparing the employee's performance to the standard.

F I G U R E 16–3   Frequently Used Methods for Setting Work Standards

METHOD	AREAS OF APPLICABILITY
Average production of work groups	When tasks performed by all individuals are the same or approximately the same.
Performance of specially selected individuals	When tasks performed by all individuals are basically the same and it would be cumbersome and time-consuming to use the group average.
Time study	Jobs involving repetitive tasks.
Work sampling	Noncyclical types of work where many different tasks are performed and there is no set pattern or cycle.
Expert opinion	When none of the more direct methods (described above) applies.

standards must be viewed by the affected employees as being fair. The most serious criticism of work standards is a lack of comparability of standards for different job categories.

Essay Appraisal

Essay appraisal – the employer/ rater describes the employee's performance in written narrative form.

The **essay appraisal** method requires the rater to describe an individual's performance in written narrative form. Instructions are often provided to the rater as to the topics that should be covered. A typical essay appraisal question might be: Describe, in your own words, this employee's performance, including quantity and quality of work, job knowledge, and ability to get along with other employees. What are the employee's strengths and weaknesses? The primary problem with essay appraisals is that their length and content can vary considerably, depending on the rater. For instance, one rater may write a lengthy statement describing an individual's potential and little about past performance. On the other hand, another rater might concentrate on the individual's past performance. Thus, essay appraisals are difficult to compare. The writing skill of the appraiser can also affect the appraisal. An effective writer can make an average employee look better than the actual performance warrants.

Critical-Incident Appraisal

Critical-incident appraisal – employer/rater keeps a diary of employees performance on the job including specific satisfactory and unsatisfactory incidences.

The **critical-incident appraisal** method requires the rater to keep a written record of incidents as they occur, involving job behaviors that illustrate both satisfactory and unsatisfactory performance of the person being rated. The incidents as they are recorded over time provide a basis for evaluating performance and providing feedback to the employee.

The main drawback to this approach is that the rater is required to jot down incidents regularly; this can be burdensome and time-consuming. Also, the definition of a critical incident is unclear and may be interpreted differently by different people. It is felt that this method can lead to friction between the manager and employees when the employees feel that the manager is keeping a "book" on them.

Graphic Rating Scale

Graphic rating scale – requires the employer/rater to indicate on a scale where the employee rates on work-related factors.

With the **graphic rating scale** method, the rater assesses an individual on factors such as quantity of work, dependability, job knowledge, attendance, accuracy of work, and cooperativeness. Graphic rating scales include both numerical ranges and written descriptions. Figure 16–4 gives an example of some of the items that might be included on a graphic rating scale that uses written descriptions.

F I G U R E   16-4   Sample Items on a Graphic Rating Scale Evaluation Form

Quantity of work (the amount of work an individual does in a workday)

( )	( )	( )	( )	( )
Does not meet minimum requirements.	Does just enough to get by.	Volume of work is satisfactory.	Very industrious, does more than is required.	Superior work production record.

Dependability (the ability to do required jobs with a minimum of supervision)

( )	( )	( )	( )	( )
Requires close supervision; is unreliable.	Sometimes requires prompting.	Usually completes necessary tasks with reasonable promptness.	Requires little supervision, is reliable.	Requires absolute minimum of supervision.

Job knowledge (information that an individual should have on work duties for satisfactory job performance)

( )	( )	( )	( )	( )
Poorly informed about work duties.	Lacks knowledge of some phases of job.	Moderately informed, can answer most questions about the job.	Understands all phases of job.	Has complete mastery of all phases of job.

Attendance (faithfulness in coming to work daily and conforming to work hours)

( )	( )	( )	( )	( )
Often absent without good excuse, or frequently reports for work late, or both.	Lax in attendance or reporting for work on time, or both.	Usually present and on time.	Very prompt, regular in attendance.	Always regular and prompt, volunteers for overtime when needed.

Accuracy (the correctness of work duties performed)

( )	( )	( )	( )	( )
Makes frequent errors.	Careless, often makes errors.	Usually accurate, makes only average number of mistakes.	Requires little supervision, is exact and precise most of the time.	Requires absolute minimum of supervision, is almost always accurate.

The graphic rating scale method is subject to some serious weaknesses. One potential weakness is that raters are unlikely to interpret written descriptions in the same manner, due to differences in background, experience, and personality. Another potential problem relates to the choice of rating categories. It is possible to choose categories that have little relationship to job performance or to omit categories that have a significant influence on job performance.

Checklist

In the **checklist** method, the rater answers yes or no to a series of questions concerning the employee's behavior. Figure 16-5 lists some typical questions. The checklist can also have varying weights assigned to each question.

Normally, the scoring key for the checklist method is kept by the human resource department; the rater is generally not aware of the weights associated

Checklist — employer/rater answers yes or no to a series of questions concerning the employee's behavior.

F I G U R E 16–5 Sample Checklist Questions

	YES	NO
1. Does the individual lose his or her temper in public?	———	———
2. Does the individual play favorites?	———	———
3. Does the individual praise employees in public when they have done a good job?	———	———
4. Does the employee volunteer to do special jobs?	———	———

with each question. But because raters can see the positive or negative connotation of each question, bias can be introduced. Additional drawbacks to the checklist method are that it is time-consuming to assemble the questions for each job category, a separate listing of questions must be developed for each different job category, and the checklist questions can have different meanings to different raters.

Behaviorally Anchored Rating Scales (BARS)

Behavior anchored rating scale (BARS) – method of performance appraisal that focuses on functional behaviors required to successfully perform a job.

The **behaviorally anchored rating scale (BARS)** method of performance appraisal is designed to assess behaviors required to successfully perform a job. The focus of BARS (and to some extent, the graphic rating scale method and checklist method) is not on performance outcomes but on functional behaviors demonstrated on the job. The assumption is that these functional behaviors will result in effective performance on the job. Managers at Work 16–2 shows how General Electric (GE) has attempted to overcome this problem in one of its performance appraisal systems.

Job dimension – broad categories of duties and responsibilities that make up a job.

To understand the use and development of BARS, several key terms must be clearly understood. First, most BARS use the term **job dimension** to mean those broad categories of duties and responsibilities that make up a job. Each job is likely to have several job dimensions, and separate scales must be developed for each one.

Figure 16–6 illustrates a BARS written for the job dimension found in many managerial jobs of planning, organizing, and scheduling project assignments and due dates. Scale values appear on the left side of the table and define specific categories of performance. Anchors, which appear on the right side of the table, are specific written statements of actual behaviors that, when they are exhibited on the job, indicate the level of performance on the scale opposite that particular anchor. As the anchor statements appear beside each of the scale values, they are said to "anchor" each of the scale values along the scale.

Rating performance using BARS requires the rater to read the list of anchors on each scale to find the group of anchors that best describes the employee's job behavior during the period being reviewed. The scale value opposite that group of anchors is then checked. This process is followed for all the

MANAGERS AT WORK 16-2

Performance Appraisal at GE's Circuit Protective Devices Department

In designing a new performance appraisal system for its Circuit Protective Devices Department, GE decided that the system should evaluate job behavior and job results separately. In other words, the evaluation was to address what was done separately from how it was done. What was done is evaluated by comparing work plans with accomplishments over the assessment period. The manager and employee complete work plans at the beginning of the performance period. Before the performance appraisal review, the employee documents actual accomplishments, which the manager then assesses and discusses with the employee.

How the work was done is evaluated in a job behaviors section of the appraisal document. This section consists of variables with descriptions of desired business behaviors. No point values are assigned to the various descriptions. Rather, space is provided for the manager to write down specific examples of the behaviors. The behavior section serves as an agenda for discussion of the employee's behavior.

Source: Adapted from Robert J. Butler and Lyle Yorks, "A New Appraisal System as Organizational Change: GE's Task Force Approach," *Personnel*, January–February 1984, pp. 34–36.

identified dimensions on the job. A total evaluation is obtained by combining the scale values checked for all the different job dimensions.

BARS are normally developed through a series of meetings attended by both managers and job incumbents. Three steps are usually followed:

1. Managers and job incumbents identify the relevant job dimensions for the job.
2. Managers and job incumbents write behavioral anchors for each of the job dimensions. As many anchors as possible should be written for each dimension.
3. Managers and job incumbents reach a consensus concerning the scale values that are to be used and the grouping of anchor statements for each scale value.

The use of BARS can result in several advantages. First, BARS are developed through the active participation of both managers and job incumbents. This increases the likelihood that the method will be accepted. Second, the anchors are developed from the observations and experiences of employees who actually perform the job. Finally, BARS can be used for providing specific feedback concerning an employee's job performance.

FIGURE 16–6   Example of a Behaviorally Anchored
Rating Scale

SCALE VALUES	ANCHORS
7 [ ] Excellent	Develops a comprehensive project plan, documents it well, obtains required approval, and distributes the plan to all concerned.
6 [ ] Very good	Plans, communicates, and observes milestones; states week by week where the project stands relative to plans. Maintains up-to-date charts of project accomplishments and backlogs and uses these to optimize any schedule modifications required. Experiences occasional minor operational problems but communicates effectively.
5 [ ] Good	Lays out all the parts of a job and schedules each part; seeks to beat schedule and will allow for slack. Satisfies customers' time constraints; time and cost overruns occur infrequently.
4 [ ] Average	Makes a list of due dates and revises them as the project progresses, usually adding unforeseen events; instigates frequent customer complaints. May have a sound plan, but does not keep track of milestones; does not report slippages in schedule or other problems as they occur.
3 [ ] Below average	Plans are poorly defined, unrealistic time schedules are common. Cannot plan more than a day or two ahead, has no concept of a realistic project due date.
2 [ ] Very poor	Has no plan or schedule of work segments to be performed. Does little or no planning for project assignments.
1 [ ] Unacceptable	Seldom, if ever, completes project, because of lack of planning, and does not seem to care. Fails consistently due to lack of planning and does not inquire about how to improve.

Source: C. E. Schneier and R. W. Beatty, "Developing Behaviorally Anchored Rating Scales (BARS)," *Personnel Administrator*, August 1979, p. 60.

One of the major drawbacks to the use of BARS is that they take considerable time and commitment to develop. Furthermore, separate forms must be developed for different jobs.[3]

Forced-Choice Rating

Forced-choice rating—employer/rater ranks a set of statements describing how an employee has carried out his responsibilities. The statements are usually assigned weights unknown to the rater; human resource department usually applies the weights and computes the scores.

Many variations of the **forced-choice rating** method exist. However, the most common practice requires the rater to rank a set of statements describing how an employee carries out the duties and responsibilities of the job. (Figure 16–7 illustrates a group of forced-choice statements.) The statements are nor-

F I G U R E 16–7   Sample Forced-Choice Set of Statements

Instructions: Rank the following statements according to how they describe the manner in which this employee carries out duties and responsibilities. Rank 1 should be given to the most descriptive, and Rank 4 to the least descriptive. No ties are allowed.

RANK	DESCRIPTION
————	Has complete mastery of all phases of job.
————	Shows superior ability to express self.
————	Requires close supervision.
————	Careless and makes recurrent errors.

mally weighted, and the weights are not generally known to the rater. After the rater ranks all of the forced-choice statements, the human resource department applies the weights and computes a score.

This method attempts to eliminate rater bias by forcing the rater to rank statements that may be seemingly indistinguishable or unrelated. However, it has been reported that the forced-choice method tends to irritate raters, who feel they are not being trusted. Furthermore, the results of the forced-choice appraisal can be difficult to communicate to employees.

Ranking Methods

When it becomes necessary to compare the performance of two or more individuals, **ranking methods** can be used. Three of the more commonly used ranking methods are alternation, paired comparison, and forced distribution.

Ranking methods – used to compare the performances of two or more individuals.

Alternation Ranking. Using this ranking method, the names of the individuals who are to be rated are listed down the left side of a sheet of paper. The rater is then asked to choose the most valuable employee on the list, cross that name off the left-hand list, and put it at the top of the column on the right side of the paper. The rater is then asked to select and cross off the name of the "least valuable" employee from the left-hand column and move it to the bottom of the right-hand column. The rater then repeats this process for all of the names on the left-hand side of the paper. The resulting list of names in the right-hand column gives a ranking of the employees from most to least valuable.

Paired Comparison Ranking. This method is best illustrated with an example. Suppose a rater is to evaluate six employees. The names of these individuals are listed on the left side of a sheet of paper. The rater then compares the first employee with the second employee on a chosen performance criterion, such as quantity of work. If the rater feels that the first employee has produced more work than the second employee, a check mark would be placed by the first employee's name. The first employee would then be compared to the third, fourth, fifth, and sixth employee on the same performance criterion. A check mark would be placed by the name of the employee who had produced the most work in each of these paired comparisons. The process is repeated until each worker is compared to every other worker on all of the chosen performance criteria. The employee with the most check marks is considered to be the best performer. Likewise, the employee with the least number of check marks is the lowest performer. One major problem with the paired comparison method is that it becomes unwieldy when comparing large numbers of employees.

Forced Distribution. This method requires the rater to compare the performance of employees and place a certain percentage of employees at various performance levels. It assumes that the performance level in a group of employees will be distributed according to a bell-shaped, or "normal," curve. Figure 16–8 illustrates how the forced-distribution method works. The rater is required to rate 60 percent of the employees as meeting expectations, 20 percent as exceeding expectations, and 20 percent as not meeting expectations.

One problem with the forced-distribution method is that in small groups of employees, a bell-shaped distribution of performance may not be applicable. Even where the distribution may approximate a normal curve, it is probably not a perfect curve. This means that some employees will probably not be rated accurately. Also, ranking methods are dramatically different from the other methods in that one individual's performance evaluation is a function of the performance of other employees in the job.

F I G U R E   16–8   Forced Distribution Curve

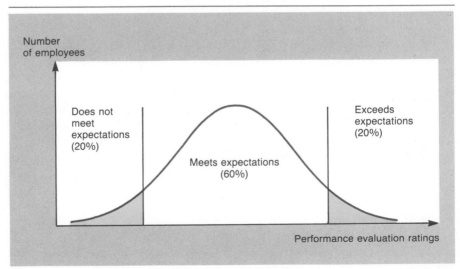

POTENTIAL ERRORS IN PERFORMANCE APPRAISALS

Several common errors have been identified in performance appraisals. **Leniency** is the grouping of ratings at the positive end instead of spreading them throughout the performance scale. **Central tendency** is the rating of all or most employees in the middle of the scale. Leniency and central tendency errors make it difficult if not impossible to separate the good performers from the poor performers. In addition, these errors make it difficult to compare ratings from different raters. For example, it is possible for a good performer who is evaluated by a manager committing central tendency errors to receive a lower rating than a poor performer who is rated by a manager committing leniency errors.

Another common error in performance appraisals is the **halo effect.**[4] This occurs when managers allow a single prominent characteristic of an employee to influence their judgment on each separate item in the performance appraisal. This often results in the employee receiving approximately the same rating on every item.

Personal preferences, prejudices, and biases can also cause errors in performance appraisals. Managers with biases or prejudices tend to look for employee behaviors that conform to their biases. Appearance, social status, dress, race, and sex have influenced many performance appraisals. Managers have also allowed first impressions to influence later judgments of an employee. First impressions are only a sample of behavior; however, people tend to retain these impressions even when faced with contradictory evidence.

Leniency – instead of spreading ratings throughout the performance scale they are grouped at the positive end.

Central tendency – where ratings for all or most employees are positioned in the middle of the scale.

Halo effect – occurs when managers let one prominent characteristic of an employee dominate their judgment on some or all traits.

OVERCOMING ERRORS IN PERFORMANCE APPRAISALS

As can be seen from the above discussion, the potential for errors in performance appraisals is great. One approach to overcoming these errors is to make refinements in the design of appraisal methods. For example, it could be argued that the forced-distribution method of performance appraisal attempts to overcome the errors of leniency and central tendency. In addition, behaviorally anchored rating scales are designed to reduce halo, leniency, and central tendency errors, because managers have specific examples of performance against which an employee is to be evaluated. Unfortunately, because refined instruments frequently do not overcome all the obstacles, it does not appear likely that refining appraisal instruments will totally overcome errors in performance appraisals.

A more promising approach to overcoming errors in performance appraisals is to improve the skills of raters. Suggestions on the specific training that should be given to raters are often vague, but they normally emphasize that

MANAGERS AT WORK 16–3

Performance Appraisal Training at Martin Marietta

Martin Marietta has developed a modular training program to teach its managers how to conduct performance appraisals. The program consists of the following five training modules:

Module 1: Introduction

1. Course objectives.
2. Outline.
3. Definition of terms.

Module 2: Purpose of performance appraisal

1. Purpose.
2. Legalities.
3. Uses of performance appraisal information in other areas of human resource management.
4. Attitude and approaches.
5. Performance appraisal and compensation.

Module 3: Components of a performance appraisal

1. Orientation.
2. Incident files.
3. Counseling sessions.
4. Self-appraisal.
5. Job description.
6. Objectives.
7. Job factors/competencies.
8. Development needs and actions.
9. Consistent documentation.
10. Summary and rating.

Module 4: Process of performance appraisal

1. Overview.
2. Techniques.

Module 5: Performance appraisal role play and practice

Source: Adapted from Virginia Bianco, "In Praise of Performance," *Personnel Journal,* June 1984, pp. 40–44.

raters should be given training to observe behavior more accurately and judge it fairly. One study found that training raters in how to keep a diary of critical incidents significantly reduced leniency and halo errors.[5]

More research is needed before a definitive set of topics for rater training can be established. However, at a minimum, raters should receive training in: (1) the performance appraisal method(s) used by the company; (2) the importance of the rater's role in the total appraisal process; (3) the use of performance appraisal information; and (4) the communication skills necessary to provide feedback to the employee. Managers at Work 16–3 outlines the topics covered in Martin Marietta's performance appraisal training program.

PROVIDING FEEDBACK THROUGH THE APPRAISAL INTERVIEW

After one of the previously discussed methods for developing an employee's performance appraisal has been used, the results must be communicated to the employee. Unless this interview is properly conducted, it can and frequently does result in an unpleasant experience for both manager and employee.

Some of the more important factors influencing success or failure of appraisal interviews are:

1. The more employees participate in the appraisal process, the more satisfied they are with the appraisal interview and with the manager, and the more likely are performance improvements objectives to be accepted and met.

2. The more a manager uses positive motivational techniques (e.g., recognizing and praising good performance), the more satisfied the employee is likely to be with the appraisal interview and with the manager.

3. The mutual setting by the manager and the employee of specific performance improvement objectives results in more improvement in performance than does a general discussion or criticism.

4. Discussing and solving problems that may be hampering the employee's current job performance improve the employee's performance.

5. Areas of job performance needing improvement that are most heavily criticized are less likely to be improved than similar areas of job performance that are less heavily criticized.

6. The more employees are allowed to voice their opinions during the interview, the more satisfied they feel with the interview.

7. The amount of thought and preparation employees independently devote before the interview increases the benefits of the interview.

8. The more the employee perceives that performance appraisal results are tied to organizational rewards, the more beneficial is the interview.

Many of the variables that have been identified and associated with positive outcomes from performance appraisal interviews are behaviors and skills that can be taught to managers responsible for conducting the interviews. The human resource department should play a key role in the development and implementation of these training programs.

PERFORMANCE APPRAISAL AND THE LAW

Title VII of the Civil Rights Act permits the use of a bona fide performance appraisal system. Performance appraisal systems are not generally considered to be bona fide when their application results in adverse effects on minorities, women, or older employees.

A number of court cases have ruled that performance appraisal systems used by organizations were discriminatory and not job related. In one case involving layoffs, *Brito et al.* v. *Zia Company,*[6] Spanish-surnamed workers were reinstated with back pay because the company had used a performance appraisal system of unknown validity in an uncontrolled and unstandardized manner. In *Mistretta* v. *Sandia Corporation,* performance appraisals were used as the main basis of layoff decisions affecting a disproportionate number of older employees.[7] The judge awarded the plaintiffs double damages plus all court costs. Generally, it can be stated that performance appraisal systems may be illegal if: the method of appraisal is not job related; performance standards are not derived through careful job analysis; the number of performance observations is inadequate; ratings are based on an evaluation of subjective or vague factors; raters are biased; or rating conditions are uncontrolled or unstandardized.

Many suggestions have been offered for making performance appraisal systems more legally acceptable. Some of these include: (1) providing written instructions to raters for the completion of evaluations; (2) deriving the content of the appraisal system from job analysis; and (3) ensuring that the results of the appraisals are reviewed by employees.[8] Unfortunately, it appears that appraisal systems in many organizations lag behind these requirements.[9] Human resource departments must play a key role in the development and implementation of effective and legal performance appraisal systems.

REWARDING EMPLOYEES

The previously described systems and methods of appraising employee performance are useful only if they are closely tied to the organization's reward system. Appraising performance without having a system that ties the results of the appraisal to the organization's reward system creates an environment where employees are poorly motivated. The purpose of the remainder of this chapter is to describe systems used by organizations to reward employees.

COMPENSATION

Compensation – the extrinsic rewards employees receive in exchange for their work.

Compensation refers to the extrinsic rewards that employees receive in exchange for their work. Usually, compensation is composed of the base wage or salary, any incentives or bonuses, and any benefits. The base wage or salary is the hourly, weekly, or monthly pay that employees receive for their work.

F I G U R E 16–9   Components of Employee Compensation

BASE WAGE OR SALARY	INCENTIVES	BENEFITS
Hourly wage	Bonuses	Paid vacation
Weekly, monthly, or annual salary	Commissions	Health insurance
	Profit sharing	Life insurance
Overtime pay	Piece-rate plans	Retirement pension

Incentives are rewards offered in addition to the base wage or salary and are usually directly related to performance. Benefits are rewards that employees receive due to their employment and position with an organization. Paid vacations, health insurance, and retirement plans are examples of benefits. Figure 16–9 presents some examples of the different types of compensation. An organization's **compensation system** consists of the policies, procedures, and rules that it follows in determining employee compensation.

Compensation system—policies, procedures, and rules the organization uses to determine employee compensation.

The Importance of Fair Pay

Employee motivation is closely related to the types of rewards offered and their method of disbursement. There is much debate over the motivational aspect of pay. But there is little doubt that inadequate pay can have a very negative impact on an organization. Figure 16–10 presents a simple model of the reactions of employees dissatisfied with their pay. According to this model, pay dissatisfaction can influence people's feelings about their jobs in two ways: (1) it can increase the desire for more money; (2) it can lower the attractiveness of the job. An individual with an increased desire for more money is likely to engage in actions that can increase pay. These actions might include joining a union, looking for another job, performing better, or going on strike. Except for performing better, all of the actions are generally classified by management as being undesirable. Better performance happens only in those cases where pay is perceived as being directly related to performance.

On the other hand, when the job becomes less attractive, the employee is more likely to be absent or tardy and become dissatisfied with the job itself. Thus, while its importance may vary somewhat from situation to situation, pay satisfaction can and usually does have a strong impact on both individual and organizational performance.

Pay Equity

The question of fair pay involves two general factors: (1) what the employee is being paid for doing his or her job compared to what other employees in

F I G U R E **16–10**   Model of the Consequences of Pay Dissatisfaction

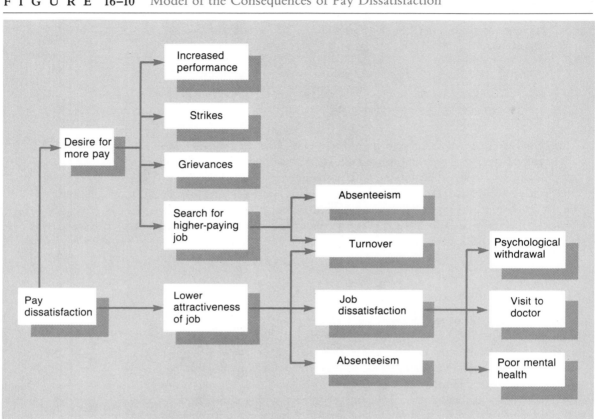

Source: E. E. Lawler III, *Pay and Organizational Effectiveness: A Psychological View* (New York: McGraw-Hill, 1971), p. 253.

Internal equity – what an employee is paid compared to what other employees in the organization are paid to do their jobs.

External equity – what employees are paid compared to employees performing similar jobs in other organizations.

the same organization are being paid to do their jobs **(internal equity);** and (2) what employees in other organizations are being paid for performing similar jobs **(external equity).** It is not at all unusual for an individual to feel good about external equity and bad about internal equity, or vice versa. For example, employees may feel very good about their pay compared to what their friends working in other organizations are making. However, a person may be very unhappy about his or her pay relative to the pay of several other people in the same organization.

If organizations are to avoid discontent with pay, employees must be convinced that both internal and external equity exist. A sound job evaluation system is usually the best method for ensuring internal equity. External equity is usually established through wage surveys.

FIGURE 16–11 Potential Uses of Job Evaluations

To provide a more workable internal wage structure to simplify and make rational the relatively chaotic wage structure resulting from chance, custom, and such individual factors as favoritism.

To provide an agreed-upon device for setting rates for new or changed jobs.

To provide a means whereby realistic comparisons may be made of the wage and salary rates of different organizations.

To provide a base for measuring individual performance.

To reduce grievances over wage and salary rates and provide an agreed-upon means for solving those disputes.

To provide incentives for employees to strive for higher-level jobs.

To provide facts for wage negotiations.

To provide facts on job relationships for use in selection, training, transfers, and promotions.

Source: Adapted from David W. Belcher, *Compensation Administration,* © 1974, pp. 91–92. Reprinted by permission of Prentice-Hall, Inc., Englewood Cliffs, N.J.

JOB EVALUATION

Job evaluation is a systematic determination of the value of each job in relation to other jobs in the organization. It is used for designing a pay structure, not for appraising the performance of employees. The general idea is to list a job's requirements and contribution to the organization and then to classify it according to its importance. For instance, a design engineer's job would be more complex and potentially contribute more than that of an assembler of the designed product. Although both jobs are important, the relative worth of each must be established. The main purpose of job evaluation is to establish the relative worth of jobs; however, it can serve several other purposes. Figure 16–11 presents a list of potential uses.

The first step in a job evaluation program is to gather information on the jobs in question. Normally, information comes from current job descriptions. If they do not exist, then it is usually necessary to analyze the jobs and create up-to-date descriptions. Then, the factor or factors are identified that will be used in determining the worth of different jobs to the organization. Factors often used are skill, responsibility, and working conditions.

The job evaluation process also involves developing and implementing a plan for using the chosen factors to evaluate the relative worth of the different jobs. Such a plan should always place jobs requiring more of the factors at a higher level in the job hierarchy than jobs requiring fewer of the factors.

It is expensive and difficult to keep job evaluations up to date. For example, the content of management and professional jobs can change significantly as

Job evaluation – systematic determination of the value of each job in relation to other jobs in the organization.

incumbents change. Also, job evaluation and performance appraisal should not be confused. Job evaluation enables management to establish salary ranges for different jobs within an organization. Where an employee falls within a salary range should be determined by performance as rated by the performance appraisal process.

WAGE SURVEYS

Wage survey – survey of selected organizations to provide a comparison of reliable information on the policies, practices, and methods of payment.

Wage surveys are performed to collect reliable information on the policies, practices, and methods of wage payment from selected organizations in a given geographic location or particular type of industry so that comparisons can be made. Wage surveys are the primary method used to ensure external equity in an organization's wage and salary system. Data may be gathered from a variety of sources. The Bureau of Labor Statistics of the U.S. Department of Labor regularly publishes wage data broken down by geographic area, industry, and occupation. Industry and employee associations sometimes conduct surveys and publish their results. Trade magazines also may contain wage survey information. Beside using these sources, many organizations design and conduct their own surveys. To design a wage survey, the jobs, area, and organizations to be studied must be determined, as must the method for gathering data.

A geographic area, an industry type, or a combination of the two may be surveyed. The size of the geographic area, the cost-of-living index for the area, and similar factors define the scope of the survey. The organizations to be surveyed are often competitors or others who employ similar types of workers. The most important and most respected organizations in the area should be chosen from among those willing to cooperate.

The three basic methods of collecting wage data are personal interviews, telephone interviews, and mailed questionnaires. The most reliable and most costly method is the personal interview. Mailed questionnaires are probably used most often. However, they should only be used to survey jobs that have a uniform meaning throughout the industry. If there is any doubt concerning the definition of a job, the responses may be unreliable. Another potential problem with mailed questionnaires is that they can be answered by someone who is not thoroughly familiar with the wage structure. The telephone method, which yields quick but often incomplete information, may be used to clarify responses to mailed questionnaires.

PAY SECRECY

Some organizations have a policy of keeping pay-related information secret. Pay secrecy is usually used to avoid any discontent that might result from employees knowing what others are being paid. Further, many employees (especially high achievers) feel strongly that their pay is nobody else's business.

Pay secrecy makes it difficult for employees to determine whether pay is related to performance. Also, it does not eliminate pay comparisons, but it may: (1) cause employees to overestimate the pay of their peers, and (2) cause employees to underestimate the pay of supervisors. Both situations can cause unnecessary feelings of discontent.

A good compromise on the issue of pay secrecy is to disclose the pay ranges for various job levels within the organization. This approach clearly gives the general ranges of pay for different jobs without telling just what any specific employee makes.

INCENTIVE PAY PLANS

Incentive pay plans relate pay to performance in order to reward above-average performance rapidly and directly. Good performance can be rewarded through the base wage or salary structure. But these rewards are often subject to delays and other restrictions. Therefore, they often are not viewed by the recipients as being directly related to performance. Incentive pay plans attempt to strengthen the performance–reward relationship and thus motivate the affected employees.

There are two basic requirements for an effective incentive plan.[10] First, if incentives are to be based on performance, then employees must feel that performance is accurately and fairly evaluated. Naturally, this is easier in some situations than in others. For example, the performance of a commissioned salesperson is usually easy to measure. On the other hand, the performance of a middle manager is often difficult to measure. A key issue in performance measurement is the degree of trust in management. If the employees distrust management, then it is almost impossible to establish a sound performance appraisal system.

The second requirement is that incentives (rewards) must be based on performance. This may seem obvious, yet it is often violated. Employees must see a relationship between what they do and what they get. Individual-based incentive plans require that employees perceive a direct relationship between their own performance and the rewards that follow. Group-based plans require employees to perceive a relationship between the group's performance and the subsequent rewards of the group's members. Furthermore, the group members must believe that their individual performances have an impact on the group's overall performance. Organization-based plans have the same basic requirements as group plans. Employees must see a relationship between the organization's performance and their individual rewards. Also, employees must believe that their individual performances affect the performance of the organization. Managers at Work 16–4 shows how incentives are at work in China.

MANAGERS AT WORK 16–4

Cotton Mills and Incentives in the People's Republic of China

Cotton Textile Mill No. 4 of Northwest China sits in the middle of Xian, a city of 2.5 million, some 550 miles southwest of Beijing. Xian enjoys a measure of fame as the site of a fascinating archaeological find—thousands of life-sized terra cotta warriors and horses guarding the tomb of Qin Shi Huangdi, an emperor who ruled in the third centruy B.C. and is credited with unifying China.

Cotton Textile Mill No. 4 has more than a touch of an American company town of yesteryear about it. Besides several manufacturing buildings, the compound boasts company-operated stores, apartment buildings, schools, and a medical clinic. Other paternalistic "fringes" abound. Company-sponsored recreational activities for workers range from a variety of athletic events, through amateur singing, dancing and opera performances, to a library. If a worker wants a big-ticket item but lacks the cash to buy, the company store will work out an installment plan.

The company also has an incentive pay plan. The average bonus comes to 20 yuan a month. This sum may seem low, but it takes on considerable luster when one learns that the average monthly wage at Mill No. 4 runs to only 60 yuan. For outstanding work, an employee may get a bonus as high as 30 to 40 yuan.

Source: Adapted from Edward R. Cony, "Beansprout Capitalism," *Barron's*, June 14, 1982, pp. 20, 32.

SUMMARY

LEARNING OBJECTIVE 1

Define Performance Appraisal.

Performance appraisal is a process that involves determining and communicating to an employee how he or she is performing the job and (ideally) establishing a plan of improvement.

LEARNING OBJECTIVE 2

Define Performance.

Performance refers to the degree of accomplishment of the tasks that make up an individual's job.

LEARNING OBJECTIVE 3

Explain the Determinants of Performance.

Job performance is the net effect of an employee's efforts as modified by abilities and role (or task) perceptions.

LEARNING OBJECTIVE 4

List and Define the Nine Major Performance Appraisal Methods.

1. Management by objectives consists of establishing clear and precisely defined statements of objectives for the work that is to be done by an employee; developing an action plan indicating how these objectives are to be achieved; allowing the employee to implement this action plan; measuring objective achievement; taking corrective action, when necessary; and establishing new objectives for the future.

2. The work standards approach involves setting a standard or expected level of output and then comparing each employee's performance to standard.

3. The essay appraisal requires the rater to describe an individual's performance in written narrative form.

4. The critical-incident appraisal method requires the rater to keep a written record of incidents as they occur, involving job behaviors that illustrate both satisfactory and unsatisfactory performance of the person being rated.

5. The graphic rating scale requires the rater to assess an individual on factors such as quantity of work, dependability, job knowledge, attendance, accuracy of work, and cooperativeness.

6. The checklist method requires the rater to answer yes or no to a series of questions concerning the employee's behavior.

7. The behaviorally anchored rating scale (BARS) method is designed to assess behaviors required to successfully perform a job.

8. The forced-choice rating method requires the rater to rank a set of statements describing how an employee carries out the duties and responsibilities of the job.

9. Ranking methods (alternation, paired comparison, and forced distribution) require that the rater compare the performance of an employee to the performance of other employees.

LEARNING OBJECTIVE 5

Discuss the Common Errors in Making Performance Appraisals.

Leniency is the grouping of ratings at the positive end instead of spreading them throughout the performance scale. Central tendency is the rating of all or most employees in the middle of the performance scale. The halo effect occurs when managers allow a single prominent characteristic of an employee to influence their judgment on each separate item in the performance appraisal.

LEARNING OBJECTIVE 6

List Some Suggestions for Making Performance Appraisal Systems More Acceptable Legally.

Suggestions include providing written instructions to raters for the completion of evaluations; deriving the content of the appraisal system from job analysis; and ensuring that the results of the appraisals are reviewed by employees.

LEARNING OBJECTIVE 7

Define Compensation.

Compensation refers to the extrinsic rewards that employees receive in exchange for their work.

LEARNING OBJECTIVE 8

Explain Pay Equity.

Pay equity consists of: (1) what the employee is being paid for doing his or her job compared to what other employees in the same organization are being paid to do their jobs (internal equity); and (2) what employees in other organizations are being paid for performing similar jobs (external equity).

LEARNING OBJECTIVE 9

Define Job Evaluation.

Job evaluation is a systematic determination of the value of each job in relation to other jobs in the organization.

LEARNING OBJECTIVE 10

Describe Wage Surveys.

Wage surveys are performed to collect reliable information on the policies, practices, and methods of wage payment from selected organizations in a geographic location or particular type of industry so that comparisons can be made.

REVIEW QUESTIONS

1. Define performance appraisal.
2. What is performance? What factors influence an employee's level of performance?
3. Give at least three uses of performance appraisal information.
4. Describe the following methods used in performance appraisal:

a. Management by objectives.
b. Work standards.
c. Essay.
d. Critical-incident.
e. Graphic rating scale.
f. Checklist.
g. Behaviorally anchored rating scale.

    h. Forced-choice rating.
    i. Ranking methods.
5. Define the following types of performance appraisal errors:
    a. Leniency.
    b. Central tendency.
    c. Halo effect.
6. Outline some of the conditions associated with the success or failure of appraisal interviews.

7. Describe some of the conditions that might make a performance appraisal system illegal.
8. Define the three basic components of compensation and give examples of each.
9. What is job evaluation?
10. What are wage surveys and how might they be conducted?
11. What are two basic requirements for an incentive plan to be effective?

DISCUSSION QUESTIONS

1. Describe your thoughts on discussing salary raises and promotions during the performance appraisal interview.
2. Was your last exam a performance appraisal? Use your last exam to discuss both the reasons for using performance appraisals and their limitations.
3. It has been said that incentive plans only

work for a relatively short time. Do you agree or disagree? Why?
4. Suppose your organization's recently completed wage survey showed that pay rates of several jobs were either less than or more than they should be. How might you bring these jobs into line?

REFERENCES & ADDITIONAL READINGS

[1] Mary Zippo and Marc Miller, "Performance Appraisal: Current Practices and Techniques," *Personnel,* May–June 1984, pp. 57–59.

[2] Ibid., p. 58.

[3] For a further discussion of BARS, see P. O. Kingstrom and A. R. Bass, "A Critical Analysis of Studies Comparing Behaviorally Anchored Rating Scales (BARS) and Other Rating Formats," *Personnel Psychology* 34 (1981), pp. 263–89.

[4] For a more in-depth discussion of the halo effect, see R. Jacobs and S. W. J. Kozlowski, "A Closer Look at Halo Error in Performance Ratings," *Academy of Management Journal,* March 1985, pp. 201–12.

[5] H. J. Bernardin and M. R. Buckley, "Strate-

gies in Rater Training," *Academy of Management Review* 6 (1981), pp. 205–12.

[6] *Brito et al.* v. *Zia Company,* 478 F.2d. 1200 (1973).

[7] H. B. Winstanley, "Legal and Ethical Issues in Performance Appraisals," *Harvard Business Review,* November–December 1980, p. 188.

[8] H. S. Field and W. H. Holley, "The Relationship of Performance Appraisal System Characteristics to Verdicts in Selected Employment Discrimination Cases," *Academy of Management Journal,* June 1982, pp. 399–402.

[9] Ibid., p. 403.

[10] J. G. Goodale and M. W. Mouser, "Developing and Auditing a Merit Pay System," *Personnel Journal,* May 1981, p. 391.

INCIDENT

Does Money Motivate?

About four months ago, Judy Holcomb was promoted to supervisor of the Claims Department for a large, Eastern insurance company. It is now time for all supervisors to make their annual salary increase recommendations. Judy doesn't feel comfortable in making these recommendations since she has only been in her job for a short time. To further complicate the situation, the former supervisor has left the company and is unavailable for consultation.

There are no formal company restrictions on the kind of raises that can be given, but Judy's boss has said that the total amount of money available to Judy for raises would be 8 percent of Judy's payroll for the past year. In other words, if the sum total of the salaries for all of Judy's employees was $100,000, then Judy would have $8,000 to allocate for raises. Judy is free to distribute the raises just about any way she wants, within reason.

Summarized below is the best information on her employees that Judy can find from the files of the former supervisor of the Claims Department. This information is supplemented by feelings Judy has developed during her short time as supervisor.

John Thompson. John has been with Judy's department for only five months. In fact, he was hired just before Judy was promoted into the supervisor's job. John is single and seems to be a carefree bachelor. His job performance, so far, has been above average, but Judy has received some negative comments about John from his co-workers. Present salary, $18,000.

Carole Wilson. Carole has been on the job for three years. Her previous performance appraisals have indicated superior performance. However, Judy does not feel that the previous evaluations are accurate. She feels that Carole's performance is, at best, average. Carole appears to be well liked by all of her co-workers. Just last year, she became widowed and is presently the sole support for her five-year-old child. Present salary: $19,000.

Evelyn Roth: Evelyn has been on the job for four years. Her previous performance appraisals were all average. In addition, she had received below-average increases for the past two years. However, Evelyn recently approached Judy and told her that she feels she was discriminated against in the past due to both her age and sex. Judy feels that Evelyn's work so far has been satisfactory but not superior. Most employees don't seem to sympathize with Evelyn's accusations of sex and age discrimination. Present salary: $17,000.

Jane Simmons. As far as Judy can tell, Jane is one of her best employees. Her previous performance appraisals also indicate that she is a superior performer. Judy knows that Jane badly needs a substantial salary increase due to some personal problems. In addition, all of Judy's employees are aware of Jane's problems. She appears to be well respected by her co-workers. Present salary: $18,500.

Bob Tyson.   Bob has been performing his present job for eight years. The job is very technical, and he would be difficult to replace. However, as far as Judy can discern, Bob is not a good worker. He is irritable and hard to work with. In spite of this, Bob has received above-average pay increases for the past two years. Present salary: $20,000.

Questions

1. Indicate the size of the raise that you would give each of these employees.

2. What criteria did you use in determining the size of the raise?

3. What do you think would be the feelings of the other people in the group if they should find out what raises you recommend?

4. Do you feel that the employees would eventually find out what raises others received? Would it matter?

EXERCISE

Developing a Performance Appraisal System

A large public utility has been having difficulty with its performance evaluation program. The organization has an evaluation program by which all operating employees and clerical employees are evaluated semiannually by their supervisors. The form that they have been using is given in Exhibit 1. It has been in use for 10 years. The form is scored as follows: excellent = 5; above average = 4; average = 3; below average = 2; and poor = 1. The scores for each facet are entered in the right-hand column and are totaled for an overall evaluation score.

In the procedure used, each supervisor rates each employee on July 30 and January 30. The supervisor discusses the rating with the employee and then sends the rating to the personnel department. Each rating is placed in

E X H I B I T 1   Performance Evaluation Form

PERFORMANCE EVALUATION

Supervisors: When you are asked to do so by the personnel department, please complete this form on each of your employees. The supervisor who is responsible for 75 percent or more of an employee's work should complete this form on him or her. Please evaluate each facet of the employee separately.

FACET	RATING					SCORE
Quality of work	Excellent	Above average	Average	Below average	Poor	
Quality of work	Poor	Below average	Average	Above average	Excellent	
Dependability at work	Excellent	Above average	Average	Below average	Poor	
Initiative at work	Poor	Below average	Average	Above average	Excellent	
Cooperativeness	Excellent	Above average	Average	Below average	Poor	
Getting along with co-workers	Poor	Below average	Average	Above average	Excellent	

Total _____

Supervisor's signature _____

Employee name _____

Employee number _____

the employee's personnel file. If promotions come up, the cumulative ratings are considered at that time. The ratings are also supposed to be used as a check when raises are given.

The system was designed by Joanna Kyle, the personnel manager who retired two years ago. Her replacement was Eugene Meyer. Meyer graduated 15 years ago with a degree in commerce from the University of Texas. Since then, he's had a variety of experiences, mostly in utilities. For about five of these years, he did personnel work.

Meyer has been reviewing the evaluation system. Employees have a mixture of indifferent and negative feelings about it. An informal survey has shown that about 60 percent of the supervisors fill the forms out, give about three minutes to each form, and send them to personnel without discussing them with the employees. Another 30 percent do a little better. They spend more time completing the forms but communicate about them only briefly and superficially with their employees. Only about 10 percent of the supervisors seriously try to do what was intended.

Meyer also found out that the forms were rarely used for promotion or pay raise decisions. Because of this, most supervisors may have felt the evaluation program was a useless ritual. Where he had been previously employed, Meyer had seen performance evaluation as a much more useful experience, which included giving positive feedback to employees, improving future employee performance, developing employee capabilities, and providing data for promoting and compensation.

Meyer has not had much experience with design of performance evaluation systems. He feels he should seek advice on the topic.

Write a report summarizing your evaluation of the strengths and weaknesses of the present appraisal system. Recommend some specific improvements or data-gathering exercises to develop a better system for Meyer.

17 Understanding Work Groups

LEARNING OBJECTIVES

*After studying this chapter,
you should be able to:*

1 Compare the following: group, formal work group, and informal work group.

2 Describe the role of a manager as a linking pin.

3 Define team building.

4 Explain group norm and group cohesiveness.

5 Define conformity.

6 Discuss idiosyncrasy credit.

7 Describe a quality circle.

Joe Marm was a young second lieutenant serving in South Vietnam. In the fall of 1965, he grabbed up two side arms and a pile of grenades and ran up a hill alone. He attacked and destroyed a machine gun nest killing eight Viet Cong. Afterwards, Lieutenant Marm was recommended for the Congressional Medal of Honor for his heroic actions. When asked why he had made the attack on his own, Marm replied, "What would the fellows have thought of me if I had been afraid to do it?"

NEW YORK TIMES ★

T he above quote describes the effect of a group on one individual. The importance of belonging to a group and its effect on human behavior in organizations was emphasized early by Elton Mayo in the famous Hawthorne Studies. He concluded that much of human behavior and attitudes can be explained by looking at the informal work group rather than at individuals themselves.[1] The major conclusion reached by the Hawthorne researchers was that workers react to the psychological and social conditions at work as well as to the physical conditions, and that group pressures directly affect an individual's actions. A significant contribution of these studies was the recognition that an organization consists of individuals, groups, and intergroup relations and that these components greatly influence the productivity and stability of the organization.

Group – number of persons who interact with one another on a face-to-face basis over a span of time and perceive themselves to be a group.

Primary Group – has all the characteristics of a group but also has feelings of loyalty, comradeship, and a common sense of values among its members.

WORK GROUPS DEFINED

A **group** is a small number of people who communicate with one another often on a face-to-face basis over a span of time and who perceive themselves to be a group. Thus, small size, face-to-face communication, and awareness that a group exists are all characteristics of a group.

Sociologists have further refined the definition of groups by distinguishing between a small group and a primary group. A small group must merely have all of the traits outlined in the previous paragraph. A **primary group,** in addition to the above traits, must have feelings of loyalty, comradeship, and a common sense of values among its members. Therefore, all primary

★ Source: *New York Times,* November 17, 1966.

MANAGERS AT WORK 17–1

Work Cells at Wang Laboratories

Work cells at Wang Laboratories are used to do away with the traditional concept of assembly-line production. Wang calls the approach the production module concept. Under the production module concept specific groups of employees are organized into work teams that manufacture designated products from beginning to end in work cells.

Wang contends that these work cells cut costs and improve productivity. Two reasons are given by Wang for these improvements. First, work cells can build a single unit in a few hours while a set of assembly lines can be delayed if just one step is off schedule. Second, work cells are more flexible than the standard assembly line, since they involve only one product and a few people. Thus, if a product is discontinued, the cost of new equipment and retraining is far less for a small group than for an entire production department.

Source: Adapted from "Work Cells: A Unique Approach," *Management Review,* March 1985, p. 9.

---

groups are small groups, but all small groups are not necessarily primary groups. Both types of groups exist within organizations.[2]

In this chapter, the term **work groups** will be used to describe groups in organizations. A further distinction will be made between formal and informal work groups. Formal work groups result primarily from the organizing function of management. Generally, **formal work groups** are defined by officially prescribed relationships between employees and a prescribed plan of effort directed toward the attainment of specific objectives.

Two popular forms of formal work groups are command groups and task groups. These groups can be either small or primary. Command groups are almost always shown on an organization chart. The vice presidents reporting to the president comprise a command group. The department heads reporting to a vice president comprise another command group. A task group is formed by employees who collaborate in order to accomplish a work task assigned by the organization. Engineers working on a particular project and committees are both examples of task groups. Managers at Work 17–1 describes Wang Laboratories' work cells which are a formal work group.

Overlapping the formal work groups in organizations are **informal work groups.** These groups are not defined by the organizing function of management. Yet, all organizations have them. Groups of employees that regularly lunch together and office "cliques" are examples of informal work groups.

Work groups – describes groups in organizations.

Formal work groups – have a defined structure and are formally recognized by the organization.

Informal work groups – result from personal contacts and interactions of people; usually not formally recognized by the organization.

F I G U R E   17–1   Linking-Pin Concept

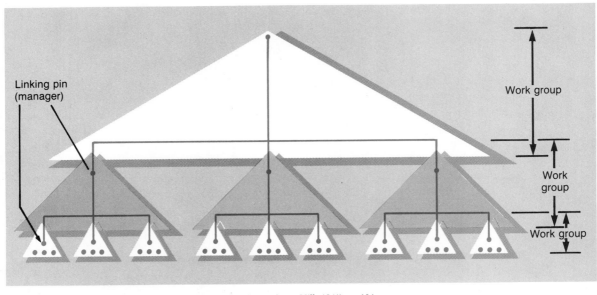

Source: Rensis Likert, *New Patterns of Management* (New York: McGraw-Hill, 1961), p. 104.

THE LINKING-PIN CONCEPT

Rensis Likert has proposed the linking-pin concept to describe management's role in work groups. Likert suggests that an individual's interactions with the organization should contribute to maintaining a sense of personal worth and importance. Both formal and informal work groups are important sources of satisfaction in maintaining an employee's sense of personal worth and importance. Likert concludes:

> Management will make full use of the potential capacities of its human resources only when each person in an organization is a member of one or more effectively functioning work groups that have a high degree of group loyalty, effective skills of interaction, and high performance goals.[3]

Likert further contends that management should consciously try to build these groups. Managers have overlapping group memberships and link these groups to the total organization. Thus, the manager is viewed as a linking pin in the organization. The linking-pin concept is depicted in Figure 17–1.

Team building – work group develops awareness of conditions that keep it from functioning effectively and takes action to eliminate these conditions.

TEAM BUILDING

Building the kind of work groups that Rensis Likert described is often called team building. **Team building** is a process that involves the work group

F I G U R E   17–2   Suggestions for Effective Team Building

1. Establish a working environment that is considered to be fair and equitable by employees.

2. Practice participation—listen to employees' ideas and get them involved in planning.

3. Show the employees that you, the manager who represents higher levels of management, also see issues from the employees' side.

4. Attempt to gain acceptance as the group's leader.

developing an awareness of those conditions that keep it from functioning effectively and then requires the work group to take action to eliminate those conditions.

To build an effective team, the manager must establish a working environment that is seen as fair and equitable. This cannot be done by one manager alone. All levels of management must contribute. However, if a manager does not establish this environment in the work unit, the efforts of higher levels of management will usually be wasted. Second, employee participation in working out changes, and keeping them informed about what is taking place, also helps build an effective team.

An effective manager also attempts to see and understand issues from the employees' point of view. However, the manager needs to be careful here. One who is always siding with the employees and taking an attitude of "it's us against them" can create a negative environment. The point is not to side with employees against management but to attempt to understand the issues from the employees' point of view.

Finally, the manager should strive to gain acceptance as the group's leader. Certainly, a manager has formal authority that is delegated from higher levels of management. However, formal authority does not guarantee effective team building. Figure 17–2 summarizes these suggestions for effective team building. Managers at Work 17–2 illustrates the results of team building at Ford Motor Company.

WHY INFORMAL WORK GROUPS EXIST

Work is a social experience and provides an opportunity for employees to fulfill many needs. When people are brought together in an office or plant, they interact and work together in their formal job duties. Friendships naturally emerge out of these continuous contacts and from areas of common interest. Mutual interests, friendships, and the need to fulfill social needs are three reasons that help to explain both the formation of informal work groups and the desire of employees to become members of such groups.

MANAGERS AT WORK 17–2

Ford's Team Taurus Concept

Under Ford's Team Taurus concept, design, manufacturing, processing, and assembly preparations for building the Taurus were carried out concurrently rather than sequentially. Ford management asked employees involved in all steps of manufacturing the car to participate in the design and engineering of the Taurus.

Ford had never done this before, but it has resulted in tremendous efficiencies and team spirit. This allowed Ford to build prototypes of the Taurus seven months earlier than they normally would have been built.

Legal and safety personnel were part of the team. Since the Taurus has a seven- or eight-year life cycle, these people were asked to anticipate the future legal and safety requirements of the car. As a result many anticipated requirements have been built into the car.

Source: Adapted from Richard Johnson, "Ford Team Taurus Concept Is Blue Print for Future Cars," *Automotive News,* May 6, 1985, p. 2.

Informal work groups provide a sense of security to the individual members, because group members usually exhibit a strong sense of loyalty and share common values. Further, membership in informal work groups facilitates social interaction and affiliation and fosters a feeling of pride or esteem by enabling an individual to be part of the in-group. One of the reasons why informal work groups evolve is to satisfy many of the needs that were described in the need hirarchy in Chapter 14.

Physical work conditions can also encourage the formation of informal work groups. People in close proximity to each other are almost forced to interact. The arrangement of furniture, desks, and offices can either encourage or discourage the formation of informal work groups. Generally, a work setting which facilitates social interaction increases the likelihood not only that an informal work group will exist but also that new employees will join.

Technology, which is closely aligned with physical work conditions, also heavily influences informal work group formation. Technology, in this broad sense, refers to how the overall work flows through the organization. The technology of an organization positions people in the work system, prescribes their activities, determines their interactions, and thus influences work group formation.

Like technology, management can influence the formation of informal work groups. For instance, suppose management decides to organize on a functional basis—accounting department, marketing department, and so forth. This facilitates the formation of informal work groups comprised of people performing similar functions. If, on the other hand, management organizes by product, customer, or geographical area, then people performing different functions are likely to form into groups.

In addition, the style of leadership employed by a manager can influence the formation of informal work groups. For instance, an autocratic manager and a participative manager can cause entirely different informal work group behavior.

In summary, there are many reasons for the formation of informal work groups within organizations. The reasons discussed here are by no means mutually exclusive or all-inclusive. The important point to remember is that overlapping the formal work groups in an organization are informal work groups which can have a significant impact on both individual and organizational performance.

FACTORS COMMON TO ALL INFORMAL WORK GROUPS

Once informal groups are formed, they evolve in such a manner that they take on a life of their own, separate and distinct from the work processes in which they originated. Informal group development is viewed as a self-generating process: Individuals who are formally required to interact with each other soon build favorable sentiments toward certain people. These sentiments serve to facilitate interactions and activities—eating lunch together, discussing problems, etc.—above and beyond those required by the job description. Simultaneously, these individuals become closer, and the group becomes an identifiable entity rather than just a collection of people. Over time, the informal group develops a set way of doing things and possesses several factors which seem to be common to all informal work groups. The implications of these factors for effective management can be better understood by examining them in more detail.

Group Norms

Group norms are the informal rules that a group adopts to regulate and regularize group members' behavior.[4] The various forms of informal group norms are limitless. One example of informal group norms that relates to the workplace is setting certain performance levels that may be either above, below, or the same as those set by management. Playing a joke or trick on all new employees is another example. Unfortunately, little is known about what factors determine whether an informal group will establish pro- or antiorganization norms.[5] However, a significant factor that determines whether group norms are closely adhered to by group members is the group's cohesiveness.[6]

Group norms – informal rules that a group adopts to regulate members' behavior.

Group Cohesiveness

Group cohesiveness – degree of attraction each member has for the group.

Group cohesiveness basically refers to the degree of attraction that each member has for the group, or the "stick-togetherness" of the group. Cohesiveness is important for the group, because the greater the cohesiveness of the group, the more likely are members to pursue group norms and not individual norms. That is, the greater the cohesiveness, the greater the individual members' conformity to group norms.

One variable affecting the cohesiveness of the group is its size. As discussed earlier, individuals in the group must interact in order for the group to exist; this interaction requirement limits the size of the group. Group cohesiveness decreases as the size of the group increases. It is possible to specify an upper limit on the size of informal work groups. However, the interaction requirement generally limits the size of the group to a maximum of 15 to 20 members. If the informal work group becomes larger than 20, subgroups begin to form.

The success and status of the informal group also play an important part in group cohesiveness. The more successful a group is in achieving its goals, the more cohesive the group becomes. The relationship is circular in that success breeds cohesiveness and cohesiveness, in turn, breeds more success. Numerous factors contribute to the status of work groups. Some of these include: the skill required in performing the job (skilled versus semiskilled jobs); opportunities for promotion (some groups develop reputations such as "the way to the top is through marketing"); the degree of supervision required (groups requiring less supervision have a higher status); and the type of work that is performed by the group (the more dangerous or more financially rewarding the work, the greater the status). Several other factors can also contribute to the status of the group. However, the important point is that groups that are successful in achieving their goals and that have higher status generally exhibit more cohesiveness.

Outside pressures, stability of membership, ability to communicate, and degree of physical isolation also influence group cohesiveness. For instance, if management's demands or requests are perceived by informal work groups as threats, group cohesiveness increases to offset the perceived threat. Higher cohesion results from stable membership in the group, because the group members have a longer time to know each other, to learn the norms of the group, and to learn how to behave according to group norms. Production lines and office layouts designed to inhibit conversation can reduce group cohesiveness. And coal miners, in their geographical isolation from the rest of the country, have demonstrated in numerous strikes the cohesiveness that can result from physical isolation from other groups.

Group cohesiveness has significance to managers. If the goals of a highly cohesive group are compatible with the organization's productivity goals, then the group's output will be above average. However, if the group's goals are incompatible with the organization's performance goals, the group's output will be below average.

Other variables can also influence the degree of group cohesiveness.[7] Figure 17–3 summarizes many of the conditions that can either increase or decrease group cohesiveness.

F I G U R E 17–3   Conditions for Increasing or Decreasing Group Cohesiveness

INCREASING COHESIVENESS

1. Smaller groups tend to have more cohesiveness. When the group becomes too large (generally larger than 20), subgroups begin to form.

2. The success and prestige of the group increases cohesiveness. Groups that are successful in achieving their goals are more cohesive. Higher-status groups are also more cohesive.

3. Physical isolation from other groups increases group cohesiveness.

4. The group becomes more attractive for individuals who gain prestige or status within the group.

5. Cohesiveness is higher under conditions where group members are in cooperative relationships than under conditions where there is internal competition.

6. When group members can fulfill more needs through participating in the group, the attraction of the group increases.

7. When the group is attacked from the outside, the cohesiveness usually increases as the members deal with the external threat. When the group shares a common fate as a result of external attack, the reaction is usually to focus the group's resources on protecting the group. The response to an outside threat is reflected in the statement, "United we stand, divided we fall."

DECREASING COHESIVENESS

1. When interpersonal conflict results from members' disagreements over ways to achieve group goals or solve group problems, the attractiveness of the group decreases. Members of highly cohesive groups may often have disagreements, but they try to eliminate the disagreements quickly.

2. If participation in the group results in unpleasant experiences for an individual, the attractiveness of the group decreases. When group activities result in embarrassment for an individual, the individual's attraction is usually reduced.

3. If membership in the group places limits on the individuals' participation in other activities or groups, cohesiveness may be lowered. In other words, if the group restricts the freedom of its members' activities outside the group, the attraction of the group may decrease.

4. If conditions exist in the group which prevent or restrict effective communication, cohesiveness decreases. Reduced communication may result if some members are too dominating or if some members are unpleasant or obnoxious in their communication behavior.

5. The cohesiveness may be reduced if group members feel the activities involve too great a personal risk. The risks could be physical danger or psychological threats. Risk could involve the group's engaging in activities which individuals feel may be illegal or immoral. Risk could involve group actions in an organization that the individual feels might result in getting disciplined or fired.

6. If the evaluation of the group by outsiders who are respected becomes negative, this can result in the group becoming unattractive to its members.

Source: Adapted from Dan L. Costley and Ralph Todd, *Human Relations in Organizations,* 2nd ed. (St. Paul, Minn.: West Publishing, 1983). Copyright © 1983 by West Publishing Company. Reprinted by permission. All rights reserved.

Group Leadership

Informal group leadership has been the subject of numerous research studies. Two of the general conclusions reached regarding informal group leadership are:

1. The group selects as its leader the individual it perceives to have the most competence in helping the group achieve its objectives.
2. The group selects as its leader the individual with strong communication skills, especially in the areas of setting objectives for the group, giving direction, and summarizing information for the group.[8]

It may also be that many informal work groups require two leaders—a task and a social leader. The task leader pushes the group toward the accomplishment of its objectives; the social leader is primarily concerned with maintaining harmony within the group.

CONFORMITY AND INFORMAL WORK GROUPS

The earlier sections of this chapter were designed to give an understanding of the nature of informal work groups in organizations. The purpose of this section is to examine the role of informal work groups in obtaining conformity of individuals to group norms.

Conformity –
degree to which group members accept and abide by the norms of the group.

Conformity is the degree to which the members of a group accept and abide by the norms of the group. It is situationally determined: Conformity in one situation might be viewed as deviant behavior in another. Probably the most important variable in the situation is the individual's relationships with other people and their relationships with each other. Thus, the group defines conformity for any given situation.

Knowing that the group defines conformity does not offer much help to practicing managers. Managers need to know how the group maintains conformity and the effect it has on the individual in the group.

Group Pressures on the Individual

Informal work groups seek to control the behavior of their members for many reasons. One reason the group desires uniform, consistent behavior from each member is so that other members can predict with reasonable certainty how the individual member will behave. This certainty is necessary in order to achieve some degree of coordination in working toward the group's goals. On the other hand, groups are organizations in and of themselves; as a result, conformity is often required in order to maintain the group. Individualistic behavior among group members can threaten the survival of the group by causing internal dissension. Individual members tend to conform to group norms under the following conditions:

1. When the norm is congruent with the personal attitudes, beliefs, and behavioral predispositions of the members.
2. When the norm is inconsistent with the personal attitudes, beliefs, or behavioral predispositions, but strong pressures to comply are exerted by the group, and the rewards of complying are valued or the sanctions imposed for noncompliance are devalued.[9]

One study on the influence of group pressures on individuals placed college students in groups of seven to nine people.[10] Group members were told that they would be comparing lengths of lines on white cards. Figure 17–4 shows the cards and lines. The subjects in the study were then asked to pick the line on the second card that was identical in length to the line on the first card.

In the experiment, all but one member of each group were told to pick one of the two wrong lines on Card 2. In addition, the uninformed member of the group was positioned to always be one of the last individuals to respond. Under ordinary circumstances, mistakes on the line selection occur less than 1 percent of the time. However, in this experiment, the uninformed member made the wrong selection in 36.8 percent of the trials.

An uninformed member confronted with only a single individual who contradicted the choice continued to answer correctly in almost all trials. When the opposition was increased by two, incorrect responses increased to 31.8 percent.

The experiment demonstrated that the group's behavior affected the behavior of the individual members; although some individuals remained independent in their judgments, other acquiesced on almost every judgment. Over all, group pressure caused individuals to make incorrect judgments in over

F I G U R E 17–4 Cards in Asch Experiment

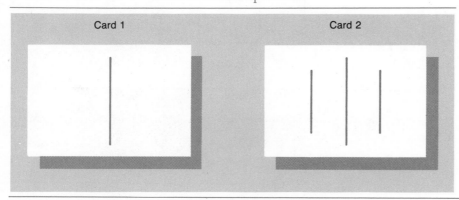

one third of the cases. The experiment also showed that the more members that disagreed with the individual, the more likely the individual was to succumb to the judgment of the group.

Lester Coch and John R. P. French conducted a classic study on the influence of groups at Harwood Manufacturing Company, a textile firm in Marion, Virginia. Figure 17–5 illustrates a major finding of their study. In this case, a woman textile worker started to exceed the group norm of 50 units per day. On the 13th day, the group began to exert pressure on the woman and her output was quickly reduced to conform with the group norm. On the 20th day, the group was disbanded by moving all group members except the woman to other jobs. Once again, her production quickly climbed to almost double the group norm.

Individuals Who Deviate from Group Norms

While evidence of conformity abounds in all group situations, there are also those members who deviate from group norms and are allowed to do so by

F I G U R E 17–5 Effect of Group Norms on Member Productivity

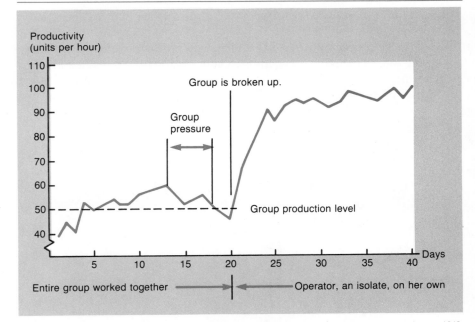

Source: Lester Coch and J. R. P. French, Jr., "Overcoming Resistance to Change," *Human Relations*, 1948, pp. 519–20.

group members. Certain members who have made or are making significant contributions to the group's goals are allowed to take some liberties within the group. This phenomenon has been called **idiosyncrasy credit.**[11]

People who contribute a great deal to the group also play a major role in developing group norms. Consequently, the group's norms largely reflect the attitudes of the major givers. This means that those who accumulate the most idiosyncrasy credit do not have to use it; the group norms largely reflect their own attitudes. People who make large contributions to the group are allowed to deviate from the group norms, but they are not likely to do so because of the similarity between their norms and group norms.

Conversely, those members who make little or no contribution to the group must learn to conform to norms which they had little or no part in establishing. Conformity, therefore, may be more difficult and more rigorously demanded from these members.

> **Idiosyncrasy credit** – form of credit or liberties a group gives to certain members who make a significant contribution to the group's goals.

MANAGEMENT AND INFORMAL WORK GROUPS

As this chapter has discussed, much individual behavior is influenced by the informal work groups to which individuals belong. Unfortunately, many managers view informal work groups as being only negative toward organizational objectives. As summarized in Figure 17–6, however, informal work groups can be beneficial to management. In order to realize the potential benefits outlined there, the manager must be aware of the impact of informal work groups on individuals. Figure 17–7 indicates several key factors the manager should keep in mind in dealing with informal work groups.

F I G U R E 17–6   Potential Benefits from Informal Work Groups

1. Informal work groups blend with the formal organization to make a workable system for getting work done.
2. Informal work groups lighten the workload for the formal manager and fill in some of the gaps in the manager's abilities.
3. Informal work groups provide satisfaction and stability to employees.
4. Informal work groups provide a useful channel of communication in the organization.
5. The presence of informal work groups encourages managers to plan and act more carefully than they would otherwise.

Source: Keith Davis, *Human Behavior at Work,* 6th ed. (New York: McGraw-Hill, 1981), pp. 275–76.

F I G U R E 17–7   Key Factors in Dealing with Informal Work Groups

1. Participation in groups is a basic source of social need satisfaction for employees.

2. Informal groups try to protect their members and provide security. They will try to protect members from perceived threats from management.

3. Groups develop communication systems to provide information that members want. If management does not provide the information employees want, the informal group will try to obtain it.

4. Both formal and informal groups obtain status and prestige within an organization. Groups may use their status and prestige as a power base to influence others in the organization.

5. Groups develop and enforce norms for the behavior of members. The group norms may be supportive of management or may work against management objectives.

6. The more cohesive a group, the more control it has over the behavior of its members. The highly cohesive group can produce high achievement of organizational goals. But it can work just as effectively against organizational objectives when the group opposes management.

7. Both formal and informal groups within an organization establish roles that affect the activities and responsibilities of members. Accepting role responsibilities in an informal group may require that an individual violate the role expectations of management.

Source: Reproduced by permission from *Human Relations in Organizations* by Dan L. Costley and Ralph Todd. Copyright © 1978, West Publishing Company. All rights reserved.

F I G U R E 17–8   Potential Benefits of a Quality Control Circle

1. Problems—including some that have existed for years—do get solved.

2. Employees participate in changing things for the better.

3. Employees and managers broaden and develop as they receive special training and put it into practice.

4. Morale improves and is maintained as people become involved in helping to improve their work life and fulfill their potential.

5. The channel for upward and downward communication is strengthened.

6. Greater trust is built between levels in the organization and among units.

7. Managers are relieved of many worries and concerns without releasing control or having any of their authority diluted.

8. They are relatively inexpensive to start.

9. They can evolve into other forms of employee participation.

Source: Adapted from Rich Tewell, "How to Keep Quality Circles in Motion," *Business*, January–March 1982, pp. 48–49; Edward E. Lawles III and Susan A. Mohrman, "Quality Circle after the Fad," *Harvard Business Review*, January–February 1985, pp. 65–71.

MANAGERS AT WORK 17–3

Quality at Paul Revere Insurance Companies

Paul Revere Insurance Companies has used a modification of the quality circle concept to help solve the problem of increasing both the quality and productivity of the white-collar industry.

At Paul Revere, everyone from the president to the most recently hired clerk is on a quality team. The quality teams have an average of 10 members and are a near mirror of the organizational structure. In virtually all cases, the quality team leader is the formal work unit manager.

The results of this effort have been impressive. In 1984, 4135 ideas originated by employees on quality teams at all levels were implemented, with annualized savings in excess of $3.2 million. When fully implemented, the ideas are expected to account for another $6 million in savings. The improvements that emerged range from mundane administrative procedures to complex, insurance-particular ideas.

Source: Adapted from Patrick L. Townsend, "The Policy Is Quality," *Best's Review (Life/Health Insurance Edition)*, Vol. 85, May 1985, p. 104.

Quality Circle

A relatively new use of a formal work group is the quality circle, which orginated in Japan. A **quality circle** is composed of a group of employees (usually from 5 to 15 people) who are members of a single work unit, section, or department. The unit's supervisor or manager is usually included as a member of the quality circle. These employees have a common bond; they perform a similar service or function by turning out a product, part of a product, or a service. Membership in a quality circle is almost always voluntary. The basic purpose of a quality circle is to discuss quality problems and to generate ideas that might help improve quality.

A quality circle usually begins by exposing the members to specialized training relating to quality. Meetings of a quality circle are normally held once or twice per month and last for one to two hours. After the initial training, a quality circle begins by discussing specific quality problems which are brought up by either management representatives or by the circle members. Staff experts may be called upon by the circle as needed. Figure 17–8 outlines the major benefits of a quality circle. As with other forms of participative management, the underlying objective of quality circles is to get employees actively involved. Managers at Work 17–3 describes the positive impact that quality circles have had at Paul Revere Insurance Companies.

Quality circle – members of a work unit who meet on a regular basis to discuss quality problems and generate ideas for improving quality.

SUMMARY

LEARNING OBJECTIVE 1

Compare the following: Group, Formal Work Group, and Informal Work Group.

A group is a small number of people who communicate with one another often on a face-to-face basis over a span of time and who perceive themselves to be a group. Formal work groups are defined by officially prescribed relationships between employees and a prescribed plan of effort directed toward the attainment of specific objectives. Informal work groups overlap the formal work groups and are illustrated by the groups of employees that regularly lunch together and office "cliques."

LEARNING OBJECTIVE 2

Describe the Role of a Manager as a Linking Pin.

Managers have overlapping group memberships and should serve to link these groups to the total organization.

LEARNING OBJECTIVE 3

Define Team Building.

Team building is a process that involves the work group in developing an awareness of those conditions that keep it from functioning effectively and then requires the work group to take action to eliminate those conditions.

LEARNING OBJECTIVE 4

Explain Group Norm and Group Cohesiveness.

Group norms are the informal rules that a group adopts to regulate and regularize group members' behavior. Group cohesiveness refers to the degree of attraction that each member has for the group, or the "stick-togetherness" of the group.

LEARNING OBJECTIVE 5

Define Conformity.

Conformity is the degree to which the members of a group accept and abide by the norms of the group.

LEARNING OBJECTIVE 6

Discuss Idiosyncrasy Credit.

Certain members of a group who have made or are making significant contributions to the group's goals are allowed to take some liberties within the group. This phenomenon has been called idiosyncrasy credit.

LEARNING OBJECTIVE 7

Describe a Quality Circle.

A quality circle is composed of a group of employees (usually from 5 to 15 people) who are members of a single work unit, section or department and who have as their basic purpose to discuss quality problems and to generate ideas that might help improve quality.

REVIEW QUESTIONS

1. Define the following terms:
   a. Group.
   b. Small group.
   c. Primary group.
   d. Work group.
2. What is team building?
3. Outline some of the reasons why informal work groups exist in organizations.
4. What is a group norm?
5. What is group cohesiveness?
6. Describe some of the variables that affect the cohesiveness of a group.
7. What is conformity?
8. Describe the results of two studies dealing with the influence of groups on individual behavior.
9. What is idiosyncrasy credit?
10. What is a quality circle?

DISCUSSION QUESTIONS

1. Do you think it is possible to eliminate entirely the need for informal work groups?
2. Discuss the following statement: Goals of informal work groups are never congruent with the goals of the formal organizations.
3. Some employees are described as "marching to the beat of a different drummer." In light of the discussion of this chapter, what does this statement mean to you?
4. Why do you feel that quality circles are effective?

REFERENCES & ADDITIONAL READINGS

[1] Elton Mayo, *The Human Problems of an Industrial Civilization* (Cambridge, Mass.: Harvard University Graduate School of Business Administration, 1946).

[2] For an analysis on the impact of group size and absenteeism, see "Group Size and Absenteeism Rates: A Longitudinal Analysis," *Academy of Management Journal,* December 1982, pp. 921–27.

[3] Rensis Likert, *New Patterns of Management* (New York: McGraw-Hill, 1961), p. 104.

[4] Daniel C. Feldman, "The Development and Enforcement of Group Norms," *Academy of Management Review* 9 (January 1984), p. 47.

[5] J. Richard Hackman, "Group Influences on Individuals," in *Handbook of Industrial and Organizational Psychology,* ed. Marvin D. Dun-

nette (New York: John Wiley & Sons, 1983), p. 1517.

[6] Ibid.

[7] For a further discussion of components of group cohesion, see Joseph P. Stokes, "Components of Group Cohesion: Intermember Attraction, Instrumental Value, and Risk Taking," *Small Group Behavior,* May 1983, pp. 163–73.

[8] Beatrice Schultz, "Predicting Emergent Leaders: An Exploratory Study of the Salience of Communicative Functions," *Small Group Behavior,* February 1978, pp. 109–14.

[9] Hackman, "Group Influences," p. 1503.

[10] Solomon Asch, "Opinions and Social Pressure," *Scientific American,* November 1955, pp. 31–34.

[11] E. P. Hollander, "Conformity, Status, and Idiosyncrasy Credit," *Psychological Review* 65 (January 1958), pp. 117–27.

INCIDENT

One of the Gang?

Recently, Gary Brown was appointed as the supervisor of a group of machine operators in which he was formerly one of the rank and file employees. When he was selected for the job, the department head told him the former supervisor was being transferred because he could not get sufficient work out of the group. He said also that the reason Gary was selected was because he appeared to be a natural leader, that he was close to the group, and that he knew the tricks they were practicing in order to restrict production. He told Gary that he believed he could lick the problem and that he would stand behind him.

He was right about Gary knowing the tricks. When he was one of the gang, not only did he try to hamper the supervisor, but he was the ringleader in trying to make life miserable for him. None of them had anything personally against the supervisor; all of them considered it a game to pit their wits against his. There was a set of signals to inform the boys that the supervisor was coming so that everyone would appear to be working hard. As soon as he left the immediate vicinity, everyone would take it easy. Also, the operators would act dumb to get the supervisor to go into lengthy explanations and demonstrations while they stood around. They complained constantly and without justification about the materials and the equipment.

At lunchtime, the boys would ridicule the company, tell the latest fast one they had pulled on the supervisor, and plan new ways to harrass him. All this seemed to be a great joke. Gary and the rest of the boys had a lot of fun at the expense of the supervisor and the company.

Now that Gary has joined the ranks of management, it is not so funny. He is determined to use his managerial position and knowledge to win the group over to working for the company instead of against it. Gary knows that, if this can be done, he will have a top-notch group. The operators know their stuff, have a very good team spirit, and, if they would use their brains and efforts constructively, could turn out above-average production.

Gary's former buddies are rather cool to him now; but this seems to be natural, and he believes he can overcome it in a short time. What has him concerned is that Joe James is taking over his old post as ringleader of the group, and the group is trying to play the same tricks on him as they did on the former supervisor.

Questions

1. Did the company make a good selection in Gary?

2. What suggestions would you make to Gary?

3. Are work groups necessarily opposed to working toward organizational goals? Explain.

EXERCISE

Crash Project

Y ou are told that you and your work group have two weeks to implement a new program. You feel two weeks are insufficient and that you and your employees would virtually have to work around the clock to complete it in that time. Morale has always been high in your group; yet you know that some people just don't like overtime. As you think about how best to handle the situation, you consider these alternatives:

1. Tell your group that the company is being pretty unreasonable about this. "I don't see what the big rush is. But it's got to be done, so let's all pitch in and help, shall we?"
2. Tell your group that you have told Bob Smith (your boss) that you have a superb group of people and that "if anyone in the company could get the job done, we could."
3. Tell the group that your job is on the line and that if they want you around for awhile, they will have to make a heroic effort.
4. Tell your group that you don't want to hear any griping. This is the nature of the job, and anyone who feels that he or she can't devote the extra time had better start looking for another job.
5. Tell the group that the job must be done and ask them to make suggestions on how it can be completed within the deadline.

Other alternatives may be open to you, but assume that these are the only ones you have considered.

WITHOUT DISCUSSION with anyone, decide which of these approaches you would take and be prepared to defend your choice.

18 Managing Conflict and Stress

LEARNING OBJECTIVES

*After studying this chapter,
you should be able to:*

1 Define conflict.

2 Discuss the useful effects of conflict.

3 List the stages of conflict development.

4 Explain the basic perspectives for
analyzing conflict.

5 Name five methods of resolving
interpersonal conflict.

6 Define stress.

7 Define burnout.

8 Describe some strategies for reducing
stress and burnout.

As conflict—difference—is here in the world, as we cannot avoid it, we should, I think, use it. Instead of condemning it, we should set it to work for us. Why not? What does the mechanical engineer do with friction? Of course, his chief job is to eliminate friction, but it is true that he also capitalizes friction. The transmission of power by belts depends on friction between the belt and the pulley. The friction between the driving wheel of the locomotive and the track is necessary to haul the train. All polishing is done by friction. The music of the violin we get by friction. We left the savage state when we discovered fire by friction. We talk of the friction of mind on mind as a good thing. So in business, too, we have to know when to try to eliminate friction and when to try to capitalize it, when to see what work we can make it do.

MARY PARKER FOLLET *

*C*onflict in organizations is often assumed to be unnatural and undesirable—to be avoided at all costs. Conflict can lead to rigidity in the system in which it operates, distort reality, and debilitate the participants in the conflict situation. Therefore, many organizations approach the management of conflict with the following situations:

1. Conflict is avoidable.
2. Conflict is the result of personality problems within the organization.
3. Conflict produces inappropriate reactions by the persons involved.
4. Conflict creates a polarization within the organization.

However, conflict is perfectly natural and should be expected to occur. The key point in the study of conflict is not that it is natural or unavoidable. But, as Mary Parker Follet states in the above quote, management must know when to eliminate conflict and when to build on it.

WHAT IS CONFLICT?

Conflict – overt behavior in which one party seeks to advance its own interests in its relationship with others.

Conflict is overt behavior in which one party seeks to advance its own interests in its relationship with others. Conflict begins when one party perceives that

* Mary Parker Follet, "Constructive Conflict," in *Dynamic Administration*, ed. Henry C. Metcalf and L. Urwick (New York: Harper & Row, 1940), pp. 30–31.

a second party has frustrated or is about to frustrate some concern of the first party.[1] The parties involved denote social units in a conflict situation. They can be individuals, groups, organizations, or nations.

Today's managers must accept the existence of conflict and realize that to attempt to stop all conflict is a mistake. The general consensus today is that conflict itself it not undesirable, rather, it is a phenomenon that can have constructive or destructive effects. How positive the effect of the conflict is often depends on the participant's own point of view. However, the results of a conflict should also be evaluated from the organization's point of view.

For example, in a struggle between two people for a promotion, the winner will probably feel that the conflict was most worthwhile, while the loser will probably reach the opposite conclusion. However, the impact of the conflict on the organization must also be considered. If the conflict ends in the selection and promotion of the better person, then the effect is good from the organization's viewpoint. If, by competing, the parties have produced more or made improvements within their areas of responsibility, then the effect is also positive. At the same time, there may be destructive effects. The overall work of the organization may have suffered during the conflict. The loser may resign or withdraw as a result of the failure. The conflict may become chronic and inhibit the work of the organization. In extreme cases, the health of one or both of the participants may be adversely affected.

The destructive effects of conflict are often obvious. The constructive effects may be more subtle. The manager must be able to see these constructive effects and to weigh them against the costs. Some potentially useful effects of conflict are:

1. Conflict energizes people. Even if not all of the resulting activity is constructive, it at least wakes people up and gets them moving.
2. Conflict is a form of communication; the resolution of conflict may open up new and lasting channels.
3. Conflict often provides an outlet for pent-up tensions, resulting in catharsis. With the air cleansed, the participants can again concentrate on their primary responsibilities.
4. Conflict may actually be an educational experience. The participants may become more aware and more understanding of their opponents' functions and the problem with which they must cope.

The potential for conflict depends on how incompatible the goals of the parties are, the extent to which the required resources to achieve the objectives are scarce and shared, and how interdependent the task activities are. The potential for conflict is great at all levels of the organization. Managers at Work 18–1 illustrates how conflict erupts at the top of organizations.

MANAGERS AT WORK 18–1

Feuding at the Top

Statistics aren't readily available on the frequency of feuding by CEOs and their presidents. However, the departure items in *The Wall Street Journal* column ("Who's News—Management Personal Notes") suggest that CEO-president feuding is not all that uncommon. For example, in 1985 Capitol Air's president resigned over differences with the CEO. Apple Computer cofounder Wozniak left the firm, citing disagreements.

Jesse Warner, former chairman of GAF Corp. went through half a dozen presidents until he solved his problem simply by eliminating the position of president. Former CBS Chairman William Paley went through four presidents. One of those quit before Paley could fire him over a dispute involving the company's cable programming.

Source: Adapted from Bruce A. Jacobs, "Trouble at the Top," *Industry Week,* May 13, 1985, pp. 70–72.

PROGRESSIVE STAGES OF CONFLICT

A manager must be aware of conflict's dynamic nature. Conflict does not usually appear suddenly. It passes through a series of progressive stages as tensions build. These stages of development are:

1. Latent conflict: At this stage, the basic conditions for conflict exist but have not yet been recognized.
2. Perceived conflict: The cause of the conflict is recognized by one or both of the participants.
3. Felt conflict: Tension is beginning to build between the participants, although no real struggle has yet begun.
4. Manifest conflict: The struggle is under way, and the behavior of the participants makes the existence of the conflict apparent to others who are not directly involved.
5. Conflict aftermath: The conflict has been ended by resolution or suppression. This establishes new conditions that will lead either to more effective cooperation or to a new conflict that may be more severe than the first.

Conflict does not always pass through all of these stages. And those in conflict may not be at the same stage simultaneously. For example, one participant could be at the manifest state of conflict while the other is at the perceived stage.

ANALYZING CONFLICT

Conflict can be analyzed from two basic perspectives. One approach sees conflict as a process internal to the individual (intrapersonal conflict). The other views it as external to the individual—individual versus individual, individual versus group, group versus group, organization versus organization, or any combination of these. External conflict is of three general types: structural, interpersonal, and strategic. The following sections examine intrapersonal, structural, and strategic conflict in more detail.

Intrapersonal Conflict

Intrapersonal conflict is internal to the individual. It is probably the most difficult form of conflict to analyze. Basically, it relates to the need-drive-goal motivational sequence (see Figure 18–1) discussed in Chapter 14.

Intrapersonal conflict can result when barriers exist between the drive and the goal. This often leads to frustration for the person involved. Such conflict may also result when goals have both positive and negative aspects and when competing and conflicting goals exist. Figure 18–2 illustrates how it can occur in the motivational sequence.

Frustration. **Frustration** results when a drive or motive is blocked before the goal is reached. Barriers can be either overt (rules and procedures) or covert (mental hang-ups). When a drive is blocked, people tend to react with defense mechanisms, which are behaviors used to cope with frustration. Figure 18–3 lists some typical defense mechanisms.

Responses to frustration vary and can be expressed through withdrawal behavior (higher absenteeism and turnover rates), aggression (sabotage and other destructive work acts), excessive drinking, drug abuse, and more subtle responses such as ulcers or heart trouble.

> **Intrapersonal conflict** –internal to the individual; relates to the need-drive-goal motivational sequence.

> **Frustration** –sults when a drive or motive is blocked before the goal is reached.

F I G U R E 18–1 The Motivation Sequence

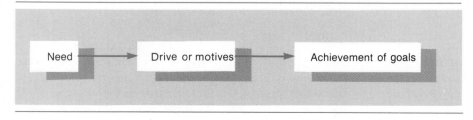

F I G U R E 18–2   Sources of Intrapersonal Conflict

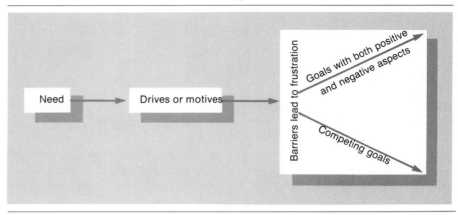

Goal Conflict. **Goal conflict** occurs when a goal has both positive and negative features or when two or more competing goals exist. Basically, three forms of conflicting goals exist:

1. Muturally exclusive positive goals. Goal conflict results when a person is motivated toward two or more positive, mutually exclusive goals at the same time. Selecting an academic major is an example of this type of conflict. Economics, law, and medicine may all have positive aspects, but all cannot be pursued at once. Often, this form of conflict can be resolved by making a decision rather quickly, thereby ending the conflict.

2. Positive-negative goals. Conflict that exists when a person tries to achieve a goal that has both positive and negative effects. To pursue a top management position, people must often sacrifice their own time and time with their family. Thus, the goal of being a successful business leader can have both positive and negative aspects.

3. Negative-negative goals. Here the person tries to avoid two or more negative, mutually exclusive goals. Someone may dislike his or her job but finds quitting and looking for another job even less attractive. The likely outcome of this conflict is frustration.

Goal conflict forces the person to make a decision. Decision making often creates a feeling of conflict within the individual. A person feeling such disharmony, called **dissonance,** will always attempt to reduce it.

Structural (Functional) Conflict

Structural (functional) conflict results from the organizational structure and is relatively independent of the individuals occupying the roles within the structure. The marketing and production departments in Figure 18–4, for example, may have structural conflict. The marketing department, being

Goal conflict – results when a goal has both positive and negative features or when two or more competing goals exist.

Dissonance – feeling of disharmony within an individual.

Structural (functional) conflict – results from the organizational structure; relatively independent of the individuals occupying the roles within the structure.

F I G U R E 18–3   Reactions to Frustration

ADJUSTIVE REACTIONS	PSYCHOLOGICAL PROCESS	ILLUSTRATION
Compensation	Individual devotes himself to a pursuit with increased vigor to make up for some feeling of real or imagined inadequacy.	Zealous, hardworking president of the Twenty-Five Year Club who has never advanced very far in the company hierarchy.
Conversion	Emotional conflicts are expressed in muscular, sensory, or bodily symptoms of disability, malfunctioning, or pain.	A disabling headache keeping a staff member off the job the day after a cherished project has been rejected.
Displacement	Redirects pent-up emotions toward persons, ideas, or objects other than the primary source of the emotion.	Roughly rejecting a simple request from a subordinate after receiving a rebuff from the boss.
Fantasy	Daydreaming or other forms of imaginative activity provide an escape from reality and imagined satisfactions.	An employee's daydream of the day in the staff meeting when he corrects the boss' mistakes and is publicly acknowledged as the real leader of the group.
Negativism	Active or passive resistance, operating unconsciously.	The manager who, having been unsuccessful in getting out of a committee assignment, picks apart every suggestion that anyone makes in the meetings.
Rationalization	Justifies inconsistent or undesirable behavior, beliefs, statements, and motivations by providing acceptable explanations for them.	Padding the expense account because "everybody does it."
Regression	Individual returns to an earlier and less mature level of adjustment in the face of frustration.	A manager, having been blocked in some administrative pursuit, busies himself with clerical duties or technical details more appropriate for his subordinates.
Repression	Completely excludes from consciousness impulse, experiences, and feelings which are psychologically disturbing because they arouse a sense of guilt or anxiety.	A subordinate "forgetting" to tell his boss the circumstances of an embarrassing situation.
Resignation, apathy, and boredom	Breaks psychological contact with the environment, withholding any sense of emotional or personal involvement.	Employee who, receiving no reward, praise, or encouragement, no longer cares whether or not he does a good job.
Flight or withdrawal	Leaves the field in which frustration, anxiety, or conflict is experienced, either physically or psychologically.	The saleman's big order falls through, and he takes the rest of the day off; constant rebuff or rejection by superiors and colleagues pushes an older worker toward being a loner and ignoring whatever friendly gestures are made.

Source: Timothy W. Costello and Sheldon S. Zalkind, *Psychology in Administration: A Research Orientation* (Englewood Cliffs, N.J.: Prentice-Hall, 1963), pp. 148–49. Copyright © 1963 by Prentice-Hall, Inc. Reprinted by permission of the publisher.

F I G U R E   18–4   Functional Organization Structure

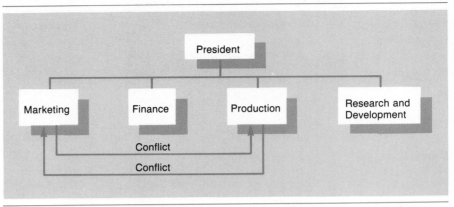

customer-oriented, may believe that some exceptions can and should be made in production for the sake of current and future sales. The production department may view such exceptions as unreasonable and not in the best interests of the organization. Hence, a structural conflict occurs. Various types of structural conflict are discussed in the following sections.

Goal segmentation and rewards. Each functional unit of an organization has different functional goals. These can cause conflict which, when it emerges, may seem to be personality clashes. The classical problem of inventory levels shows this dilemma. The marketing department would like to keep finished-goods inventories high to supply all of the customers' need on short notice. The finance department would like to keep inventories low because of the cost of maintaining these inventories. Another illustration of this dilemma concerns the product line. Marketing would like to carry a product line composed of all shapes, sizes, and colors. Because of the problems involved in producing multiple shapes, sizes, and colors, the production department would prefer one basic product. The end result in either case is often a conflict between departments.

The reward system is a key method to reduce this type of conflict. A reward system that stresses the separate performance of the departments feeds the conflict. However, rewarding the combined efforts of the conflicting departments reduces the conflict.

Mutual departmental dependence. Sometimes, two departments or units of an organization are dependent on one another for the accomplishment of their respective goals; a potential for structural conflict is then present. For instance, the marketing department's sales depend on the volume of production from the production department; at the same time, the production department's quotas are based on the sales of the marketing department. This type of mutual dependence exists in many organizations.

Unequal departmental dependence. Often, departmental dependence is unequal and fosters conflict. In most organizations, for instance, staff groups are more dependent on line groups. The staff generally must understand the problems of the line, cooperate with the line, and sell their ideas to the line. However, the line does not have to reciprocate. One tactic in this form of conflict is an attempt by the more dependent unit to interfere with the work performance of the independent group. Under this tactic, the more dependent group hopes that the other group will cooperate once they realize how the dependent group can hinder their progress.

Functional unit and the environment. Functional units obviously perform different tasks and cope with different parts of the environment. Research has shown that the more the environments served by functional units differ, the greater the potential for conflict. Paul Lawrence and Jay Lorsch have developed four basic dimensions to describe these differences: (1) structure—this refers to the basic type of supervisory style employed; (2) environment orientation—this refers to the orientation of the unit to the outside world; (3) time-span orientation—this refers to the unit's planning-time perspectives; (4) interpersonal orientation—this refers to the openness and permissiveness of interpersonal relationships.[2]

Lawrence and Lorsch applied their scheme to six organizations in the plastics industry. The results are shown in Table 18–1: The environmental differences are a primary cause of structural conflict. Coordinating the activities of departments such as applied research, sales, and production is harder due to these differences.

Role dissatisfaction. Role dissatisfaction may also produce structural conflict. Professionals in an organizational unit who receive little recognition and have limited opportunities for advancement may initiate conflict with other units. Purchasing agents often demonstrate this form of conflict.

Role dissatisfaction and conflict often result when a group that has low perceived status sets standards for another group. For example, within academic institutions, administrators—who may be viewed by the faculty as having less status—often set standards of performance and make administrative decisions that affect the faculty.

T A B L E 18–1 Differences Related to Environment of Departments

DEPARTMENTS	DEGREE OF STRUCTURAL FORMALITY	ORIENTATION TOWARD ENVIRONMENT	ORIENTATION TOWARD TIME	INTERPERSONAL ORIENTATION*
Fundamental research	Medium (4)†	Technoeconomic and scientific	Long	Task (2)
Applied research	Medium (3)	Technoeconomic	Long	Relationship (3)
Sales	High (2)	Market	Short	Relationship (4)
Production	Highest (1)	Technoeconomic	Short	Task (1)

* Fiedler's questionnaire discussed in Chapter 15 was used in this analysis.
† Numbers refer to the relative ranking of the departments in that dimension.
Source: P. R. Lawrence and J. W. Lorsch, "Differentiation and Integration in Complex Organizations," *Administrative Science Quarterly* 12 (1967), pp. 16–22.

Role ambiguity. Ambiguities in the description of a particular job can lead to structural conflict. When the credit or blame for the success or failure of a particular assignment cannot be determined between two departments, conflict is likely to result. For instance, improvements in production techniques require the efforts of the engineering and production departments. After the improvements are made, credit is difficult to assign; thus, conflict often results between these two departments.

Common resource dependence. When two organizational units are dependent on common but scarce resources, potential for conflict exists. This often occurs when two departments are competing for computer time. Each obviously feels that its projects are more important.

Communication barriers. Semantic differences can cause conflict. For instance, purchasing agents and engineers generally use different language to describe similar materials, which lead to conflict.

Communication-related conflict also occurs when a physical or organizational barrier to effective communication exists. Company headquarters and branch offices frequently suffer from this problem. Figure 18–5 summarizes types of structural conflict.

Interpersonal Conflict

Interpersonal conflict – between two or more individuals; can be caused by many factors.

Interpersonal conflict may result from personality conflicts as well as from structural conflict and many other factors. Interpersonal conflicts occur when barriers to communication exist between the involved parties. These barriers are often harder to overcome than the communication barriers discussed earlier as structural conflict. Communication barriers often create what is called *pseudo-conflict*. This results when participants in a group fail to reach a group decision because of their failure to exchange information, opinions, or ideas. Although the group may really be in complete agreement, the situation has all the symptoms of a conflict caused by differences of opinion.

A second major cause of interpersonal conflict occurs when individuals are dissatisfied with their roles as compared to the roles of others. An employee may be compatible with both his or her manager and fellow employees. However, when a peer is promoted to a management job, the employee may no longer accept his or her role in relation to the former peer.

Opposing personalities often cause conflict situations. Some people simply rub each other the wrong way. The extrovert and the introvert, the boisterous and the reserved, the optimist and the pessimist, the impulsive and the deliberate—these are but a few possible combinations that might bother each other.

Finally, there are special prejudices based on personal background or ethnic origin that cause conflict. This, of course, includes racial and religious conflicts; but there are also other, more subtle, prejudices. Examples include the college graduate versus the person with less education, the married versus the divorced person, or the longtime employee versus the new hire.

F I G U R E 18–5　Summary of Types of Structural Conflict

TYPE	EXAMPLE
Mutual departmental dependence	Marketing department's sales are dependent on the volume of production from the production department.
Unequal departmental dependence	Staff departments are generally more dependent on line departments.
Goal segmentation and rewards	Different inventory levels are desired by different functional departments.
Functional unit and environment	The environment faced by an applied research department and a sales department are different and can lead to conflict between these departments.
Role dissatisfaction	Professionals in an organizational unit who receive little attention.
Ambiguities	When the credit or blame for the success or failure of a particular assignment cannot be determined between two departments.
Common resource dependence	Two departments competing for computer time.
Communication barriers	Semantic differences. Purchasing agents and engineers may use different language to describe similar materials, and conflict can result from those semantic differences.

Unlike structural conflicts, where both parties are actively involved, interpersonal conflicts may be one-sided. One of the parties may be totally unaware of the existing conflict.

Strategic Conflict

Intrapersonal, structural, and interpersonal conflicts are usually not planned. They simply develop as a result of existing circumstances. **Strategic conflicts** are often started purposely; they are sometimes fought with an elaborate battle plan. Such conflicts usually result from the promotion of self-interests on the part of an individual or group. There is a clear goal and those who stand in the way are the adversary. In organizations, the goal is usually to gain an advantage over the opponent within the reward system. The potential reward may be a bonus or commission, a choice assignment, a promotion,

Strategic conflict – results from promotion of self-interests by an individual or group; often deliberately planned.

or an expansion of power. Whatever it is, usually only one of the participants will receive it (or the greatest portion of it).

The vice presidents of an organization may find themselves in a strategic conflict situation as the retirement of the president nears. An overly ambitious vice president, in an attempt to better his or her personal chances for the presidency, may create a strategic conflict with one or more of the other vice presidents. Stratetic conflict can also occur between departments within a university when a new course is offered and two or more departments feel that they should be teaching a particular course.

Strategic conflict does not always imply that the participants are dishonest or unethical. Indeed, rewards are there to be pursued with vigor. But such conflicts can degenerate into unfair play because the participants cannot resist temptation.

Because it is usually impossible to isolate a single cause, few conflicts fit neatly into one of the above categories. Nevertheless, they do provide a useful framework for analyzing conflict.

MANAGING CONFLICT

There are five general methods of solving interpersonal conflict situations: (1) withdraw one or more of the participants; (2) smooth over the conflict and pretend it does not exist; (3) compromise for the sake of ending the conflict; (4) force the conflict to a conclusion by third-party intervention; and (5) have a confrontation between the participants in an effort to solve the underlying source of conflict. Confrontation, or problem solving, is generally considered to be the most effective method of resolving conflict, while forcing the conflict to a conclusion has been found to be the least effective method.

Much structural conflict results from interdependencies inherent in the organizational structure. Some of this conflict potential may be removed by decoupling the conflicting parties: reduce their common resource dependencies; give each control over their own resources; introduce large buffer inventories; or invoke impersonal, straightforward rules for resource allocation. Decoupling may also occur by duplicating facilities for dependent departments. But this approach may be too expensive for the organization. One approach to reducing interdependencies is the use of a "linking" position between depending departments. The purpose is to ease communication and coordination between interdependent and potentially conflicting departments. Another way is to design the work flow so the system reflects more logical and complete work units where responsibility and authority are more consistent. Lastly, the matrix organization can offer a means for constructive confrontation, which (as stated earlier) is the most effective method of conflict resolution.

F I G U R E   18–6   Model for Conflict Management

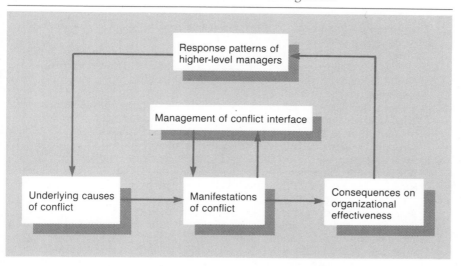

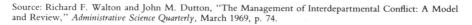

Source: Richard F. Walton and John M. Dutton, "The Management of Interdepartmental Conflict: A Model and Review," *Administrative Science Quarterly*, March 1969, p. 74.

A Model for Conflict Management

A general model for managing conflict in organizations is shown in Figure 18–6. This model views the conflict situation from two perspectives. The first views the manager as an intervening force in the conflict cycle. The second involves the response patterns of higher-level managers.

The Conflict Interface. Management of the conflict interface is based on monitoring the behavior of the participant(s) as the conflict develops. The objective of the manager is not to resolve the conflict but to act as a referee and counselor in helping the participant(s) reach an acceptable solution. Understanding the type of conflict—intrapersonal, structural, interpersonal, strategic—and the stage of the conflict cycle will aid the manager. Figure 18–7 lists key questions that a manager should address to apply the concepts presented in this chapter to the resolution of a conflict situation.

To maximize the constructive aspects of the conflict and to speed its resolution while minimizing the destructive consequences, the manager should also know the following ground rules for verbal confrontations:

1. Review past actions and clarify the issues before the confrontation begins.
2. Communicate freely; do not hold back grievances.
3. Do not surprise the opponent with a confrontation for which the individual is not prepared.

F I G U R E 18–7   Key Questions to Be Answered in Conflict Resolution

1. What perceived loss or threat of loss has led each party to perceive a conflict?
2. How does each party define the conflict issue?
   Does each party have an accurate perception of the other's concerns? Is the issue posed superficially rather than in terms of underlying concerns?
   Would alternative definitions of the issue be more helpful in suggesting integrative solutions to the conflict?
3. How does each party pursue his or her objectives in dealing with the other party?
   What is his or her underlying orientation in approaching the conflict issue—competitive, collaborative, sharing, avoidance, accommodative?
   What assumptions underlie the individual's choice of strategies and tactics?
4. How is each party's behavior influenced by the behavior of the other?
   What ongoing dynamics seem to be producing the escalation or deescalation?
   Is each party aware that the other's behavior is partly a response to his or her own?
   What efforts are the parties making to manage their own conflict?
5. If things proceed as they are, what are likely to be the short-term and long-term results—both substantive and emotional?
   What foreseeable effects will this episode have upon subsequent episodes?
6. Does the general makeup of either party predispose him or her toward the use of specific conflict-handling modes?
   Are those predispositions compatible with the requirements of his or her position?
   To what extent could a person's behavior be changed through training experiences?
7a. Is either party acting as representative for a larger set of individuals?
   What expectations do they have of the representative's behavior?
   How much power do they have over this person?
   To what extent can they monitor his or her negotiation behavior?
7b. Who are the other, relatively neutral, onlookers?
   What sort of behavior will they encourage or discourage?
   How much power do they have over the parties?
8. What is the relative importance and frequency of competitive issues versus common problems in the relationship as a whole?
   To what extent have resource scarcities created conflict of interest between the parties?
   In what ways have differentiated responsibilities created conflict of interest?
9a. Are there many rules which dictate or constrain settlements on specific issues?
   To what extent are the parties free to problem-solve on important issues?
9b. How are the behaviors of the parties shaped by the format of their negotiations?
   How frequently do the parties interact?
   When and where are meetings held?
   What are the number and composition of people present?
   How formally are the negotiations conducted?
9c. What provisions are there for involving third parties?
   Are skilled third parties available to help the parties resolve their own disputes?
   Does the larger system have provisions for terminating conflict episodes by imposing settlements when the parties deadlock?

Source: Kenneth Thomas, "Conflict and Conflict Management," in *Handbook of Industrial and Organizational Psychology,* ed. Marvin D. Dunnette (New York: John Wiley & Sons, 1983).

4. Do not attack the opponent's sensitive spots that have nothing to do with the issues of the conflict.

5. Keep to specific issues; do not argue aimlessly.

6. Maintain the intensity of the confrontation and ensure that all participants say all that they want to say. If the basic issues have been resolved at this point, agree on what steps are to be taken toward resolving the conflict.

Besides acting as referees in enforcing these rules, managers can give valuable assistance to the participant(s) without interfering with their responsibility to resolve the conflict. Managers can help the participants understand why the conflict exists and what underlying issues must be resolved. They can also help obtain information that may be needed to reach a solution. In interpersonal conflict, managers can regulate somewhat the frequency of contacts between the participants and perhaps establish a problem-solving climate when they meet. A manager's most important contribution, however, is to keep the individuals working toward a true resolution of the conflict. Confrontation of the conflict situation within the guidelines developed above should encourage constructive conflict within the organization.[3]

Responses of Higher-Level Managers. The second level of conflict management concerns the responses of higher-level managers to the conflict's consequences for the ongoing work of the organization. If the conflict itself or the nature of its aftermath has made conditions intolerable, management must step in and make whatever decisions and changes are needed to restore order. The resulting actions either force a resolution to the conflict or change the solution that has been reached.

Such intervention is often regarded as arbitrary by the participant(s), especially by those who do not receive a favorable decision. In such cases, the intervening authority must not give the impression that the action has been taken because either or both of the participants have failed; rather, an immediate or different solution is in the best interest of the organization. There should be no doubt that the solution is final and that the conflict has been concluded.

MANAGING STRESS

Just as conflict is an integral part of organizational life, so is stress. Stress is part of living and can contribute to personal growth, development, and mental health. However, excessive and prolonged stress generally becomes quite negative. Stress of this type can be related to health problems such as insomnia, asthma, ulcers, and heart disease.[4] Managers at Work 18–2 shows some recent court decisions on job-related stress.

Stress involves an interaction between a person and an environment. The potential for **stress** exists when an environmental situation presents a demand threatening to exceed a person's capabilities and resources for meeting it,

Stress – results when an environment presents a demand threatening to exceed the person's capabilities and resources for meeting it.

MANAGERS AT WORK 18–2

Stress Claims Making Business Jumpy

Helen J. Kelly, a Raytheon employee with 22 years seniority, suffered a nervous breakdown when she was told she would be transferred to another department. The Massachusetts Supreme Court ruled four to three that she was entitled to workers' compensation benefits. Her breakdown was a personal injury arising out of and in the course of her employment, the court explained. Kelly collected $40,000.

Harry A. McGarrah, an Oregon deputy sheriff, blamed his depression on the belief that his supervisor was persecuting him. The Oregon Supreme Court upheld his claim for workers' compensation benefits. He collected $20,000.

Source: Adapted from Resa W. King and Irene Pave, "Stress Claims Are Making Business Jumpy," *Business Week,* October 14, 1985, p. 152.

under conditions where the person expects a substantial difference in the rewards and costs resulting from meeting the demand versus not meeting it.

Sources of Stress

Stress can result from many factors. Some of the more common sources of employee stress are a job mismatch, conflicting expectations, role ambiguity, role overload, fear/responsibility, working conditions, working relationships, and alienation. Each of these is described more fully in Figure 18–8.

Burnout

One reaction to stress is a phenomenon that has been described as burnout. Many writers view burnout and stress as being synonymous. However, for the purposes of this book, **burnout** is a person's adaptation not only to stress but also to a variety of work-related and personal factors. In burnout, work is no longer a meaningful experience to the burned-out person.[5] Burned-out people often show a combination of the following behavioral tendencies: to blame others in the organization for their burnout, to complain bitterly about aspects of work which in the past were not areas of concern, to miss work because of nonspecific and increasingly prevalent illness, to daydream or sleep on the job, to be the last to come to work and the first to leave, to bicker with co-workers or seem uncooperative, and to become increasingly isolated from others. Figure 18–9 charts the path to professional burnout.

Burnout – adaptation an individual makes not only to stress but also to a variety of work-related and personal factors; work is no longer meaningful.

FIGURE 18–8 Common Sources and Suggested Causes of
Organizational Stress

COMMON SOURCES	SUGGESTED CAUSES
Job mismatch	Job demands skills or abilities that the employee does not possess (job incompetence).
	Job does not provide opportunity for the employee to fully utilize skills or abilities (underutilization).
Conflicting expectations	The formal organization's concept of expected behavior contradicts the employee's concept of expected behavior.
	The informal group's concept of expected behavior contradicts the employee's concept.
	The individual employee is affected by two (or more) strong influences.
Role ambiguity	Employee is uncertain or unclear about how to perform on the job.
	Employee is uncertain or unclear about what is expected in the job.
	Employee is unclear or uncertain about the relationship between job performance and expected consequences (rewards, penalities, and so forth).
Role overload	Employee is incompetent at job.
	Employee is asked to do more than time permits (time pressure).
Fear/responsibility	Employee is afraid of performing poorly or failing
	Employee feels pressure for high achievement.
	Employee has responsibility for other people.
Working conditions	The job environment is unpleasant; there is inadequate lighting or improper regulation of temperature and noise, for example.
	The requirements of the job may unnecessarily produce pacing problems, social isolation, and so forth.
	The machine design and maintenance procedures create pressure.
	The job involves long or erratic work hours.
Working relationships	Individual employees have problems relating to, and/or working with, superiors, peers, and/or subordinates.
	Employees have problems working in groups.
Alienation	There is limited social interaction.
	Employees do not participate in decision making.

Source: Adapted from Charles R. Stoner and Fred L. Fry, "Developing a Corporate Policy for Managing Stress", *Personnel*, May–June 1983, p. 70.

FIGURE 18–9   The Path to Professional Burnout

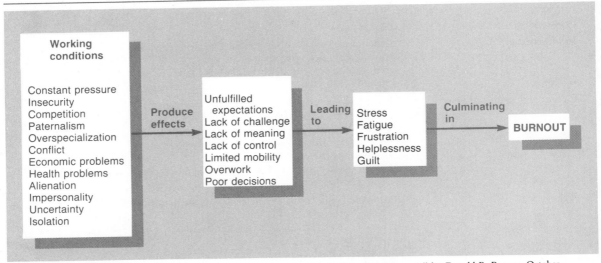

Source: Reprinted by permission from *Business* Magazine, "Helping Employees Cope with Burnout," by Donald P. Rogers, October–December 1984. Copyright © 1984 by the College of Business Administration, Georgia State University, Atlanta.

Relaxation response – trains a person to control major muscle groups.

Biofeedback – monitoring devices that give feedback on the degree of relaxation or tension of various muscle groups.

Autogenic training – much like self-hypnosis; helps individuals gain control over their physiology through passive concentration.

Meditation techniques – focus attention on a constant object such as one's breath or a repetitive syllable.

Strategies for Reducing Stress and Burnout

Several strategies are used to reduce stress and burnout. The first involves self-help approaches; one of the most frequently mentioned is proper exercise and diet. Activities include exercising, paying attention to diet and nutrition, getting the proper amounts of sleep, and engaging in leisure activities.

Other self-help approaches to stress reduction include relaxation response, biofeedback, autogenic training, and meditation. **Relaxation response** is trained control of major muscle groups. A person learns to tense and relax each set of muscles for a short period while breathing deeply and regularly. In **biofeedback,** monitoring devices give feedback on the degree of relaxation of various muscle groups. The device is used first to learn to recognize the degrees of relaxation or tension in various muscle groups. Subsequently, the person learns to relax muscles without the aid of the monitoring devices. **Autogenic training** is closely related to self-hypnosis; it helps individuals gain control over their physiology through passive concentration. Finally, **meditation techniques** are relaxing methods that focus attention on a constant object such as one's breath or a repetitive syllable.[6]

Self-help stress reduction programs may not deal with the root of the problem causing the stress. For example, stress caused by a job mismatch may be reduced by some of the self-help approaches. However, organizationally supported training and education may be necessary to minimize or fully overcome this type of stress. Figure 18–10 lists specific actions to help overcome organizationally induced stress for individuals.

F I G U R E 18–10   Actions for Reducing Stress at the Individual Level

STRESS DIMENSION	CORRECTIVE METHOD	POSSIBLE ACTION PROGRAMS
Job mismatch	Placement	Relocate, transfer.
	Training	Set up programs to build and develop particular skills.
	Education	Set up formal program to enhance overall aptitude and ability.
Conflicting expectations	Communication	Establish clear picture of the organization's role and help employee realize how to fulfill this role.
	Training	Set up programs to build and develop skills that will enable the employee to fulfill role.
Role ambiguity	Communication	Clearly explain the nature of job dimensions and expectations.
Role overload	Training and education	Develop skills to weaken cause of job incompetence. Set up time management programs to deal more effectively with time pressures.
Fear/responsibility	Training	Develop skills to address problem areas more confidently.
	Counseling	Help the employee understand and deal constructively with underlying fears and apprehension.
Working conditions	Counseling	Help employee deal with behavioral difficulties (isolation feelings, for example).
	Communication	Help employee understand justification for work process and how employee fits into overall process.
Working relationships	Training	Set up encounter and team-building sessions.
	Counseling	Deal with personality conflicts, social isolates, and so forth.
	Communication	Develop better communication practices within groups. Help supervisors and subordinates learn to relate more effectively to each other.
Alienation	Counseling	Help employees deal constructively with their feelings.
	Communication	Provide avenues for upward communication, participation, and involvement.

Source: Adapted from Charles R. Stoner and Fred L. Fry, "Developing a Corporate Policy for Managing Stress," *Personnel,* May–June 1983, p. 72.

F I G U R E   18–11   Actions for Reducing Stress at the Organizational Level

STRESS SOURCE	CORRECTIVE METHOD	POSSIBLE ACTION PROGRAMS
Job mismatch	Job redesign	Set up job enrichment programs.
	Personnel evaluation	Improve selection and placement procedures.
	Training	Institute job-related skills training.
	Communication	Provide counseling to explore causes of conflict.
Conflicting expectations	Communication	Examine and reduce misunderstandings that may cause conflict.
	Job redesign	Schedule, for example, flexitime, 4-day weeks, job sharing, and so forth to deal with particular conflict areas (that is, working woman versus family, work versus leisure).
	Personnel evaluation	Improve selection and placement (transfer, for example).
Role ambiguity	Communication	Provide more accurate job descriptions.
	Structure	Define responsibilities and authority structure more precisely.
Role overload	Job redesign	Change work floor, layout, or process.
	Structure	Rewrite job description.
Fear/responsibility	Training	Train in decision-making skills
	Communication	Provide counseling programs for dealing with underlying problems.
Working conditions	Job redesign	Change physical conditions and work routine (rotate jobs, change hours of work, give relaxation breaks and "stress days" off, for example).
Work relationships	Training	Develop human relations skills; provide training to build more cohesive, team-oriented work groups.
	Communication	Set up various counseling programs.
Alienation	Training	Help with career planning.
	Job redesign	Provide job enrichment programs.
	Structure	Utilize formal structural design that is most conducive to situation and individual needs (for example, use project or matrix format).
	Rewards	Alter methods and timing of payment; aim incentives more directly at employees' needs and expectations.
	Communication	Provide for participation by employees.

Source: Adapted from Charles R. Stoner and Fred L. Fry, "Developing a Corporate Policy for Managing Stress," *Personnel,* May–June 1983, p. 73.

Frontlines

EMPOWERMENT

Managers who exemplify empowerment encourage their employees to come up with innovative ideas and to run with them. According to Robert Waterman's *The Renewal Factor,* organizations that cultivate this managerial style are willing to give up a measure of control in order to gain control over what really counts: results. If you want to move forward, treat every member of your staff as a creative source. "When people are treated as the main engine rather than interchangeable parts of the corporate machine, motivation, creativity, and quality well up," writes Waterman. (Chapter 10)

CREATIVE MANAGEMENT

The best way to manage creative people is to manage them hardly at all, suggests *Interaction/Insight, The Management Psychology Letter.* Imaginative people, though vital to an organization, often think and work differently from most employees. Since they frequently produce their best efforts in fits and starts, allow them more freedom to work at their own pace. Also, suggests the newsletter, go easy on labeling their results as right

DRUG TESTING WITHOUT ABUSE

Employee drug abuse costs some companies a bundle. But administering a drug testing program could cost you even more. That's because some employees see them as an egregious infringement of their privacy, and they're suing left and right. In 1985, for example, a computer programmer, fired from a San Francisco company after refusing to be tested, sued her former employer for wrongful termination. She claimed that the company had threatened her right to privacy.

"There is no other area on the corporate front today where lawsuits are filed more frequently and expensively than

Courtesy of Texas Instruments Incorporated.

or wrong. By lending a sympathetic ear and acting as a sounding board, help them reach the right conclusions on their own. (Chapters 10 and 15)

in employee privacy," says Brian Zevnik, editor-in-chief of the Alexander Hamilton Institute, a New York publishing company. While the legal causes of action may range from discrimination and defamation to wrongful termination, the litigatible theme remains the same—your employees' right to privacy.

Take heart. A company can still protect itself from costly litigation, even though drug-testing laws vary from state to state. The Alexander Hamilton Institute, which recently published a book entitled *Privacy in the Workplace,* suggests taking the following steps before administering any drug testing:

- ■ Limit your initial testing to very special situations—for example, those in which workers' jobs involve a significant risk to other employees or to the public at large.

- ■ Test only when there is strong evidence of abuse, such as impaired job performance.

- ■ Be certain that the employee is aware that he is being tested specifically for drugs.

- ■ Keep all test results confidential.

- ■ Confirm all positive results by giving the employee an alternate test. Because some of the less expensive drug tests have a high error rate, a more accurate test should be conducted on those who test positively.

- ■ Offer rehabilitation, through an employee-assistance program, to those who test positive. If they refuse, you can take further action. (Chapters 3 and 12)

EMPLOYEE COMMITMENT

D eveloping committed employees begins with a manager's personally orienting each new recruit, according to *Management World*. Since employee discontent often arises out of confusion, managers should take several hours to explain carefully what a new employee needs to know about company policies and procedures. It is also important to introduce new staff members to their new co-workers. The idea is to instill an immediate sense of belonging in the new employee and to demonstrate signs of your commitment to him. (Chapter 13)

Courtesy of Steve Leonard
©1988.

PERSONAL MOTIVATION

S ometimes motivating an employee takes more than bonuses and raises. The most lasting forms of motivation are personal rewards that directly affect a worker's dignity and self-esteem, according to *May Trends*. Some examples include inviting an employee to lunch to let him know how much you appreciate his work, or offering personal congratulations in the form of handwritten notes or special awards like plaques or trophies. These personal gestures show an employee you have a sincere and intimate interest in his growth. (Chapter 14)

Courtesy of Tenneco, Inc.

THE SPECIFICS OF FEEDBACK

F eedback is most useful when it is descriptive, not evaluative, according to *Management Solutions*. You should tell an employee exactly what he did rather than simply making a judgment or broad generalization. For example, telling someone he is bad-mannered is not as effective as pointing out that he has interrupted three people in the past half hour. Even though both statements are true, the latter is apt to get the most results. Value judgments only confuse the issue. (Chapters 13 and 5)

Courtesy of International Business Machines Corporation.

EARNING TRUST

E mployee loyalty doesn't always come automatically—most managers have to earn it. According to *The Effective Executive* newsletter, one way to gain trust from your workers is to solicit constructive criticism. Employees who feel comfortable enough to voice their complaints are much more likely to trust their superiors. Try to let them know that you're open to negative as well as positive feedback, and accept the criticisms graciously. (Chapter 15)

Courtesy of International Business Machines Corporation

One way to gain trust from your workers is to solicit constructive criticism.

CONFLICTING OPTIONS

C onflicts are often difficult to resolve because each side feels a resolution will come only after one side gives in to the other. The trick is to keep the lines of communication constantly open. *Behavioral Sciences Newsletter* offers some suggestions that can be effective even if followed by only one party in the dispute:

1. Stay in contact with the conflicting party.
2. Remain actively involved in any discussion with him. Describe your view of the problem without blaming or criticizing, and listen closely to his views.
3. Offer sincere conciliatory gestures such as empathizing, expressing regret, or conceding a contested point until a compromise can be reached. (Chapter 18)

DYING LOYALTY

T he chaotic, often transient environment created by takeovers, mergers, and acquisitions is making corporate loyalty a thing of the past. According to a recent survey conducted by *Industry Week* magazine, 71.3 percent of those polled agreed that loyalty on the job was "virtually disappearing." More than half (57.3 percent) said that they were less loyal to their company than they were just five years ago. Almost three fourths of those polled (73 percent) said that their company is less loyal to them than it was five years ago. (Chapter 19)

RECENT SURVEY RESULTS ON JOB LOYALTY

71.3%	Disappearing Job Loyalty
57.3%	Less Employee Loyalty
73%	Less Company Loyalty

SUPER BRAT

While other 23-year-olds are scrambling to rise out of entry-level jobs, Michael Dell is already a self-made man. Four years ago he founded PC's Limited, now Dell Computer Corporation, one of the fastest-growing manufacturers of IBM-compatible personal computers. The company grossed $69 million in 1986, and sales topped $160 million in 1987. Light-years ahead of his competitors, Dell runs his 82,000-square-foot plant with just-in-time inventory, and he abides by the zero defect approach to production. "Why store parts for 100,000 computers when I can only produce only 400 a day? And why must I expect that a certain percentage of our machines will not work when they roll off the assembly line?" The just-in-time approach gives Dell's company crucial mobility. Because he sinks very little money into parts, Dell can phase out old products to make way for the new in a matter of days, without great losses. As for zero defect, Dell knows he'll never eliminate mistakes, but that's his goal. By the time parts are assembled into completed computers, they've been checked out eight times. (Chapter 21)

Michael Dell, founder of PC's Limited

Light-years ahead of his competitors, Dell runs his 82,000-square-foot plant with just-in-time inventory, and he abides by the zero defect approach to production.

SUCCESS STORIES

Black & Decker: Sells a wide range of construction and home-maintenance products. *Installed E-mail service between headquarters and field sales staff.*

Result: Instead of returning unsold inventory to B&D, distributors around the country could communicate and ship products directly to areas that needed them. Swapping of returned goods increased by 70 percent, preventing lost profits of $70,000. **One-year ROI:** 530 percent. **Five-year ROI:** 2,300 percent. (Chapter 22)

MANAGERS AT WORK 18–3

Stanford University Hospital

The pressure-filled and emotional atmosphere in an acute-care hospital like Stanford University Hospital makes its staff members, especially its nurses, good candidates for burnout. The Stanford approach is an example of what managers and their organizations can do to identify and deal with stress.

First, a questionnaire was administered to 129 intensive care unit (ICU) nurses to determine the nature of their stress. An analysis of the questionnaires revealed the following ranking for the primary stressors:

1. Conflicts with staff, physicians, administrators, and residents.
2. Dealing with the deaths of patients and the unnecessary prolongation of life.
3. Problems with the management of the unit.
4. Physical work environment.

Some of the actions taken to deal with these stressors included:

1. Developing and conducting workshops dealing with conflict resolution.
2. Developing and conducting workshops on death and bioethics.
3. Intensified recruitment and retention efforts to improve inadequate-staffing problems, and options in work scheduling offered to nurses.
4. Remodeling of physical plant.

Finally, a full-time nurse consultant was hired to help the nurses deal with their stress when it happened. One result of this program has been that attrition rate among Stanford ICU nurses has declined by 18 percent.

Source: Adapted from June T. Biley and Duane D. Walker, "Rx for Stress: One Hospital's Approach," *Supervisory Management,* August 1982, pp. 32–37.

Finally, if the undesirable effects of stress are widespread in an organization or work group, organizationwide corrective actions are necessary. Figure 18–11 outlines specific action programs to reduce stress at the organizational level. Managers at Work 18–3 shows one organization's approach for reducing stress.

Stress can never be entirely eliminated. As mentioned previously, some stress actually produces positive results. Effectively using the techniques described in this chapter should help to reduce the negative aspects of stress.[7]

▰/ S U M M A R Y

LEARNING OBJECTIVE 1

Define Conflict.
Conflict is overt behavior in which one party seeks to advance its own interests in its relationship with others.

LEARNING OBJECTIVE 2

Discuss the Useful Effects of Conflict.
Some potentially useful effects of conflict are: it energizes people; it is a form of communication; it often provides an outlet for pent-up tensions, resulting in catharsis; and it may actually be an educational experience.

LEARNING OBJECTIVE 3

List the Stages of Conflict Development.
The stages of conflict development are latent conflict, perceived conflict, felt conflict, manifest conflict, and conflict aftermath.

LEARNING OBJECTIVE 4

Explain the Basic Perspectives for Analyzing Conflict.
Conflict can be analyzed from two basic perspectives. One approach sees conflict as a process internal to the individual (intrapersonal conflict). The other views it as external to the individual—individual versus individual, individual versus group, group versus group, organization versus organization, or any combination of these. External conflict is of three general types: structural, interpersonal, and strategic.

LEARNING OBJECTIVE 5

Name Five Methods of Resolving Interpersonal Conflict.
There are five general methods of resolving interpersonal conflict: (1) withdraw one or more of the participants; (2) smooth over the conflict and pretend it does not exist; (3) compromise for the sake of ending the conflict; (4) force the conflict to a conclusion by third-party intervention; and (5) have a confrontation between the participants in an effort to solve the underlying source of conflict.

LEARNING OBJECTIVE 6

Define Stress.
Stress involves interaction between a person and an environment. The potential for stress exists when an environmental situation presents a demand that threatens to exceed a person's capabilities and resources for meeting it, under conditions where the person expects a substantial difference in the rewards and costs resulting from meeting the demand versus not meeting it.

LEARNING OBJECTIVE 7

Define Burnout.
Burnout is a person's adaptation not only to stress but also to a variety of work-related and personal factors.

LEARNING OBJECTIVE 8

Describe Some Strategies for Reducing Stress and Burnout.
One self-help approach for reducing stress and burnout is proper exercise and diet. Other self-help approaches to stress reduction include relaxation response, biofeedback, autogenic training, and meditation.

REVIEW QUESTIONS

1. What two basic viewpoints can be used to analyze conflict?
2. What causes intrapersonal conflict?
3. What are some typical defense mechanisms used when an individual is frustrated?
4. Describe three forms of goal conflict.
5. Name at least four types of structural conflict.
6. What are some of the causes of interpersonal conflict?
7. What is strategic conflict?
8. Describe some of the useful effects of conflict.
9. Identify the five stages of conflict.
10. What are some methods that can be used to resolve conflict?
11. Describe in detail a model for managing conflict in organizations.
12. Outline some key questions that need to be answered in conflict resolution.
13. Outline several common sources of stress.
14. What is burnout?
15. What is relaxation response? Biofeedback? Autogenic training? Meditation?

DISCUSSION QUESTIONS

1. Discuss the following statement: Every manager should attempt to avoid conflict at all times.
2. Do you agree or disagree with this statement: Conflict is inevitable. Discuss.
3. How can managers reduce destructive stress in organizations?
4. Describe how you would handle the situation in which you have two people working for you who "just rub each other the wrong way."

REFERENCES & ADDITIONAL READINGS

[1] See Kenneth Thomas, "Conflict and Conflict Management," in *Handbook of Industrial and Organizational Psychology,* ed. Marvin D. Dunnette (New York: John Wiley & Sons, 1983).

[2] P. R. Lawrence and J. W. Lorsch, *Organization and Environment* (Boston: Harvard Business School Division of Research, 1967).

[3] For more information, see D. Tjosvold, "Implications for Controversy Research for Management," *Journal of Management* 11 (Fall–Winter 1985), pp. 21–37.

[4] See John M. Ivancevich, Michael T. Matteson, and Cynthia Preston, "Occupational Stress, Type A Behavior, and Physical Well-Being," *Academy of Management Journal,* June 1982, pp. 373–91.

[5] Morley D. Glicken and Katherine Jantia, "Executives under Fire: The Burnout Syndrome," *California Management Review,* Spring 1982, p. 67. See also Donald P. Rogers, "Helping Employees Cope with Burnout," *Business,* October–December 1984, pp. 3–7.

[6] Much of the material in this paragraph was drawn from Heather R. Sailer, John Schlacter, and Mark R. Edwards, "Stress: Causes, Consequences, and Coping Strategies," *Personnel,* July–August 1982, pp. 39–40.

[7] See also Saroj Parasuraman and Joseph A. Alutto, "Sources and Outcomes of Stress in Organization Settings: Toward the Development of a Structural Model," *Academy of Management Journal* 27 (June 1984), pp. 330–50.

INCIDENT

The Young College Graduate and the Old Superintendent

Situation: You are a consultant to the manager of a garment manufacturing plant in a small southern town. The manager has been having trouble with two employees: Ralph, the plant superintendent, and Kevin, the production scheduler. Ralph is 53 years old and has been with the company since he was released from military duty after World War II. He started in the warehouse with a sixth-grade education and worked his way up through the ranks. Until recently, Ralph handled—along with his many other duties—the production scheduling function. He was proud of the fact that he could handle it all "in my head." As the volume of production and the number of different products grew, however, the plant manager felt that significant savings could be attained through a more sophisticated approach to scheduling. He believed that he could save on raw materials by purchasing in larger quantities, and on production setup time by making longer runs. He also wanted to cut down on the frequency of finished-goods stock-outs; when backlogs did occur, he wanted to be able to give customers more definite information as to when goods would be available. He wanted to have a planned schedule for at least two months into the future, with daily updates.

Kevin is 24 years old and grew up in the Chicago area. This is his first full-time job. He earned a master of science degree in industrial engineering from an eastern engineering school. He jumped right into the job and set up a computer-assisted scheduling system, using a time-sharing service with a teletype terminal in his office. The system is based on the latest production scheduling and inventory control technology. It is very flexible and has proven to be quite effective in all areas that were of interest to the plant manager.

Plant Manager: Sometimes I just want to shoot both Ralph and Kevin. If those two could just get along with each other, this plant would run like a well-oiled machine.

Consultant: What do they fight about?

Manager: Anything and everything that has to do with the production schedule. Really trivial things in a lot of cases. It all seems so completely senseless!

Consultant: Have you tried to do anything about it?

Manager: At first, I tried to minimize the impact of their feuds on the rest of the plant by stepping in and making decisions that would eliminate the point of controversy. I also tried to smooth things over as if the arguments were just friendly disagreements. I thought that after they had a chance to get accustomed to each other, the problem would go away. But it didn't. It got to the point that I was spending a good 20 percent of my time stopping their fights. Furthermore, I began to notice that other employees were starting to take sides. The younger people seemed to support Kevin; everybody else sided with Ralph. It began to look as if we might have our own little war.

Consultant: What's the current situation?

Manager: I finally told them both that if I caught them fighting again, I would take very drastic action with both of them. I think that move was a mistake though, because now they won't even talk to each other. Kevin just drops the schedule printouts on Ralph's desk every afternoon and walks away. Ralph needs some help in working with those printouts, and Kevin needs some feedback on what's actually going on in the plant. Frankly, things aren't going as well production spacewise now as when they were at each other's throats. And the tension in the plant as a whole is even worse. They are both good people and outstanding in their respective jobs. I would really hate to lose either of them, but if they can't work together, I may have to let one or both of them go.

Questions

1. Why is this conflict occurring?
2. What method did the manager use in dealing with this conflict situation? Was it effective?
3. Recommend an approach for resolving the conflict.

EXERCISE

Conflict over Quality

This morning, your department completed a large order and turned it over to quality control. The quality control manager has just come to tell you that she must tighten up on inspection standards because a number of complaints have been received from the field. She feels the order must be reworked by your department to pass inspection. You try to convince her to impose the stricter standards only on future lots, but she refuses.

Reworking these units will set you back a couple of days in your production schedule. This you can explain to your superiors. But the costs, which will be charged to your budget, will be much more difficult to explain later on.

As you reflect on what has happened, you are clearly annoyed. You decide something must be done, and you see your alternative as follows:

1. You can calm down, issue instructions to rework the units, and do the best you can with the budgeting and scheduling problems.
2. You can send the quality control manager a memo clearly outlining the cost considerations and ask her to help you find a solution.
3. You can call the quality control manager and ask for a meeting at her earliest convenience to discuss the situation further.
4. You can go to the plant manager to whom both of you report, point out the budgeting and scheduling difficulties, and request that old standards be applied this one last time.
5. You can tell the quality control manager that if she does not go along with your suggestion to impose the stricter standards only on future production, you will no longer be able to lend her one of your operators for inspection work when she needs one.

Other alternatives may be open to you, but assume that these are the only ones you have considered. WITHOUT DISCUSSION with anyone, choose one of them and be prepared to defend your choice.

19 Managing Change and Culture

LEARNING OBJECTIVES

After studying this chapter,
you should be able to:

1 Recount the three major categories of organizational change.

2 List four different reasons why employees resist change.

3 Identify several prescriptions for reducing resistance to change.

4 Summarize the four phases of an organizational development (OD) program.

5 Specify four of the most frequently used methods for intervention/education in an organizational development program.

6 Define corporate culture.

7 Describe the different factors that can contribute to an organization's culture.

8 Describe the four generic types of organizational culture.

The serious business of modern American culture is that of taming, harnessing, subduing, tempering, rationalizing, and understanding the powerful and mystifying thing that we believe to be within us and around us, and to animate all things—which we call "nature." Our personal and collective values are all measured by this enterprise, whether we speak of health, sanity, performance, sportsmanship, morality, or progress. Our collective culture is a vast accumulation of material and spiritual achievements and resources stemming from the conquest of nature and necessary to the continuance of this effort. It includes the substantial foundations of our cities and economic life, the massive banks of "information" and "knowledge" that fill our libraries and computers, the triumphs of art and science, and the arcane and ubiquitous labyrinths of technology. These are our heritage, our property, our life and our work, and our means of carrying forth our ideals and commitments.

ROY WAGNER ★

T he two major topics of this chapter—organizational change and organizational culture—are inextricably related. Both of these topics have recently been pushed to the forefront in management circles. The many reasons for heightened interest in these topics all relate to the increasing rate of change in today's world. The following analogy shows the rate of change in the modern world:

Suppose that we reduce to 12 months the total duration of the known period of history of man: some 30,000 years. In these 12 months which represent the life of all our ancestors from the Stone Age until the present, it is toward the 18th of October that the Iron Age begins. On the 8th of December, the Christian era begins.

On the 29th of December, Louis XVI ascends the throne of France. What mechanical power does mankind possess at that epoch? Exactly the same as that which the caveman had possessed plus whatever he was able to derive from draft animals after the invention of the yoke.

On the 30th of December, in the first 18 minutes of the morning, Watt invents the steam engine. Later that same day, at 4 P.M., the first railway begins to operate.

And thus we reach the last day of the year. The 31st of December. Before daybreak, Edison invents the first incandescent lamps. By early afternoon, Bleriot crosses the English Channel. And not until mid- to late afternoon does World War I begin. At this late hour, Western man disposes of ⁸⁄₁₀ of a horsepower. This is notable and brutal progress because:

★ Reprinted from *The Invention of Culture*, rev. ed. by Roy Wagner, p. 140, by permission of The University of Chicago Press. © 1981 by (The University of Chicago Press).

MANAGERS AT WORK 19–1

A Changing Business Environment

In *Megatrends,* author John Naisbitt notes that one of the most significant changes of the 1970s was the move away from a focus on the national economy toward a focus on the world economy. During the 1950s and 60s, U.S. productivity growth increased more than 3 percent per year. In 1960, the United States had a 25 percent share of the world market in manufacturing, and American companies produced 95 percent of the automobiles, steel, and consumer electronic goods sold in the United States. But the United States, the world, and the world economy have changed. During the 1970s, U.S. productivity growth fell to 1 percent per year and in some years actually declined. In 1979, the U.S. share of world manufacturing was 17 percent, and American companies produced 79 percent of the automobiles, 86 percent of the steel, and less than 50 percent of the consumer electronic goods sold in the United States. In 1985, the U.S. share of world manufacturing was 14 percent, and American companies produced 14 percent of the automobiles, 75 percent of the steel, and less than 40 percent of the consumer electronic goods sold in the United States.

Source: Adapted from John Naisbitt, *Megatrends* (New York: Warner Books, 1982), pp. 55–56.

During the whole year, he has lived with only $\frac{1}{10}$ of a horsepower. In one day, he has multiplied it by 8; but only five hours suffice to bring this figure to 80.

The following events take place during the last few minutes of the day: The first atomic bomb explodes, Neil Armstrong walks on the moon, and 50 million computers are in use.[1]

The faster rate of change forced organizations to adapt at an equally increasing rate. Managers at Work 19–1 describes several recent worldwide changes that have affected modern organizations. At this point, organizations first discovered that they could not always change their cultures as quickly as desired. Because of the problem, increasing attention has been focused on the study of organizational culture.

MANAGING CHANGE

As suggested by the analogy in the opening paragraph of this chapter, organizations today are beset by change. Many managers find themselves unable to cope with an environment or an organization which has become substantially different from the one in which they received their training and gained their early experience. Other managers find difficulty in transferring their skills to a new assignment in a different industry. A growing organization, a new assignment, and changing customer needs all may be encountered by today's managers. If managers are to be successful they must be able to adapt to these changes.

Technological changes – such things as new equipment and new processes.

Environmental changes – all non-technological changes that occur outside the organization.

Internal changes – budget adjustments, policy changes, personnel changes, and the like.

Change as it applies to organizations can be classified into three major categories: (1) technological, (2) environmental, and (3) internal to the organization. **Technological changes** are such things as new equipment and new processes. The technological advances since World War II have been dramatic, with computers being the most notable. **Environmental changes** are all those nontechnological changes that occur outside the organization. New government regulations, new social trends, and economic changes are all examples of environmental change. **Changes internal** to the organization include such things as budget adjustments, policy changes, and personnel changes. Figure 19–1 illustrates the three major categories of change.

Any of the types of changes previously discussed can greatly impact on a manager's job. Different people react in different ways to changes, and this complicates the manager's job. The next section discusses possible employee reactions to change.

F I G U R E 19–1 Types of Changes Affecting Organizations

TECHNOLOGICAL	ENVIRONMENTAL	INTERNAL
Machines	Laws	Policies
Equipment	Taxes	Procedures
Processes	Social trends	Methods
Automation	Fashion trends	Rules
Computers	Political trends	Reorganization
New raw materials	Economic trends	Budget adjustment
	Interest rates	Restructuring of jobs
	Consumer trends	Personnel
	Competition	Management
	Suppliers	Ownership
	Population trends	Products/Services sold

Employee Reactions to Change

How an employee perceives a change greatly affects how that person reacts to the change. While many variations are possible, there are four basic situations that can occur:

1. If employees cannot foresee how the change will affect them, they will resist the change or be neutral at best. Most people shy away from the unknown. The attitude often is that the change may make things worse.

2. If it is clearly seen that the change does not fit employees' needs and hopes, they will resist the change. In this instance, employees are confident that the change will make things worse.

3. If employees see that the change is going to take place regardless, they may first resist and then resign themselves to the change. The first reaction is to resist. Once the change appears inevitable, employees often see no other choice but to go along with the change.

4. If employees view the change as in their best interests, then they will be motivated to accept it. The key here is for the employees to feel sure that the change will make things better.

Note that three out of four of these situations result in some form of resistance to change. Also, the way in which employees resist change can vary greatly. For example, an employee may mildly resist by not acting interested in the change. At the other extreme, an employee may resist by trying to sabotage the change.

Resistance to Change

Most people profess to be modern and up-to-date. However, they still resist change. This is most true when the change affects their jobs. Resistance to change is a natural, normal reaction. It is not a reaction reserved only for troublemakers.

Resistance to change may be very open, or it may be very subtle. The employee who quits a job because of a change in company policy is showing resistance to change in a very open and explicit manner. Another employee who stays but becomes very sullen is resisting in a more passive manner.

Barriers to Change. There are many reasons why employees resist change. Some of the reasons found most often are discussed below.

1. Fear of the unknown. It is natural human behavior for people to fear the unknown. With many changes, the outcome is not foreseeable. When it is, the results are often not made known to all of the affected employees. For example, employees may worry about and resist a new computer if they are not sure what its impact will be on their jobs. Similarly, employees may resist a new manager simply because they don't know what to expect. A related fear is the uncertainty that employees may feel about working in a changed environment. They may fully understand a change, yet really doubt whether they will be able to handle the change. For example, an employee may resist a change in procedure because of a fear of not being able to master it.

2. Economics. Employees fear any change that they think threatens their job or income. The threat may be real or only imagined. In either case, the result is resistance. For example, a salesperson who believes that a territory change will result in less income will resist the change. Similarly, production workers will oppose new standards that they believe will be harder to achieve.

3. Inconvenience. Many changes result in personal inconveniences to the affected employees. If nothing else, they often have to learn new ways. This may mean more training, school, or practice. In either case, the employee will probably be inconvenienced. A common reaction by employees is, "it isn't worth the extra effort required."

4. Threats to interpersonal relations. The social and interpersonal relationships between employees can be quite strong. These relationships may appear unimportant to everyone but those involved. For example, eating lunch with a particular group may be very important to the involved employees. When a change, such as a transfer, threatens these relationships, the affected employees often resist. Employees naturally feel more at ease when working with people whom they know well. Also, the group may have devised methods for doing their work based on the strengths and weaknesses of group members. Any changes in the group would naturally disrupt the routine.

Reducing Resistance to Change

Most changes come from management. The way in which management implements a change often has great impact on acceptance of the change. Several suggestions for reducing resistance to change are prescribed in Figure 19–2 and discussed in the following paragraphs.

F I G U R E 19–2   Suggestions for Reducing Resistance to Change

Build trust.
Discuss upcoming changes.
Involve the employees in the changes.
Make sure the changes are reasonable.
Avoid threats.
Follow a sensible time schedule.
Implement in the most logical place.

Build trust. If employees trust and have confidence in management, they are much more likely to accept change. If there is an air of distrust, change is likely to be strongly resisted. Trust does not come overnight; it is built over a period of time. Management's actions determine the degree of trust among employees. If employees see management as fair, honest, and forthright, trust develops. If they feel that management is always trying to put something over on them, they will not exhibit trust. Managers can go a long way toward building trust if they discuss upcoming changes with the employees and if they actively involve the employees in the change process.

Discuss upcoming changes. Fear of the unknown is one of the major barriers to change. This fear can be greatly reduced by discussing any upcoming changes with the affected employees. During this discussion, the manager should be as open and honest as possible. The manager should explain not only what the change will be but also why the change is being made. The more background and detail the manager gives, the more likely that the change will be accepted by the employees. The manager should also outline the impact of the change on each affected employee. (Everyone is mainly interested in how the change will affect them personally.) A critical requirement for success is that managers give employees a chance to ask questions. Regardless of how thorough the explanation might be, employees usually have questions. Managers should try to answer each question as fully as possible.

Involve the employees. Another way to reduce resistance to change and build trust is to involve employees in the change process. While not always possible, it can be very effective. It is only natural for employees to want to go along with a change they have helped implement. A good approach is to ask for employee ideas and input as early as possible in the change process. In other words, don't wait until the last minute to ask the employees what they think; ask them as soon as possible. When affected employees have been involved in a change from or near the beginning, they will most often actively support the change. The psychology involved here is simple: Few people oppose something they have helped develop.

Make sure the changes are reasonable. The manager should always do everything possible to ensure that any proposed changes are reasonable. Often, proposals for changes come from other parts of the organization. These proposals are sometimes not reasonable, because the originator is unaware of all the pertinent circumstances. It then becomes the manager's job to do what can be done to straighten out such a situation.

Avoid threats. The manager who attempts to force change through the use of threats is taking a negative approach. This is likely to decrease rather than increase employee trust. Most people resist threats or coercion. A natural reaction is, "this must be bad news if it requires a threat." Even though threats may get results in the short run, they are often damaging in the long run. Such tactics usually have a negative impact on employee morale.

Follow a sensible time schedule. A manager can often influence the timing of changes. Some times are doubtless better than others for making certain changes. The week before Christmas, for instance, would usually not be a good time to make a major change. Similarly, a major change should normally not be attempted during the height of the vacation season. The manager can often provide valuable insight into the proper time for a change. If nothing else, the manager should always use common sense when proposing a time schedule for implementing a change.

Implement in the most logical place. Managers often have some choice as to where a change takes place. For example, a manager usually decides who will get a new piece of equipment. Those who make it a point to know their employees usually have a pretty good idea as to who will most likely be adaptable to change and who will not. Changes should, where possible, be made in such a way so as to minimize their effect on interpersonal relationships. Attempts should be made not to disturb smooth-working groups. The effect of a change on social relationships should also be considered.

All of the above suggestions require planning for successful implementation. Unfortunately, many managers do not plan for change but rather merely react to it.

Planned Change

Program of planned change – deliberate design and implementation of a structural innovation, a new policy or goal, or a change in operating philosophy, climate, and style.

Many times the need for a change can be foreseen and plans made. It is desirable then to develop a program of planned change. A **program of planned change** has been defined as "the deliberate design and implementation of a structural innovation, a new policy or goal, or a change in operating philosophy, climate, and style."[2] A program of planned change is most needed when the change will pervade most or all of the organization, as opposed to only a small segment of it.

A program of planned change usually involves a change agent—the person responsible for coordinating and overseeing the change process. A change agent can be an employee of the organization or an outside consultant.

Implementing a planned change. Basically, three elements of an organization can be altered to make a change: its organizational structure, its technology, and/or its human resources.[3] Usually, a change in one affects the others. For example, a structure change in the form of a reorganization would impact on the organization's human resources.

Structural and technological changes would be fairly simple to make except for their impact on the organization's human resources. One of the primary approaches used to change an organization's human resources is organizational development.

ORGANIZATIONAL DEVELOPMENT

Organizational development (OD) – organizationwide, planned effort managed from the top, to increase organizational performance through planned interventions.

Organizational development (OD) is an organizationwide, planned effort managed from the top, with a goal of increasing organizational performance through planned interventions in the organization. In particular, OD looks at the human side of organizations. It seeks to change attitudes, values, and management practices in an effort to improve organizational performance. The ultimate goal of OD is to structure the organizational environment so that managers and employees can use their skills and abilities to the fullest.

An OD effort starts with a recognition by management that organizational performance can and should be improved. Following this, most OD efforts include the following phases:

1. Diagnosis.
2. Change planning.

3. Intervention/education.
4. Evaluation.

Diagnosis involves gathering and analyzing information about the organization to determine the areas in need of improvement. Information is usually gathered from employees through the use of questionnaires or attitude surveys. Change planning involves developing a plan for organization improvement based on the obtained data. This planning identifies specific problem areas in the organization and outlines steps that are to be taken to resolve the problems. Intervention/education involves the sharing of diagnostic information with the people who are affected by it and helping them to realize the need for change. The intervention/education phase often involves the use of outside consultants working with individuals or employee groups. It can also involve the use of management development programs. The evaluation phase in effect repeats the diagnostic phase. In other words, after diagnosis, strategy planning, and education, data is gathered to determine the effects of the OD effort on the total organization. This information can then lead to more planning and education. Each of these phases is discussed in greater depth in the following sections.

Diagnosis – gathering and analyzing information about an organization to determine areas in need of improvement or change.

Diagnosis

The first decision to be made in the OD process is whether the organization has the talent and available time necessary to conduct the diagnosis. If not, the alternative is to hire an outside consultant. Once the decision has been made regarding who will do the diagnosis, the next step is to gather and analyze information. Some of the most frequently used methods for doing this are discussed below.

1. Review available records. The first step is to review any available records or documents that might be pertinent. Personnel records and financial reports are two types of generally available records that can be useful.

2. Survey questionnaires. The most popular method of gathering data is through questionnaires filled out by employees. Usually the questionnaires are intended to measure employee attitudes and perceptions about certain work-related factors.

3. Personal interviews. Under this approach, employees are individually interviewed regarding their opinions and perceptions and certain work-related factors. This method takes more time than the survey questionnaire method but can result in better information.

4. Direct observation. Under this method, the person conducting the diagnosis observes firsthand the behavior of organizational members at work. One advantage of this method is to see what people actually do as opposed to what they say they do.

Change Planning

The data collected in the diagnosis stage must be carefully interpreted to determine the best plan for organizational improvement. If a similar diagnosis has been done in the past, it can be revealing to compare the data and look for any obvious differences. Because much of the collected data is based on personal opinions and perceptions, there will always be areas of disagreement. The key to interpreting the data is to look for trends and areas of general agreement. The end result of the change planning process is to identify specific problem areas and to outline steps for resolving the problems.

Intervention/Education

The purpose of this phase is to share the information obtained from the diagnostic phase with the affected employees and to help them realize the need for change. A thorough analysis in the change planning phase often results in the identification of the most appropriate intervention/education method to be used. Some of the most frequently used intervention/education methods are discussed below.

Direct feedback – change agent communicates the information gathered through diagnosis directly to the affected people.

Direct feedback. With the **direct feedback** method, the change agent communicates the information gathered in the diagnostic and change planning phases to the involved parties. The change agent describes what was found and what changes are recommended. Workshops are then often conducted to initiate the desired changes.

Team building – work group develops awareness of conditions that keep them from functioning effectively and takes action to eliminate these conditions.

Team building. The objective of this method is to increase the group cohesiveness and general group spirit. **Team building** stresses the importance of working together. Many of the methods discussed in Chapter 17 are used to build teams. Some of the specific activities used include: (1) clarifying employee roles; (2) reducing conflict; (3) improving interpersonal relations; and (4) improving problem-solving skills.[4]

Sensitivity training – method used in OD to make one more aware of oneself and one's impact on others.

Sensitivity training. **Sensitivity training** is designed to make one more aware of oneself and one's impact on others. Sensitivity training involves a group, normally called a training group or T-group, which meets and has no agenda or particular focus. Normally, the group has between 10 and 15 people who may or may not know each other. With no planned structure and/or no prior common experiences, the behavior of individuals in trying to deal with the lack of structure becomes the agenda. While engaging in group dialogue, members are encouraged to learn about themselves and others in the nonstructured environment.

Although sensitivity training sessions have no agenda, there is a desired pattern of events. The group meets with no directive leadership patterns, no authority positions, no formal agenda, and no power and status positions. Therefore, a vacuum exists. Nonevaluative feedback received by individuals on their behavior from other group members is the method of learning. From this feedback and from limited guidance by the trainer, a feeling of mutual trust follows. Openness and mutual trust emerge as the members of the group serve as resources to one another. Collaborative behavior develops. Finally, the group explores the relevance of the experience as it relates to the organization.

Sensitivity training has been both passionately criticized and defended as to its relative value for organizations. In general, the research shows that people with sensitivity training tend to show increased sensitivity, more open communication, and increased flexibility.[5] However, these same studies indicate that it is difficult to predict exactly the outcome of sensitivity training for any one person. The outcomes of sensitivity training are beneficial in general, but the impact of such training for any one person cannot be predicted.

Grid OD training. **Grid OD training** is an extension of the Managerial Grid, which was discussed in Chapter 15. The methods used in grid OD training can be divided into six phases:[6]

Grid training – method used in OD to make managers and organizations more team oriented.

1. Laboratory-seminar training: Designed to introduce the participant to the Managerial Grid concepts and material. Each manager determines where he or she falls on the Managerial Grid.
2. Team development: Involves establishing the ground rules and relationships necessary for 9,9 management.
3. Intergroup development: Involves establishing the ground rules and relationships necessary for 9,9 management for group-to-group working relationships.
4. Organizational goal setting: Management by objectives is used to establish individual and organizational goals.
5. Goal attainment: Goals established in phase 4 are pursued.
6. Stabilization: Changes brought about by the other phases are evaluated, and an overall evaluation of the program is made.

As with sensitivity training, grid OD training has met with mixed success in organizations. Little research has been conducted on grid training; more is needed before conclusions can be drawn regarding its effectiveness.[7]

Evaluation

Probably the most difficult phase in the OD process is the evaluation phase.[8] The basic question to be answered is: Did the OD process produce the desired results? Unfortunately, many OD efforts begin with admirable but overly vague objectives such as improving the overall health, culture, or climate of an organization. Before any OD effort can be evaluated, explicit objectives must be determined. Objectives of an OD effort should be outcome-oriented and they should lend themselves to the development of measurable criteria.

A second requirement for evaluating OD efforts is that the evaluation effort be methodologically sound. Ideally an OD effort should be evaluated using hard, objective data. One approach is to compare data collected before

MANAGERS AT WORK 19–2

Organization Development at SAS

When Jan Carlzon came to Scandinavian Airlines (SAS) in 1981, the company had lost $20 million in that year. Carlzon produced a $54 million profit the next year. Carlzon was able to produce such a turnaround by changing the organization's outlook toward customer service. Prior to Carlzon, SAS was very rigid and its employees could do little more than follow rules and regulations. Through an organizationwide effort involving individual and group counseling, Carlzon was able to heighten employees' sensitivity to customer needs. At the same time, Carlzon gave lower-level employees more authority and responsibility so that they could better satisfy customers. For example, employees making announcements over the plane's public address system were encouraged to improvise and change the previously rigid script to make it more interesting to the passengers. According to Carlzon, "You can get people to develop their skills not by steering them with fixed rules but by giving them the total responsibility to achieve a specified result."

Source: Adapted from Jan Carlzon, "Moments of Truth," *Industry Week,* July 27, 1987, pp. 40–44.

the OD intervention against data collected after the OD intervention. An even better approach is to compare "before" and "after" data with similar data from a control group. When using this approach, two similar groups are identified—an experimental group and a control group. The OD effort is then implemented with the experimental group but not with the control group. After the OD invervention has been completed, the before and after data from the experimental group is compared with the before and after data from the control group. This approach helps to rule out changes that might have occurred as a result of factors other than the OD intervention.

From a practical standpoint, it may be desirable to use different personnel for evaluating an OD effort than those that implemented the effort. The potential problem is that those who implemented the effort may not be capable of objectively evaluating the effort. Managers at Work 19–2 describes a recent OD effort at Scandinavian Airlines (SAS).

MANAGEMENT ORGANIZATION CULTURE

The word *culture* is derived in a roundabout way from the latin verb *colere,* which means "to cultivate."[9] In later times, the word *culture* came to indicate a process of refinement and breeding in domesticating some particular crop. The modern-day meaning draws upon this agricultural derivation: It relates to society's control, refinement, and domestication of itself. A contemporary definition of **culture** is "the set of important understandings (often unstated) that members of a community share in common."[10]

Culture in an organization compares to personality in a person. Humans have fairly enduring and stable traits which help them protect their attitudes and behaviors. So do organizations. In addition, certain groups of traits or personality types are known to consist of common elements. Organizations can be described in similar terms. They can be warm, aggressive, friendly, open, innovative, conservative, and so forth. An organization's culture is transmitted in many ways, including long-standing and often unwritten rules, shared standards about what is important, prejudices, standards for social etiquette and demeanor, established customs for how to relate to peers, subordinates, and superiors, and other traditions that clarify to employees what is and is not appropriate behavior. Thus, **corporate culture** communicates how people in the organization should behave, by establishing a value system conveyed through rites, rituals, myths, legends, and actions. Simply stated, corporate culture means "the way we do things around here."[11]

> Culture – set of important understandings (often unstated) that members of a community share in common.

Cultural Forms of Expression

Culture has two basic components: (1) substance, the meanings contained in its values, norms, and beliefs; and (2) forms, the practices whereby these meanings are expressed, affirmed, and communicated to members.[12] Figure 19–3 defines many most often encountered forms of cultural expression.

> Corporate culture – communicates how people in an organization should behave, by establishing a value system conveyed through rites, rituals, myths, legends, and actions.

How Does Culture Originate?

There is no question that different organizations develop different cultures. Figure 19–4 summarizes certain cultural characteristics of some well-known companies. What causes an organization to develop a particular type of culture? Many trace their culture to one person who provided a living example of the major values of the organization. Robert Wood Johnson of Johnson & Johnson, Harley Procter of Procter & Gamble, Walt Disney of Walt Disney Productions, and Thomas J. Watson, Sr., of IBM all left their imprints on the organizations they headed. Research indicates, however, that fewer than half of a new company's values reflect the values of the founder or chief executive. The rest appear to develop in response both to the environment in which the business operates and to the needs of the employees.[13] Four separate factors contribute to an organization's culture: its history, its environment, its selection process, and its socialization processes.[14]

History. Employees are aware of the organization's past, and this awareness builds culture. Much of the "way things are done" is a continuation of how

F I G U R E   19–3   Frequently Encountered Forms of
Cultural Expression

FORM	DEFINITION
Rite	Relatively elaborate, dramatic, planned sets of activities that consolidate various forms of cultural expressions into one event, which is carried out through social interactions, usually for the benefit of an audience.
Ceremonial	System of several rites connected with a single occasion or event.
Ritual	Standardized, detailed set of techniques and behaviors that manage anxieties but seldom produce intended, technical consequences of practical importance.
Myth	Dramatic narrative of imagined events, usually used to explain origins or transformations of something. Also, an unquestioned belief about the practical benefits of certain techniques and behaviors that is not supported by demonstrated facts.
Saga	Historical narrative describing the unique accomplishments of a group and its leaders—usually in heroic terms.
Legend	Handed-down narrative of some wonderful event that is based in history but has been embellished with fictional details.
Story	Narrative based on true events—often a combination of truth and fiction.
Folktale	Completely fictional narrative.
Symbol	Any object, act, event, quality, or relation that serves as a vehicle for conveying meaning, usually by representing another thing.
Language	A particular form or manner in which members of a group use vocal sounds and written signs to convey meanings to each other.
Gesture	Movements of parts of the body used to express meanings.
Physical setting	Those things that suround people physically and provide them with immediate sensory stimuli as they carry out culturally expressive activities.
Artifact	Material objects manufactured by people to facilitate culturally expressive activities.

Source: Harrison M. Trice and Janice M. Beyer, "Studying Organizational Cultures through Rites and Ceremonials," *Academy of Management Review* 9, no. 4 (1984), p. 655.

things have always been done. The existing values which may have been established originally by a strong leader are constantly and subtly reinforced by experiences. The status quo is also protected by the human tendency to embrace beliefs and values fervently and to resist changes. Executives for Walt Disney productions reportedly pick up litter on the grounds unconsciously, because of the Disney vision of an immaculate Disneyland.

Environment. Because all organizations must interact with their environments, the environment has a role in shaping their cultures. In the case of

AT&T (see Managers at Work 19–3), the highly formalized and risk-adverse culture was in large part a product of the regulatory environment in which it operated for so long. No longer sheltered by its monopoly power, the culture must change. The question is whether the change can come fast enough to ensure success and survival.

Staffing. Organizations tend to hire, retain, and promote persons who are similar to current employees in important ways. A person's ability to fit in can be important in these processes. This "fit" criterion ensures that current values are accepted and that potential challengers of "how we do things" are screened out. For example, organizations are often as interested in the way applicants dress and handle themselves as in their work experiences.

Entry socialization. While an organization's values, norms, and beliefs may be widely and uniformly held, they are seldom written down. The new employee, least familiar with the culture, is most likely to challenge it. It is, therefore, important to help the newcomer adopt the organization's culture. Companies with strong cultures attach great importance to the process of introducing and indoctrinating new employees. This process is called the **entry socialization** process. Entry socialization not only reduces threats to the organization from newcomers; it also lets newly hired employees know what is expected of them. It may be handled in a formal or informal manner, as well as on an individual or group basis.

Entry socialization – adaption process by which new employees are introduced and indoctrinated into an organization.

F I G U R E   19–4   Culture Characteristics of Some Well-Known Companies

COMPANY	CHARACTERISTICS
IBM	Concern for marketing drives a service philosophy that is almost unparalleled. The company maintains a hot line around the clock, seven days a week, to service its products.
ITT	Financial discipline demands total dedication. Once, an executive phoned former chairman Harold Geneen at 3 A.M. to beat out the competition in a merger deal.
Digital Equipment Corporation	Emphasis on innovation creates freedom with responsibility. Employees are allowed to set their own hours and working styles, but they are expected to show evidence of progress.
Delta Air Lines	Focus on customer service produces a high degree of teamwork. Employees will gladly substitute in other jobs to keep planes flying and baggage moving.
Atlantic Richfield Company	Emphasis on entrepreneurship encourages individual action. Operating employees have the autonomy to bid on promising fields without getting approval from top management.

Source: Adapted from "Corporate Culture: The Hard-to-Change Values that Spell Success or Failure," *Business Week*, October 27, 1980, pp. 148.

MANAGERS AT WORK 19–3

Culture Change—by Choice or by Force

A company may be forced to reevaluate its culture following an upheaval in its environment or may choose to alter its culture as part of a planned strategic change. Before their court-ordered breakup in January 1984, AT&T had a strong corporate culture that focused on delivering reliable, inexpensive phone service. Now AT&T is in the middle of what one insider termed "a cultural train wreck." The company culture that advocated consensus decision making, lifetime employment, promotion from within, and pride in service—all within the regulated environment of guaranteed profits—is now suffering in the aftermath of the divestiture. The company is now having to come to terms with a highly competitive market, a declining reputation for quality service, poor employee morale, and a totally new organization structure.

In contrast, Johnson & Johnson, the maker of Band-Aids, baby shampoo and Tylenol, is undergoing a company-initiated culture change. For years, J&J has been a strong example of a market-driven, decentralized organization with 170 virtually autonomous "companies." As part of a diversification effort, J&J acquired 25 companies in 5 years. Many of the companies are in high-technology health care markets such as surgical lasers and magnetic resonance scanners. However, changing the company's mix of businesses has been easier than changing management attitudes. Marketing and sales are unaccustomed to selling products that are used more than once, and management is unaccustomed to the cooperation among units that now seems to be necessary.

For AT&T and J&J, how well they adapt their cultures to their new environments will determine the ultimate success of the organizations.

Sources: Jeremy Main, "Waking Up AT&T: There's Life after Culture Shock," *Fortune,* December 24, 1984, pp. 66–74; "Changing a Corporate Culture," *Business Week,* May 14, 1984, pp. 130–38.

Identifying Culture

Researchers have identified seven characteristics that taken together capture the essence of an organization's culture:[15]

1. *Individual autonomy:* The degree of responsibility, independence, and opportunities for exercising initiative that individuals in the organization have.

2. *Structure:* The number of rules and regulations and the amount of direct supervision that is used to oversee and control employee behavior.

3. *Support:* The degree of assistance and warmth provided by managers to their subordinates.

4. *Identification:* The degree to which members identify with the organization as a whole rather than with their particular work group or field of professional expertise.

5. *Performance-reward:* The degree to which reward allocations (i.e., salary increases, promotions) in the organization are based on performance criteria.

6. *Conflict tolerance:* The degree of conflict present in relationships between peers and work groups, as well as the willingness to be honest and open about differences.

7. *Risk tolerance:* The degree to which employees are encouraged to be aggressive, innovative, and risk seeking.

Each of these traits should be viewed as existing on a continuum that ranges from low to high. A picture of the overall culture can be formed by appraising an organization on each of these.

There are as many distinct cultures as there are organizations. Most can be grouped into one of four basic types, determined by two factors:[16] (1) the degree of risk associated with the organization's activities and (2) the speed with which organizations and their employees get feedback indicating the success of decisions. Figure 19–5 shows in matrix form the four generic types of cultures.

F I G U R E 19–5 Generic Types of Organization Cultures

		Degree of Risk	
		High	Low
Speed of feedback	Rapid	Tough-Guy, Macho Culture	Work-Hard/Play-Hard Culture
	Slow	Bet-Your-Company Culture	Process Culture

Tough-guy, macho culture. This type of culture is characterized by individualists who regularly take high risks and get quick feedback on whether their answers are right or wrong. Teamwork is not important, and every colleague is a potential rival. In this culture, the value of cooperation is ignored; there is no chance to learn from mistakes. It tends to reward employees who are

Tough-guy, macho culture – characterized by individuals who take high risks and get quick feedback on whether their answers are right or wrong.

Work-hard/ play-hard culture —encourages employees to take few risks and to expect rapid feedback.

Bet-your-company culture — requires big-stakes decisions; considerable time passes before the results are known.

Process culture — involves low risk with little feedback; employees focus on how things are done rather than on the outcomes.

temperamental and shortsighted. *Examples:* Big advertising campaigns, the fall television season, an expensive construction project, a high-budget film.

Work-hard play-hard culture. The work-hard play-hard culture encourages employees to take few risks and to expect rapid feedback. In this culture, activity is the key to success. Rewards accrue to persistence and the ability to find a need and fill it. Because of the need for volume, team players who are friendly and outgoing thrive. *Examples:* Sales organizations of all types, including retail stores, door-to-door sales, and mass-consumer sales.

The bet-your-company culture. These cultures require big-stakes decisions, with considerable time passing before the results are known. Pressures to make the right decisions are always present in this environment. *Examples:* Capital goods companies, oil companies, investment banks, architectural firms.

Process culture. This culture involves low risk coupled with little feedback; employees must focus on how things are done rather than the outcomes. Employees in this atmosphere become cautious and protective. Those who thrive are orderly, punctual, and detail oriented. *Examples:* Banks, insurance companies, government agencies, utilities.

These generic types are often not detailed enough to apply to an organization without some modifications. In fact, within an organization, there may be a mix of cultures. For example, sales may be closer to the work-hard/play-hard designation; research and development may be closer to a bet-your-company situation. While these generic cultures help to identify major types of cultural orientation, they represent only a starting point.

Use of Consultants versus Inside Diagnosis

Examinations of culture by consultants run the risk of being superficial; but they can still be useful. Information can come from the physical setting, public statements of the organization, the way the organization greets outsiders, how people in the organization spend their time, and what employees say about the company. The major advantage of an outside diagnosis is the likelihood of objectivity.

Insiders have the chance to make a more detailed study of culture but may find it hard to be objective. They must be careful to observe rather than judge. The insider can examine career paths, tenure in jobs, specific issues which consume the time of employees, and the anecdotes and stories that are passed around.

Changing Culture

Implicit in this discussion has been the fact that strong cultures can contribute greatly to an organization's success. The opposite is also true: Weak cultures

FIGURE 19–6   Characteristics of a Weak Culture

They have no clear values or beliefs about how to succeed in their business.

They have many beliefs as to how to succeed but cannot agree on which are most important.

Different parts of the organization have fundamentally different beliefs about how to succeed.

Those that personify the culture are destructive or disruptive and don't build upon any common understanding about what is important.

The rituals of day-to-day organizational life are disorganized and/or working at cross-purposes.

Source: Terrence E. Deal and Allan A. Kennedy, *Corporate Cultures: The Rites and Rituals of Corporate Life* (Reading, Mass.: Addison-Wesley Publishing, 1982), pp. 135–36.

can inhibit success. Figure 19–6 summarizes some characteristics of a weak culture.

Executives who have successfully changed organization cultures estimate that it usually takes from 6 to 15 years.[17] Because organization culture is difficult and time-consuming to change, any attempts should be well thought out. Allen Kennedy, an expert on organization culture, believes that there are only five reasons to justify a large-scale cultural change.[18]

1. The organization has strong values that don't fit a changing environment.
2. The industry is very competitive and moves with lightning speed.
3. The organization is mediocre or worse.
4. The organization is about to join the ranks of the very large companies.
5. The organization is small but growing rapidly.

As we saw earlier, in Managers at Work 19–3, some organizations attempt to change their culture only when they are forced to; others anticipate a necessary change. While massive cultural reorientation may be unreasonable in most situations, it is still possible to strengthen or "fine-tune" the current situation. A statement of corporate mission consistently reinforced by systems, structures, and policies is a useful tool for strengthening the culture.

Because of the cost, time, and difficulty involved in changing culture, many people believe it is easier to change (physically replace) the people. This view assumes that most organizations promote people who fit the prevailing norms of the organization. Therefore, the easiest if not the only way to change an organization's culture is to change its people. Managers at Work 19–4 describes how new leadership is changing the culture at GE.

MANAGERS AT WORK 19–4

The Changing Culture at General Electric

Culture clash, in the case of Jack Welch, can take the form of one person versus a good portion of a newly acquired division or company. Known for a trim, no-nonsense style of management, Welch has clashed with the more laid-back style of management to be found at some organizations.

Since taking over the top spot at General Electric (GE) in 1981, Welch has taken major steps to change its culture. Welch has moved GE out of old standby businesses such as housewares and televisions and into other riskier, more profitable, businesses like broadcasting, investment banking, and high-tech manufacturing. Welch has shed the

company of 100,000 employees—about 25 percent. This included reducing the support staff from 1,700 to approximately 1,000. Welch believes that the key to success is to create a culture of "winaholics." He has attempted to do this by giving managers more authority and fostering feelings of trust and candor. Obviously when jobs are eliminated, not everyone is happy. Only time will tell just how successful Welch's new culture will be.

Source: Adapted from Aaron Bernstein and Zachary Schiller, "Jack Welch: How Good a Manager?" *Business Week,* December 14, 1987, p. 95.

SUMMARY

This chapter attempts to develop an understanding of how today's rate of change affects organizations and presents several methods for implementing change and reducing resistance to change. Organizational development is discussed in depth as a method of introducing change. Corporate culture is defined and different types of cultures are described.

LEARNING OBJECTIVE 1

Recount the Three Major Categories of Organizational Change.

The three major categories or types of change are: (1) technological, (2) environmental, and (3) internal to the organization.

LEARNING OBJECTIVE 2

List Four Different Reasons Why Employees Resist Change.

There are many reasons why employees resist change. Four of the most frequently encountered reasons include: (1) fear of the unknown, (2) economics, (3) inconvenience, and (4) threats to interpersonal relations.

LEARNING OBJECTIVE 3

Identify Several Prescriptions for Reducing Resistance to Change.

Just as there are many reasons why employees resist change, there are also many approaches for reducing resistance to change. Several suggestions for reducing resistance to change include: (1) building trust between management and employees; (2) discussing upcoming changes with affected employees; (3) involving employees in the change process as early as possible; (4) making sure the proposed changes are reasonable; (5) avoiding threats; (6) following a sensible time schedule for implementing the change; and (7) implementing the change in the most logical place.

LEARNING OBJECTIVE 4

Summarize the Four Phases of an Organizational Development (OD) Program.

Most OD efforts include a diagnosis phase, a change/planning phase, an intervention/education phase, and an evaluation phase. Diagnosis involves gathering and analyzing information to determine the areas of the organization in need of improvement. Change planning involves developing a plan for organization improvement. Intervention/education involves the sharing of diagnostic information with the people who are affected by it and helping them to realize the need for change. The evaluation phase attempts to determine the effects that the OD effort has had on the organization.

LEARNING OBJECTIVE 5

Specify Four of the Most Frequently Used Methods for Intervention/Education in an Organizational Development Program.

Four of the most popular OD intervention/education methods are: (1) direct feedback, (2) team building, (3) sensitivity training, and (4) grid training.

LEARNING OBJECTIVE 6

Define Corporate Culture.

Corporate culture communicates how people in the organization should behave, by establishing a value system conveyed through rites, rituals, myths, legends, and actions. Simply stated, corporate culture means, "the way we do things around here."

LEARNING OBJECTIVE 7

Describe the Different Factors That Can Contribute to an Organization's Culture.

There are at least four separate factors that can contribute to an organization's culture: its history, its environment, its selection process, and its socialization processes. In most cases an organization's culture originates with its history and environment and is reinforced by its staffing decisions and the socialization processes.

LEARNING OBJECTIVE 8

Describe the Four Generic Types of Organizational Culture.
The tough-guy macho culture is characterized by individualists who regularly take high risks and get quick feedback on whether they are right or wrong. The work-hard/play-hard culture encourages employees to take few risks and to expect rapid feedback. The bet-your-company culture requires big-stake decisions with considerable time lags before the results are known. The process culture involves low risk coupled with little feedback; employees must focus on how things are done rather than the outcomes.

REVIEW QUESTIONS

1. Name the three major categories of change that apply to organizations.
2. Describe the four basic reactions of employees to change.
3. Name four common barriers (reasons for resistance) to change.
4. Discuss seven methods or approaches for reducing resistance to change.
5. What is a program of planned change?
6. What is organizational development (OD)? Describe the following techniques used in OD:

   a. Sensitivity training.
   b. Grid training.

7. What are the organizational characteristics which determine corporate culture?
8. How is corporate culture originated and maintained?
9. Name and briefly define the four generic types of corporate culture.
10. Under what circumstances might a change in corporate culture be attempted?

DISCUSSION QUESTIONS

1. Take a position and be prepared to defend it with regard to the following statement: Most people resist change, not because the change is harmful but because they are lazy.
2. Do you agree with this statement: Everyone should be exposed to sensitivity training at some point in his or her career. Explain.
3. Choose a not-for-profit organization of which you are a member (church, sorority, campus club, professional group) and analyze its culture. How is your behavior as a member shaped by the culture? How are expectations transmitted to new members?
4. Pick an actual organization or industry that you think will need to change its culture if it is to thrive in the future (like AT&T in Managers at Work 19–3). Be prepared to explain why you feel this change must occur.

REFERENCES & ADDITIONAL READINGS

[1] Adapted from R. Nordling, "Social Responsibilities of Today's Industrial Leader," quoting Jean Predseil, *S.A.M. Advanced Management Journal,* April 1957. © 1957 by Society for Advancement of Management, pp. 19–20.

[2] John M. Thomas and Warren G. Bennis, eds., *The Management of Change and Conflict* (New York: Penguin Books, 1972), p. 109.

[3] Harold J. Leavitt, "Applied Organization Change in Industry; Structural, Technical, and Human Approaches," in *New Perspectives in Organization Research,* ed. W. W. Cooper, H. J. Leavitt, and M. W. Shelly II (New York: John Wiley & Sons, 1964), pp. 55–71.

[4] Arthur G. Bedeian, *Management* (Hinsdale, Ill.: Dryden Press, 1986).

[5] Michael Beer, "The Technology of Organization Development," in *Handbook of Industrial and Organizational Psychology,* ed. Marvin D. Dunnette (New York: John Wiley & Sons, 1983), p. 941; and Michael Beer, *Organization Change and Development: A Systems View* (Santa Monica, Calif.: Goodyear Publishing, 1980), pp. 194–95.

[6] Robert R. Blake, Jane S. Mouton, Louis B. Barnes, and Larry E. Greenes, "Breakthrough in Organization Development," *Harvard Business Review,* November–December 1964, pp. 137–38.

[7] Beer, "The Technology of Organization Development," p. 943; John M. Nicholas, "Evaluation Research in Organizational Change Interventions: Considerations and Some Suggestions," *Journal of Applied Behavioral Science,* January–March 1979, pp. 23–40.

[8] Much of this section is drawn from David E. Terpstra, "The Organization Development Evaluation Process: Some Problems and Proposals," *Human Resource Management,* Spring 1981, p. 24.

[9] Roy Wagner, *The Invention of Culture,* rev. ed. (Chicago: University of Chicago Press, 1981), p. 21.

[10] Vijay Sathe, "Implications of Corporate Culture: A Manager's Guide to Action," *Organizational Dynamics,* Autumn 1983, p. 6.

[11] Terrence E. Deal and Allan A. Kennedy, *Corporate Cultures: The Rites and Rituals of Corporate Life* (Reading, Mass.: Addison-Wesley Publishing, 1982), p. 4.

[12] Harrison M. Trice and Janice M. Beyer, "Studying Organizational Cultures through Rites and Ceremonials," *Academy of Management Review* 9, no. 4 (1984), p. 645.

[13] "The Corporate Culture Vultures," *Fortune,* October 17, 1983, p. 72

[14] Stephen P. Robbins, *Essentials of Organizational Behavior* (Englewood Cliffs, N.J.: Prentice-Hall, 1984), pp. 174–76.

[15] S. P. Robbins, *Essentials of Organizational Behavior,* © 1984, p. 171. Reprinted by permission of Prentice-Hall, Inc., Englewood Cliffs, N.J.

[16] Deal and Kennedy, *Corporate Cultures,* p. 107.

[17] This section is drawn from Deal and Kennedy, *Corporate Cultures,* pp. 129–35.

[18] "The Corporate Culture Vultures," p. 70.

INCIDENT

The Way We Do Things

The Fitzgerald Company manufactures a variety of consumer products for sale through retail department stores. For over 30 years, the company has held a strong belief that customer relations and a strong selling orientation are the keys to business success. As a result, all top executives have sales backgrounds and spend much of their time outside the company with customers. Because of the strong focus on the customer, management at Fitzgerald emphasizes new-product development projects and growth in volume. The company rarely implements cost reduction or process improvement projects.

Between 1968 and 1978 Fitzgerald's 10 percent share of the market was the largest in the industry. Profitability was consistently better than the industry average. However, in the last 10 years, the markets for many of Fitzgerald's products have matured, and Fitzgerald has dropped from market share leader to the number three company in the industry. Profitability has steadily declined since 1983 although Fitzgerald offers a more extensive line of products than any of its competitors. Customers are complaining that Fitzgerald's prices are higher than those of other companies.

In June 1988, Jeff Steele, the President of Fitzgerald Company, hired Valerie Stevens of Management Consultants, Inc. to help him improve the company's financial performance. After an extensive study of Fitzgerald Company and its industry group, Valerie met with Jeff and said, "Jeff, I believe the Fitzgerald Company may have to substantially change the way it does business."

Questions

1. Describe the corporate culture at the Fitzgerald Company.

2. What does Valerie mean when she says the Fitzgerald Company may have to change the way it does business? What are some of the necessary changes?

3. Discuss the problems the company may encounter in attempting to implement changes.

EXERCISE

Resisting Change

O ne of the problems you face involves mistakes being made by employees who perform a particular operation. The same mistakes seem to occur in more than one department. You feel that a training program for the people concerned will help reduce errors.

You are aware, however, that your supervisors may defend existing procedures simply because the introduction of training may imply criticism of the way they have been operating. You realize, too, that the supervisors may fear resistance by employees afraid of not doing well in the training program. All in all, you plan to approach the subject carefully.

1. Add to the agenda of your weekly staff meeting a recommendation that training be undertaken to help reduce errors.
2. Talk to all your supervisors individually and get their attitudes and ideas about what to do before bringing the subject up in the weekly staff meeting.
3. Ask the corporate training staff to come in, determine the training needs, and develop a program to meet those needs.
4. Since this training is in the best interests of the company, tell your supervisors that they will be expected to implement and support it.
5. Appoint a team to study the matter thoroughly, develop recommendations, then bring it before the full staff meeting.

Other alternatives may be open to you, but assume that these are the only ones you have considered. WITHOUT DISCUSSION with anyone, choose one of them and be prepared to defend your choice.

CASE

Chick-fil-A★

Chick-fil-A is a breast of chicken sandwich—garnished with a pickle and served on a fresh, buttered bun—around which a whole enterprise has been built. The fast-food restaurant chain is also called Chick-fil-A. Founded by S. Truett Cathy in 1967, Chick-fil-A had 345 outlets from coast to coast by 1986. In 1986, Nationwide sales reached $181 million, up $20 million over the previous year. Average outlet sales of $540,000 were recorded. Average operator income was more than $50,000 per year. All of this was accomplished within the fast-food industry, which is quickly maturing and marked with tremendous competition in all of its segments. Chick-fil-A's high-quality, tasty breast of chicken sandwich recipe and other homemade accompaniments like fresh lemonade and lemon pie have resulted in so much financial success that 90 percent of financing for each new unit is generated internally.

Chick-fil-A is a special business entity in many ways. Its consistent record of success in the highly competitive fast-food business stems from various factors which involve all of Chick-fil-A's people. Basic to this is Truett Cathy's personality, which has greatly contributed to the people orientation at Chick-fil-A. First, Cathy is a Christian businessman with a deep religious faith. The corporate purpose statement of the enterprise reads: To glorify God by being faithful stewards of all that is entrusted to us. To have a positive influence on all who come into contact with Chick-fil-A. Cathy is quick to tell anyone who questions the Christian orientation of the firm that a "business run by Christian principles" does not require that you be a Christian. What it does mean is to believe in service and in helping others. His whole life is a demonstration of this orientation.

One example of Cathy's people orientation is the pleasant surroundings at Chick-fil-A corporate headquarters. The 110,000-square-foot building, featuring an 80-foot atrium lobby and a five-story spiral staircase, cost $7.5 million. Each floor opens into the lobby, which is topped by a clear, skylighted roof. Two glass elevators ride up the outside of the elevator shaft. Mr. Cathy wanted the building to blend into its peaceful surroundings, and it seems to almost be lost among the surrounding trees. It is hard to believe that a busy major highway is nearby. The setting, with its emphasis on nature and open space, makes both staff and visitors feel right at home at Chick-fil-A headquarters.

★ This case was prepared by Jean Marie Hanebury, Salisbury State University, Salisbury, Md. Used by permission.

Truett Cathy is committed to the quality of his product and to the excellence of his company. At the same time, he has spent as much time as possible helping others to develop their potential. Most fast-food operations have grown through the franchise system. For a hefty fee, franchisees buy into such successful chains as McDonald's, Burger King, and Mrs. Winner's Chicken. In contrast, Chick-fil-A has used the people orientation of the founder. Their unique system, called the owner-operator system, is structured in a rather unusual manner. Going back to his experience as a young family man trying to make a living and to have a happy family life, Mr. Cathy incorporated his own philosophy into the conception of how his restaurants would be organized and staffed. His son Dan puts it this way: "Dad's vision is all based on his prior restaurant experience. You can handle any other pressure if you don't have financial pressure. Consequently, the Chick-fil-A system is designed to relieve our owner-operators from financial burdens and requires the initial investment of just $5,000."

For the initial $5,000 investment, an operator is completely trained in the operations end of the business. New operators are guaranteed a minimum income of $20,000 for each of the first two years. After this initial period, they are guaranteed $12,000 plus 50 percent of the net profits. The parent company receives 15 percent of gross sales each year, and 3.25 percent of sales are used in the national advertising program. All of these monies are spent back in the local markets. There are also three or four national advertising campaigns per year.

Additionally, hundreds of thousands of pounds of chicken are given away in front of stores each year. A minimum of 100 pounds is distributed at *each* location each month. Owner-operators are free to decide how their share of the advertising budget should be spent—on newspaper ads, free coupons given out at the location, or other promotions. This allows the feeling of autonomy that is emphasized in the loose-tight approach that marks Chick-fil-A's people-oriented business plan.

Each owner-operator must be ready and willing to invest long hours to make the restaurant unit a success. The units operate six days each week. It is a cardinal rule with Truett Cathy that no Chick-fil-A will be open on Sunday; the only operator to violate this dictum is no longer with the company. The average operator can reasonably expect to make $50,000 after five years with the enterprise. In 1985, 39 of the owner-operators made more than $70,000.

One of Chick-fil-A's rules forbids multiple ownership. Cathy and his staff feel that each operator can manage just one Chick-fil-A. "Absentee ownership just doesn't work," he firmly asserts. "Each operator must run his own store. Taking on more than one would disturb [the manager's] effectiveness." President James Collins sees this philosophy as another key to success. At the same time, unit managers are encouraged to make as much money as possible from *their own unit* each year. In fact, owner-operators can and do make more money each year than most of the headquarters staff.

Part of the people philosophy at Chick-fil-A is attracting the right people to do the best job. Previous restaurant experience is not a governing criteria for selection. Truett Cathy often says, "You can train anyone to cook chicken and make coleslaw. But it is more important to carefully select the person you train, because everything else follows that initial personnel decision." Basic work habits and work attitudes must be established and reinforced. "When you have high expectations people will do their best," is one way to sum up how things are done at Chick-fil-A. Another analogy often used by the founder and his corporate headquarters staff is that of the well-trained sports team. "It's like a football team; if you pick the right players and inspire them to hard work, they will be doing their very best for the team."

Such people epitomize both the corporate staff and the owner-operators at Chick-fil-A. Someone with entrepreneurial spirit, a successful track record, a stable family background, and a history of community service is a prime candidate. Huie Woods, senior director of human resources, reiterates the philosophy: "The boss insists that human resources are the most important asset that we have. If you are right at the people end of the business, you can't fail."

Most emphasized is the selection end of this human resource process. All selections are made at the Atlanta headquarters, where much time is spent reviewing applications for staff and owner-operator positions. People with goals and values akin to those of the founder and other key managerial personnel are sought, as they are thought to exemplify the corporate purpose of Chick-fil-A.

The initial investment to become an owner-operator is small; yet Cathy has often helped finance candidates if they show potential. It is not unusual for an employee who started out making coleslaw at a Chick-fil-A location after school to aspire to and become an owner-operator.

Chick-fil-A offers owner-operators a special benefit package. Ongoing management training is one facet of the package. As noted in the 1983 annual message: "Every February, Chick-fil-A invites operators and their spouses to an expense-paid, five-day seminar at a luxury resort. For 1984, we held the seminar at the Southampton Princess Hotel in Bermuda." These yearly retreats are not just state-of-the-business reports, operational workshops, and new marketing plans. A large part of each meeting is spent on awards ceremonies. Operators are encouraged to get to know one another and their spouses so that they might enjoy the camaraderie of sharing with old and new friends.

An incentive package includes the Symbol of Success program: Operators who increase their restaurant sales by 40 percent or more are awarded the use of a new Lincoln Continental Mark VII for one year. If the operators continue the 40 percent sales growth through another year, the car is theirs to keep.

Lines of communication are also kept open between the owner-operators and corporate headquarters. Two house organs, *Chick-fil-A Operator Newsletter* and *Chicken Chatter,* keep the Chick-fil-A "family" in touch with each other. Operators are encouraged to share promotional ideas and get reports on new corporate directions. Personal milestones such as new babies, marriages, and other personal or family triumphs are shared in this manner.

There are usually only one or two full-time employees other than the operator at each location. In many instances, the operator's spouse or another family member makes up the core of the crew, other employees are called "crew members." Eighty percent of the employees are students. They are part-time employees with an average work week of 20 hours. Again, a people orientation makes the crew another ingredient in Chick-fil-A's recipe for success.

Owner-operators make all hiring decisions when it comes to the crew. They staff their own location and decide how much to pay each worker. Using tested methods developed over the years by the headquarters staff, each location trains its own crew. Dan Cathy, director of operations, described the kind of young people that Chick-fil-A operators attract: "Lots of these youngsters are class leaders. They are the kind of young people who attract other prospective employees. It is also not unusual for brothers and sisters to follow one another into the Chick-fil-A ranks. We have had as many as three members of the same family as crew members at the same time." This is the kind of relationship corporate and local managers strive to develop. It exemplifies the team and family spirit that Chick-fil-A emphasizes.

A friendly atmosphere is important at Chick-fil-A restaurants, so new crew members are introduced to public contact gradually. Almost all Chick-fil-A restaurants are located in regional malls where there is a heavy traffic of customers who want friendly service and tasty food. Pleasing the customer is another key to success, and Chick-fil-A crew members must keep that in mind.

Each new employee participates in an individual "Crew Member Training Program." Dan Cathy sees the crew member training as a "fulfilling experience. For many, Chick-fil-A is their first business exposure. Having the privilege of taking an active involvement in crew members' development is a great responsibility." Goals are set for each new employee. One of the corporate goals mentioned again and again in training manuals is to "provide a system of recognition and incentives to motivate crew members to constantly strive for increased levels of performance and productivity."

Student workers are offered special incentives to stay and grow with Chick-fil-A. Students who work an average of 20 hours a week for a period of two years or more and maintain a C average or better, receive a $1,000 scholarship to the college of their choice. More than $4 million in scholarships have been awarded since 1973.

A milestone was set for Chick-fil-A crew members in 1984: Chick-fil-A and Berry College—a four-year liberal arts institution located in Rome, Georgia—entered into a scholarship grant program. The founder of Berry College, Martha Berry, and Truett Cathy espouse the same goals.: To excel in work and study and to take pride in a job well done. Approximately 1,500 students from all over the United States and several foreign countries make up the student body at Berry.

The new joint grant program allows about 75 young people from Chick-fil-A restaurants nationwide to be housed in the Berry Academy, a former secondary school located near the main campus. To be eligible for this new program, crew members must have worked for Chick-fil-A for at least six months. They must apply and be accepted for admission to Berry before receiving approval from corporate headquarters to enter the grant program. Plans are made for more opportunities for individual growth and leadership development through company-sponsored recreational, academic, and religious programs.

Truett Cathy's President's Message of 1984 closed with these words: "The time is coming when a large number of operators and staff will come from this pool of young people who work in Chick-fil-A restaurants. For instance, one new Chick-fil-A operator, age 22, has nine years of experience with the company already. He started out as a crew member at age 13, wiping tables after school." A tremendous responsibility comes with the more conventional rewards of being a successful business manager. At Chick-fil-A, top management feels a responsibility to operators, crew members, corporate personnel, and the public in general. They have a strong commitment to people. In fact, it is said that they don't bring in an operator or a member of the staff unless it is a person they want to be with until "one of us retires or dies!"

5 Controlling Skills

SECTION 4		SECTION 5	
Human Relations Skills 14 Motivating 15 Leading 16 Appraising and Rewarding Performance 17 Work Groups 18 Conflict and Stress 19 Change and Culture	Management Foundation	**Controlling Skills** 20 Controlling 21 Operations Control 22 Management Information Systems	Improved Organizational Performance

This final section of the book, Section 5, is concerned with the controlling aspects of management. Management control involves all of the things that managers do to ensure that things are progressing according to plans.

Chapter 20 introduces the controlling function. The reasons for management control are discussed along with the requirements of a control system. Several management control methods and techniques are explained and illustrated.

Chapter 21 deals with the controlling function as it applies to operations management. The point is stressed that an organization's operating system must be properly controlled. Operations control, inventory control, and quality control are all discussed.

The final chapter of this text, Chapter 22, discusses management information systems. This chapter is designed to develop an understanding of the role that computerized information systems play in modern organizations.

20 Controlling: Comparing Actual Results to Planned Results

LEARNING OBJECTIVES

After studying this chapter,
you should be able to:

1 Explain why management controls are necessary.

2 Describe a feedback system.

3 Discuss the basic requirements of the control process.

4 Identify the factors that impact on how much control should be exercised in an organization.

5 Differentiate between the two kinds of control methods.

6 List several control methods or systems commonly used by managers.

In many circumstances, the more managers attempt to obtain and exercise control over the behavior of others in the organization, the less control they have. Furthermore, often the less control they have, the more pressure they feel to exert greater control, which in turn often decreases the amount of control they have, etc., etc.

G E N E   D A L T O N   A N D   P A U L   L A W R E N C E *

Control – process of ensuring that organizational activities are going according to plan; accomplished by comparing actual performance to predetermined standards or objectives, then taking action to correct for any deviations.

The basic premise of organizations is that all activities will function smoothly; however, the possibility of this being false gives rise to the need for control. **Control** simply means knowing what is actually happening in comparison to preset standards or objectives. The purpose of all management controls is to alert the manager to a problem or a potential problem before it becomes critical. Control is accomplished by comparing actual performance to predetermined standards or objectives and then taking action to correct any deviations from the standard. However, as the above quote implies, control is a sensitive and complex part of the management process.

Controlling is similar to planning. It addresses these basic questions: Where are we now? Where do we want to be? How can we get there from here? But controlling takes place after the planning is completed and the organizational activities have begun. Controlling is after the fact; planning is before the fact. This does not mean that control is practiced only after problems occur; it can be preventive. Control decisions can also affect future planning decisions.

WHY PRACTICE MANAGEMENT CONTROL?

As stated above, management controls alert the manager to potentially critical problems. At top management levels, a problem occurs when the organization's goals are not being met. At middle and lower levels, a problem occurs when the objectives for which the manager is responsible are not being met. These may be departmental objectives, production standards, or other performance indicators. All forms of management controls are designed to give the manager information regarding progress. The manager can use this information to:

1. *Prevent crises.* If a manager does not know what is going on, it is easy for small, readily solved problems to turn into crises.

* Gene Dalton and Paul Lawrence, *Motivation and Control in Organizations* (Homewood, Ill.: Richard D. Irwin, 1971), p. 5.

MANAGERS AT WORK 20–1

Loan Losses Indicate a Lack of Control

The old familiar names at the top of the banking world are being replaced in many cases by regional banks. One of the reasons is that many regional banks have higher stock market values, which gives these regional banks the edge in acquiring other institutions and makes it easier for them to raise money. The lower stock value of many of the older, larger, money-centered banks is the result of problem assets on their books. In previous years, bank management did not adequately control loan portfolios, and a large percentage of bad loans were made either to Third World governments or to single industries. To make matters worse, many corporations now find they can get needed funds by going direct and issuing commercial paper, rather than using the money-centered banks as they did in the past. The end result is that the larger banks are left to handle the riskiest clients who cannot get money elsewhere. It is also interesting to note that the regional banks get some of their strength from consumer banking, an area that many of the larger banks have not pursued in the past.

Source: Adapted from Sarah Bartlett, "Banking's Balance of Power Is Tilting toward the Regionals," *Business Week,* April 7, 1986, pp. 56–64.

2. *Standardize outputs.* Problems and services can be standardized in terms of quantity and quality through the use of good controls.
3. *Appraise employee performance.* Proper controls can provide the manager with objective information about employee performance.
4. *Update plans.* Remember (from Chapter 7) that the final step in the planning process is to control the plan. Controls allow the manager to compare what is happening with what was planned.
5. *Protect an organization's assets.* Controls can protect assets from inefficiency, waste, and pilferage.

Managers at Work 20–1 describes how a lack of loan control by large banks has greatly altered the banking industry.

TWO CONCERNS OF CONTROL

In controlling, the manager must balance two major concerns: stability and objective realization. To maintain stability, the manager must be sure that the organization is operating within its established boundaries of constraint.

The boundaries of constraint are determined by policies, budgets, ethics, laws, and so on. The second concern, objective realization, requires constant monitoring to ensure that enough progress is being made toward the established objectives.

A manager may become overly worried about one concern at the expense of the other. Most common is a manager who becomes preoccupied with the stability of the operation and neglects the goal. Such behavior can lead to a lot of activity but very little output—a manager obsessed with the manner or style with which a job is done is an example. On the other hand, a manager may lose sight of stability and have glamorous but short-lived success. A manager who sets production records by stopping safety checks is an example of this behavior.

THE MANAGEMENT CONTROL PROCESS

Figure 20–1 is a simple model of the management control process. Outputs from the activity are monitored by some type of sensor and compared to preset standards (normally set during the planning process). The manager acts as the regulator; he takes corrective action when the outputs do not meet the standards. The manager's actions may be directed at the inputs to the activity or at the activity itself.

Feedback (closed) system – where outputs from the system affect future inputs or future activities of the system.

Such a system, where outputs from the system affect future inputs or future activities of the system, is called a **feedback, or closed, system.** In other words, a feedback system is influenced by its own past behaviors.[1] The heating system of a house is a common example of a mechanical feedback system. The thermostat sensor compares the temperature resulting from heat previously generated by the system to some predetermined standard (the desired temperature setting) and responds accordingly.

Feedback is a vital part of the control process. Although preventive, before-the-fact steps can often aid the control process, total control cannot be practiced without feedback. Managers may receive and act on facts about the inputs or the activity itself. But in the end, they must know what is happening in the organization; feedback gives them this information.

Three Requirements for Control

The process of control has three basic requirements: (1) establish standards; (2) monitor results and compare to standards; and (3) correct deviations. The first (setting standards) comes from the planning process, while the latter two (monitoring and correcting) are unique to the control process. All three are essential to having effective control.

Standard – value used as a point of reference for comparing other values.

Setting Standards. A **standard** is a value used as a point of reference for comparing other values. Standards, when used in management controls, come

F I G U R E   20–1   The Control Process

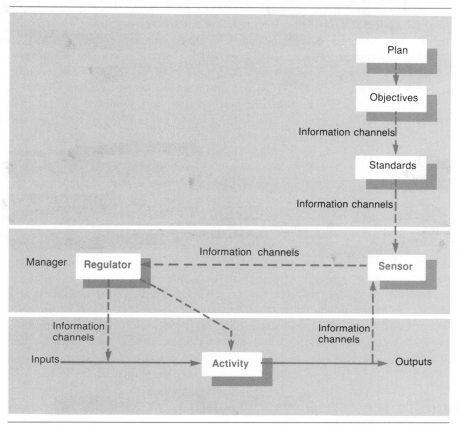

directly from objectives. As such, a standard outlines what is expected of the job and/or individual. In some instances, objectives may be used directly as standards. In other instances, performance indicators may be derived from the objectives. In either case, standards should be easy to measure and define. The more specific and measurable an objective is, the more likely that it can be directly used as a standard. Standards may deal with output per hour, quality level, inventory level, or other indicators of individual and/or organizational performance. The same guidelines presented in Chapter 7 for setting objectives should be followed for setting standards.

Monitoring Performance. Obviously, the entire control system is no better than the information on which it operates—and much of this information is gathered from the monitoring process. Monitoring is often considered to be synonymous with control. In fact, it is only part of the total control process. The main purpose of monitoring performance is to isolate problem areas. The type of standard used often dictates the type of checks to be made. Once actual performance has been checked and compared to standards, the proper corrective action can be taken.

The major problem in monitoring performance is deciding when, where, and how often to inspect or check. Checks must be made often enough to provide needed information. However, some managers become obsessed with the checking process. Monitoring can be expensive if overdone, and it can result in adverse reactions from employees. Timing is equally important. The manager must recognize a problem in time to correct it. For example, inventory control personnel must reorder stock before it has been depleted. Several techniques for monitoring performance are presented later in this chapter.

Correcting for Deviations. All too often, managers set standards and monitor results but do not follow up with actions. The first two steps are of little value if corrective action is not taken. It is entirely possible that the action that is needed may be to maintain the status quo. Action of this type would depend upon standards being met in a satisfactory manner. If standards are not being met, the manager must find the cause of the deviation and correct it. It is not enough simply to eliminate the problem itself or treat only the symptoms. This action compares to replacing a car battery when the real problem is a faulty generator. In a short time, the battery will go dead again. It is also possible that a careful analysis of the deviation will require a change in the standard. The standard may have been improperly set, or conditions may have changed so as to require a change. Figure 20–2 lists some potential causes of deviations between desired and actual performance.

F I G U R E 20–2   Potential Causes of Performance Deviations

Faulty planning.
Lack of communication within the organization.
Need for training.
Lack of motivation.
Unforeseen forces outside the organization, such as government regulation
   or competition.

Managers at Work 20–2 describes how Sony has finally taken action and moved into the VHS videotape recorder market.

Control Tolerances

Actual performance rarely conforms exactly to standards or plans. A certain amount of variation will normally occur. Therefore, the manager must set limits on the acceptable degree of deviation from standard. In other words, how much variation from standard is tolerable? The manner in which the

MANAGERS AT WORK 20–2

Sony: Better Late than Never?

Sony Corporation finally decided to add a VHS model videotape recorder to its line of home entertainment products. It has been clear for many years that VHS was becoming the dominant format in home video. Even so, Sony offered only its own Beta format recorders until recently.

Though the company has indicated that it will not abandon the Beta format, it clearly needed to offer VHS to round out its line and try and win over many of the VHS customers. Many people believe that Sony let the situation get out of hand and that they should have gotten in the VHS market sooner.

Source: Adapted from Jeffrey A. Tannenbaum, "Sony to Begin Selling VCRs in VHS Format," *The Wall Street Journal,* January 12, 1988, p. 39.

---

manager sets **control tolerances** depends on the standard being used. If the activity being monitored lends itself to numerical measurement, statistical control techniques can be used. Often, the manager must make subjective judgments as to when the system or factor being monitored is out of control. One element influencing how much deviation is acceptable is the risk of being out of control and not knowing it. In general, the lower the risk, the wider the tolerances. Figure 20–3 illustrates the idea of control tolerances. Note that the tolerance levels may be formalized, or they may merely exist in the mind of the manager. The important point is that the manager must develop some guidelines as to what deviation is acceptable (in control) and what is not acceptable (out of control).

Control tolerances – variation from the standard that is acceptable to the manager.

How Much Control?

When deciding how much control should be exercised in an organization, two major factors must be appraised: (1) economic considerations, and (2) behavioral considerations.

Economic Considerations. Installing and operating control systems cost money. A good quality control system, for instance, requires additional labor, if nothing else. The equipment costs of sophisticated electronic and mechanical control systems can be very high. Ideally, control systems should be installed as long as they save more than they cost. Figure 20–4 shows the general

FIGURE 2 0-3   Control Tolerance Limits

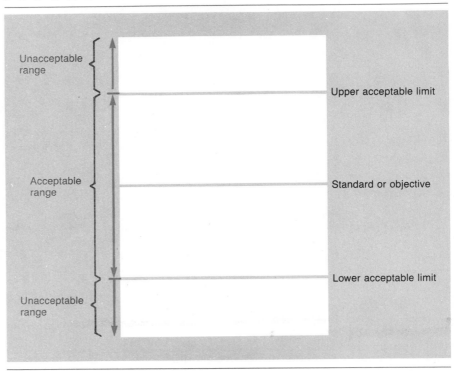

relationship between control costs and the benefits gained. It makes several points:

- There is some **optimum amount of control** (point A).
- There is some **minimum amount of control** necessary before the benefits of more control outweigh the costs (point B).
- There is some **maximum amount of control** which, if exceeded, can be very costly (point C).

The costs of implementing a control system can usually be estimated or calculated much more accurately than the benefits. For example, it is difficult to quantify and measure the true benefits of a quality control system. A good quality control system supposedly increases goodwill; but how does one measure this attribute? The decision is obviously much easier when the costs of not maintaining control are either very high or very low. Despite the measurement problems, management should regularly undertake such a study to ensure that gross misapplications do not occur.

Behavioral Considerations. Managers need to be aware of the possible impact of the control system on employees. Most people do not like to work where they feel that their every move is being watched or questioned. Still,

F I G U R E 20–4 General Relationship between Control Cost and Benefits

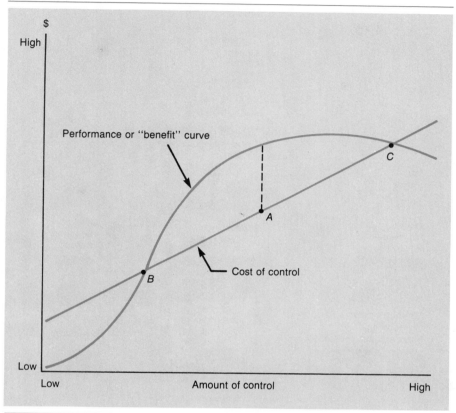

very few people like to work where there is no control: an absence of control creates an environment in which people do not know what is expected of them.

Many managers have a tendency to increase controls whenever things are not going according to plan. Figure 20–5 shows a simplified version of a model developed by Alvin Gouldner which explains this behavior.

Gouldner's model begins with top management's demand for control over operations. This is attempted through the use and enforcement of general and impersonal rules about work procedures. These rigid rules are meant to be guides for the behavior of the organization members; they also have the unintended effect of showing minimum acceptable behavior. In organizations where there is little congruence between individual and organizational objectives or there is not a high acceptance of organizational objectives, the effect is a reduction of performance to the lowest acceptable level—people not highly committed to organizational objectives will perform at the lowest acceptable

F I G U R E 20–5   Simplified Gouldner Model of Organization Control

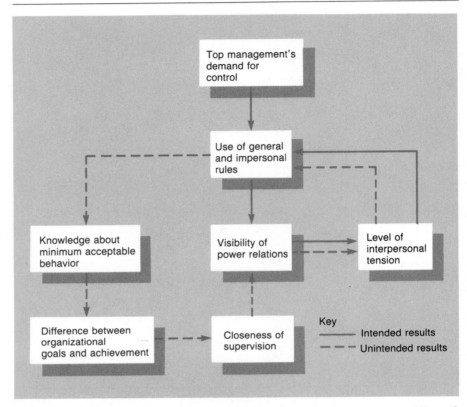

Source: James G. March and Herbert A Simon, *Organizations* (New York: John Wiley & Sons, 1958), p. 45.

level. Managers view such behavior as the result of inadequate control; they therefore respond with closer supervision. This increases the visibility of power, which in turn raises the level of interpersonal tension in the organization. Raising the tension level brings even closer enforcement of the general and impersonal formal rules. Hence, the cycle repeats itself. The overall effect is increased control, increased interpersonal tension, and a lowering of performance.

One problem in deciding the right degree of control is that different people react differently to similar controls. Research has suggested that reactions differ according to personality and prior experiences.[2] Problems can occur from unforeseen reactions to control because of both compliance and resistance.[3] Problems from compliance arise when people adhere to the prescribed behavior even when it is inappropriate. The salesperson who will not vary from prescribed procedures in order to satisfy a customer complaint is a common example of this. Problems resulting from resistance to controls arise when individuals attempt to preempt, work around, or sabotage the controls.

MANAGERS AT WORK 20-3

Drug Testing: Rights versus Efficiency

As more and more companies have become aware of the extent to which employees use drugs, they have also learned that drug abuse can have serious negative effects on employees. Employee behavior on the job can be greatly compromised through the use of drugs, even if the drugs were used the evening before. In addition to concern about potential safety problems as a result of drug use, there is a general concern about lessened efficiency for all business activities. Many employers are trying to develop a use without infringing on individual freedoms. Basically this boils down to a matter of management control versus employee rights. It is believed that this matter will be unfolding for many years to come as the courts and lawmakers decide how far management should go.

Source: Adapted from Janice Castro, "Battling the Enemy Within," *Business Week*, March 17, 1986, pp. 52–61.

Distorting a report or padding the budget is a form of control resistance.

Several things can be done to lessen negative reactions to controls. Most are based on good common sense. However, they require a real effort by the manager to carry out. The tendency is to take these suggestions for granted. They are:

1. Make sure the standards and associated controls are realistic. Standards set too high or too low turn people off. Make the standards attainable but challenging.

2. Involve subordinates in the control-setting process. Many of the behavioral problems associated with controls result from a lack of understanding of the nature and purpose of the controls. It is natural for people to resist anything new, especially if they do not understand why it is being used. Solicit and listen to suggestions from employees.

3. Use controls only where needed. As suggested by the Gouldner model, there is a strong tendency to overcontrol, to be sure that all bases are covered. Periodically evaluate the need for different controls. A good rule of thumb is to evaluate every control at least annually. Things change, which makes certain controls obsolete. Remember, overcontrol can produce some very negative results. Managers at Work 20–3 summarizes the extreme sensitivity involved in attempting to control employee drug use. Managers at Work 20–4 describes the reaction of businesses to new controls by the Indonesian government.

MANAGERS AT WORK 20–4

Too Much Government Control?

In Indonesia, the government passed a law which requires video movies to be packaged in colored containers. The color of the container indicates to the audience that it is permitted to rent and view each cassette. The law was passed in 1984 but was not actively enforced until 1987. Even though they had three years notice, many video shop owners still have large inventories of movies in the now illegal black cassettes. These owners feel that this intrusion into their operation is excessive government control.

Source: Adapted from Richard Borsuk, "It's So Simple: The Blue Movies Are Those in the Red Containers," *The Wall Street Journal,* January 12, 1988, p. 39.

Where Should Control Reside?

For years, it was believed that control in organizations was a fixed commodity that should rest only in the hands of top management. This viewpoint naturally favored a highly centralized approach to decision making and controlling. However, as decentralized organizations have become more and more common, controls have been pushed further and further down the hierarchy. It is now recognized that where the controls reside is an important factor in how much control is desirable.

Evidence favors relatively tight controls as long as they are placed as far down in the organization as possible.[4] This approach has several advantages: (1) it keeps higher-level managers from getting too involved in details; (2) it shows why the control is necessary; and (3) it elicits commitment from lower-level managers. When controls are spread through many levels of an organization, caution must be taken to ensure that there are no disagreements about how the controls are distributed.

CONTROL METHODS AND SYSTEMS

Behavior (personal) control—based on direct, personal surveillance.

Output (impersonal) control—based on the measurement of outputs.

There are two kinds of control methods: behavior control or output control. **Behavior (or personal) control** is based on direct, personal surveillance. The first-line supervisor who maintains a close personal watch over subordinates is using behavior control. **Output (or impersonal)** control is based on the measurement of outputs. Tracking production records or sales figures are examples of output controls.

Research has shown that these two categories of control are not substitutes for each other in the sense that a manager uses one or the other.[5] The evidence suggests that output control occurs in response to a manager's need to provide an accurate measure of performance. Behavior control is exerted when performance requirements are well known and personal surveillance is needed to promote efficiency and motivation. Thomas Peters and Robert Waterman strongly emphasize the need for managers at all levels to take a hands-on approach to managing.[6] By hands-on, they mean regularly mixing with subordinates and visiting them at their workplaces. Thus, organizations need to use a mix of output and behavior controls; each serves different organizational needs.

One of the most common mistakes made by managers is to assume that a new method or system of control itself will solve problems. Methods and systems, by themselves, cannot control anything! But together with good administration and intelligent interpretation, these methods and systems do provide control. The most appropriate control system is often worthless if not properly administered. Furthermore, an appropriate control system that is properly administered can only produce information that requires intelligent interpretation. Thus, the methods and systems discussed in this section should not be viewed as solutions to control problems; rather they are aids in the control process. Also note that many control tools (such as budgets) are developed as part of the planning process but are used on a regular basis as part of the control process.

Before, Concurrent, or After-the-Fact? In general, methods for exercising control can be described as either before-the-fact, concurrent, or after-the-fact. **Before-the-fact control** methods, sometimes called steering controls, attempt to prevent a problem for occurring. Requiring prior approval for purchases of all items over a certain dollar value is an example. **Concurrent controls,** also called screening controls, focus on things that happen as the inputs are being transformed into outputs. They are designed to detect a problem as it occurs. Personal observation of customers being serviced is an example of a concurrent control. **After-the-fact control** methods are designed to detect an existing or potential problem before it gets out of hand. Written or periodic reports represent after-the-fact control methods. As suggested by Figure 20–1, most controls are based on after-the-fact methods.

Budgets

Budgets are probably the most widely used control devices. A **budget** is a statement of expected results or requirements expressed in financial or numerical terms. Budgets express plans, objectives, and programs of the organization in numerical terms. Preparation of the budget is primarily a planning function (see Chapter 7); however, its administration is a controlling function.

Many different types of budgets are in use (Figure 20–6 outlines some of

Before-the-fact (steering) control — method of exercising control to prevent a problem from occurring.

Concurrent (screening) control — focus on process as it occurs, designed to detect a problem when it happens.

After-the-fact control — designed to detect a problem or potential problem before it gets out of hand.

Budget — statement of expected results or requirements expressed in financial or numerical terms.

FIGURE 20–6   Types and Purposes of Budgets

TYPE OF BUDGET	BRIEF DESCRIPTION OR PURPOSE
Revenue and expense budget.	Provides details for revenue and expense plans.
Cash budget.	Forecasts cash receipts and disbursements.
Capital expenditure budget.	Outlines specific expenditures for plant, equipment, machinery, inventories, and other capital items.
Production, material, or time budget.	Expresses physical requirements of production, or material, or the time requirements for the budget period.
Balance sheet budgets.	Forecasts the status of assets, liabilities, and net worth at the end of the budget period.

the most common types). Some may be expressed in terms other than dollars; equipment budgets may be expressed in numbers of machines. Material budgets may be expressed in pounds, pieces, gallons, and so on. Budgets not expressed in dollars can usually be translated into dollars for inclusion in an overall budget.

While budgets are useful for planning and control, they are not without their dangers. Perhaps the greatest danger is inflexibility. This is a special threat to organizations operating in an industry with rapid change and high competition. Rigidity in the budget can also lead to ignoring organizational goals for budgetary goals. The financial manager who won't go $5 over budget in order to make $500 is a classic example. Budgets can hide inefficiencies. That a certain expenditure has been made in the past often becomes justification for continuing it when the situation has greatly changed. And managers may pad budgets because they will be cut by superiors. Since the manager is never sure of how severe the cut will be, the result is often an inaccurate if not unrealistic budget.

Flexible Budgets. In order to overcome many of the shortcomings resulting from inflexibility, **flexible (variable) budgets** are designed to vary with the volume of sales or some other measure of output. Because of their nature, flexible budgets are generally limited to expense budgets. The basic idea is to allow material, labor, advertising, and other related expenses to vary with the volume of output. Because the actual level of sales or output is usually not known in advance, flexible budgets are more useful for evaluating what the expenses should have been under the circumstances; they have limited value as planning information for the overall budgeting program. Table 20–1 illustrates a simplified flexible budget.

Zero-Base Budgeting. **Zero-base budgeting** is one approach to budgeting that has received attention over the last several years. It requires each manager

Flexible (variable) budget – allows certain expenses to vary with the level of sales or output.

Zero-base budgeting – where the manager must build and justify each area of a budget. Each activity is identified, evaluated, and ranked by importance.

T A B L E 20–1 Simplified Flexible Budget

Sales (in units)	5,000	6,000	7,000	8,000	9,000
Product cost	$10,000	$12,000	$14,000	$16,000	$18,000
Advertising cost	5,000	5,000	6,000	6,000	7,000
Shipping costs	5,000	5,500	6,000	6,500	7,000
Sales commissions	2,500	3,000	3,500	4,000	4,500
Budgeted expenses	$22,500	$25,500	$29,500	$32,500	$36,500

to justify an entire budget request in detail, from scratch: the burden of proof is on each manager to justify why any money should be spent.[7] Under zero-base budgeting, each activity under a manager's discretion is identified, evaluated, and ranked by importance. Then, each year, every activity in the budget is on trial for its life and is matched against all the other claimants for an organization's resources.

Direct Observation

A store manager's daily tour of the facility; a company president's annual visit to all branches; a methods study by a staff industrial engineer—all of these are examples of control by direct observation. Although it is time-consuming, personal observation is sometimes the only way to get an accurate picture of what is really happening. One hazard is that employees may misinterpret a superior's visit and consider such action meddling or eavesdropping. Also behaviors change when people are being watched or monitored. Another potential inaccuracy lies in the interpretation of the observation. The observer must be careful not to read into the picture events that did not actually occur. Visits and direct observation can have very positive effects when viewed by the workers as a display of the superior's interest. Managers at Work 20–5 describes how the founder of McDonald's, the late Ray Kroc, used this method of control.

Written Reports

Written reports can be prepared on a periodic or "as necessary" basis. There are two basic types of written reports, analytical or informational. Analytical reports interpret the facts they present; informational reports only present the facts. Preparing a report is a four- or five-step process, depending on whether it is informational or analytical. The steps are: (1) planning the attack on the problem; (2) collecting the facts; (3) organizing the facts; (4) interpreting the facts (this step is omitted with informational reports); and (5) writing the report.[8] Most reports are prepared for the benefit of the reader, not the writer. The reader wants useful information not previously available.

MANAGERS AT WORK 20–5

Controlling through Active Involvement in Operations Details

Ray Kroc, the late founder of McDonald's Corporation, was involved in every aspect of the operations of the McDonald's fast-food business. Known as a "detail person," Ray Kroc was personally involved in setting quality and housekeeping standards, suggesting menu changes, making purchasing decisions, and performing store inspections. When potential new store sites were identified, Kroc would drive around the area and visit the local shops to see how a McDonald's store would do there. In the early 1960s Kroc proposed that the company hold classes for new operators and managers to teach them "McDonald's method of providing services." According to Ray Kroc, "If I had a brick for every time I've repeated the phrase 'Q, S, C, and V' (quality, service, cleanliness, and value), I think I'd probably be able to bridge the Atlantic Ocean with them."

Source: Adapted from Ray Kroc, "Grinding It Out: The Making of McDonald's" (Chicago: Regnery, 1977), p. 85.

The need for a report should be carefully evaluated. Periodic reports have a way of continuing long past their usefulness. Such unnecessary reports are a waste of organizational resources. Another tendency—even with necessary reports—is to include much useless information.

Audits

Audit – method of control normally involved with financial matters; also can include other areas of the organization.

Management audit – attempts to evaluate the overall management practices and policies of the organization.

Audits can be conducted either by internal or external personnel. External audits are normally done by outside accountants and are limited to financial matters. Most are done to certify that the organization's accounting methods are fair, consistent, and conform to existing practices. Most outside audits do not delve into nonfinancial matters such as management practices. The internal audit, similar to the external audit, is performed by the organization's own personnel.

When an audit looks at areas other than finances and accounting, it is known as a management audit. **Management audits** attempt to evaluate the overall management practices and policies of the organization. They can be conducted by outside consultants or inside staff; however, a management audit conducted by inside staff can easily result in a biased report.

Break-even charts depict graphically the relationship of volume of operations to profits. The break-even point (BEP) is the point at which sales revenues exactly equal expenses. Total sales below the BEP result in a loss; total sales above the BEP result in a profit.

Figure 20–7 shows a typical break-even chart. The horizontal axis represents output, the vertical axis represents expenses and revenues. It is not required, but most break-even charts assume that there are linear relationships and all costs are either fixed or variable. Fixed costs do not vary with output, at least in the short run. They include rent, insurance, and administrative salaries. Variable costs vary with output. Typical variable costs include direct labor and materials. The purpose of the chart is to show the break-even point and the effects of changes in output. A break-even chart is useful for showing whether revenue and/or costs are running as planned.

Break-even chart – depicts graphically the relationship of volume of operations to profits.

Time-Related Charts and Techniques

Gantt charts, the critical path method (CPM), and the program evaluation and control technique (PERT) (described in Chapter 9 and its Appendix) are

F I G U R E 20–7 Break-Even Chart

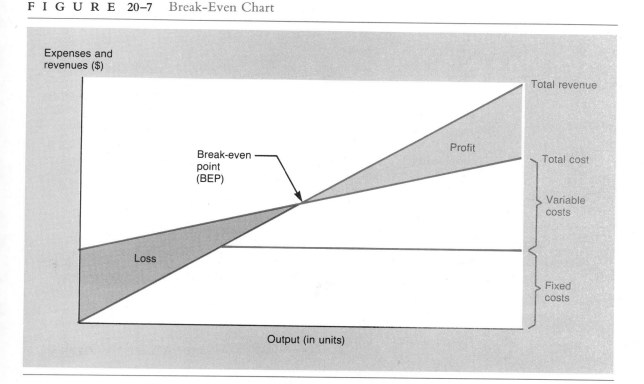

tools used to plan and schedule. These same tools can also be used for controlling once the plans have been put into action. By tracking actual progress compared to planned progress, activities that fall behind schedule can quickly be spotted.

Management by Objectives (MBO)

Management by objectives (MBO) was discussed in Chapter 7 as an effective means for setting objectives. As discussed in Chapter 16, it also can be used for control purposes. As with many of the control techniques discussed in this chapter, the development of an MBO system is part of the planning function. However, once MBO is implemented, it is used for control purposes.

Management Information Systems

In recent years, the term management information system (MIS) has become popular. A MIS is a formal system for providing information to managers. While not essential, most management information systems include the use of a computer. The basic idea behind each MIS is to provide information in a systematic and integrated manner, rather than in a sporadic and piecemeal manner. A good MIS aids managerial control by giving managers better information on a timely basis. Chapter 22 is devoted entirely to MIS.

▰ S U M M A R Y

This chapter offers a definition of management control and discusses the major elements of the managerial control process. The economic and behavioral aspects of a management control system are developed. Finally an introduction and description of several specific management control methods and techniques are presented.

LEARNING OBJECTIVE 1

Explain Why Management Controls Are Necessary.
  The overriding purpose of all management controls is to alert the manager to a problem or a potential problem before it becomes critical. Specifically, management controls can be used to: (1) prevent crises, (2) standardize outputs, (3) appraise employee performance, (4) update plans, and (5) protect an organization's assets.

LEARNING OBJECTIVE 2

Describe a Feedback System.
  Any system where the outputs from the system affect future inputs or future activities of the system is called a feedback or closed system; in other words, a feedback system is influenced by its own past behavior.

LEARNING OBJECTIVE 3

Discuss the Basic Requirements of the Control Process.

The control process has three basic requirements: (1) establish standards, (2) monitor results and compare to standards, and (3) correct for any deviations between the standard and actual results.

LEARNING OBJECTIVE 4

Identify the Factors That Impact on How Much Control Should Be Exercised in an Organization.

When deciding how much control should be exercised in an organization, two major factors must be appraised: (1) economic considerations and (2) behavioral considerations.

LEARNING OBJECTIVE 5

Differentiate between the Two Kinds of Control Methods.

Control methods can be either of two kinds: (1) behavior control or (2) output control. Behavior (or personal) control is based on direct, personal surveillance. Output (or impersonal) control is based on the measurement of outputs.

LEARNING OBJECTIVE 6

List Several Methods or Systems Commonly Used by Managers.

Many control methods or systems are in use today. Some of the most popular control methods/systems include all types of budgets, direct observations, written reports, audits, break-even charts, time-related charts/techniques, management by objectives, and various management information systems.

REVIEW QUESTIONS

1. What is management control? What are the two major concerns in management control?
2. Describe a model of the management control process.
3. Outline the three basic requirements of control.
4. How much control should be exercised in an organization?
5. Describe the two categories of control methods.

6. Describe the following control methods and systems:
   a. Budgets.
   b. Direct observation.
   c. Written reports.
   d. Audits.
   e. Break-even charts.
   f. Management by objectives.
   g. Management information systems.

DISCUSSION QUESTIONS

1. What factors should you consider before installing tighter controls? How might you evaluate these factors?
2. If you were implementing a new control system designed to check more closely the expenses of your salespeople, what actions might you take in order to minimize negative reactions?

3. Why are many managers reluctant to take the actions necessary to correct for deviations?
4. How should you deal with managers who are so "married" to their departmental budget that they will not let you spend $1 in order to make $10?

REFERENCES & ADDITIONAL READINGS

[1] Jay W. Forrester, *Principles of Systems,* 2nd ed. (Cambridge, Mass: Wright-Allen Press, 1968), pp. 1–5.

[2] For a discussion of some relevant studies, see Arnold S. Tannenbaum, "Control in Organizations: Individual Adjustment in Organization Performance," *Administrative Science Quarterly,* September 1962, pp. 241–46; Klaus Bartolke, Walter Eschweiler, Dieter Flechsenberger, and Arnold J. Tannenbaum, "Worker Participation and the Distribution of Control as Perceived by Members of Ten German Companies," *Administrative Science Quarterly* 27 (1982), pp. 380–97.

[3] Gene W. Dalton and Paul R. Lawrence, *Motivation and Control in Organizations* (Homewood, Ill.: Richard D. Irwin, 1971), p. 8.

[4] Timothy J. McMahon and G. W. Perritt, "Toward a Contingency Theory of Organizational Control," *Academy of Management Journal,* December 1973, pp. 624–35.

[5] William G. Ouchi and Mary Ann Maguire, "Organizational Control: Two Functions," *Administrative Science Quarterly,* December 1975, pp. 559–71; William G. Ouchi, "The Transmission of Control through Organizational Hierarchy," *Academy of Management Journal,* June 1978, pp. 174–76.

[6] Thomas J. Peters and Robert H. Waterman, Jr., *In Search of Excellence* (New York: Harper & Row, 1982), pp. 279–91.

[7] Stanton C. Lindquist and R. Bryant Mills, "Whatever Happened to Zero-Base Budgeting?" *Managerial Planning,* January–February 1981, pp. 31–35.

[8] C. W. Wilkinson, Dorothy Wilkinson, and Gretchen Vik, *Communicating through Letters and Reports,* 9th ed. (Homewood, Ill.: Richard D. Irwin, 1986).

INCIDENT

Mickey Mouse Controls

Bill: Hey, John, I could sure use some help. We regional supervisors are caught in the middle. What do you do about all this red tape we're having to put up with? The accounting department is all bothered about the way people are padding their expenses and about the cost of luncheons and long-distance calls. You know—their answer is nothing but more red tape.

John: Well, Bill, I don't know. I'm feeling the heat too. Upper management wants us to maintain our contacts with our brokers and try to get the money out in loans. So we push the district supervisors to see our best contacts or at least call them frequently. Yet lately, I've been having a heck of a time getting my men reimbursed for their expenses. Now the accounting department is kicking because we spend a few bucks taking someone to lunch or making a few long-distance calls.

Bill: I really don't know what to do, John. I'll admit that some of my people tend to charge the company for expenses that are for their personal entertainment. But how can I tell whether they're buttering up a broker or just living it up on the company? The accounting department must have some receipts and records to support expenses. Yet I think that getting a receipt from a parking lot attendant is carrying this control stuff too far. As a matter of fact, the other day, I caught a taxi at the airport and failed to get a receipt—I'll bet I have a hard time getting that money from the company even if I sign a notarized affidavit.

John: Well, the way I handle those things is to charge the company more for tips than I actually give—and you know they don't require receipts for tips. I just don't know how to decide whether those reimbursement receipts that I sign for my boys are legitimate. If I call a guy up and ask him about some items on a reimbursement request, he acts as though I'm charging him with grand larceny. So far, I've decided to sign whatever requests they turn in and leave the accounting department to scream if it wants to. The trouble is that I don't have any guidelines as to what is reasonable.

Bill: Yeah, but I don't want to ask questions about that because it would just result in more controls! It isn't up to me to be a policeman for the company. The accounting department sits back looking at all those figures—it should watch expenses. I ran into someone from the department the other day on what she called an internal audit trip, and she told me that they aren't in a position to say whether a $40 lunch at a restaurant is necessary to sell a loan. She said that the charge was made by one of my men and that I should check it out! Am I a regional production man or am I an accountant? I've got enough to do meeting my regional quota with my five district sales people. I can't go snooping around to find out whether they're taking advantage of the company. They may get the idea that I don't trust them, and I've always heard that good business depends on trust. Besides, our department makes the company more money than any other one. Why shouldn't we be allowed to spend a little of it?

John: Well, I say that the brass is getting hot about a relatively small problem. A little fudging on an expense account isn't going to break the company. I learned the other day that the accounting department doesn't require any receipts from the securities department people. They just give them a per diem for travel and let them spend it however they want to, just so long as they don't go over the allotted amount for the days that they're on trips.

Bill: Now that sounds like a good idea. Why can't we do that? It sure would make my life easier. I don't want to get a guilt complex about signing reimbursement requests that may look a little out of line. Why should I call a district man on the carpet for some small expense he swears really was the reason that he got the deal? Production is our job, so why can't the company leave us alone? They should let us decide what it takes to make a deal. If we don't produce the loans, we should catch flak about something that's important—not about these trifling details.

John: Bill, I've got to run now. But honestly, if I were you, I wouldn't worry about these Mickey Mouse controls. I'm just going to do my job and fill in the form in order to stay out of trouble on the details. It's not worth getting upset about.

Questions

1. Has the company imposed overly restrictive controls?

2. Do you think the company has a good conception of control tolerances?

3. What should Bill do?

EXERCISE

Staying on Budget

A s manager of the Ace Division of the Triple-A Company, you agreed to the following budget at the beginning of the current fiscal year: This budget was based on forecasted sales of 30,000 units during the year.

Fixed costs	$80,000
Subcontracting costs (variable, per unit)	4
Other variable costs (per unit)	2
Sales price	10

You are six months into the fiscal year and have collected the following sales data:

MONTH	ACTUAL SALES (UNITS)
1	2,000
2	2,200
3	1,700
4	1,800
5	2,300
6	2,200

By shopping around, you have been able to hold your subcontracting costs to an average of $3.60 per unit. The fixed and other variable costs are conforming to budgets.

A. What was the forecast break-even point in sales for the Ace Division?
B. What is the revised break-even point?
C. What trends in the above information, if any, concern you?
D. Based on the preceding information, prepare a one-page report for your boss, summarizing the current status of the Ace Division.

21 Operations Control

LEARNING OBJECTIVES

*After studying this chapter,
you should be able to:*

1 List the basic requirements for controlling
operating costs.

2 Recount the major reasons for carrying
inventories.

3 Differentiate between dependent and
independent demand inventory items.

4 Describe the ABC classification system
for managing inventories.

5 Explain the fixed-order quantity method
and the fixed-order period method for
ordering inventory.

6 Summarize the economic order quantity
(EOQ) concept.

7 Describe the basic purposes of material
requirements planning (MRP).

8 List several of the ways that the quality of
an organization's goods and services can
affect the organization.

9 Identify and define the two major types
of quality control.

While the achievement of a steady state level of system performance implies that design and start-up problems have been solved, it does not mean that the pressure is off the production manager. Regardless of how careful the planning, few systems of any complexity can be expected to operate indefinitely without encountering some type of malfunction that must be corrected. This is true not only for the physical production process but for the production management system that monitors that process as well. Indeed, while machinery may produce scrap or break down, thus necessitating repairs, the operating and control system that governs the use of the machinery may provide faulty information and incorrect decisions, requiring that it, too, be overhauled.

RICHARD B. CHASE AND NICHOLAS J. AQUILANO*

P roduct design, physical layout, and other design–related topics were discussed in Chapter 9. Unfortunately, designing an effective operating system does not in itself ensure that the system will operate efficiently. As indicated in the above quote, after the system has been designed and implemented, the day–to–day operations must be controlled. The system processes must be monitored; quality must be maintained; inventories must be managed; and all of this must be accomplished within cost constraints. In addition to ensuring that things do not get out of control, good operations control can be a substitute for resources. For example, good inventory control can reduce the investment cost in inventories. Similarly, good quality control can reduce scrap and wasted materials, thus reducing costs.

Effective operations control is attained by applying the basic control concepts discussed in Chapter 20 to the operations function of the organization. Operations controls generally relate to one of three areas: costs, inventories, or quality.

CONTROLLING OPERATION COSTS

Making sure that operating costs do not get out of hand is one of the primary jobs of the operations manager. The first requirement for controlling costs is to understand fully the organization's accounting and budgeting systems. The budgeting process was introduced in Chapter 7 and discussed further in Chapter 20. Operations managers are primarily concerned with costs relating

* Richard B. Chase and Nicholas J. Aquilano, *Production and Operations Management: A Life-Cycle Approach*, 4th ed. (Homewood, Ill.: Richard D. Irwin, 1985), p. 579.

to labor, materials, and overhead. Figure 21–1 describes the major components of each of these costs. **Variable overhead expenses** change with the level of production or service. **Fixed overhead expenses** are those that do not change appreciably with the level of production or service.

Normally, operations managers prepare monthly budgets for each of the major cost areas. Once these budgets have been approved by higher levels of management, they are put into effect. By carefully monitoring the ensuing labor, material, and overhead costs, the operations manager can compare actual costs to budgeted costs. The methods used for monitoring costs naturally vary, but they typically include direct observation, written reports, break-even charts, etc.

Usually, a cost control system only indicates when a particular cost is out of control; it does not address the question of *why* it is out of control. For example, suppose an operations manager determines from the monthly cost report that the labor costs on product X are exceeding budget by 20 percent. The manager must then attempt to determine what is causing the cost overrun. The causes could be many: unmotivated employees, several new and untrained employees, low-quality raw materials, equipment break-down, etc.

Determining the cause may require only a simple inspection of the facts, or it may require an in-depth analysis. Whatever the effort required, the operations manager must ultimately identify the source of the problem and then take the necessary corrective action. If the same cost problems continue to reoccur, chances are that the manager has not correctly identified the true

Variable overhead expenses – those that are assumed to change in proportion to the level of production or service.

Fixed overhead expenses – those that do not change appreciably with fluctuations in level of production or service.

F I G U R E 21–1 Budget Costs: The Basis for Cost Control

TYPE OF COST	COMPONENTS
Direct labor	Wages and salaries of workers who are engaged in the direct generation of goods and services. This typically does not include wages and salaries of support personnel.
Materials	Cost of materials which become a tangible part of finished goods and services.
Production overhead—variable	Training new employees, safety training, supervision and clerical, overtime premium, shift premium, payroll taxes, vacation and holiday, retirement funds, group insurance, supplies, travel, repairs and maintenance.
Production overhead—fixed	Travel, research and development, fuel (coal, gas, or oil), electricity, water, repairs and maintenance, rent, depreciation, real estate taxes, insurance.

Source: From *Production and Operations Management* by Norman Gaither. Copyright © 1980 by The Dryden Press. Reprinted by permission of the publisher.

MANAGERS AT WORK 21–1

Cost Control at Polygram

In 1985, Polygram Records, Inc. sales exceeded $800 million, making it one of the six largest record companies in the United States. April 1983 saw Polygram make the first step toward generating major cost savings. This was accomplished by closing two of its three regional U.S. distribution centers and consolidating its operations in Indianapolis. The trade-off of slightly higher transportation costs against greatly reduced inventory has produced considerable savings. Another cost-cutting technique adopted by Polygram was to consolidate and pool its distribution. In 1977, Polygram shipped its products daily from its distribution centers to its markets. Later, the frequency was reduced to three times weekly, and subsequently to twice weekly. Polygram estimates that this reduction in shipping frequency has saved approximately $1 million.

Source: "Savings to Hit Record Levels at Polygram," *Traffic Management,* May 1986, pp. 66–68.

cause of the problem or that the necessary corrective action has not been taken. Managers at Work 21–1 describes how Polygram Records, Inc. has implemented certain cost control measures.

INVENTORY CONTROL

Inventory – quantity of raw materials, in-process goods, or finished goods on hand; serves as a buffer between different rates of flow associated with the operating system.

Normally inventories are associated with manufacturing and product producing organizations. However, inventories are in reality a major concern for many organizations that are generally considered to be service companies. For example, managers of restaurants are continually faced with decisions relating to how many foodstuffs to keep on hand. Inventory decisions are also important to most retail businesses. Banks must maintain inventories of cash and office supplies.

Inventories serve as a buffer between different rates of flow associated with the operating system. **Inventories** can generally be classified into one of three categories, depending on their respective location within the operating system: (1) raw material, (2) in-process, or (3) finished goods. Raw-material inventories serve as a buffer between purchasing and production. In-process inventories are used to buffer differences in the rates of flow through the various production processes. Finished-goods inventories act as a buffer between the final stage of production and shipping. Figure 21–2 illustrates these relationships.

Inventories add flexibility to the operating system and allow the organization to do the following:

1. Purchase, produce, and ship in economic lot sizes rather than in small jobs.
2. Produce on a smooth, continuous basis even though the demand for the finished product or raw material may fluctuate.
3. Prevent major problems when forecasts of demand are in error or when there are unforeseen slowdowns or stoppages in supply or production.

When making inventory decisions, management must answer three basic questions: (1) What items should be carried in inventory? (2) When should the items be ordered? (3) How many of the selected items should be ordered and carried?

If it were not so costly, every organization would attempt to maintain very large inventories in order to facilitate purchasing, production scheduling, and distribution. However, there are many costs associated with carrying inventory. Potential inventory costs include such factors as insurance, property taxes, storage costs, obsolescence costs, spoilage, and the opportunity cost of the money invested in the inventory. The relative importance of these costs depends on the specific inventory being held. For example, with women's fashions, the obsolescence costs are potentially very high. Similarly, the storage costs might be very high for dangerous chemicals. Thus, management must continually balance the costs of holding the inventory against the costs of running short of raw materials, in-process goods, or finished goods. Managers

F I G U R E 21–2   Inventories as Buffers between Different Rates of Flow

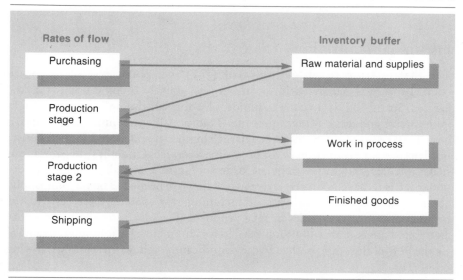

MANAGERS AT WORK 21–2

Service Merchandising in the Computer Age

Prior to the introduction of computers, service merchandising was simply worded as "rack jobbing." This operation involved wholesale routemen traveling from store to store, taking down restocking orders and then passing on the message to the various suppliers.

With the emergence of computer-monitored inventories using universal bar codes (introduced by McKesson Corporation) there is faster restocking of shelves and fewer low-turnover items. This is particularly cost effective when the operation involves very thin gross margins in retailing. This activity is carried out by a store clerk, who strolls down the aisles in a department store, sweeping a 12-inch electronic wand across shelves stacked with items ranging from hairpins to automobile engine oil. The scanner registers the additional needs into a computerized system. This data is then passed on to the McKesson warehouse. Within 48 hours, the items are delivered to the department store. McKesson distributes about 26,000 different nongrocery items to more than 18,000 supermarkets, convenience outlets, and neighborhood food stores.

Source: "Billion-Dollar Brainstorm," *Forbes,* October 19, 1987.

at Work 21–2 describes how McKesson Corporation implemented a computerized system for controlling inventories of grocery items.

Just-in-Time Inventory Control

Just-in-time inventory control (JIT) – inventory control system that schedules materials to arrive and leave at the right time.

The **just-in-time inventory control (JIT)** is a philosophy of inventory control that was pioneered in Japan but has recently become popular in the United States. JIT is actually a philosophy for scheduling so that the right items arrive and leave at the right time. Traditionally, incoming raw materials have been ordered in relatively few large shipments and stored in warehouses until needed for production or for providing a service. Under JIT, organizations make smaller and more frequent orders of raw materials. The basic idea under JIT is to have materials arrive just as they are needed. The JIT philosophy applies not only to inventories of incoming raw materials but also to the production of subassemblies or final products. The idea here is to not produce an item or subassembly until it is needed for shipment. The obvious advantage to the JIT philosophy is that it can significantly reduce inventory carrying costs.

Independent versus Dependent Demand Items

The types of inventory systems that are appropriate depend on whether the demand for the inventory items is independent or dependent. **Independent demand items** are finished goods or other end items. For the most part, independent demand items are sold or shipped out as opposed to being used in making another product. Examples of independent demand environments include most retail shops, book publishing, and hospital supplies.[1] **Dependent demand items** are typically subassemblies or component parts which will be used in making some finished product. In these cases the demand for the items depends on the number of finished products being produced. An example is the demand for wheels for new cars. If the car company plans to make 1,000 cars next month, it knows that it must have 5,000 wheels on hand (allowing for spares). With independent demand items, forecasting plays an important role in inventory stocking decisions. With dependent demand items, inventory stocking requirements are determined directly from the production plan.[2] Managing inventories for independent demand items is discussed in the next section of this chapter, followed by a discussion of managing inventories for dependent demand items.

Independent demand items – finished goods ready to be shipped out or sold.

Dependent demand items – subassembly or component parts used to make a finished product. Their demand is based on the number of finished products being produced.

Inventory Considerations for Independent Demand Items

This section discusses models, techniques, and approaches that are useful for managing inventories for independent demand items.

ABC Classification System.

One of the simplest and most widely used systems for managing inventories is the ABC approach. The **ABC classification system** is a method of managing inventories based on the total value of their usage per unit of time. In many organizations, a small number of products or materials, Group A, accounts for the greatest dollar value of the inventory. The next group of items, Group B, accounts for a moderate amount of the inventory value; and Group C accounts for a small amount of the inventory value. This concept is illustrated in Figure 21–3. The dollar value reflects both the cost of the item and its usage rate. For example, an item might be put into Group A through a combination of either low cost and high usage or high cost and low usage.

ABC Classification system – method of managing inventories based on their total value.

The purpose of grouping items in this way is to establish appropriate control over each item. Generally, the items in Group A are monitored very closely; the items in Group B are monitored with some care; and the items in Group C are only checked occasionally. Items in Group C are usually not subject to the detailed paperwork of items in Groups A and B. In an automobile service station, gasoline would be considered a Group A item and would be monitored daily. Tires, batteries, and transmission fluid would be Group B items and might be checked weekly or biweekly. Valve stems, windshield wiper blades, radiator caps, hoses, fan belts, oil and gas additives,

F I G U R E 21–3   ABC Inventory Classification (*Inventory Value for Each Group versus the Group's Portion of the Total List*)

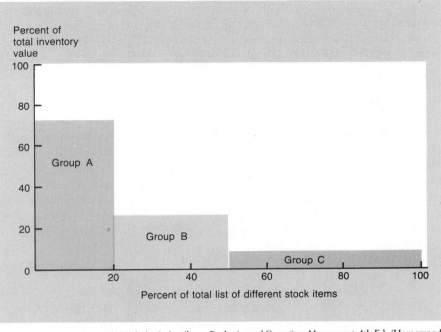

Source: Richard B. Chase and Nicholas J. Aquilano, *Production and Operations Management,* 4th Ed. (Homewood, Ill.: Richard D. Irwin, 1985), p. 511.

car wax, and so forth would be Group C items and might be checked and ordered only every two or three months.[3]

One potential shortcoming of the ABC method is that although the items in Group C might have very little cost/usage value, they may be critical to the operation. It is possible, for instance for a very inexpensive bolt to be vital to the production of a costly piece of machinery. One way to handle items like this is to designate them as Group A or B items regardless of their cost/usage value. The major advantage of the ABC method is that it concentrates on controlling those items that are most important to the operation.

Reorder Point and Safety Stock. After the decision has been made concerning the selection of items to be carried in inventory, a decision must be made concerning when to order each item. There are two basic methods for determining when to order: the fixed-order quantity method and the fixed-order period method. Under the **fixed-order quantity method,** illustrated in Figure 21–4, orders are placed whenever the inventory reaches a certain predetermined level, regardless of how long it takes to reach that level. In Figure 21–4, orders would be placed at time T_1, T_2, T_3, and T_4 under the

Fixed-order quantity method – orders are placed whenever the inventory reaches a certain predetermined level, regardless of how long it takes to reach that level; assumes continual monitoring of levels.

F I G U R E 21–4 Fixed-Order Quantity Method of Reordering

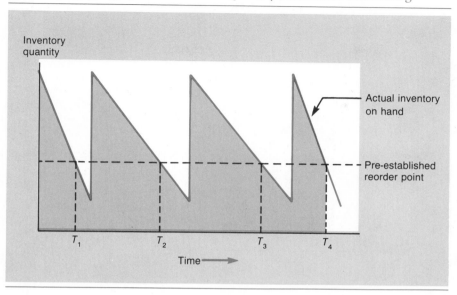

fixed-order quantity method. Thus, the time between orders can vary depending on the demand. Fixed-order quantity systems usually assume continual monitoring of inventory levels. This is not an unrealistic assumption today, since many organizations have computerized inventory records.

Under the **fixed-order period illustrated** in Figure 21–5, restocking orders are placed at predetermined, regular time intervals regardless of how much inventory is on hand. With this method, the amount ordered rather than the time between orders can vary, depending on the demand. The fixed-order period method requires that inventory be tallied only at the designated review periods. Both the fixed-order quantity method and the fixed-order period methods have certain advantages. The fixed-order period method is easier to administer because orders can be placed on a regular basis and inventory does not have to be continually counted. However, supplies in the fixed-order period method are more likely to run out if demand goes up unexpectedly. The fixed-order quantity method has the advantage of having all orders be of an equal and economical size. In general, the fixed-order period method lends itself to inventories where it is more desirable to physically count inventory on a regular periodic basis, such as in many small retail stores. The fixed-order quantity method lends itself to inventories that are easily computerized and can be continually monitored, such as with most wholesale suppliers.

Most organizations maintain **safety stocks** to accommodate unexpected changes in demand and supply and to allow for variations in delivery time. The optimum size of the safety stock is determined by the relative costs of a stock-out of the item versus the costs of carrying the additional inventory. The cost of a stock-out of the item is very often difficult to estimate. For

Fixed-order period method – orders are placed at predetermined regular time intervals regardless of inventory in stock.

Safety stocks – inventory maintained to accommodate unexpected changes in demand and supply and to allow for variations in delivery time.

F I G U R E   21–5   Fixed–Order Period Method of Reordering

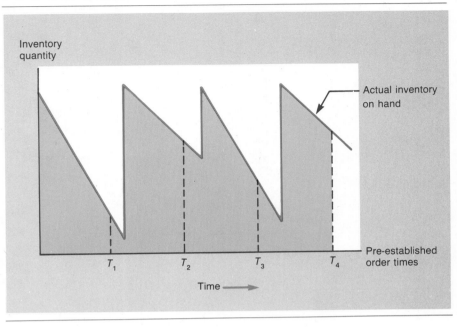

example, the customer may go elsewhere rather than wait for the product. If the product is available at another branch location, the stock-out cost may be simply the cost of shipping the item from one location to another.

The Order Quantity. Determining the amount to order is a decision that goes hand-in-hand with determining the reorder point. Most materials and finished products are consumed one by one or a few units at a time; however, because of the costs associated with ordering, shipping, and handling inventory, it is usually desirable to purchase materials and products in large lots or batches.

When determining the optimum number of units to order, the ordering costs must be balanced against the cost of carrying the inventory. Ordering costs include such things as the cost of preparing the order, shipping costs, and setup costs. Carrying costs include storage costs, insurance, taxes, obsolescence, and the opportunity costs of the money invested in the inventory. The smaller the number of units ordered, the lower the carrying costs (because the average inventory held is smaller) but the larger the ordering costs (because more orders must be placed). The optimum number of units to order, referred to as the **economic order quantity (EOQ),** is determined by the point where ordering costs equal carrying costs, or where total cost (ordering costs plus carrying costs) is at a minimum. Figure 21–6 graphically shows the inverse relationship between ordering costs and carrying costs. The total cost curve is found by vertically summing the ordering cost curve and the carrying

Economic order quantity (EOQ) – optimum number of units to order at one time.

F I G U R E 21-6   Inventory Costs versus Order Size

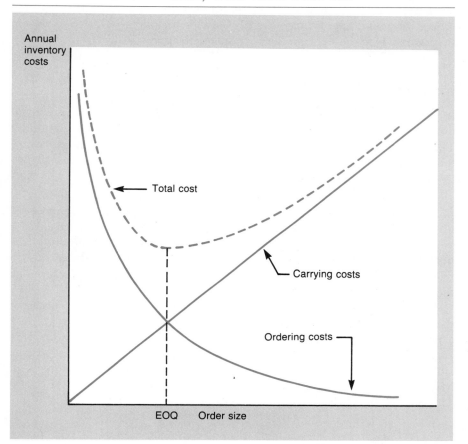

cost curve. The lowest point on the total cost curve corresponds to the point where ordering costs equal carrying costs and determines the economic order quantity.

The greatest weakness of the EOQ approach is the difficulty in accurately determining the actual carrying and ordering costs. However, research has shown that the total costs associated with order sizes that are reasonably close to the economic order quantity do not differ appreciably from the minimum total costs associated with the EOQ.[4] Thus, as long as the estimated carrying and ordering costs are "in the ball park," meaningful results can be obtained using this approach. Variations of this basic model have been developed for taking into account such things as purchase quantity and other special discounts.

EOQ analysis is directly compatible with the fixed-order quantity method of reordering. Although the quantity ordered varies under the fixed-order period method, EOQ analysis can still be used to help set up the times between the designated order periods. The idea behind this approach is to calculate the average number of days required between orders so that the expected order size would approximate the EOQ. This method would work only in situations where the demand does not fluctuate appreciably.

Managing Inventories for Dependent Demand Items

Managing inventories for dependent demand items is basically a process of insuring that the right numbers of items are available at the right times. Thus in addition to determining the number of units needed, the timing of their need is also critical.[5] Material requirements planning is a system designed to deal with these problems.

Material re-quirements planning (MRP) – dependent inventory planning and control system that schedules the right amount of materials needed to produce the final product on schedule.

Material Requirements Planning (MRP). **Material requirements planning (MRP)** is a special type of inventory system in which the needed amount of each component of a product is figured on the basis of the amount of the final product to be produced. When each component is needed depends on when the final assembly is needed and the lead time required to incorporate the component into the assembly.

The purpose of MRP is to get the right materials to the right places at the right time. It does little good to have some of the parts needed to produce a product if the organization does not have all of them. Because carrying parts that are not being used is costly, the idea behind MRP is to provide either all or none of the necessary components. Some of the advantages of MRP are outlined in Figure 21–7.

F I G U R E 21–7 Potential Advantages of Material Requirements Planning

1. It reduces the average amount of inventory for dependent-demand items (raw material, parts, and work-in-process inventory).
2. It improves work flow, resulting in reduced elapsed time between the start and finish of jobs.
3. It enables delivery promises to be more reliable.
4. It minimizes parts shortages.
5. It keeps priorities of work items up-to-date so that shopwork is more effective and appropriate.
6. It helps plan the timing of design changes and aids in their implementation.
7. It can simulate and evaluate changes in the master schedule.
8. It tells management ahead of time if desired delivery dates appear achievable.
9. It changes (expedites or deexpedites) due dates for orders.
10. It facilitates capacity requirements planning.

Source: James B. Dilworth, *Production and Operations Management,* 2nd ed. (New York: Random House, 1983), p. 261.

MANAGERS AT WORK 21–3

Importance of MRP for Ames Rubber

Materials Requirement Planning (MRP) is as important to the supplier as it is to the buyer. Ames Rubber Corporation, a 38-year-old company in Hamberg, New Jersey, employs 750 workers who engineer and produce high technology and precision rubber-based parts for manufacturers of office automation equipment. Ames plants in Hamberg and Wantage, N.J. produce and ship more than 1.5 million parts each year to their various customers. Ames uses a high-volume job shop which produces 17,000 different elastomeric parts, metal parts, and assemblies per year (an average production run is 250 parts). The parts are ordered by the buyers with zero defects on a prearranged delivery schedule. In 1980, an internal audit at Ames revealed some problems which had resulted from rapid sales growth: excessive deadlines, poor customer service, late deliveries, helter-skelter purchasing, excess and obsolete inventories, and poor enforcement of vendor delivery schedules. Ames subsequently worked out a "purchasing reorganization action plan" using MRP. This plan resulted in the clarification of major procurement objectives; development of policies for quality, quantity, and price; establishment of ground rules for vendor selection and a review of the role of the computer in purchasing. By gearing its material requirements planning to that of the buyer's, Ames has been able to reduce its problems and keep pace with its rapid growth.

Source: "Working with MRP at the Company in the Middle," *Purchasing,* July 11, 1985, pp. 80–86.

Almost all MRP utilizes a computer. This is not because there are complex equations to solve. The computer has the ability to store inventory records, production sequences, and production lead times and then rapidly convert this data into period-by-period production schedules and inventory levels. For example, if a manufacturer needs to have 100 end items assembled and ready for shipment by June, the company may need to order some subcomponents in April and make some additional subcomponent orders in May. Use of an MRP system allows a production planner to take the requirements for end-items and "back schedule" the production and ordering of subcomponents. The MRP printout would show when and how much of each subcomponent is needed in order to meet the end-item production requirements. Of course, many versions of MRP programs are available. Managers at Work 21–3 describes how MRP is used at Ames Rubber Corporation.

QUALITY CONTROL

Quality – for the operations manager, quality is determined in relation to the specifications or standards set in the design stages, the degree or grade of excellence specified.

Quality control – process of ensuring or maintaining a certain level of quality for materials, products, or services.

Quality is a relative term that means different things to different people. The consumer who demands quality may have a completely different concept than the operations manager who demands quality. The consumer is concerned with service, reliability, performance, appearance, and so forth. The operations manager's primary concern is that the product or service specifications be achieved, whatever they may be. For the operations manager, quality is determined in relation to the specifications or standards set in the design stages. Figure 21–8 lists some specific reasons for maintaining **quality control.**

There are many ways that the quality of an organization's goods and services can affect the organization. Some of the most important of these are: (1) reputation, (2) liability, (3) costs, and (4) productivity.[6] The reputation of an organization is often a direct reflection of the perceived quality of its goods and/or services. In today's legalistic environment, an organization's liability exposure can be significant and the associated costs can be high. For example, it is not unusual for a physician's malpractice insurance to cost upwards of $40,000 per year. Higher quality goods/services generally have less liability exposure than lower quality goods/services. In addition to liability costs, quality can affect other costs. Other potential costs impacted by quality include scrap costs, rework costs, warranty costs, repair costs, replacement costs and other similar costs. Productivity and quality are often closely related.[7] Poor-quality equipment, tools, parts, or subassemblies can cause defects which have a negative affect on productivity. Similarly, high-quality equipment, tools, parts, and subassemblies can have a positive impact on productivity. For example, consider how much more productive a typist can be with a word processor than with a manual typewriter.

F I G U R E   21–8   Reasons for Maintaining Quality Control

1. Maintain certain standards (such as with interchangeable replacement parts).
2. Meet customer specifications.
3. Meet legal requirements.
4. Find defective products which can be reworked.
5. Find problems in the production process.
6. Grade products (such as lumber or eggs).
7. Provide performance information on individual workers and departments.

Because of the many different ways that quality can affect an organization, it is often difficult to determine precisely the costs associated with different quality levels. Also, it must be realized that consumers and customers are only willing to pay for quality up to a point. For example, a cook may be willing to purchase a 3-speed mixer with a five-year guarantee; however, the same cook may not be willing to pay substantially more for a 20-speed,

MANAGERS AT WORK 21-4

Quality Control in the Hotel Industry

In 1981, after 16 years as a five-star, five-diamond resort, the Boca Raton Hotel and Club lost one of the stars. In early 1982, management began development of a comprehensive quality assurance (QA) program. Management stated exactly what it wanted from a QA program—to reduce employee turnover, increase positive guest comments, improve labor productivity, and make quality the responsibility of every employee.

The quality assurance program involved forming QA committees, preparing detailed performance standards for every position at the resort, analyzing the types and costs of errors that occurred during operation, and recommending procedure changes in order to avoid errors.

The program was a success. Negative guest complaints dropped from 28 percent to 5 percent in the first three months after the program was implemented. Employee turnover dropped from 117 percent in 1981 to 50 percent in 1983. Total cost savings exceeded $1 million. In 1983, the Boca Raton Hotel and Club regained its fifth star.

Source: W. Gerald Glover, R. Scott Morrison, Jr., and Alfred C. Briggs, Jr., "Making Quality Count: Boca Raton's Approach to Quality Assurance," *Cornell Hotel and Restaurant Administration Quarterly,* May 1984, pp. 39–45.

lifetime-guaranteed mixer. Once a policy decision has set the desired level of quality, the operations manager is responsible to ensure that the stated level of quality is achieved. Managers at Work 21–4 describes the results of a program to raise the level of quality of a major resort hotel. Managers at Work 21–5 describes the emphasis that GM (General Motors Corporation) is currently putting on quality.

Quality Checkpoints

If the desired level of quality is to be attained in the final product or service, checks or inspections may be required at several different points in the operating system. Figure 21–9 shows some of the more frequent inspection points in a manufacturing system. The first inspection point is when the raw materials are received. The quality of the raw materials must be compatible with the quality desired in the final product. The incoming materials should be checked for quality, quantity, and possible damage.

Depending on the operation to be performed, it may be desirable to inspect the materials again before they enter the operation. This is especially likely if the operation is costly or irreversible (such as with silverplating).

MANAGERS AT WORK 21–5

GM to Work for Better Quality

Humility is a rare commodity; and rarer still for giants. GM (General Motors Corporation), the world's largest industrial company, is now learning humility the hard way. Like a fashion designer vainly trying to dictate hemlines to women, GM has watched its sales and market share slide for more than a year as buyers purchase competitor's products. Plagued by charges of look-alike styling, reliability problems, and being the industry's highest cost producer, GM's new president, Robert C. Stempel, is fighting back. Admitting that he is "less a stylist than a nuts-and-bolts engineer," Stempel has vowed not to try and tell the customer what he or she wants. In addition, Stempel is focusing on the reliability problem. Unfortunately GM has talked about reliability before while still turning out unreliable cars. According to Stempel, GM can only win back customers by "producing our best every day and making sure each (car buyer's) experience is a good one." The only way to do that, Stempel knows, is to avoid quality compromises. The big question is whether Stempel can pull it off.

Source: "It's Time for a Tune-Up at GM," *Business Week,* September 7, 1987, pp. 22–23.

Other checks may take place prior to operations which cover or camouflage defects in the process. For example, painting may temporarily camouflage a flaw which resulted from an earlier operation.

A final inspection should take place before the product or service is distributed to the customer. This provides a check on the end product or service. It should be stressed that the optimum location and number of checkpoints depend on two separate costs: inspection cost and the cost of passing a defective. As the number of inspection locations increases, so do the inspection costs; however, the probability of passing on a defect decreases.

Types of Quality Control

Product quality control – relative to inputs or outputs of the system. Used when quality is evaluated with respect to a batch of existing products or services.

Figure 21–10 suggests that variations in quality can occur in the inputs to the operating system, in the transformation operations, or in the final product or service. Quality control relating to the inputs or outputs of the system is referred to as **product quality control.** Product quality control is used when the quality is being evaluated with respect to a batch of products or services that already exists, such as incoming raw materials or finished goods. Product quality control lends itself to acceptance sampling procedures in which some

F I G U R E 21–9 Potential Quality Control Checkpoints

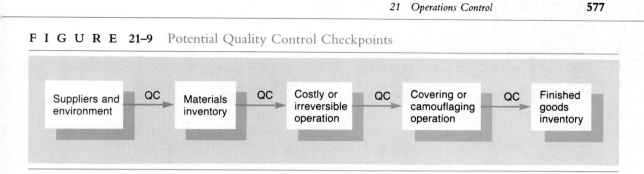

portion of a batch of outgoing items (or incoming materials) is inspected in an attempt to ensure that the batch meets specifications with regard to the percentage of defective units which will be tolerated in the batch. Under acceptance sampling procedures, the decision to accept or reject an entire batch is based on a sample or group of samples.

Quality control relating to the control of a machine or an operation during the production process is called process control. Under process control, machines and/or processes are periodically checked to detect significant changes in the quality produced by the process. When necessary, adjustments are made to bring the machines or processes back under control. Process control is used to prevent the production of defectives, whereas product control is used to detect the presence of defectives.

F I G U R E 21–10 Mean Chart

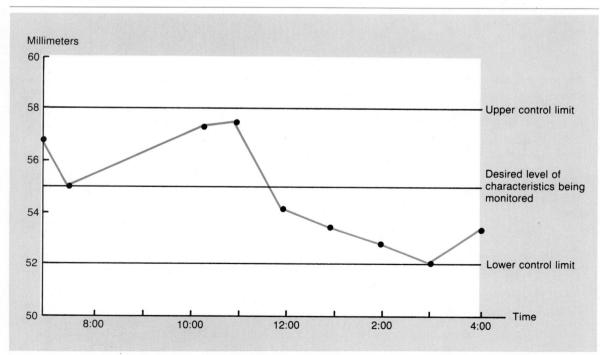

Acceptance Sampling

Acceptance sampling is a method of predicting the quality of a batch or large group of products from an inspection of a sample or group of samples taken from the batch. Acceptance sampling is used for one of three basic reasons: (1) The possible losses or costs of passing defective items are not great, relative to the cost of inspection—it would not be appropriate to inspect every match produced by a match factory. (2) Inspection of some items requires destruction of the product being tested—as is the case when testing flash bulbs. (3) Sampling usually produces results more rapidly than does a census.

The procedure followed in acceptance sampling is to draw a random sample, of a given size, from the batch or lot being examined. The sample is then tested and analyzed. If more than a certain number (determined statistically) are found defective, the entire batch is rejected; it has an unacceptably large percentage of defective items. Because of the possibility of making an incorrect inference concerning the batch, acceptance sampling always involves risks. The risk that the producer is willing to take of rejecting a good batch is referred to as the producer's risk. The risk of accepting a bad batch is referred to as the consumer's risk. Obviously, one would desire to minimize both the producer's risk and the consumer's risk. However, the only method of simultaneously lowering both of these risks is to increase the sample size—which also increases the inspection costs. Therefore, the usual approach is to decide the maximum acceptable risk for both the producer and the consumer and to design the acceptance sampling plan around these risks.

Process Control Charts

A **process control chart** is a time-based, graphic display which shows whether a machine or process is producing output at the expected quality level. If a significant change in the variable being checked is detected, the machine is said to be out of control. Control charts do not attempt to show why a machine is out of control, only if it is out of control.

The most frequently used process control charts are called mean and range charts. Mean charts (also called X-charts) monitor the mean or average value of some characteristic (dimension, weight, etc.) of the items produced by a machine or process. Range charts (also called R-charts) monitor the range of variability of some characteristic (dimension, weight, etc.) of the items produced by a machine or process.

The quality control inspector, using control charts, first calculates the desired level of the characteristic being measured. The next step is to calculate statistically the upper and lower control limits, which determine how much the characteristic can vary from the desired level before the machine or process is considered to be out of control. Once the control chart has been set up, the quality control inspector periodically takes a small sample from the machine or process outputs. Depending on the type of chart being used, the mean or range of the sample is plotted on the control chart. By plotting the results of each sample on the control chart, it is easy to identify quickly any abnormal trends in quality. A sample mean chart is shown in Figure 21–10.

A mean or range chart used by itself can easily lead to false conclusions. For example, the upper and lower control limits for a machined part might be 0.1000 millimeter and 0.0800 millimeter, respectively. A sample of four parts of 0.1200, 0.1100, 0.0700, and 0.0600 would yield an acceptable mean of 0.0900; yet, every element of the sample is out of tolerance. For this reason, when monitoring variables, it is usually desirable to use mean and range charts simultaneously to ensure that a machine or process is under control.

S U M M A R Y

This chapter emphasizes the importance of properly controlling operating systems and the application of control concepts to these systems. In addition, cost control, inventory control, and quality control are introduced and discussed.

L E A R N I N G   O B J E C T I V E 1

Understand the Basic Requirements for Controlling Operating Costs.

The first requirement for controlling costs is to understand the organization's accounting and budgeting system. Once the budgets have been put into effect, they must be carefully monitored for any unexpected cost variances. Any cost variances that are detected must then be analyzed to determine the cause.

L E A R N I N G   O B J E C T I V E 2

Recount the Major Reasons for Carrying Inventories.

Inventories add flexibility to the operating system and allow the organization to do the following:

1. Purchase, produce, and ship in economic lot sizes rather than in small jobs.
2. Produce on a smooth, continuous basis even though the demand for the finished product or raw material may fluctuate.
3. Prevent major problems when forecasts of demand are in error or when there are unforeseen slowdowns or stoppages in supply or production.

L E A R N I N G   O B J E C T I V E 3

Differentiate between Dependent and Independent Demand Inventory Items.

Dependent demand items are typically subassemblies or component parts which will be used in making some finished product. In these cases the demand for the items depends on the number of finished products being purchased. Independent demand items are finished goods or other end items. For the most part, independent items are sold or shipped as opposed to being used in making another product.

LEARNING OBJECTIVE 4

Describe the ABC Classification System for Managing Inventories.

The ABC classification system is a method of managing inventories based on the total value of their usage per unit of time. In many organizations, a small number of products, Group A, accounts for the greater dollar value of the inventory. The next group of items, Group B, accounts for a moderate amount of the inventory value; and Group C accounts for a small amount of the inventory value. The purpose of grouping items in this way is to establish appropriate control over each item. Generally, the items in Group A are monitored very closely; the items in Group B are monitored with some care; and the items in Group C are only checked occasionally.

LEARNING OBJECTIVE 5

Explain the Fixed-Order Quantity Method and the Fixed-Order Period Method for Ordering Inventory.

Under the fixed-order quantity method, orders are placed whenever the inventory reaches a certain predetermined level, regardless of how long it takes to reach that level. Thus, the time between orders can vary depending on the demand. Fixed-order quantity systems usually assume continual monitoring of inventory levels. Under the fixed-order period method, restocking orders are placed at predetermined, regular time intervals regardless of how much inventory is on hand. With this method, the amount ordered rather than the time between orders can vary, depending on the demand. The fixed-order period method requires that inventory be tallied only at the designated review periods.

LEARNING OBJECTIVE 6

Summarize the Economic Order Quantity (EOQ) Concept.

When determining the optimum number of units to order, the ordering costs must be balanced against the cost of carrying the inventory. Ordering costs include such things as the cost of preparing the order, shipping costs, and setup costs. Carrying costs include storage costs, insurance, taxes, obsolescence, and the opportunity costs of the money invested in the inventory. The smaller the number of units ordered, the lower the carrying costs (because the average inventory held is smaller) but the larger the ordering costs (because more orders must be placed). The optimum number of units to order, referred to as the economic order quantity (EOQ), is determined by the point where ordering costs equal carrying costs, or where total cost (ordering costs plus carrying costs) is at a minimum.

LEARNING OBJECTIVE 7

Describe the Basic Purposes of Material Requirements Planning (MRP).

Material requirements planning (MRP) is a special type of inventory system in which the needed amount of each component of a product is figured on the basis of the amount of the final product to be produced. When each component is needed depends on when the final assembly is needed and the lead time required to incorporate the component into the assembly. The purpose of MRP is to get the right materials to the right places at the right time.

LEARNING OBJECTIVE 8

List Several of the Ways That the Quality of an Organization's Goods and Services Can Affect the Organization.

There are many ways that the quality of an organization's goods and services can affect the organization. Some of the most important of these are: (1) reputation, (2) liability, (3) costs, and (4) productivity.

LEARNING OBJECTIVE 9

Identify and Define the Two Major Types of Quality Control.

The two major types of quality control are product quality control and process control. Product quality control is used when the quality is being evaluated with respect to a batch of products or services that already exist, such as incoming raw materials or finished goods. Under process control, machines and/or processes are periodically checked to detect significant changes in the quality produced by the process.

REVIEW QUESTIONS

1. Name the three major categories of costs that operations managers are usually concerned about from a control standpoint. Give several examples of each category.
2. What is the difference between fixed and variable overhead expenses?
3. What are the purposes of inventories?
4. What is just-in-time inventory control?
5. Explain the difference between independent and dependent demand items.
6. How does the ABC classification system work?
7. Describe two basic methods for determining reorder points.
8. What is the purpose of carrying safety stock?
9. What costs affect the economic order quantity?
10. What is material requirements planning (MRP)?
11. Define quality.
12. List five possible reasons for quality control.
13. At which points in a manufacturing system might quality checks be appropriately performed?
14. What is a process control chart?

DISCUSSION QUESTIONS

1. Discuss the production control problems that can arise when demand is continually changing.

2. It has been said that good inventory management can make the difference between success and failure in certain industries. Name several industries in which this statement is particularly applicable and discuss the reasons for your answer.

3. Since the cost of a stock-out of an inventory item is usually very difficult to estimate, how can the safety stock level be determined with any accuracy?

4. Since quality is a relative concept, how does a manager ever know if the quality level is optimum?

REFERENCES & ADDITIONAL READINGS

[1] Richard B. Chase and Nicholas J. Aquilano, *Production and Operations Management: A Life Cycle Approach,* 4th ed (Homewood, Ill.: Richard D. Irwin, 1985), p. 481.

[2] William J. Stevenson, *Production/Operations Management* (Homewood, Ill.: Richard D. Irwin, 1982), p. 385.

[3] Chase and Aquilano, *Production and Operations Management,* p. 530.

[4] John F. Magee, "Guides to Inventory Policy: I. Functions and Lot Size," *Harvard Business Review,* January–February 1956, pp. 49–60.

[5] Chase and Aquilano, *Production and Operations Management,* p. 511–12.

[6] Stevenson, *Production/Operations Management.*

[7] Ibid.

INCIDENT

The Purchasing Department

The buyers for a large airline company were having a general discussion with the manager of purchasing in her office Friday afternoon. The inspection of received parts was a topic of considerable discussion. Apparently, several parts had recently been rejected six months or more after being received. Such a rejection delay was costing the company a considerable amount of money, since most of the items were beyond the standard 90-day warranty period. The current purchasing procedures state that the department using the parts is responsible for the inspection of all parts, including stock and nonstock items. The company employs an inspector who is supposedly responsible for inspecting all aircraft parts, in accordance with FAA regulations. However, the inspector has not been able to check those items purchased as nonaircraft parts, because he is constantly overloaded. Furthermore, many of the aircraft parts are not being properly inspected because of insufficient facilities and equipment.

One recent example of the type of problem being encountered was the acceptance of a batch of plastic forks that broke readily when in use. The vendor had shipped over a hundred cases of the forks of the wrong type. Unfortunately, all the purchase order specified was "forks." Another example was the acceptance of several cases of plastic cups with the wrong logo. The cups were subsequently put into use for in-flight service and had to be used, since no other cups were available. A final example was the discovery that several expensive radar tubes in stock were found to be defective and with expired warranty. These tubes had to be reordered at almost $900 per unit.

It was apparent that the inspection function was inadequate and unable to cope with the volume of material being received. Purchasing would have to establish some guidelines as to what material should or should not be inspected after being processed by the material checker. Some of the buyers felt that the material checker (who is not the inspector) should have more responsibility than simply checking quantity and comparing the packing sheet against purchase orders. Some believed that the checker could and should have caught the obvious errors in the logo on the plastic cups. Furthermore, if the inspector had sampled the forks, they would have been rejected immediately. As for the radar tubes, they should have been forwarded by the inspector to the avionics shop for bench check and then placed in stock. Some buyers felt that the inspector should be responsible for inspection of all materials received, regardless of its function or usage. It was pointed out, however, that several landing gears had been received from the overhaul/repair vendor and tagged by the inspector as being acceptable. These gears later turned out to be defective and unstable and had to be returned for repair. This generated considerable discussion concerning the inspector's qualifications, testing capacity, workload, and responsibility for determining if the unit should be shop checked.

Much of the remaining discussion centered around what purchasing should recommend for the inspection of material. One proposal was that everything received be funneled through the Inspection Department. Another proposal was that all material be run through inspection except as otherwise noted on the purchase order. Other questions were also raised. If purchasing required all material to be inspected, would this demand additional inspection personnel? Who would be responsible for inspection specifications? Furthermore, who should determine what items should be shop checked?

The meeting was finally adjourned until the following Friday.

Questions

1. What do you think of the current system of inspection?

2. Do you think the inspector is at fault?

3. What would you suggest at the meeting next Friday?

EXERCISE

Out of Control?★

Situation 1

The manager of a fast-food hamburger chain must ensure that the hamburger that is advertised as a quarter-pounder is actually 4 ounces, more or less. The company policy states that the quarter-pounder must come within ³⁄₁₀ of an ounce (.3 oz.) of being 4 ounces in order to be used. The chart below reflects the expected weight of the patty (4 oz.), the upper control limit (4.3 oz.) and the lower control limit (3.7 oz.). A sample of patties has been taken each day for the last eight days and the average weight recorded for each day is recorded on the chart below.

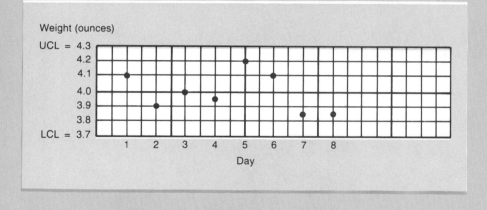

A. Should the pattie preparation process be investigated?
B. Why do you think so?

Situation 2

You are the owner of a car repair shop that specializes in tune-ups. On each work order, the mechanic records the time at which he began the tune-up and the time when finished. From these data, you can determine how long each mechanic spends on each job. You expect each job to take around 40 minutes; however, you know that if someone was in a great hurry, the job could be done in as few as 20 minutes. Also, you believe that under no

★ This exercise is adapted from Henri L. Tosi and Jerald W. Young, *Management Experiences, and Demonstrations* (Homewood, Ill.: Richard D. Irwin, 1982), pp. 45–47.

circumstances should a tune-up take over one hour. A recently hired mechanic has recorded the times shown on the chart below for his last 11 tune-up jobs:

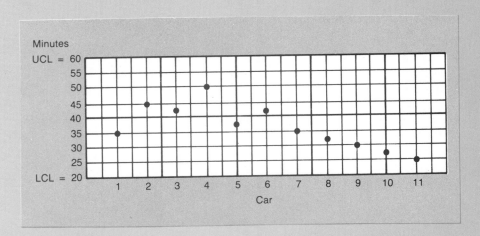

A. Should you have a talk with this person? Is there a problem?

B. Why do you think so?

22 Management Information Systems

LEARNING OBJECTIVES

After studying this chapter,
you should be able to:

1 Recount the general evolution of computers since the early 1960s.

2 Define a management information system (MIS) and distinguish between data and information.

3 Differentiate between operational and strategic MIS.

4 Describe the basic components of an MIS.

5 Summarize the steps in the design phase of MIS development.

6 Summarize the steps in the implementation phase of MIS development.

7 List several strategies for overcoming potential organization and people-related problems with designing and implementing MIS.

8 Describe an information center.

If the aviation industry had developed at the same rate as electronic data processing, we would have landed people on the moon less than six months after the Wright brothers made their first flight at Kitty Hawk. If the cost of a 1955 Cadillac (introduced about the same time as computers were introduced in business) had been reduced as much as that of computer memories while efficiencies were raised to an equal degree, the Cadillac would now cost $5 and go 20,000 mph.

JAMES A. SENN*

*S*uccessful implementation of the basic planning, organizing, and controlling functions of management requires that managers have adequate information: managers must first identify and then acquire the necessary information. Identifying and acquiring adequate information have historically been two of the biggest challenges of managers.

The advent and maturing of electronic computers have greatly altered not only the availability of information but also the manner by which it is identified and acquired. The purpose of this chapter is to introduce and give an overview of information systems that can be especially useful to managers.

THE INFORMATION EXPLOSION

Until the past 25 or so years, managers almost never felt that they had enough information to make decisions. Of course, information has always been available, but it has not always been so easy to obtain, synthesize, and analyze. In the 1950s, a manager could always send a team of researchers to the local library; even then, much of the data would not be current. Other available information sources included the radio, newspapers, and professional meetings and publications. Contrast that scenario with today! Today's managers are often burdened, not with a lack of information, but rather from information overload. **Information overload** occurs when managers have so much information that they have trouble distinguishing between the useful and the useless information.

Information overload – occurs when managers have so much information available that they have trouble distinguishing between the useful and the useless information.

The Computer Evolution

The first electronic computer, the ENIAC, was developed by the University of Pennsylvania in conjunction with the U.S. Army Ordnance Corps. The

*James A. Senn, *Information Systems in Management,* 2nd ed. (Belmont, Calif.: Wadsworth, 1982), p. 83.

MANAGERS AT WORK 22–1

Micros versus Mainframes

In 1984, sales of microcomputers surpassed those of mainframes for the first time. Current estimates forecast that microcomputer systems will be outselling mainframe systems by 65 percent a year by 1991. The development of microprocessor chips used in microcomputers has made this possible. Microprocessor chips are now vastly more powerful than just a few years ago. In 1987 both Intel and Motorola came out with new chips that could process twice as much data as the fastest microcomputers of only a year earlier. It has been estimated that enough personal computers (microcomputers) would have been sold by the end of 1987 to handle something like 20 trillion instructions per second. In comparison, it has also been estimated that all the IBM and IBM-compatible mainframes in operation in the United States at the same time would have enough combined processing power to perform only about 145 billion instructions per hour.

Source: Adapted from John W. Veritz and Goeff Lewis, "Computers: The New Look," *Business Week,* November 30, 1987, pp. 112–23.

ENIAC was 8 feet high, 8 feet long, weighed 30 tons, and required about 174,000 watts of power to run.[1] On the average, it took about two days to set up ENIAC to carry out a program.

In the 1960s, large and very costly **mainframe computers** (such as the IBM 360 series) were in use by only the very largest companies and government organizations. Not only was the hardware for these systems expensive but they also required highly paid operators, service personnel, programmers, and systems specialists. Because of the physical size and costs of these systems, they were almost always highly centralized and, more often than not, considered an extension of the accounting function.

The large computers were followed by the **minicomputers** of the 1970s. The minicomputers were much smaller in size and cost and they were often programmed to do specific functions for a specific business activity. Minicomputers ushered in the concept of distributed data processing—each operational area of an organization has control of its own computer to better respond to the needs of the area.

The decentralization first made possible by minicomputers has been taken even further by the microcomputer or personal computer. For just a few hundred dollars, a manager today can buy a **microcomputer** capable of processing mammoth amounts of data—and it occupies no more space than a typewriter! Managers at Work 22–1 discusses the growth of microcomputers.

Mainframe computer – large computer system, typically with a separate central processing unit.

Minicomputer – small (desk size) electronic, digital, stored-program, general purpose computer.

Microcomputer – very small computer, ranging in size from a "computer on a chip" to a small typewriter-size unit.

MANAGERS AT WORK 22-2

Computers Go to the Movies

Traditionally, owners of movie theaters have kept up with inventories by manually counting and recording the appropriate items. This system works well for a single or a very small group of theaters. However, as the number of theaters and auditoriums in a chain grows, management can easily lose control of inventories. In order to better control inventories and reduce other costs, many theater chains have turned to computers. At many theaters, a personal computer quite literally "runs the show" by controlling the projectors. Computerized ticket machines and multifunction cash registers at the concession stand are all tied into a central computer at the theater. Daily sales data and other information are easily tabulated and cross-referenced. This information is then transmitted to the home office for further analysis.

Source: Adapted from Jimmy Summers, "At What Point Do the Advantages Begin?" *Boxoffice,* December 1987, pp. 61–62.

User-friendly computer – requires very little technical knowledge to use.

The phenomenal improvements in computer hardware have been accompanied by improvements in software and user compatibility. Modern computers are much more **user-friendly** than those of the past. Managers today do not need to know sophisticated programming languages and computer jargon to use computers.

Computer technology improvements have also created some new problems for managers. Diverse computers and communication technologies provide a wide array of information at many different levels in the organization. Therefore, it is no longer possible to place the information function neatly on the organization chart.[2] The need to integrate and coordinate information in an organization has led to the development of systems for doing just that. Managers at Work 22–2 describes how movie theaters are now using computers as a part of their everyday operations.

Data – raw material from which information is developed; it is composed of facts that have not been interpreted.

Information – data that have been interpreted and that meet the need of one or more managers.

WHAT IS A MANAGEMENT INFORMATION SYSTEM?

Before defining management information systems (MIS), it is necessary to define some other, basic terms first. Many people make a clear distinction between the terms data and information. **Data** is the raw material from which **information** is developed; data is composed of facts that describe people, places, things, or events and that have not been interpreted.[3] Data that has been interpreted and that meets the needs of one or more managers are information.[4]

In simple terms, a **management information system (MIS)** is an integrated approach for providing interpreted and relevant data that can be used to help managers make decisions. An MIS should interpret, should organize, and should filter data so that it reaches managers in an efficient and timely manner.

MIS can be viewed as a computer-based system or, more broadly, as the total communication system—including oral, published, and database information storage and retrieval.[5] In the broader sense, management information systems have existed for many years. However, in most people's minds and in this chapter, the term MIS implies the use of computers to process data at some point in the system.

Recognizing that most MIS involves the computer, it is important to note that MIS is not the same as data processing. **Data processing** is the capture, processing, and storage of data, whereas MIS uses that data to produce information for management.[6] In other words, data processing provides the database of the MIS.

Transaction-processing systems substitute computer processing for manual recordkeeping procedures. Examples include payroll, billing, and inventory record systems. By definition, transaction processing requires routine and highly structured decisions. It is actually a subset of data processing. Therefore, an organization can have a very effective transaction-processing system and not have an MIS. Figure 22–1 shows the relationships between MIS, data processing, and transaction processing. Managers at Work 22–3 describes how some hospitals are using MIS to help control costs.

> **Management information system (MIS)** – integrated approach for providing interpreted and relevant data that can help managers make decisions.

> **Data processing** – capture, processing, and storage of data.

> **Transaction-processing systems** – substitutes computer processing for manual recordkeeping procedures.

Operational versus Strategic MIS

Historically, MIS has been used mostly to assist managers in making operational decisions. Recently, however, MIS has begun to help managers with more strategic decisions. **Operational MIS** basically provides information to assist in making decisions about current operations; **strategic MIS** is more concerned with decisions that affect the accomplishment of long-range objectives.

The following example should help distinguish between operational and strategic MIS.[7] Several discount department store chains have changed from centralized to point-of-sale warehousing by using strategic MIS. They designed their MIS to focus on inventory management and make sure that all stores are well stocked at all times. This nearly eliminates the cost of central warehousing. On the other hand, an operational MIS plan would focus on reducing central-warehousing costs. Many people contend that MIS must move from

> **Operational MIS** – basically provides information to assist in making decisions related to current operations.

> **Strategic MIS** – concerned with decisions that affect the organization's long-range objectives.

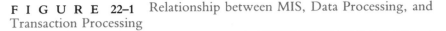

F I G U R E 22–1 Relationship between MIS, Data Processing, and Transaction Processing

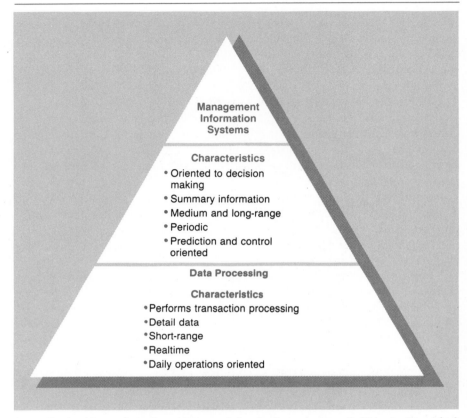

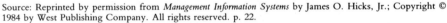

mainly an operations orientation to a more strategic orientation if organizations are to remain competitive.

Decision Support Systems (DSS)

Decision support systems (DSS) – extension of an MIS; provides information for making decisions and becomes a part of the process.

Management information systems do not make decisions for managers. Rather, they provide information to assist managers in making decisions. **Decision support systems (DSS)** not only provide inputs to the decision process; they actually become a part of the process.[8] Thus, a DSS may be viewed as an extension of an MIS. Decision support systems allows a manager to use computers directly to retrieve information for decisions on semistructured problems. Such problems contain some elements that are well defined and can be quantified and some that are not. Examples of decisions that lend themselves to DSS include plant locations, acquisitions, and new products/services.

MANAGERS AT WORK 22–3

Management Information System Helps Hospitals Control Costs

The federal government has created a new medicare fixed-fee system that is forcing hospitals to do a better job of keeping track of costs. If the cost of treating a patient exceeds the fixed fee for that particular disease, the hospital takes a loss. If the cost is less than the fixed fee, the hospital keeps the difference. As such, hospitals now have a real initiative to keep costs down and to know exactly what goes into the cost of treating each patient. Hospital administrators are turning to computers to help them structure and maintain the extensive information files needed to better control costs.

At Arnot Ogden Memorial Hospital in Elmira, New York, treatment information, prescription records, supply charges, and room charges are all recorded by patient number in a computerized file. The hospital can then track costs by patient, by doctor, and by disease. The specific cost information can then be used to spotlight everything from doctors who order more tests than average to supplies that are too costly. According to Phillip D. Cusans, the president and CEO of Stamford Hospital in Connecticut, hospitals are "making an investment in information."

Source: Adapted from "The Medicare Squeeze Pushes Hospitals into the Information Age," *Business Week,* June 18, 1984, pp. 87, 90.

MIS Components

Hardware – actual computer and its peripheral equipment.

Software – instructions and programs used to run a computer.

Programmer – writes instructional programs that tell computers what to do.

Systems analyst – studies a potential computer application and determines the type of programs needed.

Certain basic components are needed for a successful MIS.[9] The actual computer, known as **hardware,** is one requirement. The selection is abundant and continues to expand.

All computers need instructions or programs to run them. These instructions and programs are referred to as **software.** Software can be purchased off the shelf for most applications. However, some organizations elect to write their own software. This can require anything from a single programmer to several programmers and systems analysts. **Programmers** are the people who write the instructional programs that tell the computer what to do. **Systems analysts** study a potential computer application and determine the type of programs needed. Systems analysts basically serve as intermediaries between the users and the programmers.

Database – contains the data required to meet the user's need; usually, readily accessible information about the organization's operations.

A third necessary component is the database. A **database** includes the data needed by the user. Usually a database has information about the organization's operations. It is stored so as to be readily accessed. Information for a database can be very expensive.

The final necessary component of the system is the management staff and executive leadership. Other components can produce information; but this information must be used by information-oriented managers. They must know what information they need and how to use it. And they must be willing to make the effort needed to improve the information and the MIS itself. Top managers or executives must actively endorse and support the MIS. If the middle- and lower-level managers see that top management is really not committed to the MIS, the system will surely fail. Figure 22–2 summarizes the necessary components of a successful MIS.

F I G U R E 22–2   MIS Components Using a Microcomputer-Board System

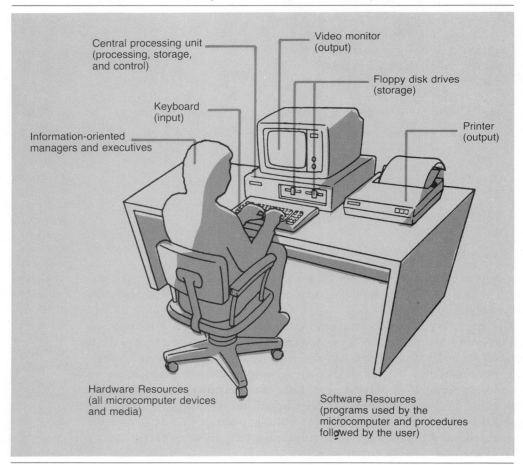

DEVELOPING AN MIS

The development of an MIS consists of the design phase and the implementation phase. Each is discussed in the following sections.[10]

The Design Phase

Designing an MIS includes everything that occurs prior to buying the equipment and putting the new MIS into operation. The design phase involves the following steps:

1. Identify the needs of managers. What problems do managers encounter? What are their informational needs? The most common and possibly most effective method for determining such needs is to interview the different managers. Once this information has been collected, it should be classified as either: (1) important enough or used often enough to be provided by the MIS, or (2) used so rarely that it is cheaper to search for it when it is needed.

2. Set objectives for the system. The objectives of the MIS should be expressed in writing. They should be based upon the managers' needs, the associated costs, and the expected benefits of the system. Remember that an MIS cannot be all things to all people. The MIS objectives should, above all else, help the organization achieve its objectives and mission.

3. Prepare a project proposal. The project proposal should contain both a general description of why the system is needed and an estimate of its cost and implementation schedule. The project proposal is used by top management to evaluate whether to pursue the project.

4. Prepare a conceptual design of the MIS. The conceptual design specifies the main subsystems and components, the arrangement and relationships of these subsystems, the general nature of the inputs and outputs, and the anticipated performance of the MIS. The major purpose of the conceptual design is to consider and evaluate alternative concepts.

5. Prepare a detailed design. The detailed design extends the conceptual design. It includes a detailed narrative, charts, tables, and diagrams for setting up the proposed MIS. The detailed design should provide all the technical information necessary to implement the system. Figure 22–3 gives the steps in the design phase and some examples of each step.

The Implementation Phase

Designing an MIS can be an expensive and lengthy process. Turning the design into a working system can be even more difficult and expensive.[11] Implementation includes the purchase and integration of the resources necessary to form a working MIS, as well as testing and actually putting the system into operation. Specifically, implementation consists of the following steps:

1. Acquiring the necessary facilities, equipment, and personnel.
2. Training the personnel.

F I G U R E 22–3 Steps in MIS Design

STEP	EXAMPLES
1. Find out the *information needs* of all managers.	Study the position description for the marketing manager. This manager states a need for monthly information about sales by product and area for the company and for competitors.
2. Write down the *objectives* of the MIS, based upon the needs of all managers, the costs, and the anticipated benefits.	One objective will be to supply managers with productivity analyses at the end of each month. Another objective will be to make financial and cost reports available within three days after the end of each month.
3. Prepare a *plan* and *proposal* for the design of MIS, including schedule and estimated cost.	A revised financial and new marketing MIS will be completed in preliminary form by May 17, 1985. The estimated cost is $57,500.
4. Prepare a preliminary, *conceptual* design of the MIS.	A table listing each manager, their responsibilities, their information needs, and source of such information. An outline of files and records. General computer configuration.
5. Prepare the *detailed* design of all aspects of the MIS.	Specific report received by each manager. The customer-record file. A flowchart of the environmental scanning system. Computer programs. Hardware architecture. (Obviously, the detailed design of the MIS is a very lengthy document.)

Source: Robert G. Murdick, *MIS Concepts and Design,* © 1980, pp. 17–18. Reprinted by permission of Prentice-Hall, Inc., Englewood Cliffs, N.J.

3. Conversion from the old to the new MIS (if an old one existed).

4. Testing the new MIS.

5. Operating the MIS.

6. Evaluating the MIS to see if it is doing what it was designed to do.

Once an MIS operates as designed, it must be maintained. Needed changes in procedures or the structure of the data files must be made to handle changing inputs and management needs. Managers at Work 22–4 describes some of the problems that the Chinese government has encountered in its attempt to install management information systems.

Organization/People Strategies

Discussion of both the design and implementation phases focused on the technical requirements of each phase. However, merely attending to these

MANAGERS AT WORK 22–4

China Encounters Problems with MIS

In its efforts to modernize industry, the Chinese government has found the use of management information systems (MIS) to be very helpful. However, even though the government set up large MIS systems, they are only available to those who can read and write in English. American software suppliers have had a hard time converting MIS programs for use in the Chinese language because the Chinese alphabet has more than 10,000 characters.

Estimates are that it could take up to 10 years for the conversion of English to Chinese characters to take place.

Additionally, the keyboards on most computers must be adapted so individual characters can be created. This is usually accomplished by simultaneously pressing several keys. Such multiple keystrokes greatly slow down the inputting of information, but the prospect of having more than 10,000 individual characters on one keyboard is not seen as a solution either.

Source: Adapted from Irwin Greestein, "Software Conversion Stalls China 10 Years," *MIS Week,* October 26, 1987, pp. 1, 48.

does not ensure that the MIS will work. In fact, a recent study reported that "for the MIS practitioner, the research results in this area carry a clear message—worry less about how up-to-date your hardware is and whether or not the latest database system is in place, and worry more about how user interaction takes place, how employees are managed, and how computer resources are allocated within the organization."[12]

A successful MIS must have the cooperation of many groups of people. So certain organization and people-related factors must be considered. The following strategies have been suggested to overcome potential organization- and people-related problems.[13]

1. Get top management involved. Top management must be committed to MIS if the system is to be successful. Not only must they approve the expenditures (which may be significant); they also must outwardly exhibit interest in the project. Subordinates sense when their superiors are genuinely interested in a project, and they act accordingly.

2. Determine if there is a felt need for the system. Make sure that the ultimate users and those who must provide inputs to the MIS feel the need for it. One helpful approach is to make sure that the users understand how the system can help them.

3. Get the users involved. Most people resist change. One of the best ways to overcome this is to involve the users in the project as early as possible. Ask for their ideas and keep them fully informed as to what is going on. Involving users early in the design phase will also help ensure that the system will be compatible with the different users' needs and their organizational constraints.

4. Provide training and education. Users must be taught how to input data and how to get answers from the system. In addition, training should include educating users in the overall purpose of the system, what it is supposed to do, how it does it, why it needs to be done, and who must do it.

5. Consider user attitudes. Studies have shown that user attitudes have a great impact on system effectiveness, especially when use of the system is mandated.[14] It is helpful to establish rewards for successful implementation of the system. These rewards do not have to be monetary but can be some form of recognition or other type of extrinsic reward.

6. Keep the interface simple. Even when the system is complex, the interface with users should be kept as simple as possible. Usually, users do not need to see the complex flow-diagrams and programming of the system design. Systems that appear very complicated to users often frighten them and make them leery of the entire system.

7. Let the ultimate users (managers) determine information usefulness. MIS designers should remember that what counts is what the users think is important. If users feel the information is neither useful nor important for making decisions, the system implementation will likely fail.

All of the above strategies are closely related to each other. They are not necessarily sequential but rather may be used at the same time. Also, they not only apply to the initial implementation but should be regularly reviewed and used to improve the system after it is operational. Figure 22–4 summarizes the above strategies.

F I G U R E   22–4   Organization/People Strategies for Implementing an MIS

1. Get top management involved.
2. Ascertain that there is a felt need for the system.
3. Get the users involved.
4. Provide training and education.
5. Consider user attitudes.
6. Keep the interface simple.
7. Let the ultimate users determine information usefulness.

INFORMATION CENTERS

Learning to interact with their companies' computer systems is a major problem for many of today's managers. Most managers do not have the time or interest to become experts in data processing. What managers want and need is to be able to gain direct access to data without becoming frustrated and confused.

Many companies—such as Exxon, Standard Oil of California, Bank of

America, and New York Telephone—have formed internal **information centers.** There managers can learn how to interact with their information systems from staff specialists whose job it is to train and support noncomputer people.[15] Typically, a manager contacts the center and describes the problems encountered and the type of information needed. A center consultant then works one-on-one with the manager, showing how to access needed data and use the software to get the desired information. The key to the information center concept is that managers use a hands-on approach and learn how to generate their own reports.

Information centers – in-house centers that companies establish to teach their managers to use their information systems.

CRITICISMS OF MIS

There is little doubt that an MIS can have a very positive effect on organizational performance. Yet, it is still subject to frequent criticism. Much criticism relates to shortfalls in methods of implementation. Figure 22–5 mentions some of the most frequent criticisms of MIS.

F I G U R E 22–5   Criticisms of MIS

WEAKNESS	CRITICISM
Inadequate information	Managers often complain that they do not get the information they need but they do get much information that is irrelevant.
Ignorance about what managers actually do	Understanding a manager's job is a natural prerequisite to providing that manager with useful information.
Centralized control of MIS	There is a tendency to centralize the development of an MIS. However, because of the large number and variety of activities that go on in an organization, this frequently leads to problems.
Complex user procedures	The rule of thumb is to keep the system as simple and user-friendly as possible.
Poor communication	Any system is almost doomed to failure if there is not open communication between the users and those responsible for developing the MIS.

Source: David Lynch, "MIS: Conceptual Framework, Criticisms, and Major Requirements for Success," *Journal of Business Communication,* Winter 1984, pp. 23–25.

Another frequent criticism of computers is that they often have a negative effect on the individuality of people.[16] Computers are often accused of dehumanizing and depersonalizing certain activities. Similarly, computerized systems frequently appear overly rigid and inflexible. For example, almost everyone has read of a story about some innocent person receiving an erroneous million-dollar billing from a computer! Yet another related criticism of computers is that they can be used to invade personal privacy and even to commit crimes such as illegal transfers and withdrawals of money.

While it is true that computerized systems can be depersonalizing and inflexible, they do not have to be. Technology has advanced to the point where it is now possible to have very "people-oriented" and "user-friendly" systems.[17] The trend toward these user-friendly systems should accelerate in the future. As far as the invasion of personal privacy and computer crimes, there are currently laws to deter these activities. New technology is also making these activities much more difficult.

COMPUTER ETHICS

As briefly discussed above, computers can be misused to the detriment of individuals and to society as a whole. The ethical climate of the organization as a whole should establish the framework for any decisions relating to computer ethics. In other words, ethical conduct related to computers should not be any different than any other ethical conduct in an organization. The Association for Computing Machinery (ACM) has developed some specific guidelines for ethical conduct related to the development and operation of computer-based information systems. These guidelines are summarized in Figure 22–6.

F I G U R E 22–6   The Code of Ethics of the Association for Computing Machinery (ACM)

CANON 1
An ACM member shall act at all times with integrity.

Ethical Considerations
An ACM member shall properly qualify himself when expressing an opinion outside his areas of competence. A member is encouraged to express his opinion on subjects within his area of competence.

An ACM member shall preface any partisan statements about information processing by indicating clearly on whose behalf they are made.

An ACM member shall act faithfully on behalf of his employers and clients.

CANON 2

An ACM member should strive to increase his competence and the competence and prestige of the profession.

Ethical Considerations
An ACM member is encouraged to extend public knowledge, understanding, and appreciation of information processing, and to oppose any false or deceptive statements relating to information processing of which he is aware.

F I G U R E 22–6 *(concluded)*

An ACM member shall not use his professional credentials to misrepresent his competence.

An ACM member shall undertake only those professional assignments and commitments for which he is qualified.

An ACM member shall strive to design and develop systems that adequately perform the intended functions and that satisfy his employer's or client's operational needs.

An ACM member should maintain and increase his competence through a program of continuing education encompassing the techniques, technical standards, and practices in his fields of professional activity.

An ACM member should provide opportunity and encouragement for professional development and advancement of both professionals and those aspiring to become professionals.

CANON 3

An ACM member shall accept responsibility for his work.

Ethical Considerations

An ACM member shall accept only those assignments for which there is reasonable expectancy of meeting requirements or specifications, and shall perform his assignments in a professional manner.

CANON 4

An ACM member shall act with professional responsibility.

Ethical Considerations

An ACM member shall not use his membership in ACM improperly for professional advantage or to misrepresent the authority of his statements.

An ACM member shall conduct professional activities on a high plane.

An ACM member is encouraged to uphold and improve the professional standards of the Association through participation in their formulation, establishment, and enforcement.

CANON 5

An ACM member should use his special knowledge and skills for the advancement of human welfare.

Ethical Considerations

An ACM member should consider the health, privacy, and general welfare of the public in the performance of his work.

An ACM member, whenever dealing with data concerning individuals, shall always consider the principle of the individual's privacy and seek the following:
    To minimize the data collected.
    To limit authorized access to the data.
    To provide proper security for the data.
    To determine the required retention period of the data.
    To ensure proper disposal of the data.

Source: James A. O'Brien, *Informaton Systems in Business Management,* 5th ed. (Homewood, Ill.: Richard D. Irwin, 1988), p. 611.

CAUTIONS CONCERNING MIS

Tremendous strides have been made regarding computers and management information systems. Still, managers must realize that technology will never replace certain aspects of a manager's job. Managers must surely become familiar with and be able to use computerized information systems. Yet, they must guard against being too dependent upon any computer system. In fact, it has been said that "too many cut-and-dried computer printouts have usurped the human aspect and put forth the fallacy that a corporation is equal to (and not more than) the sum of its parts."[18] Thomas Peters and Robert Waterman emphasize this same point in their book *In Search of Excellence* by attacking the tendency of many managers to become "overly rational."[19] Information systems can be of tremendous help in making managerial decisions. But the fact remains that successful management is still heavily dependent on human interaction.

S U M M A R Y

The purpose of this chapter is to develop an understanding of the role that computerized information systems play in modern organizations. This chapter introduces management information systems (MIS), presents a series of steps for successfully implementing an MIS, and discusses potential pitfalls and cautions relating to MIS. The focus of the chapter is not to introduce any specific MIS systems or technology but rather to develop a general appreciation of what an MIS can do for managers.

LEARNING OBJECTIVE 1

Recount the General Evolution of Computers Since the Early 1960s.

In the 1960s, large and costly mainframe computers were used almost exclusively by very large companies and governments. In the 1970s the large computers were followed by minicomputers which were much smaller in size and cost. Minicomputers ushered in the concept of distributed data processing. Personal computers are relatively inexpensive, take up very little space, and can process large amounts of data.

LEARNING OBJECTIVE 2

Define a Management Information System (MIS) and Distinguish between Data and Information.

A management information system (MIS) is an integrated approach for providing interpreted and relevant data that can help managers make decisions. The term MIS usually implies that computers are used at some point in the system to process data. Data is the raw materials from which information is developed; data is composed of facts that describe people, places, things, or events and that have not been interpreted. Data that has been interpreted and that meets the needs of one or more managers is information.

LEARNING OBJECTIVE 3

Differentiate between Operational and Strategic MIS.

Operational MIS provides information to assist in making decisions about current operations. Strategic MIS is more concerned with decisions that affect the accomplishment of long-range objectives.

LEARNING OBJECTIVE 4

Describe the Basic Components of an MIS.

The actual or physical computer is known as hardware. The instructions and programs used to run the computer are called software. The data needed by the user to run the system is referred to as a database. The final component of an MIS is the management staff and executive leadership.

LEARNING OBJECTIVE 5

Summarize the Steps in the Design Phase of MIS Development.

The design phase of MIS development involves five steps: (1) identifying the needs of managers; (2) setting objectives for the system; (3) preparing a project proposal; (4) preparing a conceptual design of the MIS; and (5) preparing a detailed design.

LEARNING OBJECTIVE 6

Summarize the Steps in the Implementation Phase of MIS Development.

The implementation phase of MIS development includes the purchase and integration of the resources necessary to form a working MIS, as well as testing and actually putting the system into operation. Specifically, implementation involves six steps: (1) acquiring the necessary facilities, equipment, and personnel; (2) training the personnel; (3) converting from the old to the new MIS (if an old one existed); (4) testing the new MIS; (5) operating the MIS; and (6) evaluating the MIS.

LEARNING OBJECTIVE 7

List Several Strategies for Overcoming Potential Organization and People-related Problems with Designing and Implementing MIS.

Some of the strategies available for overcoming organization and people-related problems that can plague an MIS are: (1) involving top management in the project; (2) determining if there is a felt need for the system; (3) getting the users involved; (4) providing training and education for the users; (5) fostering positive user attitudes; (6) keeping the interface simple; and (7) letting the ultimate users (managers) determine information usefulness.

LEARNING OBJECTIVE 8

Describe an Information Center.

An information center is an in-house center that a company establishes to teach its managers how to use its information systems. Typically an information systems professional works one-on-one with a manager showing him or her how to use a particular system or part of a system.

REVIEW QUESTIONS

1. Define information overload.
2. What is distributed data processing?
3. Distinguish between data and information.
4. What is a management information system (MIS)?
5. How does a transaction-processing system differ from an MIS?
6. Contrast operational MIS with strategic MIS.
7. What is a decision support system (DSS)?
8. What are the four basic components of an MIS?
9. Name the five basic steps involved in designing an MIS?
10. What steps are involved in implementing an MIS?
11. Briefly describe seven organization and people-related strategies that should be considered when developing an MIS.
12. What is an information center?
13. Summarize at least six criticisms that are frequently made about management information systems.

DISCUSSION QUESTIONS

1. How would you respond to the following statement: Learning about management information systems should be reserved for computer specialists?
2. When you go into a fast-food store and the salesperson keys your order into the cash register, how might this information be used as part of an MIS?
3. Assume your boss has just assigned you a special project to introduce all middle and top managers (a total of 20 managers) to personal computers. Describe in outline form how you might go about this project. Assume that none of the managers has ever worked with a personal computer.
4. Why do you think that some people like to talk about computers and MIS as if you have to be a genius to work with them?

REFERENCES & ADDITIONAL READINGS

[1] Stan Augarten, *Bit by Bit: An illustrated History of Computers* (New York: Ticknor & Fields, 1984), pp. 124–25, 128.

[2] Herbert R. Brinberg, "Effective Management of Information: How to Meet the Need of All Users," *Management Review,* February 1984, p. 11.

[3] David Lynch, "MIS: Conceptual Framework, Criticisms and Major Requirements for Success," *Journal of Business Communication,* Winter 1984, p. 20.

[4] Ibid.

[5] James O. Hicks, Jr., *Management Information Systems: A User Perspective* (St. Paul, Minn.: West Publishing, 1984), p. 21.

[6] "Using MIS Strategically," *Management Review,* April 1984, p. 5.

[7] For example, see F. Warren McFarlan, "Information Technology Changes the Way You Compete," *Harvard Business Review,* May–June 1984, pp. 98–103.

[8] James A. Senn, *Information Systems in Management,* 2nd ed. (Belmont, Calif.: Wadsworth, 1982), p. 284.

[9] This section is adapted from Raymond McLeod, Jr., *Management Information System,* 2nd ed. (Chicago: Science Research Associates 1983), pp. 16–17.

[10] Much of the material in the following two sections is drawn from Robert G. Murdick, *MIS Concepts and Design* (Englewood Cliffs, N.J.: Prentice-Hall, 1980), pp. 16–18, 210–11, 308–31.

[11] Ibid., p. 308.

[12] Paul H. Cheney and Gary W. Dickson, "Organizational Characteristics and Information Systems: An Exploratory Investigation," *Academy of Management Journal,* March 1982, pp. 181–82.

[13] Jugoslan S. Multinovich and Vladimir Vlahovich," A Strategy for a Successful MIS/DSS Implementation," *Journal of Systems Management,* August 1984, pp. 8–16.

[14] For example, see D. Robey, "User Attitudes and Management Information System Use," *Academy of Management Journal* 22, no. 3 (1979), pp. 527–38.

[15] William Clarke, "How Managers with Little DP Know-How Learn to Go Online with the Company Data Base," *Management Review,* June 1983, pp. 9–11. Much of this section is based on this article.

[16] James A. O'Brien, *Information Systems in Business Management,* 5th ed. (Homewood, Ill.: Richard D. Irwin, 1988), p. 604.

[17] Ibid.

[18] Robert E. McGarrah, "Ironies of Our Computer Age," *Business Horizons,* September–October 1984, p. 34.

[19] Thomas J. Peters and Robert Waterman, Jr., *In Search of Excellence* (New York: Harper & Row, 1982), pp. 29–54.

INCIDENT

Overburdened with Paperwork

Frank Bierman is a pharmacist and owner of a small, suburban drugstore. In recent years, his business has grown to the point where he could live comfortably—if he could just relax! Every working hour of every day he works at a breakneck speed just to fill prescriptions and keep up with all of the drugstore records.

When a customer wants a prescription filled, Frank pulls the customer's chart from a file cabinet and scans it for any potential drug interactions. He then types a prescription label that lists the patient's name, prescription number, name of the medicine, dosage, quantity, and the name of the prescribing physician. Finally, he fills the prescription, prepares a sales slip, and accepts payment.

During his few slow periods, Frank updates the customers' chart by hand with the same information that is printed on the prescription label. He also has to prepare his third-party billing forms. "Third-party billing" involves billing insurance companies directly for those customers who are covered by medicare, medicaid, or special group insurance programs. If a customer has a charge account with the store, Frank "files" a copy of the sales slip in a shoe box. Once a month, he and his wife spend an entire weekend totaling accounts, writing out bills, and addressing envelopes in order to bill customers. Frank has two clerks working in the store. They make deliveries and wait on customers, but they do not help Frank with the paperwork.

With all of the paperwork, Frank never leaves the store at closing time and rarely has a work-free weekend. He has been reading in the trade journals about small computer systems for retail drugstores that can help the pharmacist manage all of the drug, patient, and billing information. Frank thinks maybe a computer system could help him get control of the paperwork in his store.

Questions

1. What are Frank's information needs?

2. Assume you are Frank Bierman and that you have decided to look into purchasing a small computer system. Write a list of objectives that you would like for this system to achieve. Make any assumptions you feel are necessary, but note them in your answer.

EXERCISE

Recall★

Your instructor will read several series of digits to you. Listen carefully to each number. *When told to do so,* recall the digits and record them on a sheet of paper in their proper order as shown by the spaces provided below. Remember, do not write down the numbers until your instructor tells you to.

	Did You Get It Correct?	
	Yes	No
String 1: ── ── ── ── ── ── ── ── ── ── ── ── ──	──	──
String 2: ── ── ── ── ── ── ── ── ── ── ── ── ──	──	──
String 3: ── ── ── ── ── ── ── ── ── ── ── ── ──	──	──
String 4: ── ── ── ── ── ── ── ── ── ── ── ── ──	──	──
String 5: ── ── ── ── ── ── ── ── ── ── ── ── ──	──	──
String 6: ── ── ── ── ── ── ── ── ── ── ── ── ──	──	──

Compare the following sets of outcomes by noting whether you get the string correct or not.

COMPARISON I

Did you get String 1 correct?   Yes   No
Did you get String 2 correct?   Yes   No
Did you get String 3 correct?   Yes   No
How are 1, 2, and 3 different? _____
How does this show? _____
_____

COMPARISON II

Did you get String 3 correct?   Yes   No
Did you get String 5 correct?   Yes   No
How are Strings 3 and 5 different? _____
What does this show? _____
_____

COMPARISON III

Did you get String 4 correct?   Yes   No
Did you get String 6 correct?   Yes   No
How are Strings 4 and 6 different? _____
What does this show? _____
_____

★ This exercise is adapted from Henry J. Tosi and Jerald W. Young, *Management Experiences and Demonstrations* (Homewood, Ill.: Richard D. Irwin, 1982), pp. 154–55.

CASE

The Norge Division of Magic Chef

T he Norge corporation was incorporated in January 1927 in Michigan for the manufacture of Norge electric refrigeration units. At the end of 1927, Norge had 200 employees on the payroll and owned the entire common stock of Detroit Gear & Machine Company. As of the end of December 1928, two years after its inception, Norge owned approximately $1.0 million worth of fixed assets. However, Norge was to remain as a distinct corporate entity for only two years.

In July 1929, Norge Corporation was acquired by Borg-Warner through an exchange of stock. Borg-Warner was incorporated on May 9, 1928, in Illinois and within a decade had a long string of acquisitions in its pocket. After its takeover by Borg-Warner, the Norge Division, headquartered in Detroit, had a product line consisting of household appliances (refrigerators, electric ranges, gas ranges, washers, irons, electric room heaters) and commercial refrigerating equipment.

Since 1946, Norge has been one of Herrin, Illinois' major industries. Built by Borg-Warner, the plant at Herrin began with the production of wringer washers. In 1952, the first automatic washer came off the line. Both wringer and automatic washers were manufactured through most of the 1960s.

In October 1967, Borg-Warner relocated and incorporated in Delaware as successor to the original company. The control of Norge changed hands once again on July 1, 1968, when Borg-Warner sold its Norge Division to Fedders Corporation for $20 million cash, $16.8 million worth of subordinated notes, and 21,000 shares of Fedders common stock. Fedders was established in 1896 and incorporated on April 21, 1931, in New York. Fedders' product line consists of refrigeration equipment, radiators, and oil coolers for the automotive industry and compressors for refrigerators and air-conditioning applications.

Until 1968, only wringer and automatic washers were built at Norge in Herrin. At that time, Norge was also operating a dryer manufacturing branch in Effingham, Illinois. By 1971, Fedders had relocated the dryer branch to Herrin.

---

* Written by Nancy Owens and Lawrence R. Jauch. Address reprint requests to: Lawrence R. Jauch, Biedenharn Professor of Management, Northeast Louisiana University, Monroe, La. 71209-8813. © N, Owens and L. R. Jauch.

Another landmark in the vicissitudes of Norge was its acquisition by Magic Chef, Inc. on April 2, 1979. Magic Chef was founded in 1916 as Dixie Foundry and incorporated in Delaware in 1932. Magic Chef adopted its present name in 1960. Magic Chef bought the Norge Division from Fedders Corporation for $9.9 million cash and the assumption of a $3.2 million short-term note.

When Magic Chef acquired Norge, the company was greatly in need of investments in plant and equipment. The machinery was old and run-down. There was even some questions as to whether Norge could actually be made into a profitable venture. However, Skeet Rymer, Chairman of Magic Chef, determined that the benefits outweighed the costs, mainly for three reasons: acquisition of Norge would make Magic Chef a full-line manufacturer of appliances; the purchase price was a bargain; and synergism would exist between Norge and Admiral (the other company acquired by Magic Chef in 1979) because both had a relationship with Montgomery Ward.

Although much progress has been made, many problems still exist at Norge. Capital expenditures have been made, but not to the degree necessary for Norge to become competitive.

According to *Business Week* (June 20, 1983), when Norge was purchased, the laundry-appliance producer was in desperate need of new production machinery and tooling. Magic Chef had invested $4 million–$7 million annually in Norge, but that had not been enough to turn it around. After two years of marginal profitability, Norge lost $8 million in 1982. Profitability improved in 1983, and management is optimistic for the future; however, the company admits it may be several years before it can make reasonable earnings.

In addition, Norge has had to spend money that could have been utilized for plant and equipment on maintaining standards established by the Illinois Environmental Protection Agency (IEPA). For example, Norge has had some problems with waste disposal. In June 1982, the city of Herrin levied a fine against Norge of $500 for producing a "shock load" to the city's sewer system. A shock load kills treatment chemicals and shuts down the plant temporarily. Apart from this, a shock load constitutes a violation of IEPA regulations for which the city is held responsible. A sewer plant operator said the plant cannot handle grease, iron, and nickel wastes and that some combinations, such as sulfuric and nickel sulfate, are hazardous. A city official alleged that Norge's waste-disposal practices destroyed the sewer-system bacteria balance.

Following complaints from the city of Herrin, the company assigned one full-time employee to monitor the discharge problem. Norge uses a million gallons of water per day, three-fourths of which is discharged into the sewer system. Total water usage for the city of Herrin averages roughly 2.7 million gallons on a weekday.

Since complaints began pouring in from the city, Norge drew up elaborate plans to prevent certain metals from being discharged into the system. For example, a change in the painting system would cut down the quantities of nickel and zinc discharged.

NORGE TODAY

Still located in Herrin, Illinois, Norge currently builds and designs both washers and dryers. All major fabricated products are made at the Norge plant to ensure that Norge's quality standards are met and maintained.

In addition to the Norge brand, Norge also produces washers and dryers for customers such as Magic Chef, Admiral, Crosley, Western Auto, and Montgomery Ward. The relationship with Montgomery Ward is one that dates back more than 25 years. About half of the appliances manufactured by Norge go to Montgomery Ward, the second largest marketer of private-label laundry equipment.

Western Auto, which sells Norge's Citation Brand, is the company's next largest customer. Western Auto maintains 3,500 independent dealers located nationwide but concentrated mostly in the Midwest and Southeast.

Norge-brand appliances are also marketed through independent wholesale distributors who sell to local dealers. This appliance line includes coin-operated and commercial machines.

Products distributed under the Magic Chef line are marketed by a mass sales force. About 150 district managers call directly on retail accounts, thereby eliminating the wholesale step.

The Norge company occupies over 33 acres in Herrin, with nearly 1 million square feet of office plant and warehouse facilities. It is the largest industrial employer in southern Illinois, and is therefore most important to the southern Illinois economy. The plant's annual payroll is between $17 million and $20 million, with several million more spent on local purchases. Conversely, the people of southern Illinois are improtant to Norge. About 53 percent of the employees have been with the company for 10 years or more. Approximately 12 percent of the employees turn in perfect attendance records annually. The company rewards such accomplishments; those with perfect attendance are treated to a banquet and cash bonuses. Norge also holds listening sessions once a week, meeting with different employees to hear their gripes and comments.

Children of Norge employees are eligible for college scholarships, and companywide contests such as a bingo games based on safety records provide diversions from the everyday work pace.

Management at Norge feels that it is important to keep the employee involved. Carpenter describes his management style as "participative." This contrasts with the style that was in effect during the period when Norge had first been acquired by Magic Chef. Carpenter felt the early managers were very professional and capable; however, they lacked some of the hands-on experience necessary to do the job.

The change in management style brought a new way of thinking to Norge. Norge had been losing a lot of money. It was also having some problems with the Montgomery Ward relationship stemming from pricing policies. The new management implemented a strategy of realistic pricing to turn the firm around. Carpenter simply stated that Norge would no longer produce a product that would not make money. If products were unprofitable, they would be dropped.

NORGE IN THE LAUNDRY INDUSTRY

Norge has traditionally been in sixth place in terms of market share for washers and dryers. Efforts are being made to gain market share; however, competition in the industry is fierce. Norge is challenged by White Consolidated (ECI), General Electric, and Maytag, particularly for the Montgomery Ward business. In fact, just recently Montgomery Ward has made arrangements to sell the Maytag brand of washers and dryers in its stores.

Norge has lost some ground here because some of its costs are too high. Its product lines are generally two to three years behind competitors in terms of innovative features. In 1982, the company lost substantial sums of money. The following problems contributed to the loss and also to Norge's inability to be competitive: the recessionary period of 1982 made for a bad business year; and Norge had problems keeping costs under control. Norge's operations are fairly labor intensive compared to others in the industry. Material usage was not as efficient as possible; too much paint and steel were used, resulting in excessive costs.

The year 1983 marked a turning point. The company did in fact make a profit. Substantial sums were being invested to help Norge maintain this turnaround. The focal point of these investments lay in the area of quality. Management at Norge felt that heavy capital investment coupled with high volume was needed for Norge to become competitive. Management expressed the opinion that the quality of Norge products was near average. The general feeling was that the customers in Norge's target market would be willing to pay a premium for quality. Norge was spending money in the area of research and development, as well as in the production process, searching for ways to improve quality. In addition to improving quality, Norge was also attempting to reduce the size of its products while maintaining capacity. Norge-produced washers and dryers had the largest capacity in the industry.

Quality improvement is the first and foremost objective at Norge at the present time. The company is currently undertaking a new plan with respect to quality assurance/control. The focus will be on prevention rather than control or appraisal. The idea is to find the source of the problems in the products and prevent them from occurring rather than inspect and appraise the product and fix the problem after it has occurred.

The quality-assurance function at Norge may be divided into three categories: prevention, appraisal, and failure. Traditionally, Norge has concentrated primarily on appraisal and failure and paid little attention to prevention. Jim Thompson, Director of Quality Assurance, has suggested that the key ingredient to success is appropriate training of employees, although all Norge executives do not share that opinion. He feels that not enough emphasis is placed on quality in many education systems. Employees are well trained in product engineering and manufacturing, but room for improvement exists in the area of quality control.

Thompson feels that quality needs to be built into the development and product-design processes. Instead of simply scanning the design and giving approval, management needs to get more actively involved. Analysis of what could go wrong is needed here.

Among concerns of Norge executives are problems related to Norge product design, vendor relations, and manufacturing difficulties due to an antiquated plant. These problems generally manifest themselves in the form of mechanical failure as measured by service-call rates. To become more competitive, product redesign was instituted, but this led to field failure problems. The system of quality assurance of Norge is intended to provide better information to the plant about what is happening in the field. Staff increases have been made in an attempt to achieve this goal.

In addition to actual quality improvements, management at Norge also feels that perception of quality is very important for a successful company turnaround. The marketplace must be aware that efforts are being made to improve the quality at Norge.

The Appendix provides an illustration of the recently developed Quality Assurance Plan at Norge, which is a prime vehicle to implement the new quality-oriented strategy.

THE FUTURE FOR NORGE IN THE LAUNDRY BUSINESS

Many uncertainties exist with respect to forecasting U.S. appliance sales for the years 1984 through 1987. Much hinges on the success of "Reaganomics," reducing inflation, bringing down interest rates, and the success of the new tax incentives.

If an economic recovery does occur on schedule, and if interest rates decline to and remain at a reasonable level, many economists feel housing starts will increase greatly, which will in turn cause an increase in demand for major home appliances.

In addition to demand spurred by housing starts, the appliance industry is one that is greatly affected by replacement-type demand. High saturation has taken place in the market for washers and, to a lesser extent, dryers; but as these older products reach the end of their useful lives, demand for replacement products will occur.

It remains to be seen whether Norge will be able to make substantial quality improvements that its customers will be able to perceive. It is also unknown whether those customers will be willing to pay a premium price for higher quality. It will also be interesting to see if Magic Chef will invest the money needed to revitalize an older plant in a state with high labor costs to maintain its position as a full-time appliance provider. If, indeed, high volumes are necessary to become a lower-cost producer, it is questionable as to whether the expected demand for appliance replacements will be sufficient to allow the high-quality strategy to work effectively.

APPENDIX: NORGE DIVISION QUALITY ASSURANCE STRATEGIC PLAN

Current Quality Conditions

Norge quality is perceived by some to be below the industry average, and significant improvement is needed to increase market share and reduce overall quality costs. Some comments can be made about our current status:

- Service-call rates (SCR) on washers and dryers exceed that of competitors.
- Internal scrap and rework is excessive and averages more than 10 percent of direct labor.
- Warranty costs are excessive.
- Material handling in the plant contributes to excessive scrap and rework.
- Vendor components contribute significantly to field and internal failure, and not enough attention is provided in this area.
- Final testing is weak and does not provide adequate testing to screen out all functional defects to meet SCRs desired.

Quality Costs

Currently, total quality cost per unit produced is about $10. The three areas of quality costs are listed below.

Prevention. All of the efforts/components of quality costs to prevent failure/defects.

Appraisal. All of the efforts/components of quality costs to find the defects.

Failure. All of the efforts/components of quality costs to fix/pay for the failure.

In 1983, substantial sums were spent for prevention, appraisal, and failure. Norge (like many manufacturing companies) spends too much of the quality-cost dollar on appraisal and failure and too little on prevention. The overall quality-assurance strategy in the coming years will be to reduce appraisal and failure costs and increase prevention costs. As the increased dollars used for prevention take effect, overall quality costs will be reduced, and appraisal and failure costs will decline. Norge's overall objectives, strategies, and action plans are given below.

Objective—Washers

Reduce the service call rates by 5 percent in fiscal year (FY) 1984, another 5 percent by FY 1985, and another 10 percent by FY 1986.

Strategy

Develop an organization to identify and correct defects contributing to excessive failure.

Action Plans

1. Appoint a special SCR team to identify and correct defects contributing to the excessive SCR rate. Group responsible: Quality Assurance.
2. Establish a stronger field-failure investigation, analysis, and reporting function that will provide direction to the SCR committee. Group responsible: Quality Assurance.
3. Develop a strong quality-engineering organization to develop more effective quality systems and controls on new and existing products. Group responsible: Quality Assurance.
4. Establish a formal field-test program on all major washer changes. Units to be moved from a standard production run and not lab-built units. Group responsible: Quality Assurance.
5. Direct resources in product engineering to quality improvement with special emphasis on the transmission. Group responsible: Product Engineering.
6. Develop a program to report the SCR rates more widely to the organization. Solicit more employee involvement. Group responsible: Quality Assurance.
7. Originate a vendor quality-improvement program with more travel to suppliers by a quality-assurance representative to conduct quality-systems' surveys and develop supplier corrective action. Group responsible: Quality Assurance.
8. Install an automated washer test facility to replace the existing test tunnel. Group responsible: Quality Assurance/Manufacturing Services/Engineering.
9. Improve communications with hourly employees concerning quality and determine attitudes on quality of hourly and salaried employees. Group responsible: Quality Assurance/Personnel.
10. Initiate a "Whisper Quiet" program and reduce the noise level in the washer significantly. Group responsible: Quality Assurance/Product Engineering/Manufacturing Services.

Objective—Dryer

Reduce the SCR by 10 percent or more by 1985.

Strategy

Quality engineer the new 27″ dryer to provide quality controls that detect defects early and support the SCR rate objectives.

Action Plans

1. Assign a quality engineer to reevaluate the quality planning to date and assure that effective controls are in place. Group responsible: Quality Assurance.
2. Provide a new 27″ dryer that is more reliable than the existing design. Group responsible: Product Engineering/Manufacturing Services/ Quality Assurance.
3. Provide a new dryer tunnel that significantly improves testing and screens out all defects. Group responsible: Quality Assurance/Manufacturing Services.
4. Develop a supplier quality-surveillance program to control supplier quality effectively. Group responsible: Quality Assurance.

Objective—Very High Quality (VHQ)

Provide a unit to the market place that has a superior quality with a SCR that is less than 10 percent, excluding customer-responsible service calls.

Strategy

Provide superior product and quality engineering to assure that the unit is designed to provide a high quality and reliability level and that controls are in place to maintain the integrity of the design.

Action Plans

1. Provide additional controls and testing of vendor components such as the timer, pressure switch, mixing-valve motor, selection switch, solenoid, thermostat control, gas valve, and ignitor. Group responsible: Quality Assurance/Purchasing.
2. Build a test facility to 100 percent test each unit in five complete cycles.
3. Provide a dedicated line to produce the VHQ with specially trained operators. Group responsible: Manufacturing Services.

Objective—Scrap and Rework (Washer and Dryer)

Reduce scrap and rework to specified levels by year end.

Strategy

Aggressively pursue the causes of scrap and rework and develop corrective action. Find the causes, fix them, and keep them fixed.

Action Plans

1. Provide additional plant conveyor systems to prevent handling damage of parts in the following areas: washer-parts delivery; dryer-parts delivery; receiving; machine shop; porcelain. Group responsible: Manufacturing Services.

2. Continue to utilize a scrap-reduction team coordinated by Quality Assurance with appropriate functions represented. Aggressively pursue the principle "find the cause—fix it." Group responsible: Quality Assurance.

3. Improve paint and porcelain systems. Group responsible: Manufacturing Services/Quality Assurance.

4. Upgrade in-process gauging on machinery to provide operator control in the machine shop, press room, and tub and basket production area. Group responsible: Quality Assurance.

5. Provide dedicated presses for cabinet bodies, washer lids, dryer front panels, dryer tops, and dryer bases. Group responsible: Manufacturing Services.

Glossary of Key Terms

ABC classification system—Method of managing inventories, based on their values. (p. 567)

Abilities—Stable personal characteristics used in performing job tasks. (p. 422)

Acceptance sampling—Statistical method of predicting the quality of a batch or large group of products by inspecting a sample or group of samples. (p. 578)

Achievement-power-affiliation theory—Holds that people have three needs—achievement, power, and affiliation; the level of intensity varies among individuals; people are motivated in situations that allow them to satisfy their most intense need(s). (p. 374)

Activity scheduling—Develops the precise timetable to be followed in producing a product or service. (p. 231)

Administrative skills—Involve understanding and performing the organizing, staffing, and controlling functions of management. (p. 13)

Affirmative action plan—Written document outlining specific goals and timetables for remedying past discriminatory actions. (p. 311)

After-the-fact control—Designed to detect a problem or potential problem before it gets out of hand. (p. 549)

Age Discrimination in Employment Act of 1968—Amended in 1978; protects individuals from 40 to 70 years of age from discrimination in hiring, retention, compensation, and other conditions of employment. (p. 307)

Aggregate production planning—Concerned with overall operations and balancing major sections of the operating system; matches resources with demands for goods and services. (p. 227)

Apprenticeship training—Used in skilled trades; trainee works under the guidance of a skilled worker. (p. 339)

Assembly chart—Depicts the sequence and manner in which components of a product or service are assembled. (p. 229)

Assessment center—Evaluates an individual's potential as a manager and determines the person's development needs based on his or her reactions in a simulated, "real world" environment. (p. 347)

Audit—Method of control normally involved with financial matters; also can include other areas of the organization. (p. 552)

Authority—Right to issue directives (command) and expend resources. (pp. 254, 394)

Autocratic leader—Makes most decisions for the group. (p. 397)

Autogenic training—Much like self-hypnosis; helps individuals gain control over their physiology through passive concentration. (p. 490)

Before-the-fact (steering) control—Method of exercising control to prevent a problem from occurring. (p. 549)

Behavior (personal) control—Based on direct, personal surveillance. (p. 548)

Behaviorally anchored rating scale (BARS)—Determines employee's level of performance; based on whether specific job behaviors are present. (p. 428)

Bet-your-company culture—Requires big-stakes decisions; considerable time passes before the results are known. (p. 518)

Biofeedback—Monitoring devices give an individual feedback on the degree of relaxation or tension of various muscle groups. (p. 490)

Board of directors—Carefully selected committee that reviews major policy and strategy decisions proposed by top management. (p. 288)

Bottom-up management—Philosophy popularized by William B. Given that encouraged widespread delegation of authority to solicit the participation of all employees from the bottom to the top. (p. 45)

Brainstorming—Involves presenting a problem to a group and allowing them to produce a large quantity of ideas for its solution; no criticisms are allowed initially. (p. 149)

Brainwriting—Group is presented with a problem situation and members anonymously write down ideas, then exchange papers with others who build upon ideas and pass them on until all have participated. (p. 151)

Break-even chart—Depicts graphically the relationship of volume of operations to profits. (p. 553)

Budget—Statement of expected results or requirements expressed in financial or numerical terms. (p. 549)

Burnout—Adaptation an individual makes to stress and work-related and personal factors; results in a situation where work is no longer meaningful. (p. 488)

Business game—Classroom training that provides the setting of a company and its environment and requires team players to make operating decisions. (p. 345)

Business strategies—Focus on how to compete in a given business. (p. 177)

C

Captains of industry—Dominated and built corporate giants during the last 25 years of the 19th century; included John D. Rockefeller, James B. Duke, Andrew Carnegie, Cornelius Vandervilt, and others. (p. 32)

Cascade approach—Ensures that the objectives of individual units within the organization are in phase with the major objectives of the organization. (p. 169)

Case study—Classroom training where students analyze real or hypothetical situations and suggest what to do and how to do it. (p. 344)

Central tendency—Tendency to rate all or most employees in the middle of the performance rating scale. (p. 433)

Centralization—Little authority is delegated to lower levels of management. (p. 255)

Checklist—Performance appraisal in which the rater answers yes or no to questions about the behavior of the person being rated. (p. 427)

Civil Rights Act of 1964—Title VII of this act eliminates discrimination in employment based on race, color, religion, sex, or national origin in organizations that conduct interstate commerce. (p. 305)

Clifford Trust—Company turns over some of its assets for a set time period during which all of the income earned on the assets goes to charity. (p. 92)

Coaching—Management development conducted on the job, where experienced managers advise and guide trainees in solving managerial problems. (p. 343)

Coercive power—Based on fear. (p. 394)

Committee—Organization structure in which a group of people are formally appointed, organized, and superimposed on the line or line and staff structure to consider or decide certain matters. (p. 286)

Communication—Transfer of information that is meaningful to those involved; the transmittal of understanding. (p. 102)

Comparative advantage—Country produces those goods and services it can produce more efficiently or cheaply than other countries. (p. 62)

Compensation—Extrinsic rewards employees receive in exchange for their work. (p. 436)

Compensation system—Policies, procedures, and rules the organization uses to determine employee compensation. (p. 437)

Concurrent (screening) control—Focus on process as it occurs, designed to detect a problem when it happens. (p. 549)

Conflict—Overt behavior in which one party seeks to advance its own interests in its relationship with others. (p. 474)

Conformity—Refers to the degree to which group members accept and abide by the norms of the group. (p. 460)

Consumer Product Safety Act of 1972—Protects consumers against unreasonable risks of injury associated with consumer products. (p. 89)

Consumerism—Social movement that seeks to redress the perceived imbalance in the marketplace between buyers and sellers. (p. 89)

Contingency approach to leadership—Holds that the most effective style of leadership depends on the particular situation. (p. 402)

Contingency approach to management—Theorizes that different situations and conditions require different management approaches. (p. 48)

Contingency approach to organization structure—States that the most appropriate structure depends on the technology used, the rate of environmental change and other dynamic forces. (p. 291)

Continuous flows—Operating system used by companies that produce large amounts of similar products/services flowing through similar stages of the operating system. (p. 219)

Control (controlling)—Management function that measures performance against an organization's objectives, determines causes of deviations, and takes corrective action when necessary. (pp. 10, 538)

Control tolerances—Acceptable variation from the standard that is acceptable to the manager. (p. 543)

Corporate culture—Communicates how people in an organization should behave, by establishing a value system conveyed through rites, rituals, myths, legends, and actions. (p. 513)

Corporate philanthropy—Donations of money, property, or work by organizations to needy persons or for social purposes. (p. 92)

Corporate strategies—Address what businesses an organization will be in and how resources will be allocated among those businesses. (p. 177)

Council on Environmental Quality—Assists and advises the president on environmental issues. (p. 90)

Creativity—Thinking process that produces an idea or concept that is new, original, useful, or satisfying to its creator or to someone else. (p. 148)

Criterion—Measure of job success or performance.

Critical-incident appraisal—Method in which the rater records incidents of both positive and negative employee behavior and uses them to evaluate performance. (p. 426)

Culture—Set of important beliefs, key values, and understandings (often unstated) that members of a community share in common. (pp. 65, 513)

Customer departmentation — Organizational units based on division by customers served. (p. 277)

D

Data—Raw material from which information is developed; composed of facts that have not been interpreted. (p. 592)

Database—Contains the data required to meet the user's need; usually, readily accessible information about the organization's operations. (p. 596)

Data processing—Capture, processing, and storage of data. (p. 593)

Decentralization—A great deal of authority is delegated to lower levels of management. (p. 255)

Decision making—In its narrowest sense, is the process of choosing from among various alternatives. (p. 139)

Decision-making skills—Involve searching the environment for conditions requiring a decision, developing and analyzing possible alternatives, and selecting a course of action. (p. 13)

Decision process—Three stages are intelligence, design, and choice. (p. 138)

Decision support systems (DSS)—Extension of an MIS; provides information for making decisions and becomes a part of the process. (p. 594)

Democratic leader—Guides and encourages the group to make decisions. (p. 397)

Departmentation—Grouping activities into related work units. (p. 275)

Dependent demand items—Subassembly or component parts used to make a finished product. Their demand is based upon the number of finished products being produced. (p. 567)

Diagnosis—Gathering and analyzing information about an organization to determine areas in need of improvement or change. (p. 509)

Direct feedback—Change agent communicates the information gathered through diagnosis directly to the affected people. (p. 510)

Dissonance—Feeling of disharmony within an individual. (p. 478)

Downward communication—Transmitting information from higher to lower levels of the organization through the chain of command. (p. 114)

E

Economic order quantity (EOQ)—Optimum number of units to order at one time. (p. 570)

Effort—Energy (physical and/or mental) used by an individual in performing a task. (p. 422)

Entrepreneur—Person who conceives the product or service idea, starts the organization, and builds it to the point where additional people are needed. (p. 17)

Entry socialization—Adaptation process by which new employees are introduced and indoctrinated into an organization. (p. 515)

Environmental changes—All nontechnological changes that occur outside the organization. (p. 504)

Environmental impact statement (EIS)—Written report required of federal government agencies on proposed actions that affect the human environment. (p. 91)

Environmental Protection Agency (EPA)—Interprets and administers the environmental protection policies of the federal government. (p. 92)

Equal employment opportunity—Right of all people to work and advance on the basis of merit, ability, and potential. (p. 306)

Equal Pay Act of 1963—Became effective June 1964; prohibits wage discrimination on the basis of sex. (p. 305)

Essay appraisals—The employer/rater describes the employee's performance in written narrative form. (p. 426)

Ethics—Standards or principles of conduct that govern the behavior of an individual or a group of individuals. (p. 93)

Evaluation phase—Third phase in strategic management, where the implemented strategic plan is monitored, evaluated, and updated. (p. 198)

Event outcome forecasts—Try to predict the outcome or result of a highly probable future event. (p. 204)

Event timing forecasts—Try to predict when a known event will occur. (p. 204)

Exception principle—States that managers should concentrate on matters that deviate significantly from normal and let subordinates handle routine matters. Also called management by exception. (p. 265)

Executive champion—Shields a new product or idea from the organization's natural tendency to reject new products or ideas. (p. 20)

Expert power—Based on the special skill, expertise, or knowledge of an individual. (p. 395)

Export-import manager—Serves a group of exporting/importing organizations and handles all activities involved in the exporting/importing of their goods or services. (p. 63)

Exporting—Selling an organization's goods or services to another country. (p. 63)

External environment—In management process, factors outside the organization that affect it and its business. (p. 201)

External equity—What employees are paid compared to employees performing similar jobs in other organizations. (p. 438)

F

Fair Packaging and Labeling Act of 1967—Regulates labeling procedures for businesses. (p. 89)

Feedback—Flow of information from receiver to sender that indicates if message was received as intended by the sender. (p. 540)

Feedback (closed) system—Where outputs from the system affect future inputs or future activities of the system. (p. 110)

Fixed overhead expenses—Those that do not change appreciably with fluctuations in level of production or service. (p. 563)

Fixed-order period method—Orders are placed at predetermined regular time intervals regardless of inventory in stock. (p. 569)

Fixed-order quantity method—Orders are placed whenever the inventory reaches a certain predetermined level, regardless of how long it takes to reach that level; assumes continual monitoring of levels. (p. 568)

Flat structure—Organization with few levels and relatively large spans of management at each level. (p. 285)

Flexible (variable) budget—Allows certain expenses to vary with the level of sales or output. (p. 550)

Flow process chart—Outlines what happens to a product or service as it progresses through the facility. (p. 229)

Forced-choice rating—Requires rater to rank a set of statements describing how an employee carries out the duties and responsibilities of the job. (p. 430)

Foreign Corrupt Practices Act of 1977—Prohibits American companies operating abroad from bribing foreign officials, political candidates, and party leaders; requires company's books and records to accurately and fairly reflect transactions. (p. 93)

Foreign exchange rate—The rate of exchange for one currency to another currency, e.g., French francs to American dollars. (p. 66)

Formal plan—Written, documented plan developed through an identifiable process. (p. 182)

Formal work groups—Have a defined structure and are formally recognized by the organization. (p. 453)

Formulation phase—First phase in strategic management where the initial strategic plan is developed. (p. 198)

Frustration—Intrapersonal conflict that results when a drive or motive is blocked before the goal is reached. (p. 477)

Functional departmentation—Organizational units are defined by the nature of the work. (p. 275)

Functional plans—Originate from the functional areas of an organization like production, marketing, finance, and personnel. (p. 183)

Functional strategies—Concerned with the activities of the different functional areas of a business. (p. 177)

Functions of management—Activities a manager performs in doing the work of management: planning, controlling, organizing, staffing, and leading. (p. 10)

G

Geographic departmentation—Organizational units are defined by territories. (p. 277)

Goal (objectives)—Statement designed to give an organization and its members direction and purpose. (p. 168)

Goal conflict—Intrapersonal conflict that results when a goal has both positive and negative features or when two or more competing goals exist. (p. 478)

Godfather—Typically an aging leader in the organization who provides the role model for championing. (p. 20)

Gordon technique—Aid to producing creative ideas in which only the group leader knows the exact nature of the real problem and uses a key word to describe the problem area as a starting point for exploring solutions. (p. 150)

Grand strategy—Describes the way the organization will pursue its objectives, given the threats and opportunities in the environment and its own resources and capabilities. (p. 177)

Grapevines—Informal channels of communication resulting from casual contacts in various organizational units. (p. 118)

Graphic rating scale—Requires rater to indicate on a scale where the employee rates on work-related factors. (p. 426)

Grid training—Method used in organizational development to make managers and organizations more team oriented. (p. 511)

Group—Number of persons who interact with one·another over a span of time on a face-to-face basis and perceive themselves to be a group. (p. 452)

Group cohesiveness—Degree of attraction each member has for the group. (p. 458)

Group norm—Informal rules that a group adopts to regulate members' behavior. (p. 457)

H

Halo effect—Occurs when managers allow a single prominent characteristic to dominate their judgment of all traits, or allow general impression of employee to influence judgment on separate items of a performance appraisal. (pp. 318, 433)

Hardware—Actual computer and its peripheral equipment. (p. 595)

Hawthorne studies—A series of experiments conducted in 1924 at the Hawthorne Plant of Western Electric of Cicero, Illinois: production increased in no relationship to environment but rather to psychological and social conditions. (p. 41)

Hierarchy of needs—Maslow's five levels of individual needs: physiological, safety, social, esteem or ego, and self-actualization. (p. 371)

Horizontal (lateral) communication—Transmitting information across the lines of the formal organization's chain of command. (p. 117)

Host country—Country in which a foreign organization does business. (p. 64)

Human asset accounting—Measuring the costs incurred by organizations in recruiting, hiring, training, and developing their human assets. (p. 330)

Human relations skills—Involve understanding human behavior and being able to work well with people. (p. 13)

Human resource forecasting—Process that determines future human resource needs. (p. 304)

Human resource planning (HRP)—Process of getting the right number of qualified people into the right jobs at the right time. (p. 302)

I

Idiosyncrasy credit— Form of credit or liberties a group gives to certain members who make significant contributions to the group's goals. (p. 463)

Implementation phase—Second phase in strategic management, where the strategic plan is put into effect. (p. 198)

Importing—Purchasing goods or services from foreign countries. (p. 63)

In-basket technique—Classroom training where trainee is required to handle a manager's mail and phone calls and react accordingly. (p. 344)

In Search of Excellence—Book by Thomas J. Peters and Robert H. Waterman, Jr., identifies 36 companies with an excellent 20-year performance record over a 20-year period. The authors formulated eight characteristics of excellence after interviewing each company. (p. 49)

Incident method—Form of case study where students are given the general outline of a situation and are given additional information only as they request it. (p. 344)

Independent demand items—Finished goods ready to be shipped out or sold. (p. 567)

Informal organization—Aggregate of the personal contacts and interactions and the associated groupings of people working within the formal organization. (p. 252)

Informal work groups—Result from personal contacts and interactions of people within formal work groups; usually not formally recognized by the organization. (p. 453)

Information—Data that have been interpreted and that meet the need of one or more managers. (p. 592)

Information centers—In-house centers that companies set up to teach their managers how to use their information systems. (p. 601)

Information overload—Occurs when managers have so much information available that they have trouble distinguishing between the useful and the useless information. (p. 590)

Innovation—Process of applying a new and creative idea to a product, service, or method of operation. (p. 148)

Input-output scheme—List desired output, then list all steps required to attain this. Steps are then discussed and their desirability prioritized until one output emerges. (p. 151)

Intermittent flow—Operating system used when customized products and services are produced. (p. 219)

Internal changes—Budget adjustments, policy changes, personnel changes, and the like. (p. 504)

Internal equity—What an employee is paid compared to what other employees in the organization are paid to do their jobs. (p. 438)

Interpersonal communication—Communication between individuals. (p. 103)

Interpersonal conflict—Between two or more individuals, can be caused by many factors. (p. 482)

Intrapersonal conflict—Internal to the individual; relates to the need-drive-goal motivational sequence. (p. 477)

Intuitive approach to decision making—Making decisions based on hunches and intuition. (p. 144)

Inventory—Quantity of raw materials, in-process goods, or finished goods on hand; serves as a buffer between different rates of flow associated with the operating system. (p. 564)

J

Job analysis—Determining, through observation and study, information relating to the nature of a specific job. (p. 303)

Job content—Aggregate of all the work tasks the jobholder may be asked to perform. (p. 225)

Job depth—Freedom of employees to plan and organize their own work, to work at their own pace, and to move around and communicate as desired. (p. 254)

Job design—Designates specific work activities of an individual or group of individuals. (p. 225)

Job description—Written statement that identifies the tasks, duties, activities, and performance results required in a specific job. (p. 303)

Job dimension—Broad categories of duties and responsibilities that make a job. (p. 428)

Job enlargement—Making a job structurally larger by giving an employee more similar operations or tasks to perform. (p. 375)

Job enrichment—Upgrading a job with factors like more meaningful work, recognition, responsibility, and opportunities for advancement. (p. 375)

Job evaluation—Systematic determination of the value of each job in relation to other jobs in the organization. (p. 439)

Job method—Manner in which the human body is used, workplace arrangement, and design of the tools and equipment used. (p. 225)

Job rotation—Requires employee to learn several different jobs in a work unit or department and perform each for a specified time period. (pp. 343, 375)

Job satisfaction—An individual's general attitude about the job. (p. 381)

Job scope—Number of different types of operations performed on the job. (p. 253)

Job specification—Written statement that identifies the abilities, skills, traits, or attributes necessary for a particular job. (p. 303)

Judeo-Christian ethic—Generally, the basis of Western ethical codes; primary goal is love, including love of God and neighbor. (p. 93)

Jury of executive opinion—Managers get together and share opinions—from these a forecast is devised. (p. 205)

Just-in-time inventory control (JIT)—An inventory control system that schedules materials to arrive and leave at the right time. (p. 566)

L

Laissez-faire leader—Allows individuals in the group to make the decisions. (p. 397)

Leader—Occupies the central role in a leadership situation and has the ability to influence the behavior of others in a given situation. (p. 392)

Leader Behavior Description Questionnaire (LBDQ)—Developed at Ohio State University and designed to determine how successful leaders carry out their activities. (p. 397)

Leadership—Process of influencing the behavior of other members of the group. (p. 392)

Leading—Management function that directs and channels human behavior toward the accomplishment of objectives. (p. 10)

Legitimate power—Based on one's position in an organization. (p. 394)

Leniency—Grouping performance ratings at the positive end instead of spreading them over the performance scale. (p. 433)

Level of aspiration—Level of performance a person expects or hopes to attain. (p. 147)

Life-cycle theory of leadership—Holds that the maturity level of the followers determines the most appropriate leadership style for a situation. (p. 406)

Line and staff structure—Organization structure that results when staff specialists are added to a line organization. (p. 280)

Line functions—Functions and activities directly involved in producing and marketing the organization's goods or services. (p. 280)

Line structure—Organization structure with direct vertical links between the different levels of the organization. (p. 278)

Long-range objectives—Objectives that extend beyond the current fiscal year of the organization; they must support and not conflict with the organizational mission. (p. 271)

Long-range plans—Generally start at the end of the current year and extend into the future. (p. 182)

M

Mainframe computers— A large computer system, typically with a separate central processing unit. (p. 591)

Management—Process that involves guiding or directing a group of people toward organizational goals or objectives. (p. 8)

Management audit—Attempts to evaluate the overall management practices and policies of the organization. (p. 552)

Management by objectives (MBO)—Superior and subordinate jointly define the objectives and responsibilities of the subordinate's job; superior uses them to evaluate subordinate's performance; subordinate's rewards are directly related to performance. Also called goal-setting approach to performance appraisal. (pp. 173, 424)

Management development—Concerned with developing the experience, attitudes, and skills necessary to become or remain an effective manager. (p. 341)

Management functions—Activities a manager performs in doing the work of management: planning, controlling, organizing, staffing, and leading. (p. 10)

Management information system (MIS)—Integrated approach for providing interpreted and relevant data that can help managers make decisions. (p. 593)

Management theory jungle—Term developed by Harold Koontz; refers to the division of thought that resulted from the multiple approaches to studying the management process. (p. 47)

Managerial Grid®—Two-dimensional framework characterizing a leader according to concern for people and concern for production. (p. 400)

Material requirements planning (MRP)— A dependent demand inventory planning and control system that schedules the right amount of materials needed to produce the final product on schedule. (p. 572)

Matrix structure—Hybrid organization structure in which individuals from different functional areas are assigned to work on a specific project or task. Also called project form of organization. (p. 282)

Maximax approach—Sometimes called optimistic or gambling approach, to select the alternative whose best possible outcome is the best of all possible outcomes for all alternatives. (p. 141)

Maximin approach—To compare the worst possible outcomes for each of the alternatives and select the one which is least bad. This is a pessimistic approach. (p. 142)

McCormick multiple-management plan—Developed by Charles McCormick; uses participation as a training and motivational tool by selecting promising young employees from various company departments to form a junior board of directors. (p. 44)

Meditation techniques—Focus attention on a constant object such as the breath or a repetitive syllable. (p. 490)

Microcomputers—A very small computer, ranging in size from a "computer on a chip" to a small typewriter-size unit. (p. 591)

Minicomputers—A small (desk size) electronic, digital, stored-program, general purpose computer. (p. 591)

Mission (purpose)—Defines the basic purpose(s) of an organization—why the organization exists. (p. 169)

Motivation—Causative sequence concerned with what activates, directs, and sustains human behavior: needs → drives or motives → goal attainment. (p. 369)

Motivation-maintenance theory—States that all work-related factors can be grouped into one of two categories: *maintenance factors,* which will not produce motivation but can

prevent it, and *motivators,* which can encourage motivation. (p. 374)

Multinational corporation (MNC)—Any business organization that maintains a production, assembly, sales, or service presence in two or more countries. (p. 68)

N

National Environmental Policy Act of 1969—Committed the federal government to preserving the country's ecology, established a White House Council on Environmental Quality, and required filings of environmental impact statements. (p. 90)

Need hierarchy theory—Based on the assumption that individuals are motivated to satisfy a number of needs and that money can satisfy only some of these needs. (p. 371)

Nominal grouping technique (NGT)—Highly structured technique for solving group tasks; minimizes personal interactions to encourage activity and reduce pressures toward conformity. (p. 151)

Nonverbal communication—Conscious or unconscious behavior of the individual sending a message that is perceived consciously or unconsciously by the receiver. (p. 111)

O

Objectives (goals)—Statements outlining what you are trying to achieve; they give an organization and its members direction. (p. 168)

Occupational Safety and Health Act (OSHA) of 1970—Designed to reduce job injuries; established specific federal safety guidelines for almost all U.S. organizations. (p. 226)

On-the-job training (OJT)—Normally given by a senior employee or supervisor; trainee is shown how to perform the job and allowed to do it under the trainer's supervision. (p. 336)

Operating system—Consists of the processes and activities necessary to transform various inputs into goods and/or services. (p. 217)

Operational MIS—Basically provides information to assist in making decisions relating to current operations. (p. 593)

Operational or tactical planning—Presupposes a set of objectives handed down by a higher level in the organization and determines ways to attain them. (p. 183)

Operations management—Application of basic management concepts and principles to the segments of the organization that produce the goods or services. (p. 216)

Operations planning—Designing the systems of the organization that produce goods or services; planning the day-to-day operations within these systems. (p. 216)

Optimizing—Practice of selecting the best possible alternative. (p. 147)

Organization—Group of people working together in a concerted or coordinated effort to attain objectives. (p. 252)

Organization structure—Framework that defines the boundaries of the formal organization and within which the organization operates. (p. 274)

Organizational communication—Occurs within the formal organization structure. (p. 11)

Organizational development (OD)—Organization-wide, planned effort managed from the top, to increase organizational performance through planned interventions. (p. 508)

Organizational morale—Individual's feeling of being accepted by, and belonging to, a group of employees through common goals, confidence in the desirability of these goals and progress toward them. (p. 381)

Organizing—Management function that groups and assigns activities and provides the authority necessary to carry out the activities. (pp. 10, 252)

Orientation—Introduction of new employees to the organization, their work unit, and their job. (p. 331)

Orientation kit—Packet of written information given to a new employee to supplement the verbal orientation program. (p. 331)

Output (impersonal) control—Based on the measurement of outputs. (p. 548)

P

Parent organization—Organization that extends its operations beyond its nation's boundaries. (p. 64)

Parity principle—States that authority and responsibility must coincide. (p. 258)

Path-goal theory of leadership—Holds that the leader's role is to increase personal payoffs to subordinates for work-goal attainment, make the path to payoffs easier, and increase the opportunities for satisfaction enroute; the effectiveness of such efforts depends on the situation. (p. 406)

Perception—Refers to how a person processes a message; is influenced by the person's personality and previous experience and is unique for each individual. (p. 105)

Performance—Degree of accomplishment of the tasks that make up an individual's job. (p. 421)

Performance appraisal—Process of determining and communicating to employees how they are performing on the job and establishing a plan of improvement. (p. 420)

Period of solidification—Occurred in the 1920s and 1930s; management became recognized as a discipline. (p. 40)

Peter principle—Idea, popularized by Lawrence Peter, that managers tend to be promoted to their level of incompetence. (p. 300)

Physical layout—Process of planning the optimum physical arrangement of facilities—including personnel, operating equipment, storage space, office space, materials-handling equipment, and room for customer or product movement. (p. 223)

Planning—Process of deciding what objectives to pursue during a future time period and what to do to achieve those objectives. (pp. 10, 168)

Planning skills—Involve deciding what objectives to pursue during a future time period and how to achieve those objectives. (p. 15)

Policies—Broad, general guides to action which relate to objective attainment. (p. 177)

Polygraph—Device that records physical changes in the body as test subject answers questions; also known as lie detector. (p. 315)

Power—Ability or capacity to influence another to do something that the person would not otherwise do; ability to command or apply force; not necessarily accompanied by authority. (pp. 254, 393)

Preference-expectancy theory—Holds that motivation is based on a combination of the individual's expectancy that increased effort will lead to increased performance, which will lead to rewards, and the individual's preference for those rewards. (p. 376)

Primary group—Meets all the characteristics of a group but also has feelings of loyalty, comradeship, and a common sense of values among its members. (p. 452)

Principle—Accepted rule of action. (p. 14)

Principle of bounded rationality—Assumes that people have the time and cognitive ability to process only a limited amount of information upon which to base decisions. (p. 146)

Problem solving—The process of determining the appropriate responses or actions necessary to alleviate a problem. (p. 139)

Procedures—Series of related steps or tasks expressed in chronological order to achieve a specific purpose. (p. 178)

Process approach to management—Focuses on the management functions of planning, controlling, organizing, staffing, and leading. (p. 46)

Process control chart—Time-based graphic display that shows if a machine or process is producing items that meet preestablished specifications. (p. 578)

Process culture—Involves low risk with little feedback; employees focus on how things are done rather than on the outcomes. (p. 518)

Process physical layout—Equipment or services of a similar functional type are arranged or grouped together. (p. 224)

Process selection—Specifies in detail the processes and sequences required to transform inputs into products or services. (p. 220)

Product champion—Fanatic who believes in the specific product or idea that he or she has in mind. (p. 20)

Product departmentation—All activities necessary to produce and market a product or service are under one manager. (p. 276)

Product physical layout—Equipment or services are arranged according to the progressive steps by which the product is made or the customer is served. (p. 224)

Product quality control—Relative to inputs or outputs of the system. Used when quality is evaluated with respect to a batch of existing products or services. (p. 576)

Production planning—Concerned primarily with aggregate production planning, resource allocation, and activity scheduling. (p. 227)

Productivity—Output per person-hour of input. (p. 9)

Professional manager—Career manager who does not necessarily have an ownership interest in the organization and who realizes a responsibility to employees, stockholders, and the public. (p. 43)

Program of planned change—Deliberate design and implementation of a structural innovation, a new policy or goal, or a change in operating philosophy, climate, and style. (p. 508)

Programmed instruction — Classroom training in which material is presented in text form or on computers; students must answer questions correctly before advancing. (p. 339)

Programmer—Writes instructional programs that tell computers what to do. (p. 595)

Promotion—Moving an employee to a job with higher pay, status, and performance requirements. (p. 321)

Punishment—Either the application of negative stimulus or the removal of a pleasant environment as a consequence of behavior. (p. 379)

Q

Quality—For the operations manager, quality is determined in relation to the specifications or standards set in the design stages, the degree or grade of excellence specified. (p. 574)

Quality circle—Members of a work unit who meet on a regular basis to discuss quality problems and generate ideas for improving quality. (p. 465)

Quality control—Process of ensuring or maintaining a certain level of quality for materials, products, or services. (p. 574)

Quotas—Establish the maximum quantity of a product that might be imported (or exported) during a given time period. (p. 67)

R

Ranking methods—Performance appraisal in which the performance of an individual is ranked relative to the performance of others. (p. 431)

Rational approach to decision making—Involves these steps: recognize the need for a decision; establish, rank, and weigh criteria; collect data; identify alternatives; evaluate alternatives; and make the final choice. (p. 145)

Recruitment—Process of seeking and attracting a supply of people from which qualified candidates for job vacancies can be selected. (p. 308)

Referent power—Based on the charismatic traits or characteristics of an individual. (p. 395)

Rehabilitation Act of 1973—Prohibits discrimination in the hiring of the handicapped by federal agencies and federal contracters. (p. 307)

Reinforcement theory—Motivation approach based on the idea that behavior that appears to lead to a positive consequence tends to be repeated, while behavior that appears to lead to a negative consequence tends not to be repeated. (p. 378)

Relaxation response—Trains a person to control major muscle groups. (p. 490)

Resource allocation—Efficient allocation of people, materials, and equipment in order to meet the demand requirements of the operating system. (p. 228)

Responsibility—Accountability for the attainment of objectives, the use of resources, and the adherence to organizational policy. (p. 254)

Reverse discrimination—Alleged preferential treatment for one group (minority or female) over another group (male white) rather than merely providing equal opportunity. (p. 311)

Reward power—Based on an individual's ability to provide rewards for compliance with his or her wishes. (p. 394)

Risk-averting approach—To choose the alternative with the least variation among its possible outcomes. It makes for more effective planning. (p. 142)

Role—Organized set of behaviors belonging to an identifiable job. (p. 11)

Role (task) perceptions—The activities and behavior that people believe are necessary to perform job tasks. (p. 422)

Role playing—Trainees learn by acting out assigned roles in a realistic situation. (p. 344)

Routing—Finds the best path and sequence of operations for attaining a desired level of output with a given mix of equipment and personnel. (p. 228)

Rules—Guidelines that require specific and definite actions be taken or not taken in a given situation. They permit no flexibility or deviation. (p. 179)

S

Safety stocks—Inventory maintained to accommodate unexpected changes in demand and supply and to allow for variations in delivery time. (p. 569)

Satisficing—Selecting the first alternative that meets the decision maker's minimum standard of satisfaction. (p. 147)

Scalar principle—States that authority in the organization flows, one link at a time, through the chain of managers ranging from the highest to lowest ranks. Also called chain of command. (p. 261)

Scanlon plan—Incentive plan developed in 1938 by Joseph Scanlon to give workers a bonus for tangible savings in labor costs. (p. 46)

Scientific management—Philosophy of Frederick W. Taylor that sought to increase productivity and make the work easier by scientifically studying work methods and establishing standards. (p. 34)

Self-fulfilling prophecy (Pygmalion in management)—Describes the influence of one person's expectations on another's behavior. (p. 396)

Semantics—Science or study of the meaning of words and symbols. (p. 104)

Sensitivity training—Method used in organizational development to make one more aware of onself and one's impact on others. (p. 510)

Separation—Voluntary or involuntary termination of an employee. (p. 321)

Short-range objectives—Generally tied to a specific time period of a year or less and are derived from an in-depth evaluation of long-range objectives. (p. 171)

Short-range plans—Generally cover up to one year. (p. 182)

Situation of certainty—Occurs when a decision maker knows exactly what will happen and can calculate the precise outcome for each alternative. (p. 140)

Situation of risk—Occurs when the decision maker is aware of the relative probabilities associated with each alternative. (p. 141)

Situation of uncertainty—Occurs when a decision maker operates without knowing the relative probabilities associated with the respective alternatives. (p. 141)

Skills inventory—Contains basic information on all employees of an organization. (p. 303)

Social audit—Attempt to report in financial terms the expenditures and investments made by an organization for social purposes. (p. 87)

Social responsibility—Moral and ethical content of managerial and corporate decisions over and above the pragmatic requirements imposed by legal principle and the market economy. (p. 82)

Society of Consumer Affairs Professionals in Business (SOCAP)—Promotes professionalism among consumer affairs managers. (p. 90)

Sociotechnical approach—Approach to job design that considers both the technical system and the accompanying social system. (p. 226)

Software—Instructions and programs used to run a computer. (p. 595)

Soldiering—Describes the actions of employees who intentionally restrict output. (p. 33)

Span of management—Number of subordinates a manager can effectively manage. Also called span of control. (p. 262)

Staff functions—Advisory and supportive in nature; designed to contribute to the efficiency and maintenance of the organization. (p. 280)

Staffing—Management function that determines human resource needs; recruits, selects, trains, and develops human resources for jobs created by an organization. (pp. 10, 302)

Standard—Value used as a point of reference for comparing other values. (p. 540)

Statistics and mathematical methods—Data is gathered and interpreted. Requires expertise in math, statistics, and the computer; can be expensive. (p. 205)

Strategic conflict—Results from promotion of self-interests by an individual or group; often deliberately planned. (p. 483)

Strategic management—Process through which top management determines the long-run direction and performance of an organization by ensuring careful formulation, proper implementation, and continuous evaluation of plans and strategies. (p. 195)

Strategic MIS—Concerned with decisions that affect the organization's long-range objectives. (p. 593)

Strategic planning—Covers a relatively long period of time; affects many parts of the organization; includes the formulation of objectives and the selection of the means by which they are to be attained. (pp. 183, 198)

Strategy—Outlines the fundamental steps management plans to undertake in order to reach an objective or set of objectives. (p. 176)

Stress—Results when an environment presents a demand threatening to exceed the person's capabilities and resources for meeting it. (p. 487)

Structural (functional) conflict—Result of the organizational structure; relatively independent of the individuals occupying the roles within the structure. (p. 478)

Synetics—Requires the participants to fantasize about how a particular problem could be solved if there weren't any fiscal or technical constraints. Often, at least one or two of these absurd solutions can be refined into quite practical solutions. (p. 152)

Systems analyst—Studies a potential computer application and determines the type of programs needed. (p. 595)

Systems approach to management—Views the human, physical, and informational facets of the manager's job as linking together to form an integrated whole. (p. 48)

T

Tall structure—Organization with many levels and relatively small spans of management. (p. 285)

Tariffs—Government-imposed taxes charged on goods imported into, or exported from, a country. (p. 67)

Team building—Work group develops awareness of conditions that keep them from functioning effectively and takes action to eliminate these conditions. (pp. 454, 510)

Technical skills—Involve specialized knowledge, analytical ability within that specialty, and the ability to use tools and techniques of that specific discipline. (p. 13)

Technological changes—Such things as new equipment and new processes. (p. 504)

Test reliability—Consistency or reproducibility of the results of a test. (p. 314)

Test validity—Extent to which a test measures what it purports to measure (generally, how well it predicts future job success or performance). (p. 314)

Tests—Provide a sample of behavior that is used to draw inferences about the future behavior or performance of an individual. (p. 313)

Theory X and Theory Y—Terms coined by Douglas McGregor to describe assumptions made by managers about basic human nature. (p. 395)

Theory Z—Japanese management style which features lifetime employment, limited promotions, nonspecialized careers, and collective decision making. (p. 72)

Time series forecasts—Basing a prediction or trend upon historical data. (p. 204)

Tough-guy, macho culture—Characterized by individualists who take high risks and get quick feedback on whether their answers are right or wrong. (p. 517)

Traditional theory of motivation—Based on the assumption that money is the primary motivator: if the reward is great enough, employees will produce more. (p. 370)

Training—Learning process that involves the acquisition of skills or concepts to increase employee performance. (p. 335)

Trait theory—Holds that certain physical and psychological characteristics, or traits, differentiate leaders from their groups. (p. 396)

Transaction-processing systems—Substitutes computer processing for manual record-keeping procedures. (p. 593)

Transfer—Moving an employee to another job at about the same level, with about the same pay, performance requirements, and status. (p. 320)

Truth in Lending Act of 1967—Regulates the extension of credit to individuals. (p. 89)

U

Understudy assignments — On-the-job training where an individual, designated as the heir to a job, learns the job from the present jobholder. (p. 342)

Unity-of-command principle—States that an employee should have one and only one immediate manager. (p. 260)

Upward communication—Originates at the lower levels of the organization and flows toward the top. (p. 115)

User-friendly computer—Requires very little technical knowledge to use. (p. 592)

V

Value—Conception, explicit or implicit, defining what an individual or group sees as desirable. People are not born with values; they acquire and develop them later in life. (p. 154)

Variable overhead expenses—Those that are assumed to change in proportion to the level of production or service. (p. 563)

Vestibule training—Procedures and equipment similar to those used in the actual job are set up in a special working area called a vestibule. (p. 338)

W

Wage survey—Survey of selected organizations to provide a comparison of reliable information on policies, practices, and methods of payment. (p. 440)

Work groups—Describes groups in organizations. (p. 453)

Work-hard / play-hard culture — Encourages employees to take few risks and to expect rapid feedback. (p. 518)

Work standards approach—A form of goal setting that involves setting a standard or expected level of output and then comparing each employee's level to the standard. (p. 425)

Z

Zero-base budgeting—Where the manager must build and justify each area of a budget. Each activity is identified, evaluated and ranked by importance. (p. 550)

NAME AND COMPANY INDEX

SUBJECT INDEX